BUILDING SYSTEMS FOR INTERIOR DESIGNERS

BUILDING SYSTEMS FOR INTERIOR DESIGNERS

CORKY BINGGELI A.S.I.D.

JOHN WILEY & SONS, INC.

Published by John Wiley & Sons, Inc., Hoboken, New Jersey
Published simultaneously in Canada

For general information on our other products and services or for technical support, please contact our Customer Care Department within the United States at (800) 762-2974, outside the United States at (317) 572-3993 or fax (317) 572-4002.

Wiley also publishes its books in a variety of electronic formats. Some content that appears in print may not be available in electronic books. For more information about Wiley products, visit our web site at www.wiley.com.

Library of Congress Cataloging-in-Publication Data:
Binggeli, Corky.
  Building systems for interior designers / Corky Binggeli.
       p. cm.
    ISBN 0-471-41733-5 (alk. paper)
    1. Buildings—Environmental engineering.   2. Buildings—Mechanical equipment—
Design and construction.   3. Buildings—Electric equipment—Design and construction.
  I. Title.
    TH6014 .B56 2003
    696—dc21
                                                          2002003197

Printed in the United States of America

10 9 8 7 6 5 4 3 2 1

To my mother,
who taught me to love learning,
and
to my father,
who showed me how buildings are made.

CONTENTS

PREFACE

The inspiration for *Building Systems for Interior Designers* came when I tried to teach interior design students about all the ways buildings support our activities and physical needs—without an adequate textbook. I needed an approach that supported the special concerns of the interior designer, while connecting those issues to the work of the rest of the building design team. I had researched building systems in a number of excellent texts intended for architecture, engineering, and even hospitality management students, but I had found that none of those texts taught the necessary combination of related subjects in adequate depth without an emphasis on calculations and formulas.

Interior design has a relatively short history as a profession requiring special training and demanding technical expertise. Over the past half-century, design professionals have evolved from decorators working primarily in private residences to critical contributors in the design of commercial and residential buildings. We are expected to apply building codes and to work closely with engineers and architects. To do this, we must understand what the other members of the design team have to say, how they approach the design process, and how they document their work.

The more we know about the process of designing and constructing a building, the more effective impact we can have on the results. To cite one example from my own largely commercial interior design practice, my discussion with the mechanical engineer on a spa project of alternate methods of supplying extra heat to a treatment room resulted in a design that improved both our client's heating bills and his customers' experience.

The approach of architects and engineers to building design has changed from one of imposing the building on its site to one of limiting the adverse impact of the building on the environment by using resources available on site. Sustainable design requires that we select materials wisely to create healthy, safe buildings that conserve energy. Sustainable design solutions cut across disciplines, and successful solutions arise only when all the members of the design team work together. As interior designers, we can support or sabotage this effort. We must be involved in the project from the beginning to coordinate with the rest of the design team. That means we must understand and respect the concerns of the architects and engineers, while earning their respect and understanding in return.

Building Systems for Interior Designers is intended primarily as a textbook for interior design students. The style strives for clarity, with concepts explained simply and delivered in everyday language. Enough technical information is offered to support a thorough understanding of how a building works. The illustrations are plentiful and designed to convey information clearly and visually. I have kept in mind the many students for whom English is a second language—as well as the common technophobes among us—as I wrote and illustrated this text. Featured throughout the book are special "Designer's Tips." Look for this icon to find helpful professional advice on a wide range of topics.

Building Systems for Interior Designers covers some subjects, such as heating and air-conditioning systems, that are rarely included in other parts of an interior designer's education. Other areas, such as lighting, typically have entire courses devoted to them, and are given a less thorough treatment here. While some topics, such as acoustics or fire safety, are intimately tied to the work of the interior designer, others, such as transportation systems, involve the interior designer less directly, or may be absent from some projects altogether. This text assumes that the reader has a basic knowledge of building design and construction, but no special training in physics or mathematics. I have sought to cover all the related systems in a building in sufficient depth to provide the reader with a good general understanding, while avoiding repetition of material most likely covered in other courses and texts.

As the book has evolved, it has become obvious that this material is also valuable for people involved in making decisions about the systems in their own buildings, whether they are homeowners or facilities managers. Practicing interior designers and architects will also find *Building Systems for Interior Designers* a useful reference when checking facts and researching options. Interior designers preparing for the National Council for Interior Design Qualification (NCIDQ) professional certification exam will also benefit from this text.

Building Systems for Interior Designers has evolved from an initial set of lecture notes, through an illustrated outline, to classroom handouts of text and illustrations, and finally into a carefully researched and written illustrated text. In the process, I have enriched my own understanding of how buildings support our needs and activities, and this understanding has in turn benefited both my professional work as an interior designer and my continuing role as a teacher. It is my hope that, through this text, I will pass these benefits along to you, my readers.

Corky Binggeli A.S.I.D.
Arlington, Massachusetts
2002

ACKNOWLEDGMENTS

This book owes its existence to the support and talents of many people. In targeting the needs of interior designers, I began by researching the materials already available for students of architecture and engineering. I am especially indebted to the Ninth Edition of *Mechanical and Electrical Equipment for Buildings* by Benjamin Stein and John S. Reynolds (John Wiley & Sons, Inc., NY, 2000), whose comprehensive and clear coverage of building systems was both a standard for excellence and a source for accurate information.

I would never have started on the road to writing this text without the encouragement of Professor Rose-Mary Botti-Salitsky IDEC, IIDA of Mount Ida College, and of Thomas R. Consi Ph.D. at the Massachusetts Institute of Technology, a dear friend whose faith in my ability far exceeds my own. Professor Allan Kirkpatrick of Colorado State University shared his contacts and experience as a textbook author, providing the critical link to making this book a reality.

A number of friends and professional colleagues reviewed the manuscript before submission and offered extremely helpful comments on content and clarity. These include Felice Silverman IIDA of Silverman Trykowski Associates, Josh Feinstein L.C. of Sladen Feinstein Integrated Lighting, Associate Professor Herb Fremin of Wentworth Institute of Technology, and Edward T. Kirkpatrick Ph.D., P.E. Additional technical review was provided by Professor Arlena Hines ASIS, IDEC of Lansing Community College, Professor Novem Mason of the University of North Carolina at Greensboro, Professor Joyce Rasdall of Southeast Missouri State University, Jeff Barber AIA of Gensler Architecture, and Professor Janine King of the University of Florida. Their professional perspectives and teaching experience helped keep the text accurate and focused on the prospective reader, and their enthusiasm and encouragement were wonderfully motivating.

I would also like to thank the staff at John Wiley & Sons, Inc., whose professionalism, support, and good advice guided my efforts. Executive Editor Amanda Miller and Developmental Editor Jennifer Ackerman worked closely with me to see that the text and illustrations reflected the intended content and spirit that I envisioned.

Finally, I am deeply indebted to my husband, Keith Kirkpatrick, who read and commented on every word of the text and who reviewed all of the illustrations as well. This book is a testament to his patience, insight, diligence, and steadfast support in a thousand small ways.

THE BIG PICTURE

Natural Resources

● ● ●

Like our skins, a building is a layer of protection between our bodies and our environment. The building envelope is the point at which the inside comes into contact with the outside, the place where energy, materials, and living things pass in and out. The building's interior design, along with the mechanical, electrical, plumbing, and other building systems, creates an interior environment that supports our needs and activities and responds to the weather and site conditions outdoors. In turn, the environment at the building site is part of the earth's larger natural patterns.

THE OUTDOOR ENVIRONMENT

The sun acting on the earth's atmosphere creates our climate and weather conditions. During the day, the sun's energy heats the atmosphere, the land, and the sea. At night, much of this heat is released back into space. The warmth of the sun moves air and moisture across the earth's surface to give us seasonal and daily weather patterns.

Solar energy is the source of almost all of our energy resources. Ultraviolet (UV) radiation from the sun triggers photosynthesis in green plants, which produces the oxygen we breathe, the plants we eat, and the fuels we use for heat and power. Ultraviolet wavelengths make up only about 1 percent of the sun's rays that reach sea level, and are too short to be visible. About half of the energy in sunlight that reaches the earth arrives as visible wavelengths. The remainder is infrared (IR) wavelengths, which are longer than visible light, and which carry the sun's heat.

Plants combine the sun's energy with water and turn it into sugars, starches, and proteins through photosynthesis, giving us food to eat, which in turn builds and fuels our bodies. Humans and other animals breathe in oxygen and exhale carbon dioxide. Plants supply us with this oxygen by taking carbon dioxide from the air and giving back oxygen. Besides its roles in food supply and oxygen production, photosynthesis also produces wood for construction, fibers for fabrics and paper, and landscape plantings for shade and beauty.

Plants transfer the sun's energy to us when we eat them, or when we eat plant-eating animals. That energy goes back to plants when animal waste decomposes and releases nitrogen, phosphorus, potassium, carbon, and other elements into the soil and water. Animals or microorganisms break down dead animals and plants into basic chemical compounds, which then reenter the cycle to nourish plant life.

The heat of the sun evaporates water into the air, purifying it by distillation. The water vapor condenses as it rises and then precipitates as rain and snow, which clean the air as they fall to earth. Heavier particles fall out of the air by gravity, and the wind dilutes and distributes any remaining contaminants when it stirs up the air.

The sun warms our bodies and our buildings both directly and by warming the air around us. We depend on the sun's heat for comfort, and design our buildings to admit sun for warmth. Passive and active solar design techniques protect us from too much heat and cool our buildings in hot weather.

During the day, the sun illuminates both the outdoors and, through windows and skylights, the indoors. Direct sunlight, however, is often too bright for comfortable vision. When visible light is scattered by the atmosphere, the resulting diffuse light offers an even, restful illumination. Under heavy clouds and at night, we use artificial light for adequate illumination.

Sunlight disinfects surfaces that it touches, which is one reason the old-fashioned clothesline may be superior to the clothes dryer. Ultraviolet radiation kills many harmful microorganisms, purifying the atmosphere, and eliminating disease-causing bacteria from sunlit surfaces. It also creates vitamin D in our skin, which we need to utilize calcium.

Sunlight can also be destructive. Most UV radiation is intercepted by the high-altitude ozone layer, but enough gets through to burn our skin painfully and even fatally. Over the long term, exposure to UV radiation may result in skin cancer. Sunlight contributes to the deterioration of paints, roofing, wood, and other building materials. Fabric dyes may fade, and many plastics decompose when exposed to direct sun, which is an issue for interior designers when specifying materials.

All energy sources are derived from the sun, with the exception of geothermal, nuclear, and tidal power. When the sun heats the air and the ground, it creates currents that can be harnessed as wind power. The cycle of evaporation and precipitation uses solar energy to supply water for hydroelectric power. Photosynthesis in trees creates wood for fuel. About 14 percent of the world's energy comes from biomass, including firewood, crop waste, and even animal dung. These are all considered to be renewable resources because they can be constantly replenished, but our demand for energy may exceed the rate of replenishment.

Our most commonly used fuels—coal, oil, and gas—are fossil fuels. As of 1999, oil provided 32 percent of the world's energy, followed by natural gas at 22 percent, and coal at 21 percent. Huge quantities of decaying vegetation were compressed and subjected to the earth's heat over hundreds of millions of years to create the fossilized solar energy we use today. These resources are clearly not renewable in the short term.

LIMITED ENERGY RESOURCES

In the year 2000, the earth's population reached 6 billion people, with an additional billion anticipated by 2010. With only 7 percent of the world's population, North America consumes 30 percent of the world's energy, and building systems use 35 percent of that to operate. Off-site sewage treatment, water supply, and solid waste management account for an additional 6 percent. The processing, production, and transportation of materials for building construction take up another 7 percent of the energy budget. This adds up to 48 percent of total energy use appropriated for building construction and operation.

The sun's energy arrives at the earth at a fixed rate, and the supply of solar energy stored over millions of years in fossil fuels is limited. The population keeps growing, however, and each person is using more energy. We don't know exactly when we will run out of fossil fuels, but we do know that wasting the limited resources we have is a dangerous way to go. Through careful design, architects, interior designers, and building engineers can help make these finite resources last longer.

For thousands of years in the past, we relied primarily upon the sun's energy for heat and light. Prior to the nineteenth century, wood was the most common fuel. As technology developed, we used wind for transportation and processing of grain, and early industries were located along rivers and streams in order to utilize waterpower. Mineral discoveries around 1800 introduced portable, convenient, and reliable fossil fuels—coal, petroleum, and natural gas—to power the industrial revolution.

In 1830, the earth's population of about 1 billion people depended upon wood for heat and animals for transportation and work. Oil or gas were burned to light interiors. By the 1900s, coal was the dominant fuel, along with hydropower and natural gas. By 1950, petroleum and natural gas split the energy market about evenly. The United States was completely energy self-sufficient, thanks to relatively cheap and abundant domestic coal, oil, and natural gas.

Nuclear power, introduced in the 1950s, has an uncertain future. Although technically exhaustible, nuclear resources are used very slowly. Nuclear plants contain high pressures, temperatures, and radioactivity levels during operation, however, and have long and expensive construction periods. The public has serious concerns over the release of low-level radiation over long periods of time, and over the risks of high-level releases. Civilian use of nuclear power has been limited to research and generation of electricity by utilities.

Growing demand since the 1950s has promoted steadily rising imports of crude oil and petroleum products. By the late 1970s, the United States imported over 40 percent of its oil. In 1973, political conditions in oil-producing countries led to wildly fluctuating oil prices, and high prices encouraged conservation and the development of alternative energy resources. The 1973 oil crisis had a major impact on building construction and operation. By 1982, the United States imported only 28 percent of its oil. Building designers and owners now strive for energy efficiency to minimize costs. Almost all U.S. building codes now include energy conservation standards. Even so, imported oil was back up to over 40 percent by 1989, and over 50 percent in 1990.

Coal use in buildings has declined since the 1990s, with many large cities limiting its application. Currently, most coal is used for electric generation and heavy industry, where fuel storage and air pollution problems can be treated centrally. Modern techniques scrub and filter out sulfur ash from coal combustion emissions, although some older coal-burning plants still contribute significant amounts of pollution.

Our current energy resources include direct solar and renewable solar-derived sources, such as wind, wood, and hydropower; nuclear and geothermal power, which are exhaustible but are used up very slowly; tidal power; and fossil fuels, which are not renewable in the short term. Electricity can be generated from any of these. In the United States, it is usually produced from fossil fuels, with minor amounts contributed by hydropower and nuclear energy. Tidal power stations exist in Canada, France, Russia, and China, but they are expensive and don't always produce energy at the times it is needed. There are few solar thermal, solar photovoltaic, wind power or geothermal power plants in operation, and solar power currently supplies only about 1 percent of U.S. energy use.

Today's buildings are heavily reliant upon electricity because of its convenience of use and versatility, and consumption of electricity is expected to rise about twice as fast as overall energy demand. Electricity and daylight provide virtually all illumination. Electric lighting produces heat, which in turn increases air-conditioning energy use in warm weather, using even more electricity.

Only one-third of the energy used to produce electricity for space heating actually becomes heat, with most of the rest wasted at the production source.

Estimates of U.S. onshore and offshore fossil fuel reserves in 1993 indicated a supply adequate for about 50 years, with much of it expensive and environmentally objectionable to remove. A building with a 50-year functional life and 100-year structural life could easily outlast fossil fuel supplies. As the world's supply of fossil fuels diminishes, buildings must use nonrenewable fuels conservatively if at all, and look to on-site resources, such as daylighting, passive solar heating, passive cooling, solar water heating, and photovoltaic electricity.

Traditional off-site networks for natural gas and oil and the electric grid will continue to serve many buildings, often in combination with on-site sources. On-site resources take up space locally, can be labor intensive, and sometimes have higher first costs that take years to recover. Owners and designers must look beyond these immediate building conditions, and consider the building's impact on its larger environment throughout its life.

THE GREENHOUSE EFFECT

Human activities are adding greenhouse gases—pollutants that trap the earth's heat—to the atmosphere at a faster rate than at any time over the past several thousand years. A warming trend has been recorded since the late nineteenth century, with the most rapid warming occurring since 1980. If emissions of greenhouse gases continue unabated, scientists say we may change global temperature and our planet's climate at an unprecedented rate.

The greenhouse effect (Fig. 1-1) is a natural phenomenon that helps regulate the temperature of our planet. The sun heats the earth and some of this heat, rather than escaping back to space, is trapped in the atmosphere by clouds and greenhouse gases such as water vapor and carbon dioxide. Greenhouse gases serve a useful role in protecting the earth's surface from extreme differences in day and night temperatures. If all of these greenhouse gases were to suddenly disappear, our planet would be 15.5°C (60°F) colder than it is, and uninhabitable.

However, significant increases in the amount of these gases in the atmosphere cause global temperatures to rise. As greenhouse gases accumulate in the atmosphere, they absorb sunlight and IR radiation and prevent some of the heat from radiating back out into space, trapping the sun's heat around the earth. A global rise

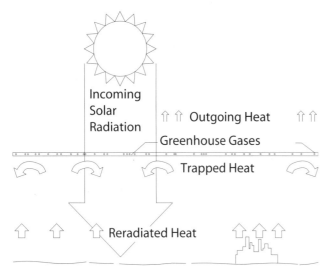

Figure 1-1 The greenhouse effect.

in temperatures of even a few degrees could result in the melting of polar ice and the ensuing rise of ocean levels, and would affect all living organisms.

Human activities contribute substantially to the production of greenhouse gases. As the population grows and as we continue to use more energy per person, we create conditions that warm our atmosphere. Energy production and use employing fossil fuels add greenhouse gases. A study commissioned by the White House and prepared by the National Academy of Sciences in 2001 found that global warming had been particularly strong in the previous 20 years, with greenhouse gases accumulating in the earth's atmosphere as a result of human activities, much of it due to emissions of carbon dioxide from burning fossil fuels.

Since preindustrial times, atmospheric concentrations of carbon dioxide have risen over 30 percent and are now increasing about one-half percent annually. Worldwide, we generate about 20 billion tons of carbon dioxide each year, an average of four tons per person. One-quarter of that comes from the United States, when the rate is 18 tons per person annually. Carbon dioxide concentrations, which averaged 280 parts per million (ppm) by volume for most of the past 10,000 years, are currently around 370 ppm.

Burning fossil fuels for transportation, electrical generation, heating, and industrial purposes contributes most of this increase. Clearing land adds to the problem by eliminating plants that would otherwise help change carbon dioxide to oxygen and filter the air. Plants can now absorb only about 40 percent of the 5 billion tons of carbon dioxide released into the air each year. Making cement from limestone also contributes significant amounts of carbon dioxide.

Methane, an even more potent greenhouse gas than carbon dioxide, has increased almost one and a half times, and is increasing by about 1 percent per year. Landfills, rice farming, and cattle raising all produce methane.

Carbon monoxide, ozone, hydrofluorocarbons (HFCs), perfluorocarbons (PFCs), chlorofluorocarbons (CFCs), and sulfur hexafluoride are other greenhouse gases. Nitrous oxide is up 15 percent over the past 20 years. Industrial smokestacks and coal-fired electric utilities produce both sulfur dioxide and carbon monoxide.

The Intergovernmental Panel on Climate Change (IPCC), which was formed in 1988 by the United Nations Environment Program and the World Meteorological Organization, projected in its *Third Assessment Report (2001)* (Cambridge University Press, 2001) an average global temperature increase of 1.4°C to 5.8°C (2.5°F–10.4°F) by 2100, and greater warming thereafter. The IPCC concluded that climate change will have mostly adverse affects, including loss of life as a result of heat waves, worsened air pollution, damaged crops, spreading tropical diseases, and depleted water resources. Extreme events like floods and droughts are likely to become more frequent, and melting glaciers will expand oceans and raise sea level 0.09 to 0.88 meters (4 inches to 35 inches) over the next century.

OZONE DEPLETION

The human health and environmental concerns about ozone layer depletion are different from the risks we face from global warming, but the two phenomena are related in certain ways. Some pollutants contribute to both problems and both alter the global atmosphere. Ozone layer depletion allows more harmful UV radiation to reach our planet's surface. Increased UV radiation can lead to skin cancers, cataracts, and a suppressed immune system in humans, as well as reduced yields for crops.

Ozone is an oxygen molecule that occurs in very small amounts in nature. In the lower atmosphere, ozone occurs as a gas that, in high enough concentrations, can cause irritations to the eyes and mucous membranes. In the upper atmosphere (the stratosphere), ozone absorbs solar UV radiation that otherwise would cause severe damage to all living organisms on the earth's surface. Prior to the industrial revolution, ozone in the lower and upper atmospheres was in equilibrium. Today, excessive ozone in the lower atmosphere contributes to the greenhouse effect and pollutes the air.

Ozone is being destroyed in the upper atmosphere, however, where it has a beneficial effect. This destruction is caused primarily by CFCs. Chlorofluorocarbons don't occur naturally. They are very stable chemicals developed in the 1960s, and they can last up to 50 years. Used primarily for refrigeration and air-conditioning, CFCs have also been used as blowing agents to produce foamed plastics for insulation, upholstery padding, and packaging, and as propellants for fire extinguishers and aerosols. In their gaseous form, they drift into the upper atmosphere and destroy ozone molecules. This allows more UV radiation to reach the surface of the earth, killing or altering complex molecules of living organisms, including DNA. This damage has resulted in an increase in skin cancers, especially in southern latitudes. The Montreal Protocol on Substances that Deplete the Ozone Layer, signed in 1987 by 25 nations (168 nations are now party to the accord), decreed an international stop to the production of CFCs by 2000, but the effects of chemicals already produced will last for many years.

SUSTAINABLE DESIGN STRATEGIES

Sustainable architecture looks at human civilization as an integral part of the natural world, and seeks to preserve nature through encouraging conservation in daily life. Energy conservation in buildings is a complex issue involving sensitivity to the building site, choice of appropriate construction methods, use and control of daylight, selection of finishes and colors, and the design of artificial lighting. The selection of heating, ventilating, and air-conditioning (HVAC) and other equipment can have a major effect on energy use. The use of alternative energy sources, waste control, water recycling, and control of building operations and maintenance all contribute to sustainable design.

The materials and methods used for building construction and finishing have an impact on the larger world. The design of a building determines how much energy it will use throughout its life. The materials used in the building's interior are tied to the waste and pollution generated by their manufacture and eventual disposal. Increasing energy efficiency and using clean energy sources can limit greenhouse gases.

According to Design Ecology, a project sponsored by Chicago's International Interior Design Association (IIDA) and Collins & Aikman Floorcoverings, "Sustainability is a state or process that can be maintained indefinitely. The principles of sustainability integrate three closely intertwined elements—the environment, the economy, and the social system—into a system that can be maintained in a healthy state indefinitely."

Environmentally conscious interior design is a practice that attempts to create indoor spaces that are environmentally sustainable and healthy for their occupants. Sustainable interiors address their impact on the global environment. To achieve sustainable design, interior designers must collaborate with architects, developers, engineers, environmental consultants, facilities and building managers, and contractors. The professional ethics and responsibilities of the interior designer include the creation of healthy and safe indoor environments. The interior designer's choices can provide comfort for the building's occupants while still benefiting the environment, an effort that often requires initial conceptual creativity rather than additional expense.

Energy-efficient techniques sometimes necessitate special equipment or construction, and may consequently have a higher initial cost than conventional designs. However, it is often possible to use techniques that have multiple benefits, spreading the cost over several applications to achieve a better balance between initial costs and benefits. For example, a building designed for daylighting and natural ventilation also offers benefits for solar heating, indoor air quality (IAQ), and lighting costs. This approach cuts across the usual building system categories and ties the building closely to its site. We discuss many of these techniques in this book, crossing conventional barriers between building systems in the process.

As an interior designer, you can help limit greenhouse gas production by specifying energy-efficient lighting and appliances. Each kilowatt-hour (kWh) of electricity produced by burning coal releases almost 1 kg (more than 2 lb) of carbon dioxide into the atmosphere. By using natural light, natural ventilation, and adequate insulation in your designs, you reduce energy use.

Specify materials that require less energy to manufacture and transport. Use products made of recycled materials that can in turn be recycled when they are replaced. It is possible to use materials and methods that are good for the global environment and for healthy interior spaces, that decrease the consumption of energy and the strain on the environment, without sacrificing the comfort, security, or aesthetics of homes, offices, or public spaces.

One way to reduce energy use while improving conditions for the building's occupants is to introduce user-operated controls. These may be as low-tech as shutters and shades that allow the control of sunlight entering a room and operable windows that offer fresh air and variable temperatures. Users who understand how a building gets and keeps heat are more likely to conserve energy. Occupants who have personal control are comfortable over a wider range of temperatures than those with centralized controls.

Using natural on-site energy sources can reduce a building's fossil fuel needs. A carefully sited building can enhance daylighting as well as passive cooling by night ventilation. Good siting also supports opportunities for solar heating, improved indoor air quality, less use of electric lights, and added acoustic absorption.

Rainwater retention employs local water for irrigation and flushing toilets. On-site wastewater recycling circulates the water and waste from kitchens and baths through treatment ponds, where microorganisms and aquatic plants digest waste matter. The resulting water is suitable for irrigation of crops and for fish food. The aquatic plants from the treatment ponds can be harvested for processing as biogas, which can then be used for cooking and for feeding farm animals. The manure from these animals in turn provides fertilizer for crops.

Look at the building envelope, HVAC system, lighting, equipment and appliances, and renewable energy systems as a whole. Energy loads—the amount of energy the building uses to operate—are reduced by integration with the building site, use of renewable resources, the design of the building envelope, and the selection of efficient lighting and appliances. Energy load reductions lead to smaller, less expensive, and more efficient HVAC systems, which in turn use less energy.

Buildings, as well as products, can be designed for recycling. A building designed for sustainability adapts easily to changed uses, thereby reducing the amount of demolition and new construction and prolonging the building's life. With careful planning, this strategy can avoid added expense or undifferentiated, generic design. The use of removable and reusable demountable building parts adds to adaptability, but may require a heavier structural system, as the floors are not integral with the beams, and mechanical and electrical systems must be well integrated to avoid leaks or cracks. Products that don't combine different materials allow easier separation and reuse or recycling of metals, plastics, and other constituents than products where diverse materials are bonded together.

The Leadership in Energy and Environmental Design System

The U.S. Green Building Council, a nonprofit coalition representing the building industry, has created a comprehensive system for building green called LEED™, short for Leadership in Energy and Environmental Design. The LEED program provides investors, architects and designers, construction personnel, and building managers with information on green building techniques and strategies. At the same time, LEED certifies buildings that meet the highest standards of economic and environmental performance, and offers professional education, training, and accreditation. Another aspect of the LEED system is its Professional Accreditation, which recognizes an individual's qualifications in sustainable building. In 1999, the LEED Commercial Interior Committee was formed to develop definitive standards for what constitutes a green interior space, and guidelines for sustainable maintenance. The LEED program is currently developing materials for commercial interiors, residential work, and operations and maintenance.

Interior designers are among those becoming LEED-accredited professionals by passing the LEED Profes-

---

When a New York City social services agency prepared to renovate a former industrial building into a children's services center, they sought a designer with the ability to create a healthy, safe environment for families in need. Karen's awareness of the ability of an interior to foster a nurturing environment and her strong interest in sustainable design caught their attention. Her LEED certification added to her credentials, and Karen was selected as interior designer for the project.

The building took up a full city block from sidewalk to sidewalk, so an interior courtyard was turned into a playground for the children. The final design incorporated energy-efficient windows that brought in light without wasting heated or conditioned air. Recycled and nonpolluting construction materials were selected for their low impact on the environment, including cellulose wall insulation and natural linoleum and tile flooring materials. Karen's familiarity with sustainable design issues not only led to a building renovation that used energy wisely and avoided damage to the environment, but also created an interior where children and their families could feel cared for and safe.

sional Accreditation Examination. More and more architects, engineers, and interior designers are realizing the business advantages of marketing green design strategies. This is a very positive step toward a more sustainable world, yet it is important to verify the credentials of those touting green design. The LEED Professional Accreditation Examination establishes minimum competency in much the same way as the NCIDQ exam seeks to set a universal standard by which to measure the competency of interior designers to practice as professionals. Training workshops are available to prepare for the exam.

Receiving LEED accreditation offers a way for designers to differentiate themselves in the marketplace. As green buildings go mainstream, both government and private sector projects will begin to require a LEED-accredited designer on the design teams they hire.

The LEED process for designing a green building starts with setting goals. Next, alternative strategies are evaluated. Finally, the design of the whole building is approached in a spirit of integration and inspiration.

It is imperative to talk with all the people involved in the building's design about goals; sometimes the best ideas come from the most unlikely places. Ask how each team member can serve the goals of this project. Include the facilities maintenance people in the design process, to give feedback to designers about what actually happens in the building, and to cultivate their support for new systems. Goals can be sabotaged when an architect, engineer, or contractor gives lip service to green design, but reacts to specifics with "We've never done it that way before," or its evil twin "We've always done it this way." Question whether time is spent on why team members can't do something, or on finding a solution—and whether higher fees are requested just to overcome opposition to a new way of doing things. Finally, be sure to include the building's users in the planning process; this sounds obvious, but it is not always done.

In 1999, the U.S. government's General Services Administration (GSA) Public Building Service (PBS) made a commitment to use the LEED rating system for all future design, construction, and repair and alterations of federal construction projects and is working on revising its leases to include requirements that spaces leased for customers be green. The Building Green Program includes increased use of recycled materials, waste management, and sustainable design. The PBS chooses products with recycled content, optimizes natural daylight, installs energy-efficient equipment and lighting, and installs water-saving devices. The Denver Courthouse serves as a model for these goals. It uses photovoltaic cells and daylighting shelves, along with over 100 other sustainable building features, enabling it to apply for a LEED Gold Rating.

The ENERGY STAR® Label

The ENERGY STAR® label (Fig. 1-2) was created in conjunction with the U.S. Department of Energy (DOE) and the U.S. Environmental Protection Agency (EPA) to help consumers quickly and easily identify energy efficient products such as homes, appliances, and lighting. ENERGY STAR products are also available in Canada. In the United States alone in the year 2000, ENERGY STAR resulted in greenhouse gas reductions equivalent to taking 10 million cars off the road. Eight hundred and sixty four billion pounds of carbon dioxide emissions have been prevented due to ENERGY STAR commitments to date.

The ENERGY STAR Homes program reviews the plans for new homes and provides design support to help the home achieve the five-star ENERGY STAR Homes rating, by setting the standard for greater value and energy savings. ENERGY STAR–certified homes are also eligible for rebates on major appliances.

The program also supplies ENERGYsmart computer software that walks you through a computerized energy audit of a home and provides detailed information on energy efficiency. The PowerSmart computer program assesses electric usage for residential customers who use more than 12,000 kW per year, and can offer discounts on insulation, refrigerators, thermostats, and heat pump repairs. ENERGY STAR Lighting includes rebates on energy-efficient light bulbs and fixtures. The program offers rebates on ENERGY STAR-labeled clothes washers, which save an average of 60 percent on energy costs and reduce laundry water consumption by 35 percent.

Beyond Sustainable Design

Conservation of limited resources is good, but it is possible to create beautiful buildings that generate more energy than they use and actually improve the health of

Figure 1-2 ENERGY STAR label.

their environments. Rather than simply cutting down on the damage buildings do to the environment, which results in designs that do less—but still some—damage, some designs have a net positive effect. Instead of suffering with a showerhead that limits the flow to an unsatisfactory minimum stream, for example, you can take a guilt-free long, hot shower, as long as the water is solar heated and returns to the system cleaner than it started. Buildings can model the abundance of nature, creating more and more riches safely, and generating delight in the process.

Such work is already being done, thanks to pioneers like William McDonough of William McDonough + Partners and McDonough Braungart Design Chemistry, LLC, and Dr. David Orr, Chairman of the Oberlin Environmental Studies Program. Their designs employ a myriad of techniques for efficient design. A photovoltaic array on the roof that turns sunlight into electric energy uses net metering to connect to the local utility's power grid, and sells excess energy back to the utility. Photovoltaic cells are connected to fuel cells that use hydrogen and oxygen to make more energy. Buildings process their own waste by passing wastewater through a manmade marsh within the building. The landscaping for the site selects plants native to the area before European settlement, bringing back habitats for birds and animals. Daylighting adds beauty and saves energy, as in a Michigan building where worker productivity increased, and workers who had left for higher wages returned because, as they said, they couldn't work in the dark. Contractors welcome low-toxicity building materials that don't have odors from volatile organic compounds (VOCs), and that avoid the need to wear respirators or masks while working.

William McDonough has been working on the Ford River Rouge automobile plant in Oregon to restore the local river as a healthy, safe biological resource. This 20-year project includes a new 55,740 square meter (600,000 square ft) automobile assembly plant featuring the largest planted living roof, with one-half million square feet of soil and plants that provide storm water management. The site supports habitat restoration and is mostly unpaved and replanted with native species. The interiors are open and airy, with skylights providing daylighting and safe walkways allowing circulation away from machinery. Ford has made a commitment to share what they learn from this building for free, and is working with McDonough on changes to products that may lead to cars that actually help clean the air.

The Lewis Center for Environmental Studies at Oberlin College in Oberlin, Ohio, represents a collaboration between William McDonough and David Orr. Completed in January 2000, the Lewis Center consists of a main building with classrooms, faculty offices, and a two-story atrium, and a connected structure with a 100-seat auditorium and a solarium. Interior walls stop short of the exposed curved ceiling, creating open space above for daylight.

One of the project's primary goals was to produce more energy than it needs to operate while maintaining acceptable comfort levels and a healthy interior environment. The building is oriented on an east-west axis to take advantage of daylight and solar heat gain, with the major classrooms situated along the southern exposure to maximize daylight, so that the lighting is often unnecessary. The roof is covered with 344 square meters (3700 square ft) of photovoltaic panels, which are expected to generate more than 75,000 kilowatt-hours (kW-h) of energy annually. Advanced design features include geothermal wells for heating and cooling, passive solar design, daylighting and fresh air delivery throughout. The thermal mass of the building's concrete floors and exposed masonry walls helps to retain and reradiate heat. Overhanging eaves and a vinecovered trellis on the south elevation shade the building, and an earth berm along the north wall further insulates the wall. The atrium's glass curtain wall uses low-emissivity (low-e) glass.

Operable windows supplement conditioned air supplied through the HVAC system. A natural wastewater treatment facility on site includes a created wetland for natural storm water management and a landscape that provides social spaces, instructional cultivation, and habitat restoration.

Interior materials support the building's goals, including sustainably harvested wood; paints, adhesives, and carpets with low VOC emissions; and materials with recycled contents such as structural steel, brick, aluminum curtain-wall framing, ceramic tile, and toilet partitions. Materials were selected for durability, low maintenance, and ecological sensitivity.

The Herman Miller SQA building in Holland, Michigan, which remanufactures Herman Miller office furniture, enhances human psychological and behavioral experience by increasing contact with natural processes, incorporating nature into the building, and reducing the use of hazardous materials and chemicals, as reported in the July/August 2000 issue of *Environmental Design & Construction* by Judith Heerwagen, Ph.D. Drawing on research from a variety of studies in the United States and Europe, Dr. Heerwagen identifies links between physical, psychosocial, and neurological-cognitive well-being and green building design features.

Designed by William McDonough + Partners, the 26,941 square meter (290,000 square ft) building houses a manufacturing plant and office/showroom. About 700 people work in the manufacturing plant and offices, which contain a fitness center with basketball court and exercise machines overlooking a country landscape, and convenient break areas. Key green building features include good energy efficiency, indoor air quality, and daylighting. The site features a restored wetlands and prairie landscape.

Although most organizations take weeks to months to regain lost efficiency after a move, lowering productivity by around 30 percent, Herman Miller's performance evaluation showed a slight overall increase in productivity in the nine-month period after their move. On-time delivery and product quality also increased. This occurred even though performance bonuses to employees decreased, with the money going instead to help pay for the new building. This initial study of the effects of green design on worker satisfaction and productivity will be augmented by the "human factors commissioning" of all of the City of Seattle's new and renovated municipal buildings, which will be designed to meet or exceed the LEED Silver level.

Building Site Conditions

The way sunlight moves around a building site influences the way the building is positioned, the size and location of windows and skylights, the amount of daylighting, and the design of mechanical and natural heating and cooling systems. The distance above or below the equator determines how sunlight moves across the site (Figs. 2-1, 2-2). The amount of sunlight that reaches the site depends on its altitude above sea level, how close it is to bodies of water, and the presence of shading plants and trees.

Fountains, waterfalls, and trees tend to raise the humidity of the site and lower the temperature. Large bodies of water, which are generally cooler than the land during the day and warmer at night, act as heat reservoirs that moderate variations in local temperatures and generate offshore breezes. Large water bodies are usually warmer than the land in the winter and cooler in the summer.

Forests, trees, other buildings, and hills shape local wind patterns. The absorbency of the ground surface determines how much heat will be retained to be released at night, and how much will be reflected onto the building surface. Light-colored surfaces reflect solar radiation, while dark ones absorb and retain radiation. Plowed ground or dark pavement will be warmer than surrounding areas, radiating heat to nearby surfaces and creating small updrafts of air. Grass and other ground covers lower ground temperatures by absorbing solar radiation, and aid cooling by evaporation.

LOCAL CLIMATES

Local temperatures vary with the time of day and the season of the year. Because the earth stores heat and releases it at a later time, a phenomenon known as thermal lag, afternoon temperatures are generally warmer than mornings. The lowest daily temperature is usually just before sunrise, when most of the previous day's heat has dissipated. Although June experiences the most solar radiation in the northern hemisphere, summer temperatures peak in July or August due to the long-term effects of thermal storage. Because of this residual stored heat, January and February—about one month past the winter solstice—are the coldest months. It is usually colder at higher latitudes, both north and south, as a result of shorter days and less solar radiation. Sites may have microclimates, different from surrounding areas, which result from their elevation, closeness to large bodies of water, shading, and wind patterns.

Cities sometimes create their own microclimates with relatively warm year-round temperatures produced

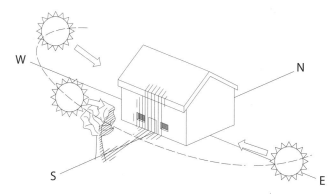

Figure 2-1 Sun angles in northern latitudes.

by heat sources such as air conditioners, furnaces, electric lights, car engines, and building machinery. Energy released by vehicles and buildings to the outdoors warms the air 3°C to 6°C (5°F–11°F) above the surrounding countryside. The rain that runs off hard paved surfaces and buildings into storm sewers isn't available for evaporative cooling. Wind is channeled between closely set buildings, which also block the sun's warmth in winter. The convective updrafts created by the large cities can affect the regional climate. Sunlight is absorbed and reradiated off massive surfaces, and less is given back to the obscured night sky.

CLIMATE TYPES

Environmentally sensitive buildings are designed in response to the climate type of the site. Indigenous ar-

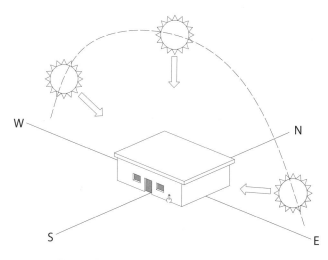

Figure 2-2 Sun angles in tropical latitudes.

chitecture, which has evolved over centuries of trial and error, provides models for building in the four basic climate types.

Cold Climates

Cold climates feature long cold winters with short, very hot periods occurring occasionally during the summer. Cold climates generally occur around 45 degrees latitude north or south, for example, in North Dakota. Buildings designed for cold climates emphasize heat retention, protection from rain and snow, and winter wind protection. They often include passive solar heating, with the building encouraging heat retention without mechanical assistance.

In cool regions, minimizing the surface area of the building reduces exposure to low temperatures. The building is oriented to absorb heat from the winter sun. Cold air collects in valley bottoms. North slopes get less winter sun and more winter wind, and hilltops lose heat to winter winds. Setting a building into a protective south-facing hillside reduces the amount of heat loss and provides wind protection, as does burying a building in earth. In cold climates, dark colors on the south-facing surfaces increase the absorption of solar heat. A dark roof with a steep slope will collect heat, but this is negated when the roof is covered with snow.

Temperate Climates

Temperate climates have cold winters and hot summers. Buildings generally require winter heating and summer cooling, especially if the climate is humid. Temperate climates are found between 35 degrees and 45 degrees latitude, in Washington, DC, for example. South-facing walls are maximized in a building designed for a temperate region. Summer shade is provided for exposures on the east and west and over the roof. Deciduous shade trees that lose their leaves in the winter help to protect the building from sun in hot weather and allow the winter sun through. The building's design encourages air movement in hot weather while protecting against cold winter winds (Fig. 2-3).

Hot Arid Climates

Hot arid climates have long, hot summers and short, sunny winters, and the daily temperatures range widely between dawn and the warmest part of the afternoon.

Figure 2-3 Building in a temperate climate.

Arizona is an example of a hot arid climate. Buildings designed for hot arid climates feature heat and sun control, and often try to increase humidity. They take advantage of wind and rain for cooling and humidity, and make the most of the cooler winter sun.

Windows and outdoor spaces are shaded from the sun, and summer shade is provided to the east and west and over the roof. Enclosed courtyards offer shade and encourage air movement, and the presence of a fountain or pool and plants increases humidity. Even small bodies of water produce a psychological and physical evaporative cooling effect. Sites in valleys near a watercourse keep cooler than poorly ventilated locations. In warm climates, sunlit surfaces should be a light color, to reflect as much sun as possible.

Hot Humid Climates

Hot humid climates have very long summers with slight seasonal variations and relatively constant temperatures. The weather is consistently hot and humid, as in New Orleans. Buildings designed for hot, humid climates take advantage of shading from the sun to reduce heat gain and cooling breezes. East and west exposures are minimized to reduce solar heat gain, although some sun in winter may be desirable. Wall openings are directed away from major noise sources so that they can remain open to take advantage of natural ventilation. If possible, the floor is raised above the ground, with a crawl space under the building for good air circulation.

THE SITE

The climate of a particular building site is determined by the sun's angle and path, the air temperature, humidity, precipitation, air motion, and air quality. Building designers describe sites by the type of soil, the characteristics of the ground surface, and the topography of the site.

Subsoil and topsoil conditions, subsurface water levels, and rocks affect excavations, foundations, and landscaping of the site. Hills, valleys, and slopes determine how water drains during storms and whether soil erosion occurs. Site contours shape paths and roadway routes, may provide shelter from the wind, and influence plant locations. Elevating a structure on poles or piers minimizes disturbance of the natural terrain and existing vegetation.

The construction of the building may alter the site by using earth and stone or other local materials. Construction of the building may bring utilities to the site, including water, electricity, and natural gas. Alterations can make a positive impact by establishing habitats for native plants and animals.

The presence of people creates a major environmental impact. Buildings contribute to air pollution directly through fuel combustion, and indirectly through the electric power plants that supply energy and the incinerators and landfills that receive waste. Power plants are primary causes of acid rain (containing sulfur oxides) and smog (nitrogen oxides). Smoke, gases, dust, and chemical particles pollute the air. Idling motors at drive-up windows and loading docks may introduce gases into building air intakes. Sewage and chemical pollutants damage surface or groundwater.

Other nearby buildings can shade areas of the site and may divert wind. Built-up areas upset natural drainage patterns. Close neighbors may limit visual or acoustic privacy. Previous land use may have left weeds or soil erosion. The interior of the building responds to these surrounding conditions by opening up to or turning away from views, noises, smells, and other disturbances. Interior spaces connect to existing on-site walks, driveways, parking areas, and gardens. The presence of wells, septic systems, and underground utilities influences the design of residential bathrooms, kitchens, and laundries as well as commercial buildings.

Traffic, industry, commerce, recreation, and residential uses all create noise. The hard surfaces and parallel walls in cities intensify noise. Mechanical systems of neighboring buildings may be very noisy, and are hard to mask without reducing air intake, although newer equipment is usually quieter. Plants only slightly reduce the sound level, but the visually softer appearance gives a perception of acoustic softness, and the sound of wind through the leaves helps to mask noise. Fountains also provide helpful masking sounds.

As you move up and down a site or within a multistory building, each level lends itself to certain types of uses. The sky layer is usually the hardest to get to and offers the most exposure to wind, sun, daylight, and rain. The near-surface layer is more accessible to people and activities. The surface layer encourages the most frequent public contact and the easiest access. The subsurface layer confers isolation by enclosure and provides privacy and thermal stability, but may have groundwater problems.

Wind and Building Openings

Winds are usually weakest in the early morning and strongest in the afternoon, and can change their effects and sometimes their directions with the seasons. Evergreen shrubs, trees, and fences can slow and diffuse winds near low-rise buildings. The more open a windbreak, the farther away its influence will be felt. Although dense windbreaks block wind in their immediate vicinity, the wind whips around them to ultimately cover an even greater area. Wind speed may increase through gaps in a windbreak. Blocking winter winds may sometimes also block desirable summer breezes. The wind patterns around buildings are complex, and localized wind turbulence between buildings often increases wind speed and turbulence just outside building entryways.

Openings in the building are the source of light, sun, and fresh air. Building openings provide opportunities for wider personal choices of temperature and access to outdoor air. On the other hand, they limit control of humidity, and permit the entry of dust and pollen. Window openings allow interior spaces to have natural light, ventilation, and views. Expansive, restricted, or filtered window openings reveal or frame views, and highlight distant vistas or closer vignettes.

Water

Rainwater falling on steeply pitched roofs with overhangs is collected by gutters and downspouts and is carried away as surface runoff, or underground through a storm sewer. Even flat roofs have a slight pitch, and the water collects into roof drains that pass through the interior of the building. Drain leaders are pipes that run vertically within partitions to carry the water down through the structure to the storm drains. Interior drains are usually more expensive than exterior gutters and leaders.

Rainwater can be retained for use on site. Roof ponds hold water while it slowly flows off the roof, giving the ground below more time to absorb runoff. The evaporation from a roof pond also helps cool the building. Water can be collected in a cistern on the roof for later use, but the added weight increases structural requirements.

Porous pavement allows water to sink into the earth rather than run off. One type of asphalt is porous, and is used for parking lots and roadways. Low-strength porous concrete is found in Florida, but wouldn't withstand a northern freeze-thaw cycle. Incremental paving consists of small concrete or plastic paving units alternating with plants, so that rainwater can drain into the ground. Parking lots can also be made of open-celled pavers that allow grass or groundcover plants to grow in their cavities.

Sites and buildings should be designed for maximum rainfall retention. In some parts of North America, half of residential water is consumed outdoors, much of it for lawn sprinklers that lose water to evaporation and runoff. Sprinkler timing devices control the length of the watering cycle and the time when it begins, so that watering can be done at night when less water evaporates. Rain sensors shut off the system, and monitors check soil moisture content. Bubblers with very low flow rates lose less water to evaporation. With drip irrigation, which works well for individual shrubs and small trees, a plastic tube network slowly and steadily drips water onto the ground surface near a plant, soaking the plants at a rate they prefer. Recycled or reclaimed water, including graywater (wastewater that is not from toilets or urinals) and stored rain, are gradually being allowed by building codes in North America.

Animal and Plant Life

Building sites provide environments for a variety of plant and animal life. Bacteria, mold, and fungi break down dead animal and vegetable matter into soil nutrients. Insects pollinate useful plants, but most insects must be kept out of the building. Termites may attack the building's structure. Building occupants may welcome cats, dogs, and other pets into a building, but want to exclude nuisance animals such as mice, raccoons, squirrels, lizards, and stray dogs. You may want to hear the birds' songs and watch them at the feeder while keeping the cardinals out of the kitchen.

Grasses, weeds, flowers, shrubs, and trees trap precipitation, prevent soil erosion, provide shade, and deflect wind. They play a major role in food and water cycles, and their growth and change through the seasons help us mark time. Plants near buildings foster privacy, provide wind protection, and reduce sun glare and heat. They frame or screen views, moderate noise, and visually connect the building to the site. Plants improve air quality by trapping particles on their leaves, to be washed to the ground by rain. Photosynthesis assimilates gases, fumes, and other pollutants.

Deciduous plants grow and drop their leaves on a schedule that responds more to the cycles of outdoor temperature than to the position of the sun (Figs. 2-4, 2-5). The sun reaches its maximum strength from March 21 through September 21, while plants provide the most shade from June to October, when the days are warmest. A deciduous vine on a trellis over a south-facing window grows during the cooler spring, shades the interior during the hottest weather, and loses its leaves in time to welcome the winter sun. The vine also cools its immediate area by evaporation. Evergreens provide shade all year and help reduce snow glare in winter.

The selection of trees for use in the landscape should consider their structure and shape, their mature

Figure 2-5 Deciduous shade tree in winter.

height and the spread of their foliage, and the speed with which they grow. The density, texture, and color of foliage may change with the seasons. For all types of plants, requirements for soil, water, sunlight, and temperature range, and the depth and extent of root structures are evaluated. Low-maintenance native or naturalized species have the best chances of success. To support plant life, soil must be able to absorb moisture, supply appropriate nutrients, be able to be aerated, and be free of concentrated salts.

Trees' ability to provide shade depends upon their orientation to the sun, their proximity to the building or outdoor space, their shape, height, and spread, and the density of their foliage and branch structure. The most effective shade is on the southeast in the morning and the southwest during late afternoon, when the sun has a low angle and casts long shadows.

Air temperatures in the shade of a tree are about 3°C to 6°C (5°F–11°F) cooler than in the sun. A wall shaded by a large tree in direct sun may be 11°C to 14°C (20°F–25°F) cooler than it would be with no shade. This temperature drop is due to the shade plus the cooling evaporation from the enormous surface area of the leaves. Shrubs right next to a wall produce similar results, trapping cooled air and preventing drafts from infiltrating the building. Neighborhoods with large trees have maximum air temperatures up to 6°C (10°F) lower than those without. Remarkably, a moist lawn will be 6°C to 8°C (10°F–14°F) cooler than bare soil, and 17°C (31°F) cooler than unshaded asphalt. Low growing, low-maintenance ground covers or paving blocks with holes are also cooler than asphalt.

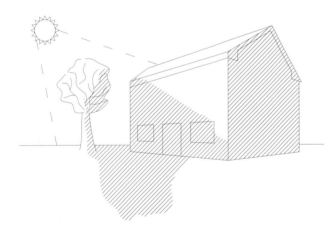

Figure 2-4 Deciduous shade tree in summer.

Designing for Building Functions

•••

The earliest shelters probably provided only a bit of shade or protection from rain, and were warmed by a fire and enclosed by one or more walls. Today we expect a lot from our buildings, beginning with the necessities for supporting human life. We must have clean air to breathe and clean water to drink, prepare food, clean our bodies and our belongings, and flush away wastes. We need facilities for food preparation and places to eat. Human body wastes, wash water, food wastes, and rubbish have to be removed or recycled.

As buildings become more complex, we expect less protection from our clothing and more from our shelters. We expect to control air temperatures and the temperatures of the surfaces and objects around us for thermal comfort. We control the humidity of the air and the flow of water vapor. We exclude rain, snow, and groundwater from the building, and circulate the air within it.

Once these basic physical needs are met, we turn to creating conditions for sensory comfort, efficiency, and privacy. We need illumination to see, and barriers for visual privacy. We seek spaces where we can hear clearly, yet which have acoustic privacy.

The next group of functions supports social needs. We try to control the entry or exit of other people and of animals. Buildings facilitate communication and connection with the world outside through windows, telephones, mailboxes, computer networks, and video ca-

bles. Our buildings support our activities by distributing concentrated energy to convenient locations, primarily through electrical systems.

The building's structure gives stable support for all the people, objects, and architectural features of the building. The structure resists the forces of snow, wind, and earthquake. Buildings protect their own structure, surfaces, internal mechanical and electrical systems, and other architectural features from water and precipitation. They adjust to their own normal movements without damage to their structure or contents. They protect occupants, contents, and the building itself from fire. Buildings support our comfort, safety, and productive activity with floors, walls, stairs, shelves, countertops, and other built-in elements.

Finally, a building capable of accomplishing all of these complex functions must be built without excessive expense or difficulty. Once built, it must be able to be operated, maintained, and changed in a useful and economical manner.

THE BUILDING ENVELOPE

The building envelope is the transition between the outdoors and the inside, consisting of the windows, doors, floors, walls, and roofs of the building. The envelope encloses and shelters space. It furnishes a barrier to rain and protects from sun, wind, and harsh temperatures. Entries are the transition zone between the building's interior and the outside world.

Traditionally, the building envelope was regarded as a barrier separating the interior from the outdoor environment. Architects created an isolated environment, and engineers equipped it with energy-using devices to control conditions. Because of the need to conserve energy, we now see the building envelope as a dynamic boundary, which interacts with the external natural energy forces and the internal building environment. The envelope is sensitively attuned to the resources of the site: sun, wind, and water. The boundary is manipulated to balance the energy flows between inside and outside.

This dynamic approach leads the architect to support proper thermal and lighting conditions through the design of the building's form and structure, supported by the mechanical and electrical systems. Engineers design these support systems with passive control mechanisms that minimize energy consumption.

A building envelope can be an open frame or a closed shell. It can be dynamic and sensitive to changing conditions and needs, letting in or closing out the sun's warmth and light, breezes and sounds. Openings and barriers may be static, like a wall; allow on–off operation, like a door; or offer adjustable control, like venetian blinds. The appropriate architectural solution depends upon the range of options you desire, the local materials available, and local style preferences. A dynamic envelope demands that the user understand how, why, and when to make adjustments. The designer must make sure the people using the building have this information.

BUILDING FORM

Energy conservation has major implications for the building's form. The orientation of the building and its width and height determine how the building will be shielded from excess heat or cold or open to ventilation or light. For example, the desire to provide daylight and natural ventilation to each room limits the width of multistory hotels.

 At the initial conceptual design stage, the architect and interior designer group similar functions and spaces with similar needs close to the resources they require, consolidating and minimizing distribution networks. The activities that attract the most frequent public par-

ticipation belong at or near ground level. Closed offices and industrial activities with infrequent public contact can be located at higher levels and in remote locations. Spaces with isolated and closely controlled environments, like lecture halls, auditoriums, and operating rooms, are placed at interior or underground locations. Mechanical spaces that need acoustic isolation and restricted public access, or that require access to outside air, should be close to related outdoor equipment, like condensers and cooling towers, and must be accessible for repair and replacement of machinery.

Large buildings are broken into zones. Perimeter zones are immediately adjacent to the building envelope, usually extending 4.6 to 6 meters (15–20 ft) inside. Perimeter zones are affected by changes in outside weather and sun. In small buildings, the perimeter zone conditions continue throughout the building. Interior zones are protected from the extremes of weather, and generally require less heating, as they retain a stable temperature. Generally, interior zones require cooling and ventilation.

BETWEEN FLOORS AND CEILINGS

A plenum is an enclosed portion of the building structure that is designed to allow the movement of air, forming part of an air distribution system. The term plenum is specifically used for the chamber at the top of a furnace, also called a bonnet, from which ducts emerge to conduct heated or conditioned air to the inhabited spaces of the building. It is also commonly used to refer to the open area between the bottom of a floor structure and the top of the ceiling assembly below. In some cases, air is carried through this space without ducting, a design called an open plenum.

Building codes limit where open plenum systems can run in a building, prohibit combustible materials in plenum spaces, and allow only certain types of wiring. Equipment in the plenum sometimes continues vertically down a structurally created shaft. The open plenum must be isolated from other spaces so that debris in the plenum and vertical shaft is not drawn into a return air intake.

The area between the floor above and ceiling below is usually full of electrical, plumbing, heating and cooling, lighting, fire suppression, and other equipment (Fig. 3-1). As an interior designer, you will often be concerned with how you can locate lighting or other design elements in relation to all the equipment in the plenum.

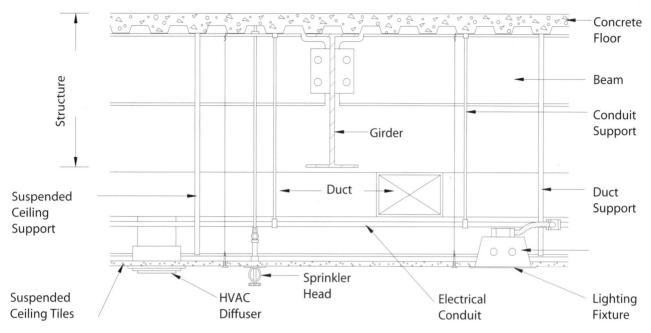

Figure 3-1 Floor/ceiling assembly.

SERVICE CORES

In most multistory buildings, the stairs, elevators, toilet rooms, and supply closets are grouped together in service cores. The mechanical, plumbing, and electrical chases, which carry wires and pipes vertically from one floor to the next, also use the service cores, along with the electrical and telephone closets, service closets, and fire protection equipment. Often, the plan of these areas varies little, if at all, from one floor to the next.

Service cores may have different ceiling heights and layouts than the rest of the floor. Mechanical equipment rooms may need higher ceilings for big pipes and ducts. Some functions, such as toilets, stairs, and elevator waiting areas, benefit from daylight, fresh air, and views, so access to the building perimeter can be a priority.

Service cores can take up a considerable amount of space. Along with the entry lobby and loading docks, service areas may nearly fill the ground floor as well as the roof and basement. Their locations must be coordinated with the structural layout of the building. In addition, they must coordinate with patterns of space use and activity. The clarity and distance of the circulation path from the farthest rentable area to the service core have a direct impact on the building's safety in a fire.

There are several common service core layouts (Fig. 3-2). Central cores are the most frequent type. In high-rise office buildings, a single service core provides the maximum amount of unobstructed rentable area. This allows for shorter electrical, mechanical, and plumbing runs and more efficient distribution paths. Some buildings locate the service core along one edge of the building, leaving more unobstructed floor space but occupying part of the perimeter and blocking daylight and views. Detached cores are located outside the body of the building to save usable floor space, but require long service runs. Using two symmetrically placed cores reduces service runs, but the remaining floor space loses some flexibility in layout and use.

Multiple cores are sometimes found in broad, low-rise buildings. Long horizontal runs are thus avoided, and mechanical equipment can serve zones with different requirements for heating and cooling. Multiple cores are used in apartment buildings and structures made of repetitive units, with the cores located between units along interior corridors.

BUILDING MATERIALS

The selection of building materials affects both the quality of the building itself and the environment beyond the building. When we look at the energy efficiency of a building, we should also consider the embodied energy used to manufacture and transport the materials from which the building is made.

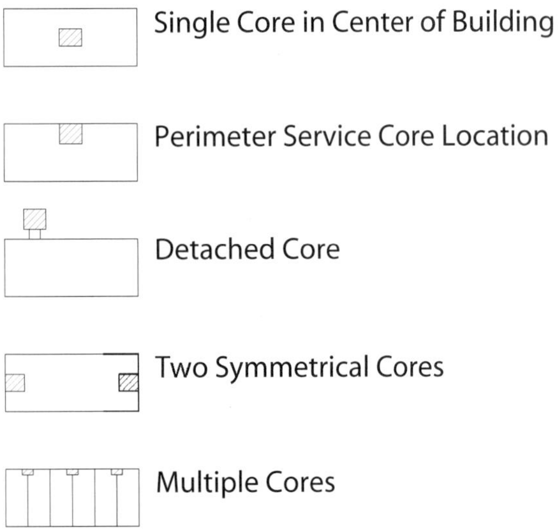

Single Core in Center of Building

Perimeter Service Core Location

Detached Core

Two Symmetrical Cores

Multiple Cores

Figure 3-2 Service core locations.

Power plants that supply electricity for buildings use very large quantities of water, which is returned at a warmer temperature, or as vapor. Mechanical and electrical systems use metals and plastics, along with some clay. These materials are selected for their strength, durability, and fire resistance, as well as their electrical resistance or conductivity. Their environmen-tal impact involves the energy cost to mine, fabricate, and transport them.

THE DESIGN TEAM

In the past, architects were directly responsible for the design of the entire building. Heating and ventilating consisted primarily of steam radiators and operable windows. Lighting and power systems were also rela-tively uncomplicated. Some parts of buildings, such as sinks, bathtubs, cooking ranges, and dishwashers, were considered separate items in the past, but are now less portable and more commonly viewed as fixed parts of the building. Portable oil lamps have been replaced by lighting fixtures that are an integral part of the build-ing, tied into the electrical system.

Today, the architect typically serves as the leader and coordinator of a team of specialist consultants, includ-ing structural, mechanical, and electrical engineers, along with fire protection, acoustic, lighting, and eleva-tor specialists. Interior designers work either directly for the architect as part of the architectural team, or serve as consultants to the architect. Energy-conscious design requires close coordination of the entire design team from the earliest design stages.

The Human Body and the Built Environment

• • •

Buildings provide environments where people can feel comfortable and safe. To understand the ways building systems are designed to meet these needs, we must first look at how the human body perceives and reacts to interior environments.

MAINTAINING THERMAL EQUILIBRIUM

Our perception that our surroundings are too cold or too hot is based on many factors beyond the temperature of the air. The season, the clothes we are wearing, the amount of humidity and air movement, and the presence of heat given off by objects in the space all influence our comfort. Contact with surfaces or moving air, or with heat radiating from an object, produces the sensation of heat or cold. There is a wide range of temperatures that will be perceived as comfortable for one individual over time and in varying situations. We can regulate the body's heat loss with three layers of protection: the skin, clothing, and buildings.

The human body operates as an engine that produces heat. The fuel is the food we eat, in the form of proteins, carbohydrates, and fats. The digestive process uses chem-

icals, bacteria, and enzymes to break down food. Useful substances are pumped into the bloodstream and carried throughout the body. Waste products are filtered out during digestion and stored for elimination.

The normal internal body temperature is around 37°C (98.6°F). The internal temperature of the human body can't vary by more than a few degrees without causing physical distress. Our bodies turn only about one-fifth of the food energy we consume into mechanical work. The other four-fifths of this energy is given off as heat or stored as fat. The body requires continuous cooling to give off all this excess heat.

An individual's metabolism sets the rate at which energy is used. This metabolic rate changes with body weight, activity level, body surface area, health, sex, and age. The amount of clothing a person is wearing and the surrounding thermal and atmospheric conditions also influence the metabolic rate. It increases when we have a fever, during continuous activity, and in cold conditions if we are not wearing warm clothes. Our metabolic rates are highest at age 10, and lowest in old age. The weight of heavy winter clothing may add 10 to 15 percent to the metabolic rate. Pregnancy and lactation increase the rate by about 10 percent.

The amount of heat our bodies produce depends on what we are doing. An average-sized person who

70 W

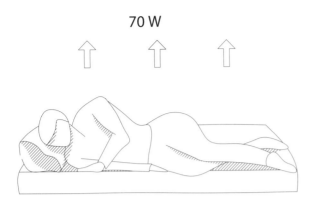

Figure 4-1 Resting person.

200 W

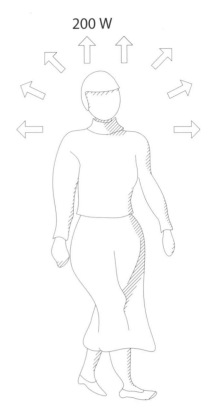

Figure 4-3 Person walking.

is resting gives off about the same amount of heat as a 70-watt (70-W) incandescent lightbulb (Fig. 4-1). When that person is sitting at a desk, the heat generated rises to about that of a 100-W lightbulb (Fig. 4-2). The same person walking down the street at two miles per hour generates around the amount of heat given off by a 200-W lightbulb (Fig. 4-3). During vigorous exercise, the amount rises to between 300 and 870 W (Fig. 4-4). This is why a room full of people doing aerobic exercise heats up fairly quickly.

The set of conditions that allows our bodies to stay at the normal body temperature with the minimal amount of bodily regulation is called thermal equilibrium. We feel uncomfortable when the body works too hard to maintain its thermal equilibrium. We experience thermal comfort when heat production equals heat loss. Our mind feels alert, our body operates at maximum efficiency, and we are at our most productive. As designers of interior spaces, our goal is to create environ-

300-870 W

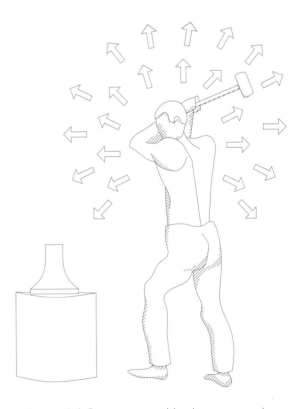

Figure 4-4 Person engaged in vigorous exercise.

100 W

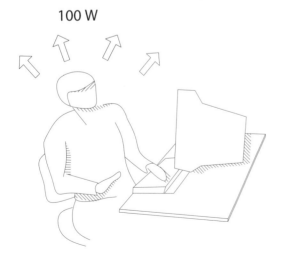

Figure 4-2 Person working at desk.

ments where people are neither too hot nor too cold to function comfortably and efficiently.

Studies have shown that industrial accidents increase at higher and at lower than normal temperatures, when our bodies struggle to run properly. When we are cold, we lose too much heat too quickly, especially from the back of the neck, the head, the back, and the arms and legs. When the body loses too much heat, we become lethargic and mentally dull. The heart pumps an increased amount of the blood directly to the skin and back to the heart, bypassing the brain and other organs. This puts an increased strain on the heart. Because we transfer heat from one part of the body to another through the bloodstream, it is sometimes difficult to figure out where the heat loss is actually occurring. We may need to wear a hat to keep our feet warm!

Our skin surface provides a layer of insulation between the body's interior and the environment, about equal in effect to putting on a light sweater. When the body loses more heat to a cold environment than it produces, it attempts to decrease the heat loss by constricting the outer blood vessels, reducing the blood flow to the outer surface of the skin. Goose bumps result when our skin tries to fluff up our meager body hairs to provide more insulation. If there continues to be too much heat loss, involuntary muscle action causes us to shiver, which increases heat production. We fold our arms and close our legs to reduce exposed area. When the level of heat loss is too great, muscle tension makes us hunch up, a strained posture that produces physical exhaustion. Ultimately, when deep body temperatures fall, we experience hypothermia, which can result in a coma or death. The slide toward hypothermia can be reversed by exercise to raise heat production, or by hot food and drink and a hot bath or sauna.

When we get too hot, the blood flow to the skin's surface increases, sweat glands secrete salt and water, and we lose body heat through evaporation of water from our skin. Water constantly evaporates from our respiratory passages and lungs; the air we exhale is usually saturated with water. In high humidity, evaporation is slow and the rate of perspiration increases as the body tries to compensate. When the surrounding air approaches body temperature, only evaporation by dry, moving air will lower our body temperature.

Overheating, like being too cold, increases fatigue and decreases our resistance to disease. If the body is not cooled, deep-body temperature rises and impairs metabolic functions, which can result in heat stroke and death. We will be looking at strategies for designing spaces that allow occupants to keep warm or cool enough to function in comfort.

EARS AND EYES

The buildings we design should help us use our senses comfortably and efficiently. We can easily block out unwanted sights by closing our eyes or turning away, but we can't stop our ears from hearing, and we receive unwanted sounds with little regard for the direction we face. Loud sounds can damage our hearing, especially over time. We have trouble hearing sounds that are much less intense than the background noise. The art and science of acoustics addresses how these issues affect the built environment.

Our eyes can be damaged if we look even quickly at the sun, or for too long at a bright snow landscape or light-colored sand. Direct glare from lighting fixtures can blind us momentarily. Interior designers should avoid strong contrasts that can make vision difficult or painful, for example, a very bright object against a very dark background or a dark object against light. Low illumination levels reduce our ability to see well. The adjustment to moderately low light levels can take several minutes, an important consideration when designing entryways between the outdoors (which may be very bright or very dark) and the building's interior. Lighting levels and daylighting are important parts of interior design.

OTHER HUMAN ENVIRONMENTAL REQUIREMENTS

We need a regular supply of water to move the products of food processing around the body. Water also helps cool the body. We need food and drinking water that is free from harmful microorganisms. Contaminated food and water spread hepatitis and typhoid. Building systems are designed to remove body and food wastes promptly for safe processing. We look at these issues in Part II of this book, on Water and Wastes.

We must have air to breathe for the oxygen it contains, which is the key to the chemical reactions that combust (burn) the food-derived fuels that keep our body operating. When we breathe air into our lungs, some oxygen dissolves into the bloodstream. We exhale air mixed with carbon dioxide and water, which are produced as wastes of combustion. Less than one-fifth of the air's oxygen is replaced by carbon dioxide with each lungful, but a constant supply of fresh air is required to avoid unconsciousness from oxygen depletion and carbon dioxide accumulation. Building ventilation systems assure that the air we breathe indoors is fresh and clean.

The human body is attacked by a very large assortment of bacteria, viruses, and fungi. Our skin, respiratory system, and digestive tract offer a supportive environment for microorganisms. Some of these are helpful, or at least benign, but some cause disease and discomfort. Our buildings provide facilities for washing food, dishes, skin, hair, and clothes to keep these other life forms under control. Poorly designed or maintained buildings can be breeding grounds for microorganisms. These are issues for both the design of building sanitary waste systems and indoor air quality (IAQ).

Our buildings exclude disease-carrying rodents and insects. Pests spread typhus, yellow fever, malaria, sleeping sickness, encephalitis, plague, and various parasites. Inadequate ventilation encourages tuberculosis and other respiratory diseases. Adequate ventilation carries away airborne bacteria and excess moisture. Sunlight entering the building dries and sterilizes our environment.

Our soft tissues, organs, and bones need protection from hard and sharp objects. Smooth floor surfaces prevent trips and ankle damage. Our buildings help us move up and down from different levels without danger of falling, and keep fire and hot objects away from our skin. The interior designer must always be on the alert for aspects of a design that could cause harm from falling objects, explosions, poisons, corrosive chemicals, harmful radiation, or electric shocks. By designing spaces with safe surfaces, even and obvious level changes, and appropriately specified materials, we protect the people who use our buildings. Our designs help prevent and suppress fires, as well as facilitating escape from a burning building.

SOCIAL REQUIREMENTS

Buildings give us space to move, to work, and to play. Our residential designs support family life with a place for the reproduction and rearing of children, preparing and sharing food with family and friends, studying, and communicating verbally, manually, and electronically. We provide spaces and facilities to pursue hobbies and to clean and repair the home. Our designs create opportunities to display and store belongings, and many of us now work at home, adding another level of complexity to these spaces. The spaces we design may be closed and private at times, and open to the rest of the world at others. We design buildings that are secure from intrusion, and provide ways to communicate both within and beyond the building's interior. We provide stairways and mechanical means of conveyance from one level to another for people with varied levels of mobility.

Our designs also support all the social activities that occur outside of the home. We provide power to buildings so that workshops, warehouses, markets, offices, studios, barns, and laboratories can design, produce, and distribute goods. These workplaces require the same basic supports for life activities as our homes, plus accommodations for the tasks they house. Humans also gather in groups to worship, exercise, play, entertain, govern, educate, and to study or observe objects of interest. These communal spaces are even more complex, as they must satisfy the needs of many people at once.

C h a p t e r

5

Building Codes

●●●

When people gather together for activities, building functions become more complex, and there is a greater chance that someone will be injured. Governments respond to concerns for safety by developing building codes. These codes dictate both the work of the interior designer and architect, and the way in which the building's mechanical, electrical, plumbing, and other systems are designed and installed.

Around 1800, many of the larger U.S. cities developed their own municipal building codes in response to a large number of building fires. In the middle of the nineteenth century, the National Board of Fire Underwriters provided insurance companies with information for fire damage claims, resulting in the National Building Code in 1905. This became the basis for the three model codes we use today.

The Building Officials Code Administrators International (BOCA) publishes the *BOCA National Building Code* (NBC). The Southern Building Code Congress International (SBCCI) publishes the *Standard Building Code* (SBC), and the International Conference of Building Officials (ICBO) publishes the *Uniform Building Code* (UBC). Each state or community either adopts one of these three model codes or bases its own code on one of them. Because different parts of the United States have their own environmental and climatic issues that

affect building construction, each model code is somewhat different from the others.

For interior design use, the three model building codes are very similar. Each includes chapters relating to the design of the building's interiors, including Use or Occupancy Classifications, the Special Use or Occupancy Requirements, and the Types of Construction sections. You will find yourself referring often to the sections covering Fire-Resistant Materials and Construction, Interior Finishes, Fire Protection Systems, Means of Egress, and Accessibility when laying out spaces and selecting materials.

The *ICC International Performance Code* (IPC) is a fourth model building code that attempts to unify code requirements across geographic barriers. Introduced by the International Codes Council (ICC) in 2002, the IPC is in the process of being adopted by states and other jurisdictions.

The model building codes frequently refer to other codes and standards. Each model code organization also publishes other codes, including a plumbing code, a mechanical code, a fire prevention code, and an existing structures code.

The jurisdiction of a project is determined by the location of the building. A jurisdiction is a geographical area that uses the same codes, standards, and regulations. A jurisdiction may be as small as a township or as large as an entire state.

Most jurisdictions have strict requirements as to who can design a project and what types of drawings are required for an interior project. Often, drawings must be stamped by a licensed architect or licensed engineer registered within the state. In some cases, interior designers are not permitted to be in charge of a project, and may have to work as part of an architect's team. Some states may allow registered interior designers to stamp drawings for projects in buildings with three or fewer stories and below a certain number of square feet. Working out the proper relationships with the architects and engineers on your team is critical to meeting the code requirements.

Another important task is keeping current on code requirements. Some states have statewide codes based on a model code, while others have local codes, and sometimes both state and local codes cover an area. Not every jurisdiction updates its codes on a regular basis, which means that in a particular jurisdiction, the code cited may not be the most current edition of that code. The designer must check with the local jurisdiction for which codes to follow. When codes are changed, one or more yearly addenda are published with the changes, and incorporated in the body of the code when the next full edition of the code is published. Designers must make provisions for acquiring these addenda, through a code update subscription service or other notification process.

CODE OFFICIALS

The codes department is the local government agency that enforces the codes within a jurisdiction. The size of the codes department varies with the size of the jurisdiction it serves. A code official is an employee of the codes department with authority to interpret and enforce codes, standards, and regulations within that jurisdiction. The plans examiner (Fig. 5-1) is a code official who checks plans and construction drawings at both the preliminary and final permit review stages of the project. The plans examiner checks for code and standards compliance, and works most closely with the designer.

The fire marshal usually represents the local fire department. The fire marshal checks drawings with the plans examiner during preliminary and final reviews, looking for fire code compliance.

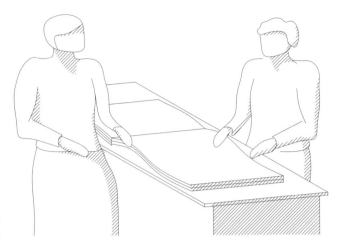

Figure 5-1 Reviewing plans.

The building inspector visits the project job site after the building permit is issued, and makes sure all construction complies with the codes as specified in the construction drawings and in code publications.

SPECIAL CODES AND THE INTERIOR DESIGNER

In addition to the basic building code, jurisdictions issue plumbing, mechanical, and electrical codes. Interior designers are not generally required to know or to research most plumbing or mechanical code issues. On projects with a major amount of plumbing or mechanical work, registered engineers will take responsibility for design and code issues. On smaller projects, a licensed plumber or mechanical contractor will know the codes. However, the interior designer needs to be aware of some plumbing and mechanical requirements, such as how to determine the number of required plumbing fixtures.

The interior designer often meets with the architect and engineers in the preliminary stages of the design process to coordinate the interior design with new and existing plumbing, mechanical, and electrical system components. The location of plumbing fixtures, sprinklers, fire extinguishers, air diffusers and returns, and other items covered by plumbing and mechanical codes must be coordinated with interior elements. The plumbing, mechanical, and electrical systems are often planned simultaneously, especially in large buildings. Vertical and horizontal chases are integrated into building cores and stairwells. Suspended ceiling and floor systems house mechanical, electrical, and plumbing components. The locations of these components affect the selection and placement of finished ceiling, walls, and floor systems. We look at the details of this coordination in other parts of this book.

STANDARDS AND ORGANIZATIONS

Codes cite standards developed by government agencies, trade associations, and standard-writing organizations as references. A standard may consist of a definition, recommended practice, test method, classification, or required specification.

The National Fire Protection Association (NFPA) was formed in 1896 to develop standards for the early use of sprinklers to put out fires. The NFPA develops and publishes about 250 standards in booklet form. The *Life Safety Code* and the *National Electric Code* (NEC) are both NFPA publications that provide guidelines for fire safety. The NFPA establishes testing requirements covering everything from textiles to fire fighting equipment to the design of means of egress.

The American National Standards Institute (ANSI) originated in 1918 to coordinate the development of voluntary standards and approve standards developed by other organizations, with an eye to avoiding duplications and establishing priorities. The standards developed by ANSI were the first to focus on achieving independence for people with disabilities by focusing on accessible features in building design, and provided a basis for the Americans with Disabilities Act (ADA).

The American Society for Testing and Materials (ASTM) dates to 1898, and its standards are used to specify materials and assure quality. The ASTM methods integrate production processes, promote trade, and enhance safety. While ASTM's 69 volumes of standards include all types of products, a separate two-volume set of about 600 standards covers the building construction industry.

In 1959, the American Society of Heating, Refrigeration, and Air-Conditioning Engineers (ASHRAE) was formed to sponsor research projects and to develop performance level standards for heating, ventilating, and air-conditioning (HVAC) and refrigeration systems. Mechanical engineers and refrigeration specialists and installers use ASHRAE standards. As an interior designer, you will typically not need to refer to ASHRAE standards. However, Provision 90A: *Energy Conservation in New Building Design*, is the basis of most building code energy provisions in the United States, and will affect the total amount of energy use permitted for lighting, heating, and cooling, and other functions in the projects you design.

Underwriters Laboratories (UL) is a testing agency that tests products, systems, and materials, and determines their relationship to life, fire, casualty hazards, and crime prevention. Underwriters Laboratories, Inc. lists all the products it tests and approves in product directories. You will find UL tags on many household appliances, as well as on lighting and other electrical fixtures. Interior designers will find the *Building Materials, Fire Protection Equipment*, and *Fire Resistance* directories the most useful. Codes will require UL testing and approval for certain products, and you should specify tested products when they are required.

FEDERAL REGULATIONS

The federal government regulates the building of federal facilities, including federal buildings, Veterans Administration hospitals, and military establishments. The construction of federal buildings is typically not subject to state or local building codes and regulations. The federal government issues regulations for government built and owned buildings, similar to the model codes. On a particular project, the authorities involved may opt to comply with stricter local requirements, so the designer must verify what codes apply.

There are over 1000 separate codes and a wide variety of federal regulations. In an effort to limit federal regulation, the Consumer Product Safety Commission encourages industry self-regulation and standardization, and industry groups have formed hundreds of standards-writing organizations and trade associations representing almost every industry.

Congress can pass laws that supersede all other state and local codes and standards. The *Federal Register* publishes federal regulations daily. They are collected in the *Code of Federal Regulations*, which is revised annually. The Occupational Safety and Health Act (OSHA), Federal Housing Act (FHA), and Americans with Disabilities Act (ADA) are examples of congressionally passed laws with wide implications for interior designers and architects.

Occupational Safety and Health Administration

In 1970, the Occupational Safety and Health Act established the Occupational Safety and Health Administration (OSHA) as a branch of the Department of Labor responsible for protecting employees in the workplace. This administration adds to code requirements by regulating the design of buildings and interior projects where people are employed, in order to ensure the safety of employees in the workplace. Contractors and subcontractors on construction projects must strictly adhere to OSHA requirements. The regulations put forth by OSHA stress safe installation of materials and equipment in order to create a safe work environment for construction workers and for future building occupants. Interior designers should be aware that these regulations exist and that they affect the process of building construction and installation of equipment and furnishings.

Americans with Disabilities Act

The term "accessible" in building codes refers to handicapped accessibility as required by codes, the Americans with Disabilities Act (ADA), and other accessibility standards. The Departments of Justice and Transportation developed the provisions of the ADA, which was passed by Congress in 1990 and became enforceable in 1992 and 1993. In addition, some states also have their own accessibility standards.

The ADA is a comprehensive civil rights law with four sections. Title I protects individuals with disabilities in employment. Title II covers state and local government services and public transportation. Title III covers all public accommodations, defined as any facility that offers food or services to the public. It also applies to commercial facilities, which are nonresidential buildings that do business but are not open to the general public. Title IV deals with telecommunications services, and requires telephone companies to provide telecommunications relay services for individuals with hearing and speech impairments. Titles III and IV affect the work of interior designers most directly, and we refer to ADA provisions throughout this book.

The regulations included in Title III have been incorporated into the *Americans with Disabilities Act Accessibility Guidelines* (ADAAG). The text of the ADAAG is law, but its appendix, which offers helpful information on interpretation and compliance, is not binding. The ADAAG deals with architectural concerns such as accessible routes and the design of restrooms for wheelchair access. Communication issues covered include alarms systems and signage for people with vision and hearing impairments.

All new buildings with public accommodations and/or commercial facilities must conform to specific ADAAG requirements. This includes a wide range of project types, including lodging, restaurants, hotels, and theaters. Shopping centers and malls, retail stores, banks, places of public assembly, museums, and galleries are also covered. Libraries, private schools, day care centers, and professional offices are all included. State and local government buildings and one- and two-family dwellings are not required to conform.

The requirements of the ADA are most stringent for new buildings or additions to existing buildings. The laws are not as clear concerning renovation of existing buildings and interiors. When an existing building is renovated, specific areas of the building must be altered to conform to ADA requirements. These alterations are limited to those deemed readily achievable in terms of structure and cost. Exemptions may be made for undue burden as a result of the difficulty or expense of an alteration. These situations are determined on a case-by-case basis by regulatory authorities or the courts, and often involve difficult judgment calls. For example, if a restaurant must add an elevator in order to expand into a second floor space, will the added seating create enough income to offset the cost of the alterations? If the business expands but doesn't provide access for people who aren't able to use stairs, they risk the bad publicity and embarrassment of a lawsuit and perhaps a public protest, and the even greater cost of retrofitting the space after the initial renovation. Sometimes there is no fair and easy answer.

Federal Housing Act

The U.S. Department of Housing and Urban Development (HUD) enforces the Federal Housing Act, which prohibits discrimination and provides protection for people with disabilities and for families with children. It applies to housing with four or more units. Such buildings must have public and common areas accessible to people with disabilities. At least the ground floor units must be accessible and must meet specific construction requirements. The FHA is essentially a residential version of the ADA.

The three model code organizations recognize the *One and Two Family Dwelling Code* (OTFDC). This is not a federal regulation, but has been adopted by many jurisdictions in the United States. The OTFDC is the main code used for construction of single and duplex family residences.

Part

II

WATER AND WASTES

Chapter 6

Sources of Water

Water makes up most of our bodies and also most of what we eat. In addition to the water we drink, the average home in the United States uses 53 liters (14 gallons) per person each day for washing clothes and dishes, and 79 liters (21 gallons) a day for bathing and personal hygiene. The typical home flushes 121 liters (32 gallons) per day down the toilet. That adds up to 958 liters (253 gallons) of water each day (Figs. 6-1, 6-2, 6-3). As interior designers, we want to help our clients conserve water while maintaining a good quality interior environment. In order to understand the role of water in the design of our buildings, let's start by looking at how we use it and where it comes from.

Water holds heat well and removes large quantities of heat when it evaporates. Because water will vaporize at skin temperatures, our bodies use evaporation to give off excess heat.

We associate water psychologically with cooling, and find water and splashing brooks or fountains refreshing. We employ sprays of water, evaporative coolers, and cooling towers to cool our buildings. We protect our buildings from fire with a system of very large pipes and valves that deliver water quickly to sprinkler systems.

In the past, communities used a municipal fountain or well as a water supply, and its sculptural form and central location made it the community's social hub. Today, a fountain or pool in the town center or in a shopping mall becomes a meeting place.

We celebrate the importance of water in our lives with ceremonial uses, which influence our feelings about the presence of water in our buildings. Christian churches practice baptism with water, sometimes including complete immersion of the person being baptized. The Jewish tradition includes ritual purification baths. Catholic churches have containers for holy water at their entrances, and pools are found in the forecourts of Islamic mosques.

Rivers and seas have historically connected countries. With the advent of the industrial revolution, factories were located along rivers to take advantage of water for power and for transportation. We use water to generate electricity at hydroelectric plants.

Water is often the focus of landscaping, inside or outside of the building. Reflections in water contrast with plantings and ground covers, and the sparkle, sound, and motion of water attract our attention. Water in a garden supports the growth of desirable plants and animals. Traditional Islamic architectural gardens in arid regions take advantage of small, tightly controlled channels to bring water into the center of buildings.

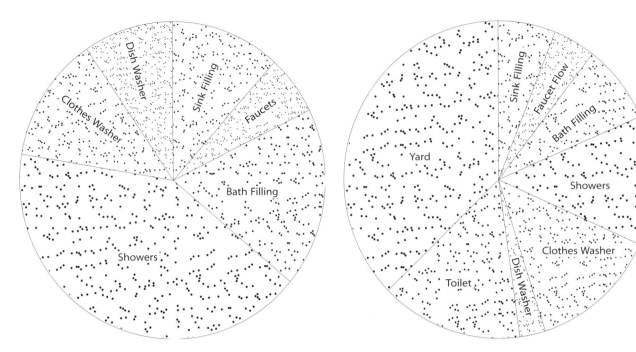

Figure 6-1 Residential hot water use.

Figure 6-3 Residential hot and cold water use combined.

THE HYDROLOGIC CYCLE

The total amount of water on the earth and in the atmosphere is finite, unless little icy comets melt in our atmosphere and contribute a small additional amount. The

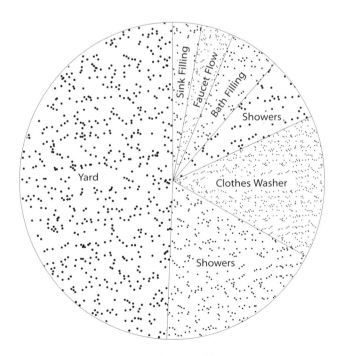

Figure 6-2 Residential cold water use.

water we use today is the same water that was in Noah's proverbial flood. Ninety-nine percent of the earth's water is either saltwater or glacial ice. A quarter of the solar energy reaching the earth is employed in constantly circulating water through evaporation and precipitation, in a process known as the hydrologic cycle (Fig. 6-4).

The most accessible sources of water for our use are precipitation and runoff. Rain, snow, and other precipitation provide a very large but thinly spread supply of relatively pure water. Precipitation can be captured on a local basis in cisterns (containers for rainwater), a strategy that is rarely used in the United States but widely found in other parts of the world where rains are rare and water is precious. Water that runs off the earth's surface results in a more concentrated flow that is more easily captured in cisterns or ponds. Any daily precipitation that doesn't evaporate or run off is retained as soil moisture. After plants use it to grow, it evaporates back into the atmosphere.

Groundwater sinks into the soil and fills the open spaces with water. The upper surface of the groundwater is called the water table. Groundwater makes up the majority of our water supply. It can also be used to store excess building heat in the summer for use in the building in winter. Groundwater can harm building foundations when it leaks into spaces below ground.

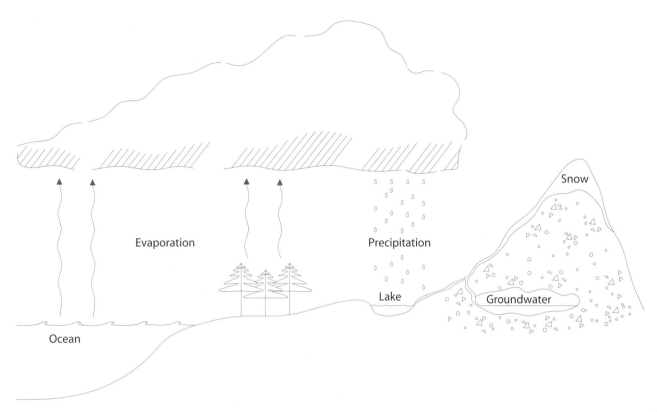

Figure 6-4 The hydrologic cycle.

RAINWATER

The earliest agrarian societies depended upon rain for agriculture. Historically, rain falling in the countryside ran into creeks, streams, and rivers, and rivers rarely ran dry. Rainfall was absorbed into the ground, which served as a huge reservoir. The water that accumulated underground emerged as springs and artesian wells, or in lakes, swamps, and marshes. Most of the water that leaked into the ground cleansed itself in the weeks, months, or years it took to get back to an aquifer, which is a water-bearing rock formation.

Early towns developed near rivers for access to transportation and wells. Streets sloped to drain in the river, which ran to river basins and the sea. Later on, marshy areas were filled in and buildings were built, along with paved streets and sidewalks. Storm sewers and pumping stations were constructed to carry away the water. The rapid runoff increased the danger of flooding, and concentrated pollutants in waterways. Water ran out of the ground into overflowing storm sewers, without recharging groundwater levels.

Today, subdivisions slope from lawns at the top to street storm drains at the bottom. Once water enters a storm drain, it dumps out in rivers far away from where it started. Huge amounts of storm water also leak into sewer pipes that mix it with sewage and take it even farther away to be processed at treatment plants. The result is a suburban desert, with lawns that need watering and restricted local water supplies.

In most of the United States, the rainwater that falls on the roof of a home is of adequate quality and quantity to provide about 95 percent of indoor residential water requirements. However, a typical U.S. suburban household could not meet all its water needs with rain off the roof without modifying the members' water use habits. Rainwater can make a major contribution to the irrigation of small lawns and gardens when a rain barrel below a downspout or cisterns located above the level of the garden collect and store water for later release.

For centuries, traditional builders have incorporated rainwater into their designs. In the world's drier regions, small cisterns within the home collect rainwater to supplement unreliable public supplies. With the advent of central water and energy supplies in industrial societies, rainwater collection and use became less common. It has become easier to raise the funds (with costs spread to consumers in monthly bills) to build a water treatment plant with the related network of pipes than to convince individuals to collect, store, and recycle their own water. An individual who chooses to use rainwater to flush toilets must pay for this private system up front, and continue to pay through taxes for municipal water treatment, so conservation can add expense.

Designing buildings to hold onto even a part of the 50 to 80 percent of rainwater that drains from many communities requires a radical rethinking of how neighborhoods are built. Recently, progress has been made in designing building sites to improve surface and groundwater qualities. The community master plan for the Coffee Creek Center, a new residential development located 50 miles southeast of Chicago, was completed in 1998 by William McDonough + Partners. Coffee Creek itself is being revived with deep-rooted native plants that build healthy and productive soil and assure biological resiliency and variety. A storm water system makes use of the native ecosystem to absorb and retain rainwater, while wastewater will be treated on site, using natural biological processes in a system of constructed wetlands.

In Bellingham, Massachusetts, workers are ripping up unnecessary asphalt to let rainwater into the ground. Concrete culverts are being replaced with tall grasses to slow runoff from parking lots. Cisterns under school roofs will catch rainwater for watering lawns. Tiny berms around a model home's lawn are designed to hold water until it is absorbed into the ground, and a basin under the driveway will catch water, filter out any motor oil, and inject the water back into the lawn.

In Foxborough, Massachusetts, the Neponset River is being liberated from under the grounds of Foxborough Stadium. The Neponset was partially buried in culverts in the late 1940s, and weeds and debris choked the remaining exposed portion. Plastic fencing and hay bales appeared to imprison the stream in an attempt to halt erosion. The river is now being freed into a 20-meter (65-ft) wide channel and wetlands corridor on the edge of the new stadium complex, creating a 915-meter (3000-ft) riverfront consisting of an acre of open water, four acres of vegetated wetland, and three acres of vegetated upland. The new 68,000-seat Gillette Stadium will use graywater to flush the toilets that football fans use on game days. Storm basins that drain into retention ponds filter out the oil, salt, and antifreeze that collect in parking areas. The project also includes a 946,000-liter (250,000-gallon) per day wastewater treatment facility and extensive use of recycled construction materials.

Acid rain, a result of air pollution in the northeastern United States, Canada, and some other parts of the world, makes some rainwater undesirable. Dust and bird droppings on collection surfaces and fungicides used for moss control can pollute the supply. Steep roofs tend to stay cleaner and collect less dirt in the rainwater.

PROTECTING THE WATER SUPPLY

Individual water use has increased dramatically in the recent past. People in Imperial Rome used about 144 liters (38 gallons) a day, and the use in London in 1912 was only 151 liters (40 gallons) per person. Just before World War II, typical daily use in American cities was up to about 435 liters (115 gallons). By the mid-1970s, Los Angeles inhabitants were using 689 liters (182 gallons) per person each day.

Our current practices use large amounts of high-quality water for low-grade tasks like flushing toilets. Better conservation practices reserve high-quality water for high-quality tasks like drinking and preparing food, reduce overall use, and recycle water for lower quality uses.

The increasing population and consumption per person puts pressures on the limited supply of clean water, threatening world health and political stability. When people upstream use more than their share of water, people downstream suffer. Agriculture and industry use very large quantities of water. Building and landscape designs often disregard water conservation to make an impression through water use. Extravagant watering of golf courses and swimming pools in desert areas flaunt an affluent lifestyle at the expense of other priorities. Water pumped out of coastal areas pulls saltwater into freshwater aquifers.

As the world's water use rose from about 10 to 50 percent of the available annual water supply between 1950 and 1980, available potable water declined rapidly. Potable water is water that is free of harmful bacteria and safe to drink or use for food preparation. The water carried from the public water supply to individual buildings in water mains—large underground pipes—must be potable.

Protecting and conserving our clean water supplies is critical to our health. Until recently, a reliable supply of clean water was not always available, and epidemic diseases continue to be spread through unsanitary water supplies. Water from ponds or streams in built-up areas is unsafe to drink, as it may contain biological or chemical pollution.

Bacteria were unknown to science until discovered in Germany in 1892. In 1817, thousands of people in India died from cholera. The epidemic spread to New

York City by 1832, causing panic. A breakthrough came in 1854, when a London physician showed that local cases could be traced to one water pump that had been contaminated by sewage from a nearby house. Cholera remains a great danger today, with an epidemic originating in Indonesia in 1961 traveling slowly around the world to reach Latin America in 1991.

In 1939, typhoid carried through the water supply killed 30 people at an Illinois mental hospital. Typhus and enteritis sickened people in Rochester, New York, when polluted river water was accidentally pumped into supply mains in 1940. As recently as 1993, cryptosporidiosis microorganisms in a poorly maintained public water supply in Milwaukee, Wisconsin, killed 104 people and made 400,000 people ill.

Proper collection, treatment, and distribution of water protect our supplies. Rainwater has almost no bacteria, and only small amounts of minerals and gases. Many communities collect clean water from rain running down mountainsides into valleys in reservoirs. They limit human access to these areas to avoid contamination. Large aqueduct pipes carry the water from the reservoir to communities, usually by gravity flow. Communities without access to relatively uninhabited mountain areas make do with water of less purity from rivers, or tap underground water flows with wells.

The availability of clean water determines where homes and businesses are located, and how many people can live in or visit an area. Water from wells and mountain reservoirs needs relatively little treatment. River water is sent through sand filters and settling basins, where particles are removed. Additional chemical treatment precipitates iron and lead compounds. Special filters are used for hydrogen sulfide, radon, and other dissolved gases. Finally, chlorine dissolved in water kills harmful microorganisms. The result is an increased supply of clean water to support the development of residential and commercial construction.

WATER SUPPLY SYSTEMS

Water mains (Fig. 6-5) are large pipes that transport water for a public water system from its source to service connections at buildings. A service pipe installed by the public water utility runs from the water main to the building, far enough underground so that it doesn't freeze in winter. Within the building or in a curb box, a water meter measures and records the quantity of water passing through the service pipe and usually also monitors sewage disposal services. A control valve is lo-

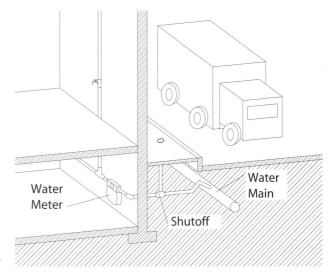

Figure 6-5 Public water supply.

cated in the curb box to shut off the water supply to the building in an emergency or if the building owner fails to pay the water bill. A shutoff valve within the building also controls the water supply.

In rural areas and in many small communities, each building must develop its own water supply. Most rely on wells, supplemented by rainwater and by reliable springs where available.

Wells

Wells supply water of more reliable quantity and quality than a rainwater system. Water near the surface may have seeped into the ground from the immediate area, and may be contaminated by sewage, barnyards, outhouses, or garbage dumps nearby. Deep wells are expensive to drill, but the water deep underground comes from hundreds of miles away, and the long trip filters out most bacteria. Well water sometimes contains dissolved minerals, most of which are harmless. Hard water results from calcium salts in the water, which can build up inside hot water pipes and cause scaling. Hard water can also turn soap into scum. A water softener installed on the pipe leading to the hot water heater will help control it.

Well water is usually potable, if the source is deep enough. It should be pure, cool, and free of discoloration and odor problems. The local health department will check samples for bacterial and chemical content before use. Wells are sunk below the water table so that they are not affected by seasonal fluctuations in the water level. Pumps bring the water from the well to the surface, where it is stored in tanks under constant pressure to compensate for variations in the flow from the well. The water can be filtered and chlorinated at this point. Pumps and pressure tanks are usually housed in outbuildings kept above freezing temperatures.

The use of water should be related to its quality. Almost every North American building has potable water. In most buildings, the majority of this clean water is used to carry away organic wastes.

When water is used efficiently and supplied locally, less water is removed from rivers, lakes, and underground aquifers. Less energy and chemicals are required for treatment and delivery, and less storm water is wasted and discharged to pollute rivers, eliminating the need for additional expensive water treatment plants. Interior designers can help to conserve clean water by specifying efficient fixtures and considering the use of recycled water where appropriate.

Municipal Water Supply Systems

The water in a community's water mains is under pressure to offset friction and gravity as it flows through the pipes. The water pressure in public water supplies is usually at or above 345 kilopascals (kPa), which is equal to 50 lb per square in. (psi). This is also about the maximum achieved by private well systems, and is adequate pressure for buildings up to six stories high. For taller buildings, or where the water pressure is lower, water is pumped to a rooftop storage tank and distributed by gravity, a system called gravity downfeed. The water storage tank can also double as a reserve for a fire protection system.

Once the water is inside the building, its pressure is changed by the size of the pipes it travels through. Bigger pipes put less pressure on the water flow, while small pipes increase the pressure. If the water rises up high in the building, gravity and friction combine to decrease the pressure. The water pressure at individual fixtures within the building may vary between 35 and 204 kPa (5–30 psi). Too much pressure causes splashing; too little produces a slow dribble. Water supply pipes are sized to use up the difference between the service pressure and the pressure required for each fixture. If the pressure is still too high, pressure reducers or regulators are installed on fixtures.

Water Quality

●●●

Whether you are working on a new building or a renovation, problems may arise with the quality of the water. Pesticides, cleaning solvents, and seepage from landfills pollute groundwater in some rural areas of the United States (Fig. 7-1). In urban areas, the level of chlorine added to prevent bacterial contamination sometimes results in bad tasting water and deterioration of pipes and plumbing fixtures.

Electric power plants discharge great amounts of waste heat into water, which can change biological and chemical conditions and threaten fish. Steel, paper, and textiles are the most polluting industries. The textile industry employs large quantities of water in fiber production and processing and in fabric finishing, especially dyeing. As a designer, you have the power to avoid products whose manufacturing includes highly toxic technologies, and to seek out ones with low environmental impact.

WATER QUALITY CHARACTERISTICS

How do you tell whether the water you drink is safe? Communities routinely check on the quality of their municipal water supplies. If a home or business owner is unsure whether his or her building's supply meets safety standards, a government or private water quality analyst will provide instructions and containers for taking samples, and assess the purity of the water supply. The analyst's report gives numerical values for mineral content, acidity or alkalinity (pH level), contamination, turbidity, total solids, and biological purity, and an opinion on the sample's suitability for its intended use.

Physical Characteristics

Even though cloudy or odd-smelling water may not actually be harmful to drink, we generally object to these physical characteristics. Turbidity—a muddy or cloudy appearance—is caused by suspended clay, silt, or other particles, or by plankton or other small organic material. Color changes can be due to dissolved organic matter, such as decaying vegetation, or other materials like rust. Like turbidity, color changes don't usually threaten health. Unpleasant taste and odor can be caused by organic materials, salts, or dissolved gases, and can often be treated after being diagnosed. Foaming is not necessarily a health threat, but may indicate concentrations of detergents present in water contaminated by domestic wastes.

Most people prefer water at a temperature of 10°C

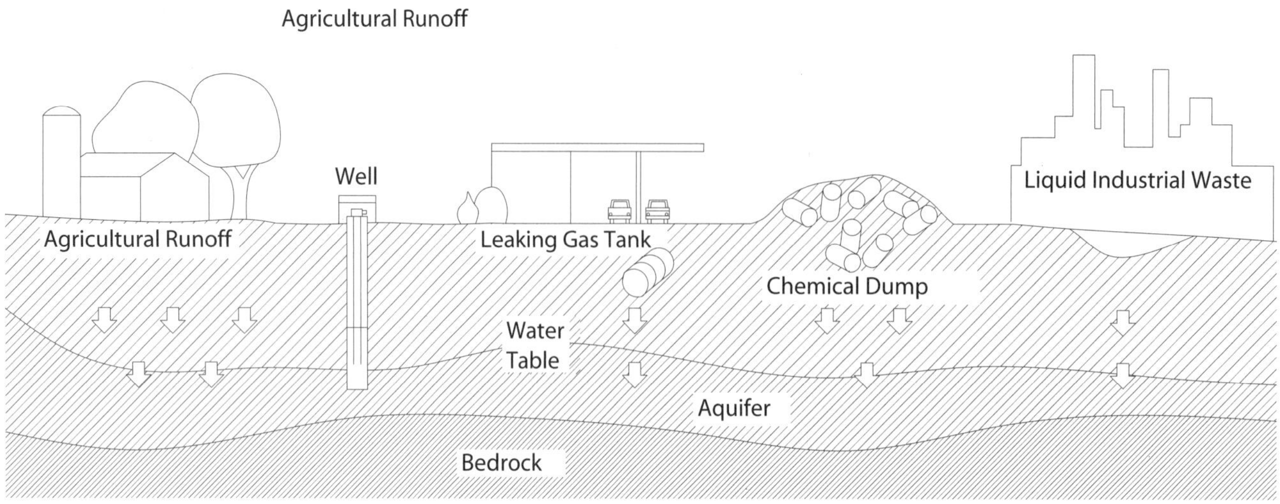

Agricultural Runoff

Figure 7-1 Groundwater contamination.

to 16°C (50°F–60°F) for drinking. When water standing in pipes becomes warmer, people often run it down the drain until it cools.

When water is piped under pressure throughout the plumbing system, air can become trapped in the water and cause cloudiness. This is only temporary and the water clears up in a short time. You can safely drink, cook with, or bathe in this water.

Chemical Characteristics

Groundwater dissolves minerals as it moves slowly down through the soil and rocks. Testing individual water supplies will detect harmful substances, corrosive chemicals, or chemicals that may stain fixtures and clothing. Corrosion produces scale that lines pipes and clogs openings. It is affected by water acidity, electrical conductivity, oxygen content, and carbon dioxide content. Acid neutralizers and corrosion inhibitors help, along with various preventive coatings and linings for pipes.

Tests for water pH determine relative alkalinity or acidity. A pH of 7 is neutral, with numbers as low as 5.5 indicating acid, corrosive conditions and as high as 9 representing alkaline conditions. If tap water stains tubs and sinks a bluish-green, it is overly acidic, and a neutralizing filter should be installed.

High alkaline or base levels entail bitter, slippery, and caustic qualities and are due to the presence of bicarbonate, carbonate, or hydroxide components. Bases have the ability to combine with acids to make salts. Hard water, caused by calcium and magnesium salts, in-

hibits the cleaning action of soaps and detergents and deposits scale inside hot water pipes and cooking utensils. The simplest way to acquire a supply of soft water for washing clothes is to collect rainwater in a cistern.

Toxic substances, including arsenic, barium, cadmium, chromium, cyanides, fluoride, lead, selenium, and silver, sometimes contaminate water. Lead poses the greatest threat to infants and young children with developing nervous systems. It is possible that lead levels in one home may be higher than levels at other homes in the same community as a result of lead solder or pipes used in the plumbing. Infants and children who drink water with high levels of lead may experience delays in their physical or mental development, showing slight deficits in attention span and learning abilities. Adults who drink this water over many years may develop kidney problems or high blood pressure. If you are concerned about a possibility of elevated lead levels in a water supply, you should have the water tested (municipal water utilities will usually do this for you). Flushing the tap for 30 seconds to two minutes before using the water will help the water supply stay fresh, but wastes a lot of water. Don't use hot water from the faucet for drinking or cooking, especially when making baby formula or other food for infants.

Arsenic occurs naturally in some water supplies. Arsenic in water can cause symptoms such as dry, hacking coughs and burning hands and feet, and increases the risk of lung, skin, or bladder cancer. A federal study in 2000 of the water supply in Fallon, Nevada, showed that customers were exposed to 90 parts per billion (ppb) of arsenic, more than any other large system. This is almost twice the standard set in 1975, and nine times the amount currently recommended by scientists and public health doctors. Even if the community supply is cleaned up, residents outside city limits rely on private wells where the arsenic frequently reaches 700 ppb and up to 2000 ppb.

Seepage of drainage from livestock manure can contaminate shallow wells with nitrates, which in high concentrations cause a condition commonly known as "blue baby" disease in infants. Wells near homes treated for termites may contain pesticides.

Chlorides from marine sediments, brine, seawater, or industrial or domestic wastes can affect the taste of groundwater. When copper enters the water supply from natural deposits or from corrosion of copper piping, it gives the water an undesirable taste.

Iron is frequently present in groundwater, or from corroded iron pipes. Changes in water speed or direction in local pipes can carry rust along. This can happen when the valves are being repaired, the system is being flushed or tested, or fire hydrants are in use. Iron produces a red, brown, or yellow color in water, and can cause brownish stains on washed clothes. Iron affects the water's taste, but it is not harmful to health.

Iron manganese is similar in color and taste to iron and acts as a natural laxative. Sulfates from natural deposits of Epsom salts or Glauber's salts are also natural laxatives. Zinc is derived from natural deposits. Zinc does not pose a health threat but leaves an undesirable taste.

Too much sodium in water may be dangerous for people with heart, kidney, or circulatory problems who need to observe low-sodium diets. Sodium can enter water through salts used for ice on roads. Some water softeners also increase sodium levels.

Biological Contaminants

Disease-producing organisms, such as bacteria, protozoa, and viruses, are sometimes found in water. A positive test for one particular kind of bacteria that is present in the fecal wastes of humans and many animals and birds—E. coli—indicates possible problems with others. Coliform bacteria, including E. coli, outnumber all other disease-producing organisms in water.

To avoid the growth of coliform bacteria, communities choose water sources without much plant or animal life, such as groundwater rather than surface water, and try to keep human activity away from watersheds (the areas that drain into the water supply) to protect

against contamination. Fertilizers and nutrient minerals from farms and lawns can encourage bacterial growth. Water stored in the dark and at low temperatures is less likely to promote bacteria. When microorganisms do get into the water supply, they are destroyed at water treatment facilities.

Sometimes microorganisms do not pose a health danger, but multiply and clog pipes and filters. They can affect the water's appearance, odor, and taste. Surface water reservoirs may contain algae. Cooling towers can also have high bacterial counts.

Radiological Characteristics

Radioactivity from mining and radioactive material used in industry, power plants, and military installations can contaminate water. Even low concentrations pose a danger because radioactive contamination accumulates in the body over time.

WATER TREATMENTS

It is best to prevent contamination of safe water supplies, and conserve them for high-quality uses. When all else fails, water is treated. Distillation, the process of heating water to produce water vapor, is a simple, low-tech way to eliminate pollution and purify water for drinking, cooking, and laboratory use. Distilled water is pure but has a flat taste.

The most important health-related water treatment is disinfection to destroy microorganisms. It is required for surface water, or for groundwater in contact with surface water. Primary water treatment begins with filtration, followed by disinfection to kill microorganisms in the water. Secondary treatment keeps the level of disinfectant high enough to prevent microorganism regrowth. Disinfection is accomplished by a variety of means, including chlorination, nanofiltration (filtration for extremely small organisms), ultraviolet (UV) light, bromine, iodine, ozone, and heat treatment.

Suspended particles and some materials affecting color or taste can be removed by filtration. Filters can also remove some bacteria, including Giardia cysts. The water is passed through permeable fabric or porous beds of filtering material.

Aeration, also called oxidation, improves taste and color and helps to remove iron and manganese. Water is sprayed or run down turbulent waterfalls to expose as much of its surface to air as possible. Sculptural waterfalls called flowforms, which have rhythmical, pulsating, or figure-8 patterns, are both efficient and beautiful. The retailer Real Goods in Hopland, California, uses flowforms as part of a recycled water irrigation system. Aeration improves the flat taste of distilled and cistern water, and removes odors from hydrogen sulfide and algae. Aeration may make the water more corrosive.

The addition of fluoride to public water supplies has greatly reduced the amount of childhood tooth decay. Once we develop our adult teeth, we no longer benefit from the fluoride, and too much fluoride can cause yellow mottling on the teeth.

Water Distribution

• • •

Throughout history, a primary concern of architects, builders, and homeowners has been how to keep water out of buildings. It wasn't until the end of the nineteenth century that supplying water inside a building became common in industrial countries. Indoor plumbing is still not available in many parts of the world today. Today, interior designers work with architects, engineers, and contractors to make sure that water is supplied in a way that supports health, safety, comfort, and utility for the client.

For indoor plumbing to work safely without spreading bacteria and polluting the fresh water supply, it's necessary to construct two completely separate systems. The first, the water supply system (Fig. 8-1), delivers clean water to buildings. The second, a system of drains, called the sanitary or drain, waste, and vent (DWV) system, channels all the waste downward through the building to the sewer below.

In small wood-frame buildings, indoor plumbing is usually hidden in floor joist and wall construction spaces. Masonry buildings require spaces that are built out with wood furring strips or metal channels to hide horizontal and vertical plumbing. In large buildings with many fixtures, piping is located in pipe chases. These are vertical and horizontal open spaces with walls (or ceiling and floor) on either side. They often have ac-

cess doors so that the pipes can be worked on without disrupting the building's occupants. The water supply plumbing and the sanitary drainage plumbing must be coordinated with the building's structure and with other building systems.

The weight of the vertical supply pipes and the water they contain is supported at each story and horizontally every 1.8 to 3 meters (6–10 ft). Adjustable hangers are used to pitch the horizontal waste pipes downward for drainage.

DISTRIBUTION SYSTEMS

In small, low buildings with moderate water use, the pressure from water mains or pumped wells is adequate to get the water to its highest point. This is called upfeed distribution. The resulting pressure is usually more than is required at the fixtures. If it causes splashing at a lavatory, a flow restrictor can be used in the faucet outlet. In medium-sized buildings where the pressure from the street main is inadequate, pumps provide extra pressure. This is referred to as pumped upfeed distribution. In hydropneumatic systems, pumps force water into sealed tanks. Compressed air then maintains the water

Figure 8-1 Water supply system.

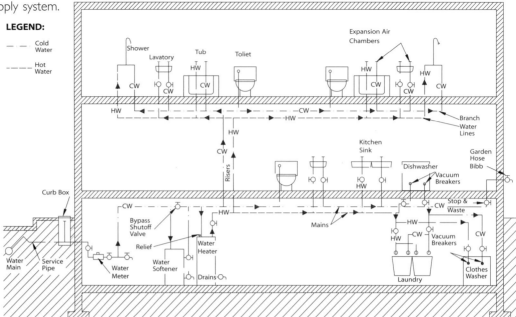

pressure. Downfeed systems raise water to storage tanks at the top of a building, from which it drops down to plumbing fixtures. The rooftop storage tanks may have to be heated to prevent freezing. The water in a rooftop storage tank is also available for fire hoses. The heavy tank requires extra structural support.

A water storage tank shares the uppermost zone in most high-rise buildings with two-story elevator penthouses, chimneys, plumbing vents, exhaust blowers, and air-conditioning cooling towers. Solar collectors for hot water heating are sometimes also on the roof. All of this equipment is usually surrounded by a band or screen two or more stories high.

SUPPLY PIPES

Lead was used for plumbing pipes by the Romans 2000 years ago, and the word "plumbing" is derived from the Latin word for lead, "plumbum." Lead pipes were used through the 1950s. As a result, the U.S. Environmental Protection Agency (EPA) is concerned even today that lead may leach out of lead pipes and copper pipes joined with lead solder and enter the water supply. Fortunately, lead on the inside surface of a pipe quickly reacts with sulfates, carbonates, and phosphates in the water to form a coating that keeps it from leaching out of the pipe. Experts believe, however, that the lead content in water is likely to exceed safe guidelines when the water is highly acidic or is allowed to sit in the lead pipes for a long time.

Plumbing supply pipes are made of copper, red brass, galvanized steel, and plastic. Galvanized steel pipe was the standard for water supply until copper took over in the 1960s. Steel pipe is strong and inexpensive, but is subject to corrosion, and eventually rusts and springs leaks. Steel pipes last from about 20 to 50 years. Mineral deposits build up inside, reducing the inside diameter and resulting in reduced water pressure at faucets.

Red brass and copper tubing offer the best corrosion resistance, with copper being less expensive, easier to assemble, more resistant to acids, and lighter weight than brass. Copper pipe lasts about twice as long as galvanized pipe. However, it costs nearly twice as much by length. Both flexible (soft temper) and rigid copper tubing can be soldered, but only the flexible copper tubing will accept compression fittings or flare fittings without soldering.

Iron (ferrous) pipes and large brass pipes use threaded connections. Copper pipes are joined with solder. Solder, which was formerly made of lead, is now a tin and antimony alloy. The molten solder is drawn into the joint. This allows piping to be set up without turning the parts to be connected, greatly facilitating installation. It also permits pipes with thin walls, because no threads have to be cut into their thickness. The smooth interiors contribute less friction to flowing water.

Plastic pipe is lightweight, low-cost, corrosion resistant, and easy to work with. It is available in flexible form for outdoor use, and as rigid pipe. Plastic pipe is made from synthetic resins derived from coal and petroleum. Rigid polyvinyl chloride (PVC, white or gray)

The design for the hair salon would involve a lot of equipment. Right from the start, Harry made sure that the engineers had spec sheets for all his client's equipment. There was just one problem. The client was looking for a special shampoo sink for the project, and was having trouble finding a supplier.

The engineer had to specify something so that the building department could review and approve the plans and the contractor could submit a bid. It was decided to specify plumbing coming up into the cabinet behind the sink, then out horizontally to the sink. The drawings were prepared and sent to the contractor and building department.

Meanwhile, the client found a supplier for the shampoo sink. Once construction began, the contractor needed the specifications on how the sink would be plumbed. Despite repeated calls to the sink supplier, Harry couldn't get technical specs for the sink.

When the sinks arrived, the contractor discovered that they were designed to be plumbed up the pedestal from the floor below. The plumbing was already installed in the cabinets behind the sink. It was possible to modify the sink to accept pipes from behind, but they would be exposed. Harry and the contractor decided to bring the plumbing from behind through a cutout in the pedestal. The exposed pipes were covered by a laminate panel to match the cabinets, giving a finished appearance and hiding the pipes.

and acrylonitrile-butadiene-styrene (ABS, black) pipes are suitable for various cold-water applications. Both ABS and PVC are thermoplastics, which can be molded under heat. Because of their sensitivity to heat, however, ABS and PVC are not used for hot water lines.

Chlorinated PVC (CPVC) pipe, which is usually cream color, may be used for hot or cold water. It is a thermoplastic and can be solvent welded, but it can be used at higher temperatures than ABS or PVC. Polybutylene (PB) pipe cannot be welded with solvent, and uses compression fittings. It is flexible, and can be snaked through walls. It is also less susceptible to damage from freezing.

More access to plastic pipes must be supplied in case fittings need to be repaired than where soldered joints are used with metal pipes. Plastic pipe used for potable water is required to have a seal from the National Sanitation Foundation (NSF). Because plastic pipes are shockproof, they are used in mobile homes where vibration would be a problem for other types of plumbing.

Engineers determine pipe sizes by the rate at which the pipes will transport water when there is the most demand. Pipes in the supply network tend to be smaller as they get farther from the water source and closer to the point of use, since not all of the water has to make the whole trip. The sizes depend on the number and types of fixtures to be served and pressure losses due to friction and vertical travel. Water flowing through a smaller pipe is under greater pressure than the same amount of water in a larger pipe. Each type of fixture is assigned a number of fixture units. Based on the total number of fixture units for the building, the number of gallons per minute (gpm) is estimated. The engineer assumes that not all the fixtures are in use at the same time, so the total demand is not directly proportional to the number of fixture units. The interior designer needs to give the engineer specific information about the number of plumbing fixtures and their requirements as early in the process as possible.

Pipes sweat when moisture in the air condenses on the outsides of cold pipes. The condensation drops off the pipes, wetting and damaging finished surfaces. Cold water pipes should be insulated to prevent condensation. Insulation also keeps heat from adjacent warm spaces from warming the water in the pipes. When pipes are wrapped in glass fiber 13 to 25 mm ($\frac{1}{2}$–1 in.) thick with a tight vapor barrier on the exterior surface, the moisture in the air can't get to the cold surface. Hot water pipes are insulated to prevent heat loss. When hot and cold water pipes run parallel to each other, they should be a minimum of 15 cm (6 in.) apart, so that they don't exchange heat.

In very cold climates, water pipes in exterior walls and unheated buildings may freeze and rupture. Avoid locating fixtures along exterior walls for this reason. If water supply pipes must be located in an exterior wall, they should be placed on the warm side (inside, in a cold climate) of the wall insulation. A drainage faucet located at a low point will allow the pipes to be drained before being exposed to freezing weather.

SUPPLY LINES AND VALVES

From a branch supply line, a line runs out to each fixture (Fig. 8-2). Roughing-in is the process of getting all the pipes installed, capped, and pressure tested before actual fixtures are installed. The rough-in dimensions for

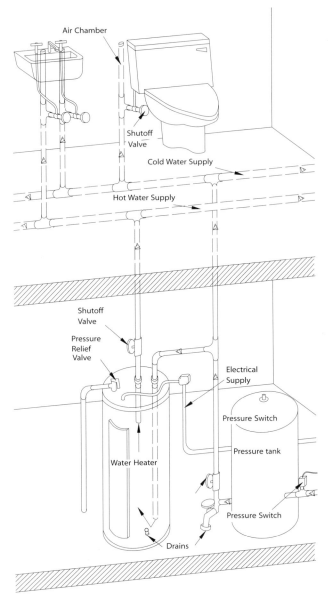

Figure 8-2 Supply plumbing.

each plumbing fixture should be verified with the fixture manufacturer so that fixture supports can be built in accurately during the proper phase of construction.

It is a good idea to have a shutoff valve to control the flow of water at each vertical pipe (known as a riser), with branches for kitchens and baths and at the runouts to individual fixtures. Additional valves may be installed to isolate one or more fixtures from the water supply system for repair and maintenance. Compression-type globe valves are used for faucets, drain valves, and hose connections.

A dead-end upright branch of pipe located near a fixture is called an air chamber. When a faucet is shut off quickly, the water's movement in the supply pipe drops to zero almost instantly. Without the air chamber, the pressure in the pipe momentarily becomes very high, and produces a sound like banging the pipe with a hammer—appropriately called water hammer—that may damage the system. The air chamber absorbs the shock and prevents water hammer.

Vacuum breakers keep dirty water from flowing back into clean supply pipes. They also isolate water from dishwashers, clothes washers, and boilers from the water supply.

CHILLED WATER

Most public buildings provide chilled drinking water. Previously, a central chiller with its own piping system was used to distribute the cold water. More recently, water is chilled in smaller water coolers at each point of use, providing better quality at less cost. A pump constantly circulates the chilled water, so you don't have to wait for the water to get cold. The chilled water piping must be covered with insulation in a vapor-tight wrap to avoid condensation.

C h a p t e r

Hot Water

Domestic hot water (DHW) is hot water that is used for bathing, clothes washing, washing dishes, and many other things, but not for heating building spaces. Domestic hot water is sometimes called building service hot water in nonresidential uses. Sometimes, when a well-insulated building uses very little water for space heating but uses a lot of hot water for other purposes, a single large hot water heater supplies both.

HOT WATER TEMPERATURES

Excessively hot water temperatures can result in scalding. People generally take showers at 41°C to 49°C (105°F–120°F), often by blending hot water at 60°C (140°F) with cold water with a mixing valve in the shower. Most people experience temperatures above 43°C (110°F) as uncomfortably hot.

Some commercial uses require higher temperatures. The minimum for a sanitizing rinse for a commercial dishwasher or laundry is 82°C (180°F). General-purpose cleaning and food preparation requires 60°C (140°F) water. Temperatures above 60°C can cause serious burns, and promote scaling if the water is hard. However, high temperatures limit the growth of the harmful bacterium *Legionella pneumophila*, which causes Legionnaire's disease. Water heaters for high temperature uses have larger heating units, but the tanks can be smaller because less cold water has to be mixed in. Some appliances, such as dishwashers, heat water at the point of use. Codes may regulate or limit high water temperatures.

Lower temperatures are less likely to cause burns, but may be inadequate for sanitation. Lower temperature water loses less heat in storage and in pipes, saving energy. Smaller heating units are adequate, but larger storage tanks are needed. Solar or waste heat recovery sources work better with lower temperature water heaters. For energy conservation, use the lowest possible temperatures.

WATER HEATERS

Water heating accounts for over 20 percent of the average family's annual heating bill. Hot water is commonly heated using natural gas or electricity. It is also possible to use heat that would be wasted from other systems, or heat from steam, cogeneration, or wood-burning systems.

Solar Water Heaters

Solar energy is often used for the hot water needs of families in sunny climates. In temperate climates with little winter sun, solar water heaters can serve as pre-heating systems, with backup from a standard system. The solar water heater raises the temperature of the water before it enters the standard water-heating tank, so that the electric element or gas burner consumes less fuel. Solar water heaters can cut the average family's water-heating bill by 40 to 60 percent annually, even in a cold climate. Heavy water users will benefit the most. Although initial costs of solar water heaters may be higher than for conventional systems, they offer long-term savings. A complete system costing under $3000 can provide two-thirds of a family's hot water needs even in New England. This is competitive with the still less expensive gas water heater. Some states offer income tax credits, and some electric utilities give rebates for solar water heaters. Solar water heaters are required on new construction in some parts of the United States.

Solar water heating isn't always the best choice. When considering a decision to go solar, the existing water heater should first be made as efficient as possible. A careful analysis of the building site will determine if there is adequate sun for solar collectors, which will need to face within 40 degrees of true south. Trees, buildings, or other obstructions should not shade the collectors between 9 a.m. and 3 p.m.

Solar water heaters use either direct or indirect systems. In a direct system, the water circulates through a solar collector (Fig. 9-1). Direct systems are simple, efficient, and have no piping or heat exchanger complications. In an indirect system, a fluid circulates in a closed loop through the collector and storage tank. With an indirect system, the fluid is not mixed with the hot water, but heat is passed between fluids by a heat exchanger. This allows for the use of nonfreezing solutions in the collector loop.

Solar water heater systems are categorized as either active or passive. In passive systems, gravity circulates water down from a storage tank above the collector. The heavy tanks may require special structural support. These systems tend to have relatively low initial installation and operating cost and to be very reliable mechanically. Active systems use pumps to force fluid to the collector. This leaves them susceptible to mechanical breakdown and increases maintenance and energy costs. Active systems are more common in the United States.

Solar energy can heat outdoor swimming pools during the months with most sun. Solar pool heating ex-

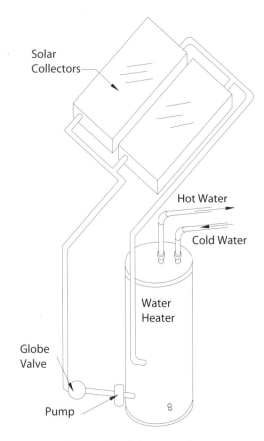

Figure 9-1 Solar water heater.

tends the swimming season by several weeks and pays for itself within two years. The pool's existing filtration system pumps water through solar collectors, where water is heated and pumped back to the pool. More complex systems are available for heating indoor pools, hot tubs, and spas in colder climates.

Heat Pump Water Heaters

A heat pump water heater takes excess heat from the air in a hot place, like a restaurant kitchen or hot outdoor air, and uses it to heat water. In the process, the heat pump cools and dehumidifies the space it serves. Because the heat pump water heater moves the heat from one location to another rather than heating the water directly, it uses only one-half to one-third of the amount of energy a standard water heater needs. Heat pump water heaters can run on the heat given off by refrigeration units such as ice-making machines, grocery refrigeration display units, and walk-in freezers.

Because a heat pump water heater uses refrigerant fluid and a compressor to transfer heat to an insulated storage tank, they are more expensive than other types of water heaters to purchase and maintain. Some units come with built-in water tanks, while others are added onto existing hot water tanks. The heat pump takes up a small amount of space in addition to the storage tank, and there is some noise from the compressor and fan.

Storage Tank Water Heaters

Residential and small commercial buildings usually use centrally located storage tank water heaters. Some buildings combine a central tank with additional tanks near the end use to help reduce heat lost in pipes. Circulating storage water heaters heat the water first by a coil, and then circulate it through the storage tank.

Storage-type water heaters are rated by tank capacity in gallons, and by recovery time, which is the time required for the tank to reach a desired temperature when filled with cold water. This shows up as the time it takes to get a hot shower after someone takes a long shower and empties the tank. Storage water heaters usually have 20- to 80-gallon capacities, and use electricity, natural gas, propane, or oil for fuel. The water enters at the bottom of the tank, where it is heated, and leaves at the top. The heat loss through the sides of the tank continues even when no hot water is being used, so storage water heaters keep using energy to maintain water temperature. The tanks usually are insulated to retain heat, but some older models may need more insulation. Local utilities will sometimes insulate hot water tanks for free. High-efficiency water heaters are better insulated and use less energy.

Tankless Water Heaters

Small wall-mounted tankless water heaters (Fig. 9-2) are located next to plumbing fixtures that occasionally need hot water, like isolated bathrooms and laundry rooms. They can be easily installed in cabinets, vanities, or closets near the point of use. Although they use a great amount of heat for a short time to heat a very limited amount of water, these tankless heaters can reduce energy consumption by limiting the heat lost from water storage tanks and long piping runs. Because they may demand a lot of heat at peak times, electric heaters are usually not economical over time where electric utilities charge customers based on demand.

These small tankless water heaters (also called instantaneous or demand heaters) raise the water tem-

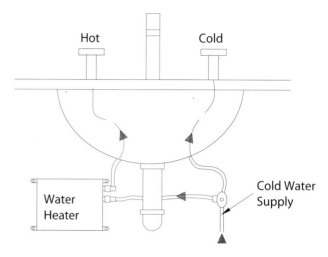

Figure 9-2 Point-of-use water heater.

perature very quickly within a heating coil, from which it is immediately sent to the point of use. A gas burner or electrical element heats the water as needed. They have no storage tank, and consequently do not lose heat. With modulating temperature controls, demand water heaters will keep water temperatures the same at different rates of flow.

Without a storage tank, the number of gallons of hot water available per minute is limited. The largest gas-fired demand water heaters can heat only 3 gallons of water per minute (gpm), so they are not very useful for commercial applications, but may be acceptable for a residence with a low-flow shower and limited demand. Gas heaters must be vented.

The largest electric models heat only 2 gpm, and are used as supplementary heaters in home additions or remote locations, or as boosters under sinks. Electric heaters require 240V wiring.

Instant hot water taps use electric resistance heaters to supply hot water up to 88°C (190°F) at kitchen and bar sinks. They are expensive and waste energy. Instant hot water dispensers require a 120V fused, grounded outlet within 102 cm (40 in.) from the hot water dispenser tank, plus a water supply.

Some tankless coil water heaters take their heat from an older oil- or gas-fired boiler used for the home heating system. The hot water circulates through a heat exchanger in the boiler. The boiler must be run for hot water even in the summer when space heating isn't needed, so the boiler cycles on and off frequently just to heat water. These inefficient systems consume 3 Btus of heat energy from fuel for each Btu of hot water they produce.

Indirect Water Heaters

Indirect water heaters also use a boiler or furnace as the heat source, but are designed to be one of the least expensive ways to provide hot water when used with a new high-efficiency boiler. Hot water from the boiler is circulated through a heat exchanger in a separate insulated tank. Less commonly, water in a heat exchanger coil circulates through a furnace, then through a water storage tank. These indirect water heaters are purchased as part of a boiler or furnace system, or as a separate component. They may be operated with gas, oil, or propane.

Integrated Water Heating and Space Heating

Some advanced heating systems combine water heating with warm air space heating in the same appliance. A powerful water heater provides hot water for domestic use and to supplement a fan-coil unit (FCU) that heats air for space heating. The warmed air is then distributed through ducts. Integrated gas heaters are inexpensive to purchase and install. They take up less space and are more efficient at heating water than conventional systems.

Water Heater Safety and Energy Efficiency

Either sealed combustion or a power-vented system will assure safety and energy efficiency in a water heater. In a sealed combustion system, outside air is fed directly to the water heater and the combustion gases are vented directly to the outside. Power-vented equipment can use house air for combustion, with flue gases vented by a fan. This is not a safe solution in a tightly sealed building.

In 1987, the National Appliance Energy Conservation Act set minimum requirements for water heating equipment in the United States. Equipment is labeled with energy conservation information. The U.S. Department of Energy (DOE) developed standardized energy factors (EF) as a measure of annual overall efficiency. Standard gas-fired storage tank water heaters may receive an EF of 0.60 to 0.64. Gas-fired tankless water heaters rate up to 0.69 with continuous pilots, and up to 0.93 with electronic ignition. The 2001 DOE standards for water heaters will increase efficiency criteria, and should result in significant utility savings over the life of gas-fired water heaters and electric water heaters.

Water heaters lose less heat if they are located in a relatively warm area, so avoid putting the water heater in an unheated basement. By locating the water heater centrally, you can cut down on heat lost in long piping runs to kitchens and bathrooms.

Existing water heaters can be upgraded for improved efficiency. By installing heat traps on both hot and cold water lines at a cost of about $30 each, you will save about $15 to $30 per year in lost heat. The cold water pipe should be insulated between the tank and the heat trap. If heat traps are not installed, both hot and cold pipes should be insulated for several feet near the water heater.

Low-flow showerheads and faucet aerators save both heat and water. United States government standards require that showerheads and faucets use less than 2.5 gpm. Low-flow showerheads come in shower massage styles. Faucets with aerators are available that use $\frac{1}{2}$ to 1 gpm. By lowering water temperatures to around 49°C (120°F), you save energy and reduce the risk of burns.

A relatively inexpensive counterflow heat exchanger can save up to 50 percent of the energy a home uses to heat water. It consists of a coil of copper tubing that's tightly wrapped around a 76- to 102-mm (3–4-in.) diameter copper pipe, and installed vertically in the plumbing system. As waste water flows down through the vertical pipe section, more than half the water's heat energy is transferred through the copper pipe and tubing to the incoming cold water. There is no pump, no storage tank, and no electricity used. The counterflow heat exchanger only works when the drain and supply lines are being used simultaneously, as when someone is taking a shower.

Spas and hot tubs must be kept tightly covered and insulated around the bottom and sides. Waterbeds are found in up to 20 percent of homes in the United States, and are sometimes the largest electrical use in the home. Most waterbeds are heated with electric coils underneath the bed. Your clients can conserve energy by keeping a comforter on top, insulating the sides, and putting the heater on a timer.

HOT WATER DISTRIBUTION

Hot water is carried through the building by pipes arranged in distribution trees. When hot water flows through a single hot water distribution tree, it will cool off as it gets farther from the hot water heater. To get hot water at the end of the run, you have to waste the cooled-off water already in the pipes. With a looped hot water distribution tree, the water circulates constantly. There is still some heat loss in the pipes, but less water has to be run at the fixture before it gets hot. Hot water is always available at each tap in one to two seconds.

Hot water is circulated by use of the thermosiphon principle. This is the phenomenon where water expands and becomes lighter as it is heated. The warmed water rises to where it is used, then cools and drops back down to the water heater, leaving no cold water standing in pipes. Thermosiphon circulation works better the higher the system goes.

Forced circulation is used in long buildings that are too low for thermosiphon circulation, and where friction from long pipe runs slows down the flow. The water heater and a pump are turned on as needed to keep water at the desired temperature. It takes five to ten seconds for water to reach full temperature at the fixture. Forced circulation is common in large one-story residential, school, and factory buildings.

Computer controls can save energy in hotels, motels, apartment houses, and larger commercial buildings. The computer provides the hottest water temperatures at the busiest hours. When usage is lower, the supply temperature is lowered and more hot water is mixed with less cold water at showers, lavatories, and sinks. Distributing cooler water to the fixture results in less heat lost along the pipes. The computer stores and adjusts a memory of the building's typical daily use patterns.

Hot water pipes expand. Expansion bends are installed in long piping runs to accommodate the expansion of the pipes due to heat.

Where the pipes branch out to a fixture, capped lengths of vertical pipe about 0.6 meters (2 ft) long provide expansion chambers to dampen the shock of hot water expansion. Rechargeable air chambers on branch lines adjacent to groups of fixtures are designed to deal with the shock of water expansion. They require service access to be refilled with air.

Waste Plumbing

Each building has a sanitary plumbing system that channels all the waste downward through the building to the municipal sewer or a septic tank below. The sanitary system begins at the sink, bathtub, toilet, and shower drains. It carries wastewater downhill, joining pipes from other drains until it connects with the sewer buried beneath the building. The sanitary system has large pipes to avoid clogs. Since the system is drained by gravity, all pipes must run downhill. Underground pipes for sewage disposal are made out of vitrified clay tile, cast iron, copper, concrete pipe, polyvinyl chloride (PVC) or acrylonitrile-butadiene-styrene (ABS) plastic. The large size of waste pipes, their need to run at a downward angle, and the expense and difficulty of tying new plumbing fixtures into existing waste systems means that the interior designer must be careful in locating toilets.

Until the advent of indoor plumbing, wastes were removed from the building daily for recycling or disposal. Historically, table scraps were fed to animals or composted. Human wastes were thrown from windows into the gutters of the street, or deposited in holes below outhouses. Urban inhabitants continued to dump sewage and garbage in gutters until the 1890s. Rural people dumped wastes into lakes, rivers, or manmade holes in the ground called cesspools, which were fed by rainwater or spring water. These cesspools generated foul smells and created a health hazard.

In the 1700s, shallow wells, springs, or streams provided potable water for farms. Widely separated dry-pit privies (outhouses) produced only limited ground pollution. By the nineteenth century, natural streams were enclosed in pipes under paved city streets. Rain ran into storm sewers and then to waterways. When flush toilets were connected to the storm sewers later in the nineteenth century, the combined storm water and sanitary drainage was channeled to fast-flowing rivers, which kept pollution levels down. Some sewers continued to carry storm water only, and separate sanitary sewers were eventually installed that fed into sewage treatment plants. Older cities still may have a combination of storm sewers, sanitary sewers, and combined sewers, in a complex network that would be difficult and expensive to sort out and reroute.

WASTE PIPING NETWORKS

With the advent of readily available supplies of water inside the house, water began to be used to flush wastes down the drain. Water pipes from sinks, lavatories, tubs, showers, water closets (toilets), urinals, and floor drains form a network drained by gravity (Fig. 10-1). In order to preserve the gravity flow, large waste pipes must run

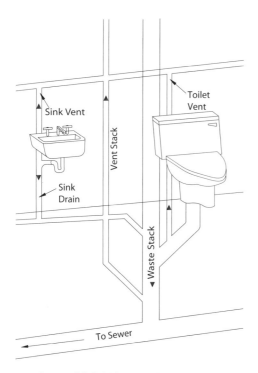

Figure 10-1 Waste piping network.

downhill, and normal atmospheric pressure must be maintained throughout the system at all times. Cleanouts are located to facilitate removal of solid wastes from clogged pipes.

Cast iron is used for waste plumbing in both small and large buildings. Cast iron was invented in Germany in 1562 and was first used in the United States in 1813. It is durable and corrosion resistant. Cast iron is hard to cut, and was formerly joined at its hub joints using molten lead. Today, cast-iron pipes use hubless or bell-and-spigot joints and fittings or a neoprene (flexible plastic) sleeve.

Plastic pipes made of ABS or PVC plastic are lightweight and can be assembled in advance. Copper pipes have been used since ancient times. Some building codes also allow galvanized wrought iron or steel pipes.

Engineers size waste plumbing lines according to their location in the system and the total number and types of fixtures they serve. Waste piping is laid out as direct and straight as possible to prevent deposit of solids and clogging. Bends are minimized in number and angled gently, without right angles. Horizontal drains should have a 1 : 100 slope ($\frac{1}{8}$ in. per foot) for pipes up to 76 mm (3 in.) in diameter, and a 1 : 50 slope ($\frac{1}{4}$ in. per foot) for pipes larger than 76 mm. These large, sloping drainpipes can gradually drop from a floor

through the ceiling below and become a problem for the interior designer.

Cleanouts are distributed throughout the sanitary system between fixtures and the outside sewer connection. They are located a maximum of 15 meters (50 ft) apart in branch lines and building drains up to 10 cm (4 in.). On larger lines, they are located a maximum of 30.5 meters (100 ft) apart. Cleanouts are also required at the base of each stack, at every change of direction greater than 45 degrees, and at the point where the building drain leaves the building. Wherever a cleanout is located, there must be access for maintenance and room to work, which may create problems for the unwary interior designer.

Fixture drains extend from the trap of a plumbing fixture to the junction with the waste or soil stack. Branch drains connect one or more fixtures to soil or waste stacks. A soil stack is the waste pipe that runs from toilets and urinals to the building drain or building sewer. A waste stack is a waste pipe that carries wastes from plumbing fixtures other than toilets and urinals. It is important to admit fresh air into the waste plumbing system, to keep the atmospheric pressure normal and avoid vacuums that could suck wastes back up into fixtures. A fresh-air inlet connects to the building drain and admits fresh air into the drainage system of the building. The building sewer connects the building drain to the public sewer or to a private treatment facility such as a septic tank.

Floor drains are located in areas where floors need to be washed down after food preparation and cooking. They allow floors to be washed or wiped up easily in shower areas, behind bars, and in other places where water may spill.

Interceptors, also known as traps, are intended to block undesirable materials before they get into the waste plumbing. Among the 25 types of interceptors are ones designed to catch hair, grease, plaster, lubricating oil, glass grindings, and industrial materials. Grease traps are the most common. Grease rises to the top of the trap, where it is caught in baffles, preventing it from congealing in piping and slowing down the digestion of sewage. Grease traps are often required by code in restaurant kitchens and other locations.

Sewage ejector pumps are used where fixtures are below the level of the sewer. Drainage from the below-grade fixture flows by gravity into a sump pit or other receptacle and is lifted up into the sewer by the pump. It is best to avoid locating fixtures below sewer level where possible, because if the power fails, the equipment shuts down and the sanitary drains don't work. Sewage ejector pumps should be used only as a last resort.

Residential Waste Piping

The waste piping for a residence usually fits into a 15-cm (6-in.) partition. In smaller buildings, 10-cm (4-in.) soil stacks and building drains are common. It is common to arrange bathrooms and kitchens back-to-back. The piping assembly can then pick up the drainage of fixtures on both sides of the wall. Sometimes an extra-wide wall serves as a vertical plumbing chase, which is a place between walls for plumbing pipes. Fitting both the supply and waste plumbing distribution trees into the space below the floor or between walls is difficult, as larger waste pipes must slope continually down from the fixture to the sewer. Some codes require that vertical vents that penetrate the roof must be a minimum of 10 cm (4 in.) in diameter, to prevent blocking by ice in freezing weather; such a requirement, of course, adds another space requirement between walls.

Large Building Waste Piping Systems

In larger buildings, the need for flexibility in space use and the desire to avoid a random partition layout means that plumbing fixtures and pipes must be carefully planned early in the design process. The location of the building core, with its elevators, stairs, and shafts for plumbing, mechanical, and electrical equipment, affects the access of surrounding areas to daylight and views.

When offices need a single lavatory or complete toilet room away from the central core (as for an executive toilet), pipes must be run horizontally from the core. In order to preserve the slope for waste piping, the farther the toilet room is located from the core, the greater amount of vertical space is taken up by the plumbing.

Wet columns group plumbing pipes away from plumbing cores to serve sinks, private toilets, and other fixtures, and provide an alternative to long horizontal waste piping runs. Wet columns are usually located at a structural column, which requires coordination with the structural design early in the design process. Individual tenants can tap into these lines without having to connect to more remote plumbing at the core of the building.

When running pipes vertically, a hole in the floor for each pipe is preferred over a slot or shaft, as it interferes less with the floor construction. Where waste piping drops through the floor and crosses below the floor slab to join the branch soil and waste stack, it can be shielded from view by a hung ceiling. An alternative method involves laying the piping above the structural slab and casting a lightweight concrete fill over it. This raises the floor 127 to 152 mm (5–6 in.). Raising the floor only in the toilet room creates access problems, so the whole floor is usually raised. This creates space for electrical conduit and to serve as an open plenum for heating, ventilating, and air-conditioning (HVAC) equipment as well.

WASTE COMPONENTS OF PLUMBING FIXTURES

Originally, the pipe that carried wastewater from a plumbing fixture ran directly to the sewer. Foul-smelling gases from the anaerobic (without oxygen) digestion in the sewer could travel back up the pipe and create a health threat indoors.

The trap (Fig. 10-2) was invented to block the waste pipe near the fixture so that gas couldn't pass back up into the building. The trap is a U-shaped or S-shaped section of drainpipe that holds wastewater. The trap forms a seal to prevent the passage of sewer gas while allowing wastewater or sewage to flow through it. Traps are made of steel, cast iron, copper, plastic, or brass. On water closets and urinals, they are an integral part of the vitreous china fixture, with wall outlets for wall-hung units and floor outlets for other types.

Drum traps are sometimes found on bathtubs in older homes. A drum trap is a cylindrical trap made from iron, brass, or lead, with a screw top or bottom. Water from the tub enters near the bottom and exits near the top, so the wastewater fills the trap and creates a water plug before flowing out. Sometimes the screw-off top, called a cleanout, is plated with chrome or brass and left exposed in the floor so it can be opened for cleaning. Drum traps can cause drainage problems because debris settles and collects in the trap. If not cleaned out regularly, these traps eventually get com-

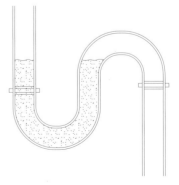

Figure 10-2 Trap.

pletely clogged up. Drum traps should be replaced during remodeling.

Every fixture must have a trap, and every trap must have a vent. Each time the filled trap is emptied, the wastewater scours the inside of the trap and washes debris away. Some fixtures have traps as an integral part of their design, including toilets and double kitchen sinks. There are a few exceptions to the rule that each fixture should have its own trap. Two laundry trays and a kitchen sink, or three laundry trays, may share a single trap. Three lavatories are permitted on one trap.

Traps should be within 0.61 meters (2 ft) of a fixture and be accessible for cleaning. If the fixture isn't used often, the water may evaporate and break the seal of the trap. This sometimes happens in unoccupied buildings and with rarely used floor drains.

VENT PIPING

The invention of the trap helped to keep sewer gases out of buildings. However, traps were not foolproof. When water moving farther downstream in the system pushes along water in front of it at higher pressures, negative pressures are left behind. The higher pressures could force sewer water through the water in some traps, and lower pressures could siphon (suck) water from other traps, allowing sewer gases to get through (Fig. 10-3).

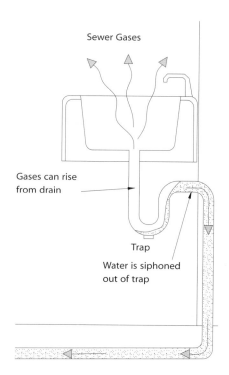

Figure 10-3 Without a fixture vent.

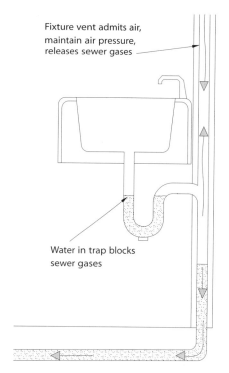

Figure 10-4 With a fixture vent.

Vent pipes (Fig. 10-4) are added to the waste piping a short distance downstream from each trap to prevent the pressures that would allow dirty water and sewer gases to get through the traps. Vent pipes run upward, join together, and eventually poke through the roof. Because the roof may be several floors up and the pipes may have to pass through other tenants' spaces, adding vent pipes in new locations can be difficult. The vent pipe allows air to enter the waste pipe and break the siphoning action. Vent pipes also release the gases of decomposition, including methane and hydrogen sulfide, to the atmosphere. By introducing fresh air through the drain and sewer lines, air vents help reduce corrosion and slime growth.

The vent pipes connect an individual plumbing fixture to two treelike configurations of piping. The waste piping collects sewage and leads down to the sewer. The vent piping connects upward with the open air, allowing gases from the waste piping to escape and keeping the air pressure in the system even. This keeps pressure on foul gases so that they can't bubble through the trap water, and gives them a local means of escape to the outdoors.

The vent must run vertically to a point above the spillover line on a sink before running horizontally so that debris won't collect in the vent if the drain clogs. Once the vent rises above the spillover line, it can run horizontally and then join up with other vents to form the vent stack, eventually exiting through the roof.

When all fixtures are on nearly the same level, a separate vertical vent stack standing next to the soil stack is not required. In one-story buildings, the upper extension of the soil stack above the highest horizontal drain connected to the stack becomes a vent called the stack vent. It must extend 31 cm (12 in.) above the roof surface, and should be kept away from vertical surfaces, operable skylights, and roof windows.

When a sink is located in an island, as in some kitchen designs, there is no place for the vent line to go up. Instead, a waste line is run to a sump at another location, which is then provided with a trap and vent. A fresh-air vent, also called a fresh air inlet, is a short air pipe connected to the main building drain just before it leaves the building, with a screen over the outdoor end to keep out debris and critters.

Chapter

11

Treating and Recycling Water

● ● ●

In the United States, each person generates almost 75,700 liters (20,000 gallons) of sewage each year. Fruits, vegetables, grains, milk products, and meats derived from nutrients in the soil are brought into cities, to be later flushed out as sewage. Some communities discharge bacteria-laden sewage into nearby lakes, rivers, or the ocean. Most cities and towns send the sewage to treatment plants, where the solid matter (sludge) settles out. The remaining liquid is chlorinated to kill bacteria and then dumped into a local waterway.

The sludge is pumped into a treatment tank, where it ferments anaerobically (without oxygen) for several weeks. This kills most of the disease-causing bacteria and precipitates out most minerals. The digested sludge is then chlorinated and pumped into the local waterway.

Waterways can't finish the natural cycle by returning the nutrients back to the soil, and end up with increasing amounts of nutrients. This nutrient-rich water promotes the fast growth of waterweeds and algae. The water becomes choked with plant growth, and the sun is unable to penetrate more than a few inches below the surface. Masses of plants die and decay, consuming much of the oxygen in the water in the process. Without oxygen, fish suffocate and die. The waterway itself begins to die. Over a few decades, it becomes a swamp,

then a meadow. Meanwhile, the farmland is gradually drained of nutrients. Farm productivity falls, and produce quality declines. Artificial fertilizers are applied to replace the wasted natural fertilizers.

Designers can step into this process when they make decisions about how wastes will be generated and handled by the buildings they design. Sewage treatment is expensive for the community, and becomes a critical issue for building owners where private or on-site sewage treatment is required. In a geographically isolated community, like Martha's Vineyard off the Massachusetts coast, restaurants have been forced out of business by the high cost of pumping out their septic tanks. One local businessman calculates that it costs him about one dollar per toilet flush, and if his septic tank fills up, he will have to shut down before it can be pumped. In 1997, Dee's Harbor Café was closed after its septic system failed, and the owner lost her life savings. Even in less remote locations, dependence on a septic tank often limits the size of a restaurant and prohibits expansion.

Sewage disposal systems are designed by sanitary engineers and must be approved and inspected by the health department before use. The type and size of private sewage treatment systems depend on the number of fixtures served and the permeability of the soil as determined by a percolation test. Rural building sites are often rejected for lack of suitable sewage disposal.

RURAL SEWAGE TREATMENT

In times past, rural wastes ended up in a cesspool, a porous underground container of stone or brick, which allowed sewage to seep into the surrounding soil. Cesspools did not remove disease-causing organisms. Within a short time, the surrounding soil became clogged with solids, and the sewage overflowed onto the surface of the ground and backed up into fixtures inside the building.

Cesspools have mostly been replaced by septic systems (Fig. 11-1). A typical septic system consists of a septic tank, a distribution box, and a leach field of perforated drainpipes buried in shallow, gravel-filled trenches. Septic tanks are nonporous tanks of precast concrete, steel, fiberglass, or polyethylene that hold sewage for a period of days while the sewage decomposes anaerobically. Anaerobic digestion produces methane gas and odor.

During this time, the sewage separates into a clear, relatively harmless effluent and a small amount of mineral matter that settles to the bottom. Soaps and slow-to-degrade fats and oils float to the top of the tank to form a layer of scum. Inlet and outlet baffles in the tank prevent the surface scum from flowing out. The liquid moves through a submerged opening in the middle of the tank to a second chamber. Here finer solids continue to sink, and less scum forms. This part of the process is known as primary treatment.

When the effluent leaves the septic tank, it is about 70 percent purified. The longer sewage stays in the tank, the less polluted is the effluent. If the building and its occupants practice water conservation, less water and wastes flow through the septic tank, the effluent stays in the tank longer before being flushed out, and it emerges cleaner. Every few years, the sludge is pumped out of the septic tank and is hauled away and processed to a harmless state at a remote plant. The methane gas and sewage odor stay in the tank.

Each time sewage flows into the tank, an equal volume of nitrate-rich water flows out and is distributed into the leach field, which provides secondary treatment. There the water is absorbed and evaporates. Nitrate-hungry microbes in the soil consume the potentially poisonous nitrates. In the process, plant food is manufactured in the form of nitrogen.

Nothing that can kill bacteria should ever be flushed down the drain into a septic system. Paints, varnishes, thinners, waste oil, photographic solutions, and pesti-

Figure 11-1 Septic system.

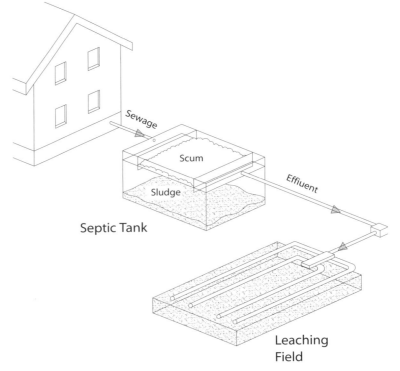

cides can disrupt the anaerobic digestion. Coffee grounds, dental floss, disposable diapers, cat litter, sanitary napkins and tampons, cigarette butts, condoms, gauze bandages, paper towels, and fat and grease add to the sludge layer in the bottom of the tank. Some systems include a grease trap in the line between the house and the septic tank, which should be cleaned out twice a year.

Trained professionals must clean the tank at regular intervals. As the sludge and scum accumulate, there is less room for the bacteria that do their work, and the system becomes less effective. If the scum escapes through the outlet baffle into the leach field, it clogs the earthen walls of the trenches and decreases the necessary absorption. Most tanks are cleaned every two to four years.

Most septic systems eventually fail, usually in the secondary treatment phase. If the septic tank or the soil in the leaching field is not porous enough, or if the system is installed too near a well or body of water, or beside a steep slope, the system can malfunction and contaminate water or soil. Most communities have strict regulations requiring soil testing and construction and design techniques for installing septic tanks. If the site can't support the septic tank, the building can't be built.

Aerobic (with oxygen) treatment units (ATUs) can replace septic tanks in troubled systems. By rejuvenating existing drainfields, they can extend the system's life. Air is bubbled through the sewage or the sewage is stirred, facilitating aerobic digestion. After about one day, the effluent moves to the settling chamber where the remaining solids settle and are filtered out. Because aerobic digestion is faster than anaerobic digestion, the tank can be smaller. However, the process is energy intensive and requires more maintenance. The effluent then moves on to secondary treatment.

Secondary treatment can use a number of different techniques, with varying impact on the building site. Disposal fields are relatively inexpensive, and do not require that the soil be very porous or that the water table be very deep below the surface. Drainlines of perforated pipe or agricultural tile separated by small openings are located in shallow trenches on a bed of gravel and covered with more gravel. The effluent runs out of these lines and through the gravel, until it seeps into the earth. The gravel's spaces hold the liquid until it is absorbed.

Buried sand filters that use sand, crushed glass, mineral tailings, or bottom ash are also used for secondary treatment. They are applied where the groundwater level is high, or in areas of exposed bedrock or poor soil. A large site area is required, but the ground surface can become a lawn or other nonpaved surface. Buried sand filters can be a remedy for failed disposal fields.

Seepage pits are a form of secondary treatment appropriate for very porous soil and a low water table only. Seepage pits can also be used as dry wells to distribute runoff from pavement gradually.

MUNICIPAL SEWAGE TREATMENT PLANTS

Larger scale sewage treatment plants continue to improve the efficiency of their processes, and municipalities are active in reducing the amount of sewage they process. Larger plants use aerobic digestion plus chemical treatment and filtration, and can produce effluent suitable for drinking. Clean effluent is pumped into the ground to replenish depleted groundwater. Digested sludge is dried, bagged, and sold for fertilizer. Some plants spray processed sewage directly on forests or cropland for irrigation or fertilizer.

ON-SITE LARGE-SCALE TREATMENT SYSTEMS

After years of sending sewage to distant treatment plants, it is becoming more common for groups of buildings to treat their wastes on site. The advantages include savings to the community, reusable treated water for landscaping and other purposes, and even pleasant and attractive outdoor or indoor environments. In some campus-type industrial, educational, or military facilities, septic tanks are installed at each building, and the outflow is combined for the secondary treatment process. Use of sand filters for secondary treatment offers simple maintenance, very low energy use, and greater available usable land area.

Constructed Wetlands

By constructing an environment that filters and purifies used water and recycles it for additional use, we can reduce municipal sewage treatment costs and support local plant and animal life. Free-surface (open) wetlands use effluents to nourish vegetation growing in soil. Human contact with these secondary treatment areas must be controlled.

The Campus Center for Appropriate Technology at Humboldt State University in Arcata, California, uses a graywater treatment marsh that consists of an open channel of water with a gravel-filled channel planted with vegetation. A primary treatment tank filters out large particles such as hair, grease, and food scraps. Water then penetrates down through the gravel in the channel. Once it reaches the end of the channel, the water is removed from the bottom of the marsh by a perforated pipe. This pipe then conveys water to the next gravel marsh box, a process that supplies it with oxygen. After treatment in the graywater marsh, water from the sinks and shower is reused on the lawns and ornamental plants. Except for periodic maintenance, very little energy is used.

Subsurface flow wetlands consist of a basin lined with large gravel or crushed rock, and a layer of soil with plants above. Plants encourage the growth of microorganisms, both anaerobic and aerobic, and bring air underwater through their roots. The effluent is then filtered through sand and disinfected. It is then safe to use for many purposes, including landscape watering. This secondary treatment option is safer for human contact, and also attracts birds. The master plan for the Coffee Creek Center southeast of Chicago features constructed wetlands for on-site treatment of wastewater from homes and businesses.

Pasveer Oxidation System

The Pasveer oxidation sewage treatment system was used by the New York Institute of Technology in Old Westbury on Long Island in New York. Purified effluent returns to the ground through 48 leaching wells under the school's athletic field. The sludge is processed using a mechanical aerator for aerobic digestion. There is no compressor, only the noise of splashing water. The process has a low profile and is screened by trees.

Greenhouse Ecosystems

Greenhouse ecosystems (Fig. 11-2) are secondary sewage treatment systems that are constructed wetlands moved indoors. Marine biologist John Todd developed *Living Machines* at Ocean Arks International. They consist of a series of tanks, each with its own particular ecosystem. The first is a stream, and the second is an indoor marsh that provides a high degree of tertiary wastewater treatment. The system costs less to construct and about the same to maintain as a conventional sewage treatment system. It uses less energy, depending upon solar energy for photosynthesis and on gravity flow. There is no need for a final, environmentally harmful chlorine treatment. The system produces one-quarter of the sludge of other systems.

These greenhouse environments are pleasant to look at and smell like commercial greenhouses. They are welcome in the neighborhoods they serve, and can save huge costs in sewer lines that would otherwise run to distant plants. Greenhouse ecosystems offer an opportunity to enrich the experience of an interior environment while solving a serious ecological problem.

Within the greenhouse ecosystems, aerobic bacteria eat suspended organic matter and convert ammonia to nitrates, producing nitrites. Algae and duckweed eat the

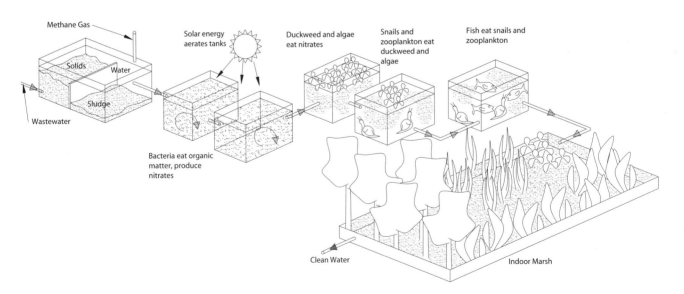

Figure 11-2 Greenhouse ecosystem.

products of the bacteria. Snails and zooplankton then eat the algae. The floating duckweed creates shade that discourages algae growth in the later stages of production. Finally, fish eat the zooplankton and snails. The systems support water hyacinth and papyrus, canna lilies, bald cypress, willows, and eucalyptus, which remove phosphorus and heavy metals during the lives of the plants, returning them to the earth when the plants die. Small fish (shiners) are sold as bait, and dead plants and fish are composted.

On-site wastewater treatment has a significant impact on the design of the building's site. Interiors are also affected, as the system may use special types of plumbing fixtures and may include indoor greenhouse filtration systems.

RECYCLED WATER

Water is categorized by its purity. Potable water has usually been treated to be safe for drinking. Rainwater offers a sporadic supply of pure water that can be used for bathing, laundry, toilet flushing, irrigation, or evaporative cooling with little or no treatment. Graywater is wastewater that is not from toilets or urinals. It comes from sinks, baths, and showers. Blackwater is water with toilet or urinal waste.

Graywater may contain soap, hair, or human waste from dirty diapers and other laundry. It can be treated and recycled for uses like toilet flushing and filtered drip irrigation. Dark graywater comes from washing machines with dirty diaper loads, kitchen sinks, and dishwashers, and is usually prohibited by codes from being reused. If graywater contains kitchen wastes, grease and food solids are a problem. Currently, few communities allow the reuse of graywater; and those that do tend to restrict its use to underground landscape irrigation for single-family houses. New York-based architect William McDonough has used gray and blackwater in designs for Eurosud-Calvission, a software research and development facility in southern France.

Future water conservation measures may include the use of water from bathing for flushing toilets, which would save 21 gallons per person each day. The 14-gallons per person used daily for laundry can help with irrigation, preferably through underground distribution systems that limit contact with people.

The Aquasaver Company in England has developed a system that diverts and cleans water from lavatories, baths, and showers for flushing toilets, washing clothes, washing cars, and irrigation. A low-pressure system installed behind panels in the bathroom pumps graywater through a series of filters, removing soaps, detergents, and other impurities. The water then goes to a storage tank in the attic or above points of use. The system uses nonhazardous cleaning agents and a network of carbon filters.

Chapter

Recycling Solid Wastes

As part of the building design team, interior designers are responsible for making sure that the solid wastes generated during construction and building operation are handled, stored, and removed in a safe, efficient, and environmentally sound way. Whether we are designing an office cubicle to include a recycling basket or making sure that an old fireplace mantle is reused rather than discarded, we can have a significant impact on how the building affects the larger environment.

Nature operates in closed cycles. One organism's waste is another's food. Nothing is really wasted except a small amount of renewable energy from the sun. Insects and microorganisms feed on the excrement and corpses of higher animals, releasing soil nutrients for plants. Dead vegetable matter is attacked, broken down, and used again.

In agrarian societies, people, along with water, air, earthworms, and bacteria, convert animal and vegetable wastes into rich soil. Sun and rain on the soil encourage plants to grow, feeding families and animals, and providing fuel for heating and cooking. Animals also provide food and clothing for people. Ashes from spent fuel and animal excrement return to replenish the soil's nutrients.

Today we discard many more materials: paper, plastics, glass, and metals; cinders, dust, dirt, and broken or worn-out machinery; kitchen garbage, and old clothes;

and industrial by-products and radioactive and chemical wastes from laboratories and industries. All of this averages out to about 45 kg (100 lb) of waste per person annually in the United States. Some of these materials, such as food scraps and paper, are links in the biological recycling chain. Some, such as metals and plastics, represent nonrenewable resources. Many waste substances contain useful energy, but separation and recycling of the mingled refuse is a Herculean task. Solid waste is the main source of land and soil pollution, next to the agricultural use of pesticides and fertilizers. Most cities burn and bury ashes, or bury the refuse itself in landfills. The organic components decompose, but glass, metals, and plastic remain.

CONSTRUCTION WASTE

It is best to reuse, then to use up, and to recycle last of all. This applies to the construction and operation of the building. As interior designers, we can work with contractors to ensure that the materials removed during renovation and the waste generated by construction has a second life, possibly by including recycling requirements in demolition specifications.

Nationwide, demolition debris adds up to 165 million tons of waste per year. Some of it, especially asphalt, concrete, bricks, and metal, is already recycled because there is a market for it, but vast amount of shingles, carpet, wallboard, doors, windows, and other pieces of homes and offices find their way into landfills because the resale and recyclable market is poor. Between 65 and 85 percent of construction debris ends up in landfills. Concrete and masonry can instead be crushed and used as aggregate for road building. Glass can be recycled into "glassphalt" road surface reflectors. Wood becomes mulch. Pulverized wood helps the composting of sludge at sewage treatment facilities.

Drywall (gypsum wallboard) disposal can pose an environmental danger. Many landfills won't accept gypsum wallboard scrap because it produces toxic hydrogen sulfide gas when buried. However, it can be recycled, with up to 85 percent of the material reused for new gypsum wallboard. Unpainted drywall can also be composted, replacing lime in the soil.

 Manufacturers currently sponsor programs that take back used carpet, which is ground up for attic insulation or recycled into new carpet. Plate glass becomes fiberglass insulation. Acoustic tiles can be recycled into new acoustic tiles.

Many new building materials can be made from recycled materials. Scrap metal containing iron is used to make reinforcing bars for concrete. Newsprint is chopped into small pieces to become cellulose insulation. Recycled plastic products include fence posts, speed bumps, deck planking, and park benches. Incinerator ash is used in nonstructural concrete. Even yogurt containers with aluminum seal scraps can become terrazzo-like floors. Look for opportunities to use recycled materials in your designs.

Demolition by hand salvage produces useful building components and even some architectural gems. The dismantling of a building generates reusable roof boards, framing lumber, and tongue-and-groove wood flooring. Doors, windows, bathroom fixtures, plywood, siding, and bricks can all be reused. Furniture, equipment, and appliances can be reused. When checking out a building for a renovation project, consider which elements can be reused in your design or salvaged for another project.

Some contractors sort excess or used building material into bins right at the site, and reuse and recycle what they can. This isn't always possible in crowded urban areas where projects take up every square inch of space. Massachusetts, Florida, North Carolina, and California have embarked on state-mandated construction recycling programs, including grants to nonprofit retailers. Despite the need to build recycling markets and

to develop strategies for dealing with wood covered with toxic lead paint, asbestos, or other nonrecyclables, construction-recycling programs promise to extend the lives of overcrowded landfills. The donated materials may also provide a tax deduction, and can help build affordable housing.

In some communities, demolition auctioneers arrange for do-it-yourselfers to deconstruct buildings by hand and take away salvageable materials. Deconstruction specialists say they can take most homes and many other buildings to their foundations, saving 80 percent or more of the material for resale or reprocessing. Some communities train welfare recipients for deconstruction jobs, which can eventually lead to carpentry apprentice programs and careers in construction. Although deconstruction takes longer than conventional demolition, the salvaged materials can often offset increased labor costs.

According to a 2001 report by the U.S. Department of Housing and Urban Development (HUD) that examines deconstruction activities in El Paso, Miami, Milwaukee, and Nashville, deconstruction fosters the creation and expansion of small businesses to handle the salvaged material from deconstruction projects. Reusing building materials can benefit the environment by diverting valuable resources from crowded landfills into profitable uses, which in turn would enable deconstruction to pay for itself by generating revenues and reducing landfill and disposal costs.

PLANNING FOR RECYCLING

The design of a building includes tracking the flow of supplies in and of refuse out. Solid wastes can take up more space than the water-borne waste systems we have discussed. The accumulation of solid wastes in a building can create fire danger, and their removal may present severe local environmental problems. The separation of solid waste to permit resource recovery has significant energy and environmental consequences. It is now common to install mechanical equipment for handling solid waste in buildings.

Since the late 1940s, the amount of packaging material used for consumer products has greatly increased. We buy food in bags and cans that we then discard. Individual packaging takes up more space in stores than does bulk storage. Wastes are stored in the home until collection day, requiring increased space allocation. It takes energy to make and transport packaging and to collect trash. Trash compactors take up space and use electricity. Landfills continue to fill up, releasing methane and leaching out chemicals.

High-grade resources are valuable materials that can be recycled. Paper and some plastics can be collected and stored within the building. Glass bottles can be returned for reuse or recycling. If recyclable materials are kept separate at the site of their use, resource recovery is much easier. Glass bottles should be washed for reuse, not broken and recycled.

Recycled paperboard (cardboard or pasteboard) saves 50 percent of the energy required to process pulp from wood. Recycled aluminum saves an astounding 96 percent of the electrical energy required for its original production. A 52-percent energy savings is achieved by recycling steel.

Wood scrap chopped into wood fiber is worth more than when it is burned as a fuel. Oriented strand board (OSB), made of wood chips and scraps, is used in the manufacture of structural insulated panels (SIPs), window frames, and other building products. Plastics are more difficult to recycle. Due to consumer preferences and regulations, recycled plastic is not often used in food-related items. Recycled plastic pellets are used in toys, building materials, and sports products. Recycled plastic bottles are used in fabrics and some carpets.

It is possible to burn for fuel some materials that are impractical to recycle. These are referred to as low-grade resources, and include gaseous wastes, liquid and semiliquid wastes, and solid wastes. Some industrial wastes give off a lot of heat when you burn them, but some are very toxic. Some cities use the heat generated by burning rubbish to fuel electric power plants or central heating installations. Trash burning is limited by environmental regulations. Burning vinyl wallcoverings poses serious environmental problems.

When composted in landfills, some of these materials produce methane gas, which can be collected for use as a high-grade fuel. Cities extract methane gas from old garbage dumps by drilling wells to tap underground pockets of decomposition gas. The quantities produced by livestock farming or sewage treatment plants are adequate to justify building gas-generating equipment. Many municipal water treatment plants are heated, illuminated, and powered by methane gas from the plants' digesters.

Incineration reduces the volume of materials that are sent to landfills. Incinerator plants are fed by dumping wastes down a chute, where they are consumed by a gas- or oil-fueled fire at the bottom. The resulting toxic ashes are then carried out of the building. Incinerators can create air pollution and are rarely installed in buildings because of the strict regulations.

Sorting and storing recyclable materials within the building requires more time and effort by the building's occupants. In an urban apartment, space and odor issues can make recycling difficult. Containers for different recyclables take up floor or cabinet space. A good community recycling program with curbside pickup helps keep accumulation down and provides some organization to the process. Some recycling programs are set up to recycle valuables in the trash automatically by mechanized sorting.

SOLID WASTE COLLECTION IN SMALL BUILDINGS

Most of the waste in a home comes from the kitchen. Finding recycling space within a pantry, air-lock entry, or cabinet or closet that opens to the outside makes daily contributions easier, facilitates weekly removal, and simplifies cleaning (Fig. 12-1).

Trash compactors take up space in the kitchen, and may have odor and noise problems. Some trash compactors have a forced-air, activated-charcoal filter to help control odors, and sound insulation to control noise. A trash compactor requires a grounded electrical outlet.

Garbage disposals are often installed below the kitchen sink, frequently along with the dishwasher. The garbage disposal grinds organic food scraps, mixes them with water, and flushes them to the sewer. Waste with less moisture goes into the garbage can. The finely chopped organic matter biodegrades better at the sewage treatment plant than it would at a landfill. However, the garbage disposal uses energy and water—2 to 4 gallons for each minute of operation. The water co-

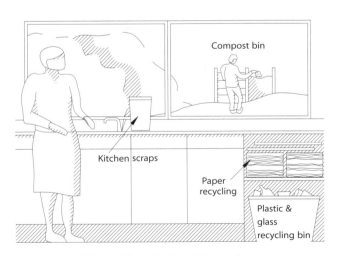

Figure 12-1 Residential recycling.

agulates grease so that it can be chopped, washes the blade, and cools the motor. More energy is used when the waste reaches the sewage treatment plant.

If you specify a garbage disposal, look for one with adequate motor horsepower and grind chamber capacity to grind quickly and efficiently. Deluxe disposal models use stainless steel extensively in the grind system to prevent corrosion. Insulated sound shells shield grind chamber noise, and some models offer a secondary sound baffle. Disposals require an electrical connection, usually a 120V, 60-Hz, AC, 15- or 20-A three-wire grounded circuit.

An alternative to the garbage disposal is the compost pile. Composting is a controlled process of decomposition of organic material. Naturally occurring soil organisms recycle nitrogen, potash, phosphorus, and other plant nutrients as they break down the material into humus. When decomposition is complete, a dark brown, powdery material called humus has been produced. As you can tell by its rich earthy aroma, the finished compost is full of nutrients essential for the healthy growth of plants and crops. Compost happens as long as there is air and water to support it.

Composting is a convenient, beneficial, and inexpensive way to handle organic waste and help the environment. Composting reduces the volume of garbage requiring disposal, saves money in reduced soil purchases and reduced local disposal costs, and enriches the soil. Self-contained units are available, and some community groups sell bins made from recycled plastics for very reasonable prices. Food wastes can be collected in a covered container beside or under the sink. Meats and animal wastes usually are not included, as they attract animals and create odors. Collected food wastes are then carried to the compost pile, where they slowly decompose into clean, rich soil for gardens. Yard wastes (leaves, grass clippings) are also added. The compost pile should have a cover, to keep out unwanted animals. The odor of a well-maintained compost pile is not unpleasant, and the compost itself has a pleasing earthy smell.

Vermiculture is a simple, if somewhat unusual, method of using worms to turn kitchen waste into extremely rich castings for use in the garden. The vericulture bin is a very effective means of reducing the amount of waste that goes into the landfill while also producing an organic fertilizer to return to the earth. Red wiggler worms are placed in one section of the worm box with wet, shredded newspaper. Food scraps from the kitchen are added to the box as they accumulate. Worms feed on fruit and vegetable peels, tea bags, coffee grounds, and pulverized eggshells, and can consume approximately half of their body weight per day. With one pound of worms, approximately one pound of soil can be removed from the box each month, while the worms stay behind to carry on the process.

Garbage compactors are designed to cut down on storage space for solid wastes. They can be used to compact separated items for recycling, such as aluminum, ferrous metals, and box cardboard. When dissimilar materials are crushed together, recycling becomes difficult. In a single family home, a garbage compactor may not save more space than it takes up, but small stores and businesses may find one beneficial.

LARGE BUILDING SOLID WASTE COLLECTION

Large apartment complexes fence in their garbage can areas to keep out dogs and other pests. This area is a good place for bins for recycling, and even a compost pile for landscaping. The solid waste storage area needs garbage truck access and noise control, and should be located with concern for wind direction to control odors.

Both the building's occupants and the custodial staff must cooperate for successful recycling in a large building. Office building operations generate large quantities of recyclable white paper, newspaper, and box cardboard, along with nonrecyclable but burnable trash, including floor sweepings. Offices also produce food scraps (including coffee grounds) and metals and glass from food containers. Dumping this all into one collection bin saves space, but with high landfill use costs, separation and recycling spaces are becoming more and more common.

The collection process for recycling in larger buildings has three stages (Fig. 12-2). First, white paper, recyclables, compostables, and garbage are deposited in separate compartments near the employees' desks. In order to make an office building recycling system work, the interior designer must often design a whole series of multiple bins and the trails that connect them. Office systems manufacturers are beginning to address some of these needs. The process often needs to be coordinated with the sources of the materials, such as paper suppliers, and with the recycling contractors who pick them up.

Next, custodians dump the separate bins in a collection cart. There are also bins for white paper in the computer and copy rooms and for compostables and garbage in the employee lunchroom. Floor sweepings

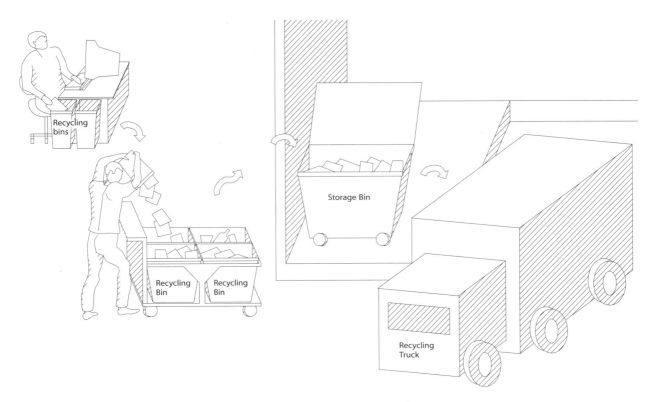

Figure 12-2 Office building recycling.

are added to the garbage. The custodians take the full cart to a service closet at the building's core and deposit each type of separated waste in a larger bin. The storage closet also has a service sink to wash the garbage bins, and may have a paper shredder.

Finally, white paper is shredded and stored for collection by recycling and garbage trucks at the ground floor service entrance, near the freight elevator. Compostables are stored or sent to a roof garden compost pile. Garbage is compacted and bagged. Compactors reduce wastes to as little as a tenth of their original volume. The storage area should be supplied with cool, dry, fresh air. Compactors and shredders are noisy and generate heat, and must be vibration-isolated from the floor. A sprinkler fire protection system may be required, and a disinfecting spray may be necessary. Access to a floor drain and water for washing is a good idea.

In some buildings, wastes are ground and transported by a system of very large vacuum pipes, which suck the wastes to a central location for incineration or compression into bales. Garbage grinders flush scraps into sewers, adding to sewage system loads.

The renovation of a late nineteenth century New York building for the National Audubon Society is an excellent example of making recycling work. Designed by the Croxton Collaborative, the eight-story building was renovated in the 1990s. The collection system uses two desktop paper trays, one for reuse and one for recycling. Central recycling points are located near four vertical chutes that pass through each floor. The chutes carry collected materials to a subbasement resource recovery center for recycling. The one for white paper is near the copier. Food wastes and soft soiled paper, returnable plastic bottles and aluminum cans, and mixed paper (colored paper, file folders, paperboard, and self-stick notes) are all collected in a pantry area near staff kitchens. Shelves in the pantry hold returnable glass bottles, coated papers (from juice and milk cartons), magazines, and newspapers.

Custodians pick up the wastebasket contents from work areas and the materials from the pantries, and take them to the subbasement to sort. In the subbasement, large movable bins collect material dropped down the chutes. Glass bottles, newspapers, and other items are boxed or baled. Recycled materials are taken to the delivery dock for pickup by recycling and garbage collectors. Organic wastes are refrigerated until enough accumulates for screening and adding to a composter. This composter is closed for odor control, but supplied with air for aerobic digestion. After about three months, the waste turns to humus and is used for a roof garden.

Food and organic waste represents a significant portion of the waste stream, and states and communities are creating opportunities for businesses to begin organic waste diversion programs. In Boston, Slade Gorton fishing company has established an effective source-separation process that captured 15 tons of fish by-products in its first two months. The Massachusetts Institute of Technology implemented a pilot source-separation system in the year 2000 in the primary on-campus dining hall. Food preparation waste from the kitchen is collected daily for composting, helping MIT to achieve its 30 percent recycling goal and reducing the cost of waste disposal. MIT is now developing plans to divert all of the school's organic waste, including yard waste and food, for composting. This will help to maximize recycling while minimizing costs, odor complaints, and the need for workers to carry all that trash.

Chapter

Plumbing Fixtures

• • •

Interior designers are often involved in the selection and specification of plumbing fixtures. Let's start our discussion of this topic with a brief look at the history of plumbing fixtures.

Indoor bathrooms were not common in homes until around 1875, but their history goes back thousands of years. Archeologists in Scotland's Orkney Islands discovered a latrine-like plumbing system dating to 8000 BC that carried wastes from stone huts to streams in a series of crude drains. Hygiene has been a religious imperative for Hindus since 3000 BC, when many homes in India had private bathroom facilities. In the Indus Valley of Pakistan, archeologists have found ancient private and public baths fitted with terracotta pipes encased in brickwork, with taps controlling the flow of water.

The most sophisticated early baths belonged to Minoan royal families. In their palace at Knossos on Crete, bathtubs were filled and emptied by vertical stone pipes cemented at their joints. These were eventually replaced by pottery pipes slotted together much like modern pipes. They provided both hot and cold water, and removed drainage waste from the royal palace. The Minoans also had the first flush toilet, a latrine with an overhead reservoir fed by trapping rainwater or by filling with buckets from a cistern.

By 1500 BC, aristocratic Egyptian homes used copper pipes for hot and cold water. Whole-body bathing was part of religious ceremonies, and priests were required to immerse themselves in cold water four times a day. The Mosaic Law of the Jews (1000–930 BC) related bodily cleanliness to moral purity, and complex public waterworks were built throughout Palestine under the rule of David and Solomon.

Bathing became a social occasion in the second century BC in Rome, when massive public bath complexes included gardens, shops, libraries, exercise rooms and lounge areas for poetry readings. The Baths of Caracalla offered body oiling and scraping salons; hot, warm, and cold tubs; sweating rooms; hair shampooing, setting, and curling areas; manicure shops; and a gymnasium. Shops sold cosmetics and perfumes. Up to 2500 members at a time visited the spas and the adjacent gallery of Greek and Roman art, library, and lecture hall. In another room, slaves served food and wine to spa visitors. All of this was only for men, but women had their own smaller spa nearby. Eventually, men and women mixed at spas, but apparently without major promiscuous behavior, a practice that lasted well into the Christian era until the Catholic Church began to dictate state policy.

All this luxury ended around 500 AD, when invading barbarians destroyed most tiled baths and terra-cotta aqueducts, leading to a decline in bathing and personal cleanliness during the Middle Ages. The Christian view at the time emphasized the mortification of the flesh, and whole-body bathing was linked to temptation and sin. Nobody bathed, but the rich used perfume to cover body odors. Outhouses, outdoor latrines and trenches, and chamber pots replaced indoor toilets. Christian prudery and medical superstitions about the evils of bathing led to an end to sanitation and the rise of disease and epidemics. In the 1500s, the Reformation's emphasis on avoiding sin and temptation led people to expose as little skin as possible to soap and water. There was almost no bathroom plumbing, even in grand European palaces. A 1589 English royal court public warning posted in the palace, and quoted in Charles Panati's *Extraordinary Origins of Everyday Things* (Harper & Row, Publishers, New York, 1987, p. 202), read, "Let no one, whoever, he may be, before, at, or after meals, early or late, foul the staircases, corridors, or closets with urine or other filth." Apparently this was quite a common problem. Around 1700, a French journal cited by the same source noted, "Paris is dreadful. The streets smell so bad that you cannot go out. . . . The multitude of people in the street produces a stench so detestable that it cannot be endured."

From medieval times on, wastes from chamber pots were tossed into streets. Legally, wastes were supposed to be collected early in the morning by night soil men, who carted them to large public cesspools, but many people avoided the cost of this service by throwing waste into the streets. Many cartoons of the period show the dangers of walking under second story windows late at night. Ladies kept to the inside of sidewalks to avoid the foul gutters.

By the 1600s, plumbing technology reappeared in parts of Europe, but indoor bathrooms did not. The initial seventeenth century construction of Versailles included a system of cascading and gushing outdoor water fountains, but did not include plumbing for toilets and bathrooms for the French royal family, 1000 nobles, and 4000 attendants who lived there.

Urbanization and industrialization in Britain in the 1700s resulted in overcrowding and squalor in cities. There was no home or public sanitation, and picturesque villages turned into disease-plagued slums. Cholera decimated London in the 1830s, and officials began a campaign for sanitation in homes, workplaces, public streets, and parks. Throughout the rest of the nineteenth century, British engineers led the western world in public and private plumbing innovations.

PLUMBING FIXTURE SELECTION AND INSTALLATION

On commercial projects, the architect and mechanical engineer usually select and specify plumbing fixtures. On residential projects, the interior designer or architect helps the client with the selection. The interior designer is often the key contact with the client for the selection of fixtures, representing their preferences and providing specification information to the engineer. Kitchen and bath designers, who usually work for businesses selling fixtures, often help owners select residential fixtures on renovation projects.

Several inspections by the local building inspector are required during the construction process, to assure that the plumbing is properly installed. Roughing-in is the process of getting all the pipes installed, capped, and pressure-tested for leaks before the actual fixtures are installed. The interior designer should check at this point to make sure the plumbing for the fixtures is in the correct location and at the correct height. The first inspection usually takes place after roughing-in the plumbing. The contractor must schedule the inspector for a prompt inspection, as work in this area can't continue until it passes inspection. The building inspector returns for a final inspection after the pipes are enclosed in the walls and the plumbing fixtures are installed.

The design of the building and the choice of fixtures affect the water and energy consumption over the life of the building. The designer can encourage conservation both by the selection of appropriate fixtures and by increasing the user's awareness of the amount of water being used.

Visible consumption measures allow the user to see how much water is being used, and to modify use patterns for better conservation. Rainwater storage tanks with visible water level indicators outside the bathroom window show how much water is used in each flush. Slightly undersized pipes allow users to hear the water flowing. This is especially useful for outdoor taps, where water may be left on.

LAVATORIES AND SINKS

Despite the hundreds of lavatory designs available in the interior design market, few consider the way our bodies work and the way we wash. Lavatories (bathroom sinks) are designed as collection bowls for water, but we use them for washing our hands, faces, and teeth quickly with running water. Because of the design of the spout, you usually have to bend at the waist and splash water upwards to wash your face. Most lavatory fittings dump running water directly down the drain. They are hard to drink from and almost impossible to use for hair washing. Most handles are hand-operated, as the name implies, and you have to move your hands out of the water stream to turn them on and off. Foot-operated controls solve this problem. The sink and adjacent counter area are often difficult to keep clean and dry.

For cleanliness and durability, lavatories must be made of hard, smooth, scrubable materials like porcelain, stainless steel, or resin-based solid surfacing materials. Look for faucet designs that are washerless, drip-free, and splash free, and made of noncorrosive materials. Models are available that have permanent lubrication, easy-to-change flow control cartridges, and controlled compression to eliminate over-tightening and wear on seals. Check for fixed faucet handle travel and features that make servicing easy.

Faucets that comply with the American with Disabilities Act (ADA) come in a variety of spout heights, and feature single-lever, easy-to-grab models, wing handles, and 4- and 5-in. blade handle designs.

Public restroom lavatories should have self-closing faucets that save water and water-heating energy. Faucet flow should be limited to a maximum of 1.9 liters (0.5 gallons) per minute. Low-flow faucets that use 1.89 to 9.46 liters (0.5–2.5 gallons) per minute employ aerators, flow restrictors, and mixing valves, which control temperatures. They function as well as or better than the 15- to 19-liter (4–5-gallon) per minute standard faucets. Low-flow aerators save up to half the amount of water used.

The term "sink" is reserved for service sinks, utility sinks, kitchen sinks, and laundry basins. Utility sinks are made of vitreous china, enameled cast iron, or enameled steel. Kitchen sinks are made of enameled cast iron, enameled steel, or stainless steel. The building code requires sinks in some locations, and local health departments may set additional requirements. Kitchen or bar sinks in break rooms and utility sinks for building maintenance are often installed even when not required by code. Kitchen sinks are limited to a maximum flow of 11.4 liters (3 gallons) per minute. Foot-operated faucets free the hands, a great convenience and water saver at kitchen sinks. The ADA sets standards for accessible kitchen sinks, including a maximum depth of 15 cm (6 in.). Service sinks, also called slop sinks, are located in janitor's rooms for filling buckets, cleaning mops, and other maintenance tasks. Wash fountains are communal hand-washing facilities sometimes found in industrial facilities.

Lavatories and other plumbing fixtures should have an air gap, a clear vertical distance between the spout of the faucet or other outlet of the supply pipe and the flood level of the receptacle. The flood level is the level at which water would overflow the rim of the plumbing fixture. Bathroom sinks have overflow ports that drain excess water before it can reach the end of the faucet. Air gaps are required to prevent the siphoning of used or contaminated water from the plumbing fixture into a pipe supplying potable water as a result of negative pressure in a pipe. Even if the water pressure fails, there is no chance of contaminated water being drawn into pipes as fresh water is drained back away from the fixture.

BATHTUBS

The Saturday night bath was an American institution well into the twentieth century. Bathing vessels were portable and sometimes combined with other furniture. A sofa might sit over a tub, or a metal tub would fold up inside a tall wooden cabinet. Homes had a bath place rather than a bathroom, and the bath and the water closet were not necessarily near each other.

Modern bathing is done on a very personal scale, in private, although tubs for two are currently in style. Social bathing is limited to recreation, not cleansing, in swimming pools, bathhouses, and hot tubs with spouts, jets, and cascades.

Standing water is good for wetting, soaping, and scrubbing, but running water is better for rinsing. We use tubs primarily for whole-body cleansing, and also for relaxing and soaking muscles. We follow a sequence of wetting our bodies, soaping ourselves, and scrubbing—all of which can be done well with standing water. Then we rinse, preferably in running water. Tubs work well in the wetting through scrubbing phase, but leave us trying to rinse soap off while sitting in soapy, dirty water. This is particularly difficult when washing hair.

Moderately priced all-in-one shower/bath enclosures in acrylic or fiberglass are very common. Fiberglass is the most cost effective, but acrylic has more durability and luster. Showers and tubs are often installed as separate entities, sometimes separated by a half wall or a door.

Tubs are often uncomfortable and dangerous for people to get into and out of. The design of the tub should ideally support the back, with a contoured surface and braces for the feet. A seat allows most of the body to be out of the water, and makes it easier to enter and leave the tub safely. A hand-held shower is very helpful for rinsing body and hair. Bathtubs are made of vitreous china, enameled cast iron, or enameled steel.

Old-fashioned cast-iron claw-foot tubs are still available. Thermaformed acrylic tub liners that can be installed over existing fixtures are a fast and economical way to upgrade a bathroom. Tubs are available with integral skirts for easy installation and removable panels for access.

For high-end designs, deeper than normal tubs made of cultured marble, fiberglass, cast iron, or acrylic may include whirlpools. Air tubs have a champagne bubble–type effect, while river jets simulate the undulating motion of white water river flow. Underwater lights, vanity mirrors, and wall-mounted CD/stereo systems with remote control are other luxurious options. Some tubs have built-in handrails and seats, while others have integrated shower or steam towers.

Clients may request big, two-person tubs with whirlpools, but often they don't use them as much as they think they will. Whirlpool baths are available in a great variety of shapes, including corner tubs 150 by 150 cm (60 by 60 in.) with built-in television monitors. Consider 183 by 107 cm (72 by 42 in.) a maximum practical size. As people become more conscious of water use, they don't necessarily want to fill up a 1136-liter (300-gallon) tub.

For safety's sake, all tubs should have integral braced grab bars horizontally and vertically at appropriate heights, and no unsafe towel or soap dishes that look like grab bars. Manufacturers offer very stylish grab bars that avoid an institutional look. Tubs should be well lit, and have easily cleaned but nonslip floors.

A shower pan that converts a standard 152-cm (60-in.) tub to a shower without moving the plumbing can improve safety. In this process, the old tub is removed and replaced with a slip-resistant shower pan. An acrylic wall surround can cover up old tile and unsightly construction work.

A single-lever faucet offers two advantages. First, the lever is easier to manipulate than round handles for those who do not have full use of their hands. Second, both temperature and flow rate can be adjusted with a single motion. To protect children and people with disabilities who have limited skin sensation, scald-proof thermostatically controlled or pressure-balanced valves should be used to control the flow of hot water.

Where a bathtub is required to be accessible, the ADA specifies the clear floor space in front of the tub, a secure seat within the tub, the location of controls and grab bars, the type of tub enclosure, and fixed/ hand-held convertible shower sprays. One of the best tub seats extends from outside the tub into the head of the tub, allowing a person to maneuver outside the tub before sliding in.

SHOWERS

Showers are seen as a quick, no-nonsense way to clean your whole body. They waste lots of fresh running water while we soap and scrub, but do an excellent job rinsing skin and hair. With luck, you get a nice invigorating massage on your back, but a real soak is impossible. If you drop the soap, you may slip and fall retrieving it. It is safer to sit when scrubbing, especially the legs and feet, so an integral seat is a good idea.

Some showerheads encourage water waste. A flow of 23 liters (6 gallons) per minute is typical, and as much as 45 liters (12 gallons) per minute was once common, using 22 liters (60 gallons) for a five-minute shower. Most codes require limited showerhead flow, with 9.5 liters (2.5 gallons) per minute being common. These low-flow showerheads can be designed in new showers or retrofitted, and save up to 70 percent when compared with standard models. Smaller pipes and heads increase the pressure, to give a satisfying shower with less water. The cost of installing low-flow faucets or showerheads results in savings of water, lower water bills, and energy savings for hot water. Domestic hot water accounts for 40 percent of U.S. energy use. An extra minute in the shower puts another 0.23 kg ($\frac{1}{2}$ lb) of carbon dioxide in the air.

When helping children bathe, you should be able to reach the controls from the outside without wetting your arm. Even with soap in your eyes, you should be able to manipulate controls from inside without seeing them. Adjustable handheld shower wall bars allow each person to adjust the showerhead to the perfect height. Shower controls and heads are available grouped together into a cleanly designed panel. Some showers feature multiple shower sprays and a steam generator. Systems that allow the sprays to be moved accommodate people of different sizes, and some systems come with programmable showerheads.

Where there is more than one shower in a public facility, the ADA requires that at least one must be accessible. There are two types of accessible showers: transfer showers and roll-in showers. Accessible showers have specified sizes, seats, grab bars, controls, curb heights, shower enclosures, and shower spray units. How the bather with disabilities will enter the shower is an important design issue, particularly if a person is in a wheelchair. For the bather who can physically transfer from a wheelchair to a shower seat, the seat and grab bars must be positioned to facilitate that entry. For those who must shower in a wheelchair, the threshold cannot be more than 25 mm ($\frac{1}{4}$ in.) high to permit roll in, and the shower floor must be sloped to contain the water.

Moderately priced shower stalls are made of fiberglass or acrylic. More upscale options include marble and other stones, larger sized ceramic tile with borders, glass block, and solid surfacing materials. Pre-plumbed, all-in-one shower enclosures that include a steam generator are also available. Shower pans are typically made of terrazzo or enameled steel and are available in solid surfacing materials as well. Barrier-free shower pans are available. Grab bars, seats, anti-scald valves, nonslip bases, and adjustable shower arms all add to safety.

Different kinds of shower seats are available—adjustable, fold-up, and stationary. Regardless of type, the seat must be installed where it will allow a seated bather to reach the showerhead, valves, and soap caddie. An adjustable showerhead can be hand-held by a seated bather or bracket-held by a standing bather.

Grab bars, positioned to help the bather enter and exit the shower, cannot extend more than 38 mm (1.5 in.) from the wall; this is to prevent a hand or arm getting caught between bar and wall. Walls behind the seat and grab bars must be reinforced to support up to 114 kg (250 lb). This is done by installing $2'' \times 4''$ or $2'' \times 8''$ blocks horizontally between framing joists. Controls should be installed above the grab bar.

Shower enclosures are usually enameled steel, stainless steel, ceramic tile, or fiberglass. Frames for shower doors come in a variety of finishes. The handle that comes with the door can be upgraded to match the bathroom decor. Etched glass doors add a design element to the bathroom. Glass panel anti-derailing mechanisms add to safety. Open, walk-in styles of showers with no doors are also an option.

Heavy glass frameless enclosures that can be joined with clear silicone are available up to 13 mm ($\frac{1}{2}$ in.) thick, although the thinner 10 mm ($\frac{3}{8}$ in.) is usually adequate. Body sprays with lots of jets pounding right at a frameless door will inevitably leak, so pointing them against a solid wall may be a better option. A vinyl gasket can deter leaks, but may defeat the visual effect of the frameless glass, and is unlikely to be effective for very long. Totally frameless enclosures always lose a certain degree of water, and glass doors generally don't keep steam in and don't retain the heat as well as framed doors. Complete water tightness may encourage mildew growth, so a vented transom above the door may be necessary.

Prefabricated modular acrylic steam rooms are available in a variety of sizes that can comfortably fit from two to eleven people. They include seating and low-voltage lighting. An average steam bath consumes less than one gallon of water. Steam generators are usually located in a cabinet adjacent to the shower enclosure, but may be located up to 6 meters (20 ft) away. Look for equipment with minimal temperature variations, an even flow of steam, quiet operation, and steam heads that are cool enough to touch. Plumbing and electrical connections are similar to those of a common residential water heater. Controls can be mounted inside or outside the steam room.

Modular saunas combine wood and glass in sizes from 122 × 122 cm (4 × 4 ft) to 366 × 366 cm (12 × 12 ft). There are even portable and personal saunas that can be assembled in minutes. Heating units are made of rust-resistant materials and hold rocks in direct contact with the heating elements. Models are available in cedar, redwood, hemlock, and aspen.

Showers may be required by code in assembly occupancies such as gyms and health clubs, and in manufacturing plants, warehouses, foundries, and other buildings where employees are exposed to excessive heat or skin contamination. The codes specify the type of shower pan and drain required.

There are alternatives to our typical showers and tubs. Traditional Japanese baths (Fig. 13-1) have two phases. You wet, soap, and scrub yourself on a little stool over a drain, rinse with warm water from a small bucket, then (freshly cleansed) you soak in a warm tub. An updated version uses a whirlpool hot tub for the soak. Locate the hot tub in a small bathhouse with a secluded view, and you approach heaven.

Figure 13-1 Traditional Japanese bath.

TOILETS, URINALS, AND BIDETS

In 1596, Queen Elizabeth had a toilet installed by Sir John Harrington, who came from Bath, giving us two euphemisms still in use today. A high water tower was located on top of the main unit, with a hand-operated tap for water flow to the tank, and a valve that released sewage to a nearby cesspool. Harrington's toilet was connected directly to the cesspool, with only a loose trapdoor in between. The queen complained about cesspool fumes in this toilet without a trap. The new toilet fell into disuse because Sir John wrote an earthy, humorous book about it, which angered the queen.

British watchmaker and mathematician Alexander Cummings put a backwards curve into the soil pipe directly underneath the toilet bowl in 1775, which retained water and cut off the smell from below. Cumming's patent application for a "stink trap" introduced the trap that has been used on all subsequent designs.

What most of us call a toilet is technically called a water closet. Toilets are not usually designed to facilitate proper washing while eliminating. A toilet seat that provides a cleansing spray is available from several American manufacturers for use on existing toilets. Bidets, which are popular in Europe and less often seen in the United States, are designed for personal cleansing. Toilets are available without a separate toilet seat, with a warmer for the seat, and with warm water within the toilet for washing.

Water closets, urinals, and bidets are made of vitreous china. Toilet bowls could never be leak proof and free of contamination until all the metal and moving parts were eliminated. In 1885, an English potter named Thomas Twyford succeeded in building the first one-piece earthenware toilet that stood on its own pedestal base. Porcelain toilets will not accumulate bacteria-harboring scratches when cleaned. His toilet design is essentially the same as the one used in the modern bathroom.

The height of the conventional toilet seat is a compromise. A lower toilet seat is healthier for the average person, as it approximates a squatting position, but is more difficult for standing male use, and for some elderly people or people with some disabilities. Higher toilets provide more support. Toilets are often used as chairs in the bathroom, and low ones are not at a comfortable chair height. The standard toilet is somewhere in between the lower and higher limits. Toilet manufacturers offer toilets with seats at the same height as a standard chair seat, marketed as comfortable for people of all ages and statures. The recommended height for a toilet that is accessible for people with disabilities is 457 mm (18 in.). Toilets are available at this height, or an existing toilet can be retrofitted with special thick seats or with a spacer ring placed between the toilet rim and a standard seat. In addition, a grab bar next to the toilet will help the user get up and down. Urinals for use by men in wheelchairs are either wall mounted at lower heights, or floor mounted.

Water closets and urinals can't be designed to have the type of air gaps found in lavatories. For example, water closets and urinals in public buildings have a supply pipe connected directly to the rim. Consequently, it is a legal requirement in most areas that at each fixture where a connection between the supply and waste plumbing is possible, a vacuum breaker must be installed on the supply line. When the pressure fails, air is allowed to enter the line, destroying the siphon action and preventing contaminated water from being sucked into the system. You may have noticed the chrome plated flush valve on every public toilet fixture; this contains the vacuum breaker. Vacuum breakers are also manufactured for outdoor faucets, where the end of a hose may be left in a swimming pool or garbage pail full of water.

Most codes require that all water closets specified for public use have elongated bowls and seats with open fronts. Specific clearances are required on each side and in front of the bowl. Automatic flushing controls add to the toilet's accessibility and keep toilets clean. They work by radiant heat from body pressure or by reflecting a light off the user and back to the control. Toilets designed for handicapped accessibility are usually wall-hung and have elongated fronts.

The ADA doesn't apply to private residences, but many designers incorporate the principles of universal design to accommodate present or future needs of their clients. The Federal Housing Act (FHA) applies to multiple unit housing built with government funds, and may require partial or full accessibility or provisions for easy conversion of some units. Structural reinforcement for future grab bars and wall-mounted water closets may be required, and is a good idea anyway.

Toilet Plumbing

Our modern toilet (water closet) emerged in the 1940s with tanks that hold about 19 liters (5 gallons) of water mounted on the backs of the bowls. When you trip the handle on the toilet, a flapper valve opens in the bottom of the tank, releasing the water to flush waste away and rinse the bowl clean. A portion of the water flows

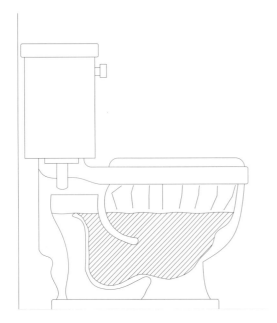

Figure 13-2 Toilet bowl.

out around the top rim, swirling to wash down the sides of the bowl (Fig. 13-2). Most of the water flows rapidly through a hole near the bowl bottom and propels waste out through the drain trap.

The volume of water needed to do a thorough job determines the size of the tank, so some tanks are bigger than others, depending on the bowl design. Once the tank empties, the flapper valve falls closed, and the tank and bowl refill from the household water supply.

Water closets have large traps that are forced to siphon rapidly during the flushing process and are refilled with fresh water to retain the seal. The water closet must be vented nearby to prevent accidental siphoning between flushes. The small supply piping available in houses can't provide the quick, ample rush of water necessary to operate a toilet's siphon trap. Instead, water is slowly collected in a tank at the back of the fixture. In public buildings with frequent flushing of toilets, slow-filling tanks could not keep up with the demand. Consequently, commercial toilet installations use larger supply pipes with special valves to regulate the strength and duration of each flush.

Toilets That Conserve Water

Approximately 70 percent of the water flushed down traditional-sized toilets isn't required for effective sewage transport. If a toilet predates 1985, it probably uses between 19 liters and 28 liters (5–7.5 gallons) per flush. The older the toilet, the more water it probably uses. Studies performed in Massachusetts show that in an average 3.2 person household where each person flushes four times a day, the 27 liters (7 gallons) per flush toilet uses 123,770 liters (32,700 gallons) of water a year. Even a 13-liter (3.5-gallon) toilet reduces water use per household to 62,074 liters (16,400 gallons) per year. Studies done at various places around the country show that toilets account for anywhere from 35 to 42 percent of all indoor household water use.

Low-consumption toilets lower building water use by 30 to 40 percent. This reduces the load on municipal sewer systems and saves fresh water supplies. Beginning in 1994, it became illegal to make or sell in the United States any toilet that uses more than 6 liters (1.6 gallons) per flush. These toilets became the center of controversy when the law got ahead of technology, resulting in steep price increases, problems with performance, and unhappy consumers. Once they decided to take a serious look at water consumption levels and water conservation, fixture manufacturers responded with only slight modifications in the basic product design. The flush valve on existing water closets was shut off prematurely, and less water was used with minimum changes to the china fixture. What resulted has contributed more to the negative impressions about 1.6 gpf (gallons per flush) low-consumption toilets than any other factor. Repeated flushing was often necessary to clean the bowl after use.

Even so, two 6-liter flushes still use less water than the former 13 liters (3.4 gallons) per flush, and most times only one flush is actually needed. Over time, manufacturers found ways to increase the swirling effect of the water and clean the bowl better. To achieve low-consumption gravity performance, the size of the trap and other openings were decreased. This resulted in a stronger siphoning action to withdraw the waste, and much improved performance. Still, there was double flushing going on, and modifications continued to be made to enlarge the trapway and water surface areas.

Although no longer legal for new installations in the United States, many older, higher consumption toilets are still in place in existing buildings. Older styles include two-piece, lower pressure models, shallow trap models, and one-piece styles that eliminate the seams between the tank and the toilet. The mechanical systems range from flush-valve commercial toilets to wash down toilets, siphon jets, siphon vortex toilets, and blowout toilets. These styles range between 9.5 liters (2.5 gallons) and 30 liters (8 gallons) per flush. Toilet dams installed in toilet tanks limit the amount of water used in existing toilets.

Watersaver toilets use 6.4 liters to 13.2 liters (1.7–3.5 gallons) of water per flush, which may not be enough of a water savings to meet strict U.S. requirements. They use a conventional flushing action, but save water by employing higher water pressure and better bowl shapes, better methods of filling and emptying, and improved trap configurations.

Some toilets conserve water by offering variable flushing controls. Dual cycle controls allow you to choose how much water you need, as do vertical flush sleeve valves. Pressure-reducing valves save water coming in on supply lines.

There are two types of ultra-low-flow (ULF) toilets currently available to homeowners that meet the legal requirements: the gravity ULF and pressurized ULF. Gravity ULF toilets have steeper-sided bowls to increase the flushing velocity. The tanks are taller and slimmer than older models, raising the water higher and increasing the flushing power. These taller tanks also hold more than 6 liters (1.6 gallons) of water, but the flush valves don't release it all, harnessing only the force of the topmost 1.6 gallons. The tank never empties its entire capacity, and it's a clever way to increase flushing power.

Pressurized ULF toilets look conventional from the outside but use a unique air-assisted flush mechanism inside the tank. The pressure-assist vessel inside the toilet's tank traps air, and as it fills with water, it uses the water supply line to compress the trapped air inside. The compressed air is what forces the water into the bowl, so instead of the pulling or siphon action of a gravity-fed toilet, the pressure-assist unit pushes waste out. This vigorous but somewhat noisy flushing action cleans the bowl better than gravity units.

Pressure-assist flushing systems (Fig. 13-3) reduce water use by elimination of leakage and double flushing. The U.S. Department of Housing and Urban Development (HUD) has calculated that a fixture can leak up to 95 liters (25 gallons) per day, depending on the age of the parts inside, but the pressure-assist unit holds the water within the tank, eliminating leaks. A larger water surface keeps the bowl cleaner, and a larger trapway and fewer bends eliminate stoppages. Because the water is contained inside the vessel within the tank, condensation doesn't form on the toilet tank. Fewer moving parts reduce maintenance.

Pressure-assist toilets install in the same space as conventional toilets, and require 138 kPa (20 pounds per square inch, psi) of water pressure, which is typical in residential housing. Pressure-assist toilets are used in homes, hotels, dormitories, and light commercial applications, and are available in handicapped accessible

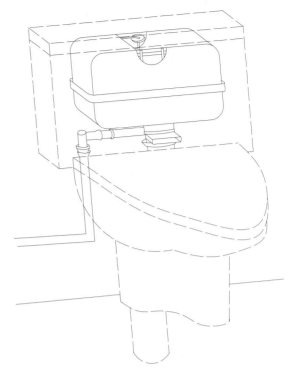

Figure 13-3 Pressure-assist toilet tank.

models. More and more states are mandating the use of pressure technology in commercial structures, primarily to prevent blockages.

In 1986, a severe drought brought the water supplies of San Simeon, California, to a severe crisis level at the same time that the wastewater treatment plant demand was reaching full capacity during the peak use season. The choices were rather grim: new, supplemental water sources, additional waste treatment capacity, or more rationing that would close some of the motel rooms that the city depended on for income. The alternative on which the city finally settled was replacing all toilets with low-consumption pressure assisted types, which reduced water consumption in the town by 39 percent compared to the older 3.5-gpf toilets. As a bonus, bowl stoppages were almost completely eliminated.

With a central compressed-air system, very low water consumption can be achieved. The Microphor flush toilet has a design with two chambers for a flush that uses only 1.4 liters (1.5 quarts) per flush. In the Envirovac system, a vacuum is used to provide a 1.4-liter flush. This system can be used in basements, as the sewer line may run horizontally or even vertically.

Some toilets use a mechanical seal rather than a water trap, and use only about 5 percent of the usual amount of water. Chemical toilets use even less.

An alternative type of toilet is made by Incinolet.

Available as a toilet or a urinal, it has no plumbing connections and reduces waste to a small volume of ash. It requires connection to electric power and a 10-cm (4-in.) diameter vent to the outside.

Composting toilets, sometimes called biological toilets, dry toilets, and waterless toilets contain and control the composting of excrement and toilet paper by aerobic bacteria and fungi. Aerobic digestion generally produces much less odor than anaerobic processes. The composting process transforms the nutrients in human excrement into forms that can be used as a soil conditioner. Composting toilets can be installed where a leaching field or septic tank, with their inherent problems and expenses, are undesirable or impractical, including areas that have placed limits on new septic systems, and in parks and nature sanctuaries.

All composting toilets require a continuous supply of room air drawn into the composting chamber and vented out through the roof to provide oxygen for the aerobic microorganisms that digest the wastes. Composting toilets eliminate or greatly reduce water for flushing but increase energy consumption, although the amount needed to run a fan and keep the compost from freezing is small, and is often supplied by a solar panel on the roof. Grates, screens, electric fans, and ventilation chimneys can provide ventilation. Airtight lids on the toilet, screens over vents, proper maintenance, and keeping kitchen scraps from the composting toilet will deter unwanted insects. Some government agencies require a permit before installing a composting toilet.

Urinals

Urinals reduce contamination from water closet seats and require only 46 cm (18 in.) of width along the wall. Urinals are not required by code in every occupancy type. They are usually substituted for one or more of the required water closets. Many bars and restaurants install urinals in addition to the number of required toilets to accommodate large crowds. The wall-hung type (Fig. 13-4) stays cleaner than the stall type, but tends to be too high for young boys and for men in wheelchairs. Where urinals are provided, the *ADA Accessibility Guidelines* (ADAAG) requires that a minimum of one of them comply with access requirements: a stall-type urinal or a wall-hung fixture with an elongated rim at a specified maximum height above the floor. Clear front space must be allowed for a front approach.

Although uncommon, urinals can be built into residential walls for pullout use, where they might be a solution to the eternal male/female toilet seat dilemma.

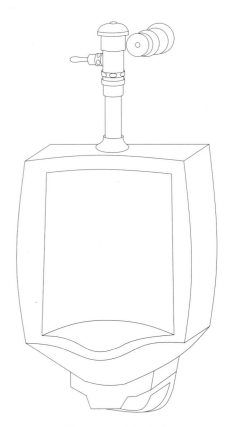

Figure 13-4 Urinal.

Waterless urinals use a floating layer of a special biodegradable and long-lasting liquid that serves as a barrier to sewer vapors in the trap while still allowing urine to pass.

PLUMBING CONSIDERATIONS FOR APPLIANCES

Although such appliances as dishwashers and clothes washers are not usually considered to be plumbing fixtures, we are including them here as an aid to interior designers, who frequently assist clients in selecting them, and who locate them on their plans. We also discuss appliances under the section on electricity.

A conventional dishwasher uses 45 to 68 liters (12–18 gallons) of water per cycle, much of it heated beyond the 49°C (120°F) household hot water supply. Optional shorter cycles use around 26 liters (7 gallons).

Washing machines use 151 liters to 208 liters (40–55 gallons) per full-size load cycle. Older-style washers with "suds savers" allowed soapy, hot wash water to be reused. Newer models have wider water quantity and temperature selections, saving water and energy. Front-loading machines greatly reduce the quantity of hot water used per wash cycle. They also give you cleaner clothes with less detergent and less energy than agitator-type machines, and reduce wear and damage to clothes.

Dishwashers and clothes washers have relatively simple plumbing requirements. Be sure to leave adequate space for access, especially in front of front-loading machines. Both dishwashers and clothes washers use vacuum breakers to prevent clean and dirty water from mixing. Kitchens need regular water supply lines for the sink and dishwasher, and waste lines for the sink, garbage disposal, and dishwasher.

FIXTURE LAYOUT AND INSTALLATION

 As with other plumbing, fixtures should never be installed in exterior walls where there is any chance of below-freezing weather. Small-scale fixture plumbing will fit into a 15-cm (6-in.) interior partition, but wall-hung fixtures require chases 46 to 61 cm (18–24 in.) thick. Plumbing chases are required where there are more than two or three fixtures. Plastic pipes are not allowed in residences in many jurisdictions.

Fixtures should be located back-to-back and one above the other wherever possible for economical installation. This allows piping space to be conserved and permits greater flexibility in the relocation of other partitions during remodeling. Wherever possible, locate all fixtures in a room along the same wall.

Bathroom fixtures should be located with space around the fixture for easy cleaning and for access for repair and part replacement. Faucets and toilet valves are subject to constant repairs, and drains must be kept free of obstructions. Waste piping clogs with hair, paper, cooking fats, and tree roots. When water supply piping fills with mineral scale, it must be replaced, which is something to be checked when the bathroom is undergoing a major renovation. Access panels may be required in the walls of rooms behind tubs, showers, and lavatories. Trenches with access plates may be required for access to pipes in concrete floors. Water heaters are especially prone to scale from mineral-rich water, and their electrical or fuel-burning components need periodic attention.

Prefabricated bathrooms are available, with manufactured assemblies of piping and fixtures. One-piece bathrooms have no seams between the fixtures and the floors. Fixture replacement is difficult and expensive, and access for plumbing repairs must be provided through adjacent rooms.

Some types of occupancies present special plumbing design challenges. Plumbing fixtures for schools should be chosen for durability and ease of maintenance. Resilient materials like stainless steel, chrome-plated cast brass, precast stone or terrazzo, or high-impact fiberglass are appropriate choices. Controls must be designed to withstand abuse, and fixtures must be securely tied into the building's structure with concealed mounting hardware designed to resist exceptional forces.

Prisons employ extreme measures to prevent plumbing fixtures from becoming weapons. Heavy-gauge stainless steel fixtures with nonremovable fittings are very expensive and require tamper-proof installation.

COMPRESSED AIR AND VACUUM LINES

In some urban locations, vacuum lines, compressed air lines, or high-pressure water mains for driving tools were once run below streets as utility systems. Today, gas, electric, and steam are the only energy utilities in common use.

An electric-powered compressor in some buildings furnishes compressed air, which is supplied through pipelines for use in workshops and factories. Compressed air is used to power portable tools, clamping devices, and paint sprayers. Air-powered tools tend to be cheaper, lighter, and more rugged than electrical tools. Vacuum lines are installed in scientific laboratory buildings.

C h a p t e r

Designing Bath and Toilet Rooms

● ● ●

The design of bathrooms and public restrooms involves not only the plumbing system, but also the mechanical and electrical systems. There are special space planning considerations in bathroom design as well, which have an impact on the plumbing layout.

DESIGNING PRIVATE BATHROOMS

The minimum code requirements for a residence include one kitchen sink, one water closet, one lavatory, one bathtub or shower unit, and one washing machine hookup. In a duplex, both units may share a single washing machine hookup. Each water closet and bathtub or shower must be installed in a room offering privacy. Some jurisdictions require additional plumbing fixtures based on the number of bedrooms. Many homes have more than one bathroom. Here are some guides to terminology and to area requirements.

The basic three-fixture bathroom with lavatory, toilet, and combination tub/shower is designed for one user at a time. You should allow a minimum of 3.25 square meters (35 square ft), although elegant master baths may be much larger. A compartmented bathroom

has the lavatory in a hallway, bedroom, or small alcove, with the toilet and bath in a separate space close by. The toilet can also be separate, with its own lavatory. Compartmented bathrooms are very convenient for couples or multiple children using the components simultaneously. They are often found in hotels. A guest bath generally includes a lavatory, toilet, and shower stall, rather than a full bathtub. You should allow a minimum of 3 square meters (30 square ft). The term half-bath refers to a lavatory and toilet, and uses about 2.3 square meters (25 square ft). The classic powder room under the stairs is a half-bath. If located near the mudroom entrance, they work very well for kids playing outdoors, allowing a quick visit without tracking dirt through the house.

Bathrooms are often the victims of the one-size-fits-all philosophy. Pullout step stools help children at lavatories. Counters and mirrors at varying heights for seated and shorter people help accommodate everyone.

Within such a usually limited space, storage can become a major problem. Families often buy toilet paper and other supplies in bulk, and need storage for at least some of these supplies within the room and the rest nearby. Towels should be stored within the room. Multiple users can leave a plethora of toiletries and grooming supplies on counters and shelves, and building in appropriate and easy to maintain storage can reduce clutter. Cleaning supplies need to be convenient but safe from small children, and preferably out of sight. The scale, toilet brush, and plunger also need to be dealt with. Specially designed accessories are available to accommodate some of these items. Designing bathroom storage that works realistically and efficiently is a challenge.

DESIGNING PUBLIC TOILET ROOMS

On many projects, the interior designer allocates the space for the public restrooms and places the fixtures. Toilet rooms in public facilities are often allotted minimal space and have to be designed with ingenuity to accommodate the required number of fixtures. The location of public restrooms should be central without being a focal point of your design.

Usually a licensed engineer designs the building's plumbing system. On small projects like adding a break room or a small toilet facility, an engineer may not be involved, and a licensed contractor will work directly off the interior designer's drawings or supply their own plumbing drawings. The design of public restrooms also involves coordination with the building's mechanical system. The type of air distribution system, ceiling height, location of supply diffusers and return grills on ceilings, walls, or floor, and the number and locations of thermostats and heating, ventilating, and air-conditioning (HVAC) zones influence the interior design.

Interior designers must be aware of the specific numbers and types of plumbing fixtures required by codes for public buildings. The model building codes that cover plumbing include the Building Officials Code Administrators International's (BOCA's) *National Plumbing Code* (NPC), the *Standard National Plumbing Code* (SPC), and the *Uniform National Plumbing Code* (UPC). These codes are geared toward plumbing engineers and professional plumbing contractors. The chapter in the codes dealing with plumbing fixtures is useful to the interior designer in determining the minimum number and types of fixtures required for particular occupancy classifications. There may be more than one code applying to a particular project, and sometimes the codes don't agree with each other.

The plumbing codes also include privacy and finish requirements and minimum clearances. The entrances to public restrooms must strike a balance between accessibility and privacy, so that they are easy to find and enter, but preserve the privacy of users. Frequently men's and women's toilet rooms are located next to each other, with both entries visible but visually separate. This avoids splitting families up across a public space, is convenient for those waiting, makes finding the restrooms easier, and saves plumbing costs. The area just outside the restroom should be designed to allow people to wait for their friends, but should avoid closed-off or dark areas where troublemakers could loiter.

Restrooms with multiple water closets must have toilet stalls made of impervious materials, with minimum clearance dimensions and privacy locks. Urinals have partial screens but do not require doors. Generally, lavatories are located closer to the door than toilets, in part to keep the most private functions out of the line of sight, and also to encourage washing after toilet use. Both men's and women's rooms should have baby-changing areas where appropriate. Some facilities, such as health clubs, have family changing and toilet rooms, small rooms designed for use by a parent or two and their children. This eliminates the dilemma of the dad with a four-year-old daughter, or the mom with a young son, especially when changing clothes.

The *Americans with Disabilities Act Accessibility Guidelines* (ADAAG) and the American National Standards Institute (ANSI) accessibility standards list access requirements, as do model codes. These requirements include minimal clearances, location requirements, and controls that are easy to use. Generally, washroom accessories must be mounted so that the part that the user operates is between 97 and 122 cm (38–48 in.) from the floor. The bottom of the reflective surface of a mirror must not be more than 102 cm (40 in.) above the floor. Grab bars must be 84 to 91 cm (33–36 in.) above the floor. Wheelchair access (Figs. 14-1, 14-2, 14-3) generally requires a 152-cm (5-ft) diameter turn circle. The turn circle should be drawn on the floor plan to show compliance. When this is not possible, a T-shaped space is usually permitted. Special requirements pertain to toilet rooms serving children aged three to twelve. States may have different or additional requirements, so be sure to check for the latest applicable accessibility codes.

The conventional height of a toilet seat is 38 cm (15 in.). The recommended height for people with disabilities is 43 to 48 cm (17–19 in.). Doors on accessible stalls should generally swing out, not in, with specific amounts of room on the push and pull sides of doors.

The ADA requires that all restrooms, even if only partially accessible, be fully accessible to the public, with adequate door width and turning space for a wheelchair.

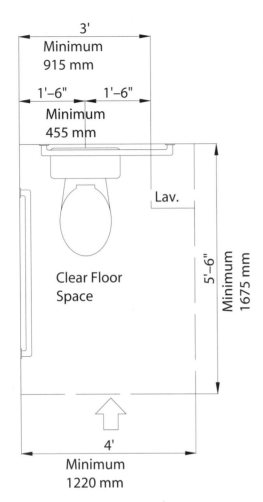

Figure 14-1 Accessible toilet stall: front approach.

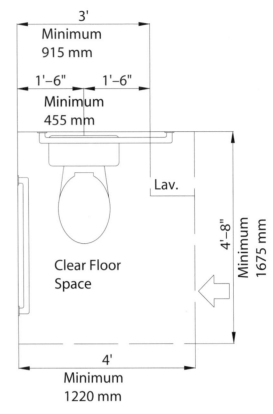

Figure 14-2 Accessible toilet stall: side approach.

A single toilet facility is usually required to be accessible or at least adaptable to use by a person with disabilities. A door is not allowed to impinge on the fixture clearance space, but can swing into a turn circle. The ADA also regulates accessories such as mirrors, medicine cabinets, controls, dispensers, receptacles, disposal units, air hand dryers, and vending machines. The heights of light switches and electrical receptacles are also specified. Where nonaccessible toilets already exist, it may be possible to add a single accessible unisex toilet rather than one per sex.

The ADA requires a minimum of one lavatory per floor to be accessible, but it is not usually difficult to make them all usable by everyone. An accessible lavatory has specific amounts of clear floor space leading to it, space underneath for knees and toes, covered hot water and drain pipes, and lever or automatic faucets. The ADA lists requirements for clearance and height.

The number of required plumbing fixtures must be

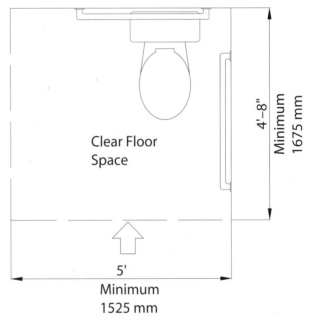

Figure 14-3 Accessible toilet stall: shorter stall with wider front.

calculated in new construction, in building additions, and when an occupancy classification changes. The number of required fixtures is based on the total number of occupants within the building or space. Typically, each floor requires a minimum of one toilet or restroom. Some tenant facilities may require their own toilet facilities, which can then be deducted from the total building requirements. The fixtures that may be required include water closets and lavatories, urinals, drinking fountains, bathtubs, showers, and washing machines. The NPC and UPC base the number of occupants on the occupant load used by the building code. The SPC requires a separate calculation. Code requirements are minimal, and buildings where many people may want to use the restrooms at the same time may want to install additional facilities.

Urinals may be required in some male restrooms depending upon the occupancy. Schools, restaurants, lounges, transportation terminals, auditoriums, theaters, and churches may have specific requirements. Facilities that tend to have heavy male restroom use, such as bars, often install additional urinals beyond the fixtures required by code.

Some occupancies with limited square footage and minimal numbers of occupants, such as small offices, retail stores, restaurants, laundries, and beauty shops, are permitted to have one facility with a single water closet and lavatory for both men and women. These facilities must be unisex and fully accessible. Adjustments may be made for facilities used predominantly by one sex if the owner can provide satisfactory data to the code officials.

In larger buildings, fixtures may be grouped together on a floor if maximum travel distances are within the limits established by code. Employee facilities can be either separate or included in the public customer facilities. It is common to share employee and public facilities in nightclubs, places of public assembly, and mercantile buildings.

Wherever there are water closets, there must be lavatories. However, lavatories are not required at the same ratio as toilets. Large restrooms usually have more water closets than lavatories.

DRINKING FOUNTAINS

Drinking fountains are not permitted in toilet rooms or in the vestibules to toilet rooms, but are often located in the corridor outside. One drinking fountain (water cooler) is typically required for each 75 occupants. In multistory buildings, each floor must have its own fountain. The ADA requires that one drinking fountain per floor be accessible. If there is only one fountain on a floor, it must have water spigots at wheelchair and standard heights. Where there are multiple drinking fountains on a floor, typically half must be accessible. Accessible fountains have controls on the front or side for easy operation, and require clear floor space for maneuvering a wheelchair. Cantilevered models require space for a front approach and minimum knee space. Freestanding models require floor space for a parallel approach.

Drinking fountains are available with filter systems that remove lead, chlorine, and sediment from the water, and remove cysts, such as cryptosporidium and Giardia as well. They use a quick-disconnect cartridge, and may have an optional audible filter monitor to indicate when the filter needs to be changed. Safety bubblers flex on impact to prevent mouth injury.

Part III

THERMAL COMFORT

Chapter

Principles of Thermal Comfort

Throughout history, people have coped with cold weather by putting on more clothes, finding a warm place, and heating their immediate surroundings with whatever energy sources were available. Over time, our tolerance for a range of indoor temperatures that changes with the seasons has become more limited. Until the 1920s, most people preferred indoor temperatures around 20°C (68°F) in winter, and tolerated higher temperatures during the summer. People would save the cost of expensive energy in winter by wearing warmer clothes. Between 1920 and 1970, energy for heating and cooling became less expensive, and people developed a preference for year-round indoor temperatures in the range of 22°C to 25.5°C (72°F–78°F).

Each of us has our own preferred temperature that we consider comfortable. Most people's comfort zone tends to be narrow, ranging from 18°C to 24°C (65°F to 76°F) during the winter. Our body's internal heating system slows down when we are less active, and we expect the building's heating system to make up the difference. The design of the heating system and the quality of the heating equipment are major elements in keeping the building comfortable. Air movement and drafts, the thermal properties of the surfaces we touch, and relative humidity also affect our comfort. The interior designer should be aware of the impact of the heat-

ing system components on the interior design, and on the comfort of the client.

Our bodies are always giving off heat. We vary individually in the amount of heat we produce and retain in our bodies. The complex physical and chemical processes involved in the maintenance of life are called our metabolism. The rate at which we generate heat is called our metabolic rate. Some people perspire more than others, and perspiration helps carry heat away from the body. The amount of insulating fat under our skin, and the ratio of skin surface area to body volume also make a difference; thinner people stay cooler than fatter people. Certain areas of our bodies are more sensitive to heat and cold than others. Our fingertips, nose, and elbows have the most heat receptors. Our upper lip, nose, chin, chest, and fingers are the areas most sensitive to cold. The temperature in the fingertips is usually in the high twenties in degrees Celsius (high eighties in degrees Fahrenheit).

When we are able to give off heat and moisture at a rate that maintains a stable, normal body temperature, we achieve a state of thermal comfort. Thermal comfort is the result of a balance between the body and its environment.

We can control our thermal comfort by becoming more active or less active, thereby speeding up or slowing down our metabolism, by wearing lighter or heavier clothing, by moving to a warmer or cooler place, or by consuming warm or cold foods. Psychological factors also influence our thermal comfort. We associate colors as being warm or cool. Smooth or airy textures suggest coolness, and fuzzy ones imply warmth. The sound of water or a breeze makes us feel cooler, while just hearing the furnace come on may help us feel warmer. We may associate bright, glaring light with heat, and shade with cooling. The movement of leaves intimates a cooling breeze, and the rattle of a window on a winter day incites chilly thoughts. Odors often create subconscious associations with environmental temperatures, such as tropical floral smells or smoky sandalwood. These conditions may or may not be accompanied by actual warmth or cooling, but psychologically contribute to our thermal sensations.

HOW BUILDINGS SUPPORT THERMAL COMFORT

We use both the heating and cooling systems of buildings to control how much heat our bodies give off. Heating systems do not usually actually raise body temperature directly, but adjust the thermal characteristics of the indoor space to reduce the rate at which our bodies lose heat. Cooling and air-conditioning systems help the body to cool more rapidly when the weather is hot. Engineers refer to heating, ventilating, and air conditioning systems and equipment with the acronym HVAC.

Men and women perceive temperatures differently. Men generally feel warmer than women when first in a room of a certain temperature, but later on feel cooler than a woman would. It takes a man about one to two hours to feel as warm or cold as a woman does in the same space. This probably accounts for the ongoing thermostat battles in many households. People at work don't seem to experience any preference between the temperatures they consider comfortable during the day or at night. Each individual has his or her own temperature sensitivities, but has consistent preferences from day to day. The same person in the same clothes will have different thermal requirements depending upon whether they are exercising vigorously, digesting a heavy meal, or sleeping. No matter what the temperature is in a space, some occupants will probably be dissatisfied.

The American Society of Heating, Refrigeration, and Air-Conditioning Engineers (ASHRAE) has published Standard 55-1992, *Thermal Environmental Conditions for Human Occupancy*, which describes the combinations of indoors space conditions and personal factors that create comfort. They looked at experimental conditions to find which combinations were acceptable to at least 80 percent of the occupants of a space. These results are based on 60 percent relative humidity, no drafts, and an activity level typical of miscellaneous office work. They reported that our sense of being warm or cool enough is a result of interactions between the temperature, thermal radiation, humidity, air speed, personal activity level, and clothing. Building occupants in typical winter clothing prefer indoors temperatures between 20°C and 24°C (68°F–74°F). When dressed in summer clothes, they prefer 23°C to 26°C (73°F–79°F) temperatures. The recommended temperature for more than one hour of a sedentary occupation is 17°C (65°F) or higher.

Since the ideal thermal conditions vary with each person and seasonally, we can only try to satisfy the majority of people. Where people remain in one location for long periods of time, as in an airplane, a theater, an office, or a workshop, we can try to give each person control over at least one element of thermal comfort. In airplanes, we have individual air vents. Small operable windows or electric heaters can help people at work. Allowing people to dress for comfort also helps. By designing interiors with a variety of conditions within one space, people can move to the area in which they are most comfortable. Sunny windows and cozy fires offer many degrees of adjustment as a person moves closer or farther away.

Our bodies become used to seasonal temperature changes. In the summer, our bodies adjust to higher outdoor temperatures. When we go into an air-conditioned interior, it takes some time for us to readjust to the lower temperatures and lower humidity. After we are in a space for a long time, as at an office where we work, the body adjusts to the conditioned interior environment. Interiors that are designed for short-term occupancy, such as stores or lobbies, should try to maintain a relatively warm, dry climate in the summer, so that our perspiration rate doesn't change dramatically when we come in from hot outdoor weather. In many commercial facilities, the HVAC system designer must compromise between the long-term needs of the employees and the short-term preferences of the more transient customers. Restaurants pose a special case. Although we tend to stay in a restaurant for a short period, our metabolic rate is increased when we digest food. Consequently, a restaurant dining room may require cooler temperatures and more humidity to balance the extra heat generated by a roomful of diners.

Restaurant designers know that the window seats are always the most popular. When Yumi visited the site for her new project the first time, she noticed that the small retail space destined to become a restaurant had metal-framed windows all across the front wall from floor to ceiling. The windows faced south, and customers would roast in the full sun all summer. To make matters worse, the local building commission would not allow exterior awnings that could provide some shade. The heating was supplied from ceiling registers, so in the winter, the windows would be cold.

Yumi started by selecting wood horizontal blinds for the window that would be left in the open (but down) position most of the time. The blinds blocked the sun's glare, while still letting the customers see out. Even more importantly, with the lights on inside at night, people passing by would be able to see into the restaurant, all the way to the back wall.

Next, Yumi designed an upholstered banquette along the windows to create a cozy seating alcove. The back of the banquette blocked the lower part of the windows, and kept both hot sun and drafts at bay. The back of the banquette was exposed to the window. Yumi commissioned a commercial artist to paint this surface in a design that warmed up the outside façade of the restaurant. This gave potential customers a glimpse of the interior design scheme. Problems solved!

The temperatures inside a building are affected by the outdoor air conditions on the exterior envelope of the building. The heat of the sun warms buildings both directly and by reradiating from the warmed earth. Warm air enters buildings through windows, doors, and the building's ventilation system. In the winter, the temperatures of building structures and contents tend to be lower than in summer at the perimeter and in the top floors of a building, where most heat is lost. The opposite is true in the summer, with the outside sun and high air temperatures having the greatest influence at the perimeter.

We generally feel uncomfortable when more heat radiates toward us from one direction than from the opposite direction, making us hot on one side and cool on the other. Most people find heat coming from the ceiling to be annoying, and prefer cool walls and ceilings. In most rooms, the rising of warm air results in higher temperatures at the ceiling than at the floor. We are more tolerant of greater temperature differences within the room when the air at the level of our heads is cooler than the air at the floor, so air-conditioning systems generally try to target the upper body zones. People also like warm, sunny walls in the winter, although they may prefer cooler walls at other times.

The heat given off by a building's occupants—their metabolic heat—affects temperatures in buildings. The heat of the people in crowded auditoriums, full classrooms, and busy stores warms these spaces. Cooking, laundry, bathing, lighting, and electrical equipment including computers are other sources of heat generation within a building. Small residential buildings usually gain less heat internally than larger office or factory buildings housing many people and lots of equipment. Such small buildings may need to turn on their heating systems sooner than larger buildings as outdoor temperatures fall.

Heat leaves buildings when heated air is exhausted or leaked to the outdoors. The building's materials also conduct heat to the outdoor air. Additional heat is radiated to cooler surfaces outdoors, and carried out with heated water into the sewers.

PRINCIPLES OF HEAT TRANSFER

In order to understand the work and priorities of mechanical engineers, we need to become familiar with the principles of heat transfer. One way to look at how heat moves from one place to another is to think of it as the energy of molecules bouncing around. Heat is transferred from one thing to another when the bouncing of the molecules causes nearby, less active molecules to start moving around too. The motion that is transferred from one bunch of molecules to another also transfers heat from the more excited group of molecules to the less excited group. A cold area is just an area with quieter molecules, and therefore with less thermal energy. A warm area is one with livelier molecules. As long as there is a temperature difference between two areas, heat always flows from a region of higher temperature to a region of lower temperature, which means that it flows from an area of active movement to one of less movement. This tendency will decrease the temperature and the amount of activity in the area with higher temperature, and increase temperature and activity in the area with the lower temperature. When there is no difference left, both areas reach a state of thermal equilibrium, and the molecules bounce around equally.

The greater the difference between the temperatures of the two things, the faster heat is transferred from one to another. In other words, the rate at which the amount of molecular activity is decreased in the more active area and increased in the quieter area is related to the amount of temperature difference between the two areas. Some other factors are also involved, such as conditions surrounding the path of heat flow and the resistance to heat flow of anything between the two areas.

Heat energy is transferred in three ways: radiation, conduction, and convection. We investigate each of these, along with evaporation, in upcoming sections.

HEAT TRANSFER AND THE BUILDING ENVELOPE

How much heat the building envelope—the construction that separates the interior spaces from the outside environment—gains or loses is influenced by the construction of the outside of the building envelope, along with the wind velocity outside the building. Each layer of material making up the building's exterior shell contributes some resistance to the flow of heat into or out of the building (Fig. 15-1). The amount of resistance depends on the properties and thickness of the materials making up the envelope. Heavy, compact materials usually have less resistance to heat flow than light ones. Each air space separating materials in the building envelope adds resistance as well. The surface inside the building also resists heat flow by holding a film of air

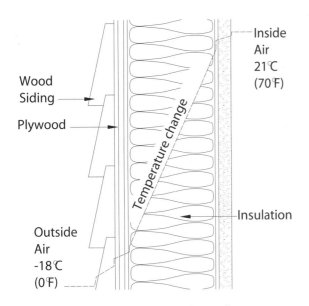

Figure 15-1 Insulated wall.

along its surface. The rougher the surface is, the thicker the film and the higher the insulation value. Think of how a very thick fur coat creates a rough insulating surface that traps a lot of air around the person wearing it.

Warmer air moving around with cooler air creates a gentle motion in otherwise still air within a room. This results in the flow of room air in contact with the inside surface of the building envelope.

Walls and roofs don't usually have uniform thermal resistance across their surfaces. Some parts, such as framing members and structural ties in metal and masonry construction, transmit heat more rapidly than others. These elements that conduct heat quickly are called thermal bridges. Thermal bridges increase heat loss significantly in an otherwise well-insulated assembly. Metal studs can also create thermal bridges. When a thermal bridge exists in a ceiling or wall, the cooler area can attract condensation, and the water can stain the interior finish. Cooler areas of the interior surface collect a thicker layer of dust because of the higher electrostatic charge that they carry in dry air. In cold weather, condensation or frost can form on interior surfaces of thermal bridges. To avoid this, insulated masonry systems use ties made of fiber composite materials with less thermal conductivity than steel.

The easiest way to control the transfer of heat through a building envelope is to control heat transfer within the building envelope itself. You can increase thermal resistance by adding insulation or reflective sheets, or by creating more air spaces. The thickness of the air space is not usually critical, but the number of air spaces makes a difference. Highly efficient insulation materials, like fiberglass batt insulation, which hold multiple air spaces within their structure, are better than empty air spaces alone. High levels of insulation maintain comfortable interior temperatures, control condensation and moisture problems, and reduce heat transmission through the envelope.

Structural insulated panels (SIPs) are now available in a wide variety of structural surfaces and interior insulation type and thickness. A single factory-built panel replaces site-built framing, and thermal performance is considerably improved because no framing members penetrate the insulated core. The typical SIP consists of two structural surfaces, often oriented-strand board (OSB), enclosing a core of either expanded polystyrene or polyisocyanurate foam between 15 and 30 cm (6–12 in.) thick. Panels are connected with plywood splines or shiplap joints that don't break the insulating layer, and their uniform thickness and construction result in sound walls without the voids common in wood framing.

So-called super insulated buildings are designed to eliminate the need for a central heating system. By using state-of-the-art energy conservation practices, little heat is lost through the building envelope, and the heat generated by cooking, appliances, lighting, and the occupant's bodies is sufficient to heat the building. A building with enough insulation and the ability to store heat well can hold a comfortable temperature overnight without additional heating. Some additional heat is usually still required to warm the building up in the morning after a cold winter night.

RADIATION

As mentioned above, the movement of energy from more active (warmer) areas to less active (cooler) areas occurs through radiation, conduction, and convection. The first of these, radiation, occurs when heat flows in electromagnetic waves from hotter surfaces through any medium, even the emptiness of outer space, to detached colder ones. With conduction, heat is transferred by contact directly from the molecules of warmer surfaces to the molecules of cooler surfaces. In convection, molecules of cooler air absorb the heat from warmer surfaces and then expand in volume, rise, and carry away the heat energy. Let's look at radiation first.

The internal energy that sets molecules vibrating sets up electromagnetic waves. Electromagnetic energy comes in many forms, including cosmic-ray photons, ultraviolet (UV) radiation, visible light, radio waves, heat, and electric currents, among others. Infrared (IR) radiation is made up of a range of longer, lower frequency wavelengths between shorter visible light and even longer microwaves. The sun's heat is mostly in wavelengths from the shorter, and hotter, end of IR radiation.

Infrared radiation is an invisible part of the light spectrum, and behaves exactly like light, that is, IR radiation travels in a straight line, doesn't turn corners, and can be instantly blocked by objects in its path. You can visualize whether radiated energy will be spread to or blocked from an object by checking whether the source object can "see" the other object through a medium that is transparent to light (air, a vacuum). Breaking the line of sight breaks the transmission path. For example, you will feel the radiated heat from a fireplace if you are sitting in a big chair facing the fire, but if you are behind the chair, the heat will be blocked (Fig. 15-2).

Your work as an interior designer can have a direct effect on how radiant heat is distributed in a space.

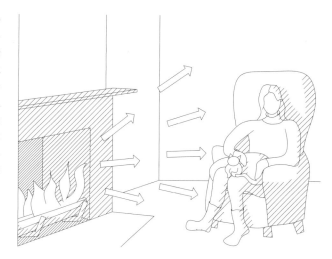

Figure 15-2 Radiation.

Buildings get heat in the shorter IR wavelengths directly from the sun. Buildings also receive thermal radiation from sun-warmed earth and floors, warm building surfaces, and even contact with human skin, all of which emit irradiation at much lower temperatures and at longer wavelengths. Radiation warms our skin when the sun strikes it, or when we stand near a fire. When we stand near a cold wall or under a cool night sky, radiation cools our skin. A cold window in a room usually has the greatest effect of draining radiated heat away from our bodies, making us feel colder. Closing the drapes blocks the heat transfer, and helps keep us warm.

Infrared electromagnetic waves are what emanate from an object and carry energy to all bodies within a direct line of sight of that object. The electromagnetic waves excite the molecules in the objects they hit, increasing the internal energy, and thereby raising the temperature. All objects give off heat in the form of IR electromagnetic radiation, and they all receive radiation from surrounding objects. When objects are close in temperature, the transfer of heat from the warmer to the cooler will be relatively slower than if there was a great difference in temperature. If two objects are at the same temperature, they will continue to radiate to each other, but no net exchange of heat takes place.

When electromagnetic waves contact an object or a medium, they are either reflected from the surface, absorbed by the material, or transmitted through the material. Different materials transmit some wavelengths of electromagnetic radiation, and reflect or absorb others. Materials that reflect visible radiation (light), such as shiny, silvered, or mirrored surfaces, also reflect radiant heat. Glass is transparent to visible light and to radiant energy from the hot sun, but is opaque to wavelengths of thermal radiation released by objects at normal earth temperatures. That is why the sun warms plants inside a glass greenhouse, but the heat absorbed and reradiated by the plants and soil can't escape back out through the glass, a situation known as the greenhouse effect. Radiation is not affected by air motion, so a breeze doesn't blow away the sunlight that pours down on your sunburned back at the beach.

How Building Materials Radiate Heat

The ways that building materials interact with the thermal radiation that reaches them is of great importance to designers. Three properties that describe these interactions with radiant heat are reflectance, absorptance, and emittance. Each of these can be influenced by the interior design of a space.

Reflectance (Fig. 15-3) refers to the amount of incoming radiation that bounces off a material, leaving the temperature of the material unchanged. If you think of radiant heat acting like visible light, a heat-reflective material is similar to a mirror. The electromagnetic waves bounce off the reflective material and don't enter it, so its temperature remains the same. New white paint will reflect 75 percent of the IR radiation striking it, as will fresh snow.

Absorptance (Fig. 15-4) is just the opposite of reflectance. An absorptive material allows thermal energy to enter, raising its temperature; when the sun shines on a stone, the stone becomes warmer. All the radiant en-

Figure 15-4 Absorptance.

ergy that reaches a material is either absorbed or reflected. Dark green grass will absorb about 94 percent of the IR radiation shining down on it. Clean asphalt and freshly tilled earth will both absorb about 95 percent.

The color of a building's surroundings and surfaces influences how much radiation is reflected, and how much is absorbed. A building painted white reflects about three-quarters of the sun's direct thermal radiation, but only about 2 percent of the longer wavelength IR radiation that bounces back onto it from its surroundings. The less intense radiation from the surrounding area tends to get absorbed by the building. For example, the heat bouncing back onto a building from a light-colored concrete parking lot outside is relatively likely to be absorbed by the building.

Once a stone has absorbed the sun's heat during the day, it will radiate that stored heat out to cooler surrounding objects through the night air. This ability of a material to radiate heat outward to other objects is called emittance (Fig. 15-5). The amount of energy available for emittance depends upon the amount absorbed, so a highly reflective material would have less absorbed energy to emit.

Black surfaces absorb and then emit the sun's heat. Sun-heated lawns and pavements emit almost as much heat to the building as if these surfaces were painted black. A building with a bright metallic exterior reflects most of the radiation emitted from the earth back out into space.

Materials can emit radiation only through a gas that is transparent to IR wavelengths (or light waves) or

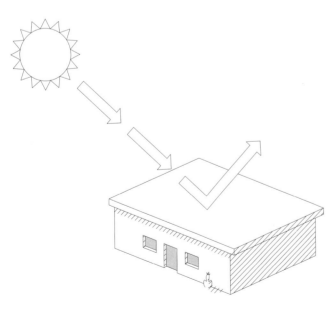

Figure 15-3 Reflectance.

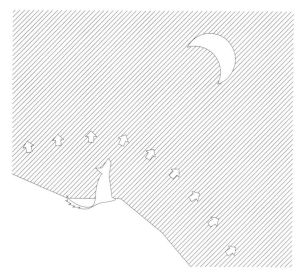

Figure 15-5 Emittance.

through a vacuum. They can't radiate heat if they are sandwiched tightly between other layers of construction materials. Metal foils are good heat conductors, but work as a mirror-like insulation to prevent radiation from being emitted when there is a space with air on one or both sides. Metal foils are often used inside walls. In cold climates, they are installed facing the warmer interior, to keep heating energy indoors. In hot climates, they are used facing the sunny outside to keep the building from heating up.

Mean Radiant Temperature and Operative Temperature

The air temperature alone doesn't adequately measure comfort in a space. Especially in spaces that use passive solar heating or passive cooling techniques, radiant temperature or air motion may be more important in creating comfort. If you are losing a lot of body heat to a cold surface nearby, you will feel chilly, even if the air temperature is acceptably high.

To try to take such conditions into account, engineers sometimes use a calculation called the mean radiant temperature (MRT) that measures the temperature of each surface in a space and determines the specific spot in the space where the MRT is to be measured. The calculation takes into account how much heat each surface emits, and how the surface's location relates to the point where the MRT is being measured. The MRT is derived by a detailed analysis and complex calculations.

A more useful measurement for determining thermal comfort is the operative temperature, which can be measured physically and doesn't involve difficult calculations. The operative temperature is essentially an average of the air temperature of a space and the average of the various surface temperatures surrounding the space.

Engineers use the MRT or operative temperature to help determine the amount of supplementary heating or cooling needed in a space. In winter, when the surfaces surrounding you are warm, the air temperature can be somewhat lower without your feeling chilled. In summer, buildings that have thick, massive walls, such as adobe houses, are likely to have cool interior surfaces, helping you keep comfortable even at higher air temperatures.

Heating Floors and Ceilings

A building's heating system can warm very large surfaces such as floors and ceilings by heating them to a few degrees above the skin temperature of your body. A cold floor gives a chill to a room, and a warm floor welcomes bare feet and a cozy feeling. The disadvantage to heating the room through heating the floor is that you can't provide enough heat to warm your body without producing hot feet. In addition, furniture blocks radiant heat to the upper body, and carpets reduce the floor's effectiveness as a heat source. Floors tend to be slow to react to changes in the demand for heat, and repair can be messy and expensive.

Systems for heating ceilings can be run at higher temperatures than those for floors, as we don't usually come in contact with ceilings. Repair and maintenance are easier, and ceilings react fairly quickly to changing demands for heat, as they usually have a lower mass than floors. However, air movement doesn't do a good job of bringing warm air downward from a ceiling, and legs and feet blocked from radiant heat by furniture may be too cold.

Small surfaces like electric filaments, gas-heated ceramic tiles, metal stoves, or fireplaces, when heated to temperatures hundreds of degrees above skin temperature, also radiate heat. Small, high-temperature IR heaters have reflectors to focus the heat. They are good for producing heat instantly and beaming it to where it is needed, and are used in large industrial buildings and outdoors. Small focused sources are more efficient than open fires or stoves, which radiate heat in all directions. The heat from these small sources feels pleasant to bare skin, and they are sometimes used in swimming pool areas, shower rooms, and bathrooms.

Creating cold surfaces is not a very successful way to make a space feel cooler, as even a moderately cold surface is moist and unpleasant in humid summer weather. This is why we don't usually actively cool ceilings and floors. Alternatives that work better are shading and insulating roofs, walls, and windows from the summer sun, and using highly reflective surface coatings on these external surfaces where practical. By using materials in the interior that heat up and cool down slowly, we can retain cool temperatures throughout the day. By opening the building to the sky at night, we can allow heat to radiate back to the cool night sky.

Averages of the surface temperatures and air temperature in a room don't tell the whole story. We may be in a room with a comfortable average air temperature, but be very hot on one side from a fireplace, and very cool on the other side facing an open window. The room's heat may be mostly up by the ceiling, leaving our feet down on the floor cold. The distribution of heated surfaces may be uneven, and large cold windows and uninsulated walls may radiate heat outside so rapidly that we feel chilly even in a room with a warm air temperature.

CONDUCTION

Conduction (Fig. 15-6) is the flow of heat through a solid material, as opposed to radiation, which takes place through a transparent gas or a vacuum. Molecules vibrating at a faster rate (at a higher temperature) bump into molecules vibrating at a slower rate (lower temperature) and transfer energy directly to them. The mol-

ecules themselves don't travel to the other object; only their energy does. When a hot pan comes in contact with our skin, the heat from the pan flows into our skin. When the object we touch is cold, like an iced drink in a cold glass, the heat flows from our skin into the glass. Conduction is responsible for only a small amount of the heat loss from our bodies. Conduction can occur within a single material, when the temperature is hotter in one part of the material than in another.

CONVECTION

Convection (Fig. 15-7) is similar to conduction in that heat leaves an object as it comes in contact with something else. In the case of convection, the transfer of heat happens by means of a moving stream of a fluid (liquid or gas) rather than another object. Our skin may be warmed or cooled by convection when it is exposed to warm or cool air passing by it. The air molecules pass by the molecules on the surface of our skin and absorb heat, and we feel cooler. The same thing happens when we run cold water over our skin. The amount of convection depends upon how rough the surface is, its orientation to the stream of fluid, the direction of the stream's flow, the type of fluid in the stream, and whether the flow is free or is forced. When there is a large difference between the air temperature and the skin temperature, plus more air or water movement, more heat will be transmitted by convection.

Convection can also heat, as well as cool. A hot bath warms us thoroughly as the heat from the water is trans-

Figure 15-6 Conduction.

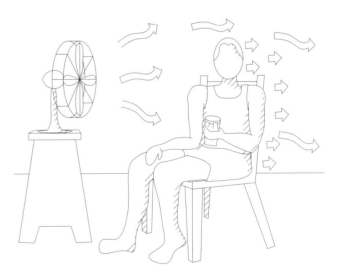

Figure 15-7 Convection.

ferred by convection to our skin. Hot air from a room's heating system flowing past us will also warm our skin.

EVAPORATION

Evaporation (Fig. 15-8) is a process that results from the three types of heat transfer (radiation, conduction, and convection). When a liquid evaporates, it removes a large quantity of heat from the surface it is leaving. For example, when we sweat, and the moisture evaporates, we feel cooler as some of the heat leaves our body. In order to understand evaporation, we need to look at the difference between latent and sensible heat. This will also be helpful later on in understanding how air-conditioning works.

The kind of heat we have been talking about up to now that comes from the motion of molecules is known as sensible heat. Sensible heat is a term to describe how excited the molecules of a material get due to radiation, the friction between two objects, a chemical reaction, contact with a hotter object, and so forth. Every material has a property called specific heat, which is how much the temperature changes due to a given input of sensible heat.

Figure 15-8 Evaporation.

Latent heat is heat that is transferred when a material changes from a solid to a liquid or from a liquid to a gas, or the other way around. So, where sensible heat is all about the motion of molecules, latent heat describes the structure of the molecules themselves. The latent heat of fusion is the heat needed to melt a solid object into a liquid. The latent heat of vaporization is the heat required to change a liquid into a gas. When a gas liquefies (condenses) or a liquid solidifies, it releases its latent heat. For example, when water vapor condenses, it gives off latent heat. The same thing happens when liquid water freezes into ice. The ice is colder than the water was because it gave off its latent heat to its surroundings.

Our bodies contain both sensible heat and latent heat. A seated man at rest in a 27°C (80°F) environment gives off about 53 watts (180 Btu) per hour of sensible heat as the warm molecules in his body bounce around. (A watt is a unit of power, and is abbreviated W. A Btu—British thermal unit—is another way to measure a unit of power. One watt is equal to 3.43 Btu.) This same fellow will simultaneously give off 44 W (150 Btu) per hour of latent heat when he perspires and the water changes from a liquid to a gas, for a total of about 97 W (330 Btu). You can visualize this amount of heat as that produced by an ordinary 100-W electrical lightbulb.

Evaporative cooling takes place when moisture evaporates and the sensible heat of the liquid is converted into the latent heat in the vapor. We lose the water and its heat from our bodies, and we feel cooler. Adding humidity to a room will decrease evaporative cooling, and is a useful technique for healthcare facilities and elderly housing, where people may feel cold even in a warm room.

Air motion increases heat loss caused by evaporation, which is why a fan can make us feel more comfortable, even if it does not actually lower the temperature of the room. This sensation is called effective temperature, producing apparently higher or lower temperatures by controlling air moisture without actually changing the temperature of the space.

Air Temperature and Air Motion

Air motion may be caused by natural convection, be mechanically forced, or be a result of the body movements of the space's occupants. The natural convection of air over our bodies dissipates body heat without added air movement. When temperatures rise, we must increase air movement to maintain thermal comfort. Insufficient air movement is perceived as stuffiness, and air stratifies, with cooler air near the floor and warmer air at the ceiling.

A noticeable amount of air movement across the body when there is perspiration on the skin is experienced as a pleasant cooling breeze. When surrounding surfaces and room air temperatures are 1.7°C (3°F) or more below the normal room temperature, we experience that same air movement as a chilly draft. Our necks, upper backs, and ankles are the most sensitive to chills. This accounts for the popularity of scarves, sweaters, and socks in the winter.

When the moving air stream is relatively cooler than the room air temperature, its velocity should be less than the speed of the other air in the room to avoid the sensation of a draft. Air velocities between 3 and 15 meters per minute or mpm (between 10 and 50 ft per minute or fpm) are generally comfortable. We sense a 2°C (1°F) for each 4.6 mpm (15 fpm) increase above a velocity of 9.2 mpm (30 fpm). Air motion is especially helpful for cooling by evaporation in hot, humid weather.

Air Temperature and Relative Humidity

Relative humidity (RH) is the ratio of the amount of water vapor actually present in air to the maximum amount that air could hold at the same time, expressed as a percentage. Hot air temperature and high RH are very uncomfortable. The higher the RH of a space, the lower the air temperature should be. RH is less critical within normal room temperature ranges.

High humidity can cause condensation problems. Humidity below 20 percent can create a buildup of static electricity and can dry out wood in furniture and interior trims.

Chapter

16

Thermal Capacity and Resistance

• • •

Thermal capacity is the ability of a material to store heat, and is roughly proportional to a material's mass or its weight. A large quantity of dense material will hold a large quantity of heat. Light, fluffy materials and small pieces of material can hold small quantities of heat. Thermal capacity is measured as the amount of heat required to raise the temperature of a unit (by volume or weight) of the material one degree. Water has a higher thermal capacity than any other common material at ordinary air temperatures. Consequently, the heat from the sun retained by a large body of water during the day will only gradually be lost to the air during the cooler night. This is why, once a lake or ocean warms up, it will stay warm even after the air cools off.

THERMAL MASS

Masses of high thermal capacity materials heat up more slowly and release heat over a longer time. A cast iron frying pan takes a while to heat up, but releases a nice even heat to the cooking food, and stays warm even when off the burner.

Materials with high thermal capacity have low thermal resistance. When heat is applied on one side of the

material, it moves fairly quickly to the cooler side until a stable condition is reached, at which time the process slows down.

Brick, earth, stone, plaster, metals, and concrete all have high thermal capacity. Fabrics have low thermal capacity. Thin partitions of low thermal capacity materials heat and cool rapidly, so the temperature fluctuates dramatically; a tin shack can get very hot in the sun and very cold at night. Insulating materials have low thermal capacity since they are not designed to hold heat; they prevent heat from passing through them by incorporating lots of air spaces between their thin fibers.

Massive constructions of materials with high thermal capacity heat up slowly, store heat, and release it slowly. Think of how a brick or stone fireplace works. The effect is to even out the otherwise rapid heat rise and fall of temperatures as the fire flares and dies. Masses of masonry or water can store heat from solar collectors to be released at night or on cloudy days.

A portion of a room's operative temperature can be composed of radiant energy stored in thermal mass. This allows changes in the room's air temperature to be evened out over time. When the air temperature of a room normally kept at 21°C (70°F) is allowed to drift down to 10°C (50°F) for the night, the room's operative temperature gradually follows down to 10°C as well.

93

If the air temperature is rapidly brought back up to 21°C, the operative temperature rises back up more gradually. The resulting lag in heating or cooling depends upon the amount of mass in the room, and its ability to give off or take on heat. The effect may take a few hours to work, or even more. This thermal lag can help moderate changes and is useful in passive solar design, but may also mean that the room won't heat back up to the desired level fast enough. Heating or cooling the room's air temperature more than the usual amount can compensate for this slow change in temperature during warm-up or cool-down periods.

High thermal mass materials can be an integral part of the building envelope, or may be incorporated into the furnishings of the space. For maximum benefit, they must be within the insulated part of the building. The building's envelope will store heat if it has a large amount of mass. This will delay the transmission of heat to the interior, resulting in a thermal lag that can last for several hours or even for days; the greater the mass, the longer the delay. Where thermal mass is used inappropriately, excessively high temperatures or cooling loads may result on sunny days, or insufficient storage may occur overnight.

The choice of whether or not to use high quantities of thermal storage mass depends on the climate, site, interior design conditions, and operating pattern of the building. High thermal mass is appropriate when outdoor temperatures swing widely above and below the desired interior temperature. Low thermal mass is a better choice when the outside temperature remains consistently above or below the desired temperature.

Heavy mud or stone buildings with high thermal mass work well in hot desert climates with extreme changes in temperature from day to night (Fig. 16-1). The hot daytime outdoor air heats the exterior face of the wall, and migrates slowly through the wall or roof toward the interior. Before much of the heat gets to the interior, the sun sets and the air cools off outside. The radiation of heat from the ground outside to the sky cools the outdoor air below the warmer temperature of the building exterior, and the warm building surfaces are then cooled by convection and radiation. The result is a building interior that is cooler than its surroundings by day, and warmer by night.

In a hot damp climate with high night temperatures, a building with low thermal capacity works best. The building envelope reflects away solar heat and reacts quickly to cooling breezes and brief reductions in air temperatures. By elevating the building above the ground on wooden poles to catch breezes, using light

Figure 16-1 Taos Pueblo, New Mexico, around 1880.

thatch for the roof, and making the walls from open screens of wood or reeds, the cooling breeze keeps heat from being retained in the building (Fig. 16-2).

In a cold climate, a building that is occupied only occasionally (like a ski lodge) should have low thermal capacity and high thermal resistance. This will help the building to warm up quickly and cool quickly after occupancy, with no stored heat wasted on an empty interior. A well-insulated frame coupled with a wood-paneled interior is a good combination.

The high thermal capacity of soil ensures that basement walls and walls banked with earth stay fairly constant in temperature, usually around 13°C to 15°C (mid-fifties in degrees Fahrenheit) year-round. Earth-

Figure 16-2 Treehouse in Buyay, Mount Clarence, New Guinea.

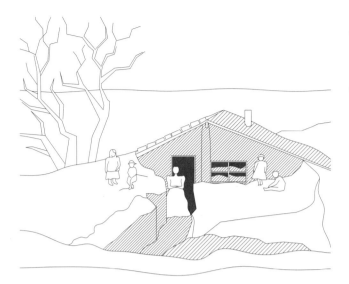

Figure 16-3 Dugout home near McCook, Nebraska, 1890s.

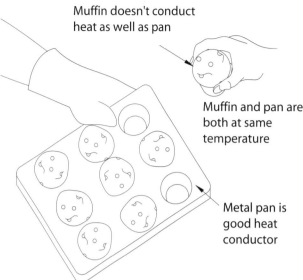

Muffin doesn't conduct heat as well as pan

Muffin and pan are both at same temperature

Metal pan is good heat conductor

Figure 16-4 Thermal conductivity.

bound walls are not exposed to extreme air temperatures in cold weather (Fig. 16-3). They should be insulated to thermal resistance values similar to the aboveground portions of the building. Burying horizontal sheets of foamed plastic insulation just below the soil's surface can minimize frost penetration into the ground adjacent to the building.

THERMAL CONDUCTIVITY

Our sense of touch tells us whether objects are hot or cold, but can be misleading as to just how hot or cold. Our senses are influenced by the rapidity with which objects conduct heat to and from our body rather than by the actual temperatures of objects (Fig. 16-4). Steel feels colder than wood at the same temperature, as heat is conducted away from our fingers more quickly by steel than by wood. This sensation is very useful to interior designers, who can specify materials that suggest warmth or coolness regardless of their actual temperatures.

If you touch a material that conducts heat rapidly—for example, a metal shelf that isn't directly in the sun—it will probably feel cool to your touch. This is because the metal will conduct the heat from your fingertips quickly away from your body and off into the surrounding air. Conductivity is a measurement of the rate at which heat will flow through a material. High conductance encourages heat transfer between a solid material and the air.

Good conductors tend to be dense and durable, and to diffuse heat readily. Smooth surfaces make better con-

tact than highly textured ones, resulting in better conduction of heat and a cooler feeling.

THERMAL RESISTANCE

Where there is a minimal amount of air motion, a wall surface will retain an insulating layer of air. The ability of this insulating air layer to resist the flow of heat away from the wall surface is called its resistance.

A good insulating material resists the conduction of heat. The higher the thermal resistance of a part of the building envelope is, the slower the heat loss. The bigger the difference between the temperature inside and outside the building is, the faster the building gains or loses heat. Designing a building's walls, roofs, and floors for the maximum amount of thermal resistance results in the best body comfort and the most energy conservation.

Solid materials have varying amounts of thermal resistance. Metals, which have very low thermal resistance, are good conductors of heat and poor thermal insulators. Masonry has moderately low resistance, and wood has moderately high resistance. Air is the best resistor of heat flow commonly found in buildings. If you keep it from moving by trapping it in a loose tangle of glass or mineral fibers, you create materials with very high thermal resistance. The fibers themselves have poor resistance to heat flow, but create resistance to air movement, and thereby trap the air for use as insulation.

When the air is disturbed, this insulating property drops to about a quarter of its value. If air circulates within a wall, a convective flow is created, which transfers heat from warmer to cooler surfaces pretty quickly.

Glass has a low resistance to heat flow, so double or triple glazing with air trapped in thin layers between sheets of glass is used for a great increase in thermal resistance. Increasing the thickness of the air space up to one inch increases the resistance slightly, as the friction between the glass surface and the air prevents convective heat flow. Spaces wider than one inch offer no additional advantage; the wider space allows convective currents, and the moving air is less effective.

Using a gas of lower thermal capacity than air can increase the thermal resistance of insulated glass. Tangles of glass fibers in the airspace also increase resistance, but block the view and reduce the amount of light transmitted. A thin metallic coating on the surface of the glass facing the airspace can reduce the emittance of the glass, and reduce the conductivity of the entire glazing assembly. Such coatings are called low emissivity coatings, or low-e coatings.

THERMAL FEEL

Interior designers can use an awareness of how we perceive the temperature of different materials to select appropriate materials for projects. A wood edge on a bar will be perceived to be warmer than a brass edge. Some of the materials we like close to our skin—wood, carpeting, upholstery, bedding, some plastics—feel warm to the touch, regardless of their actual temperature. We perceive materials to be warm that are low in thermal capacity and high in thermal resistance, and that are quickly warmed at a thin layer near their surfaces by our bodies. Materials that feel cold against the body, like metal, stone, plaster, concrete, and brick, are high in thermal capacity and low in thermal resistance. They draw heat quickly and for extended periods of time from our body because of the relatively larger bulk of cooler material.

An example of this phenomenon can be seen in the difference between a 22°C (72°F) room, which we perceive as warm, and a 22°C bath, which feels cool to us. The air is a poor conductor of heat, and has low thermal capacity, while water is the opposite. Our body gives off heat to the 22°C air at a comfortable rate, but loses heat rapidly to the 22°C water. Similarly, a carpeted floor is comfortable to bare feet at 22°C, while a concrete floor is perceived as cold.

R-VALUES

R-values measure the thermal resistance of a given material. As we discussed above, the greater the temperature difference from one side of a material to the other, the faster the heat will flow from the warmer side to the cooler side. To determine the R-value of a material, testers set up an experimental situation where heat flows through a unit of the material at the rate of one heat unit per hour. When this condition is established, the temperature on each side of the material is measured, and the R-value is an expression of that difference in temperature. R-values are used for comparing the effectiveness of solid materials as insulators, and refer to the material's resistance to heat flow.

The materials and construction assemblies used in a building's envelope affect its R-value. Different building shells vary in their ability to block heat transmission, depending upon the way they are constructed and the materials from which they are made. The structure's orientation to the sun and exposure to strong winds also influence the amount of heat that will pass through the barrier. By knowing the building's R-value, along with the desired indoor temperature and outdoor climate conditions, you can estimate the building envelope's ability to resist thermal transfer and to regulate indoor conditions for thermal comfort.

In the early 1970s, walls were often rated at around R-7, indicating that they tested out at a seven-degree difference between the two sides, compared to ratings of R-26 in 2001. Structural systems using structural insulated panels (SIPs) offer less thickness and lighter weight for walls, floors, and roofs. Structural insulated panels offer ratings around R-25, with new designs expected to be even lighter and thinner, and to have even higher ratings.

The insulating effectiveness of any airspace or air-containing building material depends upon its position and the direction of the heat flow. In the winter, heat flows up to the roof, and the warm air within the roof assembly rises to the cold upper surface, where it gives up its heat. In hot weather, the heat flow through the roof is reversed. Air warmed by the hot upper roof surface remains stratified against that surface, and heat transfer through the roof is slowed. The hot air below the roof doesn't drop to circulate with the cooler air below. A reflective foil surface will eliminate about half of the heat flowing out through roofs and walls, and about two-thirds of the heat flowing downward through floors. Foil surfaces can also reduce the transmission of heat from the sun on the roof down into the building in summer.

TYPES OF INSULATION

Insulation is the primary defense against heat loss transfer through the building envelope. The walls are the most important area to insulate, as they have the largest area. You can check if an existing building's walls are insulated by removing an electrical outlet cover and looking inside, or by drilling two 6-mm ($\frac{1}{4}$-in.) holes above one another about 100 mm (4 in.) apart in a closet or cabinet along an exterior wall, and shining a flashlight in one while looking in the other. An insulation contractor can blow cellulose or fiberglass insulation into an existing wall. To add insulation to an unheated attic without flooring, add a layer of unfaced batts about 305 mm (1 ft) deep across the joists. To insulate a space with a finished cathedral ceiling, either the interior drywall is removed to install insulation, or a new insulated exterior roof is built over the existing roof.

 Uninsulated foundation walls are responsible for as much as 20 percent of a building's heat loss. Insulating the foundation or basement floor can save several hundreds of gallons of oil or therms of gas (100,000 Btus equal 1 therm). To insulate an unheated, unfinished basement, install unfaced fiberglass batts between floor joists, supported from below with wire or metal rods as necessary. The underside of the batts can be covered with a moisture-permeable air barrier such as Tyvek® or Typar®. Insulate heated basement walls by adding frames made of 2″ × 4″ wood studs filled with fiberglass insulation against the concrete foundation walls, and covering them with drywall. Be sure to correct any drainage problems before insulating the basement.

Insulation comes in many forms. Loose-fill insulation consists of mineral wool fibers, granular vermiculite or perlite, or treated cellulose fibers. It is poured by hand or blown through a nozzle into a cavity or over a supporting membrane above ceilings on attic floors.

Foamed-in-place materials include expanded pellets and liquid-fiber mixtures that are poured, frothed, sprayed, or blown into cavities, where they adhere to surfaces. Foamed-in-place insulation is made of foamed polyurethane. By filling all corners, cracks, and crevices for an airtight seal, foamed insulation eliminates random air leakage, which can account for up to 40 percent of heating energy. Environmentally sound foamed insulation made without formaldehyde, chlorofluorocarbons (CFCs), hydrochlorofluorocarbons (HCFCs), or volatile organic compounds (VOCs) is available, and is safe for use by individuals who are chemically sensitive or suffering with allergies or asthma. Aerogel is one of the lightest existing solid materials. It is transparent and porous and contains no CFCs. Foamed into cavities, it can create walls rated up to R-32. Foamed insulation can also reduce levels of airborne sound from plumbing, outside noises, or indoor activities such as home theaters.

Flexible and semirigid insulation is available in batts and blankets. Batt insulation is made of glass or mineral wool. It comes in various thicknesses and lengths, and in 41- and 61-cm (16- and 24-in.) widths, to fit between studs, joists, and rafters in light frame construction. Batt insulation is sometimes faced with a vapor retarder of kraft paper, metal foil, or plastic sheeting, and is also used for acoustic insulation.

Rigid insulation comes in blocks, boards, and sheets and is preformed for use on pipes. It is made of plastic, or of cellular glass. Cellular glass is fire resistant, impervious to moisture, and dimensionally stable, but has a lower thermal-resistance value than foamed plastic insulation. Foamed plastics are flammable, and must be protected by a thermal barrier when used on the interior surfaces of a building.

Rigid insulation with closed-cell structures, made of extruded polystyrene or cellular glass, is moisture resistant, and may be used in contact with the earth. Such insulation is often applied to the outside of the building and covered with fabric-reinforced acrylic.

Sheets and rolls of insulation with reflective surfaces offer a barrier to radiant heat. Reflective insulation uses material of high reflectivity and low emissivity, such as paper-backed aluminum foil or foil-backed gypsum board, in conjunction with a dead-air space to reduce the transfer of radiant heat.

Gas-filled panels are a new development in insulation. Hermetically sealed plastic bags enclose honeycomb baffles of thin polymer films and a low conductivity gas such as argon, krypton, or xenon. Gas-filled panels are rated up to R-19.

Powder-evacuated panels are another new development. They combine a vacuum with a silica-based powder sealed within a multilayer gas barrier, and offer ratings of R-20 to R-25. Currently, powder-evacuated panels are expensive and subject to punctures, but continue to be developed.

Humidity

• • •

Water vapor is a colorless, odorless gas that is always present in air in widely varying quantities. The warmer the air, the more water vapor it can contain. The amount of water vapor in the air is usually less than the maximum possible, and when the maximum is exceeded, the water vapor condenses onto cool surfaces or becomes fog or rain.

As indicated earlier, relative humidity (RH) is the amount of vapor actually in the air at a given time, divided by the maximum amount of vapor that the air could contain at that temperature. For example, 50 percent RH means that the air contains half as much water vapor as it could hold at a given temperature. Colder air can hold less water vapor. If the temperature drops low enough, it reaches the dew point, which is the point at which the air contains 100 percent RH. When the RH is raised to 100 percent, as in a gym shower room or a pool area, fog is produced. Cooling below the dew point causes the water vapor—a gas—to turn into liquid droplets of fog. The vapor condenses only enough to maintain 100 percent RH, and the rest stays in the air as a gas.

People are comfortable within a wide range of humidity conditions. In the winter, relative humidity in the 20- to 50-percent range is acceptable. In summer, relative humidity can be as high as 60 percent when tem-peratures rise up to 24°C (75°F), but above that we are uncomfortable, because the water vapor (sweat) does not evaporate off our bodies well to help us cool off.

Some industrial and commercial settings, such as textile manufacturing, optical lens grinding, and food storage, require 60 percent RH. Some pharmaceutical products and the cold pressing of plywood need humidity below 20 percent. Hospitals have found that an RH of 50 to 55 percent supports the lowest amount of bacteria growth.

Humidity levels affect interior design materials. Too much moisture causes dimensional changes in wood, most plant and animal fibers, and even in masonry. Steel rusts, wood rots, and frost action causes spalling (chips or fragments breaking off) in masonry. Surface condensation damages decorative finishes and wood and metal window sashes, as well as structural members.

With the advent of smaller, tighter homes, moisture problems in residences have increased. A typical family of four produces about 11 kg (25 lb) of water vapor per day from cooking, laundering, bathing, and breathing. Humidifiers and automatic dryers give off even more. The drying of concrete slabs, masonry, or plaster in new construction, and the presence of bare earth in crawl spaces or basements add to moisture in a building.

CONDENSATION

When hot, humid air comes in contact with a cold surface, condensation forms. For example, when you take a glass of iced tea outside on a hot humid day, little drops of water will appear on the outside of the glass and run down the sides. The water vapor in the air condenses to form visible droplets of water on the cooler surface. In cold climates, water vapor can condense on the cold interior surfaces of windows. Condensation can result in water stains and mold growth.

Cooled air in summer may reach the dew point and condense on pipes and windows. Air in buildings can be cooled below the dew point by coming into contact with cold surfaces. In humid summer weather, condensation forms as "sweat" on cold water pipes, the cold-water tanks of toilets, and cool basement walls. In summer, concrete basement walls, floors, and slabs on grade that are cooled by the earth will collect condensation. Rugs on the floor or interior insulation on basement walls inhibit the rise in the concrete slab temperature and make matters worse. Both rugs and insulation may be damaged if the relative humidity is very high or if condensation occurs. Insulating the exterior or below the slab with well-drained gravel can help.

In winter, air cooled below the dew point fogs and frosts windows, and condensation can cause rust or decay when it collects under window frames. Wintertime condensation collects on cold closet walls, attic roofs, and single-pane windows.

Visible condensation can be controlled with methods that don't use additional energy (as do fans, heaters, and dehumidifiers), and that don't increase heat loss in winter and heat gain in summer. Interior surfaces should be insulated from the cold outdoors in the winter, and cold water pipes and ductwork should be insulated in the summer. Blowing warm air across perimeter windows artificially warms cold surfaces, and avoids condensation. You can use room arrangements to avoid pockets of still air and surfaces shielded from the radiant heat of the rest of the room.

In the winter, enough air motion should be provided to keep condensation from settling on cold surfaces. Reducing the amount of water vapor in the air avoids condensation in all seasons, as does ventilating moist air out of the space. When the dew point is higher outdoors than inside, ventilation rates should be reduced.

Insulated curtains that can be moved over windows can contribute to condensation problems, since the interior surface of the window is shielded from the heating source in the room and becomes cold. If warm room air can pass around or through the insulating window treatment, moisture will condense on the window. Thermal window treatments designed to seal out cold air need to be properly gasketed or sealed at the top, bottom, and sides to prevent moist room air from entering the space between the insulation and the glass, where it will condense against the cold window. The insulating material must also be impervious to moisture that might accumulate.

HIGH HUMIDITY

High summer air humidity reduces evaporation of moisture from our skin surfaces, and encourages mold and fungus growth in buildings. Refrigerant dehumidifiers are an option for spaces that don't need mechanical cooling but do need to reduce humidity.

Dehumidifiers chill air, which lowers the amount of moisture the air can hold, and thus leads to water vapor condensing on the cooling coils of the dehumidifier. The condensed water then drops off into the dehumidifier's collection container. Water accumulating in the dehumidifier may harbor disease-causing bacteria. Refrigerant dehumidifiers don't work well below 18°C (65°F), because frost forms on their cooling coils, so they might not be an appropriate choice in a cool basement.

LOW HUMIDITY

Heated winter air can be very dry, causing wood in buildings and furniture to shrink and crack. Wood shrinks in the dimension perpendicular to the grain, leaving unsightly cracks and loose furniture joints. Very low humidity causes plants to wither. Our skin becomes uncomfortable and dry, and the mucous membranes in our nose, throat, and lungs become dehydrated and susceptible to infection. Added moisture helps, as do lower air temperatures that reduce evaporation from the skin (and lower heating costs). Dry air creates static shocks. Carpeting is commercially available with a conductive material (copper or stainless steel) woven into its pile and backing that reduces voltage buildup and helps alleviate static electric shocks.

In warm-air heating systems, moisture can be added to the air as it passes through the furnace with water sprays or absorbent pads or plates supplied with water. Pans of water on radiators are an old-fashioned but effective method of raising humidity in the winter. Boiling water or washing and bathing release steam. Plants release water vapor into the air, and water evaporates from the soil in their pots. Spraying plants with a mist increases the air humidity, and the plants like it, too. We also release water vapor when we breathe.

Electric humidifiers help relieve respiratory symptoms, but may harbor bacteria or mold in their reservoirs if not properly maintained. Some humidifiers include an ultraviolet (UV) lightbulb to inhibit bacterial growth.

CONTROLLING HIDDEN MOISTURE

Indoor air in cold climates may be more humid than outdoor air, and vapors will then flow from the warmer interior to the colder exterior surfaces of the walls, ceilings, and floors. This can leave the building envelope permeated with moisture. Wet insulation becomes less effective, and dry rot, a fungus disease of timber that can cause it to become brittle and crumble into powder, can afflict wood structural members.

In hot humid climates, you need to keep the moisture from getting into the interior of the building. A drainage plane inside the exterior surfacing material, such as tarpaper, will let moisture that gets through wick away to the inside. This is safer than using a vapor barrier that may keep the moisture trapped in the wall.

When the moisture content of the air rises inside a building, it creates vapor pressure, which drives water vapor to expand into areas of lower vapor pressure like the exterior walls, seeking equilibrium. When there is moist air on one side of a wall and drier air on the other, water vapor migrates through the wall from the moist side to the drier side. Water vapor will also travel along any air leaks in the wall. Most building materials have relatively low resistance to water vapor. When the temperature at a given point within a wall drops below the dew point at that location, water vapor condenses and wets the interior construction of the wall. This condensation causes an additional drop in vapor pressure, which then draws more water vapor into the area. The result can be very wet wall interiors, with insulation materials saturated and sagging with water, or frozen into ice within the wall. The insulation becomes useless, and the heating energy use of the building increases. The wall framing materials may decay or corrode, and hidden problems may affect the building's structure. The

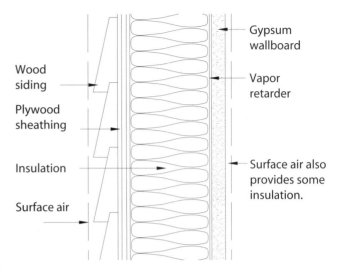

Figure 17-1 Vapor barrier.

amount of vapor pressure within a building depends on the amount of vapor produced, its inability to escape, and the air temperature.

A solid coat of exterior paint that keeps the water vapor from traveling out through the building's wall will trap vapor inside. Vapor pressure can raise blisters on a wall surface that will bubble the paint right off the wall. This is sometimes seen outside kitchens and bathrooms, where vapor pressure is likely to be highest.

By using a vapor barrier (Fig. 17-1) as close to the warm side of the building envelope as possible, this creeping water vapor can be prevented from traveling through the wall. The vapor barrier must be between the main insulating layer and the warm side of the wall. In a cold climate, the vapor barrier should be just under the plaster or paneling inside the building. In an artificially cooled building in a warm climate, the warm side is the outside.

Vinyl wallcoverings or vapor barrier paints on interior surfaces offer some protection, but don't replace the need for a vapor barrier. Aluminum-foil faced insulation is effective for thermal insulation, but does not make an adequate vapor barrier. Plastic films are tight against both moisture and infiltration. Where adding a vapor barrier to an older building is not practical, plugging air leaks in walls and applying paint to warm-side surfaces, and providing ventilation openings on cool-side surfaces clears moisture from the construction interior. Special vapor retardant interior paints are available for this purpose.

Chapter

Mechanical Engineering Design Process

The decisions made by the designers of the building's heating, ventilating, and air-conditioning (HVAC) system are crucial in determining thermal comfort, the quality of the indoor air, and the efficiency of energy use by the building. Air exchange rates affect the amount of energy used to heat or cool fresh air, and the energy lost when used air is exhausted. The American Society of Heating, Refrigerating, and Air-Conditioning Engineers (ASHRAE) requirements for ventilation include minimum rates for replacing previously circulated air in the building with fresh air.

Energy costs can be reduced or eliminated by improving building insulation, lighting design, and the efficiency of HVAC and other building equipment. Buildings that allow natural ventilation, and those that employ such techniques as heat reclamation, thermal-storage systems, and flexible air handling and chiller units lower energy use and reduce costs. The architect and engineers usually make the decisions on what systems to employ, but the responsibility for finding appropriate solutions depends on creativity and integrated efforts of the entire design team, in which the interior designer should play a significant role.

The mechanical systems of the building have their own model codes, which are geared toward professional mechanical engineers and installers. They are based on three model codes: the *Building Officials Code Administrators International* (BOCA) *National Mechanical Code* (NMC), the *Standard National Mechanical Code* (SMC), and the *Uniform National Mechanical Code* (UMC). These model codes are revised every three years.

As an interior designer, you will rarely need to refer to the mechanical codes, but you should be familiar with some of their general requirements and terms, especially those affecting energy conservation requirements. In buildings where there is a minimum of mechanical work, the mechanical engineer or contractor will work directly off the interior designer's drawings. For example, the interior design drawings may be the source for information in a renovation project where a few supply diffusers or return grilles are being added to an existing system. In any event, you may need to coordinate your preliminary design with the mechanical engineer or contractor to make sure you leave enough room for clearances around HVAC equipment.

The mechanical engineer, like the interior designer, is trying to achieve an environment where people are comfortable, and to meet the requirements of applicable codes. By calculating how much heating or cooling is needed to achieve comfort, the engineer is able to develop design strategies that affect both the architecture and the mechanical systems of the building, such as the optimal size of windows, or the relative amounts of insulation or thermal mass. The engineer will figure out how big the HVAC system components should be to provide enough heating and/or cooling for the most extreme conditions the building is likely to experience. The engineer will calculate the amount of energy used for normal conditions in a typical season and adjust the design to reduce long-term energy use. The number of people using the building both seasonally and hourly is also taken into account.

The amount of heat gained or lost from the outside environment will be considered. The materials, areas, and rates of heat flow through the building's envelope affect this calculation. The amount of fresh air introduced into the system also influences these calculations, so the engineer will look at the volumes of the spaces in the building and the rates of fresh air exchange. The engineer will suggest window locations and other design elements that minimize the heat gain within the building.

PHASES OF THE DESIGN PROCESS

The phases of the engineering design process are similar to those of architects and interior designers: preliminary design, design development, design finalization and specification, and the construction phase. During the preliminary design phase, the engineer considers the most general combinations of comfort requirements and climate characteristics. The schedule of activities that will take place in the space is listed, along with the conditions required for comfort during performance. The engineer analyzes the site's energy resources and lists strategies to design with the climate. Building form alternatives are considered and discussed with the architect. Available systems are reviewed, including both passive (nonmechanical) and active alternatives. Then the engineer figures out the size of one or more alternative systems using general design guidelines.

 In smaller buildings, the architect may do the system design. For larger, more complex buildings, the mechanical engineer will work as a team with architects, landscape architects, and the interior designer. The team approach helps to assess the value of a variety of design alternatives arising from different perspectives. When mutual goals are agreed upon early in the design process, this team approach can lead to creative innovations. The more that the siting, layout, and orientation

of the building reduces heat loss, the less energy the heating and cooling equipment consumes. Opportunities may arise for the design of the HVAC system to be expressed in the form of the building. Creative teamwork can lead to new designs that offer better environments with less energy use, and that can be applied to many other buildings later on.

During the design development phase, one alternative is usually chosen as presenting the best combination of aesthetic, social, and technical solutions for the building's program. The engineer is given the latest set of drawings and programming information for the building. The architect and engineer then establish the design conditions by listing the range of acceptable air and surface temperatures, air motions, relative humidities, lighting levels, and background noise levels for each activity to take place in the building. A schedule of operations for each activity is also developed.

By considering these activities and their schedule, the amount of heat that will be generated by the activities, and the building's orientation, the engineer then determines the HVAC zones for the building. Each of these zones has its own set of functional, scheduling, and orientation concerns that determine when and how much heating, cooling, or ventilation is needed. For each zone, the engineer establishes the thermal load (the amount of heat gained or lost) for the worst winter and summer conditions, and for average conditions during the majority of the building's operating hours. An estimate of the building's annual energy consumption may also be made at this time.

With all this detailed information in place, the engineer next selects the HVAC systems. More than one system may be used to meet different conditions in a large building. For example, one system may serve zones that are completely within the interior of the building, with a separate system for perimeter zones.

Next, the engineer identifies the components of the HVAC system, and locates them within the building. Mechanical rooms, distribution trees (vertical chases and horizontal runs of ductwork), and components like fancoil units (FCUs) under windows and air grilles within specific spaces all have to be selected and located. Sizes for these components are also specified.

Once the engineer lays out the system, it is time to coordinate conflicts with other building systems, such as the structure, plumbing, fire safety, and circulation. By drawing sections through the building, architects and engineers can identify clearance problems and see opportunities to coordinate the HVAC system with other building systems.

The process of design finalization involves the designer of the HVAC system verifying the load on each component, and the component's ability to meet this load. Then the final drawings and specifications are completed. During construction, the engineer may visit the site to assure that work is proceeding according to design, and to deal with unanticipated site conditions.

THERMAL COMFORT ZONES

The way zones for heating and cooling are set up by the mechanical engineer has implications for the architecture and interior design of the space. Zones may occupy horizontal areas of a single floor, or may be vertically connected between floors. The function of a space affects both its vertical and horizontal zoning (Fig. 18-1). Some functions may tolerate higher temperatures than others. Some functions require daylight, which may add heat to the space, while others are better off away from the building's perimeter. In some areas, such as laboratories, air quality and isolation is a major concern. The input of the interior designer can be an important component in making sure that the client's needs are met.

Zones also take into consideration the schedule of use of the space. Spaces that gain heat from daylight or electric lighting during the day only may be able to flush that heat to another space for use at night. An isolated activity with a different schedule from the rest of the building may need a separate mechanical system.

The building's orientation will also affect the HVAC zones. Exposure to daylight, direct sun, and wind all create specific heating and cooling requirements. Perimeter spaces have different needs from interior spaces.

In multistory buildings, interior spaces on intermediate floors—those spaces not at the building's perimeter or on the top or ground floors—may be able to use ventilation air as their only heating load source. These areas are so well shielded from the building's exterior that they may not need additional heat, and can be served only by cooling. The amount of electrically generated heat, plus that produced by human activity and other heat-generating sources, usually outweigh the cooling effect of the amount of outdoor air supplied by minimal ventilation, even in winter weather. In the summer, most of the interior cooling loads are generated inside the building. The perimeter areas of the building are much more weather sensitive.

HEATING AND COOLING LOADS

Heating and cooling loads are the amounts of energy required to make up for heat loss and heat gain in the building (Fig. 18-2). The rate of flow of hot or cold air coming into the building from ventilation and infiltration influences the amount of heating or cooling load. It is also dependent upon the difference in temperature and humidity between the inside and outside air. The amount of outside air coming in is expressed in liters per second (cubic feet per minute, or cfm).

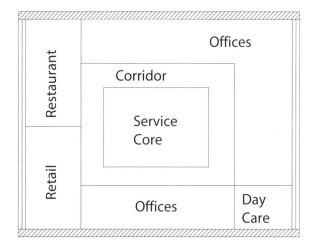

Figure 18-1 Thermal zones based on activity patterns.

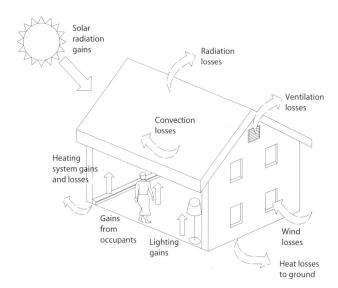

Figure 18-2 Heat gains and losses in buildings.

Heat Loss and Heating Loads

A heating load is created when a building loses heat through the building envelope. Cold outside air entering a building through ventilation, such as an open window, or as a result of infiltration, as when air leaks through cracks in the building envelope, also add to the heating load.

Convection, radiation, or conduction of heat through the building's exterior walls, windows, and roof assemblies and the floors of unheated spaces are the main sources of heat loss in cold weather. Wind passing the building both draws warm air out and forces cold air in. Infiltration of cold air through cracks in the exterior construction, especially around doors and windows contributes significant heat loss. This heat loss places a heating load on the building's mechanical system, which must make up heat in spaces that lose it through cracks and poorly insulated areas.

Energy auditors use equipment to locate air leaks and areas with inadequate insulation. They know what to look for in new and older buildings, and the cost of an energy audit is a good investment for a building owner. Some utilities will supply basic energy audits for free. Trained experts, sometimes called house doctors or home performance contractors, look at the building as a system and evaluate safety, comfort, energy efficiency, and indoor air quality. You can get a listing of qualified, trained energy auditors from your state energy office or cooperative extension service.

The most common sources of air leaks are where plumbing, wiring, or a chimney penetrates through an insulated floor or ceiling, or along the sill plate or band joist on top of the building's foundation wall. Fireplace dampers and attic access hatches are other likely suspects.

 Anywhere that walls and ceilings or floors meet or where openings pierce the building's exterior is an opportunity for air to infiltrate. Air can leak where the tops of interior partition walls intersect with the attic space and through recessed lights and fans in insulated ceilings. Missing plaster allows air to pass through a wall, as do electrical outlets and switches on exterior walls. Window, door, and baseboard moldings can leak air, as can dropped ceilings above bathtubs and cabinets. Air can also leak at low walls along the exterior in finished attics, especially at access doors, and at built-in cabinets and bureaus.

Gaps under 4 mm ($\frac{1}{4}$ in.) wide can be sealed with caulk, which is available in a variety of types for different materials. Specify caulks with 20-year flexibility lifetimes, and select either colored or paintable caulk for visible use. Avoid using the cheapest caulks, as they don't hold up well. Larger cracks and holes that are protected from the sun and moisture can be filled with expanding one-part polyurethane foam sealant. Look for a safe-for-ozone label for foam sealants without chlorofluorocarbons (CFCs).

For even larger cracks and for backing in deep cracks, specify backer rod or crack filler, usually in the form of a round 4- to 25-mm ($\frac{1}{4}$–1-in.) diameter coil made of a flexible foam material. The crack is then sealed with caulk. Rigid foam insulation or fiberglass insulation wrapped in plastic can be used for very large openings like plumbing chases and attic hatch covers. Avoid using plastic in places with high temperatures, as it may melt. Metal flashing with high temperature silicone sealants may be permitted around chimneys by some building codes.

Heat Gains and Cooling Loads

Buildings gain heat from occupants and their activities. Cooling loads are defined as the hourly rate of heat gain in an enclosed space, and are expressed in Btu per hour. Cooling loads are used as the basis for selecting an air-conditioning unit or a cooling system.

Cooling loads represent the energy needed to offset the heat gained through the building envelope in hot weather or from hot air entering by infiltration or ventilation. People's body heat, showering, cooking, lighting, and appliances and equipment use also create cooling loads.

The heat generated by lighting is often the greatest part of the total cooling load in a building. All types of electric lighting convert electrical power into light plus heat. Eventually, the light is also converted to heat within the space (think about a lamp shining on a desk and the desk becoming warmer). All the electrical power that enters a lighting fixture ends up as heat in the space.

Some of the heat from lighting is convected from the lighting fixture to the surrounding air and becomes part of the cooling load. The rest is radiated to surrounding surfaces, except for a small amount that is conducted to adjacent material. This radiated and conducted heat is then convected to the air, becoming part of the cooling load. Recessed fixtures tend to heat the surrounding structure, while hanging fixtures convey heat more directly to the air. Some fixtures are designed so that air returns through them, absorbing heat that would otherwise go into the space.

Electric, gas, or steam appliances and equipment in restaurants, hospitals, laboratories, and commercial spaces such as beauty salons and restaurants release heat to interiors. Hoods over kitchen appliances that exhaust air may reduce heat gain, but the exhausted air must be replaced with outdoor air, which may need to be cooled. Steam or hot water pipes that run through air-conditioned spaces and hot water tanks within spaces contribute to the cooling load.

In warm or hot weather, buildings gain heat by convection, radiation, and conduction through the exterior walls and window and roof assemblies. The amount of heat gain varies with the time of day, the orientation of the affected building parts to the sun, the exposure to the wind, and the amount of time it takes for the heat to reach the interior of the building (thermal lag). The heat gain from sun shining on windows varies with the orientation to the sun and the ways the windows are shaded.

In hot weather, warm makeup air enters when spaces are ventilated to remove odors or pollutants. The use of a dehumidifier to lower relative humidity (RH) in a space adds to heat gain, due to the latent heat released into the space when moist air is condensed and the heat produced by running the dehumidifier's compressor.

Measuring Heating and Cooling Loads

A degree-day is a unit used in computing heating and cooling loads, sizing HVAC systems, and calculating yearly fuel consumption. It represents one degree of difference in mean daily outdoor temperature from a standard temperature. A heating degree-day is one degree-day below the standard temperature of 18°C (65°F), and is used in estimating fuel or power consumption by a heating system. A cooling degree-day is one degree-day above the standard temperature of 24°C (75°F), and helps in calculating energy requirements for air-conditioning and refrigeration systems. Degree-day information is usually published in daily newspapers.

Systems are rated in tons of refrigeration, which is the cooling effect obtained when a ton of ice at 0°C (32°F) melts to water while at the same temperature over a period of 24 hours. It is equal to 3.5 kW (12,000 Btu/hr).

The energy-efficiency rating is an index of the efficiency of a refrigerating unit. It expresses the number of Btus removed per watt of electrical energy input.

ENERGY USE CALCULATIONS

Mechanical engineers perform load calculations to determine the correct size for heating and cooling equipment, airflow rates, and duct and pipe sizes. Architects calculate loads to make sure that the building envelope is adequately insulated, to compare alternative envelope designs, to estimate preliminary mechanical system costs, and to evaluate the potential benefits of solar energy design. Load calculations provide the basis for estimates of annual building energy use. They can become very complicated when used for detailed cost comparisons of alternative systems.

Hourly computer simulations of heating and cooling loads are necessary for accurate calculations for large industrial or commercial buildings. Calculating the hourly heating and cooling energy use for a year requires a substantial computer program. Looking at hourly solar angles and intensities and analyzing shading patterns can determine when the peak load occurs in the course of a year. However, even the best estimates are based on average weather conditions, and can't take into consideration potential problems with construction quality and unusual weather. Any computer program's results are dependent upon the assumptions of the person selecting the input data. Hourly annual calculations are not usually done for simple residences, but may be required to estimate energy use for a passive-solar heated home.

When one design costs less to install but another is more energy efficient, engineers may perform energy design value analyses. For example, an analysis may help with decisions about optimizing the quantity of insulation, choosing between double and triple glazing, selecting types of lighting, deciding on solar energy use, and balancing aesthetic considerations with their cost to the client.

There are four methods of design value analysis. The first looks at the payback period, which is the length of time required for the investment in the building to pay for itself in energy savings. This is a relatively simple method to understand, and is often used to screen out options. A second, lifecycle costing, looks at the total cost of owning, operating, and maintaining a project over its useful life, and considers salvage values and disposal costs. A third method, return on investment (ROI) considers whether the same money could be better invested elsewhere for more profit. The final method, comparative value analysis, also considers issues like improved worker efficiency, reduced air and water pollution, and appearance, and weight factors for relative importance. Then all competing designs are compared in an evaluation matrix, a graphic tool that helps the user decide on which of several complex choices to select.

Energy improvements, such as improving insulation or upgrading windows, can often be planned as part of other building renovations. The payback period for insulating oil- and gas-heated buildings is around five years, and much faster with electric heat. New energy-efficient construction typically reduces heating bills in cold climates by 75 percent. Building a super-efficient house, with R-30 walls, R-38 ceilings, and R-19 foundations, adds about $5000 to $10,000 to the cost of conventional construction, money that can be recovered in five to ten years in energy savings. Such a house also creates less environmental pollution. Look for contractors with experience in energy-efficient construction for the best ideas and workmanship.

HEATING AND COOLING SYSTEM COMPONENTS

Although we, as interior designers, don't design the HVAC system, we do have to deal with the space that components take up, their noise, their terminal outlets in occupied rooms, and the access space needed for repair and maintenance. There are three main parts to an HVAC system: the equipment that generates the heating or cooling, the medium by which the heat or cooling is transported, and the devices by which it is delivered. For example, a building might use an oil-fired boiler to generate hot water. The water is the medium that carries the heat throughout the building, and the pipes and radiators are the delivery devices.

The front end (or head end) of the system is where the energy or fuel consumption or heat collection occurs. The equipment here is selected for its capacity to offset the peak load of the zones it is serving, and to bring them back from the lower temperature that they are set at when not in use to the normal operating condition. For example, the air-conditioning equipment will be sized to cool the spaces in an office building it serves enough to counteract the hottest days that are expected. When the air-conditioning is shut off or reduced at night, the building will warm up somewhat. The equipment will need to be able to cool off the building to an acceptable temperature the next morning. The front end may consist of a central heat source, such as a furnace, a steam or hot water boiler, a solar collector, a geothermal well, or a heating water converter. The front end may also include a central cooling source like a chiller, direct expansion (DX) air conditioner, or evaporative cooler.

The conveying medium transports the heated or cooled steam, water, or air through a system of pipes or ducts throughout the building. Steam will travel under its own pressure. Air is moved by fans, and water is moved by pumps.

Terminal delivery devices are located within the spaces to be heated or cooled. The heated or cooled medium is delivered to the space by air registers and diffusers, hydronic radiators or convectors, or FCUs.

It is becoming more common for buildings to be designed for localized, rather than centralized, HVAC production and control. Multipurpose buildings with fragmented occupancy schedules call for many diverse HVAC zones. Digital control systems allow both overall building coordination and localized thermal response. Employees are more satisfied when they can control their interior environment. Self-contained package units can provide heating and/or cooling directly to the space, combining all three components in one piece of equipment.

ARCHITECTURAL CONSIDERATIONS

The design of the HVAC system affects the building's architecture and interior design. The architect must coordinate with all consultants from the beginning of the project to allow realistic space allotments for HVAC equipment. The design of the mechanical system must merge with the architectural and structural planning, and should be developed concurrently. Spaces requiring quiet, such as bedrooms and conference rooms, should be located as far away from noisy HVAC equipment as possible, both horizontally and vertically. Interior design issues, such as whether to use an open office plan with modular furniture systems or private enclosed offices, have a great impact on the mechanical system, and should be shared with the engineer early in the design process.

The mechanical engineer decides which HVAC system will be used in a large building. The mechanical engineer selects the system based on initial and life-cycle costs, suitability for the intended occupancy, availability of floor space for the required equipment, maintenance requirements and reliability of the equipment, and simplicity of the system's controls. The architect must communicate and coordinate with the engineer, and ask questions about the impact the engineering system will have on the architectural and interior design.

Together, the architect and engineer evaluate issues that affect the thermal qualities of the building, such as the amount and type of insulation and the shading of the building from the sun's heat, that influence the mechanical equipment size and fuel consumption. The architect may develop design elements that reduce the operating expenses of the system and decrease the size and initial cost of HVAC equipment, but increase the initial cost of the building's construction. The use of cost-effectiveness analyses help determine the optimal economic balance between passive (built into the building's architectural design) and active (mechanical system) approaches.

Early in the project, the architect must consider the number, position, and size of central HVAC stations, and ensure that they are located near the areas they serve and with access to outdoor air. Clearances must be allowed around the equipment for access during normal operation, inspection, routine maintenance, and repair. Plans should be made for eventual replacement of major components without substantial damage to existing building materials. Space for flue stacks, access for fuel delivery, and room for fuel storage may be needed. HVAC requirements can have a substantial impact on the space plan, ceiling heights, and other interior design issues, so getting involved early in the process is a good idea.

Mechanical rooms often take up around 5 to 10 percent of the gross building area. Furnace and boiler rooms, fan rooms, and refrigeration rooms may be separate spaces or may be combined. They may require doors of adequate width for equipment replacement, and the doors might need to be louvered to allow air to enter the space. Their size, location, and noise can be important interior design considerations.

The locations and dimensions of piping and ductwork will determine where chases must be located for clusters of piping and ductwork running vertically between floors. Ductwork, and especially areas where ducts connect, requires regular access for maintenance. Suspended ceiling grids allow easy duct access. Gypsum wallboard ceilings may require access doors at specific locations, including at all fire dampers within ducts. With proper early planning, only minor changes in the floor plan will be needed to fit in the final mechanical design.

Within occupied areas, space must be allocated along exterior walls for exposed terminal delivery devices, such as registers and diffusers. Their form and position must be coordinated with the interior design, to avoid conflicts between furniture arrangements and the location of grilles or wall-mounted units. Thermostat locations are determined by the engineer and are dependent upon the surrounding heat sources, but have a significant effect on the visual quality of the interior space. The architect is also concerned with the appearance on the exterior of the building of grilles and openings in outside walls.

Improved electronic communications networks have made possible the increasing use of residences as workspaces. Residential design has consequently become more complex, entailing office-quality lighting, new zones for heating and cooling, added electrical raceways, and improved sound isolation.

Indoor Air Contaminants

Americans spend 80 to 90 percent of their time indoors. As our buildings become more tightly controlled environments, the quality of indoor air and its effects on our health becomes an increasingly critical issue. There are over 80,000 synthetic chemicals in use today, most of which have not been tested individually or in combination for their effects on human health. Materials used in building, furnishing, and maintaining a building potentially contain many toxic chemicals.

According to the U.S. Environmental Protection Agency (EPA), indoor air in the United States is now on average two to ten times more contaminated than the air outside. The World Health Organization (WHO) asserts that 40 percent of all buildings pose significant health hazards from indoor pollution, and WHO experts have observed unusually high rates of health and comfort complaints that could be related to indoor air quality (IAQ) from occupants in up to 30 percent of new or remodeled commercial buildings.

Twenty percent of all workers report building-related irritations or illnesses. The EPA has declared poor IAQ the number one environmental health problem in the United States. According to the American Medical Association, a third of our total national health expenditure is spent on ailments directly attributable to indoor air pollution. The EPA cites an 18 percent decrease in overall worker productivity due to poor IAQ.

Three major reasons for poor IAQ in office buildings are the presence of indoor air pollution sources; poorly designed, maintained, or operated ventilation systems; and uses of the building that were unanticipated or poorly planned for when the building was designed or renovated. Interior designers play a significant role in specifying materials that may contribute to indoor air pollution. We also are key players in the renovation of buildings to new uses and to accommodate new ways of working.

Air pollution problems can start with the building's materials and finishes and/or with the construction methods used to build or renovate the building. Indoor air quality is compromised when inadequate ventilation fails to provide enough outside air. Chemicals used in cleaning and office products thus get trapped inside the building, and outdoor pollutants that enter get caught inside, adding to the problem. Mold or other microorganisms that grow, multiply, and disperse particles through heating, ventilating and air-conditioning (HVAC) systems are a significant source of IAQ problems as well. Poor design and maintenance of the HVAC system supports the growth of microorganisms.

People contribute skin scales, carbon dioxide that we exhale, and airborne particles, vapors, and gases. Cleaning, cooking, broiling, gas and oil burning, personal hygiene, and smoking all add pollutants to indoor air. Pesticides from pest management practices can also pollute the building's air. Indoor air pollutants can be circulated from portions of the building used for specialized purposes, such as restaurants, print shops, and dry-cleaning stores, into offices in the same building.

Prior to 1973, energy for buildings was relatively inexpensive, and large quantities of outdoor air were used to ventilate buildings. During the oil embargo of 1973, Americans became more aware of the limited supply of fossil fuels for energy. New energy-conserving designs were developed that often limited the amount of outdoor air entering the building, thereby saving the cost of heating or cooling this fresh air. Insulation was increased, air leakage through the building envelope was reduced, and mechanical ventilation rates were decreased. Heat exchangers were introduced to recover the heat of exhaust air.

Air quality was originally ignored in the quest to produce energy-efficient buildings, leading to concentration of contaminants at levels that threatened public health. Scientists developed new chemical compounds for use in the manufacture of synthetic building materials, in equipment inside the building, and in cleaning and maintenance products. With the decrease in fresh air entering the building, these potential air pollutants became concentrated in the indoor environment of some buildings. Some chemicals were concentrated at levels 100 times higher than would ever occur in the open air. Because updating codes takes years, and ventilation standards have changed, the code in force when an HVAC system was designed may have permitted a lower ventilation rate than the current standards.

Contaminants in buildings are so widespread that virtually every building contains one or more recognized contaminants. Asbestos and lead have been used in building products for many years in the past. Heating systems can give off carbon monoxide. Interior finishes and building materials often contain formaldehyde. Benzene and chlordane are both petroleum products found in detergents, insecticides, and motor fuels. Mercury, ozone, and radon can contaminate buildings as well. Paper copying and inks produce irritating fumes, and dust and tobacco smoke contain particles that irritate the respiratory system. Plastics can give off offensive gases. Fabrics treated with fire-retardant chemicals can cause problems for some people.

The overall result of these pollutants can be sick building syndrome (SBS), which is diagnosed when more than 20 percent of the building's occupants complain of symptoms such as headaches, upper respiratory irritation, or eye irritation, and when these symptoms disappear after leaving the building on weekends. Symptoms may also include irritation of mucous membranes, dizziness, nausea, throat irritation, and fatigue. Although the specific causes aren't identified, the symptoms coincide with time spent in a particular building and disappear once the sufferer leaves. The related term "building related illness" (BRI) is also used to describe the same range of ailments, from mild allergic reactions to more serious infections such as pneumonia; the difference is that BRI is applied to those cases where the specific cause of the ailment is known. Both SBS and BRI are largely the result of poor IAQ.

The EPA conservatively estimates the potential economic impact of employee illness and loss of productivity due to indoor air pollution to total $4.4 to $5.4 billion per year. The most susceptible people, who are also those who spend the most time indoors, include children, elderly people, and people with chronic illnesses. Contamination by multiple chemicals has an effect greater than the sum of the same chemicals individually. Allergies and asthma are rising dramatically, and may be caused by contaminants in a sick building.

Symptoms that appear suddenly after a change in the building, such as painting or pesticide application, are another indication of IAQ problems. Some individuals may be affected by IAQ problems, while others sharing the same space are not.

Frequently, IAQ problems in large commercial buildings cannot be effectively identified or remedied without a comprehensive building investigation. Diagnosing symptoms that relate to IAQ can be difficult, time consuming, and expensive. If a professional company is hired to conduct an investigation of a commercial building, the building's owner should select a company on the basis of its experience in identifying and solving IAQ problems in nonindustrial buildings, as the methodology and standards are different for industrial settings.

These investigations may start with written questionnaires and telephone consultations in which building investigators assess the history of occupant symptoms and building operation procedures. In some cases, these inquiries may quickly uncover the problem and on-site visits are unnecessary. More often, investigators will need to come to the building to conduct personal interviews with occupants, to look for possible sources of problems, and to inspect the design and operation of the ventilation system and other building features. Taking measurements of pollutants at the very low levels often found in office buildings is expensive and may not yield information readily useful in identifying problem sources. The process of solving IAQ problems that result in health and comfort complaints can be a slow one, involving several trial solutions before successful remedial actions are identified.

Unusual odors, too hot an indoor environment, improper lighting, noise, vibration, overcrowding, ergonomic stressors, and job-related psychosocial problems can all produce symptoms that are similar to those associated with poor air quality, but IAQ may not be the culprit. Because of the complexity of IAQ problems and building dynamics, as well as the potential for serious human health effects, building owners or managers who suspect IAQ problems should seek the help of competent, qualified IAQ specialists to investigate, diagnose, and mitigate problems.

 In order to improve IAQ and prevent contamination by pollutants, the building's architect, engineers, and interior designer must work together. The interior designer can specify appropriate materials, products, and equipment. You should evaluate the amount and toxicity of emissions given off during installation or use, especially where surfaces of possibly polluting materials are exposed to the air and to people. Review maintenance requirements for cleaning processes, stain resistant treatments, and waxing that emit pollutants. When the construction is complete, the interior designer should provide the building's management, users, and owners with appropriate information about maintenance requirements.

 Many of the problems people have with reactions to building contaminants begin with new or renovation construction. Renovations in occupied buildings are especially likely to introduce pollutants into the building's interior. Construction can be compartmentalized using partitions and doors with closers, and connecting plenums can be blocked. The work area must be securely isolated from other occupied spaces, and supplied with extra ventilation via window- or door-mounted fans. Keeping the construction area under negative pressure prevents contaminants from spreading throughout the building. Plugging up air-conditioning returns so that contamination from a construction area can't spread throughout the building also helps. If appropriate, construction workers should use organic vapor respirators with charcoal filters. Emphasize that complying with IAQ requirements also protects construction workers.

GASES AND PARTICLES

Indoor air contains gases and particles, some organic and some inorganic, some visible and others invisible, which may be toxic to humans—or harmless. Air normally contains about 80 percent nitrogen, 20 percent oxygen, and a small amount of carbon dioxide, along with varying amounts of particulate materials. What we experience as dust, fumes, or smoke is mostly solid particulates suspended in the air. Fumes arise as vapors from solid materials and are sometimes detectable by distinctive odors. Smoke is produced by the incomplete combustion of organic substances like tobacco, wood, coal, or oil so, as the saying goes, where there's smoke, there's fire. The air we breathe can suspend tiny living organisms, from submicroscopic viruses to pollen grains, bacteria, and fungus spores. When we sneeze, we spray droplets containing microorganisms.

Carbon Dioxide

Carbon dioxide is an odorless gas that we exhale every time we breathe. It is also produced by combustion of carbon in machinery. Carbon dioxide is always present in the air, but excess carbon dioxide causes stuffiness and discomfort. At high enough levels, it dulls our ability to think. The presence of excess carbon dioxide is used as an indicator of an inadequate ventilation rate in enclosed or high-occupancy spaces.

Where people are concentrated in confined spaces, such as theaters, the carbon dioxide produced by their respiration must be removed and replaced with oxygen by ventilation with fresh air. Concentrations of oxygen in the air below 12 percent and carbon dioxide concentrations greater than 5 percent are dangerous, even for short periods. For longer periods, even smaller carbon dioxide concentrations can cause problems.

Irritating Particles

Irritating particles in the air tend to be imperceptible at first, but your distress increases over time. Your symptoms may include itching or burning eyes, sneezing, coughing, dry nose and throat, a sore throat, or tightness in your chest. Sources of irritants can be the building itself, its equipment, or its occupants.

Several common air pollutants are the products of combustion. Outdoors, coal-burning factories, vehicle exhaust, and heating exhaust from oil, wood, or coal contribute to air pollution that contaminates the supply of air available for building ventilation. Forest fires and open incineration of trash and yard waste also generate particles that can enter buildings through poorly placed air intakes. Indoors, heating and cooking appliances add to small amounts of particles from dry-process photocopiers. The largest contributor of combustion particles in offices and residential buildings is environmental tobacco smoke inhaled by nonsmokers, which accounts for 50 to 90 percent of the total particles where smoking occurs. Combustion burners (furnaces, etc.) that are not sealed, vented, and exhausted properly can also add pollutants.

Carbon monoxide is an odorless gas produced by incomplete combustion in furnaces, stoves, and fireplaces. It is also present in automobile exhaust. It is often found near garages, combustion equipment, or indoor air contaminated with tobacco smoke. It seeps into buildings adjacent to underground or indoor garages. The U.S. Department of Energy (DOE) reports that, in many office buildings, afternoon concentrations of carbon monoxide are sometimes known to exceed the recommended daily allowance for outdoors. Carbon monoxide interferes with oxygen intake, causes headaches, dizziness, sleepiness, and muscular weakness, and at high concentrations it can cause unconsciousness and death. The symptoms of carbon monoxide poisoning are sometimes confused with the flu or food poisoning. Fetuses, infants, elderly people, and people with anemia or with a history of heart or respiratory disease can be especially sensitive to carbon monoxide exposure. Prolonged exposure decreases the oxygen-carrying capacity of the blood, resulting in shortness of breath, fatigue, and nausea.

Nitrogen oxide is a yellowish brown gas that is a product of high-temperature combustion and is found in tobacco smoke. It can cause respiratory irritation, interferes with breathing, can cause lung damage, and may suppress the immune system.

Nitrogen dioxide is a colorless, odorless gas that is used in some chemical processes as a catalyst or oxidizing agent. It irritates the mucous membranes in the eye, nose, and throat, and causes shortness of breath after exposure to high concentrations. There is evidence that high concentrations or continued exposure to low levels of nitrogen dioxide increases the risk of respiratory infection, and repeated exposures to elevated levels may lead or contribute to the development of lung disease.

Heating systems using coal and oil may generate sulfur oxides, which have been implicated in acid rain and cause damage to plants and building envelope materials. Sulfur oxides irritate the respiratory tract and complicate cardiovascular disease, causing burning eyes and reduced lung function.

Tobacco smoke, burning wood or coal, barbecuing, and burning food all produce polynuclear aromatic hydrocarbons. These are cancer-causing irritants. Irritation tends to increase with low humidity. Where smoking occurs, proper separation and isolation of spaces is a must.

Fireplaces should be carefully designed and supplied with sufficient fresh air for a proper draft. Kitchen cooking equipment, especially grilling equipment, must be properly exhausted and supplied with adequate fresh air.

Humidifiers and humidification systems spray mineral particles suspended in water mist. These may include asbestos, lead, aluminum, and dissolved organic gases present in the water source for the humidifier.

Exposure to combustion products can be reduced in homes by taking special precautions. When operating fuel-burning unvented kerosene or gas space heaters, the type of fuel used and the quality of the flame must be monitored. While this type of space heater is in use, it is recommended that a door from the room where the heater is located be opened to the rest of the house, and that a window be opened slightly. However, this is rarely done, as it allows the warm air to escape.

Install exhaust fans over gas cooking stoves and ranges and keep the burners properly adjusted to avoid exposure to pollutants during cooking. Choose properly sized new stoves that are certified as meeting EPA emission standards. Emphasize to clients that they should have central air-handling systems, including furnaces, flues, and chimneys, inspected annually, and promptly repair cracks or damaged parts. Blocked, leaking, or damaged chimneys or flues release harmful combustion gases and particles, and even fatal concentrations of carbon monoxide. Carbon monoxide detectors are inexpensive, easy to install and use, and can save lives.

Ozone

Ozone is an irritating pale blue gas composed of three oxygen atoms. It is explosive and toxic even at low concentrations. Buildings may contain ozone from copy machines, high-voltage electronic equipment, or electrostatic air cleaners. Ozone in our air supply can inflame the windpipe, resulting in wheezing, shortness of breath, dizziness, or asthma.

The risk of ozone irritation is highest in small poorly ventilated offices, even at low concentrations. A level of under 80 parts per billion (ppb) is considered normal and acceptable. Levels over 100 ppb can irritate eyes and respiratory systems, while levels over 500 ppb are considered extremely high and can result in nausea, headaches, and the increased risk of lung infections. Elevated levels near high traffic can create health problems for elderly people and people with asthma. Outdoor fumes can be drawn into buildings through poorly located intake vents.

Laser printers, photocopiers, small motors, and electronic air cleaners produce ozone. Dry-process photocopying machines also release hydrocarbons and respirable suspended particulates. Wet-process photocopiers give off aliphatic hydrocarbons and other volatile organic compounds (VOCs), as well as ozone. These emissions don't dissipate in areas with poor ventilation, and build up in large copying areas during the week. Laser and other computer printers produce hydrocarbons and ozone. Computer terminals, fax machines, and other electronic equipment and the documents they generate also emit ozone and VOCs.

 Proper maintenance and exhausting contaminated air at the source may help with these equipment sources of pollution, or the equipment may have to be removed from occupied areas. Emissions can be reduced by selecting lower-emitting equipment in consultation with the manufacturer and authorities on emissions. Minimizing the use of equipment, turning it off when possible, and educating operators on use and maintenance also help. Consolidate equipment in isolated rooms with separate exhaust and supply ducts and increased outdoor air. When equipment such as computer terminals must be near workers, locate return air ducts nearby to dilute contaminants, and make sure that operators get adequate breaks away from the equipment.

Radioactive Air Contaminants

Radioactivity in the air is not common, with one exception: radon. Radioactivity may be in the form of particles or gases. Many radioactive materials are chemically toxic in high concentrations, but the radioactivity itself is the main problem for air quality. Radioactive particles and gases can be removed from the air by filters and other devices. They release gamma radiation, which can penetrate solid walls, so areas where radioactive materials are in use require special treatment. The danger to people arises when the radioactive materials are taken into and retained inside the body.

Radioactive substances may generate enough heat to damage filtration equipment, or to spontaneously ignite. Even very low concentrations may be dangerous, and can be detected with special electronic instruments. Radioactivity must be prevented from entering sensitive facilities, like photographic plants. Where radioactivity is handled within a building, it should be removed from the air as close to its source as possible before the air is released to the outdoors. The air ducts serving spaces where X-rays and radiation therapy are used must be lined with lead to contain radiation, as must the room itself be.

Radon is a colorless, odorless radioactive gas produced by the decay of radioactive uranium. It occurs naturally in soil, groundwater, and air all over the United States. Radon can move through soil and into buildings through cracks and openings in the foundation around plumbing, especially below grade. Sometimes radon enters the home through well water. In a small number of homes, the building materials can give off radon, too. However, building materials rarely cause radon problems by themselves. Radon decays rapidly, releasing radiation as it does.

If radon becomes concentrated within a building, it may result in an increased risk of lung cancer over a long period of time. Radon breaks down into decay products that may become trapped in the lungs, releasing small amounts of radiation as they continue to deteriorate. The eventual result may be lung damage or lung cancer. The EPA conservatively estimates that radon causes about 4000 deaths per year in the United States, but suggests that the number may actually be as high as 30,000 deaths per year. Radon is the second leading cause of lung cancer after smoking.

The U.S. federal government recommends that homeowners measure the level of radon in their homes. A good time is when purchasing a new house, or renovating an old one, and as an interior designer, you are in a good position to advocate for radon testing. Testing is easy and quick. There are many kinds of inexpensive, do-it-yourself radon test kits available through the mail and in hardware stores and other retail outlets. Look for kits that are state certified or have met the requirements of some national radon proficiency program. Trained contractors can also do radon testing. Radon is detected with special instruments, which measure it in picocuries per liter (pCi/L) in air. The average outdoor level is around 0.4 pCi/L, and the EPA recommends action when indoor readings exceed this level.

Radon may be unevenly distributed in a building, depending on its concentration in the bedrock or soil under the building, and the openings to the ground and permeability of the foundation slab. Pressure differences between indoors and the area below the slab affect radon levels, as does the amount of outdoor air brought into the indoors. Sealing foundations and floor drains and ventilating the subsoil can control radon. Where the risk is high, under-slab ventilation is recommended.

Tobacco Smoke

Tobacco smoke is the most common indoor pollutant. Increasingly, people find it extremely objectionable. The isolation of the smoker doesn't help if nonsmokers breathe the same air circulated by the air-handling system, which only dilutes, but does not remove, the smoke.

Tobacco smoke is a very complicated mixture of over 4700 chemical compounds, irritating gases, and carcinogenic tar particles. Visible smoke consists of tens of trillions of fine particles of carcinogenic tar and nicotine per cigarette. Gaseous contaminants include nitrogen dioxide, formaldehyde, hydrogen sulfide, hydrogen cyanide, carbon monoxide, ammonia, and nicotine, which are extremely noxious at high concentrations. Short-term exposure is irritating to the eyes, nose, and throat. Prolonged exposure can result in death.

 Interior designers are often involved in creating segregated smoking areas. In some parts of the United States, smoking is banned from entire buildings. In other communities, smoking is allowed only in certain types of businesses, such as bars. Yet other localities require restaurants and other establishments to create separate smoking and nonsmoking sections. Often, the choice of a smoke-free environment rests with the business owner, and the interior designer is likely to have a considerable say in whether to go smoke-free. Offering customers a truly smokeless environment will often attract more people than it will drive away. Second-hand smoke is also a very real health threat to the employees of businesses where smoking is allowed.

When you do create a space for smoking, be sure you are up to date on the current local restrictions and requirements, which are subject to frequent changes and are sometimes very complex. The barriers you design between smoking and nonsmoking spaces should not only comply with the letter of the law, but also truly provide a smoke-free environment. Ceiling-hung smoke-filtering equipment does not ensure a smoke-free environment, and smoke is often drawn by the HVAC system from one area into another.

Soil Gases

Methane and other gases in the soil are released by decomposing garbage in landfills, leaking sewage lines, and toxic waste. They can be explosive or toxic, and have obnoxious odors. The history of a site should be known before building begins, and soil removed if necessary. The foundation and floor drains should be sealed, and the subsoil ventilated if there is a problem.

ODORS

Foul-smelling air is not necessarily unhealthy, but can cause nausea, headache, and loss of appetite. Even a mild but recognizable odor can make us uneasy. Our noses are more sensitive than most detection equipment available today. It is possible to detect harmful substances by their odors, and eliminate them before they reach dangerous levels.

Building intakes for outdoor air may pick up auto exhaust, furnace and industrial effluents, or smog, and bring the contamination into the building's air supply. In industrial spaces, odors arise from chemical products such as printing inks, dyes, and synthetic materials, and from manufactured products. Body odors accumulate in offices, assembly rooms, and other enclosed and densely occupied spaces. Smoking adds to the contamination of the air supply. Some materials, such as cotton, wool, rayon, and fir wood, absorb odors readily, and give them off later at varying rates, depending upon temperature and relative humidity. Occupancy odors can accumulate on furnishings and continue to be released after the people who produced them have left the space.

Some of the odors we sense indoors can come from moisture or certain kinds of metals and coatings used on air-conditioning coils. Linoleum, paint, upholstery, rugs, drapes, and other room furnishings may add odors, which tend to be reduced with lower relative humidity. Food, cooking, and the decomposition of animal and vegetable matter produce odors that may be offensive.

As our environment is freed of multiple odors, we become more sensitive to the remaining ones. The obvious presence of human body odor in a space is usually an indication of inadequate ventilation. Removing gases or vapors or reducing their concentration below perceptible levels help to control odors. We can also act to interfere with the perception of the odor. Ventilation with clean outdoor air dilutes odors. Air washers or air scrubbers are pieces of equipment that can clean away odors. Odors can be adsorbed (assimilated by the surface of a solid) by activated charcoal filters or other materials. Equipment is also available to remove odors by chemical reactions, odor modification, oxidation, or combustion.

VOLATILE ORGANIC COMPOUNDS

Volatile organic compounds (VOCs) are chemical compounds that tend to evaporate at room temperature and normal atmospheric pressure (and are thus volatile), and that contain one or more carbon atoms (and are thus called organic compounds). They are invisible fumes or vapors. Some VOCs have sharp odors, while others are detectable only by sensitive equipment. Almost any manufactured or natural product may give off VOCs in a confined space. VOCs commonly evaporate from building and furnishing products. Plywood, plastic, fibers, varnishes, coatings, and cleaning chemicals are common sources. Solvents used in paints, waxes, consumer products, and petroleum fuels all emit VOCs, many of which are toxic and can affect the central nervous system, the eyes, and the respiratory system.

As interior designers, clients sometimes call on us to minimize the use of potentially polluting materials in the spaces we design. Products sometimes advertise that they are less polluting than a competing material or even than an earlier version of the same product. In order to evaluate the claims of manufacturers for "green" products, we need to have some understanding of the components that are most likely to cause problems for sensitive users. The information that follows is intended as a reference for some of the more common chemicals, but is by no means an exhaustive list.

Most of the research on acceptable levels of VOCs has been done in industrial settings, and is influenced by what is achievable rather than what is safe based on health studies. Preliminary research suggests that the effects of various VOCs can add together to have a greater impact than the individual components separately.

Volatile organic compounds enter the air when the surfaces of solid materials evaporate or offgas at room temperatures. The list of irritating VOCs includes methane, ethane, methylene chloride, trichloroethane, chlorofluoracarbons (CFCs), hydrochlorofluorocarbons (HCFCs), hydrofluorocarbons (HFCs), formaldehyde, and hydrocarbons (HCs) such as styrene, benzene, and alcohols, all of which can be found in newly constructed or renovated spaces. Some products will offgas VOCs for a period, during which time the space must be ventilated, and then revert to a safe state.

Methylene chloride is found in paint strippers, adhesive removers, and aerosol spray paints. It is known to cause cancer in animals, and is converted to carbon monoxide in the body. Xylenes are found in varnishes and solvents for resins and enamels. Xylene is a narcotic and irritant that affects the heart, liver, kidney, and nervous system. Toluene is a petrochemical found in various adhesives and solvents and in chipboard. It is narcotic and may cause anemia. Styrene is a possible carcinogen in many paints, plastic foams, plastics, and resins.

Benzene is a respiratory tract irritant and carcinogen in cigarette smoke, automobile emissions, and in paints, stains, and varnishes used on furnishings. Ethyl benzene, which is found in some solvents, causes severe irritation to the eyes and respiratory tract. Trichloroethylene is found in furniture varnishes and may affect the control of the nervous system. It is also probably a carcinogen. Methylene chloride is a narcotic found in acoustical office partitions that can affect the central nervous system and probably also causes cancer. Methylethylketone, also called 2-butanone, is an ingredient in fiberboard and particleboard. It is an irritant and central nervous system depressant.

Tetrachloroethylene, also known as perchloroethylene, is the chemical most widely used to dry-clean fabrics and draperies. It can irritate the skin and eyes or depress the central nervous system, and has been shown to be a carcinogen in animals. People breathe low levels of this chemical both in homes where dry-cleaned goods are stored and as they wear dry-cleaned clothing. Dry-cleaners recapture the perchloroethylene during the dry-cleaning process so they can save money by reusing it, and they remove more of the chemical during the pressing and finishing processes. Some dry-cleaners, however, do not remove as much as possible all of the time. If goods with a chemical odor are returned to you repeatedly, look for a different dry-cleaner.

Paints, solvents, carpets, soft plastics, adhesives, caulks, soft woods, paper products, and cleaning and maintenance products may all emit VOCs. Building occupants may experience intoxication, loss of judgment, and panic, in addition to the symptoms typical of formaldehyde.

Most of the more serious effects are the result of exposures at levels higher than those normally expected indoors. However, some common situations are likely to cause mild to serious health effects from VOC exposure. These include installation of large volumes of new furniture or wall partitions and dry cleaning of large volumes of draperies or upholstered furniture. Large-scale cleaning, painting, or installation of wall or floor coverings also results in unusually high levels of VOCs. Temporary temperature fluctuations and inadequate ventilation can also increase VOC levels.

Both building maintenance workers and other building occupants are exposed to higher levels of VOCs when the HVAC system is shut down at night or during weekends. VOCs are not adequately cleared from the building, and the accumulation is circulated through the building when the system is turned on again.

Formaldehyde

Formaldehyde is the most widespread VOC, and a major contributor to SBS. Formaldehyde is a colorless, strong-smelling gas used in the manufacture of synthetic resins and dyes, and as a preservative and disinfectant. It is present in buildings in urea-formaldehyde foam insulation (UFFI) and in pressed wood products. The U.S. National Institute of Occupational Safety and Health has implicated formaldehyde emissions, primarily from furnishings, as the cause of 4 percent of BRIs investigated.

Because it is a gas at room temperature that dissolves readily in water, formaldehyde irritates moist body surfaces, such as the mucous membranes of the eyes, the upper respiratory tract, and the skin. Ten to twenty percent of healthy people experience nausea, vomiting, histamine allergic reactions, or asthmatic attacks when exposed to levels of formaldehyde as low as 0.03 parts per million (ppm). Healthy people can have difficulty breathing, and may cough, wheeze, and feel tightness in the chest at 5 to 30 ppm.

At high levels, formaldehyde causes tearing, burning, and stinging eyes, a tingling sensation in the nose and sneezing, and soreness and dryness in the throat. The irritation persists even after removal of the source, and can temporarily heighten sensitivity to other contaminants. Higher levels can produce pulmonary edema, lung inflammation, pneumonia, and death. Formaldehyde may also increase the risk of cancer in humans. Formaldehyde has been clearly demonstrated to have negative effects on people with chemical sensitivities.

Formaldehyde is found in particleboard, interior laminated panels, glues, fabric treatments, and paints. Interior-grade plywood or particleboard, medium-density fiberboard, insulation, and some textiles emit it. Carpeting and panelboard in new and renovated buildings may give off small quantities of formaldehyde for years. Its effects are most severe when new, but can last from a few hours to many years after installation. Areas where formaldehyde is evaporating should be thoroughly ventilated.

 Interior designers should seek alternatives to particleboard if possible, although it can be very difficult to avoid, especially on a limited budget. Seek out particleboard with lower VOCs. Some manufacturers have done emissions testing, and can provide information. Demands by architects and interior designers will encourage testing and availability of safer materials. If emissions information is not available, look for manufacturers using European standard board, or U.S. board rated "exposure one," which have lower emissions. You can also reduce exposure to formaldehyde by purchasing exterior-grade products, which emit less formaldehyde.

Particleboard should be sealed with a secure coating to encapsulate the VOCs. Some sealants are applied by the manufacturer before shipping, while others are applied on site after installation. Sealants can prevent formaldehyde release, and prevent moisture from seeping into the material. Some products react with the formaldehyde to create nonemitting or inert compounds. Thin liquid coatings that form a hard surface after curing and drying, including acid-curing lacquers, polyacrilamide, polyurethane lacquer or varnish, and latex paints, may also emit VOCs while drying, but the end effect is to seal in the long-term formaldehyde emissions. If the particleboard you specify is sealed with veneers or laminate, check that all surfaces are completely sealed, including edges, backs, under desktops or tabletops, and inside cabinets and drawers. If there are unsealed areas, request application of a liquid sealer formulated especially for formaldehyde reduction.

During the 1970s, many homeowners had urea-formaldehyde foam insulation (UFFI) installed in the wall cavities of their homes as an energy-conservation measure. However, many of these homes were found to have relatively high indoor concentrations of formaldehyde soon after the UFFI installation. Few homes are now being insulated with this product. Studies show that formaldehyde emissions from UFFI decline with time, so homes in which UFFI was installed many years ago are unlikely to have high levels of formaldehyde now.

Controlling VOCs

Some building materials may act as sponges for VOCs, absorbing them for later release. Carpeting, ceiling tiles, and freestanding partitions have high surface areas that can absorb VOCs. Rougher surfaces and lower ventilation rates increase absorption. Higher air temperatures increase VOC emissions and air concentrations. VOC emissions can be managed by limiting sources, providing proper ventilation, and controlling the relative humidity of the air.

The stability of materials has an impact on the interior air quality over an extended period. Interior design finishes that don't produce or retain dust and designs that limit open shelving or dust collecting areas help control VOC retention in the space. Durable materials, such as hardwoods, ceramics, masonry, metals, glass, baked enamels, and hard plastics, are generally low in VOC emissions. Low VOC paints are available as well. Fibers like cotton, wool, acetate, and rayon have low VOCs, but their dyes and treatments may release toxic chemicals.

Rerelease of VOCs that have been absorbed by furnishings can be controlled by using the maximum amount of outside air ventilation during and following installation of finishes and furnishings. Air should be exhausted directly to the outside rather than through the HVAC system. Ventilation should continue constantly when VOC levels are elevated. Installed materials can be protected from collecting VOC emissions from other products by sealing them in plastic vapor barriers. Fiber-lined HVAC ducts and return air plenums should also be protected, especially the exposed upper surfaces of ceiling panels and exposed spray-on insulation. Newly occupied buildings should be operated at the lowest acceptable temperatures to slow VOC emissions.

The period immediately following the finishing of the building's interior is critical for VOC exposure. Aging materials before installation may help release some of the VOCs outside of the space. If possible, occupancy should be delayed to allow for outgassing from adhesives, paints, and other materials and finishes.

In new construction, it may be possible to use a bake-out period. The unoccupied building is sealed, and the temperature is raised to around 27°C (80°F). The space is periodically completely ventilated, over a period of from 72 hours to a week. This process increases the aging rate for shorter-lived VOC sources. Baking-out must be thoughtfully planned and professionally monitored. The effectiveness of bake-out procedures are mixed, depending upon the materials and procedures involved.

BIOLOGICAL CONTAMINANTS

Most of us don't even want to think about bacteria, fungi, viruses, algae, insect parts, dead mice, and dust in the air we breathe. Yet these contaminants are all less common than human skin scales. We shed skin cells constantly from our skin and in our breath, and our environment is littered with our dead cells. It is estimated that a person sheds 40,000 biological particles containing bacteria per minute while sitting at a desk, and as many as 45 million per minute when exercising. The number of bacteria able to reproduce in an office environment is often in the range of 1000 colony-forming units per cubic meter.

Bacteria and fungi are present indoors and out, but office buildings provide an exceptionally favorable environment of high humidity and standing water in circulation and air-conditioning ducts, ceiling tiles, insulation, and even ice machines. These microorganisms release bioaerosols, which include tiny spores from molds and other fungi that float through the air and irritate skin and mucous membranes.

Mold in carpets eats skin scales, as do dust mites. Mold and dust mite excrement are two very common causes of allergies. Other biological particulates include

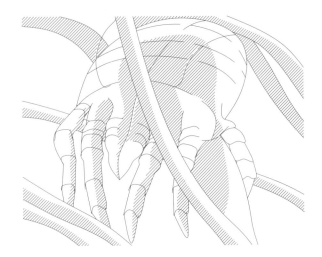

Figure 19-1 A dust mite in carpet.

pollens, spores, cat dander allergens, and finely ground food products like grains, coffee, and cornstarch. The protein in urine from rats and mice is a potent allergen. When it dries, it can become airborne.

Dust mites (Fig. 19-1) congregate where nutrients (dead skin cells) collect, in and around beds, bedding materials, in upholstered furnishings, in carpet, and in places of high human activity. They require at least 60 percent relative humidity to survive. A relative humidity of 30 to 50 percent is generally recommended for homes. Dust mites are common in both residential and commercial spaces.

Dust mites are relatively large, so they settle out of the air and usually live at floor level, only becoming airborne when the dust is disturbed. About 53 percent of allergic individuals are sensitive to household dust, and more than 37 percent are allergic to dust mite allergens. Dust mite allergens include enzymes in their feces, mite saliva, and the soluble proteins from mite body parts. Reactions include nasal inflammation, asthma, and itching, inflammation, and rash.

Nearly everything organic releases particles or microscopic bits of solid or liquid matter that can stay airborne for long periods of time. Larger particles are usually caught in the nose before they can reach the lungs. Pollen grains from weeds, grasses, and trees, which cause seasonal allergies for many people, are larger than ordinary dust particles, and can be filtered out mechanically. Most pollen grains are also hygroscopic, which means they vary in size and weight when they absorb water from humid air.

Particles less than 10 microns in diameter are known as respirable suspended particles or RSPs. (A hundred microns is about the diameter of a human hair.) When they get past the nose and invade deep into the lungs, they can cause coughing, wheezing, and respiratory tract infections. Respirable suspended particles can cause chemical or mechanical irritation of tissues, including nerve endings wherever they are deposited. They can affect respiration and aggravate cardiovascular disease. In addition, RSPs may have an impact on the immune system, and can cause changes in lung tissue, including cancer. They are linked to SBS, respiratory diseases, and asthma. They tend to affect preadolescent children, older people, and people with respiratory conditions most severely. Many people become increasingly sensitive to RSPs through repeated contact, resulting in allergic reactions.

It is often difficult to test for biological contaminants, as many of the specific test substances are not widely available, and the symptoms are varied and similar to those from other causes. Estimates of the impact of RSPs on building problems vary from 5 to 50 percent of sick building cases.

Biological contaminants need four things to grow in a building: a source, water, nutrients, and favorable temperatures. Contaminants arrive in buildings from outdoor air, and live in air-handling and humidification systems, and in building materials and furnishings. Building occupants, pets, and houseplants all contribute as sources. Water is provided by roof and plumbing leaks, vapor migration and condensation, houseplants, humidifiers, aquariums, and building occupants. Biological contaminants can eat dust, dirt, food, water, houseplants, dead plant tissue, building materials, and furnishings—almost anything you are likely to find in a building! They enjoy temperatures between 4.4°C and 37.8°C (40°F–100°F).

Biological contamination is often the result of inadequate preventive maintenance. The internal components of air-handling units, fan-coil units (FCUs), and induction units are seldom cleaned. Drain pans hold stagnant contaminated water that should be drained. Wet cooling coils and porous insulation collect dirt and debris, especially in air-conditioning systems.

Inaccessible, poorly designed mechanical systems defeat efforts at proper maintenance. Access doors to heat exchangers, air-handling units, and heat pumps may be in inaccessible locations over ceiling tiles. Air-handling units may be confined in small rooms or plenums. Fan-coil and induction units are often difficult to disassemble for cleaning. Locating an outdoor intake within 7.6 meters (25 ft) of a cooling tower or other unsanitary location allows microorganisms to enter the building. Whenever an area is flooded, cleanup must be thorough and prompt.

Moisture encourages the retention and growth of molds, fungi, viruses, and algae, and prime growth conditions often exist in heating and cooling systems. Standing warm water, as in untreated hot tubs, air-conditioning drain pans, and humidifier reservoirs, can harbor hazardous bacteria. Dead mold and other biological contaminants don't always show up on tests, so diagnosis of problems can be difficult. Filters are rarely effective for bacteria, and evaporative humidifier filters can even harbor bacteria that eat cellulose and thrive in the warm, wet environment. Air-conditioning coils can hold skin cells, lint, paper fibers, and water, a perfect environment for mold and bacteria. Building air quality specialists tell horror stories of mold-covered mechanical systems supplying the air for an entire building.

Excessive humidity in occupied spaces encourages the growth of biological contaminants. Keeping the relative humidity below 70 percent discourages fungus, and below 50 percent minimizes condensation on cold surfaces during summer months.

Contamination of the central air system and lack of proper ventilation create breeding conditions for microorganisms. Incorrectly specified building and interior materials or finishes provide homes for bacteria and fungi. For example, carpet that is not resistant to moisture can become wet in the wrong location and harbor microorganisms.

Fungus particles and dust mites grow in basements, damp carpets, bedding, fabrics, walls, ceilings, and closets. Covering beds and upholstery with barrier cloth and increasing ventilation can contain them. Borax treatments can retard fungus. Many types of bacteria and fungi produce toxic substances called endotoxins as byproducts of their metabolic processes.

Microorganisms become airborne by attaching to dust particles suspended in the air by activity nearby. Dust control, air sterilization, and carefully designed ventilation systems can help. Operating rooms may require special downdraft ventilation. The air supplied to nurseries for premature babies or to laboratories is sometimes sterilized with ultraviolet (UV) light in the ductwork, although this system is difficult to maintain. Air from high infection risk areas, like medical treatment and research areas, is normally isolated from the air supply for uninfected areas. The safety precautions taken include increasing outside air supplies, avoiding air movement from one room into another, and specifying cleaning of recirculated air.

In the 1960s, a group of American Legion members at a convention in a hotel suddenly began to die of a mysterious malady, which became known as Legionnaire's disease. This fatal respiratory illness was eventually traced to the bacterium *Legionella* growing in an improperly maintained HVAC system. *Legionella* grows in cooling towers and plumbing systems, and on other surfaces within water-containing systems. Most people have been exposed to *Legionella*, which is present in about a quarter of fresh water samples, but it rarely causes disease except under certain indoor conditions and in susceptible human hosts. Legionnaire's disease is a progressive, potentially fatal form of pneumonia that infects only about 5 percent of those who inhale droplets of water with the bacteria. Fifteen percent of those infected die of the disease. Pontiac fever is a two- to three-day-long flu-like illness also caused by *Legionella* that infects 95 percent of exposed individuals.

Legionnaire's disease continues to cause periodic deaths in poorly maintained buildings, including the Ford Motor Co.'s Cleveland Casting Plant, which was temporarily closed after an outbreak in 2001. The air-conditioning system in the new aquarium in Melbourne, Australia, was reported in 2000 to have spread the bacteria responsible for a deadly outbreak of Legionnaires' disease. Two women died, eight people were in critical condition, and 66 people were confirmed to have the disease.

Pseudomonas is responsible for humidifier fever or humidifier lung, and produces flu-like symptoms with fever, chills, difficulty breathing, muscle aches, and malaise when toxins produced by microbes are distributed through the air. The water reservoirs of humidified heating systems, air-conditioning units, cool-mist humidifiers, and evaporative air coolers can harbor pseudomonas. Humidifier fever symptoms emerge 4 to 12 hours after exposure, and then subside. Humidifier lung can cause permanent, potentially fatal changes in lung tissue with continual exposure.

Fungi are plantlike organisms that lack the chlorophyll needed for photosynthesis, and include molds, mildew, and yeasts. Mildew is a fungus that appears as a thin layer of black spots on a surface; you may see it on your shower curtain. Fungi live on decomposed organic matter or living hosts, and reproduce by spores. Some spores are dry, and can become airborne. Others are slimy, and it is these that create mold-infested building materials or furnishings implicated in SBS. They will grow on almost anything, including glass, paint, rubber, textiles, electrical equipment, mineral wool, or fiberglass duct lining materials, and the substances that hold buildings together. Molds grow where there is moisture or a relative humidity over 70 percent, often from water damage from leaks in pipes or floods or from condensation on walls and ceilings. Synthetic carpets containing large amounts of dust make excellent mold environments, especially after water damage. Spores in air-conditioning systems may contribute to SBS.

Mycotoxins are digestive by-products of fungi. Some are helpful, like penicillin, while others, like aflatoxin, are carcinogens. Some mycotoxins become toxic in combination with other substances. Fungi emit VOCs, creating a distinctive odor that is often the first indication of their presence. Ethanol is one common VOC emitted by fungi, and enhances the toxic and irritant effects of other VOCs. Exposure to fungi spores, mycotoxins, and VOCs can result in allergic reactions, which are usually hard to test for, and other immune system disorders and toxic reactions.

Free-living amoebas are microscopic protozoa that can form dormant cysts when food isn't available and hide away until times of plenty. Amoebas are implicated in some BRIs. In addition, bacteria that have been eaten by amoebas can stay alive, and are thus protected from disinfectants like chlorine. Viruses are submicroscopic organisms that reproduce in living hosts, and that can cause disease. Blue-green algae and green algae are one-celled microscopic organisms that grow in fresh or salt water and sunlight. They can be dispersed through the humidification and HVAC systems from areas of standing water.

Installing and using exhaust fans that are vented to the outdoors in kitchens and bathrooms, and venting clothes dryers outdoors can reduce moisture and cut down on the growth of biological contaminants. Ventilate the attic and crawl spaces to prevent moisture buildup. If using cool mist or ultrasonic humidifiers, clean appliances according to manufacturer's instructions and refill with fresh water daily. Thoroughly clean and dry water-damaged carpets and building materials, within 24 hours if possible, or consider removal and replacement.

Keeping the building clean limits exposure to house dust mites, pollens, animal dander, and other allergy-causing agents. As an interior designer, avoid specifying room furnishings that accumulate dust, especially if they cannot be washed in hot water. Using central vacuum systems that are vented to the outdoors or vacuums with high-efficiency filters may also be of help. Do not finish a basement below ground level unless all water leaks are patched and outdoor ventilation and adequate heat to prevent condensation are provided. Operate a dehumidifier in the basement if needed to keep relative humidity levels between 30 and 50 percent.

OTHER POLLUTANTS

As if biological contaminants and chemicals didn't pose enough of a threat to the well-being of our clients and us, there are even more dangers posed by mineral and glass fibers, lead, and pesticide residues. Renovation work in older buildings often generates exposure to problems that have been in the building for a long time. As interior designers, it is our responsibility to understand and avoid these dangers.

Mineral and Glass Fibers

The breakdown of interior duct lining and fireproofing can put fibrous mineral particles into the air. Fire-resistant acoustic tiles and fabrics can add irritating fibers as well. Mineral and glass fibers are potential irritants, burning the eyes, itching the skin, and creating a long-term risk of lung damage and cancer. They should be handled only with a respirator and gloves, should be sealed and enclosed and not disturbed in place.

Asbestos has been known since ancient times for its resistance to fire. It was used in the nineteenth century as a structural fire-resistant coating. Up until 1975, asbestos was widely used for steam pipe and duct insulation and in furnaces and furnace parts. Before 1980, acoustic tiles and fiber cement shingles and siding contained asbestos. Vinyl floor tiles made from the 1940s to the 1980s contain asbestos, as does their adhesive.

Inhalation of asbestos fibers presents a long-term risk of cancer, asbestosis (fibrous scarring of the lungs), and fluid in the lungs.

Citing the growing costs of asbestos-related lawsuits, W. R. Grace & Co. filed for Chapter 11 Bankruptcy protection in 2001. Most of the suits stem from the asbestos added to some of Grace's fire-protection products. The company stopped adding any asbestos to its products in 1973.

Asbestos fibers may still be found in existing construction, in the insulation on heating system components and other equipment, in acoustic tiles, in drywall joint-finishing material, and in textured paint purchased before 1977. Some sprayed and troweled ceiling finishing plaster installed between 1945 and 1973 also contains asbestos.

Asbestos is white, light gray, or light brown, and looks like coarse fabric or paper. It may also appear as a dense pulpy mass of light gray stucco-like material applied to ceilings, beams, and columns. Most asbestos can be left undisturbed, as long as it doesn't emit fibers into the air. Asbestos can be sealed with a special sealant, and covered with sheet metal if it is not crumbling, but it remains in place and must be dealt with later during renovation or demolition. Avoid drilling holes, hanging materials onto walls or ceilings, causing abrasion, or removing ceiling tiles below material containing as-

bestos. Wrapping can repair asbestos-covered steam lines and boiler surfaces. Asbestos in walls and ceilings can't usually be repaired, as it is difficult to keep it airtight. Enclosures are possible in small areas not likely to be disturbed, without water damage, deteriorating asbestos, or low ceilings.

Encapsulation may cost more than removal. Removal is the only permanent solution, but since it may release fibers if not done correctly, removal can be more dangerous than leaving the asbestos in place. If removal is required, get an expert to identify and remove the asbestos. Be sure that the expert you select to remove asbestos is properly certified and licensed. Investigators found five instances in Massachusetts where contractors falsely claimed in telephone listings that they were licensed. Four people were arrested in Massachusetts in 2000 for violating the state's Clean Air Act and hazardous material handling law when they removed asbestos from a school, a home, an apartment building, and two demolition sites. In one case, the homeowner used a hidden camera to discover workers ripping off pipe insulation by hand, releasing asbestos fibers into the air. The same company was working at a private elementary school nearby, where violations were also found. Another contractor knocked down two buildings that were sided with asbestos shingles, contaminating the sites. In another case, an apartment building owner hired a tenant to remove asbestos, which was then tossed into a common dumpster. The tenant did not use safety gear and was exposed to high levels of asbestos. Do not accept a contractor's assurances that he or she can take care of the asbestos problem for you, and that "we do it all the time."

Areas where asbestos is being removed must be isolated by airtight plastic containment barriers, and kept under negative pressure with high-efficiency particulate air (HEPA) filtration (which we discuss later) within the barrier. The asbestos-containing material must be wetted prior to removal and disposed of in leak-tight containers. All surfaces should be wet-mopped or HEPA vacuumed for two consecutive days after the removal is completed. The work site should be inspected and air quality tested after the work is done.

Manmade mineral fibers are generally larger than asbestos fibers, and therefore less dangerous. They are commonly found in wall insulation, ceiling tiles, and duct insulation. An initial blowout period for duct insulation removes broken fibers. Fiberglass insulation is made of glass wool. Continuous-filament fiberglass is used to reinforce plastic, and for specialty textiles and fiber optics. Mineral wool, also called rock wool and slag wool, is used for insulation and fireproofing. Manmade mineral fiber manufacturing workers have increased cancer rates.

Lead

Lead has been known and used throughout the world for over 5000 years. The Phoenicians, Egyptians, Greeks, Indians, Chinese, and later the Romans used lead vessels, water ducts, and utensils. Lead was present in most paint in the United States until it was banned in 1978 by federal law, although it had been banned in most other countries decades earlier. Until 1985, pipes and solder contained lead, as did gasoline, and it was commonly found in dust and soil near roads. Old pipes and solder should be replaced. Soil near roads or where lead paint residues may have washed off buildings should be tested before being used to grow food.

Improperly glazed ceramics and leaded crystal contain lead, and the foil on wine bottles may be lead. Lead is also used for fabricating leaded glass artwork, and should be handled and stored carefully to avoid coming in contact with children or food.

Lead poisoning is considered the number one health hazard to children under the age of seven. Young children can ingest or inhale lead-based paint chips or dust. Many cases occur in adults and children of all socioeconomic levels in buildings undergoing renovation, and during improperly conducted lead abatement procedures. Particles are suspended in the air or settle on surfaces, which can release the particles back into the air when disturbed. Carpets can collect particles. A quarter of the homes built before 1990 with shag or plush carpets that have been vacuumed with a loose belt, a full bag, or less than once a month show high levels of lead. Lead accumulates in the body. Children ingest and inhale lead through playing on floors and other dusty surfaces, and then putting their hands in their mouths.

Many American children now demonstrate some level of irreversible lead poisoning that can impair motor function and intelligence. Lead is a neurotoxin, and is especially damaging to fetuses, infants, and young children, causing learning disabilities, nausea, trembling, and numbness in the arms and legs. Lead exposure has been implicated in attention deficit disorder (ADD), impaired hearing, reading, and learning disabilities, delayed cognitive development, reduced IQ scores, mental retardation, seizures, convulsions, coma, and death. In adults, lead exposure can cause high blood pressure, and occupational exposure has been implicated in kidney disease.

Houses built prior to 1950 are likely to contain paint with high levels of lead. Lead-based paint is in three quarters of U.S. homes built prior to 1975, amounting to nearly 60 million private homes. This residential exposure accounts for 80 to 90 percent of total lead exposure. The woodwork and walls of many homes were painted with lead-based paints. It is critical that old lead paint be identified and removed, or sealed in an approved manner. As an interior designer, you are in a position to advocate for proper handling and disposal of lead paint.

A professional licensed contractor should remove lead. Occupants must be out of the building during the process, and workers must be properly protected. Lead paint should not be sanded or burned off. Moldings and other woodwork should be replaced or chemically treated. Wood floors must be sealed or covered, belongings should be removed or covered, and dust should be contained during the process. The final cleanup should be done using a HEPA vacuum.

If the condition of the lead-based painted surfaces is clean and intact and there is no cracking, peeling, blistering or flaking of existing paint, building and health authorities sometimes permit surfaces to be encapsulated, using a coating that is applied in liquid form that provides a flexible, impact-resistant barrier. These products can be used on almost any surface, including wood, concrete, brick, cement, sheetrock, plaster, or gypsum. Some coatings contain a bitter-tasting, FDA-approved ingestion deterrent to discourage oral contact or ingestion by children. Encapsulation is the most economical and simplest procedure, and does not require hazardous waste removal or relocation of building occupants. Some products are formulated for professional use only, while others are designed for homeowners and do-it-yourselfers. The effectiveness of encapsulation versus removal remains a controversial issue.

Pesticide Residues

Prior to the 1980s, buildings may have been treated with pesticides that contained toxic substances. Treatments for termites, roaches, and mice might all present problems. Basements, foundations, ceilings, wall cavities, cabinets, closets, and the soil outside foundations may contain dangerous pesticide residues. These residues may be neurotoxins, and may present a long-term risk of liver or kidney disease or cancer. If the history of the contamination is known, the materials can be identified and removed by experts. It is sometimes possible to seal the pesticides permanently.

Designing for Indoor Air Quality

•••

Asthma and allergies have reached an all-time high, especially among children. Workers struggling with multiple health problems are forced to quit their jobs and face unemployment. Public buildings are emptied of employees and require expensive and time-consuming renovations. Each year, news reports highlight schools that are unable to open in time for classes while they are stripped of contaminants. These are some of the results of poor air quality.

How does the quality of the air in buildings become a public health, public policy, and public funding issue? The building may take in contaminated outside air when air intake locations and building exhaust locations are poorly designed. Buildings designed without operable windows limit fresh air. Indoor air quality (IAQ) needs to be a priority, right from the start of the design process, through construction and continuing with proper maintenance of heating, ventilating, and air-conditioning (HVAC) equipment. You can choose what you eat and drink, but not what you breathe. You can't see contaminated air (except smoke), and you may not be aware that the air you breathe could be the cause of health problems. When the HVAC system recirculates air, the building depends heavily on filtration to preserve air quality. You can filter particles, but not gases, and masks don't work for vapors.

According to the American Society of Heating, Refrigeration, and Air-Conditioning Engineers (ASHRAE), increasing ventilation and air distribution is the best and most cost-effective way to freshen the air inside most buildings. Blowers and fans that move the air, ductwork that delivers it to the building's rooms, and vents that distribute it accomplish ventilation in a modern office building. A good ventilation design will distribute supply air uniformly, except in areas with heat- and vapor-producing office machines that require added airflow. Placing supply and exhaust vents sufficiently far apart allows fresh air to circulate more freely. ASHRAE has established a general guideline of 20 cubic feet of outside air per minute per person for an office environment to dilute building contaminants sufficiently and maintain a healthy environment.

Indoor air quality (IAQ) considerations affect the decision of whether to use local or centralized HVAC equipment. Equipment that includes individual exhaust fans may help keep some areas under low pressure and contain possible pollutants, as opposed to systems that exhaust up a very tall central stack. Local air cleaners can be selected to cope with local pollution problems. On the other hand, centralized air cleaning makes maintenance easier and encourages regular maintenance. Exterior air intakes scattered in many locations may need many small heat exchangers to temper outside air, while one large exchanger can accommodate a central intake. In practice, large buildings use a mix of local and centralized equipment.

The HVAC system can contribute to indoor air pollution. Worn fan belts and motors can emit particulates. Maintenance activities, such as changing filters, can cause sudden bursts of contaminants to flow through the system. HVAC systems can harbor a variety of biological contaminants that grow within the system and are then distributed by it. The system can draw contaminated outdoor air into the system and distribute it. The condition of the outdoor air, the location of outdoor air intakes, and the ability of the system to remove contaminants before distribution will determine the degree to which an HVAC system spreads contaminants. The HVAC system may also distribute contaminants from areas of higher concentration, such as smoking lounges or photocopying rooms, to those of lower concentration. The contaminants from one business can travel to adjoining businesses through shared HVAC systems.

Design practices that support good IAQ start with carefully locating the building on the site, and include limiting pollution at the source by selecting materials and equipment with care. The HVAC system should provide for an adequate supply of fresh air, and the filtering of both fresh and return air. Upon completion of construction, the building ventilation should be run in a flush mode to thoroughly change the air.

When looking for products that emit low amounts of volatile organic compounds (VOCs), consider how much of the surface area of the product is exposed to circulating indoor air, and how much of the product is used in the building. Seek manufacturer's information on the chemical composition of the product. Find out what is known of the toxicity or irritation potential of the major chemical constituents of the product. Try to find out how stable the product is in a warm, dry office environment, or in the intended use.

Manufacturers of office systems have published studies evaluating workstations, panels, fabrics, and coating for their impact on IAQ. Check with the suppliers of products you specify for this information.

Building materials can be tested for air quality considerations in full-scale time tests. The contractor is given a target for allowable air concentrations of various chemicals in the work to be done. Materials likely to contribute more than one-third of the allowable amount are tested as assemblies before acceptance for use in the building. This procedure shortens or avoids the 90-day flush out of the completed building with outdoor air before occupancy. Full-scale tests were used in

the U.S. Environmental Protection Agency (EPA) campus at Research Triangle Park, North Carolina, which was designed by Hellmuth, Obata + Kassabaum of Washington, DC.

Unavoidable sources of pollution should be isolated. Isolating sources of pollution can be difficult. Copying machines are essential in open offices. You should try to erect as much of a barrier as possible, and provide local ventilation to remove contaminated air immediately (Fig. 20-1). Healthcare and laboratory buildings are usually broken into clean and dirty zones, sometimes with separate circulation paths. By using higher air pressure in clean areas, airflow from dirty areas to clean ones is discouraged. Exhaust fans are installed in low-pressure spaces, to push out dirty air. The amount of clean air supplied to dirty areas is limited, to keep air pressures low. Makeup air or supply air is added from the HVAC system to the clean, higher-pressure side of the system.

Keeping the building and its equipment clean and well maintained is critical to good IAQ. Many of the cleaners that custodians use can be hazardous to their health. Toilet bowl and general-purpose cleaners can be corrosive to the eyes and skin. Glass cleaner and disinfectants may be flammable or poisonous. Metal cleaners and carpet spotters may contain cancer-causing chemicals. Cleaning agents should be carefully selected, and the building air should be flushed out after unoccupied weekends and holidays to remove accumulated pollutants from furnishings and finishes.

Some custodial companies are making a point of using environmentally preferable products (EPPs), defined as products that have a reduced effect on human health and the environment when compared with competing products. These products have reduced amounts of VOCs that contribute to respiratory and central nervous system problems. Environmentally preferable products also reduce the amount of toxins dumped down the drain.

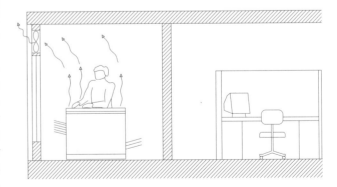

Figure 20-1 Copier isolation and exhaust.

Chemicals such as chlorine are not biodegradable and can be toxic to aquatic life.

Interior designers have a responsibility to make sure that building owners, managers, and maintenance staff understand the original IAQ design elements and principles in order to ensure benefits in the future. Maintaining and monitoring the HVAC system reduces sick building risk and assures that problems are identified and corrected at minimum expense. A broad-spectrum antimicrobial additive can help control microorganisms, as will keeping the interior clean, free of humidity, and well ventilated. The interior designer should come back to the space a few months after the construction is finished, and again a few years later, to learn how the process could be improved for future projects. The feedback of an environmental consultant is very helpful as well.

As many as one-third of schools may have unacceptable IAQ, with students and teachers complaining about headaches, asthma attacks, and fatigue from poorly ventilated classrooms or mold from leaking roofs. Many older homes contain lead paint or lead-contaminated yards in which children play. Even the small amount of mercury in a broken thermometer can lead to severe neurological damage in children.

Dr. Michael Rich, a specialist in adolescent medicine at Children's Hospital in Boston, has observed that 95 percent of his patients with asthma had elements in their environment that were precipitating asthma, elements that they knew about but didn't mention during doctor's visits. Asthma tends to be linked with poverty, and many of the obvious problems for kids with asthma are elements that are beyond their control if they are poor, such as avoiding forced-air heating or industrial fumes. Fixing the quality of housing is the first step to fixing children's health.

An EPA program to promote IAQ targets health threats to children at school, at home, and outside. Thousands of children are still threatened by lead poisoning, mercury, and bouts with asthma. In schools, the EPA program will train more officials on how to detect and fix air quality problems, and eliminate toxic chemicals in science labs. At home, a lead safety program will help to clean up lead-tainted yards and to crack down on landlords who do not get rid of lead paint or mold that can contribute to asthma. Outside, the agency will help finance and run programs to publicize air quality reports from areas with high asthma rates.

The Blackstone School, built in Boston, Massachusetts, in 1975, is one EPA success story. Higher than average asthma rates of two cases per classroom, combined with mice, mold from water leaks, and poor mainte-

nance of ductwork, made it clear that this was a sick building. After a study by the EPA, an overhaul was ordered. Pest control was introduced and the leaking roof was fixed. Grimy air ducts were cleaned, walls were washed, and light covers were cleaned regularly. Children are now healthier, and the school is safer and cleaner.

ALLERGIES AND MULTIPLE CHEMICAL SENSITIVITY

Interior designers are more and more often being called on to help people with allergies or other physical sensitivities in the design of healthy, nonpolluting homes. Businesses too are becoming more aware of the costs of sick employees, and more concerned about the health of the indoor environment. Some interior designers have made environmentally sensitive and healthy design a specialty. As our homes and workspaces are exposed to increasing levels of more exotic chemicals, it becomes ever more important that designers have the knowledge and skills necessary to create safe indoor environments. Here are a couple of examples of real people who developed serious illnesses as a result of unhealthy interior environments.

The computer programmer was a young man who prided himself on his good work habits and general good health. He had heard about people who claimed to become ill from working in a "sick building," but always thought that these folks were probably hypochondriacs or neurotics. Shortly after his office was moved into a newly renovated building, however, he began to get headaches at work. He blamed them on tension, or maybe just overwork, and continued to come to work in his new office. Gradually the headaches increased, and it would take him longer and longer after leaving work to get rid of them.

Eventually, the headaches began to occur at home or wherever the programmer went. The severity increased as well. Still, his work ethic pushed him to go to work, and he was reluctant to make a connection between his job and his health problems. Finally, with work becoming impossible due to the constant and very severe headaches, he talked to his supervisor about the problem. No, his boss was not aware of anyone else complaining of headaches.

Only later did the young man learn that other workers in other departments throughout the building were experiencing similar symptoms. Like him, most had hesitated to complain to their bosses, and most of their bosses were unaware of related problems throughout the company.

The computer programmer was forced by his health to quit his job. He now must avoid not only the contaminants introduced in the new building's construction that eventually were implicated in his problems, but many other common materials. His sensitivity to many chemicals has had a profound effect on his health, his career, and his ability to live and work where and how he likes. He now knows that people who complain of an unusual sensitivity to chemicals in their environment are not always inventing imaginary problems.

A high school teacher in Gloucester, Massachusetts, had never had allergies until her school underwent renovations. She noticed she was coughing a lot and had burning eyes in the spring of 1996, when renovations began at the school. She would come home from work exhausted, fall asleep around 4 p.m., and not wake up until the next morning. Her voice became raspy and hard to hear. Her doctor ordered her not to return to the school. She now becomes dizzy and feels ill from odors as minor as a whiff of perfume, the smell of new clothes, or the scent of a window cleaner, and must wear a microphone at work because her vocal cords are so damaged students have trouble hearing her. She and 18 other current or former staff members have filed lawsuits against the architect and contractors of the project, claiming that improperly used chemicals sensitized some staff and students so greatly they now become ill at the slightest provocation, while others developed asthma and respiratory problems. Students at the school had to be tutored off-site because of poor air quality. The city of Gloucester also sued the contractor and architect in 2000, alleging shoddy workmanship and bad design. The general contractor has also had to settle a lawsuit stemming from a botched waterproofing project at a Boston courthouse that left scores of employees ill, and was fined by the federal office of Occupational Safety and Health Administration (OSHA) for letting fumes seep into a science wing at another school in 1997.

Multiple chemical sensitivity (MCS) is a controversial illness. There is no standard medical definition, diagnosis, or cure. The Center for Disease Control doesn't recognize it, and scientists and doctors argue about whether it is a real or an imagined disorder. Disbelievers claim that those who complain of chemical sensitivities often have a history of other problems, including depression, which has led many to label MCS a psychological problem.

Multiple chemical sensitivity is usually triggered by an acute, but sometimes continuous, exposure to toxic chemicals after which one develops intolerance for lower levels of a range of substances. In other words, someone can develop MCS after one massive exposure to, say, a pesticide spraying or a chemical spill, or after years of working at a factory that uses toxic substances. Less commonly, it can result from built-up exposure to the chemicals we all come into contact with each day.

The Social Security Administration and the U.S. Department of Housing and Urban Development (HUD) now recognize MCS as a disability in the United States. It is a preventable chronic condition in which people develop increased sensitivities to synthetic chemicals or irritants. MCS is caused by acute and high-level or chronic and low-level exposure to chemicals in pesticides, petrochemicals, gas, building materials including formaldehyde, furnishings, office equipment, carpets, personal care and laundry products, biological contaminants, and other materials. People exposed to toxins may develop injuries to their nervous, endocrine, immune, and respiratory systems that make them sensitive to even minute amounts of common, synthetic chemicals. Symptoms may vary widely from person to person and may appear unrelated to one another. Continued exposure causes a person to react to many other synthetic chemicals. Symptoms may become disabling or life threatening. Multiple chemical sensitivity starts with symptoms manifesting only in the contaminated building. With continued exposure, symptoms begin to occur everywhere, including at home. The level of sensitivity increases, too, eventually leading to extreme sensitivity to a wide range of chemicals.

The source of the problem could be fireproofing on fabrics or pesticides outside an air intake. It may be made worse by the lack of operable windows to ventilate the building. Occupying a building while construction continues exposes office workers to paints and solvents, as well as many other chemicals common in construction.

When the human body's ability to react to chemicals and other substances in the environment is altered, exposure to these substances can result in illness. Allergic disorders, triggered by foods, dust, pollens, bacteria, fungi, medicines, or other chemicals, include hay fever, asthma, eczema, and contact dermatitis. Dust, irritating gases, or changes in the temperature and humidity in the indoor environment can trigger asthma attacks in allergic individuals, even without exposure to specific allergens.

The Ecology House in San Rafael, California, was designed for low-income people with MCS. The designers avoided plywood, and used Douglas fir sheathing. The floors are tiled, not carpeted. Cabinets are made of metal rather than plywood or oriented strand board (OSB). Heat is supplied by radiant hot water, rather than forced air. Painted surfaces are minimized, and no fireplaces or barbecues are allowed. Window coverings that do not collect dust are installed rather than curtains. The facility includes an airing room, where items like newspapers can be hung while ink odors evaporate.

INTERIOR DESIGN MATERIALS

We have looked at the ways IAQ can become contaminated, how that contamination affects building occupants, and how the building's design can influence IAQ. Now let's examine how interior construction and furnishing materials relate to issues of indoor air quality.

Wall and Ceiling Construction Materials

Volatile organic compound emissions from ceiling and wall materials are highest just after installation. Most wall finishes have a slow decay rate, emitting VOCs gradually for a prolonged period. Finishes that are applied wet give up their VOCs more quickly, and become inert after a shorter ventilation period.

Gypsum board may emit a wide range of VOCs, including xylenes, butylacetate, and formaldehyde during an initial outgassing period, then continue to emit VOCs at a lower rate for up to seven years. Joint compounds give off formaldehyde, toluene, ethyl-benzene, styrene, xylenes, and other VOCs. Many ceiling tiles and panels are made of fibers held in formaldehyde-based resin, and may emit formaldehyde.

Pressed Wood Products

Pressed wood products originated in Europe in the 1960s as an alternative to wood furnishings, and entered the U.S. market in the 1970s. Pressed wood products (Fig. 20-2) include particleboard, medium-density fiberboard (MDF), hardwood plywood, chipboard, and hardboard such as pegboard. These materials emit VOCs including formaldehyde, α-pinene, xylenes, butanol, butyl acetate, hexanal, and acetone.

Chemicals that emit VOCs are used in pressed wood products to provide strength and moisture resistance. Phenol-formaldehyde (PF) resins resist moisture degradation, and are used in products destined for exterior

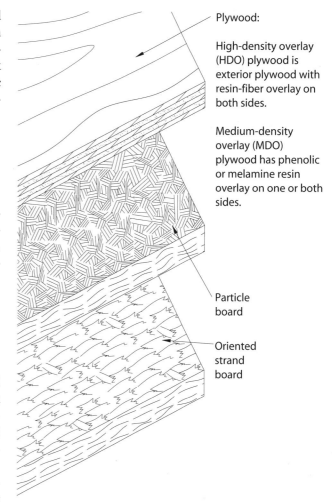

Plywood:

High-density overlay (HDO) plywood is exterior plywood with resin-fiber overlay on both sides.

Medium-density overlay (MDO) plywood has phenolic or melamine resin overlay on one or both sides.

Particle board

Oriented strand board

Figure 20-2 Plywood, particle board, and oriented strand board (OSB).

applications, as well as interior plywood and as bonding for laminates on wood and steel surfaces. Urea-formaldehyde (UF) resins are less expensive, but can only be used for interior applications. Urea-formaldehyde resins offgas 10 to 20 times as much as PF resins. They are present in particleboard and in MDF, which has the highest VOC content of the pressed wood products.

Pressed wood products are used extensively in residential and commercial interiors projects. Worksurfaces in offices account for 15 to 35 percent of the floor space. Shelving adds another 10 to 20 percent, is usually located near workers' faces, and is exposed to air on both upper and lower sides. In mobile homes, where pressed wood products cover virtually every surface within a confined space, formaldehyde is concentrated and poses an increased threat to the health of occupants. Newly constructed and furnished buildings present a greater threat than older buildings, where the VOCs have had time to dissipate. High temperatures and humidity increase the decomposition of VOCs, releasing more formaldehyde during summer months.

Particle board, also called industrial board, is made of chips and shavings of soft woods such as pine held together with UF resins and glues, which constitute 6 to 10 percent of the product's weight. Medium-density fiberboard (MDF) combines wood pieces and chips with UF adhesives and other chemicals comprising 8 to 14 percent of its weight. These are pressed together in a hot hydraulic press. Medium-density fiberboard is used for drawer fronts, cabinet doors, and furniture tops.

Hardwood plywood consists of thin sheets and veneers of hardwoods like oak and maple, held together by PF resins and glues that make up 2.5 percent of its weight. Hardwood plywoods are used for cabinets and furniture.

Chipboard is made of untreated wood fiber and paper by-products pressed together with small amounts of formaldehyde resins. Chipboard is used for the innermost layer of many modular office partitions. Hardboard is used for pegboard and other inexpensive functions. Wood fibers are pressed into a dense sheet while applying heat to allow the natural resins to hold the sheet together without glue. Relatively small amounts of formaldehyde resins are then added along with other chemicals to improve strength and moisture resistance.

Other pressed wood products, such as softwood plywood and flake strand board or OSB, are produced for exterior construction use and contain the dark, or red/black-colored PF resin. Although formaldehyde is present in both types of resins, pressed woods that contain PF resin generally emit formaldehyde at considerably lower rates than those containing UF resin. Where you are using extensive amounts of pressed wood products in an interior, investigate whether PF resin products are an option.

Since 1985, HUD has permitted only the use of plywood and particleboard that conform to specified formaldehyde emission limits in the construction of prefabricated and mobile homes. In the past, some of these homes had elevated levels of formaldehyde because of the large amount of high-emitting pressed wood products used in their construction and because of their relatively small interior space. We should note here that some natural wood products can also emit VOCs.

Flooring

Around 3 billion yards of carpet is sold each year in the United States, 70 percent of which is replacement carpet. More than 2 billion yards of carpet ends up in land-fills each year, where it remains largely intact for hundreds of years.

Carpets may emit VOCs including formaldehyde, toluene, benzene, and styrene, among others. The most common emission is from 4-phenylcyclohexene (4-PC), an odorous VOC from styrene-butadiene (SB) latex that is used to bind the carpet fibers to the jute backings. Using heat fusion bonding for carpet backing eliminates the high-VOC latex bond. Low emission carpets have fusion bonded backing and use alternative fastening systems to eliminate latex and adhesives. Emissions from 4-PC may be initially high and tend to diminish quickly. The amount of emissions varies with the carpet type. Emissions of 4-PC have been linked to headaches, runny eyes, mucous membrane irritation, dizziness, neurological symptoms, and fatigue occurring after carpet installation. Carpets require three to four weeks for outgassing, with added ventilation and an increased air exchange rate.

Carpet pads made of foamed plastic or sheet rubber are high in VOCs. Felt pads, which use recycled synthetic fibers or wool, or jute backings have low VOC emissions. Cork, which is a quick-growing natural resource, can also be used. Tacking with nail strips rather than gluing down carpet lowers emissions as well. If glue is used, it should be water based or low-toxicity. Some carpet adhesives emit xylenes, toluene, and a host of other VOCs. Adhesives often emit VOCs for up to one week.

Standard particleboard is often used as an underlayment for carpet. It can be replaced with formaldehyde-free particleboard or exterior plywood. The best option is low-density panels made from recycled paper.

Once a carpet is installed, it can continue to contribute to IAQ problems. Carpets collect dust and particles. Vacuuming with plastic bags that retain microscopic particles can contain these. The cleaning solutions used on carpeting may include highly toxic chemicals.

The Carpet and Rug Institute (CRI) has developed an Indoor Air Quality Testing Program. Environmentally responsible carpet is identified with the CRI IAQ label. New nylon formulations can be recycled into useful products. Synthetic carpet can by made from recycled post-consumer plastic, such as soda bottles. DuPont and BASF both have developed nationwide commercial carpet recycling programs. You can incorporate these programs into your projects by specifying products that have the CRI IAQ label, and checking with manufacturers about recycling.

Vinyl flooring emits VOCs. Soft vinyl used for sheet flooring, which must bend into a roll, is made from petrochemical polymers with chemicals added for flexibility, and emits large amounts of VOCs for long periods of time. Vinyl floor tiles emit formaldehyde, toluene, ketones, xylenes, and many other VOCs. Vinyl sheets and tiles are made of polyvinyl chloride (PVC) or a copolymer of vinyl chloride, a binder of vinyl resins and plasticizers, fillers, and pigments. Sheet vinyl also has a foam interlayer and a backing of organic or other fiber or plastic.

Natural linoleum, made of linseed oil, cork, tree resin, wood flour, clay pigments, and jute backing, is a durable, attractive, and environmentally friendly alternative. The linseed oil is slowly oxidized and mixed with pine resins into jelly-like slabs, then mixed with the cork and wood flour and pigment granules. It is passed through rollers onto the jute backing to form sheets, and cured in heated drying rooms. Natural linoleum is extremely long wearing, as the linseed oil continues to oxidize even after curing, creating additional chemical bonds. However, linoleum may emit VOCs including toluene, hexanal, propanal, and butyl formiate when initially installed.

Floor tile adhesives may emit toluene, benzene, ethyl acetate, ethyl benzene, and styrene. Adhesives with low VOCs are available.

The UF or polyurethane coatings on hardwood flooring emit butyl acetate, ethyl acetate, ethyl benzene, xylenes, and formaldehyde VOCs for a few days. Some of the adhesives used with wood flooring also emit VOCs.

Paints, Stains, and Other Coatings

The types of VOCs and the rate at which they are emitted by paints depend on the chemical makeup, application, indoor environment, and surface characteristics of the substrate. Water-, oil-, or solvent-based paints all emit aromatic hydrocarbons, alcohols, and aliphatic hydrocarbons. Latex- and solvent-based paints may give off benzene, toluene, xylenes, ethanol, methanol, and other VOCs. Paints can continue to emit VOCs even after drying, with water-borne paints emitting some chemicals even six months later.

Solvent-based paints contain hydrocarbons (HCs) and other VOCs, which evaporate as the paint dries. When the HCs react with sunlight and pollutants in the air, they produce ozone. Solvent-based paints require the use of hazardous solvents for thinning and cleanup. Solvent-free paints are available in Europe.

Water-based paints, like latex paints, release much lower VOCs than oil-based paints and varnishes. However, they may still be associated with irritation of mucous membranes, resulting in headaches and both acute and chronic respiratory affects. Latex paint may give off VOCs, including butanone, ethyl benzene, and toluene. Paints have information about VOCs on their labels. A rating of less than 100 grams per liter (about 13 oz per gallon) is good. Latex paints have biocides to prevent fungus growth and spoilage. Latex paints with mercury-based preservatives and antimildew agents can increase the risk of liver and kidney damage, and if inhaled, can affect the lungs and brain, but even so are less hazardous than solvent-based paints.

Most varnishes are solvent-based urethanes. They are highly noxious to handle, but stable when cured. Water-based emulsion urethanes are low-emission, and perform well. Solvents for mixing, removal, and application of paints also emit VOCs. Paint stripper emits methylene chloride.

When acid-cured or acid-catalyzed paints and coatings are applied to pressed wood surfaces, they seal in the emissions from the UF resin in the pressed wood, and the outcome is fewer VOC emissions. Acid-cured coatings do contain formaldehyde, acetone, toluene, and butanol, but their ability to seal in formaldehyde outweighs the short-lived VOCs they emit. Emissions from sprayed-on coatings decline by 90 to 96 percent during the first 16 weeks after application, and brushed-on coatings similarly decline 82 to 96 percent. Wood stains also emit a variety of VOCs, as does polyurethane varnish.

Polymer oils for floor and cabinet finishes contain formaldehyde gas. They remain toxic for several weeks after application. If you must use them, select water-based urethane, low toxic sealers, and wax finishes. Furniture polish emits a range of VOCs as well.

Increasing ventilation alone may not be enough to disperse VOCs during application of wet materials. Isolate the workspace from adjacent sections of the building. Block return registers, and open temporary local exhausts like doors and windows. Increase ventilation to other areas of the building, as well.

Wall Finishes

Wallcoverings vary in their impact on IAQ, depending upon the materials from which they are made. Metal foils have very low emissions, but present disposal problems. Vinyl and vinyl-coated wallcoverings are less stable if made of soft plastics, and have long outgassing times. Vinyl wallcoverings emit vinyl chloride monomers and a variety of other VOCs, but some studies indicate that they are responsible for only negligible amounts of vinyl chloride emissions. Both metallic and vinyl wallcoverings have highly polluting manufacturing processes.

Wallcoverings made of paper, plant fibers, silk, cotton, and similar materials may also pose problems. Wallpaper is usually made of four layers: a facing, an intermediate layer, a backing, and the paste. They may contain VOC-emitting inks, printing solvents, adhesives, binding agents, finishing compounds, resins, glues, paper, vinyl sheeting, or plasticizers. Most wallpaper now uses organic dyes and water-based inks that emit fewer VOCs. Some wallpaper emits VOCs including methanol, ethanol, toluene, xylenes, and others, and may emit far more formaldehyde than vinyl wallcoverings. Wallpaper may remain above recommended exposure limits for one to three days after installation. VOC emissions from all types of wallcoverings drop after a few days.

The adhesives used for heavy wallcoverings can be a problem. Wallpaper paste may emit a wide variety of VOCs. Low-toxic adhesives are available. Lightweight papers can be applied with light, water-based glue.

Acoustic panels, tiles, and wallcoverings are typically made with a mineral fiber or fiberglass backing with fabric coverings. They can be long-term sources of formaldehyde and other gases, and tend to retain dust. Ceiling panels of wood fibers, tapestries, or cork are better choices, if permitted by the fire codes.

Wood paneling may be made of hardwood plywood, MDF, solid hardwood, or UFFI simulated wall paneling. Depending on its composition, wood paneling may emit formaldehyde, acetone, benzene, and other VOCs, especially with higher temperatures and humidity.

Plastic or melamine panels can give off formaldehyde, phenol, aliphatic and aromatic HCs, ketones and other VOCs. Polyvinyl chloride paneling emits phenol, aliphatic and aromatic HCs, and glycol ethers and esters. Plastic tiles contain polystyrene and UF resins.

When choosing a finish, consider where and how it will be used, the client's level of concern about avoiding VOCs, whether proper ventilation will be provided before occupancy, and what alternatives exist that might have less impact on the quality of the indoor air. It is not always possible to completely avoid VOC emissions on a project, but with care and resourcefulness, you can keep high standards for appearance and maintenance, while cutting pollutants and observing budget constraints.

Fabrics and Upholstered Furniture

The chemicals used to manufacture synthetic fabrics can emit VOCs. Upholstered furniture coverings may emit formaldehyde, chloroform, methyl chloroform, and other VOCs. Polyurethane foam used in cushions and upholstered furniture emits toluene di-isocyanate (TDI)

and phenol, but emissions decrease over time. Other furniture components, such as pressed wood products, adhesives, and formaldehyde resins, emit VOCs.

Natural and synthetic fabrics are often treated with chemicals for strength, permanent press features, fire resistance, water repellant properties, and soil repellency. These treatments may emit VOCs. Formaldehyde is often used as the carrier solvent in dying fabrics and in cross-linking plant fibers to give rigidity to permanent press fabrics. Its use has decreased by up to 90 percent since 1975, but it can still contribute substantially to VOC emissions in a building. Draperies are often treated for soil, wrinkle, and fire resistance, and may emit VOCs as a result.

Modular Office Partitions

Although new office systems are less dependent on fabric-covered cubicles, the majority of offices continue to use these corporate workhorses. In fact, many offices save money and avoid adding to landfills by purchasing refurbished panels. Panels surround workers right at breathing level, and add up to large amounts of square footage. Since modular office partitions absorb pollutants and later release them back into the air, long-term use of older panels can add to their impact on IAQ.

Many modular office partitions consist of fabric attached to fiberglass batt insulation, which is bonded to a tempered hardboard or chipboard frame with vinyl acetate adhesive. A metallic outer frame and support legs complete the panel. Office partitions expose a great deal of surface to the indoor air, totaling as much as twice the floor surface area. The chipboard, hardboard, and treated fabrics they contain have a high potential for VOC emissions. The panels are in close proximity to office workers, and often nearly surround them, cutting off air circulation, and keeping the VOCs near the workers.

Modular office partitions have the highest danger for VOC emission right after installation. Manufacturers may treat the panels with chemicals for soil and wrinkle resistance just before wrapping and shipping, increasing the amount of formaldehyde and other VOCs. Methylene chloride solvents are often used to clean panels during manufacture and storage, and can be released when the panels are unwrapped and installed.

Office partitions collect air contaminants, which can be held in the fabric coverings and released later. Textured fabric surfaces can absorb VOCs emitted by carpets, paints, copying fluids, and tobacco smoke. Their absorption increases with higher temperatures and decreased ventilation, conditions that often occur in offices on weekends. Because of their low thermal mass, office partitions emit surges of VOCs whenever there is a rapid change in air temperature, as when the air-conditioning is turned back on and ventilation increased on a Monday morning.

Some manufacturers will precondition furnishings, including office partitions, during the storage, shipping, and installation process. Since most of the outgassing occurs in the first few hours, days, or weeks after removal of the packaging, VOCs can be eliminated from the site by unpacking and exposing materials before bringing them into the building.

Plastics

Technically, plastics are not solids, but viscoelastic fluids, and they evaporate. The plastics used to make wallcoverings, carpets, padding, plumbing pipes, and electric wires and their insulation emit toxic chemicals. These include nitrogen oxide, cyanide, and acid gases. Fumes can be produced by polymers or by additives used as colorants or plasticizers. Plasticizers soften plastics, making them less stable. Polyvinyl chloride plastics are safe to use, but their manufacturing process is hazardous and produces health risks. They also emit toxic fumes in fires. Most plastic laminates have very low toxicity levels. They are made from petroleum. Other chemicals have replaced chlorofluorocarbons (CFCs) for upholstery foams and insulating foams. One type of replacement, hydrochlorofluorocarbons (HCFCs), contributes to the greenhouse effect.

Plastics last for hundreds of years, and pollute both the land and the marine environment. The best solution for their disposal is recycling, which also saves raw materials and energy. Recycled plastics are used for outdoor furniture, floor tiles, carpets, and an increasing number of other products.

Adhesives, Sealants, and Coatings

Most adhesives used in the building process are solvent-based with toluene, xylene, acetone, and other hazardous solvents. Water-based adhesives are safer, but still contain some solvents, including benzene, toluene, acetone, and xylenes. The lowest toxicity is found in water-soluble casein or plain white glue.

Caulking compounds used to seal cracks and seams may emit VOCs. Silicone caulking is very safe and stable. Latex caulking is safe once cured, but some types produce odors for weeks after installation from a variety of VOCs including benzene and toluene. Uncured rubber caulkings, such as butyl caulk, acoustical sealant, and polysulfide caulk, are harmful, and may emit formaldehyde, acetic acid, toluene, xylenes, and other VOCs.

The process of painting or plating furniture can create air and water pollution and toxic waste. Coating processes are less polluting and safer. Metals can be coated with powder coating. Polymer coating has replaced cadmium plating, which produced air and water pollution. Check specifications for metal tables and chairs to see how they are coated.

MATERIALS SAFETY DATA SHEETS

Manufacturers of products that have health and safety implications are required to provide a summary of the chemical composition of the material including health risks, flammability, handling, and storage precautions. Materials Safety Data Sheets (MSDS) list all chemical constituents that make up a minimum of 1 percent of the material and are not proprietary. The sheets do not predict VOC emission rates, and you have to make assumptions about whether higher percentages of a chemical imply higher outgassing rates. It is best to require MSDS for all products and materials used indoors. If questionable components are present, you may have to obtain additional information on chemical formulations, storage, drying times, and airing procedures.

Some definitions are useful to decipher the information in an MSDS. The accepted toxicity for a hazardous material is referred to as its threshold limit value (TLV). The lower the TLV, the more toxic the material. The allowable exposure limit over a working day is called the time weighted average (TWA). The lower the TWA, the more toxic the material. The lethal dose, 50 percent (LD50) is the dose at which, when ingested, half of tested lab animals will die. (The U.S. government has recently changed its policy to permit other tests that do not result in high mortality for lab animals.) The lower the LD50, the more toxic the material. The total volatile organic content (TVOC) is the volume of the product that will evaporate over time. High TVOC adds more indoor air pollution.

INDOOR AIR QUALITY EQUIPMENT

Once the sources of IAQ problems have been removed or isolated wherever possible, increased ventilation and improved air filtration are usually the next most practical measures. The most expensive part of running a business is the cost of employing people. The projected health and productivity benefits of increasing ventilation for a large building are many times the cost. Improving air filtration also produces great benefits for each dollar spent.

Let's look at some of the building system components that address IAQ issues. We discuss these in more detail later, so consider this an introduction to some of the terminology and design considerations.

Building codes specify the amount of ventilation required for specific purposes and occupancies in terms of air change per hour, or in cubic feet per minute (cfm) per person. ASHRAE Standard 62-1989, *Ventilation for Acceptable Indoor Air Quality*, recommends 15 to 20 cfm of outdoor air per person for most applications. The mechanical engineer will use the appropriate figure to determine what equipment is needed for a specific project.

Increasing ventilation for improved air quality must strike a balance with energy conservation. Energy conservation efforts have resulted in reduced air circulation rates in many central air-handling systems. Fewer fans use less power, but distribution is poorer, and the air mix within individual spaces suffers. Individual space air-filtering equipment provides a higher circulation rate and a proper air mix. Each unit has a fan that operates with or without the central HVAC fan, and circulates air six to ten times per hour. The air is then ducted to diffusers, from which it circulates across the space to return air intakes on the opposite side of the room.

There are a number of ways that good ventilation can be assured while controlling heat loss. Heat exchangers recover heat from air that is being exhausted and transfer it to makeup outside air coming into the building, saving heating energy. By tracking occupancy patterns in the building, ventilation can be tailored to the number of people in the building at any one time. Opening outside air dampers for one hour after people leave an area for the day, where possible, can dilute large volumes of room air and dissipate collected contaminants.

Engineers find that it is easiest to get good IAQ with a heating and cooling system using forced air motion (fans and blowers), with some filtering equipment built into the air-handling equipment. Separate air-cleaning systems are commonly used with radiant heating systems. Cooling systems can use economizer cycles at night, when they vent warm indoor air to the outside, and bring in cooler outdoor air for overnight cooling. Evaporative cooling systems use a continuous flow of outdoor air where you want to add humidity to the indoor air.

The general types of technologies used by air cleaners include mechanical filters, electronic air cleaners, and hybrid filters for the capture of particles, plus gas phase filters to control odors. Air cleaners that operate by chemical process, such as ozonation, also exist. The selection of a type of air filter should depend on the intended use of the filter, as explained below.

Air filters protect the HVAC equipment and its components and the furnishings and decor of occupied spaces, and protect the general well-being of residents. They reduce housekeeping and building maintenance, as well as furnace and heating equipment fire hazards. The lower efficiency filters generally used in central HVAC systems will usually cover all of these functions except protecting the health of the occupants, for which much higher performance filtration is required. It may not always be possible to install such equipment in older existing environmental systems, so self-contained portable room air cleaners must sometimes be used to obtain sufficiently high levels of filtration effectiveness.

Residential Air Cleaners

Until recently, small, inexpensive, tabletop appliance-type air cleaners have been quite popular for residential use. They generally contain small panels of dry, loosely packed, low-density fiber filters upstream of a high-velocity fan. Tabletop units may also consist of a fan and an electronic or other type of filter. Small tabletop units generally have limited airflow and inefficient panel filters. Most tests have shown these tabletop units to be relatively ineffective. The combination of low filter efficiency and low airflow in these units causes them to provide essentially no cleaning when assessed for impact on the air of the entire room. Some of the units produce harmful levels of ozone and do not have automatic controls to limit ozone output.

Another major type of residential air cleaner is the larger but still portable device designed to clean the air in a specific size room (Fig. 20-3). Due to their larger and more effective filters or collecting plates, these portable room air cleaners are considerably more effective in cleaning the air in a room than the tabletop units and have become increasingly popular in the past several years. Room-size air cleaners are generally utilized when continuous, localized air cleaning is necessary. Most units may be moved from room to room to reduce pollutant concentration levels as needed. As with tabletop units, room units incorporate a variety of air-cleaning technologies.

Air-cleaning systems can also be installed in the central heating or air-conditioning systems of a residence or in an HVAC system. These units are commonly re-

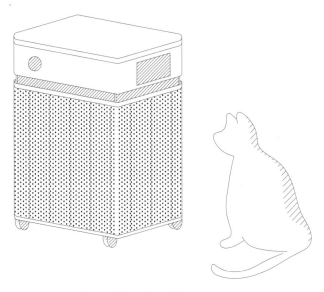

Figure 20-3 Portable air cleaner.

ferred to as in-duct units, although they are not actually located in the distribution ductwork, but rather in un-ducted return air grilles or ducted return air plenums. These central filtration systems provide building-wide air cleaning and, by continuously recirculating building air through the unit, can potentially clean the air throughout the entire air-handling system, ductwork, and rooms. However, with these types of units, the HVAC fan must be in constant operation for air clean-ing to occur, since the airborne contaminants must be captured and carried back to the centralized filter for capture and retention. Thus central filtration systems must be operated with the fan on for constant air move-ment through the HVAC system. Generally, residential HVAC systems run their fans only intermittently to maintain a comfortable indoor temperature. Research indicates that a highly efficient room unit will be more effective at removing pollutants in the room where it is located than a central filtration system.

Both outside air and recycled air must be filtered. Inadequate filtration is a result of low-efficiency filters, improper installation, or torn, clogged, or otherwise in-effective filters. Ductwork is often installed without any provision for access or cleaning, leading to a massive buildup of contamination that can spread to building occupants. Poor maintenance in the ducts puts even more demands on the filters. It is best to remove pol-lutants at the source, and therefore ASHRAE recom-mends dust collectors at the source rather than filters for dusty areas. For example, the maintenance workshop in a hotel would have a vacuum that removed sawdust immediately from the worktable, rather than a filter in the air-conditioning system that would allow the dust to spread throughout the area.

If the sources of allergy problems are present in a residence, air cleaning alone has not been proven ef-fective at reducing airborne allergen-containing particles to levels at which no adverse effects are anticipated. Cats, for example, generally shed allergen at a much greater rate than air cleaners can effect removal. Dust mites ex-crete allergens in fecal particles within the carpet or the bedding, where air cleaners are ineffective. For individ-uals sensitive to dust mite allergen, the use of imper-meable mattress coverings appears to be as effective as the use of an air-cleaning unit above the bed. Source control should always be the first choice for allergen control in residences.

If the choice is made to use an air cleaner, choose one that ensures high efficiency over an extended pe-riod of time and does not produce ozone levels above 0.05 parts per million (ppm).

Mechanical Filters

Mechanical filters may be used in central filtration sys-tems as well as in portable units using a fan to force air through the filter. Mechanical filters capture particles by straining larger and then smaller particles out of the airstream thorough increasingly smaller openings in the filter pack. Very small submicron-sized particles are captured by being drawn toward the surfaces of the fil-tration medium, where they are held by static electric charges. This is the factor responsible for the effective-ness of the highest efficiency mechanical filters' removal of submicron-sized particles. There are three major types of mechanical filters: panel or flat filters, pleated filters, and high-efficiency particulate air (HEPA) filters.

Flat or panel filters (Fig. 20-4) usually contain a low packing density fibrous medium that can be either dry or coated with a sticky substance, such as oil, so that particles adhere to it. Less-expensive lower efficiency fil-ters that employ woven fiberglass strands to catch par-ticles restrict airflow less, so smaller fans and less en-ergy are needed. The typical, low-efficiency furnace filter in many residential HVAC systems is a flat filter, 13 to 25 mm ($\frac{1}{2}$–1 in.) thick, that is efficient in collecting large particles, but removes only between 10 and 60 percent of total particles, and lets most smaller, respirable-size particles through.

Older buildings were designed with only crude panel filters in HVAC equipment. Engineers now also use a combination of high-efficiency particle filters and adsorption filters to achieve high IAQ. Panel filters are

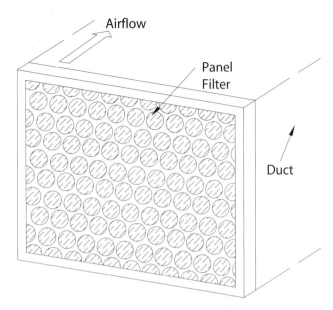

Figure 20-4 Dry mat panel air filter.

placed ahead of the HVAC unit's fan (upstream), and the high-efficiency systems are located downstream from the HVAC's cooling units and drain pans. This way, microbiological contaminants in wet components of the system are removed before they are distributed with the air through the entire building.

Not all pollutants can be removed by filters. Large sized particles are the easiest to remove, but smaller particles may be the most dangerous. Panel filters come with HVAC equipment, and are designed primarily to protect fans from large particles of lint and dust, not for proper air cleaning. Standard commercial grade filters remove 75 to 85 percent of particles from the air.

Media filters use much finer fibers. However, any increase in filter density significantly increases resistance to airflow, slowing down the air flowing through the filter. Media filters are around 90 percent efficient. They are usually a minimum of 15 cm (6 in.) deep, and have a minimum life cycle of six months. Filters, and especially media filters, require regular maintenance. If blocked, they can damage HVAC equipment, so they must be replaced frequently. Filters for large units can cover an entire wall in a room-size air-handler plenum.

The most effective approach to increasing effectiveness in a filter is to extend the surface area by pleating the filter medium. This slows down the airflow velocity through the filter and decreases overall resistance to airflow to reduce the drop in pressure. Pleated filters use highly efficient filter paper in pleats within a frame. Pleating of filter media increases the total filtering area and extends the useful life of the filter. The efficiency of pleated media filters is much higher than for other dry-type filters.

High-efficiency particulate air filters provide the best protection. Such HEPA filters were originally developed during World War II to prevent discharge of radioactive particles from nuclear reactor facility exhausts. They are now found in special air cleaners for very polluted environments, and for spaces that demand the highest quality IAQ. High-efficiency filters are used in hospitals and laboratories, as well as in portable residential air cleaners. They are generally made from a single sheet of water repellent fiber that's pleated to provide more surface area with which to catch particles. The filter is made of tiny glass fibers in a thickness and texture very similar to blotter paper. To qualify as a HEPA filter, the filter must allow no more than three particles out of 10,000 (including smaller respirable particles) to penetrate the filtration media, a minimum particle removal efficiency of 99.97 percent. Because they are more densely woven than other filters, HEPA filters require larger and more energy-intensive fans, making them more expensive and noisier. Consequently, HEPA filters are generally reserved for hospital operating rooms, manufacturing clean rooms (for example, where computer chips are made), and other especially sensitive places. HEPA filters are generally not applied to central residential HVAC systems due to their size and horsepower requirements. They need a powerful fan, leading to increased energy costs. Replacement filters range from $50 to $100, but last up to five years when used with a prefilter.

Similar HEPA-type filters with less efficient filter paper may have 55 percent efficiencies. These filters, which are still very good when compared to conventional panel type and even pleated filters, have higher airflow, lower efficiency, and lower cost than their original version.

In summary, there is little reason to use inexpensive tabletop, appliance-type air cleaners, regardless of the technology they employ. In general, high-efficiency particle collection requires larger filters or electronic air cleaners.

Electronic Air Cleaners

Electronic filters, generally marketed as electronic air cleaners, employ an electrical field to trap particles. Like mechanical filters, they may be installed in central filtration systems as well as in portable units with fans. Electronic air cleaners require less maintenance than systems with filters, but produce ozone. Air rushing through a mechanical filter produces static electricity.

Larger particles cling to the filter, which loses efficiency with more humidity and higher air velocity.

The simplest form of electronic air cleaner is the negative ion generator. A basic electronic air cleaner uses static charges to remove particles from indoor air. They operate by charging the particles in a room, which become attracted to and deposit on walls, floors, tabletops, curtains, or occupants, from which they must then be cleaned up.

More advanced units are designed to reduce soiling in a room. They generate negative ions within a space through which air flows, causing particles entrained in the air to become charged. The charged particles are then drawn back into the cleaner by a fan, where they are collected on a charged panel filter. In other ionizers, a stream of negative ions is generated in pulses, and negatively charged particles are drawn back to the ionizer. While personal air purifiers using this technology can have a beneficial effect on airborne particles, they also require frequent maintenance and cleaning.

Electrostatic precipitators are the more common type of electronic air cleaner. They employ a one-stage or a two-stage design for particle collection. In the less expensive but less effective single-stage design, a charged medium acts to both charge and collect airborne particles. This polarizes particles, which then cling to the filter material. If the field is not strong enough, many particles fail to be polarized and pass through.

In a two-stage electronic air cleaner, dirty air passes between the ionizing wires of a high-voltage power supply. Electrons are stripped from the particles in the air, leaving the particles with a positive charge (ions). The ionized particles then pass between closely spaced collector plates with opposing charges. They are repelled by the positive plates and attracted to the negative ones, where they are collected.

The advantages of electronic filters are that they generally have low energy costs because they don't create a lot of resistance. The airflow through the units remains constant, and the precipitating cell is reusable, avoiding long-term filter replacement costs. The major disadvantages are that they become less efficient with use, precipitating cells require frequent cleaning, and they can produce ozone, either as a by-product of use or intentionally. Those installed into HVAC systems have a relatively high initial cost, including expensive installation.

Hybrid Filters

Hybrid filters incorporate two or more of the filter control technologies discussed above. Some combine mechanical filters with an electrostatic precipitator or an ion generator in an integrated system or single self-contained device.

Gas Phase Filters

Compared to particulate control, gas phase pollution control is a relatively new and complex field that seeks to remove gases and associated odors. Two types of gas phase capture and control filters are chemisorption and physical adsorption.

Chemisorption occurs when the active material attracts gas molecules onto its surface, where a bond is formed between the surface and the molecule. The material that absorbs the pollutant is changed by the interaction, and requires replacement regularly.

Physical adsorption filters are used to remove gases by physically attracting and adhering a gas to the surface of a solid, usually activated carbon in the case of air filtration. The process is similar to the action of a magnet attracting iron filings. The pollutant doesn't bond with the solid, which can thus be reused. Once the gas is on the activated carbon, it moves down into the carbon particle, eventually condensing into a liquid.

Activated carbon adsorbs some gaseous indoor air pollutants, especially VOCs, sulfur dioxide, and ozone, but it does not efficiently adsorb volatile, low molecular weight gases such as formaldehyde and ammonia. Although relatively small quantities of activated charcoal reduce odors in residences, many pollutants affect health at levels below odor thresholds.

Some recently developed systems use more active particles of carbon, permanganate alumina, or zeolite that are incorporated into a fabric mat. Other adsorption filters use porous pellets impregnated with active chemicals like potassium permanganate, which react with contaminants and reduce their harmful effects.

All adsorbents require frequent maintenance, and may reemit trapped pollutants when saturated. High-quality adsorption filters are designed to be used 24 hours per day, seven days a week, for six months, at which time they must be regenerated or replaced. While effective, these filters only capture a small percentage of certain specific gases and vapors.

Air Washers

Air washers are sometimes used to control humidity and bacterial growth. In some large ventilation systems, air is scrubbed with jets of water that remove dust from the air. If the equipment is not well maintained, the moisture within the air washer can be a source of pollution.

Ozone Generators

Although it is harmful in high concentrations, ozone may be used to reduce indoor pollutants. When the two molecules that make up oxygen are broken down with an electrical discharge, the molecules end up coming back together in groups of three to form ozone molecules. Once released into the air, ozone actively seeks out pollutants, attaching itself to a wide range of contaminants including chemical gases, bacteria, mold, and mildew, and destroying them by cracking their molecular membranes. Because ozone has a very short life span—between 20 and 30 minutes—it's easy to avoid achieving the high concentrations that can damage people's health. However, some experts, including the EPA, do not agree that ozone is an effective air treatment.

Ozone generators use a chemical modification process instead of mechanical or electronic filters. Ozone has been used in water purification since 1893, and is used in cooling towers to control contaminants without negative side effects. Ozone introduced into the airstream can help control microbial growth and odors in uses such as meat storage or in fire- and flood-damaged buildings where humans are not exposed.

Appliance-sized ozone generating units have typically been marketed in the United States as air cleaners. However, the high concentration levels required for contaminant control are in conflict with potential health effects as established by the National Institute of Occupational Safety and Health, the EPA, and the U.S. Food and Drug Administration. Because of the documented health dangers of ozone, especially for individuals with asthma, and the lack of evidence for its ability to effectively clean the air at low concentrations, the American Lung Association suggests that ozone generators not be used.

Ultraviolet Light

Ultraviolet (UV) light rays kill germs and destroy the DNA structure of viruses, bacteria, and fungi. These are the same rays that emanate from the sun and kill microorganisms on laundry on a clothesline. Ultraviolet light has been used for years in hospitals to sanitize rooms and equipment, and is also effective in eliminating many odors and controlling the spread of cold

and flu viruses. However, it can be more expensive than other purification techniques.

Ultraviolet light is installed within HVAC systems to control fungi, bacteria, and viruses, helping cooling coils and drain pans stay cleaner. It works best at room temperatures and warmer, and with UV-reflective aluminum duct interiors. The lamps used for UV light take up very little space within the ductwork, and no ozone or chemicals are produced. Tube life is 5000 to 7500 hours, so if the tubes are on all the time, they need access for replacement in less than a year.

Ultraviolet lamps may also be installed directly in rooms, such as kitchens, sickrooms, or overcrowded dwellings. The lamps must be mounted high in the room and shielded from sight, as they can damage the eyes and skin. Some personal air purifiers also use UV light. Laboratory fume hoods and other IAQ equipment use a UV lamp focused on a catalyst in the presence of water vapor. This process destroys airborne microorganisms and VOCs better than chlorine.

The National Renewable Energy Laboratory is developing a process for using UV to control VOCs. Polluted air is bombarded with UV in the presence of special catalysts. The process quickly breaks down cigarette smoke, formaldehyde, and toluene into molecules of water and carbon dioxide.

Future Developments in Testing and Filters

Filter strips precoated with testing compounds that will affordably detect harmful pollutants in specific locations are being developed. Hanging these strips in a building may eliminate the need for expensive surveys and tests by air quality consultants.

Compounds that are specifically designed to target particular gases such as formaldehyde and carbon monoxide are also under development. When sprayed onto lower efficiency and carbon-activated filters, these compounds will extract the offending gases from the air through adsorption. By combining test strips with these new compounds, IAQ problems will be targeted more easily.

Central Cleaning Systems

Central cleaning systems have been used in homes and commercial buildings for years. They are essentially built-in vacuum cleaners with powerful motors. As such, they can be used to trap dirt and dust inside the power unit equipment and away from rooms where people live and work, or they can be vented outdoors, decreasing exposure for people with dust allergies. The power unit is usually installed in a utility room, basement, or garage. Tubing running under the floor or in the attic connects through the walls to unobtrusive inlets placed conveniently throughout the building. When it's time to vacuum, a long flexible hose is inserted into an inlet and the system turns on automatically. The noise is kept at the remote location of the power unit. Most power units operate on a dedicated 15-A normal residential electrical circuit, but some larger units may require heavier wiring. Systems come with a variety of hoses and brushes. Installation is simplest in new construction. With a day or two's work, a builder, a plumber, a system dealer, or even a building owner with some knowledge of electricity, can install a system. Central cleaning systems are commonly found in commercial office buildings and restaurants.

Odor Control

We perceive an odor most when we first encounter it, and then the odor gradually fades in our awareness. This is why you notice an odor more when first entering a room, but later become unaware of it. Typical office odors include tobacco smoke, body odor, grooming products (perfumes), copy machines, cleaning fluids, and outgassing from materials such as carpets, furniture, and construction materials. Testing equipment doesn't detect odors as well as your nose, so it may be difficult to test for specific sources of odors.

You can cut down on odors by increasing the rate of outdoor ventilation. In order to control human body odor, engineers recommend that three to four liters per second or L/s (6–9 cfm) of outdoor air per occupant should be added to the space. Where smoking occurs, 7 to 14 L/s (15–30 cfm) per person is required, which is bad for energy conservation in hot and cold weathers. This is yet another cost to society from smoking.

Chapter

Ventilation

Before the invention of mechanical ventilation, the common high ceilings in buildings created a large volume of indoor air that diluted odors and carbon dioxide. Fresh air was provided by infiltration, the accidental leakage of air through cracks in the building, which along with operable windows created a steady exchange of air with the outdoors. The high ceilings of older auditoriums harbor a reserve where fresh air can build up when the building is unoccupied between performances.

NATURAL VENTILATION

Natural ventilation requires a source of air of an acceptable temperature, moisture content, and cleanliness, and a force—usually wind or convection—to move the air through the inhabited spaces of a building. Air flows through a building because it moves from higher pressure to lower pressure areas. Controls are provided for the volume, velocity, and direction of the airflow. Finally, the contaminated air must be cleaned and reused or exhausted from the building.

The simplest system for getting fresh air into a building uses outdoor air for its source and wind for its power. Wind creates local areas of high pressure on the wind-

ward side of the building, and low pressure on the leeward side. Fresh air infiltrates the building on the windward side through cracks and seams. On the opposite side of the building, where pressure is lower, stale indoors air leaks back outside. Wind-powered ventilation is most efficient if there are windows on at least two sides of a room, preferably opposite each other. The process of infiltration can be slow in a tightly constructed building. Loose-fitting doors and windows result in buildings with drafty rooms and wasted energy.

Depending on the leakage openings in the building exterior, the wind can affect pressure relationships within and between rooms. The building should be designed to take advantage of the prevailing winds in the warmest seasons when it is sited and when the interior is laid out.

Very leaky spaces have two to three air changes or more per hour. Even when doors and windows are weather-stripped and construction seams are sealed airtight, about one-half to one air change per hour will occur, but this may be useful for the minimum air replacement needed in a small building. Weather-stripping materials generally have a lifespan of less than ten years, and need to be replaced before they wear out.

In convective ventilation, differences in the density of warmer and cooler air create the differences in pressure that move the air. Convective ventilation uses the principle that hot air rises, known as the stack effect. The warm air inside the building rises and exits near the building's top. Cool air infiltrates at lower levels. The stack effect works best when the intakes are as low as possible and the height of the stack is as great as possible. The stack effect is not noticeable in buildings less than five stories or about 30.5 meters (100 ft) tall. In cold weather, fans can be run in reverse to push warm air back down into the building. Fire protection codes restrict air interaction between floors of high-rises, reducing or eliminating the stack effect. To depend on convective forces alone for natural ventilation, you need relatively large openings. Insect screens keep out bugs, birds, and small animals, and admit light and air, but cut down on the amount of airflow. Systems using only convective forces are not usually as strong as those depending on the wind.

The ventilation rate is measured in liters per second (L/s) or in cubic feet per minute (cfm). It takes only very small amounts of air to provide enough oxygen for us to breathe. The recommended ventilation rate for offices is 9.44 L/s (20 cfm) of outside air for each occupant in non-smoking areas. About a quarter of this amount is required to dilute carbon dioxide from human respiration, while another quarter counteracts body odors. The remainder dilutes emissions from interior building materials and office equipment. This works out to slightly more than one air change per hour in an office with an eight-foot high ceiling. Lower ceilings create greater densities of people per volume, and require higher rates of ventilation.

Especially high rates of air replacement are needed in buildings housing heat- and odor-producing activities. Restaurant kitchens, gym locker rooms, bars, and auditoriums require extra ventilation. Lower rates are permissible for residences, lightly occupied offices, warehouses, and light manufacturing plants.

Using natural ventilation helps keep a building cool in hot weather and supplies fresh air without resorting to energy-dependent machines. However, in cold climates energy loss through buildings that leak warm air can offset the benefits of natural cooling. Careful building design can maximize the benefits of natural ventilation while avoiding energy waste.

Attic ventilation is the traditional way of controlling temperature and moisture in an attic. Ventilating an attic reduces temperature swings. It makes the building more comfortable during hot weather and reduces the cost of mechanical air conditioning. William Rose, with the Building Research Council at the University of Illinois, has been conducting some of the first research into how and why attic ventilation works.

Thermal buoyancy—the rising of warm air—is a major cause of air leakage from a building's living space to the attic, but Rose's research shows that wind is the major force driving air exchange between an attic and the outdoors, and that the role of thermal buoyancy in diluting attic air with outdoor air is negligible. Generally, we assume that warmer air rises and escapes from high vents in an attic, while cooler air enters in lower vents. Some ridge vents at the roof's peak may in fact allow air to blow in one side and out the other, without drawing much air from the attic. Ridge vents with baffles may create better suction to draw air out.

Soffit vents, which are located in the roof's overhang, work well as inlets and outlets. There's less problem with rain and snow getting in, because soffit vents point downward. Soffit vents should always be installed whenever there are high vents on ridges or gables, which pull air out of the attic. Without soffit vents, makeup air would be drawn through the ceiling below, which increases heat loss and adds moisture to the attic.

To get maximum protection, soffit vents should be located as far out from the wall as possible, so that rain or snow blowing into the soffit is less likely to soak the insulation or drywall. They should be distributed evenly around the attic, including corners. At least half of the vent area should be low on the roof. The net free area (NFA), which is stamped on the vents, indicates resistance, with higher numbers indicating less resistance and better airflow.

Rose's research shows that a ventilated attic is slightly warmer on a clear, cold night than an unvented attic. In winter, venting maintains uniform roof sheathing temperature, which reduces the likelihood that ice dams will form. Without good ventilation, warm spots form near the eaves that melt snow against the roof shingles, which can later refreeze into an ice dam. Water runs down until it is over the eaves, where it refreezes. This ice then builds up and causes the water collecting above it to seep in under the shingles and into the eaves or the house. More melting snow can build up behind the ice dam and damage the building.

Chronic ice dam problems often lead to the use of electric heater cables or snow shoveling to attempt to clear the snow out of the way. Using self-stick rubberized water and ice membranes plus roof ventilation can prevent ice dams.

Warm air rising up through plumbing, electrical, and other penetrations into the attic will also heat the roof sheathing. Adding ventilation without sealing air leaks into the attic can actually increase the amount of air leaking from the house, wasting valuable heat and potentially making ice dams worse. Air leaking out of air handlers and ducts, and heat leaving the system by conduction can be among the largest causes of heat loss and ice damming.

Heated air escaping into the roof not only contributes to ice dams and heat loss, it is also the primary means for moisture to get into attic or roof framing, where it can condense and cause mold, mildew, and structural damage to the roof. Surprisingly, much of the moisture that rises through openings around plumbing, ducts, and wires comes as water vapor in air vented from crawlspaces. Once in the attic, the air cools, allowing its water vapor to condense on roof sheathing. Ventilation alone can't take care of moisture in the attic. Keeping dampness out of the building—especially out of the basement and crawlspace—helps protect against condensation and mildew in the attic. An airtight ceiling is also important.

Installing rigid insulation in the eaves (the projecting overhang at the lower edge of a roof) reduces heat loss in the eave area. Another option is to change the framing detail to one that leaves more room between the top plate and the rafter. Cardboard or foam baffles precut to fit 16- or 24-in. on center framing can eliminate wind blowing across insulation.

Eliminate leaks that allow heated air to escape into the attic at top plates, wiring penetrations, plumbing vents, and chimney and duct chases. Recessed lights are responsible for significant heat loss; be sure to use fixtures rated for insulation contact (IC rated) and air tightness.

Heating, ventilating, and air-conditioning (HVAC) equipment and ductwork in attics will waste leaking air. If there is no alternative, all ducts should be sealed tightly and run close to the ceiling, buried in loose fill insulation to the equivalent R-value of the attic insulation.

Once you eliminate the heat loss in the attic, there is little driving force to pull air through the vents. However, code-required ventilation openings in attics and cathedral ceilings should be installed as a backup measure.

Though now valued for style, symbolism, and attractiveness, cupolas (Fig. 21-1) represented early air-conditioning. The cupola was a high point in which the hottest air in the house could collect and from which it could escape outside because hot air's natural buoyancy causes it to rise. Cooler air was in turn drawn into the house through the open windows below. This stack effect becomes most effective when there is a good source of hot air to accelerate the flow, as from an attic. When the wind was blowing briskly through the cupola, an updraft throughout the house pulled cooler air in through the windows. However, without at least a little wind, you didn't get much ventilation. Using a cupola

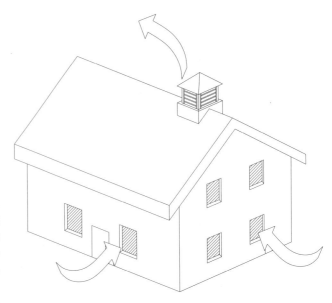

Figure 21-1 Cupola.

or ridge vents along the top of the roof will cool only the attic if there is an air and vapor barrier and blanket of insulation isolating the attic from the house below, as is customary today.

Roof windows, also called operable or venting skylights (Fig. 21-2), can create the same updraft throughout the house as an old-fashioned cupola. When shaded to keep direct sunlight out, they are one of the best natural ventilating devices available. However, their value for cooling alone does not compensate for their initial cost. Roof windows also allow moisture to escape from kitchens, baths, laundry rooms, and pool enclosures.

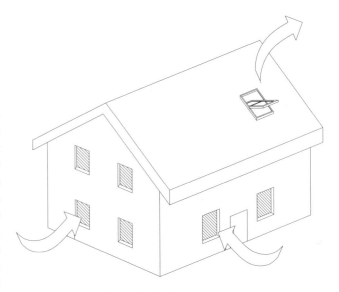

Figure 21-2 Roof window.

Roof windows are available with remote controls and rain sensors. Skylights can be prewired for sun-screening accessories, including sun-blocking shades, pleated shades, venetian blinds, or roller shades. Exterior awnings block up to 40 percent more heat than interior shades, and are available with manual and automatic controls. ENERGY STAR® skylights use low-emissivity (low-e) glass coatings, warm edge technology that ensures that the areas around the frames don't reduce the insulating properties of the glazing, and energy-efficient blinds that improve overall energy efficiency.

Roof ventilators also increase natural ventilation. Some roof ventilators are spun by the wind, drawing air from the room below. Some rely on convective flow, while some create low-pressure areas that are then filled with interior air. Wind gravity or turbine ventilators create suction when wind blows across the top of a stack, pulling air up and out of the building. Roof ventilators require control dampers to change the size of the opening as necessary.

Doors should not be relied upon for essential building ventilation unless they are equipped with a holder set at the desired angle. An ordinary door can't control the amount of air that flows past it.

In residences, ventilation is tied to the quantity of exterior windows and the amount of natural ventilation they supply. If the bathroom does not have a window, it is required to have a fan with a duct leading directly to the exterior. A window provides not only ventilation, but also daylight and possibly a room-expanding view. A percentage of the windows in a residence must be operable for ventilation and emergency egress.

William McDonough + Partners designed the offices for Gap Inc. in San Bruno, California, in 1994 around the concept that people would rather spend their day outside. Daylight, fresh air, and views of the outdoors are celebrated throughout the two-story structure. Fresh air is available through operable windows throughout the building. A raised floor provides ventilation that puts fresh air directly at the occupant's breathing level as oxygen-depleted air and indoor air pollutants are carried upward. At night, cool night air is run across the thermal mass of the slab within the raised floor. The raised floor also eliminates the need for dropped acoustic ceilings, allowing the exposed acoustical deck to reflect lighting. Through careful use of daylighting, fresh air, and other methods, the Gap office building exceeds its goal of being 30 percent more energy efficient than is required by California law, at a cost that was expected to be repaid by energy savings within six years.

The Lewis Center for Environmental Studies at Oberlin College bases ventilation rates on carbon dioxide levels in the building. As more students enter the building, the carbon dioxide levels rise, triggering the HVAC system or automatically opening clerestory windows. This ensures that the building is not being ventilated more than it needs, thus saving heating and cooling energy.

In the past, the American Society of Heating, Refrigeration, and Air-Conditioning Engineers (ASHRAE) standards for building ventilation have shown a preference for mechanical ventilation systems. In response to energy conservation issues, however, these standards have been modified, and in 2002, ASHRAE is scheduled to introduce an alternative ventilation standard for naturally ventilated buildings.

FANS

Mechanical ventilation options include unit ventilator fans on the outside wall of each room to circulate room air and replace a fraction of it with outdoor air. Window or through-wall air-conditioning units can also be run as fans. A central heating and cooling system with coils of hot or chilled water will temper the air in room ventilation units. Fixed location fans can provide a reliable, positive airflow to an interior space.

Some residences have a principal exhaust fan designed for quiet, continuous use in a central location. This whole-house ventilator (Fig. 21-3) has a motor-driven fan for pulling stale air from living areas of the

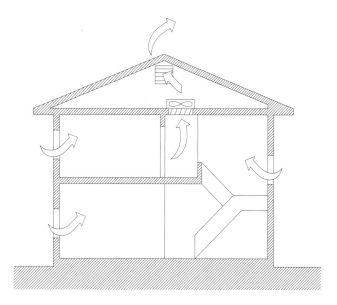

Figure 21-3 Whole house fan.

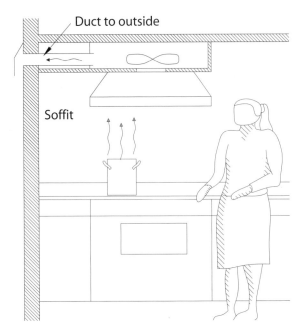

Duct to outside

Soffit

Figure 21-4 Kitchen exhaust fan.

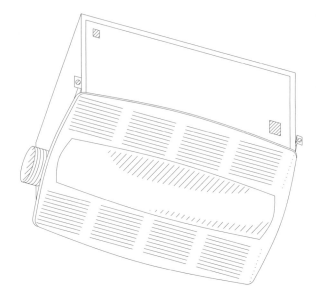

Figure 21-5 Recessed bathroom ceiling fan-light.

house and exhausting it through attic vents. Without an adequate exhaust fan, the building may not have enough air for combustion equipment, such as furnaces and stovetop barbecues, to function correctly, and fumes may not be exhausted properly. Equipment that demands a large amount of exhaust should have another fan supplying makeup air running at the same time.

Bathrooms and kitchens have exhaust fans (Fig. 21-4) to control odors and humidity. By creating negative pressures, exhaust fans help contain odors within the space where they originate. In radiant heated buildings, exhaust fans are sometimes the only source of air movement. The air that residential kitchen and bathroom fans dump outdoors is replaced by air leaking into various parts of the house. The result is a loss of heating or cooling energy.

Codes prohibit discharging exhaust fans into attics, basements, or crawlspaces. The American National Standards Institute (ANSI) and ASHRAE have jointly published ANSI/ASHRAE 90.2-1993, *Energy-Efficient Design of New Low-Rise Residential Buildings,* which requires user-controlled exhaust fans of at least 23.6 L/s (50 cfm) capacity for bathrooms, and 47.2 L/s (100 cfm) for kitchens. The intake should be as close as possible to the source of the polluted air, and the air path should avoid crossing other spaces. Kitchen fans can exhaust grease, odors, and water vapor directly above the range, with a duct vertically through the roof, directly through an exterior wall, or horizontally to the outside through a soffit above wall cabinets. Self-ventilating cooktops

may exhaust directly to the outside or, when located in an interior location, through a duct in the floor.

In bathrooms, the exhaust fan (Fig. 21-5) should be in the ceiling above the toilet and shower or high on the exterior wall opposite the door. It should discharge directly to the outside, at a point a minimum of 91 cm (3 ft) away from any opening that allows outside air to enter the building. Residential exhaust fans are often combined with a lighting fixture, a fan-forced heater, or a radiant heat lamp.

Residential fans are often very noisy, which can be an advantage when masking toilet sounds, but may be annoying at other times. Models are available with a high-efficiency centrifugal blower that provides virtually silent performance, and a lighted switch that indicates when the fan is on. Highly energy-efficient motors are available that use about a third of the electricity of standard versions, and which may qualify for local utility rebates. Some designs allow easy installation in new construction as well as retrofit applications. Models are available that activate automatically to remove excess humidity. Fluorescent or incandescent lighting fixtures, and even night-lights, are included in some designs. Fans for use over bathtubs and showers should be Underwriters Laboratories (UL) listed and connected to ground fault circuit interrupter (GFCI) protected branch circuits. Larger multiport exhaust fans are designed for larger master bathroom suites, where they can vent the toilet area, the shower, and a walk-in closet with one quiet unit. The acoustically insulated motor is mounted in a remote location, and flexible ducts are run to unobtrusive grilles at three separate areas.

Fan models are available for use in business or small offices that offer computerized operating programs to ensure regular exchanges of air. Again, quiet operation and high energy efficiency are available. In addition to ceiling mounts, exhaust fans come in models for mounting through the wall without ducting, with a concealed intake behind a central panel that can be decorated to match the room, and for moving air from one room to another through the intervening wall via grilles on both sides. Blower fans that use an activated charcoal filter to remove odors are offered in unducted models, which filter and recirculate air but do not remove the air from the room. In-line fan systems for residential and light commercial applications locate fans in flexible round ducts or rigid square and rectangular ducts to exhaust air from several rooms.

Operable exterior openings (windows or skylights) are permitted instead of mechanical fans, but must have an area of not less than one-twentieth of the floor area, and a minimal size of 0.14 square meters (1.5 square ft). If natural ventilation is used for kitchen ventilation, openings must be a minimum of 0.46 square meters (5 square ft).

Public toilet room plumbing facilities must be coordinated with the ventilation system to keep odors away from other building spaces while providing fresh air. The toilet room should be downstream in the airflow from other spaces. The air from toilet rooms should not be vented into other spaces, but exhausted outdoors. By keeping slightly lower air pressure in the toilet rooms than in adjacent spaces, air flows into the toilet room from the other spaces, containing toilet room odors. This is accomplished by supplying more air to surrounding spaces than is returned. The surplus is drawn into the toilet rooms and then exhausted. Exhaust vents should be located close to toilets and above them.

Overall room exhaust fans are also used in storage rooms, janitor's closets, and darkrooms. The amount of outdoor air supplied is slightly less than the amount exhausted, resulting in negative air pressure within the room. This draws air in from surrounding areas, preventing odors and contamination from migrating to other areas.

LOCALIZED EXHAUST SYSTEMS

Industrial process areas, laboratories, and critical medical care areas may require one or more fans and ductwork to the outside. Kitchens, toilet rooms, smoking rooms, and chemical storage rooms also should be directly exhausted to the outside. Photocopiers, blueprinting machines, and other equipment may need localized exhaust ventilation. Buildings with many exhausts have greater heating and cooling loads.

Hoods can be built over points where contamination originates. Commercial kitchen hoods collect grease, moisture, and heat at ranges and steam tables. Sometimes outside air is introduced at or near the exhaust hood with minimal conditioning, and then quickly exhausted, saving heating and cooling energy.

Since hot air rises, an overhead hood works best over a range. Fans that pull from several inches above the burner surface at the back of the stove, and downdraft fans, including those on indoor grills, require significantly more airflow to be effective. It is best to install a fan that's no bigger than needed. The Home Ventilating Institute, a fan manufacturers' trade association, recommends range hood capacity of 40 to 50 cfm per linear foot of range, or about 120 to 150 cfm for the standard 76-cm (30-in.) range. To work properly, the range hood should be at least as wide as the stove with an extra 76 to 152 mm (3–6 in.) for good measure. It should be located no more than 51 to 61 cm (20–24 in.) above the stovetop. A 51-cm deep hood will capture fumes better than the typical 43-cm (17-in.) deep models. Wall-mounted hoods are generally more effective than freestanding island hoods, because there are fewer air currents to blow fumes away from the hood. Slide-out ventilation hoods are mounted below wall cabinets, and can be vented or unvented. Some manufacturers offer hoods with dishwasher-safe grease filters. Retractable downdraft vents behind cooktop burners also have washable grease filters. Residential kitchen hoods generally require a 115V, 60-Hz, AC, 15-A grounded fused electrical supply.

The rising popularity of commercial-style ranges is partly responsible for the increasing airflow capacity of range fans. More airflow is required to remove the heat from high-output ranges and to make up for the reduced effectiveness of more stylish, slimmer hoods. High-powered kitchen range hoods may create health hazards. Typical range hoods are rated at 175 to 250 cfm. Many new fans remove air at a rate of more than 600 cfm, and some exceed 1000 cfm. These high-capacity fans are easily powerful enough to pull exhaust gases out of a fireplace, wood stove, water heater, or furnace, a problem called backdrafting. Backdrafting exposes building occupants to fumes containing carbon monoxide, oxides of nitrogen, and other pollutants. A 1994 study by the Bonneville Power Administration of new homes without special air sealing in Oregon, Washington, and Idaho showed that 56 percent of the homes could easily have backdrafting problems from typical exhaust fans.

To protect against backdrafting, you must be sure to provide a reliable source of makeup air to replace the air that is being exhausted. Suggesting that occupants open a window doesn't work well, since even if they remember to do it, they are likely to open it only a crack, especially in bad weather. According to standards established by the Canadian R-2000 program, a 200-cfm range hood would require a 61-cm (24-in.) wide window to be raised 13 cm (5 in.) to create enough ventilation area. The Uniform National Mechanical Code (UMC) contains a similar provision.

 Canada's national building code requires a separate fan wired to blow outside air into the same space when the rating of any exhaust device, including fans and clothes dryers, exceeds 160 cfm. In colder climates, preheating the incoming air can eliminate cold drafts. Range hood manufacturers may not provide an integrated makeup air solution, so the range hood installer has to find a way to activate the supply fan when the exhaust fan starts. After installation, it's important to verify that the exhaust fan is not depressurizing chimneys or flues. It is possible to get a rough idea whether backdrafting is occurring by using a stick of incense or a smoking match, closing all interior doors except between the kitchen and combustion appliances. While the fan is running, watch to see if the smoke rises up the flue. Also perform the test while the furnace blower is operating, because unbalanced air flows in ductwork can also contribute to depressurization problems. A contractor can use a pressure device called a manometer for a more exact reading.

Residential range hoods are available in a wide variety of styles and materials, including stainless steel and glass. Some models extract air almost noiselessly. Innovative self-cleaning features and lighting fixtures are included with some styles. Where hoods are installed without ducts, heavy-duty charcoal filters are advertised for ensuring the removal of smoke and odors.

Most buildings are designed to have a positive air pressure as compared to the outdoors, so that unconditioned air doesn't enter through openings in the building envelope. Corridors should be supplied with fresh air, and residential units, including apartments, condominiums, hotels, motels, hospitals, and nursing homes, should have exhausts.

Multistory buildings have chases for exhaust ducts through successive floors, which can double up with plumbing in apartments, hotels, and hospitals. Kitchen exhausts must remain separate, due to the risk of fires. In major laboratory buildings, many exhaust stacks can be seen rising high above the roof.

Chapter

22

Fenestration

●●●

The fenestration of a building—its windows, skylights, and clerestories (high windows)—greatly influences the amount of heat gain and loss, as well as the infiltration and ventilation. The proportion of glass on the exterior affects energy conservation and thermal comfort.

Windows can be used to improve energy conservation by admitting solar thermal energy, providing natural ventilation for cooling, and reducing the need for artificial illumination. The proper amount of fenestration is determined by architectural considerations, the ability to control thermal conditions, the first cost of construction versus the long-term energy and life-cycle costs, and the human psychological and physical needs for windows.

WINDOW ORIENTATIONS

In temperate northern hemisphere locations, north-facing windows lose radiated heat in all seasons, especially in winter. East-facing windows gain heat very rapidly in summer when the sun enters at a very direct angle in the mornings. South-facing windows receive solar heat most of the day in the summer, but at a low intensity, as the higher position of the sun strikes at an

acute angle. In the winter, the low sun angle provides sun to south-facing windows all day long. West-facing windows heat up rapidly on summer afternoons when the building is already warm, causing overheating. This is especially a problem when it results in hot bedrooms at night. Planting shade trees to the west and installing deep awnings over windows can help. East and west windows must be shaded in tropical latitudes. Horizontal skylights gain the most solar heat in the summer, when the sun is overhead, and the least in the winter, when the sun angle is lower.

WINDOWS AND NATURAL VENTILATION

The open position of a window determines how well it provides natural ventilation. The wind is deflected if it strikes the glass surface. The direction of wind is unpredictable, and in order to provide ventilation without cold drafts, you have to keep the wind away from people. When you want the wind to provide cooling, it needs to flow across the body. Windows with multiple positions can offer control.

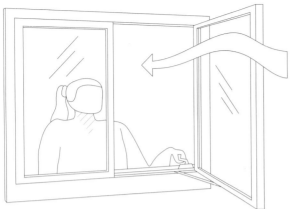

Figure 22-1 Casement window.

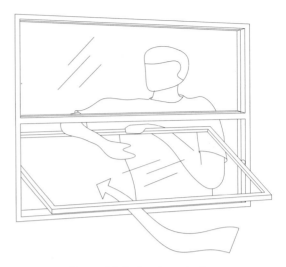

Figure 22-3 Awning window.

Fixed glazing allows heat and light to pass through, but provides no ventilation. Casement windows (Fig. 22-1) open fully, and the swing of the sash can divert a breeze into a room. Double-hung windows (Fig. 22-2) can only open half of their area, either at the top, the bottom, or part of each. Sliding windows also only allow ventilation through half of their surface area. Awning or hopper (Fig. 22-3) windows allow air through while keeping rain out. Jalousie windows are horizontal glass or wood louvers that pivot simultaneously in a common frame. They are used primarily in mild climates to control ventilation while cutting off visibility from outside. Sashes that pivot 90° or 180° about a vertical or horizontal axis at or near their centers are used in multistory or high-rise buildings. They are operated only for cleaning, maintenance, or emergency ventilation.

THERMAL TRANSMISSION

Windows and doors account for about one-third of a home's heat loss, with windows contributing more than doors. Windows should be replaced, or at least undergo extensive repairs, if they contain rotted or damaged wood, cracked glass, missing putty, poorly fitting sashes, or locks that don't work. New windows may cost $200 to $400 each, including labor for installation.

Glass conducts heat very efficiently. Glazed areas usually lose more heat than insulated opaque walls and roofs. Windows and skylights are typically the lowest R-value component of the building envelope, allowing infiltration of outdoor air and admitting solar heat. Without some kind of adjustable insulation, they are much less thermally resistant. Glazed areas at the perimeter of the building cool adjacent interior air in the winter, and the cooler, denser vertical layer of air along the glass drops to the floor, creating a carpet of cold air. The inside and outside surfaces of a pane of glass are around the same temperature, which is in turn about half way between the indoor and outdoor temperatures. Consequently, where there are windows, the temperature inside the building is strongly affected by the exterior temperature. In walls with a lot of glazing, the interior surface and air temperatures approach the exterior temperature.

Windows can give off surprisingly large amounts of heat. Each square foot of unshaded window facing east, south, or west in mid-summer admits about as much heat as one-half square foot of cast-iron radiator at full output. This is perhaps an impossible amount to cool in the summer. A similarly huge energy loss occurs in the winter.

Figure 22-2 Double-hung window.

In order to conserve energy, building codes and standards prescribe relatively small windows in relationship to residential floor areas and commercial wall areas. You may have to prove a significant benefit in order to increase these sizes. Large glass areas for daylighting increase heating requirements, but use less electricity for lighting. Less electric lighting means less heat load that must be removed by air-conditioning. Less exposed glazing is needed for daylighting in summer than in winter. All of these factors offer some options for good trade-offs, with passive solar heating or surplus heat from another source making up some of the added heating load. Increasing insulation in walls or roofs may also justify more glass areas.

When sunshine and heat transmission through glass is controlled properly, light and warmth enter the space without glare and radiant heat buildup. Solar heat gain can be collected within the space with control devices that admit heat but control glare. Where added heat is not wanted in the building's interior, it is best to use exterior controls.

The best new windows insulate almost four times as well as the best windows available in 1990. A window's solar heat gain coefficient (SHGC) is a measurement of the amount of solar energy that passes through the window. The SHGC measures how well a product blocks heat caused by sunlight, and is expressed as a number between 0 and 1. A lower SHGC means less heat gain. SHGC is particularly important in warmer climates, where you want to keep most of the heat outside. Typical values range from 0.4 to 0.9, with the higher numbers indicating more solar energy transmitted to the inside. Sunlight passing through glazing warms objects, but the radiant heat then emitted by the objects can't escape quickly back through the glazing, so the space warms up.

Solar gains through windows and skylights range from none at night to 1058 W per square meter (335 Btu per square ft) per hour. The amount of heat gain depends on the time of day, the time of the year, cloudiness, the orientation and tilt angle of the glass, the latitude of the site, and the type and number of layers of glazing. Internal and external shading devices also affect heat gain. Solar heat gain is a desirable quality for passive solar heating, but is undesirable when you want to prevent overheating in the summer.

The interior designer's choice of window frames and glazing materials can influence the interior climate. Windows and skylights are responsible for up to a quarter of the building's energy loss. All windows produced today for use in the building's exterior have two layers of glass. Using low-emissivity (low-e) coatings, which affect the windows' ability to absorb or reflect radiant energy, may cost 10 to 15 percent more, but can reduce energy loss up to 18 percent. Adding low-e coatings to all the windows in the United States would save one-half million barrels of oil per day, a reduction equal to one-third of the oil imported from the Persian Gulf.

Energy-efficient windows can reduce the cost of the building's heating, ventilating, and air-conditioning (HVAC) by minimizing the influence of outside temperatures and sunlight. This also reduces maintenance, noise, and condensation problems. Over time, the extra initial cost usually pays for itself.

Ordinary window glass passes about 80 percent of the infrared (IR) solar radiation, and absorbs the majority of longer-wave IR from sun-warmed interior surfaces, keeping the heat inside. In cold weather, it loses most of the absorbed heat by convection to the outside air. Because ordinary glazing prevents the passage of heat from sun-warmed interior surfaces back to the outdoors, greenhouses and parked cars get hot on sunny days. This principle is also used in the design of flat-plate solar collectors.

Until the 1980s, adding a second or third layer of glazing was the determining factor for energy performance in windows. Insulating glass consists of multiple layers of glass with air spaces between. Double-glazing is almost twice as efficient as single, but has no effect on air leaking through the edges of the sash. In the 1970s, triple- and even quadruple-glazed windows were introduced. Thin plastic films are sometimes used for the inner layers. The sashes of high-performance windows have double or triple gaskets. Metal sashes can be designed with thermal breaks to prevent shortcuts for escaping heat.

Edge spacers hold the panes of glass apart in insulated windows, and provide an airtight seal. Edge spacers were usually constructed of hollow aluminum channels filled with desiccant beads to absorb any small mount of moisture that gets into the window. Aluminum is highly heat conductive, and aluminum frames without thermal breaks are very inefficient. Around 1990, new better edge spacers were developed using thin-walled steel with a thermal break or silicone foam or butyl rubber. These newer edge spacers made window energy performance 2 to 10 percent more efficient. When specifying insulated windows, check warranties against seal failure, which can lead to fogging and loss of the low-conductivity gas fill. Choose windows with long warranties.

In the late 1990s, window ratings of R-1 were the norm. Today, ratings of R-6.5 or higher are possible with a second layer of glass, wider air spaces between layers, tinted, reflective, and low-e coatings, and films between glazings. Windows are available with operable blinds installed between glazing layers for sun control. So-called "smart windows" are being developed for the future that will offer variable light transmission.

A quick and inexpensive way to improve window thermal transmission is to weatherstrip all window edges and cracks with rope caulk. This costs less than a dollar per window, and the rope caulk can be removed, stored in foil, and reused until it hardens. Other types of weatherstripping cost $8 to $10 per window, but are more permanent, are not visible, and allow the window to be opened. Either compression-type or V-strip type weatherstripping is used, depending upon the type of window. The upper sash of a double-hung window can be permanently caulked if it is not routinely opened for ventilation.

Weatherstripping is available in metal, felt, vinyl, or foam rubber strips that are placed between a door or window sash and the frame. It can be fastened to the edge or face of a door, or to a doorframe and threshold. Weatherstripping provides a seal against wind-blown rain and reduces infiltration of air and dust. The material you choose should be durable under extended use, noncorrosive, and replaceable. Spring-tensioned strips of aluminum, bronze or stainless or galvanized steel, vinyl or neoprene gaskets, foam plastic or rubber strips, or woven pile strips all are options. Weatherstripping is often supplied and installed by manufacturers of sliding glass doors, glass entrance doors, revolving doors, and overhead doors. An automatic door bottom is a horizontal bar at the bottom of a door that drops automatically when the door is closed to seal the threshold to air and sound.

A separate sash, or storm window, added to a single-glazed window cuts thermal conductivity and infiltration in half. A single sash with insulated glazing plus a storm window results in one-third as much heat transmission, and half as much infiltration. Storm windows will save about 3.8 liters (1 gallon) of home heating oil per 0.09 square meters (1 square ft) of window per year in a cold climate.

The simplest storm window is a plastic film taped to the inside of the window frame, which costs only about $3 to $8 per window and will last from one to three years. The plastic is heated with a blow dryer to shrink tight. A slightly more complex interior storm window consists of a sturdy aluminum frame and two sheets of clear glazing film, creating a layer of air between them. A secondary air layer is established between the existing window and the interior storm window. The

windows are held in place by fasteners screwed into the sash or molding, and are sold as do-it-yourself kits for about $50.

Exterior removable or operable glass or rigid acrylic storms are more common than internal styles. The tightest aluminum-framed combination storm/screen windows have air leakage ratings as low as 0.01 cubic ft per minute (cfm) per foot, although some leak over 1 cfm per foot. Specify storm/screen windows rated lower than 0.3 cfm per foot. Storm-screen units are available with low-e coatings on the glass, and cost from $50 to $120 each, including labor. Aluminum frames should be tightly sealed where they are mounted to the window casings. All cracks should be caulked, but the small weep holes at the bottom edges must not be sealed to prevent moisture buildup.

Older wood-framed storm windows can be repainted and used, and may be more energy efficient than newer styles. Wood-framed storm windows have separate screens that have to be taken up and down yearly.

Double- or triple-sealed panes filled with a low-conductivity gas such as argon, krypton, carbon dioxide, or sulfur hexafluoride can reduce heat loss even further than windows with air between the glazing layers. The inert gas reduces convective currents, and the inner surface stays close to the indoor temperature, with less condensation occurring. These windows require very reliable edge seals.

Low-emittance (low-e) coatings are applied to one glass surface facing the air gap. Low-e coatings were developed and commercialized in the 1980s. They consist of thin, transparent coatings of silver or tin oxide that allow the passage of visible light while reflecting IR heat radiation back into the room, reducing the flow of heat through the window. Hard-coat low-e coatings are durable, less expensive, but less effective than soft-coat ones. Soft-coat low-e coatings have better thermal performance, but cost more, and can be degraded by oxidation during the manufacturing process. Low-e coatings reduce ultraviolet (UV) transmission, thereby reducing fading.

High-transmission low-e coatings are used in colder climates for passive solar heating. The coating on the inner glass surface traps outgoing IR radiation. Variations in design are available for different climate zones and applications. Selective-transmission low-e coatings are used for winter heating and summer cooling. They transmit a relatively high level of visible light for daylighting. The coating on the outer glazing traps incoming IR radiation, which is convected away by outdoor air. Low-transmission low-e coatings on the outer glazing reject more of the solar gain. A building may need different types of low-e coatings on different sides of the building. The south side may need low-e and high solar heat gain coatings for passive solar heating, while the less sunny north side may require the lowest U-value windows possible (U-value is discussed below). Some window manufacturers offer different types only at a premium cost.

U-Value

The National Fenestration Rating Council (NFRC) was established in 1992 to develop procedures that determine the U-value, also known as the U-factor, of fenestration products accurately. The NFRC is a nonprofit collaboration of window manufacturers, government agencies, and building trade associations that seeks to establish a fair, accurate, and credible energy rating system for windows, doors, and skylights. The U-value measures how well a product prevents heat from escaping a building. U-value ratings generally fall between 0.20 and 1.20. The smaller the U-value, the less heat is transmitted. The U-value is particularly important in cold climates.

The "U" in U-value is a unit that expresses the heat flow through a constructed building section including air spaces of 19 mm ($\frac{3}{4}$ in.) or more and of air films. After testing and evaluation of a window is completed by an independent laboratory, the manufacturer is authorized to label the product with its U-value. U-values measure whole-window conditions, not just center or edge conditions of the window.

Designers, engineers, and architects can evaluate the energy properties of windows using their U-values. Ratings are based on standard window sizes, so be sure to compare windows of the same size. The use of U-values makes heat gain and loss calculations more reliable. A U-value is the inverse of an R-value, which indicates the level of insulation, so a low U-value correlates to a high R-value.

Solar Heat Gain Coefficient (SHGC)

The U-value tells you how much heat will be lost through a given window. The NFRC also provides solar heat gain ratings for windows that look at how much of the sun's heat will pass through into the interior. Solar heat gain is good in the winter, when it reduces the load for the building's heating equipment. In the summer, however, added solar heat increases the cooling load. The solar heat gain coefficient (SHGC) is a number from 0 to 1.0. The higher the SHGC, the more solar energy passes through the window glazing and frame.

Windows for colder climates should have SHGCs greater than 0.7, while warmer climates should have lower coefficients. ENERGY STAR® products for northern climates must have a U-factor of 0.35 or less for windows and 0.45 or less for skylights. Central climate ENERGY STAR windows should have 0.40 U-factors, and SHGCs of 0.55 or less. Windows for southern, warm climates should have 0.75 U-factors, and SHGCs below 0.40 to earn the ENERGY STAR label.

SELECTING GLAZING MATERIALS

The material selected for windows and skylights should be appropriate to the amount of light that needs to pass through for its intended use. Thermal performance and life-cycle costs are important economic considerations. Strength and safety must also be considered. Sound reduction can be another important factor, and the aesthetic impact of the glazing's appearance, size, location, and framing has a major impact on the interior and exterior of the building.

The color of glazing can be critical for certain functions. Artists' studios, showroom windows, and community building lobbies all require high quality visibility between the interior and exterior. Warm-toned bronze or gray glazing can affect the interior and exterior color scheme. Tinted glazing controls glare and excess solar heat gain year round, so solar warmth is decreased in the winter as well as the summer. The tinting can also modify distracting or undesirable views. It can provide some privacy from the street for occupants, while allowing some view out when the illumination outside is substantially higher than inside during the day. Unfortunately, this effect may be reversed at night, putting occupants on display. Reflective glazing may bounce glare onto nearby buildings or into traffic.

Heat-absorbing glass is usually gray or brownish. It absorbs selected wavelengths of light. The glass absorbs about 60 percent of the solar heat, with around half of that reradiated and convected into the building's interior. Heat-reflecting glass bounces off most of the sun's heat. A large wall can reflect enough sun to overheat adjacent buildings, and cause severe visual glare in neighboring streets and open spaces.

Tinted or reflective glass is especially vulnerable to thermal stress. Warm air from a floor register can cause the glass to break from tension stresses on the glass edges.

The U-value of a wall depends primarily on the choice of glass and frame for any window in that wall, so improving the efficiency of windows is the most important thing you can do to decrease the heat loss of a wall. A typical double-glazed window has an R-value of around 2. High-performance glazings use low-e glass and heat mirror films. Low-e glazing is rated around R-3.5, and gas-filled glazing around R-5. Some super window designs add additional layers for a rating of around 5.6. Super windows use a combination of glazings and films, coatings, and inert gases with sealed, thermally broken frame construction. They can substantially lower heat flow rates, but are higher in cost.

Building codes require shatter-resistant glass in some circumstances. Tempered, laminated, or wired glass, and some plastics, may meet these requirements. Sunlight tends to deteriorate plastic glazing, and it scratches more easily than glass. Plastics may expand or contract with temperature extremes more than glass, although newer products continue to show improvements.

PLASTIC FILMS

 Plastic films glued to the inside face of window glass work like reflective and absorptive glass to intercept the sun's energy before it enters the building. The films can be reflective or darkening. Silver and gold films block out slightly more total radiated energy than visible light. Bronze and smoke colored films intercept more of the visible light. Silver film is the most effective at reflecting solar radiation, rejecting up to 80 percent. During the winter, the films reflect radiated heat back inside the room, and improve the room's operative temperature. They also reduce drafts due to cold glass surfaces and make the window glass more shatter-resistant. Tinted glass coatings are continuing to be improved, and lightly tinted coatings that reduce visibility less are available for climates with high cooling loads.

Selective-transmission films admit most of the incoming solar radiation, but reflect far-IR radiation from warm objects in the room back into the room. Glass does this to a degree anyway, but these films increase the effect. As separate sheets, these films can be applied to existing windows to reduce the amount of building heat lost through the window.

Plastic window films can cause cracking of thermal pane and other windows from thermal expansion and contraction of the self-contained insulated window units. Plastic films should not be used on tinted glass or on very large areas of glass. The films themselves are relatively fragile and have a limited service life.

WINDOW FRAMES

There are three main types of frame materials, each of which addresses aspects of the lifespan of the windows. Wood is the most common material and a moderate insulator that requires staining or painting to prevent rot from moisture buildup. It remains warm to the touch all winter, and stays at room temperature in the summer. Vinyl is usually not paintable, but offers a lifetime free of maintenance. Some radical climatic changes over time may stress vinyl to failure at the joints, allowing water penetration, although this is rare with quality manufacturers. Vinyl (PVC) frames with fiberglass can provide better insulation than wood. Aluminum frames, common in the western United States, must have a thermal break or they will conduct heat rapidly. Aluminum is lightweight and is usually not paintable, but it remains free of maintenance for its lifetime. Over the course of many years, aluminum will oxidize, leaving a dull pitted appearance. If not well insulated with a thermal break, it is very cold to the touch in winter and hot in summer.

The window's dimensions affect its energy performance. The glass, low-e coating, and gas fill work better at conserving energy than the edge spacer, sash, and frame, so the center is actually more efficient than the edges of the window. True divided lights (many small panes, each in its own frame) have a great deal more edge area per window, and are much less efficient.

The air tightness of a window frame is measured in cubic feet of air per linear foot of crack (cfm/ft) along the opening in which they are installed. The tightest windows rate 0.01 cfm/ft, with an industry standard of 0.37 cfm/ft. Better windows rate in the 0.01 to 0.06 cfm/ft range, with some as high as 1 cfm/ft. The actual performance in the building depends on the quality control at the factory and the care taken during shipping and installation. An experienced contractor is a good investment. In general, casement and awning windows are tighter than double-hung and other sliding windows, as they pull against a compression gasket.

WINDOW TREATMENTS

The type of window coverings you specify can affect the heating and air-conditioning load in a space. The location of drapery may interfere with supply air diffusers or other heating units near a window. As the interior designer, you should have the mechanical engineer or architect check the proposed type, size, and mounting of window treatments to verify that they will not create a problem with the HVAC system.

Thermal shades (Fig. 22-4) can be made in many different ways. The curtain needs to be sealed tightly against the wall, or cold air will flow out of the openings in the seal. Insulating fabric is available that is made up of a layer of cotton, then insulation, then a Mylar (plastic and aluminum material) layer that acts as a vapor barrier and reflects the IR component of heat back to the room, then more insulation. One side comes unfinished so you can add fabric to match the room's décor. The fabric can simply be wrapped around a 1″ × 2″ wood strip and stapled, and the 1″ × 2″ strip is screwed above the window, or hung from a wooden pole or other type of bar. A heavy wooden dowel is inserted at the bottom so that the curtain hangs straight. The curtain can be attached to the wall with magnets, snaps, hook-and-loop fasteners, or channels. The curtain can be rigged like a Roman shade or rolled up by hand and tied.

Draperies fitted with foam or other insulating backing can be used as thermal barriers for windows. Insulating curtains and drapes are available that fit into tracks. In-Sol Drapes, which were designed by Massachusetts-based designer Frank Bateman, use a combination of Mylar and polished aluminum to stop up to 80 percent of heat loss through windows. The reflecting material also keeps out UV radiation. Any fabric can be added to the drapery material for aesthetic purposes.

Insulating shades are available in a great variety of styles, and stop up to 80 percent of winter heat loss and 86 percent of summer heat gain. They insulate and seal a window on all four sides, providing an added R-value of 4.99. Five layers of air- and moisture-tight fabric are ultrasonically welded without perforating the internal solar barrier. Systems are available for sunrooms with straight or curved eaves and wood or aluminum framework. Skylight shades use a high temperature track and can be surface mounted or recessed into the opening of the frame. Some styles, suitable for locations where the window shade does not have to be opened and closed frequently, use hook-and-loop attachments instead of tracks. Roman shade styles can be covered in the manufacturer's or custom fabrics.

Honeycomb window shades over double-glazing offer improved winter R-values. Translucent 10-mm ($\frac{3}{8}$-in.) shades produce a rating of R-3.23, while translucent 19-mm ($\frac{3}{4}$-in.) shades are rated R-3.57, and opaque shades rate R-4.2. Cellular honeycomb shades can be mounted in tracks and can move horizontally or vertically on flat or curved surfaces. Motor or manual operation is available.

Operating insulating shutters can act as rigid window insulation. Shutters may be hinged, sliding, folding, or bi-fold. Interior shutters are usually manually operated, and exterior shutters are mechanical.

Both draperies and shutters require storage space when they are not in place across the window. An airtight seal around the edges keeps thermal performance high and prevents condensation from forming.

Mesh materials of loosely woven fiberglass fabric are designed to intercept specific percentages of sunshine. They are mounted in frames over windows, and have fairly long life spans. Mesh shades with different dot densities are specified by transmittance. They control brightness while still leaving a view to the outside.

Motorized window treatment controls are available for both residential and commercial installations, and for vertical blinds, drapery, metal or wood blinds, roller or Roman shades, and cellular shade systems. Systems for blinds offer either a single motor or separate motors for tilting and traversing, and the ability to control multiple windows with one remote. The headrail may serve

Figure 22-4 Thermal shade.

as its own valance. Factory preset limit switches make installation easier. Controls are by low-voltage modular switches or wireless remote control.

DOORS

Doors also contribute to heat loss. The entire perimeter of the door should be weatherstripped, with a door sweep at the bottom of the door. Storm doors are prob-ably not cost effective when added to old, uninsulated metal or fiberglass doors, and trapped heat may damage their plastic trim.

The NFRC has established a rating procedure for determining the thermal performance of doors and side-lights, as they have for windows. A permanent label attached to the edge of the door slab lists the certified U-factor. A temporary label also appears on the face of the door. The energy rating is listed as a U-factor, the rate of heat loss. Higher numbers mean more heat loss. The values presented include the door and its frame.

Chapter 23

Solar Heating

It is estimated that if the sunlight that reaches the earth's surface in one day were converted into useful energy forms, it would satisfy the energy needs of the world for over 50 years. The amount of sunlight falling on a building typically carries enough energy to keep the building comfortable throughout the year. The limited supply of fossil fuels encourages their conservation for uses in industry rather than as sources of building heat. Electric energy is an inefficient source of heat, and may be generated by fossil fuels or by nuclear power plants. Solar energy offers an alternative with fewer air polluting emissions and no danger of harmful radioactivity. Solar energy also offers insurance against the possibility that conventional energy technologies could suddenly become too expensive, unavailable, or undesirable for social, political, or physical reasons. The ability to produce energy on site leads to decentralization and social stability.

Despite the availability of free energy from the sun, the cost of solar systems has not been competitive with cheaper conventional fuel systems. Solar equipment tends to be relatively expensive, and solar installations have taken a long time to pay back the initial investment. Initial costs for solar collectors for heating range from $645 to $1500 per square meter ($60–$140 per square ft). Pool-heating systems run from $110 to $800

per square meter ($12–$75 per square ft). Most solar systems can handle 40 to 70 percent of the heating load for a building.

We begin this discussion of solar heating by considering the nature of this energy source. The part of the radiation from the sun that is not scattered or absorbed and that reaches the earth's surface is called direct radiation. When the sunlight has been scattered or reemitted, it is called diffuse radiation.

Solar energy comes in four useful forms. First, by providing the energy for photosynthesis, the sun maintains life by producing food and converting carbon dioxide into oxygen. Photosynthesis is also necessary for the growth of wood, and indirectly for fossil fuels, which were once living plants and animals. Second, natural daylight provides illumination both outside and inside buildings. The third form is provided when photovoltaic cells convert sunlight directly into electrical energy, and the fourth form, thermal energy, is used for space heating, domestic hot water, power generation, distillation processes, and heating of industrial processes. You could even include wind power as a fifth form, since the sun's heat drives the wind. Solar heating is primarily concerned with the sun's thermal energy, but solar designs have implications for photovoltaics, lighting, and even photosynthesis as well.

A passive solar heating system is actually the building itself, has no moving parts, and is dependent on the local site and climate conditions. Passive systems incorporate solar collection, storage, and distribution into the architectural design of the building's structure, without pumps or fans. This is accomplished by selecting the optimal location, type, and size of windows, and by employing overhangs and shading. Thermal storage mass is integrated into the building's construction. The payback cost with fuel cost savings for passive solar systems is generally one to thirteen years. Passive solar systems can present conflicts between access to the sun and space use, view, and ventilation, since collecting the sun's radiation for heating may dictate a massive wall where a window would offer a great view instead. Avoiding glare and overheating are major concerns.

Active solar heating systems offer better control of the environment within the building, and can be added onto most existing buildings. Active systems use pumps, fans, heat pumps, and other mechanical equipment to transmit and distribute thermal energy via air or a liquid. Most systems use electricity continually to operate the system. Active systems take around 30 years to pay back, but systems typically last only 20 years before major components need replacement. Many buildings use hybrid systems, with passive solar design features and electrically driven fans or pumps.

PASSIVE SOLAR DESIGNS

All-passive solar systems utilize south-facing glass or transparent plastic for solar collection. The low winter sun puts out 90 percent of its energy during the period from 9:00 a.m. to 3:00 p.m. Where other buildings or tall trees block access to the sun during this critical period, solar energy systems are not practical. The area of the glazing amounts to 30 to 50 percent of the floor area in cold climates, and 15 to 25 percent in temperate climates, depending on the average outdoor winter temperature and projected heat loss. Glazing materials must be resistant to degradation by the sun's ultraviolet (UV) rays. Double-glazing and insulation are used to minimize heat loss at night.

A second essential component of a passive solar design is the presence of thermal mass for heat collection, storage, and distribution, oriented to receive the maximum amount of solar exposure. Concrete, brick, stone, tile, rammed earth, sand, water, or other liquids can be used. The thicknesses necessary for effective thermal storage are significant: for concrete, 30 to 46 cm (12–18 in.); for brick, 25 to 36 cm (10–14 in.); for adobe, 20 to 31 cm (8–12 in.); and 15 cm (6 in.) or more of water. Some systems use materials that hold and release energy through phase changes (changing from liquid to gas, for example), like eutectic salts and paraffins. Dark-colored surfaces absorb more solar radiation than lighter ones. Vents, dampers, movable insulating panels, and shading devices can assist in balancing heat distribution.

When designing a building to take advantage of solar heating, provisions must be made to prevent overheating in warm weather. Roofs provide a barrier to excess summer solar radiation, especially in the tropics where the sun is directly overhead. The transmission of solar heat from the roof to the interior of the building can result in high ceiling temperatures. Surfaces that reflect most infrared (IR) rays heat up very little in the sun. High ceiling temperatures can be reduced with thermally resistant materials, materials with high thermal capacity, or ventilated spaces in the roof structure.

Orienting building entrances away from or protected from prevailing cold winter winds, and buffering entries with airlocks, vestibules, or double entry doors dramatically reduces the amount of interior and exterior air change when people enter. Locating an unheated garage, mudroom, or sunspace between the doors to a conditioned interior space is a very effective way to control air loss in any building.

The interior layout of a passively solar heated building should be designed at the same time as the building's siting, rough building shape, shading, and orientation for maximum compatibility. Spaces with maximum heating and lighting needs should be located on the building's south face. Buffer areas, such as toilet rooms, kitchens, corridors, stairwells, storage, garage, and mechanical and utility spaces need less light and air-conditioning, and can be located on a north or west wall. The areas with the greatest illumination level needs, for accounting, typing, reading, or drafting, should be next to windows and have access to natural lighting. Conference rooms, which need few or no windows for light and views, can be located farther away from windows. Spaces that need a lot of cooling due to high internal heat gains from activities or equipment should be located on the north or east sides of the building.

Shading

In 1960, 12 percent of all American homes had air conditioners, a figure that rose to 64 percent by the late 1980s. By 1989, air conditioners were installed in 77 percent of new single-family homes. The cost of the equipment, labor and energy involved in air-conditioning is climbing rapidly. The environmental cost of chlorofluorocarbon (CFC) refrigerants is now being felt by the refrigeration industry and by consumers. To fight these rising costs, designers and builders can look to the time before air-conditioning for natural cooling ideas. In many climates, the right combination of properly implemented natural methods can provide cooling equivalent to mechanical air-conditioning. At the very least, natural cooling allows you to install smaller cooling equipment that will run fewer hours and consume less energy.

Providing shade from the sun is essential for passively cooled buildings, and for passively heated buildings that might become overheated in hot weather. The best shading occurs before the sun's heat reaches the building. If sunrays are intercepted before passing through the glass, the air-conditioning cooling load can be cut in half, saving anywhere from 10 to 50 percent of energy costs. Place the highest priority on the surfaces that receive the most summer heat. That's usually the east and west.

Shading options, in order of effectiveness, are trees and shrubs, trellises, overhangs, awnings, shade screens, window coatings, and interior shades. Trees throw shade over the walls and roof, and will also shade driveways, sidewalks, and patios that can bounce heat to the building. Since big trees give more shade than little ones, devise a site plan that preserves as many existing trees as possible. Then plant new trees immediately after construction. Trees provide a cooling bonus. To keep themselves cool, trees pump water from the ground into their leaves. As this water evaporates from the surface of the leaves, it cools the tree. This evaporative cooling cools the surrounding area, too.

Deciduous trees are best for south yards, because their canopies are broad and dense. Deciduous shade trees and vines can provide shade for low buildings, while allowing more sunlight through when their leaves fall in the winter. Evergreens can work well for north and northwest yards.

The closer a tree is to the building, the more hours of shade it will give. To be effective, trees should be planted between 1.5 and 6 meters (5–20 ft) from the building. Shrubs offer less shading, but also cost less, reach mature size more quickly, and require less space. Shrubs can shade walls and windows without blocking roof-mounted solar panels.

Trellises are permanent structures that partially shade the outside of a building. Clinging vines growing over the trellis add more shade and evaporative cool-

Figure 23-1 Deciduous vines for seasonal shade.

ing. A special trellis to shade air conditioners, heat pumps, and evaporative coolers improves the equipment's performance. Be sure not to restrict airflow to the equipment. Fast growing vines create shade quickly, while trees can take years to provide useful shade. Deciduous vines (Fig. 23-1), such as grape, clematis, and wisteria, lose their leaves in winter, allowing the sun's heat to strike the building. Trellises and climbing plants are a design solution that's attractive and flexible.

Most homes have a built-in shading device where the roof overhangs the building. Overhangs block the high-angle, summer sun, but allow the lower winter sun to strike the building. They are only effective for the upper story of a multistory building, and don't provide relief for east and west windows. Roof overhangs or horizontal-shading devices (Fig. 23-2) at each floor of taller

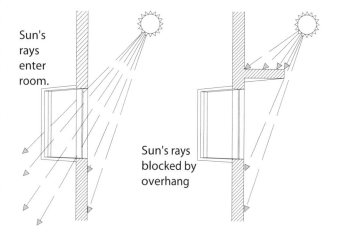

Sun's rays enter room.

Sun's rays blocked by overhang

Figure 23-2 Horizontal overhang.

buildings can block high summertime sun angles on south-facing walls, while admitting lower winter sun.

Horizontal louvers parallel to the wall permit air circulation near the wall and reduce conductive heat gain. Manual or automatic timer-controlled photoelectric controls allow the louvers to adapt to the sun's angle. Slanted louvers offer even more protection than parallel ones, with angles varying to coordinate with solar angles. Louvers hung from a solid overhang protect against low sun angles, but may interfere with the view. Vertical louvers are most effective on the east or west. Egg-crate louvers (known as *brise soleil*) combine horizontal and vertical elements to produce a lot of shade. They are very efficient in hot climates.

Outside shade screens on windows exposed to direct sunlight prevent sun from entering a window. These devices are often called sun screens, shade cloths, or solar shields. The screens are made from aluminum or plastic and are lightweight, durable, and easy to install. Unlike insect screens, shade screens are specially made to block a certain amount of the sun's energy, usually between 50 and 90 percent. The shading coefficient is the amount of heat that penetrates the screen, with lower numbers indicating that less energy gets through. While you can see through a shade screen, the view is obscured. Fixed sunshades can block sun in early spring, when it is desirable to have sun penetrate to the interior.

Adjustable sunshades, such as awnings, avoid this problem. Manual controls for adjustable sunshades are inexpensive and relatively trouble-free but require occupants to make the adjustment when necessary. Motorized devices also depend on someone to operate them, but are good for large or heavy devices in remote places, such as clerestory windows. Automatic systems with computerized controls can be set to consider the thermal needs of the entire building.

Awnings can cover individual windows or sections of outside walls, and are most effective on the south side of the building. Awnings come in a variety of shapes, sizes, and colors to match many building designs. Fixed awnings block light at a given angle, while adjustable awnings can be rolled up in the winter to allow low-angle sun to reach into the building. Awnings have the disadvantage of blocking the view from the top half of the window.

Exterior shading rejects about 80 percent of the solar energy striking the window. Interior shading devices absorb and reradiate 80 percent of it into the interior, increasing interior temperatures dramatically. Outside louvers can cool off in a breeze, while draperies become part of a heat trap, giving off radiant heat in hot weather. Interior shading devices like roller shades, blinds, and curtains, absorb solar radiation and convert it to convected heat in the interior air. They also prevent direct solar radiation from striking occupants and furnishings. Interior shades don't block sunlight as well as exterior shades. Blinds and drapes can reduce solar radiation by as much as half, depending upon their reflectivity. They also reduce visual glare from direct sunlight. Interior shading devices don't have to deal with weathering, are exposed to less dirt, and are usually easy to adjust manually.

To give the most benefit, interior shades should have a light-colored surface on the side facing the window, and be made of an insulating material. They should fit tightly to prevent air movement into the room and should cover the whole window.

Direct Gain Solar Designs

Direct gain systems (Fig. 23-3) collect heat directly within the interior space. The surface area of the storage mass, which is built into the space, accounts for 50 to 60 percent of the total surface area of the space, including interior partitions. Surfaces are constructed of concrete, concrete block, brick, stone, adobe, or other thick, massive materials. Brick veneer or clay tile over a bed of grout is an effective finish. Floors are typically slab-on-grade without carpets or rugs. The sun should strike directly or be reflected onto the massive surfaces as soon as possible after entering the space. During the winter, the warm surfaces raise the mean radiant temperature (MRT) in the room higher than the air temperature, allowing comfortable conditions at 3°C–6°C (5°F–10°F) below normal. The mass also keeps room temperatures from becoming too hot in the summer. When additional cooling is needed, ventilation is provided with operable windows and walls.

Direct gain systems are simple, and offer daylight

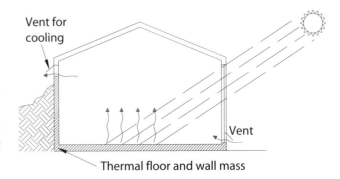

Figure 23-3 Direct gain passive solar design.

and views to the south. Site conditions and window treatments must prevent bright winter sun from creating glare. Too much heat may enter the space on sunny days. Operable window insulation at night keeps the heat inside the space. Glass filters out much of the sun's UV, but enough gets through to the interior to bleach paints, interior furnishings, and other building materials. You should select fade-resistant colors and materials if they will be exposed directly to the sun for a long time.

Daily temperatures in direct gain passive solar spaces typically fluctuate 6°C–17°C (10°F–30°F). A well-designed system can be 30 to 70 percent efficient in capturing and using the solar energy that strikes the building. Direct gain design demands skillful and total integration of all architectural elements within the space, including walls, floor, ceiling, and interior surface finishes. The patterns of sun and shade create texture and rhythm, and the shadows cast on the exterior have a strong impact on the appearance of the building facade.

Indirect Gain Designs

Indirect gain heating places a thermal storage mass between the sun and the occupied space. A sheet of glass covers an opaque wall 20 to 30 cm (8–12 in.) thick. The sun strikes the mass, where its energy is stored and slowly transferred to the interior space. The absorbed solar energy moves through the wall by conduction and then to the space by radiation and convection. The interior side of the wall must be kept free of hangings and large furniture so that radiant heat can transfer into the space. Indirect gain systems admit less daylight than direct gain systems, and offer little or no view to the south. Radiant heat continues to flow into the space in the evenings after sunny days.

Thermal storage walls are painted black on the outside surface, which is then covered with a sheet of glazing. Due to thermal lag, heat takes hours to conduct through the wall. During the hottest part of the day, some of the heat flows back out through the glass before it can be passed into the building. There may be vents at the top and bottom of the wall to circulate room air, thus delivering warmer air sooner, but this feature also adds dust and dirt to the space between the mass and the glass.

The first example of a thermal storage wall was constructed in a house built by Felix Trombe and Jacques Michel in Odeillo, France, in 1967. Openings in this 61-cm (2-in.) thick concrete Trombe wall were double-glazed. Trombe walls are a classic element in indirect gain passive solar design. Trombe walls can have large openings for daylight and view. It can be difficult to clean the airspace between the Trombe wall and the glass, and placing objects near the interior surface must be minimized.

Water walls are made of corrugated galvanized steel culverts, steel drums, or fiberglass-reinforced plastic tubes. An air space is provided for expansion of the water when heated. Water walls are opaque, and can be fitted below windows. The use of water allows convection, which moves the heat more rapidly through the wall. Steve Baer constructed a wall of 55-gallon drums filled with water and stacked horizontally at his residence in Corrales, New Mexico. The home includes adobe walls and a concrete floor. A rigid insulation panel is hinged at the bottom with its reflective surface on the interior side. It can be opened flat on the floor in front of the collector, reflecting additional sun on the system, and is folded up out of the way when not in use.

Greenhouses and sunspaces (Fig. 23-4) combine direct and indirect gain systems. When a greenhouse is used as part of a solar heating system, a masonry or water thermal wall is used between the greenhouse and the occupied space. Solar greenhouse efficiency can be as high as 60 to 75 percent. Only 10 to 30 percent of the energy entering the greenhouse is supplied to the occupied space unless an active heat storage system is used. The remainder of the heat is used to heat the greenhouse itself.

Sunspaces are glass-enclosed porches or rooms adjoining another living space, and oriented to admit large

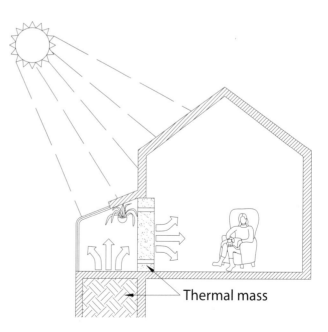

Figure 23-4 Passive solar greenhouse/sunspace.

amounts of sunlight. They are used in passive solar designs with thermal mass. Where sunspaces don't include thermal mass for night heating, and are not heated at night, they are only used as weather permits. If an insulated, lightweight frame is the common wall with the occupied space, the sunspace should contain a row of water containers along the full east-west width of the space. These containers, two times as wide as they are tall and sitting adjacent to the floor and common wall, take up much of the sunspace's floor area. Heat is transferred into the occupied space for use as it builds up in the sunspace. Greenhouses and sunspaces are easy to retrofit onto the south side of an existing building. The floor should be a thermally massive slab-on-grade, with perimeter insulation. The greenhouse or sunspace needs shading and ventilation through windows or with fans to prevent overheating.

Sunspaces, solariums, and greenhouses are available as manufactured systems with wood or metal frames, complete with glazing and flashing. A ventilating fan can be mounted on the roof or in either of the gable ends. Insulated shades and blinds that follow the slope of the roof can be operated manually or by remote control. Awning and casement sashes for ventilation, ventilated roof sashes, and doors are available from manufacturers.

Indirect gain passive solar systems are fairly versatile for retrofitting existing buildings, where they can be added to the south wall of buildings with a clear southern exposure. Their appearance may be more difficult to integrate into the building's architecture. The overall efficiency of indirect gain systems runs about 30 to 45 percent, with water walls being slightly more efficient than masonry.

Roof ponds expose water to the sun during the day. Water in large plastic bags, typically 15 to 30 cm (6–12 in.) deep, is usually supported by a metal deck roof structure, which also serves as the finished ceiling of the room below. The metal deck conducts heat from the water storage and radiates it to the space below. An insulating panel is moved mechanically with an electric motor over the roof pond at night, so that stored heat radiates downward into the space rather than up into the sky.

The roof structure must be able to support the 160- to 320-kg per square meter (32- to 65-lb per square ft) dead load of the water. Indoor masonry partitions moderate the indoor temperature fluctuations, and help support the weight of the roof. Roof ponds are limited to one-story buildings. The indoor temperatures remain very stable, in the range of 5°C to 8°C (9°F–14°F) fluctuations when using lightweight materials, and 3°C to 4°C (5°F–8°F) when masonry is used.

In summer, reversing the process allows internal heat to be absorbed during the day to be radiated to the sky at night. The outside of the water bags can be sprayed or flooded for added evaporative cooling in summer, increasing the cooling effect fourfold. The original roof pond system was built by Harold Hay in Atascadero, California, where it has provided all of the heating and cooling needs of the building since 1973.

Most glass and plastics do not pass long-wave thermal radiation, so closed windows and glass- or plastic-covered solar collectors do not radiate much heat to the night sky. Open windows work better, but if warm trees, buildings, or earth are within the radiation's path, rather than colder open sky, less heat will be removed.

Isolated Gain Designs

Isolated gain systems allow solar radiation to be collected and stored away from the space to be heated. Solar collectors can have a significant impact on the architectural design of a building, but they can be located anywhere near or on the building, such as the roof, a south wall, the ground, or even on an adjacent building. Wherever they are located, they must be exposed to the sun, so they are likely to be very visible.

Typically, solar collectors in the United States are 0.9 by 2.1 meters (3 by 7 ft). Two or three panels will provide domestic hot water for a typical family of four. Each installation should be studied to determine the optimum size of the collector array. The array size will depend on the energy load required, the amount of backup storage needed, the proposed application, and the cost of competing local energy sources. As a rule of thumb, 5 square meters (54 square ft) of collectors per residential user should be allotted for heating domestic hot water. Collectors should equal one-quarter to one-half of the internal floor area served for space heating, with even larger amounts for cooling.

South wall installations of collectors work best for space heating in northern climates, where the winter sun is very low in the sky and strikes vertical walls directly. Collectors must be kept free of snow cover.

Flat plate collectors are the more common and less expensive type of collector panels. The sun's rays pass through a cover plate and strike the blackened metal surface. This absorbent plate collects the solar radiation. Fluid circulating through tubes or channels in the plate picks up the heat and carries it to an isolated storage unit. Flat plate collectors can use both direct and diffuse solar radiation. The glazing over the absorbent plate reduces the radiation and convection heat losses to a cooler surrounding environment. These cover plates of glass, clear plastic, or fiberglass block some of the solar radiation but slow down heat loss to the environment. An insulating box contains the heat loss at the back and sides of the collector. As the sun warms air or water in the solar collector, the air or water rises either to the space where the heat is used, or to a thermally massive storage area where the heat can be stored until it is needed. Simultaneously, cooler air or water is pulled from the bottom of the thermal storage area, using a natural convection loop.

Solar-concentrating collectors use only direct solar radiation, but achieve much higher temperatures than flat plate collectors. The higher temperatures can be used for cooling or to produce steam for electrical-generation turbines. These collectors use optical lenses or reflectors to focus solar radiation onto a point much smaller than the area that receives the sun's rays, concentrating energy and producing higher temperatures. They use tracking mechanisms to follow the sun throughout the day.

Solar storage typically holds one to three days' output from collectors. Most systems need to be drained when not collecting to prevent freezing. Antifreeze and heat exchangers are also used. Some systems store heat in air spaces in a large bed of river rocks.

The reflections from solar collectors on walls and sloped roofs can produce glare into neighboring buildings. Although the heat reflected into neighboring buildings may be welcome in the winter, it adds to their cooling load in the summer. Strategically placed external projections on the building and foliage can eliminate the problem.

ACTIVE SOLAR DESIGNS

Active solar systems use solar collector panels plus circulation and distribution systems along with a heat exchanger and a storage facility to absorb, transfer, and store energy from solar radiation for building heating and cooling. Systems use air, water, or another liquid for the heat transfer medium, which carries collected heat energy from solar panels to the heat exchange equipment or storage utility for later use.

Liquid systems use pipes for circulation and distribution. They are protected from freezing with antifreeze

solutions. Aluminum pipes require the use of a corrosion-retarding additive.

Air systems use ductwork, which requires more installation space. Larger collector surfaces are also required, as air transfers heat less efficiently than liquids. Air system panels are easier to maintain, however, since leaking, corrosion, and freezing are not problems.

The storage facility for active systems holds heat for use at night and on overcast days. It is an insulated tank filled with water or other liquid, or a bin of rocks or phase-change salts for air systems.

Heat distribution in an active solar system is similar to that in a conventional heating system, using all-air or air-water delivery. A heat pump or absorptive cooling unit accomplishes cooling.

For efficiency, the building should be thermally efficient and well insulated. The siting, orientation, and window openings should take advantage of seasonal solar radiation. A backup heating system is recommended.

SOLAR WATER HEATING, COOLING, AND OTHER APPLICATIONS

Using solar energy to heat water is one of the most cost-effective solar applications. Solar water heaters manufactured as packages, including collectors, storage tank, and controls, are available in many countries worldwide.

Solar energy is also used for the heating loads of industrial processes, including drying lumber or food, chemical or metallurgical process extraction operations, food processing and cooking, curing masonry products, and drying paint. Solar cooling is used for refrigeration of food or chemical preservation.

The need for cooling with a solar design comes at the time when the greatest amount of solar energy is available. The solar energy is stored as hot water as it comes out of collectors, or as chilled water. Solar air-conditioning systems operate by absorption, by the Rankine cycle, in which solar steam turns a turbine to power an air conditioner, or by desiccant cooling, which uses dehumidification to cool. The equipment for solar cooling is expensive, so it is used only where cooling loads can't be avoided by good building design.

Part IV

HEATING AND COOLING SYSTEMS

Chapter

24

Heating Systems

• • •

Heating and cooling systems have evolved over time, as equipment has become more complex. As an interior designer, you should be aware of how heating and cooling equipment works, and be aware of how the equipment will affect your design, energy efficiency, and your client's comfort.

The Romans developed the first centralized heating systems in the first century AD. Charles Panati, in his *Extraordinary Origins of Everyday Things* (New York: Harper & Row Publishers, 1987, page 131), says that, according to the Stoic philosopher and statesman Seneca, several patrician homes had "tubes embedded in the walls for directing and spreading, equally throughout the house, a soft and regular heat." The hot exhaust from wood or coal fires in the basement was collected under the floor in an area called a hypocaust and distributed through terracotta tubes. The remains of these systems have been discovered in parts of Europe where Roman culture flourished. Unfortunately, central heating disappeared with the fall of the Roman Empire.

In the vast, drafty castles of the eleventh century, about 80 percent of the heat went up the chimneys of the huge central fireplaces while people huddled close to the fire to keep warm. Sometimes a large wall of clay and brick several feet behind the fire was used to absorb and reradiate the heat later on, but this construction was relatively rare until the eighteenth century.

In 1642, French engineers installed single-room heating systems in the Louvre in Paris that sucked room-temperature air through passages around the fire and discharged heated air back into the room. This continual reuse resulted in stale air and stuffy rooms.

The industrial revolution brought steam heat to Europe in the eighteenth century. Steam conveyed in pipes heated schools, churches, law courts, assembly halls, greenhouses, and the homes of wealthy people. The extremely hot surfaces of the steam pipes dried out the air uncomfortably and generated the odor of charred dust.

Eighteenth century America used a system similar to the Roman hypocaust. A large coal furnace in the basement sent heated air through a network of pipes with vents in major rooms. Around 1880, many buildings were converted to steam systems. A coal furnace heated a water tank, and hot air pipes carried both steam and hot water to vents connected to radiators. These steam radiators are still seen in many older homes.

FUELS

We have already discussed the most powerful heating source at our disposal: the sun. Any building heating system must start with an assessment of the available

161

free heat from the sun, and look to other fuel sources as supplements. Currently, solar energy supplies only about 2 percent of our energy needs. Our primary source of energy is fossil fuels.

Fossil fuels include gas, oil, and coal, and are the most common sources of energy for heating and cooling systems. Heating systems in the United States generate over 1 billion tons of carbon dioxide per year, and about 12 percent of the sulfur dioxide and nitrogen oxides that pollute the air. The heating system is responsible for the largest energy expense in most homes, accounting for two-thirds of the annual energy bill in colder climates. Buildings consume more than 30 percent of all energy used in the United States.

The early cave dwellers tamed fire for cooking and heating. Wood provided an easy to harvest, store, and use supply. Wood fires are so much a part of our human past that we still love to sit by a fire on a cold evening. Where properly harvested, wood is a sustainable resource. However, in desert areas, destroying the few available trees can lead to expansion of the desert and eventual famine. Wood harvesting can also result in habitat destruction and endanger the survival of forest animals.

Wood fires in fireplaces lose most of their heat up the chimney. Much of the room air goes with it, and it is sometimes in doubt whether the room actually gets warmer. Wood requires extensive storage space, which should be covered, well ventilated, and easy to access. Wood brought directly into the house from a woodpile may contain insects, making storage problematic. Incomplete combustion of wood can give off dangerous gases. Wood fires leave deposits of creosote, an oily product of burning wood tar, inside chimneys. Creosote is highly combustible, and can spontaneously erupt into a chimney fire at high temperatures. Due to this extreme hazard, chimneys must be cleaned frequently.

Wood pellets made from wood by-products offer a clean alternative to burning solid wood. Pellet stoves were introduced in 1984, and use dense pellets of quality sawdust, which is highly efficient and produces less pollution. Pellets are cleaner and need less storage space than cordwood, but are more expensive. They are automatically fed into special stoves by an electric auger.

Natural gas is the second most common heating fuel. Natural gas is usually piped thousands of miles directly from the wellhead to the consumer. Natural gas burns cleanly. Because it is delivered through a pipeline, it does not require storage space in the building. Some homes that use oil for heat use natural gas for hot water and for stoves and clothes dryers.

The odor we associate with natural gas is not its own. Odorless natural gas was in use at the New London Con-

solidated School in London, Texas, on March 18, 1937, when a spark emitted by a sander in a shop class caused a gas explosion that killed 298 students and teachers. The Texas state legislature passed a law three days later, mandating the addition of a distinctive odor to natural gas, so that leaks could be readily detected.

Gas piping systems are relatively simple. A regulator steps down the high pressure from the gas main or storage tank. A meter measures consumption, and pipes of appropriate sizes serve various appliances. The American Gas Association (AGA) conducts research and gives information on safe and efficient installation and operation of gas-fired equipment. The AGA issues standards and proposes installation requirements that usually are incorporated in major building codes.

Local gas utilities working with governmental agencies offer rebates to encourage customers to purchase and install high-efficiency gas heating systems. Equipment covered includes ENERGY STAR® hot water boilers, hot air furnaces, and steam boilers.

Propane gas is also clean burning, but slightly more expensive than natural gas. Propane and butane are petroleum gases that become liquids under moderate pressure. They are transported in pressurized cylinders that are connected to the building's gas piping. Liquefied gas is most often used for small installations in remote locations.

Oil is an efficient energy source that is delivered by truck. The size of the storage tank in the building depends on the proximity of the supplier and the space available in the building. Newer construction without basements limits space for oil tanks. Outdoor tanks sometimes leak and can contaminate soil and groundwater, so they are often allowed only in aboveground locations. Fuel oil is derived from refined crude petroleum, and is classified by its viscosity, with #2 being used in residential and light commercial burners, and #4, 5, 6, or heaver used for large commercial and industrial facilities.

Despite the fact that coal is much more plentiful than oil or gas, it is rarely used for heating new residential construction. Coal requires a complex heating system with high maintenance requirements. It is bulky, heavy, and dirty to distribute, store, and handle. Coal is difficult to burn efficiently and cleanly, and expensive emissions control equipment is mandated for air pollution abatement. Chinese cities are currently battling extreme pollution problems brought on by the extensive use of coal for heat. When coal is burned, the resulting heavy, dusty ash must be removed. Mining coal underground is dangerous and open pits destroy the countryside.

Electrical energy has the lowest installation cost of common fuels and is clean and easy to distribute within the building. However, generating electricity remotely for heat is about half as efficient as direct combustion of another fuel in the building itself. Electricity is several times more expensive than any other fuel in most parts of the world. It can be an efficient fuel when used in an electric heat pump system.

Electricity is distributed through small wires and uses relatively small, quiet equipment. The major space considerations are in larger buildings for transformers, switchgear, or large substations. Electrical billing rates, determined by a usage meter, are higher than other fuel options in most regions of the United States. When electricity is generated from fossil fuels or nuclear energy, for every unit of heat released through electric resistance into a room, two to three units are discarded into waterways and the atmosphere due to losses in electrical generation and transmission.

Water-generated power is clean and renewable, and early industrial communities were sited along rivers to use waterpower. However, the huge dams required to generate electricity from water (hydroelectric energy) can displace people from their homes, devastate vast areas through flooding, and decimate fish populations that need open rivers to spawn. A recent development by Northeastern University engineering professor emeritus Alexander Gorlov represents a new solution to the problem of how to harness hydropower without building a dam. Gorlov's helical turbine design is potentially suitable for use in most of the world's rivers, as well as in ocean channels. They have been installed in test installations in Brazil and in Vinalhaven, Maine.

Wind is slowly becoming a more popular energy source. By tying the electrical energy it produces into the electrical distribution grid, the uneven character of the wind is less of a problem. Because the cost of a windmill is about the same as the cost of a house, small-scale wind energy is not yet an efficient option. At large-scale wind farms in southern California and west Texas, wind turbines generate electricity profitably. The development of relatively small wind farms in New York State and New England is limited by siting and transmission constraints. Large offshore wind farms are popular in northern Europe, and could be located off Cape Cod and other coastal regions in the United States.

Where a large quantity of solid waste is available, useful heat can be recovered by using it as refuse derived fuel. Modern heat recovery incinerators use a high temperature process called pyrolysis to dispose of solid waste. The waste is converted to carbon dioxide, water vapor, flue gases, and ash. Pyrolysis allows the system to meet U.S. Environmental Protection Agency (EPA) emission standards, even when using pathological wastes and plastics as refuse. Hospitals generate up to 9.1 kg (20 lb) of solid waste per patient per bed day, making incineration a fuel source for space heating, hot water, sterilization, kitchens, and laundries.

An incinerator can easily be added to a boiler to serve as a supplemental source of heat. Small, preassembled domestic incinerators take up about 2.8 square meters (30 square ft) of floor space, including working room.

The earth itself gives off heat that can be tapped for use in buildings. Direct geothermal energy has been used for space heating since the nineteenth century. It is currently used in large building complexes, or through direct wells into individual buildings. Geothermal energy is used for space heating, domestic hot water, industrial processing, and occasionally for cooling.

The Lewis Center for Environmental Studies at Oberlin College uses 24 geothermal wells to heat and cool the building. Water circulates to heat pumps located in each space throughout the building. In addition, two larger pumps serve the ventilation needs for the building. Each pump is controlled individually, allowing each unit to either reject or extract heat from the circulating water as needed. This reduces energy use by enabling simultaneous heating and cooling within the building.

High-pressure city steam is available from underground mains in some urban areas. The source is usually exhaust steam from a local electrical generating plant, reheated somewhat and distributed through mains and meters to users. This by-product increases the efficiency of the generating plant's use of fuel. City steam generates no pollutants and presents virtually no fire hazard. Many large buildings use city steam for heating and absorption cooling use. High-pressure steam avoids the need to install individual boilers and chimneys in buildings. In the past, it has been used to power elevators, fans, and pumps, but these functions have now been replaced by electricity.

Biopower is the process of using plant and other organic matter to generate electricity. Biomass—plant and animal matter—has been used for lighting, cooking, and heating ever since humans first discovered fire. Biomass residue for power production comes from agricultural waste, forest products residue, urban wood waste, and energy crops such as willow, poplar, switchgrass, and eucalyptus. One-third of the electricity consumed in the state of Maine comes from biopower facilities, with the forest products industry providing the fuel. Biomass power can reduce sulfur emissions that are linked to acid rain, and reduces the amount of waste sent to landfills.

ENERGY CONSERVATION

Architects and engineers are designing buildings with systems that will eventually wean us from our dependence on nonrenewable fuels. With an eye to protecting natural resources and preserving the environment, building engineers are seeking ways to share heating and cooling tasks between mechanical systems and natural ventilation and daylighting.

ENERGY STAR certifications have been developed by the EPA and the U.S. Department of Energy (DOE) for energy-efficient furnaces, central and room air conditioners, and heat pumps. ENERGY STAR homes are identified as at least 30 percent more energy efficient than the current International Energy Conservation Code requirements.

Utility companies have realized that it costs less to offer rebates for the purchase of energy-efficient appliances than to build new power plants. Local electric utilities and some gas companies offer rebates for high-efficiency heat pumps and central air conditioners. Gas companies offer rebates for high-efficiency furnaces and boilers.

Modifying Existing Heating Systems

Many existing home heating systems dating from the 1950s and 1960s are much too large for their buildings. Consequently, they keep cycling on and off to first heat the building then allow it to cool off, a process that wastes energy. A heat loss analysis of the building can determine the proper size for the equipment.

Modifying an existing heating system can produce significant energy savings. A new, more efficient oil burner is another option. A device that senses the outdoor temperature and keeps the boiler only as hot as necessary, called a modulating aquastat, is available for hot water systems. Hot water time delay relays circulate already warmed water through radiators without turning on the boiler to heat more water. Pilotless ignition of gas heaters saves the gas used to run the pilot light. Flue economizers recover heat from hot gases that go up the flue.

Photovoltaics and Fuel Cells

The development of fuel cells and photovoltaics is offering increased energy autonomy for larger buildings. Hydrogen is being developed as a high-grade fuel, extracted from water using electricity from solar and wind sources. With an increase in the use of solar energy, half of the world energy supply is expected to come from alternatives to fossil fuels by the year 2050.

The 48-story office building constructed in 1998 at 4 Times Square in New York was designed by Fox and Fowle, Architects, P.C. to integrate a variety of energy-saving features. Photovoltaic cells in the building facade along with fuel cell power packages generate power for hot water heating and electricity. A high-performance low-emissivity (low-e) glass curtain wall and efficient lighting with occupancy sensors and controls reduce the heating and cooling loads. Fresh air is increased by more than 50 percent above the usual amount for improved indoor air quality (IAQ), and a dedicated exhaust shaft rids the building of tobacco smoke and other pollution along with excess heat. Waste chutes and storage facilities expedite recycling. Centralized, automatic building management monitors air quality floor by floor to filter air and purge the system of pollutants. Environmentally friendly building materials and maintenance feature recycled and recyclable materials and supplies, further improving air quality.

The initiation of space exploration required a compact, safe, and highly efficient source of energy for electricity, heat, and water purification. Fuel cells were developed to use stored oxygen and hydrogen to generate direct current power. They convert the chemical energy of hydrogen and oxygen into electricity and heat without combustion. Virtually no nitrous oxides or carbon monoxide are produced.

The development of building fuel cell power plants promises the potential of high-efficiency, low-pollution energy. Fuel cells are designed to run on hydrogen. When a source of hydrogen isn't available, a fuel processor uses petroleum or natural gas to make hydrogen-rich fuel for the fuel cell stack. The fuel processor also gives off by-products that are released to the air. The fuel cell uses the hydrogen to make direct current (DC) electrical energy. An inverter converts the DC energy that the fuel cell produces to alternating current (AC) for building use.

Solar energy is becoming available as electricity directly at the point of use through photovoltaic (PV) technology. Site-generated PV uses DC electrical current, which is already being used in televisions, lighting, motors, and appliances for recreational vehicles. The power is then converted to AC power and tied to the central electrical energy grid. During periods of low supply, the energy grid provides backup energy. When extra production is available on-site, the meter runs backwards, effectively selling the extra energy to the grid.

Storing Energy on Site

Energy can be generated and stored on site in several ways. With hydrogen storage, wind-generated electrical energy splits water into oxygen and hydrogen, which can be stored for future use. Solar energy is stored in thermally massive surfaces for night use. These same masses can retain the night's coolness for daytime use. Heated rainwater stored in cisterns can be kept at varied temperatures depending upon the use schedule.

FIREPLACES

Wood-heating devices are the oldest method of heating after the sun. Campfires evolved into fireplaces and eventually into the wood stove, which offers fuel efficiency within an enclosed space. Wood is popular for heating homes in regions where energy costs are high and local regulations permit burning wood. Not all fireplaces are good heaters, however, and any fireplace or wood stove requires timely maintenance if it is to remain reliable and safe.

Fireplaces and stoves can add to both indoor and outdoor air pollution, emitting carbon monoxide, irritating particles, and sometimes nitrogen dioxide. Wood smoke causes nose and throat irritation, and can trigger asthma attacks. To keep chimneys clean and minimize pollution risks, burn small hot fires, not large smoky ones, use seasoned wood, and provide adequate ventilation.

A fireplace (Fig. 24-1) is really a framed opening in a chimney, designed to hold an open fire and sustain combustion of fuel. Modern fireplaces combine masonry and steel construction; some are almost entirely steel. Fireplaces should be designed to carry smoke and other combustion by-products safely outside, and to radiate the maximum amount of heat comfortably into the room. The design must keep the fireplace adequate distances from combustible materials. Multifaced fireplaces are sensitive to drafts in a room, so avoid placing their openings opposite an exterior door.

The firebox is the chamber where combustion takes place. In traditional fireplaces, the firebox is steel, lined with noncombustible firebrick. The firebox is typically 91 or 107 cm (36 or 42 in.) wide and about 64 cm (25 in.) high. The top of the firebox tapers to a throat, a narrow opening that connects the firebox and the smoke chamber. The throat is fitted with a damper that regulates the draft in the fireplace.

The smoke chamber connects the throat to the flue of the chimney. At the bottom of the smoke chamber, a

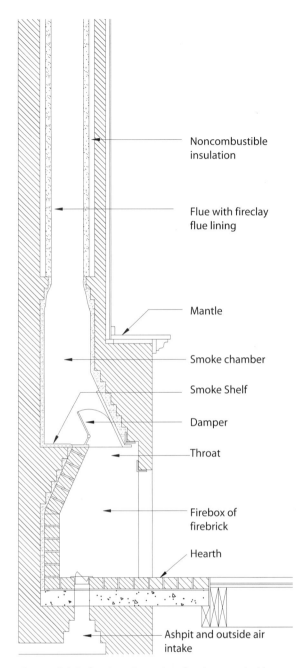

Noncombustible insulation

Flue with fireclay flue lining

Mantle

Smoke chamber

Smoke Shelf

Damper

Throat

Firebox of firebrick

Hearth

Ashpit and outside air intake

Figure 24-1 Section through a fireplace and chimney.

smoke shelf deflects downdrafts from the chimney, preventing cold air and smoke from entering the room. The flue creates a draft and carries smoke and gases of the fire safely outside. The hotter air that has been heated by the fire, being less dense than the fresh air in the chimney, rises up and out of the flue. The flue is usually a metal or tile liner inside a masonry chimney. Masonry chimneys must have a minimum of 5 cm (2 in.) clearance from combustible construction. Normally, fire stopping is provided between the chimney and wood framing.

To burn properly, a fire requires a steady flow of air. Traditional fireplaces draw the air for combustion from inside the house. A grate on the floor of the fireplace holds logs so air can stoke the fire from underneath. Other fireplaces pull in outside air through an air intake underneath the fireplace floor. A flue damper enables you to regulate the draft and can be completely closed to keep air from escaping up the flue when the fireplace is not in use.

The hearth extends the floor of the fireplace out into the room, with noncombustible material like brick, tile, or stone to resist flying sparks. Many fireplaces have an ash drop in the hearth, which can be opened to dump ashes into a pit underneath. Some also have a gas starter, which sets logs ablaze without kindling. On the wall of the room, the chimneybreast often projects a few inches into the room. A mantle may trim the top of the fireplace.

Ordinary fireplaces generate mostly radiant heat, which warms only the immediate vicinity. Heat-circulating fireplaces produce some radiant heat, but mainly warm the air that circulates around the firebox. One, and sometimes two, shells surround the firebox in a heat-circulating fireplace. A room air intake under the firebox lets cool air in. As the air absorbs heat, it rises to a warm air outlet at the top of the fireplace. Some fireplaces have a fan that increases the airflow to speed up the heat transfer. Convection currents in the room carry warm air away from the fireplace and cool air back for reheating.

Most heat-circulating fireplaces gain further efficiency by enclosing the firebox with glass doors that let you see the flames without wasting their energy in radiant heat. A damper at the bottom of the door lets you control the supply of air for combustion. Some highly efficient heat-circulating fireplaces have an outside air intake and do not require room air for combustion.

In some areas, including Washington, Colorado, and parts of California, strict environmental laws prohibit burning of wood on certain days to all but certified, clean-burning appliances, which usually means factory-built fireplaces or wood stoves. These environmental measures have cut into the number of traditional masonry fireplaces that are constructed. The relatively low cost of zero-clearance fireplaces, which don't need space between their enclosures and nearby combustible materials, also compete with traditional fireplaces, as do gas fireplaces.

In response, manufacturers have introduced clean-burning masonry fireplaces that are certified under state environmental regulations. The manufacturers supply the pieces critical to combustion efficiency, and the lo-cal dealer supplies firebrick, backup material, flue liner, and stone, along with accessories. Some of these clean burners are variations of the Rumford design that was developed in England in the later 1700s. The Rumford is a tall, shallow fireplace, about as tall as it is wide, that burns hot and easily radiates heat into the room. To prevent smoking, the fireplace is built with a rounded throat that draws air up into the smoke chamber. Some current models can be used in new construction or retrofitted into an existing fireplace.

Another design uses a standard brick fireplace on the outside and a masonry heater on the inside. Burning gases are mixed with oxygen in five separate locations in the fireplace, and the burning continues as the gases travel down hidden channels between the firebox and the chimney. The heat from the burning, which greatly reduces pollutants, is stored in the masonry mass. After the fire goes out, heat is slowly released over the ensuing 12 to 16 hours.

WOOD STOVES

Many modern wood-burning stoves are more efficient than heat-circulating fireplaces. Some stoves only radiate heat, while others also heat air passing around the firebox in convention currents. The EPA certifies prefabricated fireplaces and stoves for burning efficiency and allowable particulate emissions. New models that meet EPA requirements are quite clean burning.

A wood stove (Fig. 24-2) may be the only source of heat for a residence or small commercial building. The location of the wood stove has a significant impact on the building design. It is easier to add a freestanding stove than a built-in fireplace, but because a stove must be located at safe distances from combustible surfaces, it occupies a great deal more floor space. Noncombustible materials must be used below and around the wood stove, with a minimum clearance provided to combustible materials. Wood-burning stoves require 46 cm (18 in.) minimum between uninsulated metal chimneys and combustible wall or ceiling surfaces. The stove must be at least 91 cm (36 in.) from the nearest wall. This may be reduced to 46 cm if the wall is protected by a noncombustible heat shield or 25-mm (1-in.) clear air space.

The stove's location affects furniture arrangements and circulation paths. Areas that "see" the stove get most of the radiant heat, resulting in hot spots near the stove and cold spots where visual access is blocked. You have to leave circulation paths around hot stove surfaces. Remember also to plan space for wood storage, which

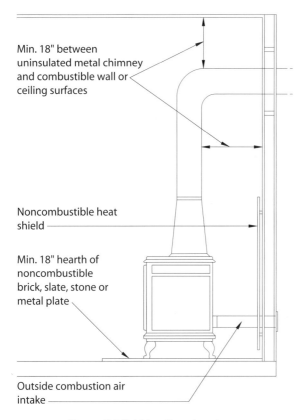

Min. 18" between uninsulated metal chimney and combustible wall or ceiling surfaces

Noncombustible heat shield

Min. 18" hearth of noncombustible brick, slate, stone or metal plate

Outside combustion air intake

Figure 24-2 Woodburning stove.

should be covered, well ventilated, accessible, and large enough for an ample supply.

Circulation stoves convert the fire's radiant heat to convected heat in the air. The hot air rises in a layer to the ceiling level. If a path exists at ceiling level between rooms, this heat can spread through a building and to upper floors. Thermally massive ceilings hold heat longer for release overnight.

Catalytic combustors on wood stoves reduce air pollution. Honeycomb-shaped ceramic disks up to 152 mm (6 in.) in diameter and 76 mm (3 in.) thick are inserted into the flue or built into the stove. The disks ignite wood smoke at a lower temperature, burning up gases and producing more heat and less creosote. Wood stoves with catalytic combustors can't burn plastic, colored newsprint, metals, or sulfur. Precision dampers and other controls let you adjust the heat output.

CHIMNEYS AND FLUES

We usually associate chimneys with fireplaces, but boilers and furnaces have chimneys too. Older, less efficient fuel-burning equipment use chimneys to carry high-

temperature flue gases. These must be isolated from combustible construction. Traditional flues are built 10 to 12 meters (35–40 ft) high to provide an adequate draft. In newer flues, fans now provide this draft.

Burning produces carbon monoxide (CO) and carbon dioxide (CO_2). Carbon monoxide is toxic and odorless and can cause death. We exhale carbon dioxide with every breath we take, but carbon dioxide can also be dangerous if it replaces the oxygen in the air we breathe. Chimneys carry these gases and other products of combustion up and out of the building.

Chimneys in homes are usually constructed of a terracotta flue lining surrounded by 8 in. of brick, with a 2-in. space between the brick and any wood. This space is filled with incombustible mineral wool. Prefabricated chimneys are replacing heavier, bulkier field-built masonry. High-efficiency boilers and furnaces remove so much heat from exhaust gases that the flues used can be smaller, and can be vented through a wall to the exterior, eliminating a chimney.

Where you have a chimney, you need a source of fresh air. Chimneys work by convection, with warmer air and gases rising up and out of the chimney. The removal of air through the chimney leaves the room with the fireplace at a lower air pressure than the outdoors. This lower pressure often draws air from the surrounding room. Oxygen is only about one-fifth of the air, so it takes a lot of air to provide enough oxygen for combustion.

This makeup air should be drawn from the outdoors, with an intake located close to the fuel burner or a duct that is connected to a more remote intake. A duct or grille draws air directly from the outdoors to the fire without passing through the room. When an intake isn't supplied, outdoor air is sucked through building cracks, creating a draft through the room that can cancel out the heat from the fireplace. If the air leaks are all plugged, the fire becomes smoky and sluggish, and the chimney won't work properly. Smoke buildup in the room depletes oxygen.

Most of the heat from a fireplace goes up the chimney, which can result in a net heat loss. The colder it is outside, the more heat is lost. Masonry masses around the fireplace can store and release some heat, especially when the fireplace is surrounded by the building and is not on an exterior wall. The American National Standards Institute (ANSI) and the American Society of Heating Refrigeration, and Air-Conditioning Engineers (ASHRAE) have jointly put forth Standard 90.2–1993, *Energy Efficient Design of New Low-Rise Residential Buildings*, which requires a tight-fitting damper, firebox doors, and a source of outside combustion air within the firebox for a safe and efficient fireplace.

MASONRY HEATERS

Masonry heaters can be used to heat an entire residence. They take up a small floor area relative to their height. An inner vertical firebox provides a hot, clean, and efficient burn. Combustible gases flow down into outer chambers, and transfer heat to external masonry surfaces. The cool room air rises when heated by the masonry. Masonry heaters provide gentle, even heat without dangerous hot surfaces. You can build a fire at dinnertime to burn until bedtime, and the heater will provide radiant heat all night without a fire.

GAS-FIRED HEATERS

Vent-free gas heating appliances include unvented, wall-mounted, and freestanding gas heaters and gas fireplaces. They require that a nearby window be kept open a couple of inches for an adequate fresh air supply to prevent oxygen depletion, which results in heat loss. Unvented gas heaters are similar to unvented kerosene heaters, which have been banned in most states for residential use. Unvented gas heaters produce nitrous oxides, which cause nose, eye, and throat irritation, along with carbon monoxide. They also produce a great deal of water vapor that can cause condensation, mildew, and rot in wall and ceiling cavities. Unvented gas heaters and gas fireplaces are prohibited in homes statewide in California, Minnesota, Massachusetts, Montana, and Alaska, and in cities throughout the United States and Canada.

Gas-fired infrared (IR) heating units are used in semioutdoor locations, like loading docks and repair shops. They use natural gas or propane. If they are vented, they can be installed in warehouse-type retail stores. Gas-fired heaters heat surfaces first, not the air, providing thermal comfort without high air temperatures. They are large and usually noisy.

Gas-fired baseboard heaters also use natural gas or propane to heat by convection and radiation. They use a built-in fan to vent directly to the outside, so they must be located at or near an external wall. Gas-fired baseboard heaters come in 1.2- and 1.9-m (4- and 6-ft) lengths.

Gas logs and gas fireplaces burn natural or propane gas to provide flames that are largely decorative, although some units also provide quiet a bit of heat. Ceramic gas logs can be hooked up to an existing gas starter in a fireplace or to a new line brought to the firebox.

Operate gas logs in fireplaces with the damper open, so carbon monoxide will vent up the chimney.

Gas fireplaces require only a small vent. Direct-vent models expel carbon monoxide out the rear, which means you can vent directly through an exterior wall and do not need to build a chimney to the roofline. Some gas fireplaces also draw combustion air from outside.

HOT WATER AND STEAM HEATING SYSTEMS

Originally, mechanical systems in buildings were designed to provide additional heat in cold weather. Cooling was taken care of by the way the building was sited, shaded, and ventilated. Our first look at mechanical systems will consider these heating-only systems. In practice today, most heating equipment is used in conjunction with cooling and ventilating equipment, which we look at later.

Hot water systems were the residential standard until about 1935. Hot water (hydronic) systems heat a building by means of water heated in a boiler and circulated by a pump through pipes to a fin-tube radiator, convector, or unit heater for heating only. Fan-coil units (FCUs) and radiant panels are used for both heating and cooling. Hydronic systems are used in residences, and in perimeter areas of commercial buildings with separate cooling-only ducted systems in the interior spaces. Steam boilers generate steam that is circulated through piping to radiators.

Frank Lloyd Wright used a hot water heating system in the Robie House in Chicago. Wall radiators were integrated below the north windows in the living room. Under floor radiators with grilles in the floor were designed for the full-height south windows, but were never installed. The boiler was located in a basement room.

In Mies van der Rohe's Farnsworth House in Fox River, Illinois, four walls of ceiling-to-floor glass presented a heating system design challenge. Radiant heating pipes were installed in the floor slab, and a boiler was located in a central utility closet.

Boilers

Boilers heat the water for recirculating hot water systems used for building heating. They can provide enough heat for entire buildings. A boiler (Fig. 24-3) is a closed arrangement of vessels and tubes in which water is

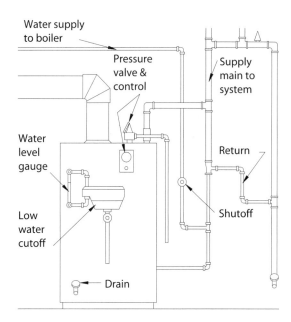

Water supply to boiler

Pressure valve & control

Supply main to system

Water level gauge

Return

Low water cutoff

Shutoff

Drain

Figure 24-3 Steam boiler.

heated or steam is generated. The type of boiler used depends on the size of the heating load, the heating fuels available, the efficiency needed, and whether the boilers are single or modular. Fuels for boilers include wood, coal, solid waste, fuel oil, gas, or electricity, and some boilers use more than one fuel. Fossil-fuel burning boilers need flues to exhaust gases, fresh air for combustion, and pollution-control equipment. A horizontal pipe carries exhaust gas from the boiler, and is connected to a vertical flue section called the stack. Boilers also need ventilation air, with an inlet and outlet on opposite sides of the room.

In older coal-fueled boilers, the coal was shoveled by hand into the boiler's firebox. Newer boilers use a mechanized stoker and automated ash-removal system. The ash is removed to a landfill, or can be used to improve the qualities of concrete. Coal boilers require antipollution equipment to control fly ash, which consists of various sizes of particles, and flue gas containing sulfur and nitrogen. Flue gases contribute to acid rain, which damages plant life and animals and erodes ancient monuments and ruins as well as modern statues and buildings. Acid rain pollutes water systems and affects tree growth.

Electric boilers eliminate the need for combustion air, flues, and air pollution in the building. However, these improvements are offset by the use of high-grade electrical energy for the low-grade task of heating. As discussed earlier, electricity is inefficient to generate, and produces pollution at the electrical generating plant. It is also expensive.

Boilers sometimes use recovered industrial waste heat to generate steam, often in combination with oil or gas. Hot water converters use a steam or hot water heat source such as geothermal, district heating, or a central steam boiler to heat hot water for building use. Hot water converters are essentially heat exchangers that transmit heat from a steam or hot water source to the water to be heated.

Boilers have safety release valves that open when vapor pressure is above a set level, allowing vapor to escape until the pressure is reduced to a safe or acceptable level. An air cushion tank, also known as a compression tank or expansion tank, is a closed tank containing air that is usually located above the boiler. Heated water expands and compresses air in the tank, which keeps the water from boiling and avoids frequent opening of the pressure relief valve.

Boiler systems require a fuel, a heat source, and a pump or fan to move the water. A distribution system, heat exchanger or terminal within the space to be heated, and a control system complete the equipment. Any heat escaping through the boiler's walls also helps heat the building. If a boiler is too small for the building, the building temperatures will be too low. Boilers that are too large waste money and space.

Cast-iron boilers are used for low-pressure steam and low-temperature hot water systems, and are generally less efficient than other types. Small steel boilers, called portable boilers, are assembled from welded steel units. They are prefabricated on a steel foundation and transported as a single package from the factory. Large boilers are installed in refractory brick settings built at the site.

Gas-fired cast-iron hot water boilers use hot gases rising through cast-iron sections to heat water inside. Additional heat is collected from a heat extractor in the flue. Oil-fired, cast-iron hot water boilers regulate the amount of air at a burner unit. The flame enters a refractory (resistant to heat) chamber, and continues around the outside of water-filled cast-iron sections.

In oil-fired steel boilers, the hot flame from burning oil produces combustion within a refractory chamber and fire tubes. The refractory chamber heats water outside the chamber. A domestic hot water coil can be connected, but this requires a larger boiler for support. An aquastat (a thermostat for water) turns on to keep the water hot. Newer, small-dimension compact boilers have high thermal efficiencies. They are available with venting options suitable for small equipment rooms.

Boilers are most efficient when in operation continuously. Modular boilers provide an efficient alternative, as sections can be used as needed, resulting in ease of maintenance and smaller size.

Gas-fired pulse boilers are even smaller and more energy efficient. They produce 60 to 70 small explosions per second, which cause the flue gases to pulse, and create a highly efficient heat transfer. Gas-fired pulse boilers operate at lower temperatures at efficiencies as high as 90 percent. They exhaust moist air, not hot smoke. To receive ENERGY STAR certification, a boiler must have an annual fuel usage efficiency of 85 percent or higher.

Steam boilers for space heating and domestic hot water are usually low-pressure. They are also used for electrical power generation for hospitals, kitchens, and industrial processes. A pressure gauge and an automatic safety control shut down boiler operation if needed, and a relief valve will blow off dangerous excess pressure. A glass water-level gauge shows the water level in the boiler and a shutoff valve in the water supply line permits water to be added manually as needed. Some boilers have an automatic water feed instead of a manual one. A low-water cutoff automatically shuts down the boiler if the water level drops too far.

With a pump added, low-pressure water systems can serve larger areas, including high-rise buildings. Medium-high-pressure steam boilers are found in high-rise buildings. High-pressure steam or water can carry more heat, allowing for smaller distribution piping for heat delivery throughout the building. High-pressure plants are more complex, and require added safety precautions and the presence of a qualified operating engineer when in use. Hot water is quieter and easier to distribute than steam.

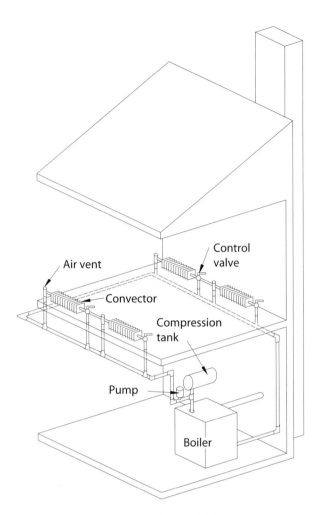

Figure 24-4 Hot water (hydronic) heating system.

Distribution Systems

In steam heating systems, steam that is produced in a boiler is circulated under pressure through insulated pipes, and then condensed in cast-iron radiators. In the radiator, the latent heat given off when the steam cools and becomes water is released to the air of the room. The condensed water then returns to the boiler through a network of return pipes. The system is reasonably efficient but difficult to control precisely, as the steam gives off its heat rapidly.

Steam pipes are larger than those for water, but smaller than air ducts. The steam moves by its own power, and the rate can't be controlled as water can. It is also harder to control temperature. The condensation of steam in pipes is noisy, and hot water systems (Fig. 24-4) are now more common than steam. In order for the condensed water to collect and drain in the steam pipes, the drainpipes must be sloped, taking up more space in construction.

The old style of cast-iron radiator, located near outside walls and under windows in every room, is not installed anymore, but are still in service in older buildings. Old-fashioned radiators are made of from 2 to 50 cast-iron sections, each with four or six tubes. Some models stand on the floor, others hang on wall brackets. Such radiators have pipes that are exposed to the room, and thus leaks in these radiators are easily repaired.

Radiators lose much heat to the adjacent exterior walls. Foil-covered cardboard radiator reflectors are available at building supply stores, and can be placed between the wall and the radiator. Keeping a radiator clean will also maximize heat reflection out into the room.

Fin-tube radiation devices, fan-coil units (FCUs), unit heaters, and IR heaters are currently used with steam. Fin-tube radiators (Fig. 24-5) are longer and smaller than the old-fashioned cast-iron radiators.

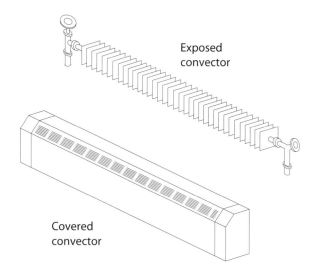

Figure 24-5 Baseboard fin tube convectors.

Radiators (Fig. 24-6) are also used in hot water systems. Hot water (or hydronic) systems are much easier to control. Only the sensible heat of the water is transmitted to the air, not the latent heat of vaporization as with steam. A very even, controlled release of heat to the air is achieved by regulating the temperature and rate of circulation of the water. Hydronic systems are silent when properly installed and adjusted, and produce comfortable heat.

Hot water baseboard and radiator systems are laid out in four different arrangements. In a series loop sys-

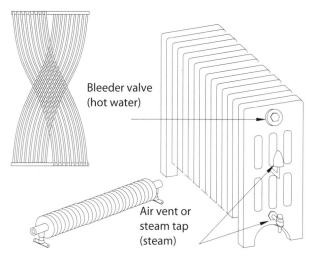

Older styles are available in many new colors.

Figure 24-6 Radiators.

tem, water flows through each baseboard or fin tube radiator at the building's perimeter in turn. The water becomes somewhat cooler by the time it gets to the end of the loop. A damper at each baseboard adjusts heat by reducing the amount of air that passes over the fins. Because all elements are turned on or off together, a series loop should only serve spaces within a single zone that share the same heating requirements.

One-pipe systems are very common. A single pipe supplies hot water from the boiler to each radiator or convector in sequence. Special fittings divert part of the flow into each baseboard. A valve at each baseboard allows for the heat to be reduced or shut off. Because it uses a little more piping than the series loop system, it is not as economical to install. Temperatures are still lower at the end of the loop, as with a series loop system.

Two-pipe systems use one pipe to supply water from the boiler to radiators or convectors, and a second pipe to return water to the boiler. In a two-pipe reverse return system, the lengths of supply and return pipes for each radiator or convector are nearly equal. The water is supplied to each baseboard or radiator at the same temperature, as the supply pipe doesn't pass through the baseboard or accept cooled return water. This system uses more pipe than a one-pipe system, increasing the cost.

In the final system, a two-pipe direct return system, a return pipe from each radiator or convector takes the shortest route back to the boiler. This diversion of most of the water before it reaches the end results in hotter spaces at the beginning and cooler spaces at the end of the run. This is a generally unsatisfactory system.

Hot water circulating through pipes causes pipe expansion, so expansion joints are inserted into long pipe runs. Clearance around all pipes passing through floors and walls is also provided to accommodate pipe expansion. Air vents keep air from accumulating at high points in the piping or at convector branches. Access is required for air vents in piping, which have to be bled—have the excess air let out—by hand. Water vents prevent water in the low points of a drained, inoperative system from freezing and bursting the tubing and fittings. A water vent is also located at the bottom of a boiler to allow it to be drained.

Natural Convection Heating Units

Radiators and convectors are used to supply heat only in residential and small light-commercial buildings. What we usually call radiators, including both fin-tube radiation devices and old-fashioned cast-iron radiators, actually use convection as their primary heating principle. There are various styles of baseboard and cabinet convection heating units used in smaller buildings. Their appearance and the space they occupy are of concern to the interior designer. When located below a window, they can affect the design of window treatments.

Radiators consist of a series or coil of pipes through which hot water or steam passes. The heated pipes warm the space by convection and somewhat by radiation. Fin-tube radiators (also called fin-tube convectors) are usually used along outside walls and below windows. They raise the temperatures of the glass and wall surfaces. Along an interior wall, a fin-tube radiator would reinforce the cold air circulation pattern in the room, and occupants would be too cold on one side and too hot on the other.

Fin-tube baseboard units have horizontal tubes with closely spaced vertical fins to maximize heat transfer to the surrounding air. The aluminum or copper fins are 5 to 10 cm (2–4 in.) square and are bonded to copper tubing. Steam or hot water circulates through the tubing. There are also electric resistance fin-tube units with an electrical element instead of the copper tubing. Cool room air is drawn in from below by convection, and rises by natural convection when heated by contact with the fins. The heated air is discharged out through a grille at the top, and more air is drawn into the bottom of the unit. Baseboard unit enclosures usually run the length of the wall, but the element inside may be shorter. They tend to be less conspicuous than cabinet-style units.

Convectors are a form of fin-tube radiator, with an output larger than a baseboard fin-tube convector for a given length of wall. Convectors are housed in freestanding, wall-hung, or recessed cabinets 61 cm high by 91 cm wide (2 by 3 ft). Air must flow freely around the units in order to be heated. Each unit has an inlet valve, which can be adjusted with a screwdriver to control the flow of water or steam. Hot-water units have bleeder valves to purge air. With the system operating, the valve can be opened with a screwdriver or key until water comes out, and then closed.

Controls

Thermostats are set to temperatures that will trigger turning the heating system on and off. If a thermostat controls both the circulation pump that distributes the heat and boiler that heats the water or steam, the system will operate almost continually in cold weather, as the average temperature in the system gradually rises.

When a thermostat controls only the boiler, with a continuous circulation pump, more energy is used for the pump but variations in the system's temperature are minimized, as are expansion noises.

RADIANT HEATING

As we have seen, thermal comfort depends on more than air temperature. The temperature of surrounding surfaces also comes into play. Warm surfaces can maintain comfort even when air temperature is lower. Radiant heating is a more comfortable way to warm people than introducing heated air into a space.

Radiant heat can be more energy efficient than hot air systems, as it transfers heat directly to objects and occupants without heating large volumes of air first. The warmer surfaces that result mean that more body heat can be lost by convection without the room becoming uncomfortably cold. As a result, the temperature of the air in the space can be kept cooler, and less heat will be lost through the building envelope.

Radiant heating systems use ceilings, floors, and sometimes walls as radiant surfaces. The heat source may be pipes or tubing carrying hot water, or electric-resistance heating cables embedded within the ceiling, floor, or wall construction. Radiant heat is absorbed by the surfaces and objects in the room, and reradiates from the warmed surfaces. Radiant panel systems can't respond quickly to changing temperature demands, and are often supplemented with perimeter convection units. Separate ventilation, humidity control, and cooling system are required for completely conditioned air.

Radiantly Heated Floors

Floors can be heated by electrical resistance wires, warm air circulating through multiple ducts, and warm water circulating through coils of pipe to warm the surfaces of concrete or plaster. Heated floors warm feet by conduction, and set up convective currents to heat the room air evenly. Tables and chairs can block IR waves coming up from a floor, thereby blocking heat to the upper body.

Without good insulation, heated floors can't provide all the heat needed in a cold climate unless the floor is brought up to a temperature too hot for feet. Rugs and carpets reduce the efficiency of heated floors. Heated floors can't react quickly to small or sudden changes in demand, due to the high thermal mass of concrete floors. Repairs are messy and expensive.

Hydronic radiant panels are better used in floors than ceilings. Hydronic radiant heating systems circulate warm water through metal or plastic pipes, either encased in a concrete slab or secured under the subfloor with conductive heat plates. They are directly embedded in concrete cast-in-place floors. Radiant coils under wood floors are quite popular. A rug or carpet over the floor will interfere with the exchange of heat. Special under-carpet pads can help with heat transfer, or higher water temperatures can be used.

The water supplied for radiant heating may be heated in a boiler, heat pump, solar collector, or geothermal system. In response to a thermostat setting, a control valve in each coil adjusts the supply water temperature by mixing it with cooler water that has been circulated already. Adjacent spaces must be insulated, as radiant panels generate very high temperatures, and there is the strong potential for great heat loss. With higher insulation, smaller panels can be used. They are usually located near exterior walls, but this may not be the case in solar-heated buildings, where they can supplement areas that aren't heated well by the sun. Copper was formerly used for the piping, but connections could fail, so synthetic one-piece systems are now used.

Electric radiant floors aren't appropriate for every home because of the cost of electricity, but they can be an excellent solution to certain design problems. Choosing the right system means knowing what you want it to do, and looking past manufacturers' claims to the system's real costs and benefits. Electric systems are easier and less expensive to install than their hydronic counterparts. They're also less expensive to design for different zones. They can be used to heat a whole house or to provide spot comfort in kitchens and baths.

Electric radiant floor elements can consist of cables coated with electrical insulation (Fig. 24-7), or of fabric mats with the cables woven into them, which are more expensive. Like hydronic tubes, electric elements are embedded in the floor system. Cables are usually embedded in a 38-mm (1.5-in.) thick slab of gypsum underlayment or lightweight concrete. As with hydronic tubing, you need to consider the ability of the framing to support the slab's weight and make adjustments to window and door heights for the slab's extra thickness.

Mats generally require less floor thickness than cables, and can often be placed in a mortar bed beneath floor tiles. This adds as little as 3 mm ($\frac{1}{8}$ in.) to the floor height. Some mats can be rolled out on the subfloor beneath a carpet and pad. Mats are available in a range of

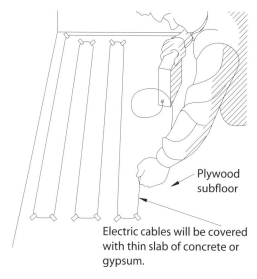

Electric cables will be covered with thin slab of concrete or gypsum.

Figure 24-7 Electric radiant floor.

standard and custom sizes and shapes. Mats heat up a tile floor faster than buried cables, but the thermal mass of the cable system will keep the floor warm for a longer period of time.

Hydronic radiant heating systems can use gas, oil, electricity, or even solar energy as their energy source. On the other hand, electric cables don't require a boiler, and may be more cost-effective for small floors. An electric system for a small bathroom could cost $300 to $400, compared to $4000 to $5000 for a hydronic system, not including fuel costs, which are generally higher for electric systems. Electric floors are often used to supplement heating systems in homes with forced-air systems. Highly efficient homes with thick insulation, airtight construction, and passive solar features may also be appropriate sites for electric floors.

Radiantly Heated Ceilings

Ceiling installations are usually preferred over floors systems. Ceiling constructions have less thermal capacity than floors, and therefore respond faster. They can also be heated to higher temperatures. The system is concealed except for thermostats and balancing valves.

The wiring for electric resistance heating can be installed in the ceiling. It is acceptable for ceilings to get hotter than walls or floors, since they are not usually touched. However, downward convection is poor and the hot air stays just below the ceiling. When the ceiling is at its warmest, the room may feel uncomfortable. Overall efficiency suffers, and cooler air may stratify at floor level. Tables and desks block heat from above, resulting in cold feet and legs.

Hidden wires in radiant ceiling systems can be punctured during renovations or repairs. Even though a plaster ceiling may have to be torn down for system repairs, the expense is less than tearing up a concrete floor. Some systems use snap-together metal components for easy maintenance.

Preassembled electric radiant heating panels (Fig. 24-8) are also available. They can be installed in a modular suspended ceiling system, or surface mounted to heat specific areas. Radiant heating panels can be installed at the edges of a space to provide additional heat with variable air volume systems. Applications include office building entryways and enclosed walkways. They are useful in hospital nurseries, and in hydrotherapy, burn, and trauma areas. Residential uses include bathrooms, above full height windows, and in other cold spots. Factory silicone sealed panels are available for use in high-moisture areas. Some panels can be silkscreened to provide an architectural blend with acoustical tiles. Custom colors are also available. Radiant heating panels operate at 66°C to 77°C (150°F–170°F).

Research has found that heating a home with ceiling-mounted radiant panels produced energy savings of 33 percent compared to a heat pump and 52 percent compared to baseboard heaters. The research project, completed in May 1994, was sponsored by the U.S. DOE, the National Association of Home Builders (NAHB) Research Center, and Solid State Heating Corporation, Inc. (SSHC), the maker of the panels used in the tests. These panels differ from other types of radiant heaters in several ways. They mount to the ceiling surface, not behind or inside gypsum board. Their lightweight construction has little thermal mass that must come up to temperature, and the textured surface adheres directly to the heating element. These characteristics make the panels able to reach operating temperature in only three to five minutes. Because the panels respond quickly, people can turn the heat on and off as they would the lights. The panels operate quietly and without air movement.

Most of the heat from radiant heating panels flows directly beneath the panel and falls off gradually with greater distance, dropping by about 5°F over the first 6 feet. This may seem like a disadvantage, but some occupants like to find a spot that is relatively cooler or warmer within the room. Proper placement of panels must be coordinated with ceiling fans, sprinkler heads, and other obstructions, which can be a problem when installing them in an existing building.

Manufactured gypsum board heating panels use an electrical heating element in 16-mm ($\frac{5}{8}$-in.) fire-rated gypsum wallboard. They are 122 cm (4 ft) wide and 183, 244, 305, or 366 cm (6, 8, 10, or 12 ft) long. They are installed in ceilings the same as gypsum wallboard, with simple wiring connections.

Radiant panels avoid some of the problems inherent with forced-air systems, such as heat loss from ducts, air leakage, energy use by furnace blowers, and inability to respond to local zone conditions. Installation costs for energy-efficient radiant panels are considerably less than the cost for a forced-air system, but radiant panels can't provide cooling, as a forced-air system can.

Embedded radiant heating systems went out of favor in the 1970s due to the expense of the large quantity of piping and ductwork, and high electrical energy costs. Malfunctions were difficult and expensive to correct. Systems were slow to react to changing room thermal demands, due to the thermal inertia of concrete slabs, so they were slow to warm up after being set back for the night.

Radiant devices are also used to melt snow on driveways, walks, and airport runways. They circulate an antifreeze solution or use electric cables. Newer products use flexible plastic piping that operates continually at around 49°C (120°F) or higher, and have a 30-year expected lifetime.

TOWEL WARMERS

Towel warmers (Fig. 24-9) are designed to dry and warm towels, and also serve as a heat source in a bathroom or spa. They are available in electronic and hydronic

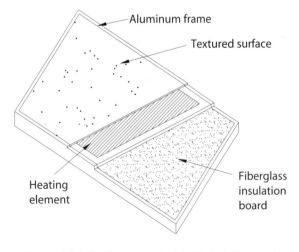

Figure 24-8 Surface-mounted radiant ceiling panel.

Aluminum frame

Textured surface

Heating element

Fiberglass insulation board

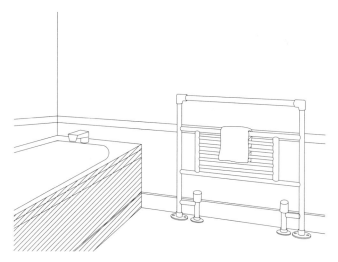

Figure 24-9 Towel warmer.

models, with a variety of styles and finishes. Electric towel warmers are easy to install and fairly flexible as to location. They should not be located where you can reach them while in bath water. Some towel warmers have time clocks to turn them on and off. Models are available that attach to a door's hinge pins, to the wall, or are free standing.

Hydronic towel warmers are connected to either the home's heating system or to a loop of hot water that circulates from the home's hot water tank. If they are connected to the heating system, the heat must be turned on for the towel warmer to operate. They are more complicated to install than electric warmers, but are more flexible in location, as they can be installed near a tub or whirlpool. Multirail towel warmers have several cross rails, allowing the towel warmer to be sized to heat the bathroom.

UNIT HEATERS

Unit heaters are used in large open areas like warehouses, storage spaces, industrial shops, garages, and showrooms, where the heating loads and volume of heated space are too large for natural convection units. Unit heaters can heat cold spaces rapidly. Smaller cabinet models are used in corridors, lobbies, and vestibules. They spread their heat over a wide area from a small number of units.

Unit heaters take advantage of natural convection plus a fan to blow forced air across the unit's heating element and into the room. The source of heat may be steam, hot water, electricity, or direct combustion of oil or gas. For direct combustion, fuel is piped directly to the unit and a flue vents to the outdoors for removal of combustion products. Through-wall models vent flue gases and introduce fresh outdoor air.

Unit heaters are made of factory-assembled components including a fan and a heating mechanism in a casing. The casing has an air inlet and vanes for directing the air out. Units are usually suspended from the roof structure or floor mounted, and located at the building's perimeter. Mounting the unit overhead saves floor space.

ELECTRIC RESISTANCE HEAT

When your feet get cold but you don't want to turn up the heat throughout the building, you might want to use an electric resistance space heater. These common, low-cost, and easy-to-install small heaters offer individual thermostatic control and don't waste heat in unoccupied rooms. However, they use expensive electricity as their fuel, so their use should be limited to spot-heating a small area for a limited time in an otherwise cool building.

The first electric room heater was patented in 1892 by the British inventors R. E. Compton and J. H. Dowsing, who had attached several turns of high-resistance wire around a flat rectangular plate of cast iron. The glowing white-orange wire was set at the center of a metallic reflector, which concentrated the heat into a beam. The success of their heater depended upon homes being wired for electricity, which was becoming more popular thanks to Edison's invention of the electric light.

In 1906, Illinois inventor Albert Marsh modified the original design with a nickel and chrome radiating element, producing white-hot temperatures without melting. In 1912, the British heater replaced the heavy cast-iron plate with a lightweight fireproof clay one, creating the first really efficient portable electric heater.

An electrical resistance system works like a toaster: wires heat up when you turn it on. Electric resistance heating takes advantage of the way electrical energy is converted to heat when it has difficulty passing along a conductor. Most of the time such a system consists of baseboard units or small, wall-mounted heaters, both of which contain the hot wires. The heaters are inexpensive and clean, and don't have to be vented. No space is used for chimneys or fuel storage.

Electric heating units designed for residential use combine a radiant heating element with a fan and a light in a ceiling-mounted unit. Some units include a nightlight as well. Bulb heaters provide silent, instant warmth using 250W R-40 IR heat lamps. Bulb heaters are available vented and unvented, and recessed or surface mounted. Auxiliary heaters are available for mounting in or on walls, and in kickspaces below cabinets.

Electrical resistance heating units (Fig. 24-10) are compact and versatile, but lack humidity and air quality controls. Electric resistance heaters use high-grade electrical energy for the low-grade task of heating. These heaters have hot surfaces, and their location must be carefully chosen in relation to furniture, drapery, and traffic patterns.

The elements of an electric resistance heating system can be housed in baseboard convection units around the perimeter of a room. Resistance coils heat room air as it circulates through the units by convection. Electric unit heaters use a fan to draw in room air and pass it over resistance-heating coils, then blow it back into the room.

Units are available that can be wall- or ceiling-mounted for bathrooms and other spaces where the floor might be wet but where quick heat for a limited time in an enclosed space is needed. Infrared heat lamps are also installed in bathroom ceilings for this purpose.

Toe space unit heaters are designed to be installed in the low space under kitchen and bathroom cabinets. Wall unit heaters are available in surface mounted or recessed styles for use in bathrooms, kitchens, and other small rooms. Fully recessed floor unit heaters are typically used where glazing comes to the floor, as at a glass sliding door or large window. Industrial unit heaters are housed in metal cabinets with directional outlets, and are designed to be suspended from the ceiling or roof structure. Quartz heaters have resistance heating ele-

ments sealed in quartz-glass tubes that produce IR radiation in front of a reflective background.

Small high-temperature IR heat sources with focusing reflectors can be installed in locations where they don't cast IR radiation shadows, such as overhead. They are useful where high air temperatures can't be maintained, as in large industrial buildings or outdoors. IR heaters are often used at loading docks, grandstands, public waiting areas, garages, and hangers. They will melt snow over limited areas.

Small IR heaters radiate a lot of heat instantly from a small area, and beam the heat where needed. High-temperature IR heaters may be electrical, gas-fired, or oil-fired. Venting is required for oil and sometimes for gas. The temperatures in the units can be greater than 260°C (500°F). Their radiant heat feels pleasant on bare skin, making these devices desirable for swimming pools, shower rooms, and bathrooms.

Portable electric resistance heaters heat a small area in their immediate vicinity without heating an entire building. However, their use as a substitute for building heating inevitably leads to deaths each year, when they are left running all night and come in contact with bedding or drapery, or where they are connected to unsafe building wiring.

There are several types of portable electric resistance heaters available today. Quartz heaters use electricity to quietly heat the floors and furniture within about 15 feet. You only feel their warmth if you stand nearby. Electrical forced air heaters are best used in a room that can be closed off. Electrical forced air heaters blow warm air and circulate it throughout a room. Ceramic forced air heaters use a ceramic heating element that is safer than other electric space heaters. Electricity heats the oil

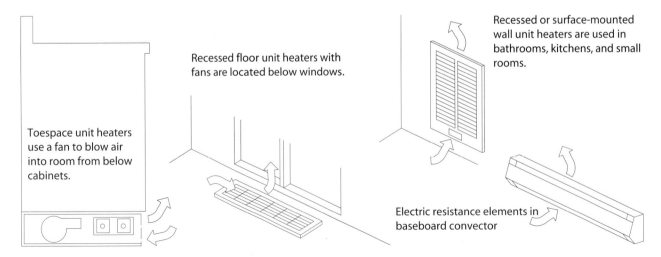

Recessed floor unit heaters with fans are located below windows.

Recessed or surface-mounted wall unit heaters are used in bathrooms, kitchens, and small rooms.

Toespace unit heaters use a fan to blow air into room from below cabinets.

Electric resistance elements in baseboard convector

Figure 24-10 Electric resistance heating.

inside oil-filled heaters to heat a room or temporarily replace a main heat source.

Electric resistance heating elements can also be exposed to the airstream in a furnace or mounted inside ductwork in forced air heating systems. Sometimes they are used to provide heat for a boiler in a hydronic heating system.

WARM AIR HEATING

Around 1900, warm air heating systems began to take the place of fireplaces. The original warm air systems used an iron furnace in the basement, which was hand-fired with coal. A short duct from the top of the sheet metal enclosing the furnace delivered warm air to a large grille in the middle of the parlor floor, with little heat going to other rooms.

Over time, oil or gas furnaces that fired automatically replaced coal furnaces, and operational and safety controls were added. Air was ducted to and from each room, which evened out temperatures and airflow. Fans were added to move the air, making it possible to reduce the size of the ducts. Adjustable registers permitted control within each room. Filters at the furnace cleaned air as it was circulated. Eventually, with the addition of both fans and cooling coils to the furnace, it became possible to circulate both hot and cold air.

During the 1960s, fewer homes were being built with basements, and subslab perimeter systems took the place of basement furnaces. The heat source was located in the center of the building's interior, where heat that escaped would help heat the house. Air was delivered from below, up and across windows and back to a central high return grille in each room. The air frequently failed to come back down to the lower levels of the room, leaving occupants with cold feet. In addition, water penetrating below the house could get into the heating system, causing major problems with condensation and mold.

Electric heating systems became popular at this time, as they eliminated combustion, chimneys, and fuel storage. Horizontal electric furnaces were located in shallow attics or above furred ceilings. Air was delivered down from the ceiling across windows, and taken back through door grilles and open plenum spaces. Heat pumps have mostly replaced less-efficient electric resistance systems.

Today, air is heated in a gas, oil, or electric furnace, and distributed by fan through ductwork to registers or diffusers in inhabited spaces. Forced-air heating is the most versatile widely used system for heating houses and small buildings. The system can include filtering,

humidifying, and dehumidifying devices. Cooling can be added with an outdoor compressor and condensing unit that supplies refrigerant to evaporator coils in the main supply ductwork. Fresh air is typically supplied by natural ventilation. Warm air distribution systems offer good control of comfort through air temperature and air volume control. The moving stream of air stirs and redistributes air in the room. Warm air systems work especially well in tall spaces where air stratifies with warm air at the top and cold air at the bottom.

Well-designed warm air heating systems are generally considered to be comfortable. The air motion in a warm air heating system can create uniform conditions and reasonably equal temperatures in all parts of the building. A forced-air (using fans) system usually burns gas or oil inside a closed chamber, called a heat exchanger, inside a furnace. A large blower located inside the furnace compartment forces cool air across the hot outer surface of the heat exchanger, heating the air. Fans move the heated air through a system of supply ducts located inside the walls and between floors and ceilings. Supply registers are equipped with dampers within the ducts that balance and adjust the system by controlling airflow. The dampers' vanes disperse the air, controlling its direction and reducing its velocity.

A separate system of exhaust ducts draws cool air back through return air grilles to be reheated and recirculated. Return air grilles are located near the floor, on walls, or on the ceiling. They can sometimes be relocated during design or renovation projects to avoid conflict with another piece of equipment. Sometimes there is no separate ductwork for the return air. Return grilles are then placed in the suspended ceiling to collect return air. The mechanical system draws return air back to a central collection point. It is then returned through ducts to the building's heating plant. This use of the space between the suspended ceiling and structural floor above as one huge return duct is referred to as a plenum return.

Filters and special air-cleaning equipment can clean both recirculated and outdoor air. The system circulates fresh air to reduce odors, and to make up for air exhausted by kitchen, laundry, and bathroom fans. The system can also add humidity as needed.

A wide variety of residential systems are available, depending upon the size of the house. The heating system must be large enough to maintain the desired temperature in all habitable rooms.

Energy-saving designs for warm air systems start with insulated windows, roof, walls, and floors, reducing the amount of heat needed. Warming the windows directly is less essential when they are well insulated, so a central furnace or heat pump connects to short ducts to the inner side of each room. Air is returned to the central unit through open grilles in doors and the furnace, or to a heat pump enclosure.

Warm air systems can be noisy. A quiet motor with cushioned mountings should be selected for the blower (fan), and it should not be located too close to the return grille to avoid noise. The blower housing should also be isolated from conduits or water piping, with flexible connections attaching equipment to ductwork. Ducts can be lined with sound absorbing materials, but care must be taken to avoid creating an environment for mold and mildew growth. Warm air distribution systems can circulate dust and contaminants as well as air through the building.

Mechanical systems all require regular maintenance for efficient operation and proper indoor air quality. The air filters of heating, ventilating, and air-conditioning (HVAC) equipment must be cleaned and replaced at regular intervals. Burners should occasionally be cleaned and adjusted for maximum efficiency of combustion. Motors, fans, pumps, and compressors should have their rubber belts checked and replaced as necessary. Ductwork may need to be vacuum cleaned.

Furnaces

Systems using air as the primary distribution fluid have a furnace as a heat-generating source, rather than the boiler used for water or steam. Warm air furnaces (Fig. 24-11) are usually located near the center of the building. The furnace is selected after the engineer determines the type of system and fuel source. Cool air returns from occupied spaces at around 16°C to 21°C (60°F–70°F) and passes through a filter, a fan or blower, and a heating chamber. When the air goes to the supply air ductwork, it is between 49°C and 60°C (120°F–140°F). The bonnet or plenum is a chamber at the top of the furnace from which the ducts emerge to conduct heated or conditioned air to inhabited spaces. The furnace may include a humidification system that evaporates moisture into the air as it passes through.

In a forced-air gas furnace, a thermostatically controlled valve feeds gas to a series of burner tubes, where it is lighted by an electric spark or pilot light flame. Air is warmed in a heat exchanger above the burners and circulated by the furnace blower. The exchanger must heat the air inside without allowing odorless, deadly carbon monoxide to get into the supply ducts, and should be checked for safety every few years. The burner and blower chambers have one or more access panels, and room must be left around the furnace for maintenance.

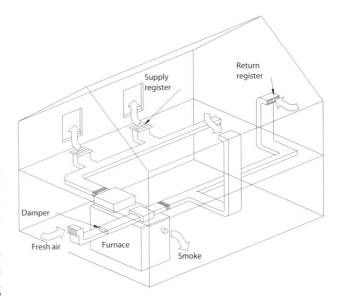

Figure 24-11 Warm air furnace and ducts.

Oil-fired forced-air furnaces are very efficient and durable, but more complicated than gas-fired furnaces. Oil is pumped from a storage tank into a combustion chamber, where it is atomized and ignited by a spark. The flame heats a heat exchanger that warms the air that is circulated through the system by a blower. If the burner fails to ignite, a safety switch opens when it senses that no heat is being produced. A second safety device is a photoelectric cell that detects when the chamber goes dark and shuts the system down. A safety note: both devices may have reset switches, which should never be pushed more than twice in succession, as excess fuel pumped into the combustion chamber could explode.

No combustion occurs in an electric forced-air furnace, so there is no flue through which heat can escape, resulting in very high efficiency. Electric furnaces are clean and simple and have fewer problems than combustion furnaces. However, even with high efficiency, the high cost of electricity may make them more expensive to operate.

In residential design, the burner is started and stopped by a thermostat, usually in or near the living room in a location where the temperature is unlikely to change rapidly, protected from drafts, direct sun, and the warmth of nearby warm air registers. When the thermostat indicates that heat is needed, the burner and blower start up. The blower continues after the burner stops, until the temperature in the furnace drops below a set point. A high limit switch shuts off the burner if the temperature is too high.

Conventional combustion techniques in furnaces are usually only around 80 percent efficient. Newer pulse-combustion and condensing combustion processes are designed to be up to 95 percent efficient, as they recover much of the heat that goes up the flue stack with other equipment. These newer furnaces have simple connections, requiring only a small vent and outside air pipes, and a condensate drain pipe. To receive Energy Star certification, a furnace must have an annual fuel usage efficiency of 90 percent. Furnaces can typically be expected to function for 15 to 20 years.

Gas and oil furnaces require combustion air and ventilation for exhausting combustion products to the outside. Gases rise up the flue from the furnace as a result of the chimney's heat and the temperature difference between the flue gases and the outside air. When either is increased, the force of the draft is increased. Flues extend past the top of the highest point of the building so combustion products are not drawn back into the building. Where the chimney is not high enough, a fan can help create the needed draft.

Energy can be recovered from exhausted air with a regenerative wheel, a rotating device of metal mesh that uses its large thermal capacity to transfer heat from one duct to another. Air-to-air heat exchangers with very large surfaces also save energy.

Heat Pumps

Heat pumps derive their name from their ability to transfer heat against its natural direction. As we know, heat normally flows from warmer to cooler areas. But any air above absolute zero always contains some thermal energy. The higher the temperature, the more energy is available. A heat pump can deliver 1.5 to 3.5 units of heat for each unit of electricity it uses. This can save 30 to 60 percent over the cost of electric heating, depending on geographic location and the equipment used. Heat pumps do this without combustion or flues.

In a heat pump (Fig. 24-12), a relatively small amount of energy is used to pump a larger amount of heat from a cold substance (the water, the ground, or outdoor air) to a warmer substance, such as the air inside the building. Heat pumps work especially well with relatively lower temperature heat sources, such as the water inside the jacket of an internal combustion engine, or warm water from a flat-plate solar collector. The heat pump increases the heat from these sources to the higher temperatures needed for space heating. Heat pumps can be part of a total energy system, concentrating waste heat from an electrical generating system to heat the same buildings served by the electrical generators. Heat pumps that pump heat from water or ground sources are more dependable than air sources in cold weather.

Heat pumps offer some energy advantages over other systems. A typical gas heating unit is about 60 to 80 percent efficient, with the rest of the energy going up the flue. Electrical resistance heating turns all the energy used into heat, but the process of creating electricity is highly inefficient. Heat pumps run at 150 to 350 percent efficiency; that means they transfer more energy than they use. They are always more efficient than electrical resistance heating in the long run, but heat pump equipment is more expensive to purchase, install, and

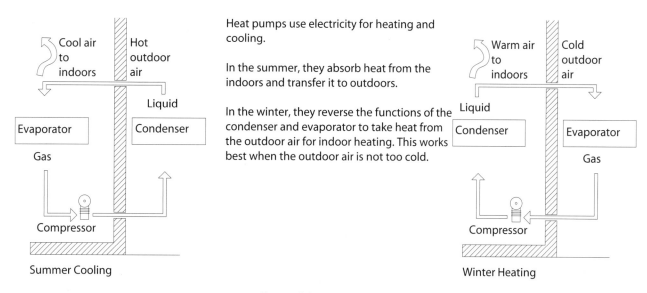

Figure 24-12 Heat pump.

maintain. Some heat pumps use the energy they generate to heat by electrical resistance, and are usually the most expensive. Other types use a refrigerant, such as HCFC-22 or one of the newer HFC alternatives, like a modern refrigerator. Air source heat pumps are not efficient where the temperature drops lower than $-7°C$ to $-1°C$ ($20°F–30°F$).

Air-to-air heat pumps use a refrigeration cycle to both heat and cool. Heat is pumped from the indoors to the outdoors in summer, and from outside to inside in winter. Air-to-air heat pumps are the most common type used in small buildings.

Air-to-water heat pumps cool and dehumidify interior spaces, with the heat going into useful water. Restaurants use air-to-water heat pumps to cool hot cooking areas, taking advantage of the hot water produced for food preparation and dishwashing. Heat pumps are also used for indoor pools, athletic facilities, small-scale industrial operations, motels and hotels, and apartment buildings.

In the heating mode, the heat pump extracts heat from outside the building and delivers it to the building, usually in conjunction with a forced warm air delivery system. When the heat pump uses air as the source of heat, the heat output and efficiency decline with colder weather. Air-to-air heat pumps operating below freezing temperatures generally rely on electric resistance heating elements for backup heating. They work best in areas with mild winters, where there is a balance between heating and cooling loads, or where electrical heating is the only option.

Water-to-air heat pumps rely on water as the source of heat and deliver warmed air to the space. Water sources have relatively consistent and high temperatures, around $10°C$ ($50°F$) in the north and $16°C$ ($60°F$) in the southern United States. If well water is used as the source, it must be treated for corrosion, which is expensive. Added to this is the cost of drilling, piping, and pumping the well.

Water source heat pump systems use an interior closed water loop to connect a series of heat pumps. One zone of the building can be heated while another is cooled, and the extra heat from the cooling process can be used to heat another area. A boiler serves as a supplementary heat source and a cooling tower rejects heat to maintain useable water temperatures within the loop. This is a good system for motels where some rooms get southern sun and some are in the shade, some are occupied and some not, and domestic hot water needs are high.

Water-to-air heat pumps use a closed piping loop, with heat rejected by one heat pump in the cooling mode being used by another in the heating mode. The water can also double as a water source for the fire suppression sprinkler system. Water-to-water heat pumps replace a boiler and chiller. Dairies use them to simultaneously cool milk and heat water for cleaning.

Ground source heat pumps (ground-to-air) are known as geothermal heat pumps or geo-exchange systems. Ground source heat pumps take advantage of the fact that underground temperatures are more constant year round than air temperatures. Geothermal heat pumps are 25 to 45 percent more efficient than air-source heat pumps. They can supply energy for heating, cooling, and domestic hot water. An environmentally safe refrigerant is circulated through a loop that is installed underground in long 1- to 2-meter (3- to 6-ft) deep trenches or vertical holes. The refrigerant takes heat from the soil in winter and discharges heat to the soil in summer. Ground source systems are out of sight and require no maintenance. Noise is confined to a compressor in a small indoor mechanical room. These systems are often used in retrofits of schools with large land areas, and when historic structures have very limited indoor mechanical equipment spaces. Ground source heat pumps are more costly and more difficult to install than air-source pumps. However, they offer life-cycle savings and low energy bills, and require less maintenance.

A geo-exchange system was installed in the 1990s in a building near Central Park in New York City. Heat was taken from two wells drilled 458 meters (1500 ft) deep into bedrock. In Cambridge, Massachusetts, a co-housing project in a densely settled urban area features 41 living units with passive solar heat and central heating and cooling via ground-source heat pumps with locally controlled thermal zones. The system is relatively quiet and avoids discharging heat in the summer and cold air in the winter.

Heat pumps are either single package (unitary) systems, where both incoming and outgoing air passes through one piece of equipment, or split systems with both outside and inside components. Single package heat pumps are usually located on roofs for unlimited access to outdoor air and to isolate noise. With split systems, the noisy compressor and outdoor air fan are outdoors, away from the building's interior.

Ducts and Dampers

Ducts are either round or rectangular, and are made of metal or glass fiber. Flexible ducting is used to connect supply air registers to the main ductwork to allow adjustments in the location of ceiling fixtures, but is not permitted in exposed ceilings. Duct sizes are selected to control air velocity. The dimensions for ducts on construction drawings are usually the inside dimensions, and you can add an extra 51 mm (2 in.) to each dimension shown to account for the duct wall and insulation. Ductwork can be bulky and difficult to house compared to piping. With early coordination, ducts can be located within joist spaces and roof trusses, and between bulky recessed lighting fixtures.

Vertical duct shafts take up about 1 to 2 square meters for every 1000 square meters of floor served. In addition, fan rooms use up 2 to 4 percent of the total floor area served, rising to 6 to 8 percent for hospitals. Fan rooms are located to serve specific zones or levels. A single air-handling unit can serve between 8 and 20 floors. The smaller the number of floors, the smaller the vertical ducts can be.

Ductwork can be concealed or exposed. Concealed ductwork permits better isolation from the noise and vibration of equipment and from the flow of air. Surfaces are less complicated to clean, and less visible. Construction can be less meticulous, and construction costs are lower. It costs more to install visually acceptable exposed ductwork than to construct a ceiling to hide standard ducts. Concealed ductwork provides better architectural control over the appearance of the ceiling and wall surfaces. Access panels and doors or suspended ceilings must provide access for maintenance.

Rectangular medium- and high-velocity ducts can transmit excessive noise if not properly supported, stiffened, and lined with sound-absorbing material. Rigid round ducts are stronger, and have better aerodynamic characteristics, so they have fewer noise problems. High-velocity ducts can route air through a terminal box, called a sound trap or sound attenuator, which is lined with an acoustic absorber, to diminish noise. Air can also be slowed down as it enters a room, reducing the noise of friction through the ducts.

Ducts should be insulated and all joints and seams sealed for energy efficiency. All hot-air ducts passing through unheated spaces should be wrapped with insulation. Foil-faced, vinyl-faced, or rigid foam insulation can be used. Duct insulation should have a minimum rating of R-5 for cold climates, and an R-8 rating is even better. All joints or seams in the insulation should be sealed with duct tape.

Ducts will conduct noise from one space to another, so they are sometimes lined with sound-absorbing material. During the 1970s, cheaply made materials prone to deterioration were used to reduce noise in high-velocity locations. Damaged or improperly stored material has also been installed in ducts. In these cases, delamination of fiberglass in the duct linings resulted in glass particles in the air. Duct linings are still in use, but

better quality materials are installed with more care. Even good quality duct linings should not be used downstream from moisture, which can encourage the growth of mold and bacteria. In difficult acoustic situations, use double-walled ducts with lining enclosed between the walls.

Airborne dust is a common source of problems in a forced-air heating system. As air is pulled through the furnace, dust will readily adhere to oily or greasy components. Because household dust usually contains atomized cooking grease, even nonoily parts acquire a coat of fuzz. This will inhibit the cooling of the components, and when motors and bearings run hot, their lives are shortened. Dust can also clog furnace filters, restricting the flow of air. This places stress on the blower motor, reducing its efficiency and making it run hotter. To avoid these problems, remind clients that the registers in each room should be vacuumed at least once a month. Remove the air return grilles and clean the return duct as far as the vacuum cleaner will reach. Also, service the furnace filter and blower regularly.

To help you know what you are looking at on a job site, here are a few duct terms. Leaders are ducts that convey warm air from the furnace to stack or branch ducts. Stacks convey warm air from the leader vertically to a register on upper floors. The tapered section of duct forming a transition between two sections with different areas is called a gathering. A boot is a duct fitting forming the transition between two sections that vary in the shape of their cross sections. Manifolds are duct components that have several outlets for making multiple connections. The cold air return is the ductwork that conveys cool air back to the furnace for reheating. An extended plenum system is a perimeter heating system in which a main duct conveys warm air to a number of branch ducts, each of which serves a single floor register.

Perimeter heating is the term for a layout of warm air registers placed in or near the floor along exterior walls. A perimeter loop system consists of a loop of ductwork, usually embedded in a concrete ground slab, for distribution of warm air to each floor register. A perimeter radial system uses a leader from a centrally located furnace to carry warm air directly to each floor register.

A damper is a piece of metal positioned in the duct to open or close the duct to the passage of air. Dampers balance the system and adjust to the occupants' needs. Balancing dampers are hand operated, and locked in position after adjustment to correctly proportion airflow to all outlets. Motorized control dampers vary airflow in response to signals from automatic control systems.

Splitter dampers and turning vanes guide air within ducts to prevent turbulence and airflow resistance by turning the air smoothly. Splitter dampers are used where branch ducts leave larger trunk ducts. Turning vanes are used at right angle turns, where space is not available for larger radius turns. The flow of air within risers can be controlled by adjusting a damper in the basement at the foot of the riser. Dampers should be labeled to indicate which rooms they serve.

Large commercial structures have fire-rated partitions, floors, and ceilings that confine fires for specified periods of time. Air ducts through a fire barrier are required by codes to have fire dampers made of fire-resistive materials. A fire damper is normally held open, but in the event of a fire, a fusible link melts, releasing the catch that holds the damper open, thus closing it automatically. This prevents the spread of fire and smoke through the system. Access doors are normally installed at fire dampers for inspection and servicing.

Supply Registers, Diffusers, and Return Grilles

Air for heating, cooling, and ventilation is supplied through registers and diffusers (Fig. 24-13). Grilles are rectangular openings with fixed vertical or horizontal vanes or louvers through which air passes. A register is a grille with a damper directly behind the louvered face to regulate the volume of airflow. The selection and placement of supply and return openings requires architectural and engineering coordination, and has a distinct effect on the interior design of the space. Registers, diffusers, and grilles are selected for airflow capacity and velocity, pressure drop, noise factor, and appearance.

The register or diffuser that introduces air into the space should create an air pattern that maintains the desired air temperature, humidity, and motion with only minor horizontal or vertical variations. Unwanted obstructions result in uneven, ineffective delivery. Thermostats should not be in the direct line of the supply air stream, or the result will be erratic operation of the system. Room air always moves toward the outlet as it is replaced by new air. This often results in smudge marks from dirt particles in heavily used or smoky spaces. If the ceiling surface is textured, the accumulation of dirt is even heavier. This is often a problem with existing ceilings in renovation projects.

Diffusers have slats set at angles for deflecting warm or conditioned air from the outlet in various directions. Ceiling diffusers spread low-velocity air out from the ceiling. They may be round, square, rectangular, or lin-

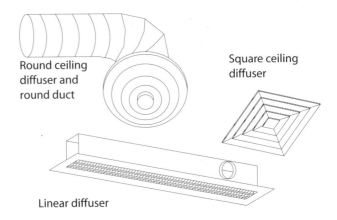

Round ceiling diffuser and round duct

Square ceiling diffuser

Linear diffuser

The slats in diffusers deflect air in various directions.

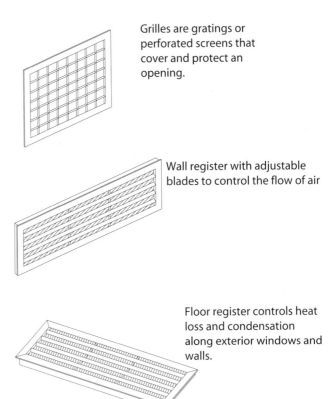

Grilles are gratings or perforated screens that cover and protect an opening.

Wall register with adjustable blades to control the flow of air

Floor register controls heat loss and condensation along exterior windows and walls.

Figure 24-13 Registers, diffusers, and grilles.

ear, or may be perforated ceiling tiles. In spaces where noise control is critical, like recording or telecasting studios, pinhole perforated diffusers can provide a large quantity of low-velocity air. Flat, linear slotted diffusers are used at the base of glass doors or windows. Careless placement of curtains, flowerpots, or other objects often obstruct floor diffusers.

Sidewall registers direct air above the space, parallel to the ceiling. Floor registers control heat loss and condensation along exterior windows and walls, and are commonly located in the floor below areas of glass. Perforated metal faceplates can be placed over standard ceiling diffusers, creating a uniform perforated ceiling. It is generally best to use a mixture of register types to accommodate both heating and cooling.

Air supply units are designed to distribute air perpendicular to the surface. The throw distance and spread or diffusion pattern of the supply outlet, as well as obstructions to the air distribution path, are considered in their placement. The throw distance is the distance a projected air stream travels from the outlet to a point where its velocity is reduced to a specified value. The air velocity and the shape of the outlet determine the throw. The spread is the extent to which projected air stream diffuses at the end of the throw. The spacing of outlets is approximately equal to their spread.

Return grilles are commonly louvered, eggcrate, or perforated designs. They may be referred to as either grilles or registers. Return grilles are connected to a duct, lead to an undivided plenum above the ceiling, or transfer air directly from one area to another.

Return grilles can be located to minimize the amount of return air ductwork. High return grilles pick up warmer air that needs less reheating. Air may circulate continuously, being warmed or cooled as needed. The slotted type of return grille is usually used in walls, and the grid type in floors. Floor grilles tend to collect dirt.

Return air inlets for heating systems are usually located near the floor and across the space from supply outlets. Return inlets for cooling are located in ceilings or high on walls to avoid removing cooled air that has just been supplied to the room. Exhaust air inlets are usually located in ceilings or high on walls, and are almost always ducted. Supply registers can also sometimes be used as return grilles.

Chapter

25

Cooling

The invention of air-conditioning has made sweltering summers more bearable. Sunbelt cities, such as Atlanta, Miami, and Houston, have grown larger thanks to air-conditioning, which has made it easier for people to live and work there year round by reducing the heat and humidity indoors. Mechanical cooling systems were originally developed as separate equipment, to be used in conjunction with mechanical heating equipment. Today, cooling equipment is often integrated into heating, ventilating, and air-conditioning (HVAC) systems, as we discuss later.

The earliest known home air-cooling systems were in use in Egypt around 3000 BC. Egyptian women put water in shallow clay trays on a bed of straw at sundown. The rapid evaporation from the water's surface and the damp sides of the tray combined with the night temperature drop to produce a thin film of ice on top, even though the air temperature was not below freezing. The low humidity aided evaporation, and the resulting cooling brought the temperature down enough to make ice.

Around 2000 BC, a wealthy Babylonian merchant developed a home air-conditioning system. At sundown, servants sprayed water on the walls and floor of a room. Evaporation plus nocturnal cooling brought relief from the heat.

Evaporative cooling was also used in ancient India. At night, wet grass mats were hung over openings on the westward side of the house. Water sprayed by hand or trickling from a perforated trough above the windows kept the mats wet through the night. When a gentle warm wind struck the cooler wet grass, evaporation cooled temperatures inside as much as 30°.

By the end of the nineteenth century, large restaurants and public places were embedding air pipes in a mixture of ice and salt, and circulating the cooled air with fans. The Madison Square Garden Theater in New York City used four tons of ice per night. None of these systems addressed how to remove humidity from warm air.

The term "air-conditioning" is credited to physicist Stuart W. Cramer, who presented a paper on humidity control in textile mills before the American Cotton Manufacturers Association in 1907. Willis Carrier, an upstate New York farm boy who won an engineering scholarship to Cornell University, produced the first commercial air conditioner in 1914. Carrier was fascinated with heating and ventilating systems. One year after his graduation from Cornell in 1902, he got his first air-cooling job for a Brooklyn lithographer and printer. Temperature and humidity fluctuations made paper expand and shrink. Ink flowed too freely or dried up, and colors varied. Carrier modified a conventional steam heater to accept cold water and fan-circulated cooled air. He calculated and balanced the air temperature and airflow, and succeeded in cooling the air and removing the humidity. Carrier is known today as the father of modern air-conditioning.

By 1919, Chicago had its first air-conditioned movie house. That same year, the Abraham & Strauss department store in New York was air-conditioned. In 1925, a 133-ton air-conditioning unit was installed in New York's Rivoli Theater. By the summer of 1930, over 300 theaters were air-conditioned, drawing in hordes of people for the cooling as well as the movie. By the end of the 1930s, stores and office buildings claimed that air-conditioning increased workers' productivity enough to offset the cost. Workers were even coming early and staying late to stay cool.

Today, cooling accounts for 20 percent of the energy use in the United States, and 40 percent in the southern states alone. One-third of the U.S. population spends substantial amounts of time in air-conditioned environments. Two-thirds of U.S. homes have air conditioners. Residential air conditioning uses almost 5 percent of all energy in the United States—over $10 billion worth—and adds about 100 million tons of carbon dioxide to the atmosphere from the electric power generation stations that use fossil fuels.

The combination of air conditioning with electric lights has had a profound effect on the design of buildings. With fewer windows needed for ventilation and daylighting, interior spaces became windowless. Less need for daylight penetration also lowered ceilings, encouraged designs with less exterior wall area, and permitted using less exterior land space for the building itself.

Although the term "air-conditioning" is often associated only with cooling, it actually has a broader meaning. Air-conditioning is the treatment of air so that its temperature, humidity, cleanliness, quality, and motion are maintained as appropriate for the building's occupants, a particular process, or some object in the space.

Engineers use some common terms when discussing air conditioning. The rate at which heat needs to be removed from air is referred to as the cooling load. The capacity of equipment is its ability to remove heat. The total load on a cooling system equals its heat gain, which is almost the same thing as saying its cooling load, although from the engineer's viewpoint there is a technical difference.

DESIGN STRATEGIES FOR COOLING

To make an air conditioner effective, you have to close yourself up tightly in your building to keep the cooled air from escaping. When you shut out the summertime heat, you shut yourself in. You miss the fresh air, the smells and sounds of the yard, and the pleasure of relaxing on a shaded deck or porch. The natural cooling features of the building can decrease your reliance on air conditioning during hot weather. By improving ventilation and air movement inside and by providing shade outside, you can conserve energy, cut utility bills, and enjoy summer more without being held hostage by the heat.

We have already looked at several design techniques that can reduce cooling loads and increase comfort. Shading with horizontal overhangs on southern exposures keeps out the sun's heat. Shaded areas on the building's face can also serve as balconies, porches, verandas, and cantilevered upper floors. Covered awnings, screens, landscaping plants, and other shading devices keep the sun's heat outside.

Cooling issues frequently have a relationship to building form and daylighting decisions. The number and location of openings that allow in the breeze, and the need to close them sometimes to retain cool air, affect the building's appearance and the amount of daylight admitted. East and west windows may be minimized to keep direct sun out of the building. The amount of exposure to daylight needed in the winter may be enough to cause overheating in the summer.

Natural ventilation offsets higher air temperatures by increased air motion. This is especially effective in humid, hot climates with little change between day and night temperatures. Building designs for natural ventilation are very open to breezes, but closed to direct sun. Such buildings are often thermally lightweight, as night air is not cool enough in some locations to remove stored daytime heat. A good design for cooling brings in outdoor air when the exterior temperature is 25°C (77°F) or lower, and closes the building up tight on hot days while opening it up at night. When designing for cooling, the need to keep hot air out is balanced by the need for fresh air and comfortable breezes.

Cross ventilation is driven by wind through windows. Buildings with narrow floor plans with large ventilation openings on both sides favor cross ventilation. This type of layout also works well for daylighting. Stack ventilation uses very low openings to admit outside air, and very high openings to exhaust rising hot air. Stack ventilation is generally weaker than cross ventilation.

The structure of the building may be able to absorb heat by day, and be flushed by cool air at night. High thermal mass cooling works well in places with warm, dry summers. The thermal mass of the building stays cool during the hot daytime, and the heat drains away slowly during the cool night. Such buildings use thermal mass on the floors, walls, or roofs. Fans are often used with high thermal mass systems. Large, high buildings with concrete structures are good candidates for high thermal mass cooling.

 In a high thermal mass design, the building needs a heat sink, a place from which heat is ejected at night. The roof can radiate heat to a cold night sky, but needs protection from exposure to the sun by day. The masonry courtyards of traditional Mediterranean buildings use *toldos*, movable shading devices that protect the courtyard floors and roofs, and open to the sky at night.

Roof ponds collect water that has been sprayed over the roof at night in a storage pond, which can also be used for passive solar heating. Sliding panels of insulation over bags of water are opened on winter days to capture the sun. On summer nights, the panels are again opened to radiate heat to the sky.

When mechanical cooling is required, sometimes it can run at night when electrical power is least expensive. Incoming air can be precooled to reduce the equipment's cooling load. For buildings with relatively short but intense peak load periods, the space, its contents, and the surrounding mass can be precooled to a desired temperature prior to occupancy. This increases the amount of heat that can be soaked up by the building when the daily heat gain is at its peak. Precooling minimizes the amount of heat released to the room air during the peak period. Precooling works where the building has high thermal storage capacity, or where the cooling system is more efficient during cooler night periods. The occupancy patterns of churches and theaters offer opportunities to use precooling.

Fans can be very effective in cooling small buildings. A person perceives a decrease of 1°C for every 2.5 meters per minute (1°F per 15 feet per minute—fpm) increase in the speed of air past the body. The air motion produced varies with the fan's height above the floor, the number of fans in the space, and the fan's power, speed, and blade size.

The American Society of Heating, Refrigerating, and Air-Conditioning Engineers' (ASHRAE's) acceptable temperature range for people wearing light summer clothes is 22°C to 26°C (72°F–78°F) at between 35 and 60 percent relative humidity. A slow-turning ceiling mounted paddle fan can extend this comfort range to about 28°C (82°F).

 The correct size for a ceiling fan is determined by the size of the room in which it is located. A 91-cm (36-in.) diameter fan is adequate for a 9-square-meter (100-square-ft) room. For a 3.9-square-meter (150-square-ft) room, use a 107-cm (42-in.) fan; for a 21-square-meter (225-square-ft) room, a 122-cm

(48-in.) fan; and for a 35-square-meter (375-square-ft) room, a 132-cm (52-in.) diameter fan. Two fans are required for rooms over 37 square meters (400 square ft).

Two out of three homes have ceiling fans, but most of these fans have inefficient blade shapes and motors. Residential ceiling fans often include incandescent lights, which increase the heat in the room. In addition, the heat from the motor adds to the room's heat, and the fan only cools you if it moves air past you.

Many people believe that using ceiling fans will reduce energy use, because occupants can raise the thermostat setting point two or three degrees thanks to the cooling effect of the air movement. A study by the Florida Solar Energy Center looked at 400 new homes in central Florida, with an average of four or five ceiling fans that operated 13 to 14 hours per day. Surprisingly, the survey and monitoring revealed no correlation between using ceiling fans and saving energy. Instead, a computer simulation showed a potential energy use increase of 10 percent. Apparently, the energy that runs all those fans exceeds the potential savings of lowering the thermostat setting.

Ceiling fans are now part of the ENERGY STAR® program for energy efficiency. New ceiling fans with aerodynamically curved fan blades are being marketed through national home building supply stores. These innovative fans are more efficient, and as a result can be run at lower speeds, saving energy. They use fluorescent lights with electronic ballasts, which are more energy efficient and produce less heat. Remote controls and temperature sensors make it easier to use the fan only when it will improve conditions in the room. When run at a low speed in the winter, a ceiling fan will bring warm air that has stratified at the ceiling back down to body level.

Attic fans decrease air-conditioning costs by reducing the temperature in the attic, and protect attic spaces from condensation damage in the winter. They are activated by heat and moisture. Some roof-mounted fans are available with energy-efficient, quiet motors. Gable fans come with louvers that can be automatically controlled, for houses without louvered vents in the attic.

Window fans should be located on the downwind side of a house, facing outward to increase air flow. Open a window in each room and leave interior doors open. Window fans don't work well in long, narrow hallways, or in buildings with many small rooms and interior partitions.

A whole house fan removes heat from a central area and exhausts it through a ventilated attic. The fan is mounted in the hallway ceiling on the top floor of the building, and blows air into the attic. It is covered on the bottom with a louvered vent. The fan develops a continuous draft that draws air in through open windows and doors and blows it out through the attic, maintaining a steady, cooling breeze throughout the house. A whole house fan costs about the same as three or four window fans. Operating the fan costs less than operating the air conditioner, so it is a good cooling alternative if the outdoor temperature isn't too high.

Whole house fans should have at least two speeds. Belt-driven models have low speed fans (700 rpm or less) for quiet operation. For proper ventilation and efficient operation, any whole house fan requires adequate, unobstructed outlets in the attic through soffits vents, grilles, or louvers, equal to 1 square foot for every 300 cubic feet per minute (cfm) of air moved. The opening size of the ventilation area in the attic, excluding the area blocked by screens or louvers, must be at least twice the free opening size of the fan. Several windows should remain open in the house when the fan is in use. The fan should have manual controls, even if it also has automatic controls, and a fusible link for shutdown in the event of fire. Careful installation will avoid vibrations.

EVAPORATIVE COOLING

When moisture is added to air, the relative humidity increases and we perceive the temperature to have decreased. This works where the air is very dry and not too hot, and requires a large quantity of water and outdoor air. For centuries, fountains have cooled courtyards in hot arid climates. Passive evaporative cooling systems can be as simple as a sprinkler on the roof of a conventional building, or as complex as a roof pond with adjustable louvers.

Outdoor conditions in about half of the United States are suitable for mechanical evaporative cooling. Known as swamp coolers or desert coolers, evaporative coolers (Fig. 25-1) are also used in high-heat applications such as restaurant kitchens. Dry fresh air from outdoors is circulated through a wet pad, where it absorbs moisture as water vapor. After use, the air exits the building through grilles or open windows. Evaporative coolers are often located on the roof. Through-wall coolers are also common.

When the outdoor air is at 41°C (105°F) and the relative humidity is a low 10 percent, evaporative cooling can produce indoor air at 26°C (78°F) and 50 percent relative humidity with only the power necessary to operate a fan. However, the fans that drive evaporative coolers are noisy, and the aroma of the wetted cooler may be unpleasant.

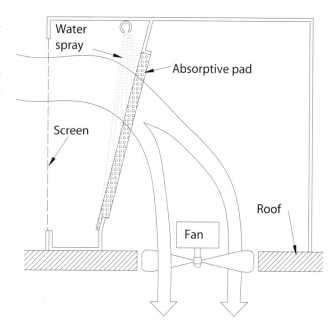

Figure 25-1 Evaporative cooler.

Misting or fogging systems make people feel cooler with no total change in the heat content of the treated air. Roof sprays have been used in the past to keep poorly insulated roofs cool. Misting can be used for small outdoor areas, such as team benches at football stadiums or refreshment pavilions. It has also been used in very large spaces in hot dry climates, including a railroad station in Atocha, Spain, and a conservatory in Michigan. Night roof spray thermal storage systems cool water on the roof at night via radiation and evaporation. The water is stored on or below the roof for use the next day in building cooling, or in a tank to precool entering air.

Indirect evaporative cooling actually uses both direct and indirect evaporative techniques, and may be combined with direct refrigerant cooling systems. Warm, dry outdoor air that has been cooled by evaporation is passed through a rock bed under a building at night. The next day, very hot dry air is cooled by passing through the rock bed, and then through an evaporative cooler.

PROCESS OF AIR-CONDITIONING

When all else fails and the outdoor temperature climbs, we must choose to suffer the heat or turn on the air-conditioning. In order to understand the discussions that take place between your client, the architect, the engineers, and the contractors, you should have a basic understanding of air conditioning.

Let's look at how an air conditioner works. A fan sucks warm indoor air across a series of coils containing refrigerants and blows it back into the room. The refrigerant absorbs heat in the evaporator and then exhausts it outside through another system of fans and coils in the condenser. When the indoor air cools, it also dehumidifies. The moisture taken out of the air condenses on the cool coils just like water collects on a glass of iced lemonade on a hot day. The water runs down a drain or drips off the air conditioner outside. The lower humidity of the conditioned air contributes to the cooling effect you feel.

Air-conditioning cools by removing sensible heat—the heat transferred by the motion of molecules—from the air. As we already know, the transfer of sensible heat requires a temperature difference between a warmer area and a cooler one. A surface, such as a coil or a cooling panel, is placed in contact with the air and kept at a temperature below that of the air by continuous extraction of heat. If the temperature of this surface is below the dew point temperature of the air, condensation will form on it. The air, in losing moisture because of the condensation, also loses latent heat—the heat transfer that takes place because of a change in the structure of the molecules. Consequently, it is both cooled and dehumidified. The condensation must be drained away from the air-conditioning equipment, so the equipment needs a drain.

A well-designed air-conditioning system must eliminate both the heat and humidity unintentionally leaking into the building or generated within it, and that introduced with air for ventilation. Engineers try to design air-conditioning systems that are large enough to assure adequate comfort, but not so large that they cycle on and off too frequently, which would wear out the equipment faster. With some equipment, excessive cycling on and off results in decreased efficiency and more energy use.

REFRIGERATION CYCLES

As we have just seen, when humid summer air is cooled to a temperature below the dew point, the condensation that forms is collected in a metal pan and drained away. The dew point is, by definition, 100 percent relative humidity, which is uncomfortable even in cooled air. Since cooler air can hold less water, cooling the air to an even lower temperature reduces the humidity level even further. When the super-cooled air is then reheated, the relative humidity at the new, desirable level is lower and more comfortable. The power for reheating the air

comes from a hot water or steam coil, and the chilled air is usually also mixed with warmer room air.

The mechanical equipment in buildings can rapidly concentrate heating and cooling on demand. In larger buildings, a central heating and cooling device is adjusted to individual spaces, or conditions are controlled within the space served. This greatly reduces the amount of distribution ducts required.

The refrigeration cycle, which is used for cooling, is also used in heating. The mechanical refrigeration equipment in HVAC systems uses two types of heat transfer processes: the compression cycle and the absorption cycle. Both of these cooling cycles have a hot side and a cold side. The cold side is used for cooling, while the hot side can provide supplemental heat in cold weather by being used as a heat pump. In large buildings, the perimeter areas may need to be heated in cool weather, while the interior spaces may need ventilation and cooling.

Compression Refrigeration

Most common home air-conditioning systems use a compressor cycle, similar to that of a refrigerator. A compressor on the outside of the house is filled with a refrigerant, which is a fluid that can change back and forth between a liquid and a gas. As it changes, it absorbs or releases heat, so that it can carry heat from inside the house to the outside. It uses a lot of electricity to take heat from the cooler inside of the house and dump it in the warmer outside.

Air conditioners work by circulating a refrigerant through two sets of coils in one continuous loop. One set, the evaporator coils, cools the room; the other set, the condenser coils, gives off heat to the outdoors. Between them, a barrier (the expansion valve) keeps the two parts from working against each other. Near the barrier and as part of the refrigerant loop is the compressor. The two fans help transfer the heat from the air to the coils, and then to the outside air.

When the condenser coils and compressor work together to remove heat from the system, it is called the compression cycle (Fig. 25-2). The compressor circulates the refrigerant and compresses it. In the compressor, heat energy is released as the refrigerant changes from vapor to a liquid state. The released heat is absorbed by cooling water and pumped from the building, or absorbed by fan-blown air and pushed to the outdoors. Heated water may be dumped into sewers, or may release heat through evaporation and convection in an outdoor cooling tower. The cooling water is then recir-

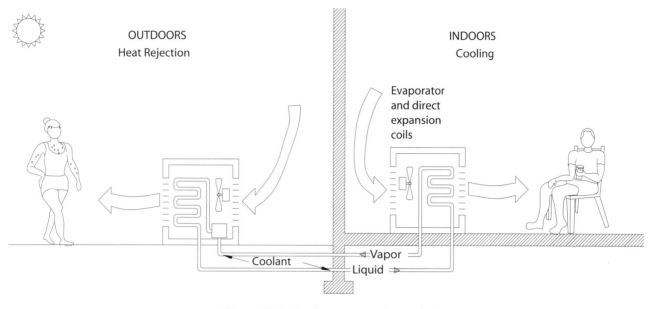

Figure 25-2 Cooling compression cycle.

culated to warm vapor emerging from the compressor to liquefy the refrigerant at fairly high pressures. The warm liquid refrigerant then passes through the expansion valve, and as it evaporates in the evaporator, it cools the chilled water system.

Compression refrigeration systems in small buildings transfer heat from one circulating water system (chilled water) to another (condenser water), and the system is referred to as a water-to-water system. Cooling takes place by changing a refrigerant from a liquid to a vapor. Heat can be extracted from water or from air.

The compression refrigeration process essentially pumps heat out of the chilled water system and into the condenser water system, continually repeating the cycle. Water or air cooled by the expansion (evaporator) coils is distributed throughout the building, absorbing heat from occupants, machinery, lighting, and building surfaces, and then returned for another chilling cycle.

With an air-to-air system, indoor air is cooled by passing over an evaporator coil in which refrigerant is expanding from liquid to gas. This direct expansion gives these evaporator coils the name DX coils. The compressor and condenser unit is often located outdoors, because it is noisy and hot. The cooled air is distributed through the ducts of a warm air heating system.

A refrigerant is a gas at normal temperatures and pressures, so it can vaporize at low temperatures. Freon, the most common refrigerant up to the 1990s, can escape into the atmosphere as chlorofluorocarbon (CFC)

gases. These CFCs have long atmospheric lives, up to 145 years for CFC-12, and lead to ozone depletion, so even with the worldwide ban on the production of CFCs in the 1990s, they will be around for a long time. Many existing older CFC chillers still haven't been replaced. In addition, there is currently a black market demand for the CFC-containing refrigerant Freon. This is despite the fact that ozone depletion increases the burning of skin by ultraviolet (UV) radiation from the sun, resulting in skin cancers, eye cataracts, and possible damage to crop production. Hydrochlorofluorocarbons (HCFCs) are still a threat to the environment but are less harmful than CFCs. Because they contain chlorine, which leads to ozone depletion, HCFCs are also being phased out.

Hydrofluorocarbons (HFCs) also pose some threat of global warming and have long atmospheric lifetimes, but have low toxicity and are nonflammable. Natural hydrocarbons (HCs) have a negligible effect on global warming and short atmospheric life. However, they are flammable and explosive. Lower-threat alternative refrigerants may use more energy, which may mean more fossil fuel use and more pollution. Production of refrigerants with photovoltaic energy is an alternative.

Ammonia is a refrigerant that is acutely toxic and flammable. Fortunately, its distinctive odor warns of leaks. Use of ammonia as a refrigerant requires regular maintenance, good ventilation, and good access and escape routes. Equipment must be kept in closed mechanical rooms.

Absorption Refrigeration

Another type of air-conditioning system uses a salt solution to cool spaces (Fig. 25-3). In the absorption cycle, water vapor is attracted to a concentrated salt solution, which absorbs water from the evaporator vessel. The water cools rapidly as it is evaporated into the evaporator vessel. The water is now diluting the salt solution in the evaporator. The diluted salt solution is drawn off from the vessel continually, sprayed into a piece of equipment called a generator that boils excess water off, and returned to repeat the absorption cycle. The steam that boils off condenses at a condenser with cool water or air, and returns to the evaporator vessel. The cooled water left in the evaporator can be tapped through a heat exchanger as a source of chilled water.

Absorption cycles are about half as efficient as compression cycles. Energy for the system can come from the sun or from high-temperature waste heat from steam or hot water. Even though an absorption cycle is less efficient, it may use less energy, since it can use lower-grade heat to run a generator, as opposed to the electricity the compression cycle uses for its compressor.

Desiccant Cooling

Cooling with desiccants does not use any refrigerants with CFCs. Desiccants are porous materials, such as silica gel, activated alumina, and synthetic polymers with a high affinity for water vapor, that lower humidity without overcooling the air. In active desiccant systems, desiccants are heated with natural gas or solar energy to drive out the moisture that they have removed from the air. Passive systems use the heat from the building's exhaust air to release and vent moisture removed from incoming air.

COOLING EQUIPMENT

Air-conditioning systems range from small window units to very large air conditioners integrated into a building's HVAC system. Some air-conditioning components are noisy, and most must be protected from excessive sun, and all use a lot of energy.

As we mentioned previously, an air conditioner em-

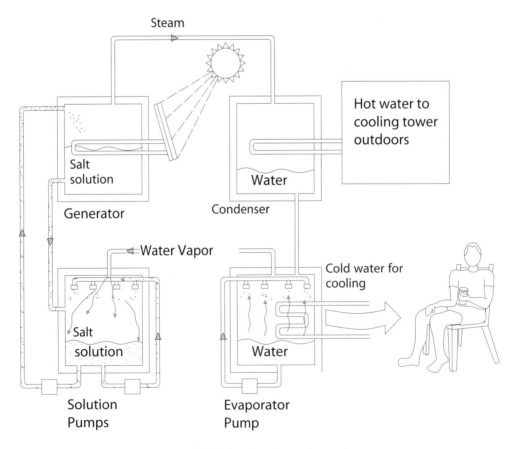

Figure 25-3 Cooling absorption cycle.

ploys a condenser, which is a heat exchanger used in a refrigeration cycle to discharge heat to the outside environment. Air-cooled condensers, which are less expensive and don't require as much maintenance as water-cooled units, are common on small refrigeration systems. Medium-sized systems may use water or air. Large condensers are water cooled for higher efficiency, but have higher installation and maintenance costs.

In the early days of air-conditioning, city-supplied water was run through water-cooled condensers to pick up waste heat before going into the sewer. This wasted water and increased the burden on the sewer system, and is now prohibited in most large communities. Today condenser water is typically recirculated through a cooling tower, where the heat is given off to the atmosphere. Evaporative condensers are a cross between a cooling tower and an air-cooled condenser. They use less energy than a water-cooled condenser with a cooling tower and are more efficient.

Packaged Terminal Air Conditioners

Packaged terminal air conditioners (PTAC) are factory-assembled units that can be added to a building as needed and located in the space to be served. Each unit contains a compressor, condenser, expansion valve, and evaporator. Available PTACs include window air conditioners, through-wall room units, and heat pumps, which we discussed earlier. Most through-wall units are located near the floor, and look like a wall mounted fan-coil unit (FCU) below the window.

PTACs are simple to install, and permit occupants to have direct thermal control of the space. They offer individual metering for separate tenants. Removal for repair or replacement is easy, and the failure of a unit affects only one room. There is no need for ductwork, a central chiller, a cooling tower, pumps, or piping, which saves space and money.

Unit Air Conditioners

Unit air conditioners are small, electrically powered PTACs mounted in windows or exterior walls. The unit air conditioner is the most common piece of mechanical equipment in the United States. They are common in new and existing rooms and buildings. Unit air conditioners are easy to select, install, and service or replace. They provide the option of separate zones for individual apartments or motel rooms. If they are turned on only as needed, they may offer energy savings.

Unit air conditioners (Fig. 25-4) are not as efficient as a larger central unit, however, especially if a fuel other than electricity would power the larger unit. They don't offer energy-conserving options like exchange of waste heat. Unit air conditioners are noisy and, due to high air velocity, can cause drafts. Sometimes the noise is welcome, as it can mask street noise. In moderate climates, air can be circulated either through cold-side or hot-side coils, using the unit as a heat pump to cool in hot weather and heat in cool weather. This doesn't work economically in very cold weather, when there is not enough heat outdoors.

In many homes, a room air-conditioning unit is installed in the window or wall with the compressor located outside. The efficiency of air-conditioning equipment is listed on an EnergyGuide label. Room air conditioners measure energy efficiency with the energy efficiency ratio (EER), which divides the cooling output in

---

The tight layout for the retail store left only one space for the cash/wrap desk to go, and that turned out to be right next to the old, ugly, and highly visible air-handling unit. Richard thought he could probably tuck the desk into the available space with enough room around it for staff and customers, and covering the unit to improve its appearance wouldn't be too difficult. The tricky parts would be providing access to the unit for repairs and maintenance, and hiding the large air intake grille.

Once Richard had worked out the space planning issues and come up with a finish materials palette, he addressed the air-handling unit. He enclosed the unit in veneer plywood stained to match the adjacent woodwork. The plywood panels were attached with screws that were covered by removable wood plugs, so that the panels could be taken down for major maintenance. They also provided a perfect spot for a sign.

The air intake grille, which was about 2 ft square and near the floor, faced directly out toward the customer side of the desk. Richard designed a counter just to the side of the unit that butted up against the front of the unit. The counter gave the store a spot for impulse and informational items adjacent to where the customers would stand, and the grille was much less visible hidden below the counter. Maintenance personnel could duck under the counter to remove the grill and replace the filter. The solution worked fine and looked great.

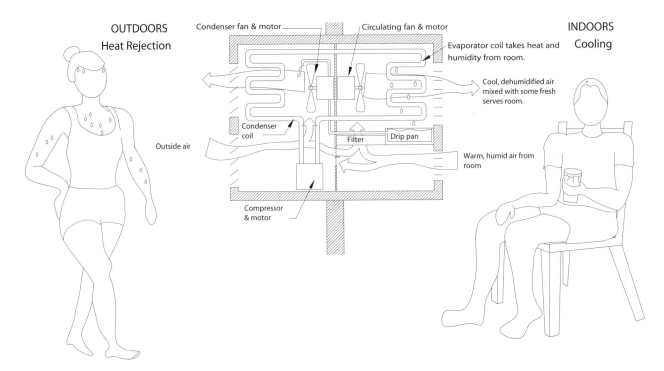

Figure 25-4 Unit air conditioner.

Btu by the power consumption. On average, the 1990 standard requires a minimum EER of about 8.6. New room air conditioners, as of October 2000, must have an average EER rating of around 10, and even stricter regulations are under consideration by the federal government.

Window air-conditioning units are also best kept out of direct sun, so east or west windows are to be avoided. The north wall of the house, or possibly the south wall, is a possibility.

Some home air conditioners save energy with a fan-only switch that allows you to use cooler, nonconditioned outside air at night. A filter check light reminder for maintenance and an automatic delay fan switch that turns the fan off a few minutes after the compressor shuts off also improve energy efficiency. Quiet operation, which is not usually rated, is a valuable feature, but you will probably have to turn the air conditioner on to check this out. Highly energy-efficient units may not dehumidify as well as less efficient units. Air conditioners must be kept clean and refrigerant must be recharged as needed to keep efficiency up.

Central Residential Air Conditioners

Some homes have central air conditioners that cool the entire house, with a large compressor unit outside. Central air conditioners are rated by the seasonal energy efficiency ratio (SEER), which takes the seasonal cooling output in Btus and divides it by the seasonal energy input in watt-hours for an average U.S. climate. Many older home central air conditioners have SEER ratings between 6 and 7. In 1988, the average SEER for central air conditioners was around 9, but the minimum requirement has been raised to 10. To earn an ENERGY STAR® certification, the air conditioner must achieve a SEER of 12 or higher.

Building codes regulate the permissible amount of energy use for residential heating and cooling systems. The American National Standards Institute (ANSI) and the American Society of Heating, Refrigeration, and Air-Conditioning Engineers (ASHRAE) have jointly put forth Standard 90.2–1993, *Energy Efficient Design of New Low-Rise Residential Building*. ASHRAE, along with Board of Standards Review (BSR) of the American National Standards Institute (ANSI) has published BSR/ASHRAE/IESNA 90.1, *Energy Standard for Buildings Except Low-Rise Residential Buildings*. These standards set minimum efficiency ratings for heating and cooling equipment.

In addition to the EER and SEER, several other ratings apply, depending upon the size and type of equipment. The annual fuel utilization efficiency (AFUE) rating is a ratio of the annual fuel output energy to annual input energy. The coefficient of performance (COP) assesses the rate of heat removal for cooling equipment, and the efficiency of heat pump systems for heating. The integrated part load value (IPLV) expresses the efficiency of air-conditioning and heat pump equipment.

The location of the air-conditioning equipment for a residence or small commercial building will frequently influence both the interior design and the landscaping close to the building. A cool, shaded outdoor location is best for the compressor. The north side of a house under trees or tall shrubs is a good choice, as long as the plantings don't block the unit's ability to dump heat. Because of exposure to direct sun, a rooftop or the east or west side of the building is usually a poor choice of location. Compressors are noisy and should be kept away from patios or bedroom windows.

Residential Heat Pumps for Air-Conditioning

In climates without extreme temperature changes, residences may employ heat pumps that can be reversed for heating the house in the winter. Residential heat pumps are electrically powered heating and cooling units. They are similar to through-wall units, but reverse the cycle to pump heat from outside in the winter. Room size heat pumps may distribute heating or cooling from water to air or from air to air. As we discussed previously, water source units are called hydronic heat pumps. They require a piping loop connected to a central boiler, and a cooling tower. Heat pumps are usually located on the south side of the building for heating and cooling, especially in cooler climates. A sunscreen can be added in the summer.

For cooling, heat pumps use a normal compressive refrigeration cycle to absorb and transfer excess heat to the outdoors. For heating, heat energy is drawn from outdoor air by switching the air heating and cooling ducts (the heat exchange functions of the condenser and evaporator remain the same).

Earth Tubes

Earth tubes cool air before it enters a building. A fan forces air through long underground tubes. These tubes are sometimes located in trenches designed for underground water lines or other purposes.

Chapter 26

Heating, Ventilating, and Air-Conditioning (HVAC) Systems

•••

Now that we have reviewed both mechanical heating and cooling systems, it is time to look at how they are used together. A heating, ventilating, and air-conditioning (HVAC) system integrates mechanical equipment into one complex system that is designed to provide thermal comfort and air quality throughout a building. The difficulty of doing this is apparent when we consider that a building may be hot from the sun on one side, colder on the other, and warm in its interior, all at the same time on a winter day. Keeping everyone inside the building comfortable while conserving energy is a formidable task.

In the 1960s, when energy costs were low, architects, engineers, and building owners didn't worry about how easily heat was transmitted through the building envelope. Dramatic architectural effects like all-glass buildings took precedence over energy conservation. Omitting roof and wall insulation minimized initial building costs. The HVAC system designer made the building comfortable by using as much mechanical equipment as necessary.

With increased fuel costs, energy has become one of the largest expenses in any building's operating budget. Some energy conservation strategies came at the expense of comfort. The better the building interior is isolated from severe outside conditions, the more comfortable the occupants remain.

The design of the building envelope influences comfort in the way it transmits heat to surfaces and slowly changes air temperature. Air and surface temperatures can often be controlled by passive design techniques. Air motion and air humidity contribute to comfortable cooling. Access to outdoor air improves air quality, and also provides daylight, view, and solar heat on cold days.

There are limits to what can be accomplished without mechanical systems. It is difficult to get the building itself to provide adequate air motion for comfort when temperatures exceed 31°C (88°F). Without some way to remove humidity from the air, most North American buildings are clammy in summer and mold becomes a serious problem. It is difficult to filter air without the use of fans. All this leaves the mechanical designer with the job of deciding whether mechanical equipment will supplement and modify conditions occasionally, always modify and control the interior environment, or permanently exclude the outdoor environment.

The temperature, humidity, purity, distribution, and motion of air within interior building spaces are all controlled simultaneously by an HVAC system. These systems use air, water, or both to distribute heating and cooling energy. Systems include furnaces that supply hot air and boilers that heat water or produce steam. Some

194

systems include electric heaters that use electrical resistance to convert electricity to heat.

The mechanical engineer selects the HVAC system based on performance, efficiency, and initial and life costs of the system. The engineer considers the availability of fuel, power, air and water, and the means for their delivery and storage. The need for access to outdoor air is taken into account. The system is evaluated for its flexibility to serve different zones with different demands. The type and layout of the distribution system for heating and cooling is reviewed, with an eye to laying out efficient, short, direct runs while minimizing the number of turns and offsets, to minimize friction losses.

The equipment of an HVAC system can take up 10 to 15 percent of the building area. The size requirements for a building depend on the heating and cooling loads. Some pieces require additional access space for service and maintenance. Codes may require mechanical areas to have noise and vibration control and fire resistant enclosures. Heavy equipment may need additional structural support.

CENTRALIZED VERSUS LOCAL EQUIPMENT

The designer of the mechanical system for a building looks at whether the building's needs are dominated by heating or by cooling concerns. Because climate is such a strong factor in small buildings and heating and cooling needs may vary room by room, localized equipment rather than a centralized system may be the better choice. A local system can respond more rapidly to individual room needs and scheduling differences. No large central equipment spaces are needed, as equipment can be distributed throughout the building or over the roof in the case of low-rise buildings. Distribution trees are shorter, and breakdowns are localized. Control systems are greatly simplified. Energy is conserved when heating and cooling is used only as needed.

On the other hand, the noise from many machines all over the building can be objectionable. The presence of maintenance workers within occupied areas can be disruptive. Multiple pieces of equipment mean many filters to clean and change to assure air quality. There is less opportunity to use waste energy than with a centralized system.

Central systems have some distinct advantages. The equipment has its own space, and does not take up room within occupied spaces. Maintenance need not interrupt room activities. Energy recovery from boilers and chillers is possible in a central equipment room. Centralized mechanical spaces concentrate the noise and heat for easier control. Air intakes can be high above street pollution, and regular maintenance of centralized air filtering equipment results in longer equipment life.

Mechanical rooms need to be centrally located near the area served, with direct access to the outside for fresh air and for installation and removal of equipment. Achieving both a central location and outside access is often difficult. Rooms for heating, cooling, and air-handling equipment need ceilings around 3.7 meters (12 ft) high.

Distribution trees of centralized systems are larger and controls are more complex than for localized systems. Breakdown of a single piece of equipment may affect the entire building. Energy is wasted when the entire system is activated to serve one zone.

INTERIOR DESIGN IMPLICATIONS

Uniformity in the design of the building has implications for the HVAC system and for the interior design of the building. Uniform ceiling heights, lighting placement, and HVAC grille locations increase flexibility in office arrangements and extend the building's useful lifespan. Four basic types of office space can be interchanged within a flexible overall plan. These include enclosed offices; bullpen offices with repeated, identical workstations with desk-height dividers; uniform open plan offices with higher partitions; and free-form open plan offices with partitions of varying heights. However, uniformity in ceiling lighting, air handling, and size can make design of connecting corridors, lounges, and other support services difficult.

On the other hand, diverse design elements require complete and detailed design of a space, but the resulting design may be a more complex and interesting building for designer, builder, and user. Variety aids user orientation and distinguishes spaces from one another.

Some spaces require diverse thermal conditions. In winter, we expect offices to be relatively warmer than circulation spaces, which are transitional from the exterior to the interior. Just like a space can seem lighter and higher if preceded by a lower, darker space, transitional spaces that are closer to outside temperatures can make key spaces seem more comfortable without extreme heating or cooling, saving energy over the life of the building.

The design of the air-circulation and ventilation system interacts with the layout of furniture. Even furniture like filing cabinets and acoustic screens less than 1.5 meters (5 ft) high can impede air circulation, especially if they extend to the floor. Some sources recommend an open space of at least 25 to 51 mm (1–2 in.) at the base for furniture pieces, with 152 mm (6 in.) allowing even better airflow. If walls or full-height partitions enclose spaces, each enclosed space should have one supply vent and one return or exhaust vent.

HVAC ZONES

The numbers and types of HVAC zones required for thermal comfort influence the selection of centralized versus local HVAC equipment systems. A zone placed away from the building envelope may not have the access to outdoor air required for a localized system. Space must be available for equipment within a local zone.

Large multipurpose buildings conventionally use a system of 16 zones (Fig. 26-1). Each function—apartments, offices, and stores—has five zones: north, east, south, and west sides, and a central core. Underground parking is the sixteenth zone. Each of these zones may encompass more than one floor. Adding in scheduling considerations may increase the number of zones. If apartments need individual controls, each apartment may become one zone.

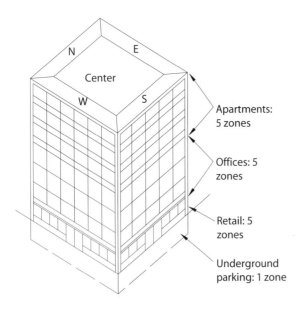

Figure 26-1 Building perimeter and interior zones.

TYPES OF HVAC SYSTEMS

There are hundreds of types of HVAC systems in use in large buildings, but most can be classified into one of four main categories. One type, direct refrigerant systems, are heating and cooling systems that respond directly to the needs of individual zones. The other three, all-air, air and water, and all-water systems, produce heating and cooling in a central location, far from some zones. Air-handling equipment for these last three systems is either central or located on each floor.

As the size of a building's structural elements has decreased due to improved material strength, the size of building mechanical systems has increased. Where smaller structural elements leave more floor area open, more flexibility in space planning is possible. Mechanical components are often located at or within structural columns. It is common to have a structural column with an air duct crossing it at the top. Because the moving parts of the mechanical system need maintenance and change with user needs but the structure rarely changes, it is impractical to wrap the mechanical system completely inside the structural envelope.

Exposing the mechanical system within the space permits easy access for maintenance, repair, and alteration. Exposed systems may add visual interest. Office buildings sometimes expose the HVAC system in corridors and service areas, but conceal it in offices. Exposed systems aid flexibility and reveal elements that users can manipulate, reminding them of the opportunity and encouraging user interaction.

A dramatic example of an exposed system is the Centre Georges Pompidou in Paris, designed by Piano + Rogers, Architects. This design competition winner houses a museum of modern art, reference library, center for industrial design, and center for music and acoustics research, and supporting services. The structural and mechanical systems, including columns, ductwork, and piping, are revealed through the building facade in a way reminiscent of the Visible Man models that show the muscles, organs, and circulatory system of the human body.

The location of centralized HVAC equipment in a large building has implications for the building's space use and function. The heat, noise, moisture, air motion, and vibration from equipment may annoy adjacent floors or neighboring buildings. Mechanical floors can be used to separate floors of apartments from floors of offices, isolating daytime-use spaces from housing used more heavily at night. Very large buildings often require several intermediate mechanical floors. Basement locations offer noise isolation, utility access, and support for heavy machinery. Rooftops provide access to air for rejecting excess heat, plus unlimited headroom. However, top floor spaces often bring top rental fees, which are lost when these spaces are devoted to mechanical equipment.

HVAC EQUIPMENT

HVAC systems are made up of a number of separate pieces of equipment, which may be combined into the comprehensive term air-handling units. Preheaters warm air that is below 0°C (32°F) to a temperature slightly above freezing before it is sent on for other processing. Blowers (fans) supply air at a moderate pressure, to create the forced drafts that operate the HVAC system. Humidifiers maintain or increase the amount of water vapor in the air. A chilled water plant powered by electricity, steam, or gas delivers chilled water to the air-handling equipment for cooling, and pumps condenser water to the cooling tower to dispose of excess heat.

The boiler generates hot water or steam for heating, and requires fuel and air supplies. Hot water (hydronic) heating is more common than steam heat today. The fan room contains air-handling equipment in large buildings. Sometimes individual fan rooms are located on each floor or in each zone. Chimneys exhaust gases from the burning fuel.

Cooling towers extract heat from the water that has been used for cooling by blowing air over the water to create water vapor and liberate the latent heat. They are typically located on the roof. Cooling towers use a huge quantity of outdoor air, and create an unpleasant microclimate, with fog in cold weather. The evaporation and exposure of water to the outdoors in hot, humid conditions leads to scaling and corrosion in pipes. The growth of bacteria and algae in cooling towers has been linked to Legionnaire's disease. Vapor from cooling towers must be isolated from fresh air intakes, neighboring buildings, and parked cars. Cooling towers are very noisy due to the forced air motion, and require acoustic isolation from the structural frame of the building. It is difficult to shield the noise and view of the cooling tower without a solid barrier that would limit access to air.

Special control equipment in HVAC systems for large buildings maintains comfort through central monitoring and coordination of equipment and building conditions. Controls increase fuel economy by running equipment in the most efficient way, and act as safety devices to limit or override mechanical equipment in emergencies. They are able to eliminate human error, and are reliable except during power failures. Controls for an HVAC system usually maintain conditions within a range called a deadband, which attempts to avoid the need for heating or cooling.

Control equipment includes controllers, actuators, limit and safety controls, and other accessories. Controllers measure, analyze, and initiate actions. Actuators get the pieces of equipment to carry out the controllers' commands. Limit and safety controls prevent damage to the equipment or the building by shutting down equipment before an emergency can occur.

Unitary Air-Handling Units

Self-contained, weatherproof units with a fan, filters, a compressor, condenser, and evaporator coils for cooling are referred to as unitary air-handling units. A unitary air-handling unit is made up of a factory-assembled unit plus a cooling compressor in a compact enclosure, which can be connected to ductwork. The unitary air-handling unit may be connected to a cooling tower or fluid cooler, or to a remote condenser. For heating, the unit may operate as a heat pump or contain auxiliary heating elements. Unitary air-handling units are powered by electricity or by a combination of electricity and gas.

Unitary air-handling units are installed on the roof directly above the space to be air-conditioned, or mounted on a concrete pad along the exterior building wall. Rooftop units may be placed at intervals along long buildings. Unitary air-handling units are self-contained, and are used where the utility services of individual tenants are metered separately. Packaged systems with vertical shafts that connect to horizontal branch ducts can serve buildings up to four or five stories high. They have a life of about 10 years and require little maintenance. Furnaces, with or without cooling coils, are also considered to be air-handling units.

The supply and return ductwork for unitary air-handling units passes horizontally through an outside wall. Split systems have an indoor module with an evaporating coil, an expansion valve, a provision for heating, and an air handler, plus a separate outdoor condensing unit with a noisy compressor and air-cooled condenser. Insulated refrigerant tubing and control wiring connect the two parts.

Computer Room Units

Computer room units use a highly reliable air-handling unit with extremely precise temperature, humidity, and dust controls for sensitive electronic equipment, all located in the space served. High-quality components, reserve capacity, and redundant components to take over in case of equipment failure add to the expense of computer room units.

Central Air-Handling Units

Central air-handling unit systems are found in large buildings with multiple zones of at least 450 square meters (5000 square ft) and in tall multistory buildings. Hospitals with stringent air quality controls use central air-handling systems exclusively. Large central air-handling unit systems require routine daily checking and regularly scheduled maintenance. They are built on site, and take longer to install than prefabricated units, but may be more energy efficient. Central air-handling systems have a 20- to 30-year life expectancy.

In air-handling unit systems for large buildings, air is passed over the air-handling unit's heat exchanger coil, which contains steam or hot water pipes. Heating is transferred to the air, then to ducts and into the spaces where it will be used.

The air distributed from the central air-handling unit ends up in the building's individual occupied spaces. Small terminal units may be mounted directly below a window or in openings in the exterior wall of each space served. Window-mounted units typically are used to retrofit existing buildings.

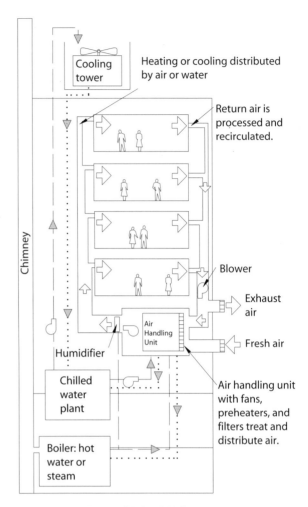

Figure 26-2 HVAC system.

DISTRIBUTION TREES

Centralized HVAC systems (Fig. 26-2) distribute heating and cooling through systems called distribution trees. Distribution trees take up a lot of space, both horizontally and vertically. They need to be coordinated with the lighting, ceiling design, and other interior design elements. Like trees in nature, distribution trees have roots—the machines heating or cooling the air or water. The trunk of the tree is the main duct or pipe from the mechanical equipment to the zone served. The tree's branches are the many smaller ducts or pipes leading to individual spaces. The leaves are the point of interchange between the piped or ducted heating or cooling and the space served. This point may be a large, bulky fan-coil unit (FCU) on an exterior wall below the window. The leaves could also be perforated ceiling tiles with thousands of small holes like an almost invisible, widely spreading grille.

A building can have one giant distribution tree, several medium-sized trees, or a veritable forest of much smaller trees. A large mechanical room is the source of all heating and cooling production, the large trunk duct, and lots of branches. Alternatively, each zone in a building can have its own mechanical system, such as a rooftop heat pump, with short trunks and few branches.

Current trends in HVAC distribution for large buildings feature decentralized air handling, with small fan rooms on each floor, resulting in smaller vertical air distribution trees. Daylighting considerations and indirect lighting for computer screens are pushing office ceilings higher. Raised floor displacement systems are being used with exposed concrete structures. It is logical to put the parts of the system that deal with sun, shade, and temperature changes at the perimeter, and to use the building core for more stable interior areas. However, perimeter distribution usually costs more to construct and must respond to the temperature extremes at the building envelope.

An HVAC system can distribute heating and cooling by means of air, water, or both. All-air systems have the largest trees, followed by air and water systems. Air systems use ducts, which are bulky and have a significant visual impact. All-water systems with local control of fresh air have the smallest distribution trees. Water systems use pipes, which take up less space, and are easier to integrate with the building's structural columns.

All-air systems provide the best comfort of these three systems. The air is heated or cooled, humidity controlled, and filtered, and fresh outdoor air is added, all under controlled conditions. Within each zone, supply registers and return grilles ensure a stream of conditioned air to all areas.

The buildings we live with today reflect a variety of historic approaches to building design for thermal comfort. Multistory buildings constructed in the late nineteenth and early twentieth centuries needed daylight and cross ventilation, and thus were designed with narrow plans and high ceilings. The Marquette Building, designed by Holabird and Roche, is a typical example of Chicago architecture of the 1890s. The architects satisfied the owners' demand that not one inch of the interior be unlighted by locating three corridors with offices on each side around a central court. Small-diameter steam or heated water distribution trees were installed at the perimeter to compensate for heat gain or loss.

With the increasing use of electric lighting and air-conditioning, floor plans became wider and large central internal areas developed. The R.C.A. Building in New York's Rockefeller Center (1931–1932) retained a slab-like floor plan to allow daylight to reach the working areas arranged around a core containing elevators and other service spaces. Central boilers, chillers, and fan rooms supplied lots of forced cooled air through bulky air distribution trees.

The advent of glass curtain walls and the slick, two-dimensional modern look in the mid-twentieth century made air-distribution trees visually intrusive, and they were pushed to the building's core. The work of Mies van der Rohe, including New York's Seagram Office Building (1958) and Chicago's Lake Shore Drive Apartments (1951), represents the epitome of this style, but there are, of course, many less distinguished examples. The extensive glass perimeters led to extreme demands in heating and cooling, and large distribution trees were installed above suspended ceilings to get the heat and air-conditioning to the building perimeter. The result was often vast, visually dull, low-ceilinged offices without daylight.

These large office buildings often had greater core than perimeter areas. The low efficiency of high lighting levels assured that this large interior always needed cooling. Air supply from suspended ceilings fell down toward the occupants. The suspended ceiling was also used for air return, either as a plenum or with ductwork. Lighting fixtures were made to serve as air supply and return fixtures. As returns, they removed most of the heat from the lighting before it was added to the office space, resulting in less work for the cooling system.

Within large office spaces, a supply diffuser and return grille circulated air to enclosed offices. Air diffusers and grilles on the ceiling allowed rearrangements of cubicles and furniture in open offices. Ceiling locations did not depend upon the exact locations of low partitions, or on whether the cubicle partitions had open spaces at the bottom or not.

Distribution trees not only spread horizontally, but vertically as well. Vertical distribution layouts affect floor space, the flexibility of the space plan, and the amount of available rental space. Vertical distribution chases are located at circulation cores, in structural elements, or at the edges of the building. Vertical distribution within internal circulation cores is common, and keeps the mechanical system away from windows. Containing vertical distribution within circulation cores also permits a flexible plan for the remainder of the floor. Usually there will be only one core vertical duct, with very large branches near the core. Due to the large size, the placement of this duct and its main branches is critical. Vertical distribution can be integrated with the building structure, with multiple trees at columns, resulting in small horizontal trees. Distribution trees may conflict with girder connections to columns, so soffits are often used to create another layer to accommodate horizontal and vertical ducts. Where horizontal distribution is at the edges of the building, it must be integrated with sun-shading devices and light shelves. Ductwork must be carefully laid out, and integrated with the structure and spaces of a building, and with the plumbing and electrical systems.

When the building's architect and engineers lay out the HVAC distribution pattern, the interior designer's work is directly affected. Ceiling heights are determined, and the transition from higher to lower spaces has a direct impact on interior volumes and relationships. Horizontal distribution takes up room at the ceiling and lowers ceiling heights, which may be an issue in daylighting design. Code-mandated building height limits may in turn limit floor to ceiling heights. Horizontal layouts are located at circulation paths, at structural elements, at the building perimeter, or in separate layers above or below other floors.

Horizontal distribution above corridors is very common, and the reduced headroom is not usually a problem. Circulation spaces are usually away from windows, so daylight is not affected. Corridors provide logical connections from one space to another, and are good paths for distribution trees. The change from lower service spaces to higher ceilings in office spaces enhances the openness of the higher spaces.

Some distribution systems run under floors rather than overhead. Underfloor HVAC supply is combined with ventilation with cool, fresh air. Instead of supplying large quantities of low-velocity air through very large ducts, a raised-floor system provides a plenum below the floor. The air is warmed by heat from lighting, people, and equipment, and rises to the ceiling. Outlets at the floor are adjustable, and easy for workers to reach.

Raised floors are built on a 0.6 by 0.6 meter (2 by 2 ft) module. The diffusing module may also contain an outlet for power and cable service. Codes may restrict the height of raised floor plenums, or require specially coated wiring within the plenum to resist wear by moving air washing over the wires for years on end. The decision to use raised floors increases the minimum floor-to-floor height in the building. In order to accommodate warm air stratification, a floor-to-floor height of at least 2.75 meters (9 ft) is recommended.

Air delivery through access-floor plenums brings cool air directly to where it's needed, and reduces energy consumption. As the chilled air delivered through the floor warms, it rises to return-air vents in the ceiling or very high on walls. In order to eliminate the suspended ceiling, the vents must be located at least 3 meters (10 ft) above the floor, and placed at fixed, regular intervals throughout the space, which might impair flexibility in room layout. Ceiling space is also generally required for lighting and sprinkler systems, unless lighting is provided indirectly and sprinklers are brought through the slab above, making reconfiguration difficult. In general, a ceiling air return requires about 15 to 20 cm (6–8 in.) of space, and the space required for ceiling-mounted light fixtures continues to diminish as very small fluorescent tubes and shallow fixtures become more common. Though underfloor systems still require a slightly greater slab-to-slab height than conventional systems, that difference is becoming very small.

The elimination of the suspended ceiling and supply ductwork also eliminates the open space above, and exposes the lighting, fire sprinkler, and public address systems below the ceiling structure. Some systems, such as public address, can puncture the structural floor and use the open space below the raised floor above.

If all the components of an underfloor system are designed, installed, and maintained properly, the system will offer as great a degree of fire protection as any other cabling system. Wiring must conform to code no matter where it's placed, and there's no reason that an underfloor system can't incorporate code-mandated smoke barriers. Noise transmission also isn't a problem, as the depth of the underfloor space and the carpet covering the floor provide acoustical insulation that's more than sufficient. Fears that an underfloor system might feel "bouncy" may have been true in the past, but today's dense, high-quality flooring products have removed this drawback.

Some contractors may not be familiar with access floors, increasing initial costs. In some installations, the need for special treatments of the perimeter cooling/heating zone can add to underfloor system expenses. Multitenant floors may require fire barriers down to the slab, which could interrupt airflow. The solution is to introduce fire dampers, but this too can be costly. Although underfloor plenums are shallow enough that neighboring tenants can't squeeze through them, they do have some security considerations. The systems must be carefully designed to preserve secure telecommunications. Wet areas with sinks and toilets must be isolated from the underfloor system.

The development of flat-screen computer technologies promises to reduce the amount of heat generated by office equipment, and offers the possibility of smaller underfloor ducts. However, this is balanced against the tendency to cram offices with more and more electronic devices and higher densities of people. It is unlikely that, in the end, new technologies will result in smaller duct sizes.

Ceiling heights are also important for distribution of air from the ceiling. Higher ceilings above cubicles allow colder air to be used, and that means smaller ducts. High ceilings also allow deeper daylight penetration and a larger pool of air, which stays fresher longer.

Sometimes the best solution for a building's HVAC system combines centralized heating and cooling equipment with local air distribution. A remote central boiler and chiller serve fan rooms on each floor. Distribution runs horizontally from the fan rooms, minimizing the bulk of the air-distribution tree.

Distribution trees can be located outside the building to save rentable floor space. However, exterior trees require expensive coverings and are more likely to gain or lose heat, increasing energy use.

ALL-AIR DISTRIBUTION SYSTEMS

Some all-air systems distribute air through a single supply duct and a single return duct. Double-duct systems use two supply ducts and a single return duct. In some smaller buildings, one system serves a single zone, and all spaces in the building receive the same air from the same source. In other, larger buildings, the system may serve a larger number of zones, with the air customized to the needs of each zone. In addition to the number of supply ducts and the number of zones, all-air distribution systems vary as to whether air temperature is controlled at a central location or at the room in which it is used.

Single-Duct Systems

Single-duct systems may serve one or many zones. In small buildings, a single-zone air-distribution system with a master thermostat regulates the temperature for the whole building. Such a system has a very low first cost.

A multizone single-duct system is a collection of up to eight single-zone systems served by one supply fan. Separate ducts from the central air-handling unit serve each zone with its own centrally conditioned air stream. Multizone systems have very large distribution trees. Energy is always being expended for ventilation, even if there is no need for heating or cooling. Multizone systems are used in medium-sized buildings or in large buildings with central equipment on each floor.

The constant air volume (CAV) system is the simplest central air-conditioning system. Single-duct CAV systems supply conditioned air at a constant temperature through a low-velocity duct system. Fans circulate air past heating and cooling coils through a duct system that delivers it to all rooms. Heated coils are active only when the building requires heat. Small systems use a firebox burning gas or oil instead. Cooling coils in residential systems can be the cool side of a refrigerant system connected directly to a compressor. In larger buildings, cooling coils carry water chilled by refrigerant coils from a nearby compression or absorption chiller. Electrically controlled dampers exhaust a percentage of air from the return ductwork, and admit an equal amount of fresh air from outdoors to ventilate the building. A single thermostat controls the entire system.

In the 1990s, single-duct, variable air volume (VAV) systems (Fig. 26-3) became the most popular. Each zone has its own thermostat that operates a damper. The dampers at terminal outlets control the flow of conditioned air to the local ductwork in that zone according to temperature requirements for each zone or space.

Single-duct VAV systems are the most common system for new institutional and office buildings where precise control is not critical. Older buildings with less

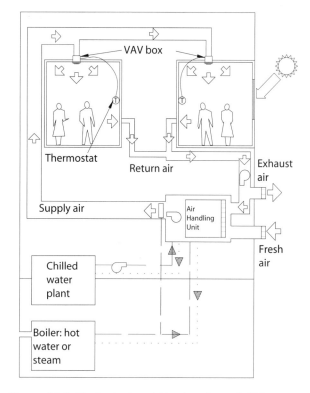

Figure 26-3 Single-duct variable air volume (VAV) system.

efficient systems can be converted to VAV to reduce energy consumption. The single duct takes up less space than multiple-duct systems. Single-duct VAV systems work better for stable interior spaces than for more variable perimeter zones. They do not work well where the internal zones generate a lot of heat. Fan-powered VAV systems use individual units that can supply heat while the main supply system is providing cooling elsewhere, and these systems improve ventilation and circulation of air. They work well with the variations in temperatures at less stable perimeter zones. The fan draws air from the ceiling or floor plenum, heating it as required. When new, cool outdoor air is reduced to a minimum, energy is saved but air quality suffers.

Terminal reheat systems offer more flexibility in meeting changing space requirements. A single duct supplies a central air stream at around 13°C (55°F) to terminals with electric or hot water reheat coils. The reheat coils regulate the temperature of the air to each individually controlled zone or space. Where water is used in the reheat coils, the system must circulate both the air and hot water to each zone. Most of the time, the 13°C air stream has been cooled from warmer air temperatures, and this wastes a lot of energy. Single-duct reheat systems have small duct networks that save space. Terminal reheat systems are more expensive to install and operate than CAV or VAV systems. They are restricted by codes and by American Society of Heating, Refrigeration, and Air-Conditioning Engineers (ASHRAE) standards to use in critical areas like laboratories, electronics factories, and hospital operating rooms.

Double-Duct Systems

Where temperatures must be closely controlled in a large number of rooms or zones, double-duct systems (Fig. 26-4) circulate both heated and cooled air to a control box in each zone. Double-duct systems offer superior comfort control and flexibility for simultaneous heating and cooling zones. Double-duct CAV systems use two supply ducts and a separate return duct. Both warm and cool air ducts supply large mixing boxes controlled by dampers. In summer, the cooling air stream is used alone, and in winter, the warming one is used. The mixing boxes proportion and blend warm and cold air to the desired temperature before delivering it to the zone or space.

Air quality in a double-duct system is controlled through positive and negative pressures. Spaces that generate odor, excess heat and humidity, or pollutants, such as kitchens, toilets, or retail pet stores, are supplied with

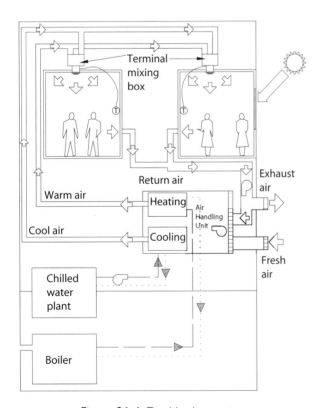

Figure 26-4 Double-duct system.

less air than adjacent spaces, resulting in lower air pressure. Air will naturally flow from higher-pressure spaces into lower-pressure ones, and the lower-pressure spaces can then be exhausted directly outdoors, keeping pollutants from spreading into adjacent spaces.

In some spaces, like shopping malls, the corridors of apartment houses, and stair towers, more air is introduced into the space than is mechanically removed. These spaces are kept under positive pressure, so that air tends not to flow into them. This pressurization helps prevent unheated or uncooled outdoor air or smoke from a fire from entering these spaces. Higher air pressures also reduce discomfort from drafts and uneven temperatures from infiltration of air through the building envelope.

Double-duct CAV systems provide the best comfort under conditions where the amount of actual heating or cooling is below the maximum for which the system was designed, as in a partially occupied room. They work less well with perimeter zones in cold climates. They are usually high-velocity systems, so smaller duct sizes can reduce installation space, but they still use a great deal more space and energy than a single-duct VAV system. The mixing boxes are also expensive and require maintenance. Double-duct systems are very expensive to install, and are usually used only in larger buildings, such as hospitals, where a variety of zones with differing needs justifies a separate CAV for each zone.

ALL-WATER DISTRIBUTION SYSTEMS

All-water systems are a simpler alternative for heating and cooling than all-air systems. The distribution trees are slim. Water systems provide temperature control only. Air quality is provided by windows or infiltration, or by a separate fresh air supply system.

Water for the HVAC system is heated in a boiler to between 71°C and 121°C (160°F–250°F). Cold water is cooled in a chiller to 4°C to 10°C (40°F–50°F). Chillers remove heat collected by a recirculating chilled water system as it cools a building. New chiller designs avoid ozone-depleting chlorofluorocarbons (CFCs) and hydrochlorofluorocarbons (HCFCs). In order to accommodate unstable energy prices, newer chillers can change quickly from electricity to natural gas.

As discussed earlier, absorption chillers use an absorptive refrigeration cycle, which is less efficient than compressive refrigeration cycle equipment. Absorption chillers are compact and have fewer moving parts, therefore requiring less maintenance, and don't use CFCs or HCFCs. They produce less vibration and are quieter as well. Centrifugal chillers use a compression refrigeration cycle and require a cooling tower.

Once the water is heated or chilled, it is then piped to a fan-coil unit (FCU) or radiant panel for both heating and cooling. An FCU contains an air filter and a fan for drawing a mixture of room air and outdoor air over coils of heated or chilled water, then blowing it back into the space.

Fan-Coil Units

A fan-coil unit (FCU) (Fig. 26-5) is a factory-assembled unit with a heating and/or cooling coil, fan, and filter. Wall, ceiling, and vertical stacking models are available. Some designs are concealed in custom enclosures, semi-recessed into the wall, or installed as floor consoles with various cabinets. Recessed units are often found along corridors. Ceiling models are available in cabinets for exposed locations, or without a cabinet for concealed mounting. They should not be mounted above solid ceilings, as the condensate drains are prone to clogging and the drain pans can overflow, requiring maintenance. One ceiling unit can be ducted to supply several adjacent small spaces. Vertical stacking units are used in multiple-floor apartment buildings, condominiums, office buildings, and hotels. They eliminate the need for separate piping risers and runouts.

Fan-coil units may have one or two coils. Those with a single coil can only heat or cool without a seasonal changeover period, but the design saves plumbing costs.

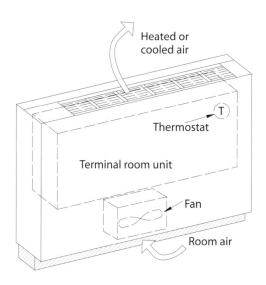

Figure 26-5 Fan-coil unit (FCU).

Heated or cooled air

Thermostat

Terminal room unit

Fan

Room air

Adding an electrical heating coil gives more versatility, and even with the electrical hookup and electricity for heat, is still less expensive than two-coil units. Units with cooling have condensate drip pans connected to drain lines. Units with a cooling coil also dehumidify. A single unit serves one or a small number of rooms. Baseboard, valance (above window), and corner FCUs are available.

Fan-coil units are a good choice for serving a large number of small, individually controlled rooms with a variety of occupants, such as hotels and motels, apartments, nursing homes, and medical centers. Since FCUs don't provide fresh air for ventilation, each space must have operable windows for ventilation. Maintenance occurs in the room, along with fan noise, and the drain pans may support bacterial growth. The filters on FCUs are relatively ineffective.

Unit ventilators are FCUs with an opening through the exterior wall for outside air. Unit ventilators offer individual temperature control in each room. They circulate only chilled or heated water from a central unit to the room. An inside damper controls the amount of fresh air. Room air plus a percentage of fresh outdoor air is filtered and passed by a heated or cooled water coil.

The opening through the wall is covered with a louvered grille, which may leak air. The result can be drafts, energy waste, and the possibility of freezing and rupturing coils. Circulation of cooled water causes condensate to form on the coil, as with other FCUs.

Unit ventilators are good for spaces with high-density occupancies and perimeter rooms without operating windows, like school classrooms, meeting rooms, and patient rooms in hospitals and nursing homes. With automatic controls and a motorized damper, unit ventilators can use an economizer cycle to save energy.

Because little air mixes between zones, FCUs provide isolation from potential air contaminants. They are easy systems to retrofit, and are often used in hotels, motels, or apartments. However, the use of all-water systems requires a lot of maintenance. Each FCU has filters that must be cleaned, and a drain pan to treat and empty. The noisy fan can provide masking noise, or may be objectionable.

Fin-Tube Radiation

An alternative to FCUs is hot water fin-tube radiation, used in a room with operable windows for ventilation. It is best to have separate internal cooling zones and perimeter heating zones. Sometimes, a single fin-tube is used to provide both heating and cooling in one space, in order to save money. Since air-cooling is best introduced into the space from above and heating works best at the base of perimeter walls below windows, when one system is used for both, the quality of thermal comfort and energy efficiency suffer. Locating the fin-tube below a window may interfere with drapery.

All-Water Piping Systems

Systems that distribute heating and cooling by means of water are configured in a variety of ways. One-pipe systems (Fig. 26-6) use less piping and cost less money to install. The same water passes through each terminal in series, becoming cooler (or warmer, when chilled water is used) as it nears the end of its run. Thermal control is very poor, particularly between different zones.

Two-pipe systems (Fig. 26-7) have separate pipes for supply and return, so each terminal draws from the supply pipe and returns water to the return pipe as needed. All terminals get water at approximately the same temperature, either all hot water, or all chilled water.

A three-pipe system distributes one pipe for heating and one pipe for cooling to each terminal. The third pipe returns all the water to both the chiller and the boiler. Mixing the hot and cold in the return pipe results in water that is too cold for the boiler, and too hot for the chiller, which wastes energy. Three-pipe systems are nearly obsolete.

The four-pipe system is the most expensive to install, but it provides year-round independent zone comfort control without energy waste. Each terminal has a chilled water supply and return and a heating water supply and return. This system can provide simultaneous heating and cooling as needed in various zones. Four-

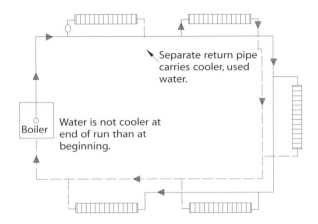

Figure 26-7 Two-pipe hydronic distribution system.

pipe systems also allow a quick seasonal changeover from heating to cooling.

AIR-WATER DISTRIBUTION SYSTEMS

Air-water systems provide superior comfort control. The water distribution tree does most of the heating or cooling. A small centrally conditioned airstream filters, controls humidity, and adds fresh air. The total distribution tree space is less than for all-air systems. Where the water distribution is either heat only or cool only, a two-pipe system is used. A four-pipe system is used where both heating and cooling are desired.

Air is not recirculated in air-water systems, making this a good choice for hospitals and other facilities where contamination may be a problem. Exhaust air is returned via return air ducts, making energy recovery possible, or is exhausted locally.

Air-water systems are often used in perimeter zones of large buildings, where the extra heating or cooling is provided by water. Single-duct VAV systems are used in the interior spaces. Air-water systems are commonly used in the perimeter zones of office buildings, hospitals, schools, apartments, and laboratories.

The first cost of both air and water supply and return trees is higher than some other systems. Space is needed for both the air ducts and water piping. Filters must be maintained within the space, and the system offers less humidity control than all-air systems. Within the space served, air-water systems may be distributed by induction systems, by fan-coil units with supplementary air, by radiant panels with supplementary air, or by a water loop heat pump.

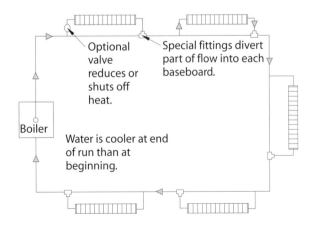

Figure 26-6 One-pipe hydronic distribution system.

Induction systems are located either above a suspended ceiling or below windows. The latter location is easier to maintain. A high-velocity, high-pressure, constant volume air supply is forced through an opening in a way that induces existing air in the room to join the new air. The air then passes over finned tubes for heating and cooling. Thermostats control the output by controlling the flow of water or flow of new air. The result is thorough circulation of room air with only a little centrally heated air.

Fan-coil units for air-water distribution systems add a fan at each unit. Fan-coil units are usually located below windows. Horizontal FCUs can be located above suspended ceilings. A supply air plenum over the corridor feeds rooms on each side. The fan moves both new and existing room air over a coil to heat or cool, circulating the air in the process. This system is widely used.

Medium-temperature radiant panels are large flat surfaces too hot to touch. They consist of prefabricated metal panels heated by electrical resistance elements or tubes with hot water circulation bonded to a radiant surface, and are mounted on walls or ceilings. Panels that circulate water also provide cooling. Radiant panels with supplementary air offset the loss from large areas of cold glass on a winter day, or when occupants are sedentary or lightly dressed, as in nursing homes. Centrally conditioned, tempered fresh supplementary air is brought to the space in a constant volume stream.

Low-temperature radiant floor, wall, and ceiling systems operate near room temperature. Heat is supplied from electrical elements, water piping, or ducts embedded in the floor or laid above the ceiling. Ceiling or wall panels may also contain cooled water, and the ceiling or wall provides a large surface for radiant heat exchange.

The radiant panel's large surface must be kept clear of obstructions, but it has the advantage that there are no volumes of visible equipment within the room. Panels need to be well insulated from adjoining spaces. Located in the ceiling, radiant panels are supplied with chilled as well as heated water. In the floor, they can provide a cooled floor in the summer and a warm one in the winter without drafts, and can be used with most floor finishes, including carpet. This can be a good option where occupants spend a lot of time at floor level, as young children or children with some disabilities may.

Water loop heat pumps are a variation on the two-pipe water distribution system. Heat pumps either draw heat from the loop to heat the space, or discharge heat into it to cool the space. In a large building in cold weather, excess interior zone heat can be used to warm perimeter spaces. In hot weather, a cooling tower is used to discharge excess heat. In cold weather, a boiler adds extra heat.

COOLING ADDED ONTO HEATING

Historically, mechanical cooling started out as retrofits to existing heating systems. Cooling coils were added to a warm air furnace, creating air-to-air refrigeration. The air was then used to cool a condenser, and indoor air was cooled directly by being passed over an evaporating coil in which a refrigerant expanded from a liquid to a gas. The resulting excess heat was moved from indoor to outdoor air. The direct cooling of air by expanding refrigerant is called direct expansion, and the cooling coils are called DX (for direct expansion) coils.

A hydronic system plus coils combines a perimeter hot water heating pipe with an overhead air-handling system. The hydronic system with coils was used in the original Levittown standardized houses on New York State's Long Island. The heat output from a boiler with a tankless coil that provides domestic hot water supplies the perimeter space heating loop and a coil in the air-handling unit of the duct system. The total heating load is met by a combination of radiant heat from the perimeter loop and heated air from the overhead air-handling system. The sharing of the heating load between these two systems provides more constant indoor temperatures. However, there is less air distribution than in conventionally ducted systems.

HEAT RECOVERY AND ENERGY CONSERVATION

The simplest form of energy conservation is insulating heating pipes with foam or fiberglass. Pipe insulation costs about $0.30 to $0.80 per foot, and saves around $0.50 per foot each year. Fiberglass pipe insulation should be at least 19 mm ($\frac{3}{4}$ in.) thick, and foam insulation 13 mm ($\frac{1}{2}$ in.) thick. Foam insulation should not be used on steam pipes, as it may melt. Steam pipes were usually asbestos-wrapped in the past, and existing ones can be left alone if they are well sealed, not flaky and not in a living space. If the white protective sheathing is damaged or missing, call a certified asbestos abatement contractor.

One way to conserve energy in a building while maintaining an adequate flow of fresh air is to use a heat exchanger, which maintains an adequate supply of fresh air without major increases in energy consumption. Heat exchangers are often included within heating and cooling systems, as part of other equipment or as separate units. In tightly built small buildings, the incoming and outgoing air streams are often adjacent to one another. By using a heat exchanger, 70 percent or more of the heat in the exhausted air can be extracted and used to preheat incoming air. For best diffusion of fresh air, the heat exchanger should be located at the central forced-air fan. Where there is no central fan, the heat exchanger should have its own fan.

There are a variety of types of heat exchangers, each with its own advantages and limitations. Air-to-air heat exchangers are not to be used on exhaust air streams with grease, lint or excessive moisture, as from cooking or clothes drying, due to risk of clogging, frosting, and fire hazards. A built-in defroster that uses energy (and thus reduces the energy saved by the heat exchanger) is required for cold winter conditions. The outdoor air intake must be carefully located, as far as possible from the exhaust air outlet and away from pollution sources such as vehicle exhaust, furnace flues, dryer and exhaust fan vents, and plumbing vents.

Another form of heat exchanger is the energy recovery ventilator (ERV), which draws air out beside a toilet, and exchanges 85 percent of the heat in this warmed air with incoming fresh air. The fresh air is mixed with some return air, fed to a heat pump above the ERV, then on to other rooms, maintaining negative pressure in the bathroom. The ERV system has been used in student apartments in Greensboro, North Carolina.

Energy transfer wheels are heat exchangers that recover heat from exhausted air in winter and cool and dehumidify incoming air in summer. Both incoming and outgoing streams of air pass through a wheel, where they are kept separate by seals and by the airflow pattern itself. Energy transfer wheels are up to 3.66 meters (12 ft) in diameter, and are 70 to 80 percent effective in reusing heating or cooling energy.

The heat pipe is a heat exchanger that uses refrigerant to dehumidify and cool incoming air before it reaches the evaporating coil of an air conditioner, and adds heat back in after use, all without any additional energy input. Refrigerant is sealed inside a bundle of tubes with radiating fins. The refrigerant alternately evaporates, condenses, and migrates by capillary action through a porous wick, within a self-contained unit. Heat pipes are 50 to 70 percent efficient, have no moving parts so require no maintenance, and have an extremely long useful life.

Another heat recovery system uses closed-loop run-around coils in the incoming and exhaust airstreams to heat a fluid that is circulated by a pump. Run-around coils transfer heat between intake and exhaust air ducts when they are rather far apart. Run-around coils are easy to retrofit in existing buildings, and recover about half of the exhaust heat. Open run-around coils use fluid sprayed on the airstreams to take heat and moisture from warm areas and release it to cool areas.

The Canadian National Research Council offers information on a "breathable wall" to be used with an exhaust air heat pump. When the heat pump takes heat from forced exhaust air for space heating or domestic hot water, the result is a house under negative pressure. Fresh replacement air then infiltrates through the outside walls. This is made possible by the breathable wall construction, a combination of fiberglass lap siding board, fiberglass insulation batts, breathable sheathing, and no vapor barrier. The slow, steady stream of cold air that enters is warmed by the insulation as it enters the house.

Economizer cycles take advantage of buildings with interior zones that need only cooling and some tempering of ventilation air, and perimeter zones that need both heating and cooling in response to conditions at the building envelope. The perimeter zones usually extend about 3 to 6 meters (10–20 ft) into the building, so small buildings may not have an identifiable interior zone.

With a well-insulated perimeter, adjusting the amount of new ventilation air can control the amount of heat removed from interior zones in cold weather. An economizer cycle uses cool outside air for neutralizing interior heat gains instead of mechanical cooling. Economizer cycles use automatically opening dampers to draw in a large amount of outside air to the ventilating system when needed to offset interior heat. Boiler flue economizers pass the hot gases from a boiler's stack through a heat exchanger. The heat is then used to preheat incoming boiler water.

CONTROLS

A thermostat (Fig. 26-8) is a temperature-activated switch that turns heating and cooling equipment on and off in order to maintain a preset temperature. Thermostats also control the flow of water to radiators and convectors. The fans that circulate warm air also use thermostats. The thermostat triggers a low-limit switch, which turns fans and pumps on for the heat-distribution system when a preset low temperature is reached. An upper-limit switch shuts off the furnace when the

Figure 26-8 Thermostat.

specified temperature is reached. A safety switch prevents fuel from flowing to the heating plant if the pilot light or fuel-ignition system is not working.

A 1° reduction in the thermostat setting can save 2 percent of the heating bill for a home. Clock thermostats set back the temperature automatically at night, and turn back up one-half hour before the occupants get up in the morning. Clock thermostats pay for themselves in about one year.

The mechanical engineer determines the location of a thermostat based on the location of surrounding heat sources. Most thermostat malfunctions result from improper location, poor maintenance, or inappropriate use of the device. To work properly, the thermostat must be mounted on an inside wall away from doors and windows, so that it will not be affected by the outside temperature or by drafts. Do not place lamps, appliances, TV sets, or heaters under the thermostat, as their heat will affect furnace operation. If the thermostat is in a location where the space's occupants usually change the temperature, it should be in an accessible location, although there is no specific requirement in the Americans with Disabilities Act (ADA).

The interior designer should make it a point to know where the thermostat is to be located, as it could end up in the middle of a featured wall, right where the designer had planned to hang a piece of art. Thermostats are available with a flush-mounted wall plate, and with remote sensing wires that could be wrapped around a picture, sculpture, molding, or other decorative element. When thermostats must be concealed for aesthetic reasons or to avoid damage, they can be located in a return air duct.

Self-contained thermostats provide inexpensive room-by-room control for water or steam distribution systems. Self-contained thermostatic control valves can be mounted directly on cast-iron radiators, fin-tube radiators, FCUs, and unit heaters. They can be retrofitted

in dormitories, apartments, and offices that have only one thermostat for each floor of the building. They provide highly cost-effective energy conservation by controlling the temperature locally, eliminating the need to open windows in overheated rooms. Self-contained microprocessor-based thermostats can be fine-tuned for flexible, simple control.

The HVAC controls for small buildings are usually thermostats. The American National Standards Institute (ANSI) and ASHRAE have published Standard 90.2–1993, *Energy Efficient Design of New Low-Rise Residential Buildings*, which set standards for thermostats. Thermostats must be able to be set from 13°C to 29°C (55°F–85°F). They must also have an adjustable deadband, the range of which includes settings at 5.6°C (10°F) increments. The deadband is a range of temperatures separating a lower temperature that triggers the heat to go on from a higher temperature that starts the cooling system.

Workstation delivery systems (Fig. 26-9) offer personalized air-distribution controls. Some systems use conditioned air supplied through conventional ceiling systems, while others supply the air from a floor, wall, or column plenum. Both types of systems utilize a large under-the-desk fan and electronics unit that requires a single utility outlet. This outlet is equipped with telescoping ducts attached to desktop diffusers to distribute the airflow as desired. Individual users can control air temperature, airflow, under-desk radiant heat, task light level, and background noise from a desktop control unit. When the West Bend Mutual Insurance Company headquarters installed 370 of these units in the early 1990s, thermal complaints were immediately cut down from 40 a day to 2 per week.

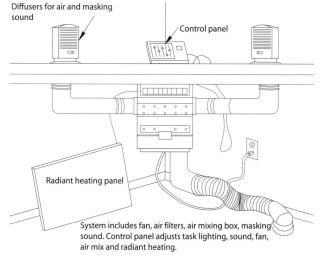

Figure 26-9 Workstation delivery system.

One workstation delivery system provides each workstation with a fan, air filters, an air mixing box, and a masking sound generator. The control panel allows adjustment of task lighting, background sound, fan speed, air mixture, and radiant heating located below the desk. Another type of system uses ductwork integral to the workstation panels. Conditioned air flows from the building's HVAC system through a control box and the ductwork, then through dampers and down into the workstation. Workers turn the control dial within their workstation to regulate the volume of conditioned air flowing into the workstation. Research by Professor Alan Hedge of Cornell University indicates that having individual control of conditioned air results in reduced stress and increased productivity.

Building management control systems are designed to meet the needs of commercial office buildings, hospitals, hotels, schools, manufacturing facilities, universities, and other specialized facilities. Systems are designed to be easy to use and to have extensive reporting capabilities. Building management systems use direct digital control (DDC), with microcontrollers on each piece of regulated equipment. The DDC system can respond to the needs of specific users. DDC systems can be integrated with energy management systems for individual buildings, as well as centralized management of individual systems in separate locations. A central controller connects the operator's workstation to other controllers that handle specific task locations, such as equipment and machine rooms. These are in turn connected to the end devices, such as motors and sensors, which produce the desired action. Systems are designed for the specific application, and the manufacturer also provides training for facility staff.

Control systems for mechanical and electrical equipment can automatically warm up or cool down rooms in time for the occupants' arrival. Central automatic systems control fresh air quantities, adjust movable sun-shading devices, and adjust the intensity of lighting, promoting the maximum amount of on-site, renewable energy use. Control systems use little space, but must be accessible for upgrades. Where buildings use automatic controls for HVAC systems, the specifications for mechanical work usually require an operating manual and orientation session for the building manager on how the system works.

Building management systems for small buildings can be activated by remote control in anticipation of the owner's arrival. Door and window locks, security cameras, lighting, and appliances can be part of a comprehensive control system.

Central logic control systems are building management systems for large buildings, and are used in most new large buildings. The goal of central logic control systems is to maintain comfort with energy conservation. They coordinate relationships between the building's structure, systems, services, and management for improved productivity and cost effectiveness. The centrally regulated HVAC is tied into the lighting, electrical power, elevators, service hot water, access control and security, telecommunications, and information management systems. These systems alert building staff to malfunctions and can learn from past practice and keep records on performance.

The fume hoods in laboratories exhaust a large quantity of air, and may need to isolate hazardous substances, toxic materials, and disease or other biological organisms. The building control system can keep the lab under positive pressure and balance the needs for isolation and fresh air.

Hotels risk energy loss in unoccupied rooms or rooms with open windows. By tying the building control system into the registration desk, the system can respond to remote unoccupied rooms and open windows. A purge mode can clear the air completely for a new occupant.

Offices use building control systems to tie together VAV supply units, ventilating windows, daylight reflectors, venetian blinds, radiant heaters, electrical lighting, and insulating shades. A control panel allows an individual worker to interact with the control system.

Building management systems that include indoor air quality (IAQ) sensors automatically measure IAQ and control outside air intake. The HVAC system is then adjusted automatically.

Very sophisticated systems are currently under development for small buildings, such as residences, retail, and commercial occupancies. In buildings with varied and unpredictable use patterns, adaptive control of home environment (ACHE) systems anticipate users' needs and save energy. These ACHE systems use a neural network that adapts to its environment and anticipates users' needs to control lighting, air temperature, ventilation, and water heating, providing just enough energy when needed. Lights are set to the minimum requirement and heated water is maintained at the minimum level to meet demands. Only occupied rooms are kept at the optimal temperature. The control framework compares the cost of energy against a level of minimal acceptable comfort. The settings develop as the building is used over time. They adjust to overrule of the minimum levels, but test that minimum occasionally to make sure that a more energy-efficient level isn't acceptable.

Building management systems are not without problems. A study of 60 new buildings found that half suffered from controls problems, 40 percent had HVAC problems, and a quarter had malfunctioning energy management systems, economizers, and variable speed drives. Most shocking of all, 15 percent had missing equipment!

VERY LARGE HEATING AND COOLING SYSTEMS

Large projects with many large buildings can be served by one central station heating and cooling plant. This offers economy of scale. The system uses very large, efficient, and well-maintained boilers and chillers. Energy is recovered through a heat exchanger, and air pollution is reduced. Noisy equipment is removed from other buildings and concentrated in the one plant.

District heating and cooling is used in Europe for residences and small commercial buildings. District steam systems serve central areas of many U.S. cities.

Cogeneration was used in paper mills in the early 1900s, but has been developed for use in hundreds of commercial, industrial, and academic buildings since the 1960s. Cogeneration plants use waste heat from a generating plant for space heating or for steam absorption cooling. The cogeneration plant recovers some of the heat wasted in the creation of electricity by steam turbines. Electricity for power and lighting is generated at the site. Cogeneration plants supply building heat in the winter and cooling in the summer.

High-temperature water and chilled water is used at Air Force bases in the United States, and at airports, in hospital complexes, and on college campuses. It uses smaller mains than steam, and water treatment and corrosion are minimal. Installation costs are greater than for steam, but operating costs are less.

ELECTRICITY

How Electrical Systems Work

Electricity is the most prevalent form of energy in a modern building. Electricity supplies electrical outlets and lighting fixtures. Ventilation, heating, and cooling equipment depends upon electrical energy. Electricity provides energy for elevators and material transporters, and energy for signal and communication equipment.

Lighting is the major user of electrical energy in most buildings. In commercial buildings, motors are the second heaviest user of electrical energy, for heating, ventilating, and air-conditioning (HVAC) systems, plumbing pumps, elevators, and most industrial processes. Working with the building's architect and engineers, you, as the interior designer, are responsible for seeing that power is available where needed for your client's equipment, and for making sure that the lighting and appliances are appropriate and energy efficient.

Until around 1870, only fire and muscle power were commonly used in buildings to perform useful work. Historically, coal and oil were burned for heat and light or converted into energy for machines that generated heat. Since the end of the nineteenth century, heat has been converted into electricity. Even nuclear energy produces heat for conversion to electricity. Converting heat to electricity is inherently inefficient, with about 60 percent of the energy in the heat wasted.

Today, electricity offers a clean, reliable, and very convenient source of energy for illumination, heating, power equipment, and electronic communication. Electricity is not usually generated on the building site. Small generating units powered by internal-combustion engines, water, sun, or wind have generally been considered expensive to buy and maintain, of limited capacity, and less reliable and efficient than central generating plants, although this is changing. Local energy generation can be noisy or smelly. The water levels, wind speeds, or sunlight levels used for local energy production tend to fluctuate and may be unable to generate a steady alternating current (AC). Private generating systems have been relegated to use as standby generators to keep critical buildings electrified during power failures, or as generators installed in large building complexes as part of a total energy system. As fuel prices rise, we are examining fuel efficiency and use more closely. Techniques for generating and storing energy are advancing, and we can look forward to a significant increase in locally produced electrical energy.

Currently, large centralized electrical generating plants are usually powered by water or steam turbines. The steam is generated by coal, oil, gas, or nuclear fuel. The efficiency of electrical generation plants rarely exceeds 40 percent, which means that one and one-half times as much heat goes up the chimney and into waterways as to transmission lines for energy. Further losses occur in the transmission lines to the user, so that the electrical energy we receive is only one-third of the initial energy available from the fuel. Compare this with modern heat-producing equipment that burns fuel in the building itself, which is generally 70 to 90 percent efficient.

PRINCIPLES OF ELECTRICITY

Electricity is a form of energy that occurs naturally only in uncontrolled forms like lightning and other static electrical discharges, or in natural galvanic reactions that cause corrosion. As Vaughn Bradshaw explains in *Building Control Systems* (New York: John Wiley & Sons, Inc., 1993, 295):

> No one knows exactly what electricity is or how it works. It does, however, behave in predictable ways, that is, when a light switch is thrown, the light consistently goes on, or if it doesn't go on, prescribed steps (such as replacing the lamp) can be taken to correct the problem. Because the experience is repeatable, observers have made up theories about what constitutes the electrical phenomenon. These theories have changed and evolved over time, and undoubtedly will continue to be improved upon.

The currently accepted theory is that electrical current consists of a flow of electrons along a conductor. The flow is induced by an imbalance of positive and negative charges. Like charges repel and opposite charges attract. Electrons, with their negative charges, are repelled by a negatively charged area and attracted to a positively charged one. When a positive area is connected to a negative area by a material that will conduct electricity, electrons flow from the negative side to the positive side.

Lightning

A lightning bolt is an instantaneous release of very high electrical potential between a rain cloud and the earth. Tall buildings and buildings in exposed locations are most susceptible to lightning strikes. It is a fallacy that lightning never strikes twice in the same spot. Tall, conductive targets get struck repeatedly. The Empire State Building in New York is hit a hundred times during an average year. Buildings are protected from lightning by pointed metal rods that connect directly with the earth through heavy electrical conductors. By leaking a charge

off their points, they neutralize electrical charges of clouds before lightning bolts even form. If lightning still strikes the building, the lightning rods and conductors offer a path to the ground of much less resistance than the building itself, thereby protecting the building.

Protection of a building against lightning strikes should be done completely and properly, with Underwriters Laboratories (UL) label equipment and a UL-approved installer. Partial protection is improper protection, and may be worse than none at all.

Circuits

When electricity flows from one point to another along a closed path (a wire, for example), the electrons flow from a point with a negative charge to one with a positive charge. Any closed path followed by an electrical current is called a circuit (Fig. 27-1). An electrical circuit is a complete conduction path that carries current from a source of electricity to and through some electrical device (or load) and back to the source. Current can't flow unless there is a closed circuit back to the source.

Electrical circuits can be arranged in a couple of different ways. In a series circuit, the parts of the circuit are connected one after another, and the resistances and voltages add up. The current is the same in all points of a series circuit. Old-fashioned Christmas tree lights that all went out when one light blew were in series. When the single light blew out, the circuit was broken, and the electricity couldn't make the trip around the circuit to light the other lights.

When two or more branches or loads in a circuit are connected between the same two points, they are

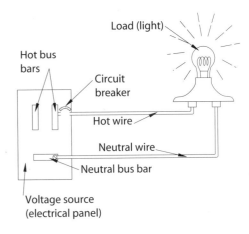

Figure 27-1 Circuit.

said to be connected in parallel. Parallel circuits are the standard arrangement in all building wiring. Each parallel group acts as a separate circuit. If one of these smaller circuits is broken, only the devices on that section are affected, and the rest of the circuit continues to circulate electricity.

Sometimes, due to worn insulation on a wire or another problem, an accidental connection is made between points on a circuit. This connection shortens the circuit and lets the electricity take a shortcut back to the source. The electricity doesn't encounter the resistance that would be in the normal wiring, and the current rises instantly to a very high level. This is called a short circuit. If the flow of electricity isn't stopped by a fuse or circuit breaker, the heat generated by the excessive current will probably start a fire.

Amps, Volts, Watts, and Ohms

This process of electricity flowing along a circuit is called electrical current, or amperage. It is measured in amperes (abbreviated amps or simply "A"), named after André Ampère, a French mathematician and physicist who lived from 1775 to 1836. Electricity flows at a constant speed, and moves virtually instantaneously. An ampere is defined as one coulomb per second flowing past a given point. To give you an idea of what this is, a coulomb is in turn defined as 6.28×10^{18} electrons—a very, very large number of very, very tiny things.

The force that drives the current is considered to be a difference in electrical voltage. The more voltage in a system, the more current flows, the more electrons move along the conductor each second, and the more amperes are measured in the circuit. A unit of voltage is called a volt (V), after Count Alessandro Volta (1745–1827), an Italian physicist and a pioneer in the study of electricity. A volt is defined as a measure of the difference in electrical potential between two points of a conductor carrying a constant current of 1 A, when the power dissipated between the two points is equal to one watt. To get an idea of how much power is in a volt, try building up a static charge by scuffing your feet on a wool carpet. You can actually generate about 400V by doing this, enough to make a visible spark jump between your finger and a metal object—or another person. A static shock has an extremely tiny current flow (amperage), so only a limited number of electrons are available to make the jump. Its effect is startling rather than harmful, despite the high voltage. However, the current flow available from the utility grid is almost unlimited, making our 120V household systems powerful and dangerous.

The electrical current could easily melt all the wiring in your home.

Well, now we have to explain what a watt is, and predictably, it is named after somebody famous, James Watt (1736–1819), a Scottish engineer who invented the modern steam engine. A watt (W) is defined as 1 A flowing under the electromotive force of 1V. This is, of course, a circular definition, but we already know that electricity is a mysterious subject. Just remember that a watt is used to measure how many electrons are passing a point, and how much force is available to move them.

Utility meters measure electrical power use in kilowatt-hours (kWh). In physics, energy is technically defined as the work that a physical system is capable of doing in changing from its actual state to a specified reference state. We define power as the ability to do work, or the rate at which energy is used in doing work. Power is energy used over time. A watt represents the rate at which energy is being used at any given moment, and 1000 W equal 1 kilowatt (kW). Electrical power is expressed in watts or kilowatts, and time is expressed in hours, so units of energy are watt-hours or kilowatt-hours (kWh). One kWh equals 1 W of power in use for 1000 hours. The amount of energy used is directly proportional to the power of a system (the number of watts) and the length of time it is in operation (hours).

The oldest and simplest method of getting electrons moving is electrochemical action. This is the method used in a dry cell or storage type battery. Chemical action causes positive charges to collect on a positive terminal, while electrons, which have negative charges, collect on a negative terminal. With nothing connected to the battery, there is a tendency for the electrified particles at the positive and negative terminals to flow. This tendency, or potential difference, is voltage. The higher the voltage, the higher the current is for a given amount of resistance. We discuss resistance shortly.

We are familiar with watts as indications of the amount of electricity a lightbulb (lamp) will use. A 60-W incandescent lamp uses 60 W of power to operate. When the lamp is placed in an electrical circuit, with voltage on one side 120V higher than voltage on the other side, then 60 divided by 120 or $\frac{1}{2}$ A of current will flow through the circuit. The current is said to be drawn through the circuit by the lightbulb, which is called the load on the circuit. When the voltage is lower, more current is needed to get the same power at a lower voltage. For example, if the voltage difference were only 12V instead of 120V, the current draw would be 60 divided by 12, or 5 A. The amount of current (number of amperes) determines the size of the wire needed for a particular use.

Electrical resistance is believed to be a form of friction on the atomic level. You can think of it as similar to friction, or like a constriction in the flow of water or another substance. Electrical current always flows through the path of least resistance. Good conductors are simply materials in which there are a lot of electrons that are free to move around, so that there isn't a lot of resistance to the electrons moving. All metals conduct electricity, although some do it better than others. Good electrical conductors include silver, gold, and platinum, with copper and aluminum almost as good, and much less expensive.

What makes a metal imperfect as a conductor is that there are internal obstacles to the free motion of electrons that can't be avoided because metals are made of atoms. These impede the flow of electrons and give rise to electrical resistance. Repeated collisions of electrons with these bumps lead to loss of energy in the form of heat. Materials with low resistances are obviously very useful as they conduct electricity more efficiently and lose less energy to heat.

In some cases, and in particular at very low temperatures, electrons can sort of team up into something like one huge lump of electrical charge that is insensitive to these little bumps and electrical resistance drops to exactly zero, an amazing phenomenon called superconductivity. An electrical current started in a superconductor will keep going forever, and superconducting cables can transmit energy with no losses at all. So far, all superconductors need to operate at very low temperatures, close to absolute zero. Whether a material that will be superconducting at room temperature is even possible is still an open question, but the search is continuing.

Insulators are materials that offer so much resistance that they virtually prevent the flow of any electricity at all, so they are used to contain electricity in its path. Glass, mica, and rubber are very good insulators, as are distilled water, porcelain, and certain synthetic materials. Rubber and plastic are used for wire coverings, porcelain is used for lamp sockets, and some switches are immersed in oil.

Electrical resistance is measured in units called ohms. An ohm is equal to the resistance of a conductor in which a potential difference of 1V produces a current of 1 A. You are probably wondering after whom the ohm was named. Georg Simon Ohm was a German physicist who lived from 1787 to 1854.

Direct and Alternating Current

There are two types of electrical current. Direct current (DC) has a constant flow rate from a constant voltage source, like a battery in which one terminal (or pole) is always positive and the other always negative. The flow is always in the same direction, or polarity. Any current in which each wire is always of the same polarity, with one wire always positive and one always negative, is a direct current. Direct current is produced in batteries and photovoltaic equipment.

With alternating current (AC), the voltage difference between the two points reverses in a regular manner. This means that the electrical current changes direction back and forth at a fixed frequency (rate). The change from positive to negative to positive again is called one cycle, and the speed with which the cycle occurs is the frequency of the current. Commercial power from utility companies in the United States and Canada is AC, typically supplied at 60 cycles per second, or 60 hertz (Hz). Many other countries supply commercial power at 50 Hz. By the way, Hertz was not the same fellow who started the rental car franchises, but Gustav Hertz, a German atomic physicist born in 1887.

Equipment made for one frequency is not compatible with any other frequency. Motors won't perform as desired at the wrong frequency, and may overheat, burn out, or have a shortened life. In AC circuits, resistance (measured in ohms) is called impedance.

The advantage of AC over DC is the ease and efficiency with which the level of voltage can be changed by transformers. Generators (Fig. 27-2) put out currents at many thousands of volts. Transformers at the generating plant further increase the voltage before the electricity is passed to the main transmission lines, to keep amperage at a minimum. When the amperage is kept low, large amounts of energy can be transmitted through small wires with minimum transmission losses.

The electricity passes through substations on its way to local transmission lines. Once the electrical energy has reached the local area, it is reduced in voltage at another transformer for distribution to buildings. The local lines have higher transmission losses per mile than the main lines, but are much shorter.

The voltage that reaches the building is still too high for consumer use, so each building or group of buildings has a small transformer to reduce the voltage still further before it enters the building. Electrical service for small buildings is provided at 230 or 240V. You have probably seen large, cylindrical transformers on utility poles that reduce the voltage for small buildings. The voltage is again reduced to around 120V for household use. Some older homes have only 120V service. Near large cities, the supply may be 120/208V. Large buildings and building complexes often buy electricity at the local line voltage and reduce it themselves with indoor transformers before use.

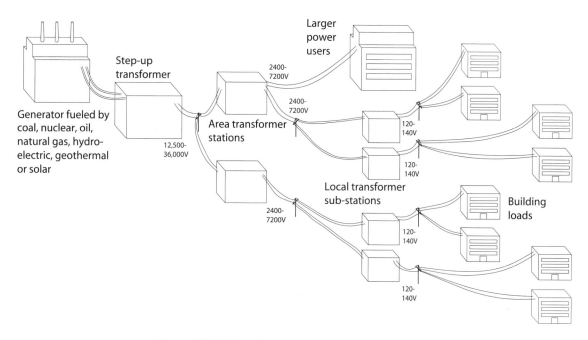

Figure 27-2 How electricity is supplied to a building.

Transformers for large buildings are usually mounted on poles or pads outside the building, or inside a room or vault. The transformer for a large building steps down 4160V service to 480V for distribution within the building. A second transformer in an electrical closet steps 480V down to 120V for receptacle outlets.

The electricity within a home may not be exactly 120 and 240V. Typically, a city dweller might have 126V at an outlet, while a suburbanite may receive only 118V. Outlets at the far end of a branch circuit have lower voltages than those near the service entrance panel, but the wiring in a home shouldn't vary by more than 4V. The minimum safe supply is 108V in order to avoid damage to electrical equipment.

ON-SITE POWER GENERATION

Up through the early twentieth century, nearly all large buildings and groups of buildings supplied their own on-site or local power. On-site generators supplied electricity for elevators, ventilators, call bells, fire alarms, and lighting. The homes of the very rich frequently had private electrical plants. The Gould estate in Lakewood, New Jersey, used two gasoline engines to power its generator dynamos, which lit the house and grounds. The estate's generator also powered a refrigerating plant and laundry, and even Mr. Gould's electric cigar lighters and Mrs. Gould's hair curler. The Vanderbilt mansion in New

York City was powered for a time by a generating plant designed by Thomas Edison, until it was removed because of the noise.

All this technology used DC electricity, which can't be transformed to different voltages, and must be generated and distributed at the voltage to be used in the building. The low voltages produced by these local DC power plants lost too much voltage to be distributed over long distances. In 1882, Edison opened the first centralized electrical utility, the Pearl Street Station in New York, which provided AC electricity to homes and shops within a one square mile area. The success of the Pearl Street Station encouraged the building of other power stations all over the United States. Purchasing power from a central source was less expensive, less noisy, and took up less space than generating it on site.

With the development and use of AC machines, electricity could be transmitted at high voltages over long distances, and an extensive distribution system came into existence. High voltage transmission reduced power losses through the wires. The high voltage was transformed down to usable voltages at the point of use. By the 1920s, larger central power stations led to lower construction and operating costs per kilowatt. Electrical power companies bought fuel under large, long-term contracts, further reducing power costs. Some on-site generation was still used where utility power was unreliable or expensive.

In the 1960s, total energy systems that produced electricity and heat simultaneously from the same fuel source came into use for shopping centers, industrial plants, community buildings, motels, hospitals, schools, and multifamily residential projects. Independent total energy systems had no connection to the local electrical utility, and had to run at a rate to meet the electrical demand even if that meant also producing more heat than needed. Excess heat was wasted through a cooling tower, in local ponds or rivers, or as steam.

In 1978, The Public Utilities Regulatory Policies Act (PURPA) decreed that utilities must buy on-site generated electricity sold by small private power producers. Local total energy systems could now be connected to the electrical utility.

Today, fuel-fired generators are used on site for emergency and standby power in hospitals and other critical processes. Larger, modular integrated utility systems (MIUS) link electrical energy production, heating and cooling, solid waste and sewage, and potable water, so that waste generated by one part of the system can be used as input by another. Such systems are often used with cogeneration plants that use one fuel source to produce more than one type of energy. Moderate-sized communities or large building complexes use MIUS to provide utility services at lower installation and operating costs, save natural resources, and minimize environmental impact.

Wind Power

Wind energy has been used for thousands of years to propel sailing ships, grind grain, and pump water. There is evidence that wind energy was used to propel boats along the Nile River as early as 5000 BC, and simple windmills were used in China to pump water in ancient times. Windmills erected as the American west was developed during the late nineteenth century pumped water for farms and ranches. Small electric wind systems were developed to generate direct electrical current by 1900, but most of these fell out of favor when rural areas became attached to the national electricity grid during the 1930s. By 1920, wind turbine generators were producing electricity in many European countries. In the United States, rural electrification in the 1950s offered electricity at rates below what could be produced locally, and the small-scale windmill became a thing of the past.

Recently, wind power has become an appealing alternative to fossil fuels, especially in countries with scarce petroleum and ample wind. The Danish Wind Turbine Manufacturers Association reports that there were over 4784 turbines in Denmark in 1997.

Modern windmills are known by many names,

among them wind turbines, wind-driven generators, and the official U.S. government term, wind energy conservation systems (WECS). Once the relatively high initial cost has been paid, the electricity is produced for free, offering a hedge against anticipated high future electrical costs. Windmills have a minimal impact on the environment and offer energy independence. The space around the wind turbines can still be used for agriculture, grazing, ranching, or most other uses. Turbines pay for themselves more quickly than most other types of energy production, and a family-size wind turbine system with tower, inverter, turbine, and accessories can pay for itself in about ten years. At remote sites without electrical service, it is more cost effective to install a windmill than to install and buy oil or natural gas for an engine generator set or to extend power from a distant utility.

There is some danger that large birds of prey, such as golden and bald eagles, will be killed by industrial wind farms, although this seems to be limited to sites along avian flyways. Noise may also be a concern, especially with large turbine blades that are close to the ground. Wind turbines are usually sited at higher elevations to catch higher-speed winds.

In addition to solar power and a backup generator, Humboldt State University's Campus Center for Appropriate Technology uses a wind turbine system to meet its energy needs. The system consists of a wind turbine on a pole, wiring, and a control box. An inverter converts the electricity from DC to AC.

Photovoltaic Cells

Photovoltaic (PV) technology converts sunlight directly into electricity. It works any time the sun is shining, but the more intense the light and the more direct the angle of the light, the more electricity will be produced. Unlike solar systems for heating water, PV technology does not use the sun's heat to make electricity. Instead, it produces electricity directly from electrons freed by the interaction of sunlight with certain semiconductor materials in the PV array.

Photovoltaic cells were developed in 1954 as an energy source for the space program. Until the 1970s, the manufacture and installation of solar energy panels was not regulated, and poor quality systems and unreliable dealers combined with lower fossil fuel prices to limit solar construction.

You've probably seen small versions of PV collectors on calculators and watches. The same type of silicon wafers that are used to make computer chips can be used to create electricity when the sun is shining on them. Photovoltaic cells are made from a very pure form of silicon, an abundant element in the earth's crust that is not very difficult to mine.

Photovoltaic cells provide direct electrical current. When enough heat or light strikes a cell connected to a circuit, the difference in voltage causes current to flow. No voltage difference is produced in the dark, so the cell only provides energy when exposed to light. A cell can be connected to a battery, to provide continuous power.

Even the best PV cells turn less than a quarter of the solar energy that strikes them into electricity, with the rest given off as heat. Commercially available cells are currently only about 10 to 12 percent efficient. New designs currently being researched are up to 18 percent efficient.

Individual PV cells are wired together to produce a PV module, the smallest PV component sold commercially, and these modules range in power output from about 10 to 300 W. Usually, individual modules are mounted onto an existing roof. Some modules can be designed directly into the roof, acting as both a roofing material and an electricity generator. To connect a PV system to a utility grid, one or more PV modules is connected to an inverter that converts the modules' DC electricity to AC electricity. The AC power is compatible with the electric grid and can be used by lights, appliances, computers, televisions, and many other devices. Some systems include batteries to provide backup power in case the utility suffers a power outage.

Small commercial and industrial PV applications include lighting, traffic counters, signaling, and fence charging. Larger systems provide electricity for residential, office, educational, and mobile electrical needs. Systems are not limited to sunny tropical areas. A solar electric system in Boston, Massachusetts, will produce over 90 percent of the energy generated by the same system in Miami, Florida. In areas with low-sun winter seasons, like New England, these systems are frequently paired with a generator or other backup systems for extra power.

Photovoltaic energy is a clean, reliable alternative for providing electrical power. It minimizes dependence on fossil fuels and reduces vulnerability to fuel price spikes. Solar energy can decrease utility bills and increase the resale value of real estate.

When the PV system generates more electricity than is needed at the site, excess energy can be fed directly onto electric lines for use by other electric customers (Fig. 27-3). Through a net-metering agreement with the electric utility, PV system owners are compensated for the excess power they produce. The PV system contractor installs an inverter that ensures that the electricity coming from the PV system is compatible with electricity coming from the power lines.

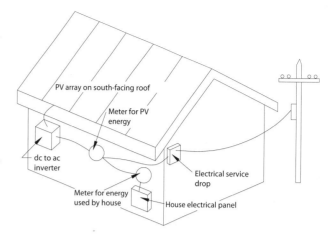

Figure 27-3 Grid connected PV system.

Stand-Alone Photovoltaic Arrays

The oldest type of PV system is the stand-alone array. Stand-alone arrays are isolated from the utility electrical grid and designed for a specific job. They are used for sign lighting, railroad crossing lights, unattended pumps and navigational aids, lighthouses, motor homes, sailboats and yachts, and isolated small residences. When a fuel-powered generator is added for a more reliable supply, the system becomes a hybrid stand-alone. Storage batteries store the excess from peak hours to use during cloudy days and at night. Because the power is DC, some uses require a DC–AC inverter to change to AC power. Fluorescent lighting fixtures are available with inverter ballasts. Some kitchen appliances and power tools may only be available for use with AC, but the number of DC-compatible appliances is increasing.

For systems that aren't attached to the utility grid, PV system batteries help smooth out supply and use patterns. In homes, PV production peaks at noon, while use peaks in the evening. Stores, shops, and cottage industries tend to have usage that coincides more closely with PV production. This reduces drain on the battery and allows less expensive batteries to be used. Batteries must be able to supply most or all of the electrical requirements for a given period, usually three days of cloudy weather. The cost of replacing the backup battery adds to the system cost over time.

Commercial Photovoltaic Applications

Until the late 1980s, PV systems had very limited applications and were generally not cost effective. In 1982, ARCO started up the first PV central power station in

San Bernardino County, California. More recently, federally financed research and development and state and federal legislation have increased the impact of PV systems on commercial electrical power. In 1990, the U.S. Department of Energy (DOE) and 20 private companies initiated the PV manufacturing technology project (PV Mat), and in 1992 the DOE sponsored PV : bonus, a building cost-sharing project. These programs reduced PV module costs by more than half and spurred development of new PV module materials, construction technologies, product forms, and PV module efficiency. Costs for the power produced dropped from around $0.50 to $1 per watt to about half that.

Many states are establishing requirements for electricity from renewable sources. By 2003, electricity suppliers in Massachusetts will be required by law to provide electricity generated from renewable sources, such as solar PV systems.

Designing Buildings for Photovoltaic Systems

PV system arrays are complete connected sets of modules mounted and ready to deliver electricity. Building mounted arrays are stationary and usually consist of flat plates mounted at an angle. Tracking arrays follow the motion of the sun, providing more contact with the solar cells.

A building with good access to the sun and a roof that faces south is ideal for installation of a PV system. Roofs that face east or west may also be acceptable. Flat roofs also work well for solar systems, because the PV array can be mounted flat on the roof facing the sky or can be mounted on frames that are tilted toward the south at the optimal angle. All or most of the sun's path should be clear and not obscured by trees, roof gables, chimneys, buildings, and other features of the building and surrounding landscape. Shade falling over part of the PV array for part of the day can substantially reduce the amount of electricity that the system will produce.

The amount of mounting space needed for the solar system is based on the size of the system. Most residential systems require between 4.6 and 19 square meters (50–200 square ft), depending on the type of PV module used and its efficiency. Composition-shingle roofs are the easiest type to work with, and slate roofs are the most difficult.

The decision to install a PV system involves several economic considerations. The connection to the electrical grid and the cost of power from the grid are basic criteria. The cost of the system components over the life of the whole installation must be added to the costs of maintenance and financing. The PV system's battery can double as an emergency source for computers and peripherals to cover grid power interruptions.

Photovoltaic panels can substitute for other construction materials, providing a cost savings. New solar electric technology has made possible a number of products that serve another building function while acting as photovoltaic cells. Building integrated PV (BIPV) elements are structures that combine PV modules into roof panels, roofing tiles, wall panels, skylights, and other building materials, replacing traditional building elements. Companies in the United States, Japan, and Europe are actively pursuing new module designs. Solar roof shingles, structural metal roofing, and architectural metal roofing are now available, along with window glass. These products use flexible, lightweight panels designed to emulate conventional roofing materials in design, construction, function, and installation. Structural metal panels are used for PV-covered parking, charging stations for electric vehicles, park shelters and other covered outdoor spaces, and for commercial buildings. PV shingles can be used in combination with conventional shingles. Custom-color crystalline solar cells, including gold, violet, and green, are becoming available. Other architectural module designs have space between the cells and opaque backings to provide diffuse daylighting along with electric production.

A single-residence PV system costs about $10 per watt of rated system capacity, including installation and all system components. A 1000-W system that would supply about one-third of the electricity for an energy-efficient home would cost approximately $10,000. With larger systems and projects where costs can be shared, the cost per watt could be reduced significantly. It currently costs from $10,000 to $40,000 to install a full solar system in a home, but rebates for up to one-half of that are currently offered in about 30 states, with more considering doing so. When purchased in quantity by a builder, solar panel systems add about $50 per month to the cost of the house, while saving from $50 to $100 in monthly electric bills.

From a long-term perspective, it does not have to cost more to build with solar. The smartest building designs will specify a tight building envelope and high-efficiency lighting and HVAC equipment. The savings from these energy-efficient measures can be used to pay for a solar investment over time. While it is common for builders and architects to focus on current equipment costs, it is critical to approach projects with a focus on the cost of both constructing and operating a building over its lifetime. States offer residential tax credits for solar applications, and there are both state and federal tax incentives available for corporations, making commercial solar applications highly attractive.

As mentioned previously, the 1978 Public Utility Regulatory Policy Act (PURPA) requires that electric utilities buy electrical power from small suppliers. The price is established at a price equal to the cost the utility avoids by not having to produce that power. This has been interpreted as the cost of the fuel alone, without consideration of the cost of additional plant construction and related expenses. Under PURPA, energy has been purchased at around three cents per kWh by the same utilities that sell energy at eight to fourteen cents per kWh. This policy has discouraged development of grid-connected PV installations.

More recently, states have adopted net-metering laws that require the utility to pay PV providers at the same rate at which it sells the electricity during PV generating hours. The energy that the customer generates and uses is credited at the rate the utility would otherwise charge that customer. Only when the customer is producing more energy than he or she uses does the utility pay at the avoided cost rate. This means that small producers get fair credit for the energy they supply themselves, and are able to sell any excess to the utility, even if at a low rate. When the PV user buys from the utility, they pay at the conventional utility rate. Thirty states offer net-metering as of 2001.

Net-metering benefits both the customer and the utility. Some utilities have instituted PV installation programs primarily for residences. The utility installs and maintains the PV system on the customer's property (usually the roof), and the customer pays a small surcharge to the utility bill. The result is an environmentally beneficial power supply.

With the metering systems currently in use and the relatively high initial product costs, PV grid-connected systems can seldom justify the cost of installation on economic grounds only, but this is changing. Some utilities allow the installation of small individual PV modules in existing conventional buildings. These PV modules plug into conventional outlets in the building and supply power to the building. The excess not used in the building is fed back to the utility via a reversible energy meter. The system can be expanded gradually without centralized installation expenses.

Two large PV installations were completed in 2001. The 49-kW system on the Field Museum of Natural History in Chicago is connected to the local utility's electricity grid, reducing the amount of power from nonrenewable, high-emissions sources during peak periods. The 200-kW system mounted on the Neutrogena Corporation headquarters in Los Angeles covers 2230 square meters (24,000 square ft) of roof area and will help reduce the company's energy consumption by about 20 percent.

At the DOE's headquarters in Washington, DC, a blank south-facing wall presents three-quarters of an acre of poured-in-place concrete to views from the National Mall. This eyesore is scheduled to become one of the largest solar installations in the world. The DOE, with the National Renewable Energy Laboratory, the American Institute of Architects, and the Architectural Engineering Institute, organized a design competition for a clean, renewable energy design. The winning design, proposed by architects at Solomon Cordwell Buenz & Associates in Chicago and engineers Ove Arup & Partners in New York, is an elegant, sweeping wall of tensioned cables, struts, and glass. The wall is a light, rigid structure that supports a PV collection system to turn solar energy into electricity, plus a solar thermal system that generates heat.

Many small projects are cropping up, such as the renovation of the Porter Square Shopping Center in Cambridge, Massachusetts, where roof-mounted PV panels provide almost all the energy needed for lighting. Another project is the Conde Nast skyscraper in New York City, where PV panels wrap the upper floors.

The National Fire Protection Association (NFPA) publishes NFPA 70, Article 690, *Solar Photovoltaic Systems*, which sets standards for PV systems. If the system is connected to the electrical grid, the local utility will have additional interconnection requirements. The electric utility will also know about the option of offering net-metering. Some homeowners' associations require residents to gain approval for a solar installation from an architectural committee, which in turn may require a system plan and agreement from neighbors. In most locations, building and/or electrical permits are required from city or county building departments. After the PV system is installed, it must be inspected and approved by the local permitting agency (usually the building or electrical inspector) and often by the electric utility as well.

More than 500,000 homes worldwide use PV to supply or supplement their electricity requirements, though all but about 10,000 are rural or remote off-grid applications. Residential and commercial BIPV are the most likely large-scale markets for PV in the developed countries. With participation of architects and building engineers, the technology is taking a progressively more sophisticated, elegant, and appropriate role in building design, putting energy-producing buildings within our reach.

Fuel Cells

Fuel cell systems are currently being developed and marketed for residential and light commercial applications in Europe beginning in mid 2003. The fuel cell units, which operate on natural gas or propane, will be used to generate electricity for backup electrical power or as primary power. Some of the fuel cells will be offered in cogeneration units, using the heat generated by the fuel cell for space heating and domestic hot water. The electricity produced will replace or reduce use of electricity from the electrical grid.

The Long Island Power Authority in New York State is connecting 75 fuel cells to its electric grid. The fuel cells are intended to add to the reliability and performance of the electrical grid system. By connecting the fuel cells directly to the transmission grid, the electricity they create will be distributed through the utility's electric transmission and distribution system.

A new 500-W residential cogeneration fuel cell system is being introduced for the Japanese residential market. The goal is an efficient, cost-effective fuel cell system using compact 1-kW and 500-W fuel cells, well suited to the residential and apartment markets in Japan, where the demand for low-power alternative energy sources is strong. The manufacturer hopes to develop a technology base for new products in the United States and Europe as well.

ELECTRICAL SYSTEM DESIGN PROCESS

Engineers start the process of designing electrical systems by estimating the total building electrical power load. They then plan the spaces required for electrical equipment such as transformer rooms, conduit chases, and electrical closets. The amount of energy a building is permitted to consume is governed by building codes. A building energy consumption analysis determines whether the building design will meet the target electrical energy budget. If not, the engineer must modify the electrical loads and reconsider the projected system criteria. The engineer will incorporate energy conservation devices and techniques and draw up energy use guidelines to be applied when the building is occupied. These techniques depend upon the day-to-day voluntary actions of the building's occupants, which are hard to determine during the planning phase.

Once the electrical load is estimated, the engineer and the utility determine the point at which the electrical service enters the building and the meter location. They decide on the type of service run, service voltage, and the building utility voltage. With the client, the engineer looks at how all areas of the building will be used and the type and rating of the client's equipment, including specific electric ratings and service connection requirements.

The electrical engineer gets the electrical rating of all the equipment from the HVAC, plumbing, elevator, interior design, and kitchen consultants. This communication is often made at conferences where the electrical consultant makes recommendations to the other specialists regarding the comparative costs and characteristics of equipment options.

The electrical engineer is responsible for determining the location and estimated size of all required electrical equipment spaces, including switchboard rooms, emergency equipment spaces, and electrical closets. Panel boards are normally located in closets but may be in corridor walls or other locations. The architect must reserve spaces for electrical equipment.

The electrical engineer, the architect, the interior designer, and the lighting designer design the lighting for the building. Plans may have to separate the lighting plan from the layouts for receptacles, data, and signal and control systems. Underfloor, under-carpet, over-ceiling wiring and overhead raceways are usually shown together on their own plan. The engineer then prepares a lighting fixture layout. All electrical apparatus is located on a plan, including receptacles, switches, and motors. Data processing and signal apparatus is located. Telecommunications outlets, network connections, phone outlets, speakers and microphones, TV outlets, and fire and smoke detectors are shown. Control wiring and building management system panels are also indicated.

Next, all lighting, electrical devices, and power equipment is circuited to appropriate panels. The engineer will detail the number of circuits needed to carry the electrical load, and the types and sizes of electrical cables and materials and electrical equipment, along with their placement throughout the building. Panel schedules are prepared that list all the circuits for each panel, including those for emergency equipment. Panel loads are computed that show how much power is circuited through each panel. The engineer prepares riser diagrams that show how wiring is run vertically, and designs the panels, switchboards, and service equipment. After computing the sizes of wiring sizes and protective equipment ratings, the engineer checks the work. The engineer then coordinates the electrical design with the other consultants and the architectural plans, and continues to make changes as needed.

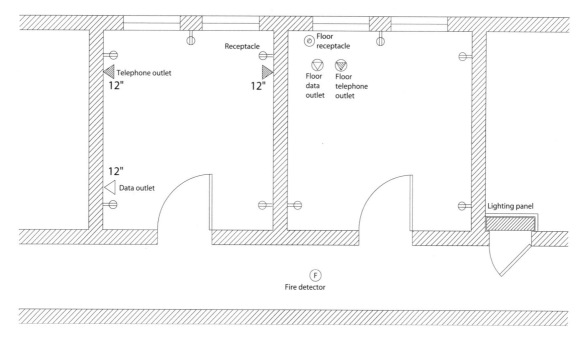

Figure 27-4 Electrical power plan.

   Interior designers are also responsible for showing electrical system information on their drawings (Fig. 27-4). The electrical engineer uses the interior design drawings to help design the electrical system. The interior design drawings often indicate all electrical outlets, switches, and lighting fixtures and their type. Large equipment and appliances should be indicated, along with their electrical requirements. Communication system equipment, like public phones, phone outlets, and related equipment, and computer outlets are shown. In new buildings, the location and size of equipment rooms, including switching rooms and electrical closets, should be coordinated with the electrical engineer.

The designer should be familiar with the location and size of the electrical panels, and with the building systems that affect the type of wiring used, such as plenum mechanical systems. The interior designer must know the locations of existing or planned receptacles, switches, dedicated outlets, and ground fault circuit interrupters (GFCIs). Lighting fixtures, appliances, equipment, and emergency electrical systems affect the interior design. You may need to coordinate the location of equipment rooms. The presence of an uninterrupted power supply or standby power supply is also important to know about.

The interior designer does not usually need to be completely familiar with the electrical code requirements, but there are several areas that may affect interior design work. Building codes set limits on the total amount of energy used by the building, including equipment and lighting, so the interior designer should be aware of energy-efficient options. The *National Electrical Code* (NEC) is also known as NFPA 70. The NEC sets the minimum standard for all electrical design for construction, and is revised every three years. It is the only model electrical code published, and is the basis for electrical codes in almost all jurisdictions. Interior designers rarely use the NEC, as it is the responsibility of the electrical engineer to design the electrical system. On smaller projects, a licensed electrical contractor will know the codes. However, since you will typically specify the location of electrical outlets and fixtures, you need to know basic code requirements. The electrical code includes restrictions on the proximity of electrical components and plumbing, for example. Standards for electrical and communications systems are set by the American National Standards Institute (ANSI), the National Electrical Manufacturers Association (NEMA), and the Underwriters Laboratories (UL). In addition, the Americans with Disabilities Act (ADA) specifies mounting heights for outlets and fixtures in handicapped accessible spaces.

Electrical Service Equipment

● ● ●

There are two separate electrical systems in most buildings. The electrical power system (Fig. 28-1) distributes electrical energy through the building. The electrical signal or communication system, which we look at later, transmits information via telephone, cable TV wires, or other separate data lines. The electrical power service from the utility line may come into the building either overhead or underground. The length of the service run and type of terrain, as well as the installation costs, affect the decision of which to use. Service voltage requirements and the size and nature of the electrical load also influence the choice. Other considerations include the importance of appearance, local practices and ordinances, maintenance and reliability criteria, weather conditions, and whether some type of interbuilding distribution is required.

Overhead service costs from 50 to 90 percent less than underground service to install, but the cost of underground service is decreasing. Overhead service is preferred for carrying high voltages over long runs and where the terrain is rocky. Access for maintenance is easier with overhead service. Wires on poles are more prone to problems in bad weather than underground cables.

Underground service is barely noticeable, very reliable, and has a long life. All this comes at a higher cost. Underground service is used in dense urban areas. The

service cables run in pipe conduits or raceways that allow for future replacement. Direct burial cable may be used for residential service connections.

SERVICE ENTRANCE

Wires called service conductors extend from the main power line or transformer to the building's service equipment (Fig. 28-2). The portion of the overhead service conductors leading from the nearest utility pole to the building is called the service drop. In a residence, you may see three cables twisted together, or in older houses, running separated. In underground systems, the portion of the service conductor extending from the main power line or transformer to the building is called the service lateral. The section of the service conductor that extends from the service drop or service lateral to the building's service equipment is called the service entrance conductor. A grounding rod or electrode is firmly embedded in the earth to establish a ground connection outside the building.

The network of wires that carry electrical current through a building stretches out from a single center, the main service panel, which is usually located where the power line enters the building. In a residence, the

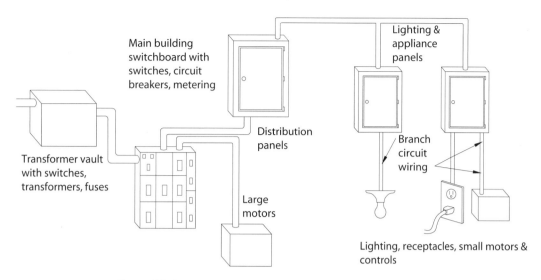

Figure 28-1 How electricity is distributed through a building.

main service panel is usually located in the basement or in a utility room. In larger buildings, this equipment is usually located in a switchgear room near the entrance of the service conductors, and is mounted on a main switchboard. The main service panel is located as close as possible to the service connection to minimize voltage drop and to save wiring. Secondary switches, along with fuses and circuit breakers for controlling and protecting the electrical power supply to a building, are also in the main service panel.

 To protect firefighters, the main service panel has a main disconnect (or service) switch. The disconnect switch must be in a readily accessible spot near where the service enters the building. Access to the main disconnect switch must not be blocked. In a residential building, the main disconnect is usually the main switch or breaker of the panel board. This may be a lever disconnect, with an external handle controlling contact with two main fuses in a cabinet. When the lever is pulled to the "off" position, the main power supply is shut off. Some residential systems have a pullout block arrangement. In this type of disconnect switch, the main cartridge fuses are mounted on one or two nonmetallic pullout blocks, and pulling firmly on the handgrips removes the blocks from the cabinet and disconnects the power. Other systems use a single main circuit breaker, which shuts off all power when switched to the "off" position. Some homes are not required by the *National Electrical Code* (NEC) to have a single main disconnect, and use a multiple breaker main. All breakers in the main section, up to a maximum of six, must be switched off to disconnect service. It is important to maintain easy access to the main disconnect.

When the voltage used by the building is different from the service voltage, a transformer is used to transform alternating current (AC) of one voltage to AC of another voltage. Transformers are not used with direct current (DC), which can only be used at its original voltage. Transformers may be pole or pad mounted outside a building or in a room or vault within the building. Step-down transformers lower voltage, and step-up transformers do the opposite. Typically, a transformer will step down incoming 1460V service to 480V for distribution within the building. Another transformer then steps down 480V to 120V for receptacle circuits. Low or secondary voltages used in buildings include 120, 208, 240, 277, and 480 volts.

Electric Meters

A watt-hour meter measures and records the quantity of electric power consumed over time. Meters are supplied by the utility, and are always placed ahead of the main disconnect switch so that they can't be disconnected. Meters are located outside at the service point or inside the building, where they must be kept readily accessible to utility personnel. Manual reading of kilowatt-hour meters of individual consumers is labor intensive. Meters are often inaccessible, and meter readers may face hostile dogs and inclement weather. Remote reading of inside meters is now common. Programmable electro-optical automatic meter-reading systems can be activated locally or from a remote location. Meter data is transferred electrically to a data processing center, where bills and load profiles are prepared, and area load

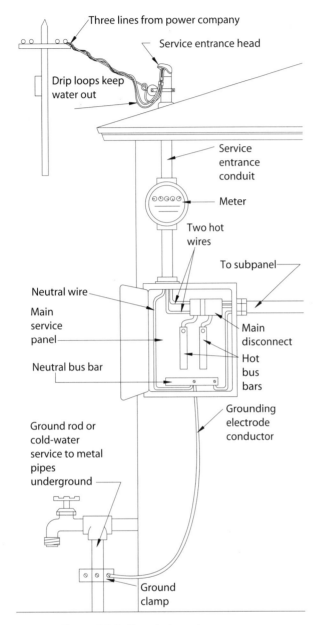

Figure 28-2 Electrical service entrance.

energy consumed in units of kilowatt-hours. In single-occupancy buildings or where the landlord pays for electrical service, there is one meter. For multitenant buildings, banks of meters are installed so that each unit is metered separately. A single meter is not allowed in new multiple dwelling constructions by federal law, as tenants tend to waste energy when they don't have to pay for it directly.

Advanced smart meters are now available that tell you how much electricity really costs right this hour or minute, and how much it would be worth to you, in real money, to conserve. Electricity prices are set largely by what it costs to produce enough electricity for the busiest few hours of the year, with prices rising dramatically when demand threatens to outstrip supply. A considerable portion of what you pay for electricity each month covers the risk of these rare price spikes and the cost of building special power plants like jet turbines and hydroelectric reservoirs that are used only rarely to cover demand peaks. If enough people had electric meters that said, in effect, you can save 25 cents by waiting until midnight to dry your clothes, demand could be measurably reduced, enough to trim price spikes significantly.

Electric utilities already offer this type of service to their largest industrial and institutional customers, giving them bounties to shut down factories or conserve power when shortages and rolling blackouts loom. Utilities are also initiating Web sites that allow participating businesses to get real-time electric price information, with incentives to cut back use when prices soar.

Companies are developing technologies for the small-user market, such as a device that connects home and business electric meters, and conceivably individual appliances, through the Internet to electric utilities. Utilities would be able to collect billing information directly over the Internet, rather than sending out meter readers. Puget Sound Energy in suburban Seattle has outfitted 1 million homes and businesses with advanced meters that take readings every 15 minutes and send them back wirelessly. Eventually, utilities may be able, with customer's approval, to control things inside the house like thermostats, electric heaters, clothes dryers, and dishwashers. This would allow consumers to save energy and electric costs without having to repeatedly check their electric meters or the utility's Web site.

Other Service Equipment

The area where a step-down transformer, meters, controls, buswork, and other equipment are located is called a unit substation or transformer load center. It

patterns can be studied. Miniature radio transmitters on the meter can be remotely activated to transmit current kilowatt-hour data, which is encoded and recorded automatically. Such meters are more expensive but are replacing conventional units, resulting in a large reduction in labor costs, and better quality and quantity of data. Even with remote readers, the meter must be available for inspection and service.

Within the meter, the electricity drives a tiny motor at a speed proportional to the rate at which current passes through the wires. The motor advances pointers on dials by means of gears, and records the quantity of may be located outdoors or indoors in a basement with ventilation, with access by authorized personnel only. Transformers produce heat, which must be either ventilated or used. They are usually located on an exterior wall, with a louver with a bird screen. Indoor locations help to avoid vandalism and hide the transformer's appearance. Transformer rooms may have to be heated in cold climates. Transformer vaults are fire-rated enclosures provided in case of rupture of an oil-filled transformer case. Transformer vaults often have to be vented to the outside with flues or ducts. When a transformer is located outdoors, no building space is required, and there is less of a heat or noise problem. Outdoor locations cost less and are easier to maintain or replace. They provide an opportunity to use low-cost, long-life, oil-filled units.

ELECTRICAL PANELS

The layout of the electrical system starts with the location of the electrical panels (Fig. 28-3). In residences, the service equipment and the building's panel board are combined in one unit. The panel board is usually located in the garage, a utility room, or the basement. It is located as close to major electrical loads as feasible, and sometimes an additional subpanel is added near kitchen and laundry loads. In apartments, panels are often located in the kitchen or in a corridor immediately adjacent to the kitchen, where they are used as the code-required means for disconnecting most fixed appliances.

In smaller commercial buildings, electrical panels may be recessed into corridor walls. In small office, retail, and other buildings, lighting panels may be mounted in a convenient area to enable the use of circuit breakers for load switching. Buildings six and more stories high use electrical closets for the panels, and risers to connect floors. Larger buildings use strategically located electrical closets to house all electrical supply equipment.

A switchboard is the main electrical panel that distributes the electricity from the utility service connection to the rest of the building. A switchboard is a large freestanding assembly of switches, fuses, and/or circuit breakers that provides switching and overcurrent protection to a number of circuits connected to a single source. Switchboards often also include metering and other instrumentation. The switchboard distributes bulk power into smaller packages and provides protection for that process. Modern switchboards are all of a type called "deadfront," where all live points, circuit breakers, switches, and fuses are completely enclosed in the metal structure. Pushbuttons and handles on the panel front control the equipment.

The NEC regulates the size of the room that contains a switchboard. When equipment is located on both sides of the room, access space is required on both sides. If the room contains a transformer also, additional space must be allowed. The room must be ventilated either directly to the outside or with ducts and fans. Smaller distribution switchboards do not require a special room, and are usually located in a wire screen enclosure with "Danger—High Voltage" signs. Switchboard rooms require exits, hallways, and hatches large enough for the installation and removal of equipment.

Low-voltage switchboards with large circuit breakers, and all high-voltage (over 600V) equipment are referred to as switchgear. In commercial, industrial, and public buildings, switchgear is usually located in the basement in a separate well-ventilated electrical switchgear room. Switchgear rooms, emergency generator rooms, and transformer vaults must be completely enclosed and must have their own emergency lighting source.

Panelboards are similar to switchboards but on a smaller scale. They accept relatively large blocks of power and distribute smaller blocks of electricity to each floor or tenant space. Within the panelboard, main buses,

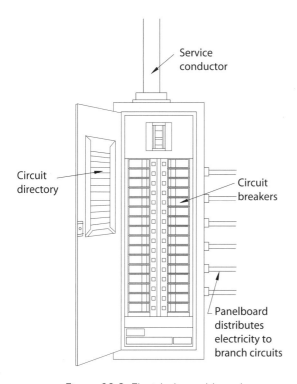

Service conductor

Circuit directory

Circuit breakers

Panelboard distributes electricity to branch circuits

Figure 28-3 Electrical panel board.

fuses, or circuit breakers feed smaller branch circuits that contain lighting, motors, and so forth. This equipment is mounted inside an open metal cabinet called a back-box, with prefabricated knockouts at the top, bottom, and sides for connecting conduits carrying circuit conductors. The panelboard may have a main circuit breaker that disconnects the entire panel in the event of a major fault. Small panels in residential work may be referred to as load centers.

One-sided panels are housed in electrical closets or cabinets placed in or against a wall. They are stacked vertically in multistory buildings. Each floor may also have one or more branch panelboards that supply electricity to a particular area or tenant. Additional distribution panels are located as needed by the loads they serve. Self-contained areas, like laboratories, should have their own panels.

ELECTRICAL CLOSETS

The space allotted for electrical closets varies to fit other architectural considerations. They are vertically stacked with other electrical closets so as not to block horizontal conduits. Outside walls or spaces adjacent to shafts, columns, and stairs are not good locations. Electrical closet spaces should not have other utilities, like piping or ducts, running through them either horizontally or vertically.

Each electrical closet has one or more locking doors. Inside is space for current and expansion panels, switches, transformers, telephone cabinets, and communications equipment. Floor slots or sleeves allow conduit and bus risers to pass through from other floors. The electrical closet must have space, lighting, and ventilation for the electrician to work comfortably and safely on installations and repairs. Electrical closets and cabinets must be fire-rated, as they are common places for fires to start, and they should not be located next to stairwells or other main means of egress. The electrical engineer is responsible for locating electrical closets, and their location will have implications for the interior designer's space plan.

ENERGY CONSERVATION AND DEMAND CONTROL

In the past, issues of energy conservation and electrical demand limitation were essentially economic decisions. Owners balanced the cost of installing control equipment against the potential for savings on electrical bills. Today, legislation mandates energy use limitations, including lighting controls in certain nonresidential buildings. The trend toward stricter regulations continues.

Energy conservation affects the work of the electrical engineer, the architect, the interior designer, and the building's owner and occupants. Conservation can start with the selection of high-efficiency motors, transformers, and other equipment. Electrical load control equipment is often necessary to meet code requirements for energy budgets. The electrical design should plan to accommodate expansion by making it simple to add additional equipment at a later date, rather than by oversizing the original equipment.

We have already looked at a number of ways to conserve electrical energy. In residential buildings with multiple tenants, individual user metering makes the tenant financially responsible for energy use. The exceptions are hotels, dormitories, and transient residences. Electrical heating elements should be avoided, as they use a high-grade resource for a low-grade task. When we discuss lighting design, we look at how remote control switching for blocks of lighting conserves energy.

Sophisticated, sensitive electronic equipment is becoming a greater part of the commercial building electric load. Computers, building automation systems, telephone automation systems, printers, fax machines, PC networks, and copiers are commonplace. This high-tech equipment can save energy by limiting space requirements, reducing the need for direct meetings, and replacing the hand delivery of documents, but it uses electricity to do these things. Look for the ENERGY STAR® symbol on computers and home office equipment, especially color monitors and laser printers.

Energy may leak from home electronics and small household appliances that require direct current, such as televisions, VCRs, cordless phones, telephone answering machines, portable tools, and rechargeable vacuum cleaners. These implements draw energy when in use and also when the power is apparently off. The average U.S. household leaks 50 W of electricity continuously, or around 440 kW-h per year. This adds up to over $3 billion in electricity in the United States per year. Televisions, VCRs, and cable boxes account for half of this, for instant-on, remote control, channel memory, and those light-emitting diode (LED) clocks that always read 12:00. Digital satellite systems also leak an average of 13 W when not in use. Direct current transformers, such as those on electric toothbrushes, draw 2 to 6 W of electric power even when not in use or when the appliance is fully charged. To encourage your client to save energy, advise them to unplug equipment that is not in use, and look for ENERGY STAR appliances, which leak less energy.

All electrical riser shafts should be sealed to avoid building heat loss. Electrical equipment should be located in the coolest possible place, preferably below grade, so that it doesn't add to the cooling load.

Electrical load control, also referred to as demand control, switches or modulates the electric load in response to a central signal. Originally, techniques for load control did not always result in financial savings. Modern miniaturized programmable control elements are more economical. For lighting, panelboards with miniaturized programmable elements are called intelligent panelboards.

Beginning in the 1980s, many utilities offered customers rebates of up to 40 percent of the cost of equipment and renovations that would reduce maximum electrical demand levels and overall energy use. By limiting the maximum amount of energy used at peak times and the overall total amount of electricity needed, utilities avoided having to invest in the construction of new power plants. Most large users invested large sums in electrical demand control and energy conservation and management equipment, resulting in lower electrical bills. Rebate policies made demand control cost-effective, and although rebate programs are no longer in effect, energy conservation equipment and techniques are now widespread. These policies led to a considerable reduction in the use of electrical power and energy nationwide.

The oldest and simplest type of utility-sponsored demand control is a utility rate schedule that varies with the time of day, offering lower rates for off-peak hours. The utility installs a free, time-controlled circuit switch for use with water heaters, well pumps, battery chargers, and so forth, where time delay is possible. The equipment is energized only during hours of low demand, which are usually mid-afternoon and after midnight.

Industrial and commercial installations may adopt user supplied demand control for a reduction of 15 to 20 percent in electric bills. The system disconnects and reconnects electrical loads to level off demand peaks. These interruptions can be very short and virtually unnoticeable. These systems control heating, ventilating, and air-conditioning (HVAC) loads, lighting loads, and process loads in small commercial, institutional, and industrial buildings. Since a person needs to determine the safety of shutting off certain other loads, essential lighting, elevators, communication equipment, computers, process control, and emergency equipment are not controlled by automatic systems. Manual systems also exist that trigger alarms indicating that it is time to connect or disconnect a load.

Intelligent panelboards are compact, centralized programmable microprocessors that provide electrical load control and switching functions directly within the panelboard, eliminating external devices and the associated wiring. The intelligent panelboard can also accept signal data from individual remote or network sources, and provide status reports, alarm signals, operational logs, and local bypass and override functions. The elimination of remote relays, relay panels, programmable time switches, and remote-control switches, and the wiring that goes with them, offsets the high initial cost of these systems. An intelligent panel board simplifies and improves facility operations and reduces maintenance costs and electric bills.

Other options for energy conservation include systems that conform to an ideal energy use curve automatically. Forecasting systems are the most sophisticated, most expensive, and most effective energy control systems for large structures with complex needs. They are part of a computerized central control facility.

Electrical Circuit Design

Once the building is connected to the community's electrical grid, you need to locate the places where you want the electricity to be available and provide a way to turn it on and off safely. During the design of a building, the electrical engineer or electrical contractor will design the type of circuiting, wire sizes, and so forth. As the interior designer, you should be familiar with the basic principles of power supply and distribution, in order to be able to coordinate interior design issues with the rest of the design team.

Because the location of outlets and switches is dependent upon the layout of furniture and intended use of the room, they are often shown on the interior design drawings. Power requirements and locations for special built-in equipment are also usually indicated on the interior design drawings. As the interior designer, you will want to approve the appearance of cover plates and other visible electrical devices.

The information the interior designer supplies is integrated into the electrical engineer's drawings. The electrical engineer will take cost and safety into consideration in the design of the electrical system. In addition to the construction cost of the system, the decisions made by the electrical engineer consider the cost of materials over the life of the building, and the cost of energy to run the system.

As you know, electricity must have a complete path or circuit from its source, through a device, and back to the source. An electrical circuit is a loop. Interrupting the circuit, as with a switch, stops the flow around the loop. When a lamp or appliance is turned on, alternating current (AC) electricity flows both ways in the loop, changing direction 60 times a second (60 cycles, or 60 hertz).

Lines from the power company run either overhead or underground to carry electricity from a transformer through the meter and into the service entrance panel. In smaller buildings, service is usually provided at 230 or 240V. Most homes have three-wire service, with two hot conductors each supplying 115 or 120V, and one neutral conductor. The actual pressure (voltage) supplied can vary between 115 and 125V within a given day.

The wires that carry the electrical service must be protected from damage within the structure of the building. In wood residential construction, a tough protective plastic sheath houses all three wires. In heavier construction, the wires are run in steel or plastic pipes called conduits. Conduits provide better protection, and new wires can be installed by pulling them through existing conduits, which can't be done with plastic-sheathed cable.

Electrical power distribution systems are designed to provide the amount of energy required at the location desired, and to do this safely. Even the smallest part of the system is connected to a powerful utility network, so the potential for physical damage, injury, and fire is always present. The solution is to isolate electrical conductors from the structure of the building, except at the specific points, such as wall receptacles, where you want contact. Insulating the conductors and putting them in protective raceways accomplishes this.

The *National Electrical Code* (NEC) sets minimum standards for electrical design for construction. Local inspection authorities visit the site at least twice during construction to determine whether the design, material, and installation techniques meet national and local code requirements. The first visit is after the raceways have been installed (called roughing-in) and before the wiring and closing-in of the walls. A second visit is made after the entire job is complete.

The quality of the installation is the responsibility of the contractor. The designer must be wary of equipment substitutions by the contractor, whose bid was submitted on the basis of the plans and specifications. The contractor should be required to supply the equipment that is specified.

GROUNDING

To receive a shock two things must occur simultaneously: you must touch a hot wire (or a metal object in contact with a hot wire) and you must be grounded (Fig. 29-1). An electrical circuit has three wires. The hot wire, which is covered by black insulation (or any color but white, green, or gray) runs side by side with the neutral and ground wires. The neutral wire has a white or gray insulation. The ground wire is either bare copper or has green insulation. Homes built before 1960 often don't have a ground wire.

The hot wire carries the electrical power generated by your local utility. It's always poised and waiting to deliver its charge from inside an outlet or behind a switch, but current won't flow and release its power until it has a way to get back to its source, and to close the loop of the circuit. The neutral wire closes the loop. When you throw a switch to turn on an electric light bulb, you are essentially connecting the hot and neutral wires together and creating a circuit for electricity to follow.

The hot wire immediately senses this path and releases its energy. If nothing impeded the current flow, most of that energy would go unused. A light bulb or other electrical device standing in the path between the hot and the neutral wire uses up virtually all the energy available in the hot wire, leaving little for the neutral wire to carry back to the source. This is why you get a shock from touching the hot wire but not the neutral one, even when current is flowing.

When you get a shock from a hot wire, your body acts like a neutral wire and completes the circuit to the damp ground you are standing on. This is because the earth itself is also an excellent path that leads back to the power source and closes the loop. In fact, the electrical system uses the earth as an alternate path for safety purposes. The neutral wire is connected to the ground at the main service panel. From the main service panel, a wire goes to a copper-coated steel rod driven deeply

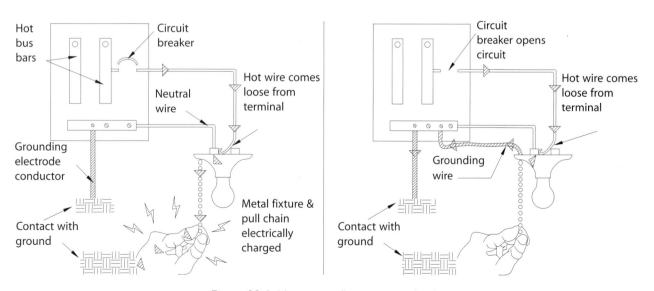

Figure 29-1 How grounding prevents shocks.

into the earth beside the building, or to a metal water pipe that enters underground in older buildings. The power source is also grounded through a wire from the transformer on the utility pole to the earth. All building wiring is grounded. If you're not in contact with the damp ground, either by touching it directly or through wires, metal pipes or damp concrete in contact with the soil, you won't get a shock.

Your body is not as good an electrical path as a wire, even though it is about 90 percent water and water can be a good conductor. Your skin thickness, muscle, and other body traits make you a poor path for electrical current. Even so, your body is very vulnerable to electrical shocks. This is because shocks kill by stopping your heart. A steadily beating heart relies on tiny electrochemical nerve pulses that carry a current in the range of 0.001 A. Even a charge as small as 0.006 A can shatter the heart's microcircuitry and disrupt its beating rhythm. Often the nerves can't stabilize quickly enough to restore the circuitry and save your life.

An electric drill draws about 3 A and an electric mixer draws about 1 A, much more than the amount it takes for a fatal disruption of the heartbeat. Fortunately, it takes a fairly high voltage to push a significant amount of current through you. Generally, you won't get a shock from circuits under 24V. Electric toys fall into this range, as do doorbells, thermostats, telephones, security systems, cable TV, and low-voltage lighting. Even within this range, however, a shock can disrupt the heartbeat of a person with a pacemaker.

The best defense against a shock when you're handling electrical devices or appliances is to make sure your body is not grounded. Remember, current will go through you only when you are a path to the ground. Don't work with electricity while standing on damp ground or damp concrete, and don't work on a metal ladder that's resting on damp materials. Using electric tools and other electrical devices around the plumbing system can be dangerous, too. All these connect you with the ground.

The NEC has introduced three features that make electrical systems safer: the equipment ground, the ground fault circuit interrupter, and polarized plugs.

The Equipment Ground

 The equipment ground is the third wire, either bare copper or having green insulation, which runs alongside the hot and neutral wires. If you haven't seen it, you'll know it's there by the type of outlets and plugs used. The equipment ground is that third prong on a three-prong plug, the one that goes into the half-round hole in an outlet. While the ground wire appeared well before the 1950s, it wasn't required in residential wiring systems by the NEC until about 1960, so older homes that haven't been remodeled probably don't have an equipment ground.

The purpose of the equipment ground is to solve the problem of electrical leaks. Usually a hot wire is covered by insulation, buried in an electrical box inside a wall, or covered by motor housings and light sockets where you can't touch it. When equipment wears out, then electricity can escape through frayed insulation.

Faulty equipment grounds are most likely to occur where vibration and other types of movement wear out a wire's insulation or break the wire itself. Old refrigerators and washing machines, which vibrate a lot, are typical culprits. So are lamps whose insulated cords harden as they age but that still receive a lot of heavy use. When such leaks occur, a hot wire can be exposed or an entire metal appliance can be electrically charged, and you risk a shock any time you touch it. Such a fault could connect the metal case of the appliance with the electrical power circuit. If you touch the now electrified metal case and a ground, like a water pipe, you would get a very nasty 120V shock. If your hands are wet when you make contact, the resulting shock could be fatal. Consequently, appliance manufacturers recommend that appliance cases be grounded to a cold water pipe, and supplied with three-wire plugs. Two of the three wires connect to the appliance, and the third to the metal case.

The ground wire runs alongside the hot and neutral wires and is attached to the metal parts of electrical boxes, outlets, and electrical tools and appliances that could carry an electrical charge should a leak occur. The ground wire siphons off those leaks by providing a good path back to the main service panel, exactly like the neutral wire. In effect, any leak that's picked up by the ground wire will probably blow a fuse or trip a breaker and shut the circuit down, signaling that you have a serious problem somewhere in the system.

To accept the three-prong plugs that accommodate the ground wire, and to provide a safe ground path, the NEC requires that all receptacles be of the grounding type, and that all wiring systems provide a ground path separate and distinct from the neutral conductor. Electrical codes require that each 120V circuit have a system of grounding. This prevents shocks from contacts where electricity and conductive materials come together, including parts of the electrical system like metal switches, junction and outlet boxes, and metal faceplates.

Where wiring travels through the building inside armored cable, metal conduit, or flexible metal conduit, the conductive metal enclosure forms the grounding system. When a metal enclosure is not used, a separate grounding wire must run with the circuit wires. Nonmetallic or flexible metallic wiring (Romex or BX) are required to have a separate grounding conductor. Nonmetallic cable already has a bare grounding wire within it. Insulated grounding conductors must have a green covering. We cover these types of wiring a little later on.

Bypassing the Equipment Ground

In an older house with two-prong outlets, we often are faced with the decision of how to plug in a three-prong plug for a microwave or other electrical device. Breaking off the third, round grounding prong or filing down the wide neutral blade of a polarized plug sabotages the equipment's safety features and increases the potential for dangerous shocks.

Replacing the old two-slot outlets with the newer, three-slot, grounded types that will accept all types of household plugs and will conveniently allow a three-prong cord to be plugged in anywhere seems like a good solution. However, since old two-wire systems do not have an equipment ground, the ground prong on the plug does not really go to ground. Installing a proper ground wire for these outlets is time consuming and costly, but if it's not done, you have created the illusion of a grounded outlet that isn't really safe.

Another way around the problem is the three-prong/two-prong adapter, more popularly known as a cheater plug. The NEC accepts this device provided you insert the screw that attaches the cover plate through the equipment ground tab. This screw connects to the metal yoke, which in turn connects to the metal electrical box. However, unless the metal electrical box has been grounded to earth, this again only creates a false impression of a safe, grounded system. This false sense of security puts you one step closer to receiving a dangerous or even fatal shock.

Safe Alternatives to Bypassing the Equipment Ground

The best solution for old, ungrounded electrical systems is to run grounded circuits from the service panel or other grounded electrical boxes to convenient parts of rooms. You can run cables up from the basement into walls or drop them down walls from the attic.

The 1993 NEC allows one exception to help resolve the grounding problem. You can substitute a ground fault circuit interrupter (GFCI) outlet for an ungrounded outlet because a GFCI behaves as though it is grounded, even if it isn't. A GFCI contains a hole for the grounding prong on three-prong plugs. It's particularly useful when you want to upgrade an old two-wire electrical system that doesn't have an equipment ground. You get safety at a bargain price—less than $10 for a GFCI versus tearing open walls to run new wiring. We discuss GFCI outlets in greater detail later on.

ELECTRICAL FIRE RISKS

The *National Electrical Code* (NEC) of the National Fire Protection Association (NFPA) defines fundamental safety measures that must be followed in the selection, construction, and installation of all electrical equipment. All inspectors, electrical designers, engineers, contractors, and operating personnel use the NEC. The NEC is incorporated into OSHA, the Occupational Safety and Health Act, and has the force of law.

The National Electrical Safety Code is published by the Institute of Electrical and Electronic Engineers (IEEE), and provides clearance for overhead lines, grounding methods, and underground construction. Many large cities, including New York, Boston, and Washington, DC, have their own electrical codes with additional regulations. The utility supplying the electrical service will also have its own standards.

The Underwriters Laboratories, Inc. (UL) establishes standards and tests and inspects electrical equipment. In addition, UL publishes lists of inspected and approved electrical equipment. Many local codes state that only electrical materials bearing the UL label of approval are acceptable.

An electrical permit is required when doing electrical work. It ensures that the work is reviewed with the local building inspector in light of local codes. The inspector will check the work to make sure it is done right.

CIRCUIT PROTECTION

Because the amperage available from the utility grid is almost unlimited, a 120V household system is powerful and dangerous. The electrical current could easily melt all the wiring in your home. Special devices that limit current are located in the main service panel. If you open up the door of your electrical panel, you will find either fuses or circuit breakers (and sometimes both), each rated to withstand a certain amount of current, usually 15 A. If the current exceeds the listed amount, the fuse will burn out (blow) or the breaker will trip, shutting off the current and protecting the wiring system from an overload. When this happens, it is a signal that you are trying to draw too much power through the wires.

Overloaded and short-circuited currents can result in overheating and fires. Circuit protective devices protect insulation, wiring, switches, and other equipment from these dangers by providing an automatic way to open the circuit and break the flow of electricity.

Fuses and Circuit Breakers

If too much current flows in a wire, it can get hot enough to set fire to surrounding material. Fuses and circuit breakers protect against this possibility by cutting off power to any circuit that is drawing excessive power. They provide an automatic means for opening a circuit and stopping the flow of electricity.

The key element in a fuse (Fig. 29-2) is a strip of metal with a low melting point. When too much current flows, the strip melts, or blows, thereby interrupting power in the circuit. When the fusible strip of metal is installed in an insulated fiber tube, it is called a cartridge tube. When encased in a porcelain cup, it is a plug fuse.

A circuit breaker (Fig. 29-3) is an electromechanical device that performs the same protective function as a fuse. A circuit breaker acts as a switch to protect and disconnect a circuit. A strip made of two different metals in the circuit breaker becomes a link in the circuit. Heat from an excessive current bends the metal strip, as the two metals expand at different rates. This trips a release that breaks

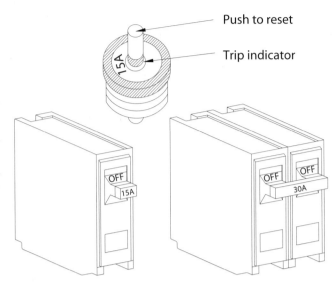

Figure 29-3 Circuit breakers.

the circuit. Commercial and industrial applications use solid-state electronic tripping control units that provide adjustable overload, short-circuit, and ground fault protection. Circuit breakers can be reset after each use, and can be used to manually switch the circuit off for maintenance work. They shut off the current to the circuit if more current starts flowing than the wire can carry without overheating and causing a fire. This may occur when too many appliances are plugged in at once, or when a short circuit occurs. Circuit breakers are easily installed as needed for various circuits in the building.

Both fuses and circuit breakers are rated in amperes and matched to the wiring they protect. Plug fuses are screwed in and are rated from 5 to 30 A, and 150V to ground maximum. Cartridge fuses are used for 30 A up to 6000 A and 600V. Cartridge fuses often show no sign of having blown. A blown screw-in fuse can generally be spotted by a blackened glass or break in the metal strip. Unlike circuit breakers, which can be reset after they trip, fuses must be replaced when they have been used to break a circuit. In neither case, however, should the circuit be reactivated until the cause of the problem has been located and fixed.

A demand for too much power, called an overcurrent, occurs when too many devices are connected to a circuit or when a failed device or loose wire causes a short circuit. Overloading the circuit with too many appliances or lighting fixtures is the commonest cause of fuses blowing repeatedly or circuit breakers tripping again and again. An overcurrent also may occur when high-wattage fixtures and appliance motors are turned on, because they momentarily need much more electricity to start than they draw when operating. If a cir-

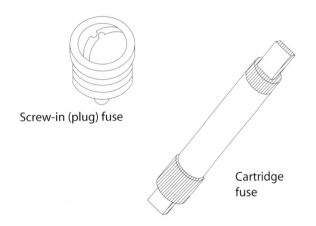

Screw-in (plug) fuse

Cartridge fuse

Figure 29-2 Fuses.

cuit is near capacity, a start-up overcurrent can blow a fuse, even though there is no real danger to the system.

Circuit breakers are built to withstand these momentary surges, but standard fuses are not. When a circuit often blows a fuse when an appliance such as a refrigerator or room air conditioner is turned on, a time-delay or slow-blow fuse can help cope with brief surge demands. Both plug and cartridge fuses are available in slow-blow designs that safely allow temporary overloads. Whether a fuse or a circuit breaker is the better choice depends on the application and on other technical considerations.

Ground Fault Circuit Interrupters

As we mentioned earlier, the NEC recognizes a ground fault circuit interrupter (GFCI or sometimes GFI) (Fig. 29-4) as a way to protect against shocks when a building's wiring is not grounded. GFCIs are actually designed for another primary use, which we now look at in more detail.

Even after ground wires were commonly installed in buildings, researchers found that shocks were still common, especially in damp or wet areas, including kitchens, bathrooms, basements, and outdoors. Plug-in devices such as hair dryers, power tools, and coffee makers that are in common use around sinks, in the basement, or out in the garage are part of the problem.

Water and electricity don't mix. Dampness in the soil or in concrete that rests in the soil makes either surface a good electrical conductor and a good ground. Metal faucets and drains are also excellent grounds, because the water supply lines and sewers that they connect with are usually underground. Shutting off a faucet with one hand while holding a faulty hair dryer with the other could be fatal.

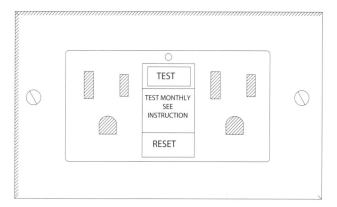

Figure 29-4 GFCI receptacle.

Unfortunately, the fuses or circuit breakers in the main service panel will not protect you from a lethal shock in such circumstances. Fuses and circuit breakers protect the wires in your house from overheating, melting the insulation, and causing a fire. They don't protect you against faults in the electrical ground.

Fortunately, the ground fault circuit interrupter, which is a special type of circuit breaker, was invented around 1970. The role of the GFCI is to protect you from a potentially dangerous shock. A GFCI device can be part of a circuit breaker or can be installed as a separate outlet.

When you leave a hair dryer with a frayed cord in a little spilled water that is in contact with the sink's metal faucet, you have the makings of a shocking situation. You could accidentally touch an exposed hot wire in the frayed cord while at the same time turning off the water faucet with your other hand. Even though the dryer is turned off, an electric current immediately flows from the cord, through your body, through the plumbing system, and eventually to ground. This is called a ground fault. It will not cause the circuit breakers or fuses in the main service panel to break the circuit, and the current will continue to flow through your body.

A GFCI instantaneously senses misdirected electrical current and reacts within one-fortieth of a second to shut off the circuit before a lethal dose of electricity escapes. When it senses a ground fault, the GFCI interrupts the circuit and switches it off.

Another function of GFCIs is to detect small ground faults (current leaks) and to disconnect the power to the circuit or appliance. The current required to trip a circuit breaker is high, so small leaks of current can continue unnoticed until the danger of shock or fire is imminent.

Ground fault circuit interrupters permit the easy location of ground faults. They are required in addition to circuit breakers in circuits where there is an increased hazard of accidental electrical shock, such as near bathroom sinks. If the GFCI senses any leakage of current from the circuit, it will disconnect the circuit instantly and completely. The GFCI does this by precisely comparing the current flowing in the hot and neutral legs of the circuit. If the amount of current is different, it means that some current is leaking out of the circuit.

Ground fault circuit interrupters have a relatively short history in the NEC. The 1971 code initially required them on circuitry controlling lights and other electrical equipment for swimming pools. It required GFCIs in outdoor locations in 1973 and at construction sites in 1974. The 1975 code required GFCI outlets in all new and remodeled bathrooms. Initial GFCI locations were undoubtedly limited to the most dangerous areas by the relatively high price of the device, about $25. As the price dropped below $10, the cost became insignificant compared to the safety gained. More recent versions of the NEC expanded GFCI requirements to include garages and basements.

The 1993 code requires GFCI protection for readily accessible outlets located outdoors, in crawl spaces and unfinished basements, and in garages. The NEC requires GFCIs in all standard 120V duplex receptacle outlets in bathrooms and kitchens. The code treats spas, hot tubs, and Jacuzzis as if they were swimming pools, and outlets, lights, and electrical equipment within a certain distance of pools all require GFCI protection. Local codes typically also require them in office break rooms, bar areas, and laundry rooms, as well as in outdoor and other damp locations. GFCIs should be used on all appliance circuits. Because lighting fixture circuits are commonly in the ceiling and are switch controlled, they are not usually required to have GFCIs.

Ground fault circuit interrupters can be installed built into a receptacle, or in an electrical distribution center in place of a circuit breaker, to protect that particular circuit. The type of GFCI that plugs into an existing outlet should only be used on a temporary basis, as on a construction site before permanent wiring is installed.

To make sure that GFCIs are working, manufacturers added the "test" and "reset" buttons that you see on them. Pushing the test button creates a small electrical fault, which the GFCI should sense and immediately react to by shutting off the circuit. The reset button restores the circuit. Repeated action by the GFCI to protect a leaking circuit will eventually wear the GFCI out. You should test your GFCIs every week and replace them immediately if they are not working properly.

BRANCH CIRCUITS

Branch circuits carry the electrical power throughout the building to the places where it will be used. After passing through the main service disconnect, each hot conductor (wire) connects to one of two hot bus bars in the distribution center. The bus bars are metal bars that accept the amount of current permitted by the main fuses or circuit breaker, and allow the circuit to be divided into smaller units for branch circuits. Each branch circuit attaches to one or both hot bus bars by means of fuses or circuit breakers.

Each 120V circuit has one hot and one neutral conductor. The hot conductor originates at the branch circuit overcurrent protective device (fuse or circuit breaker) connected to one of the hot bus bars. A 240V circuit uses both hot conductors, and originates at the branch overcurrent protective device connected to both hot bus bars.

All of the neutral conductors start at the neutral bus bar in the distribution center. All the neutral conductors are in direct electrical contact with the earth through a grounding conductor at the neutral bus bar of the service entrance panel. An overcurrent protective device never interrupts the neutral conductors, so that the ground is maintained at all times. The effect of this arrangement is that each branch circuit takes off from an overcurrent protective device and returns to the neutral bus bar.

In order to decide how many branch circuits to specify and where they should run, the electrical system designer takes into account a variety of different loads. Lighting is the first and often the greatest. Data processing equipment, convenience outlets, desktop computers and their peripherals, plug-in heaters, water fountains, and other miscellaneous electrical power users make up a second group. Heating, ventilating, and air-conditioning (HVAC) and plumbing equipment use electrical energy for motors and switches. Elevators, escalators, and material handling equipment, dumbwaiters, and trash and linen transportation systems are another group of loads. Kitchen equipment in restaurants, most hospitals, and some office, educational, and religious buildings can be a significant electrical load. In addition, some buildings contain special loads such as laboratory equipment, shop loads, display areas and display windows, flood lighting, canopy heaters, and industrial processes.

Once the electrical power requirements of various areas of the building are determined, the electrical engineer lays out wiring circuits to distribute power to points of use. Branch circuits extend from the final overcurrent device protecting a circuit to outlets served by the circuit. Each circuit is sized according to the amount of load it must carry, with about 20 percent of its capacity reserved for flexibility, expansion, and safety. To avoid excessive drops in voltage, branch circuits should be limited to less than 30 meters (100 ft) in length.

The electrical engineer will specify general-purpose circuits to supply current to a number of outlets for lighting and appliances. Manufacturers specify load requirements for lighting fixtures and electrically powered appliances and equipment, and the interior designer is often responsible for getting these specifications to the engineer. The design load for a general-purpose circuit depends on the number of receptacles served by the circuit, and on how the receptacles are used.

Branch circuits with multiple general-purpose-type 20-A outlets or multiple appliance-type outlets have a maximum 50-A capacity. Single-type outlets for specific pieces of equipment may be 200 to 300 A, depending upon the equipment needs. Lighting, convenience receptacles, and appliances should each be grouped on separate circuits. Audio equipment may need to be on the same ground as the room it is serving, to avoid interference problems. Similarly, dimmers may need to be shielded to protect sensitive electronic equipment.

Circuits are arranged so that each space has parts of different circuits in it. If receptacles within a space are located on more than one circuit, the loss of one receptacle will not eliminate all power to the space.

 The layout of the branch circuits, feeders, and panels is designed for flexibility in accommodating all probable patterns, arrangements, and locations of electrical loads. Laboratories, research facilities, and small educational buildings require much more flexibility than residential, office, and fixed-purpose industrial installations. However, with the rapid expansion of computers and other electronic equipment in home offices and small businesses, flexibility and expansion should be built into most electrical designs. It can be difficult to anticipate future uses and requirements, but an overly specific design wastes money and resources, both during initial installation and in operation.

In addition to being flexible, the building's electrical service must be reliable. The electrical service works together with the building's distribution system. The quality of the electrical utility's service is one key element in determining reliability, and the quality of the building's wiring system is the other. You can't make use of very reliable and expensive service if the power can't be reliably distributed to where it will be used. Because a system is only as reliable as its weakest element, redundant equipment is sometimes provided at anticipated weak points in the system. For especially critical loads within the system, as in healthcare facilities, the electrical system designer designates reliable power paths or provides individual standby power packages.

In addition to making sure that the electrical design is compliant with applicable codes, the system designer must prevent electrical safety hazards in the event of misuse, abuse, or failure of equipment. Large equipment may obstruct access spaces, passages, closets, and walls. Doors to rooms with electrical equipment should open out, so that a worker can't fall against a door and prevent rescue in an emergency. In some buildings, lightning protection is also a safety issue.

Economic factors influence the selection of equipment and materials for electrical systems. Equipment must function adequately and have a satisfactory appearance while minimizing costs. Where there are many competing brands and types of equipment with similar qualities, cost is the deciding factor. The initial purchase and installation cost is only one consideration. Low first cost equipment may result in higher energy costs, higher maintenance costs, and a shorter useful life. The life-cycle equipment costs over the life of the structure may make a more expensive purchase a better deal in the long run.

The calculation of energy use by electrical equipment involves complex evaluations of energy codes and budgets, energy conservation technologies, and energy controls. Buildings constructed with government participation may have energy budgets, such as a limited number of Btu per square foot per year. Some codes also require energy use calculations for heating and cooling as well as lighting equipment. Energy budgets affect electrical distribution systems, as set forth in the American Society of Heating, Refrigeration, and Air-Conditioning Engineers' (ASHRAE's) Standard 90.

Wiring and conduit are generally small and take up relatively little space in the building. Panels, motor control centers, busduct, distribution centers, switchboards, transformers, and other equipment are large, bulky, noisy, and highly sensitive to tampering and vandalism. Spaces for electrical equipment must be easy to maintain and well ventilated. They should be centrally located to limit the length of runs, and should allow room for expansion. Spaces should limit access to authorized personnel only, and should be designed to contain noise.

ELECTRICAL DESIGN FOR RESIDENCES

Residential electrical requirements are set by NFPA 70A, *Electrical Code for One & Two Family Dwellings*, which sets the distances for electrical outlets and mandates the use of GFCIs in wet locations. Electrical outlets are not permitted directly above baseboard heating units in newer buildings. Ranges and ovens, open-top gas broiler units, clothes dryers, and water heaters have their own specific code requirements or standards.

Electrical codes require that every room, hallway, stairway, attached garage, and outdoor entrance must have a minimum of one lighting outlet controlled by a wall switch. In rooms other than the kitchen and bathroom, the wall switch can control one or more receptacles for plugging in lamps rather than actual lighting outlets for ceiling- or wall-mounted lights. One lighting outlet of any type is required in each utility room, attic, basement, or underfloor space that is used for storage or that contains equipment that may require service.

The number of branch circuits required for a residence, including an allowance for expansion, is estimated by allotting one 15-A circuit per 37 to 45 square meters (400–480 square ft), or one 20-A circuit per 49 to 60 square meters (530–640 square ft) plus an allowance for expansion, with more provided as needed.

No point on a wall is permitted to be more than 1.8 meters (6 ft) from a 20-A, grounding-type convenience receptacle. Any wall 61 cm (2 ft) or more in length, including walls broken by fireplaces, must have a receptacle. You must have a receptacle within 1.8 meters (6 ft) of any door or opening, including arches but not including windows. Receptacles should not be combined with switches into a single outlet unless convenience of use dictates that the receptacle should be mounted as high as a switch. In rooms without overhead lights, provide a switch control for one-half of a receptacle intended for a lamp in an appropriate place.

Code requirements are geared to prevent us from running an octopus of appliance cords off an extension cord plugged into a single outlet. Too much power coming through a single extension cord can overheat the cord and cause a fire. The NEC requires a minimum of two 20-A appliance branch circuits exclusively for receptacle outlets for small appliances in the kitchen, pantry, breakfast and/or dining room, and similar areas, considering that any receptacle in these areas is a potential appliance outlet. Clock outlets are allowed on these circuits. All kitchen outlets intended to serve countertop areas are to be fed from at least two of these circuits, so that all countertop outlets are not lost if one circuit fails. According to the NEC, no point on the wall behind the countertop can be more than 61 cm (2 ft) from an outlet, and all countertop convenience receptacles must be GFCI types. Every counter space greater than 30 cm (1 ft) in length should have a receptacle (Fig. 29-5). With a maximum of four receptacle outlets per 20-A circuit, and an ever-increasing variety of small electrical appliances, you usually need more than two appliance circuits in the kitchen.

Dishwashers, microwaves, refrigerators, and garbage disposals each require their own separate 20-amp circuit. An electric range or oven requires an individual 50-A, 120/240V major appliance circuit. Gas appliances also require their own separate fuel lines. Receptacles behind stationary appliances like refrigerators do not count toward the 3.66-meter (12-ft) spacing requirement. Plan for a readily accessible means for disconnecting electric ranges, cooktops, and ovens within sight of these appliances. A small kitchen panel recessed into

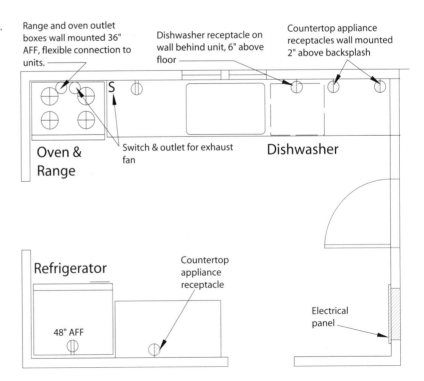

Figure 29-5 Typical kitchen power plan.

Range and oven outlet boxes wall mounted 36" AFF, flexible connection to units.

Dishwasher receptacle on wall behind unit, 6" above floor

Countertop appliance receptacles wall mounted 2" above backsplash

Oven & Range

Switch & outlet for exhaust fan

Dishwasher

Refrigerator

48" AFF

Countertop appliance receptacle

Electrical panel

the kitchen wall to control and disconnect kitchen appliances is a good idea.

In bathrooms, locate electrical switches and convenience outlets wherever needed, but away from water and wet areas. They must not be accessible from the tub or shower. All bathroom outlets should be GFCI types. Supply a minimum of one 20-A wall-mounted GFCI receptacle adjacent to the bathroom lavatory, fed from a 20-A circuit that feeds only these receptacles. Do not connect the receptacle near the lavatory to the bathroom lighting, exhaust fan, heaters, or other outlets.

Each bedroom in a house without central air-conditioning needs one additional circuit, similar to an appliance circuit, for use with a window air conditioner. Locate a pair of duplex outlets, two on each side of the bed, for clocks, radios, lamps, and electric blankets. For closets, switch controls are preferable to pull-chains, which are a nuisance but considerably cheaper.

To accommodate home offices, each study and workroom or large master bedroom should be equipped electrically to double as an office. At a minimum, allow six duplex 15- or 20-A receptacles on a minimum of two different circuits, one of which serves no other outlets, and all of which have adequate surge protection. An additional separate insulated and isolated ground wire, connected only at the service entrance, should run to boxes containing two of these receptacles, where it should be terminated, clearly marked, and labeled. This will allow special grounding receptacles if the normal receptacles have too much electrical noise for computer use. Install two phone jacks in recessed boxes, with an empty 19-mm ($\frac{3}{4}$-in.) conduit from the telephone entry service point to an empty 100-mm (4-in.) square box. The incoming telephone service lines need a surge suppressor.

The NEC requires a minimum of one 20-A appliance circuit exclusively for laundry outlets. In addition, an individual 30-A, 120/240V major appliance circuit, separate from the laundry circuit and rated for an electric dryer, must be supplied along with a heavy duty receptacle, unless it is certain that a gas dryer will be used.

Places that are often used for workshop-type activities, like garages, utility rooms, and basements, should have receptacles in appliance-type circuits, with a maximum of four receptacles per circuit. Basements are required to have a minimum of one receptacle. Receptacles in garages, sheds, crawl spaces, below-grade finished or unfinished basements, or outdoors must be GFCI types. GFCI-protected and weatherproofed receptacles must be located on the front and on the rear of the house, with a switch controlling them inside the house.

ELECTRICAL DESIGN FOR COMMERCIAL SPACES

The electrical code establishes requirements for convenience receptacles in commercial spaces. The code seeks to ensure that there are enough outlets to prevent a spaghetti-like tangle of extension cords, while respecting the total energy use in the space. An office of less than 37 square meters (400 square ft) is required to have one convenience receptacle per 3.7 square meters (40 square ft) or one per 3 meters (10 linear ft) of wall, whichever is greater. Larger offices need 10 outlets for the initial 37 square meters, with one outlet per 9.3 to 11.6 square meters (100–125 square ft) of additional space. Provide a minimum of one 20-A duplex receptacle for a computer terminal on an adjacent wall, power pole, or floor near each desk, with a maximum of six per 20-A branch circuit.

Office corridors require one 20-A, 120V receptacle for each 15.3 meters (50 linear ft) for vacuuming and waxing machines. All office electrical equipment should be specification grade.

Stores require one convenience outlet per 28 square meters (300 square ft) for lamps, show windows, and demonstration appliances. The type of store and the anticipated uses will determine locations and quantities.

Classrooms in schools need 20-A outlets wired two per circuit at the front and back of each classroom for opaque, slide, and video projectors. Side walls also need similar outlets, wired six to eight per circuit.

Computer areas in schools need to be laid out in detail, with two-section surface mounted or recessed raceways on the wall behind a row of computers, and two duplex 20-A receptacles at each computer station wired on alternate circuits. Another section of raceway for network cabling and wiring into peripherals helps contain all these frequently changed wires. Special equipment in school laboratories, shops, and cooking rooms require adequate outlets.

Public areas and corridors in schools require heavy-duty devices and key-operated switches, plastic rather than glass lighting fixtures, and vandal-proof equipment wherever possible. All electrical panels must be locked, and should be in locked closets.

ELECTRONIC EQUIPMENT PROTECTION

The sudden power increases, called surges, that momentarily disrupt a building's steady power flow can destroy many of our electrical appliances and other devices. Electrical power can jump from its normal 120V up to 400V or 500V. These electrical surges are invisible and give no warning, zipping right through the main electrical panel so fast that the circuit breakers and fuses don't notice them. Fortunately, most such surges are small and don't cause much damage. Except for the massive surge caused by a direct lightning strike, which is extremely rare, surges in the past were a minor curiosity rather than a problem.

The invention of sensitive electronic devices with microprocessors changed that. Microprocessors are found in computers, stereos, TV and VCR controls, garage door openers, telephones, and an increasing number of other common devices. Fax machines and printers are sensitive to surges. Home appliances with microprocessor controllers include ranges, dishwashers, ovens, microwaves, and clothes washers. Intercoms and security systems, plug-in radios, answering machines, smoke alarms, programmable thermostats, dimmers, and motion detectors may all have microprocessors.

Microprocessors use much less voltage than our electrical systems. Each microprocessor's built-in power supply converts 120V electricity to about 5V. Microprocessors like nice, steady current. Small changes in power, even a split-second surge, can scramble the electrical signals. A surge that slips past the power supply can destroy delicate chips and burn out circuits.

If your electrical system takes a direct hit, your electronic equipment will be destroyed, but the chances of this happening are low. It's more likely that lightning will induce a surge in your building's electrical system. A lightning strike generates a brief but very powerful magnetic field in the surrounding atmosphere. Electrical wiring from the utility pole and throughout the building acts like an antenna and picks up an electrical charge from the magnetic field as it briefly forms and collapses. The lightning does not even have to hit nearby power lines to cause damage. It could generate a charge from some distance away, and any power lines between your house and the lightning strike will conduct the surge.

Surprisingly, some of the most troublesome electrical surges come from inside the building itself. Large electric motors, like the ones in a refrigerator or air conditioner, generate a surge every time they switch on. Lightweight electric motors, like the one in a vacuum cleaner, also cause surges. The surge can run through any wire in the system in any direction and out to any device on the branch circuits. Not all of these surges are harmful, but they occur regularly as motorized appliances cycle on and off.

All computer installations, even the smallest home office, need to be protected from line transients with a surge suppressor. The multitap plug-in strips with built-in surge suppressors are inadequate unless they meet specifications for surge current, clamping voltage, and surge-energy suitable for the particular installation. Major data processing installations require additional types of treatment including voltage regulators, electrical noise isolation, filtering, and suppression, and surge suppressors.

Sensitive equipment should be isolated on separate electrical feeders. It is helpful to separate sensitive equipment physically to avoid problems from switching, arcing, and rectifying equipment. Fluorescent, mercury, sodium, and metal-halide discharge type lighting, especially with electronic ballasts, can cause interference. Separating the equipment-grounding pole of the electrical receptacle from the wiring system ground is a good idea where electronic dimmers, ballasts, and switching devices are present. These specially grounded receptacles have orange faceplates or an orange triangle on the faceplate.

There is a wide range of plug-in devices, called surge suppressors, surge protectors, or transient voltage surge suppressors (TVSS), with higher quality surge suppressors costing more. They range from cord-connected multioutlet strips to large three-phase units located at the building's service entrance. All are designed to limit a surge in voltage to a level that the protected equipment can withstand without damage. This is done by placing one or more devices in the path of the incoming voltage transient to obstruct the amount of current allowed through, or by placing devices that have a lower impedance (resistance) across an incoming power line in parallel with the protected load, so that the higher transient voltage bypasses the current coming into the building. Hybrid units combine both of these methods.

In general, look for these three things in a suppressor: a quick response time, low clamping voltage, and high energy-handling capacity. Suppression devices have to react quickly to sudden rises in voltage to prevent damage from the initial burst. Look for devices with quick response times, 10 nanoseconds (that's 10 billionths of a second) or less. That information should be stamped on the device itself or on its package.

Suppressors react to the voltage level. The clamping voltage sets the maximum voltage that the suppressor will allow through. When the voltage rises, the suppressor kicks in and diverts all voltage above the set level. Look for surge protection that clamps at 300V or less.

The longer the surge lasts, the more energy it carries, and the more energy the suppressor must divert or absorb. A suppressor will burn out immediately if the surge exceeds its energy-absorbing capability. Utility companies in many parts of the country will install a suppressor designed to absorb most lightning-induced surges for about $160. It's mounted at the electric meter or main panel and reacts relatively slowly, but it can absorb the intense energy induced by most nearby lightning strikes. You can choose this type and still install faster responding protectors to handle the residual charge that gets in, as well as lighter surges produced from inside the home.

Two other features are useful in a surge suppressor. Firstly, the suppressor should have three-line protection. That means that the device should protect all three wires—the hot, neutral, and ground—since surges can travel through any one of them. Secondly, make sure that the suppressor has some sort of indicator so you know if it is no longer working. Most suppressors can take only so many hits before they start to wear out and need replacement.

The right amount of protection involves balancing expense against efficacy. Good surge protection for even a home computer is expensive. The cost of the protection must be weighed against the cost of the equipment itself to see if it is worth protecting devices such as TVs and VCRs, as well as less expensive equipment. For a building in a region with frequent thunderstorms, such as Florida, it might be worthwhile to protect less expensive equipment too. It is worthwhile to buy good suppressors for all expensive and essential equipment. Some units suitable for small offices include a surge suppressor, line voltage conditioner, and backup battery for under $200 (Fig. 29-6). Unplugging equipment that isn't in use is a no-cost protection against surges.

Uninterruptible power supplies (UPS) are designed for computer and data processing facilities that can't tolerate power outages over 8 to 50 milliseconds (thousandths of a second) without serious risk of data loss. A UPS is an arrangement of normal and backup power supplies that transfers a facility's critical load from normal to backup mode in so short a time that no computer malfunction results. The minimum required by computer industry guidelines for computer equipment tolerance is 8.3 milliseconds. Standby power usually runs for five to ten minutes, which is enough time to shut down the equipment manually or automatically. Some industrial processes can't tolerate any shutdown, and the standby power for them is designed to run as long as needed. The selection of appropriate UPS systems can be highly complex.

Users of electronic equipment sometimes report mysterious glitches, frozen screens, locked keyboards, and other computer malfunctions that seem to come from nowhere. Many of these problems can result from irregularities in the power feeding the computer. Com-

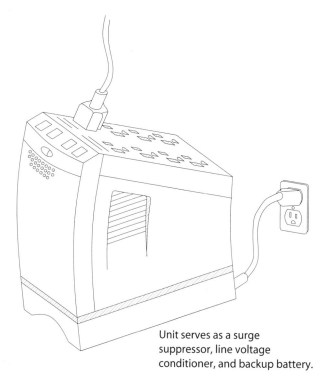

Unit serves as a surge suppressor, line voltage conditioner, and backup battery.

Figure 29-6 Power supply protection.

puters code and store information on the basis of very small changes in voltage, and any deviation from standard voltage can cause them to malfunction.

Random high-frequency voltages superimposed on the power supply voltage in the form of radio frequency interference (radio noise) and other irregularities can cause data errors in data processing equipment like computers and their peripherals. Slow voltage fluctuations can result in overheating, data loss, and premature equipment failures. Large, rapid voltage fluctuations, known as spikes and transients, can cause equipment burnout and system collapse. Electrical noise comes from electronic equipment power supplies, lighting dimmers, solid-state motor controls, and power line carrier systems (which we discuss later on). Arc welding, switching transients, and local magnetic fields can also cause problems. Noise problems respond to electrical isolation, filtering, and noise suppression.

Facilities attempt to avoid these problems by providing clean power for their electronic equipment. Clean power can be defined as any power that is within a range of 5 percent above or 10 percent below the standard 120V, and free from electrical noise generated by other machines using the circuit. A typical wall socket may supply electrical power more than 10 percent below 120V, and momentary deviations occur regularly due to outages, spikes, and electrical noise.

Many large companies offer computer grade power, which is desirable for all new office spaces and full building renovations. These power conditioning systems convert utility-supplied electric power, with its surges, spikes, radio frequency noise, and voltage fluctuations, to a pure, noiseless, accurately voltage-regulated sinusoidal waveform. Power conditioning is not the same as a UPS, which maintains power during utility failure, but both may be included in a single equipment package.

ELECTRICAL EMERGENCY SYSTEMS

Most buildings are required by code to have emergency energy sources to operate lighting for means of egress, exit signs, automatic door locks, and other equipment in an emergency. Emergency systems supply power to equipment that is essential to human life safety on the interruption of the normal supply. The NFPA governs emergency systems under several codes. The NFPA 101, 1997 *Life Safety Code*, covers emergency systems in the means of egress chapters.

Emergency lighting systems illuminate areas of assembly to permit safe exiting and prevent panic. The emergency power system provides power for the fire detection and alarm systems, and for elevators, fire pumps, and public address and communications. It allows the orderly shutdown or maintenance of hazardous processes. Building codes identify a number of building types by use, such as Residential, Assembly, and Business. Codes require that artificial lighting must be present in all exit discharges any time a building is in use, with exceptions for Residential occupancies. The intensity of emergency lighting must be at least 11 lux (one footcandle) at floor level. This can be reduced during performances at some Assembly occupancies. All exit lighting must be connected to an emergency power source that will ensure illumination for a minimum of one to one and one-half hours in case of a power failure. The code official may need to designate which exit access way must be illuminated by emergency lighting.

Standby power systems are sometimes required by code. The National Fire Protection Association's NFPA 110, *Standard for Emergency Light and Power*, and NFPA 111, *Standard on Stored Electrical Energy Emergency and Standby Power Systems*, govern standby systems. Standby systems are required for power processes and systems whose stoppage might create a hazard or hamper firefighting operations, and for safety measures. These could include HVAC systems, water supply equipment, and industrial processes whose interruption could cause safety or health hazards. Optional standby systems are installed to carry any or all loads in a facility at the discretion of the owner. They protect property and prevent financial loss in the event of a normal service interruption, and are used for critical industrial processes or where an ongoing research project can't be shut down.

Emergency systems for healthcare in most jurisdictions are governed by NFPA 99, *Standard for Health Care Facilities*. Most codes require emergency systems. Some also require standby systems for essential water systems, water treatment systems, and a few other uses. The emergency system must pick up loads within ten seconds of the power interruption. Legally required standby systems must pick up within one minute. Batteries and photovoltaic cells are major sources for emergency and standby power, which is consequently usually direct current (DC). Emergency supply batteries must have a full-load capacity of 90 minutes. An emergency or legally required standby supply with an engine-generator set must have a two-hour minimum. The wiring system for emergency power is separate from the normal power system, except where it is connected to the same equipment.

Electrical Wiring and Distribution

●●●

As you are already aware, wires that carry electrical current are called conductors. They extend from the circuit breaker boxes to individual switches, lights, and outlets. Conductors are rated in amperes for their capacity to carry current. Conductor ampacity (capacity in amperes) increases with increasing conductor size and the maximum permissible temperature of the insulation protecting the conductor. Conductors are surrounded by insulation that provides electrical isolation and physical protection. A jacket over the insulation gives added physical protection.

TYPES OF CONDUCTORS

Silver and gold are the best known materials for conducting electricity, but are very expensive. Copper is almost as good, and is commonly used for building wiring. Aluminum has about 80 percent of the conductivity of copper.

Aluminum is cheaper than copper, even when you take into account that the wire sizes need to be slightly larger. It is also lighter than copper. We don't usually think of electrical wiring as being heavy, but in large-scale installations, the weight added to the building

must be supported by the building's structure, and this adds expense to the building. In addition, heavier wiring requires more labor to transport and install, which also costs more. Consequently, aluminum is used for larger sized conductors. Copper wire is more economical in small and medium sizes, and is a better conductor.

Aluminum is difficult to splice and to join to other electrical components. Aluminum oxide, which forms within minutes on the surface of aluminum exposed to air, is an adhesive, poorly conductive film, and the interference of this corrosion with current flow can cause overheating problems and fires in buildings if connections aren't properly made to fixtures. Aluminum oxide must be removed and prevented from forming again for a good, long-life joint. The danger of fire from poor aluminum conductor connections is greatest in residential branch circuits, where unskilled homeowners may make changes. Aluminum is banned from some localities for use in branch circuits.

Even the best conductors offer some resistance to the flow of electricity, and this resistance generates heat from the flow of electrons through the conductor. The heat a current generates when flowing through a conductor is dissipated into the surrounding materials. Ampacity—the conductor's capacity to carry current—is increased with the increasing size of the conductor and with the maximum temperature permitted for the conductor's insulating material.

In the United States, standard sizes for the round cross section of conductors are set using the American Wire Gauge (AWG). The numbers run in reverse order to the size of the wire, with a smaller AWG number indicating a larger wire size. Single conductors sized No. 8 AWG and smaller are referred to as wire. Single insulated conductors No. 6 AWG or larger and several conductors of any size assembled into a single unit are called cable. Outside of the United States, the diameter of conductors is sized in millimeters (mm).

The size of the wires in an electrical system is selected according to the maximum amount of current to be carried and the length of the wire needed. Careful wire sizing avoids excessive heating of the wire and energy loss. Light duty 115V or 120V circuits use quite slender wires, similar to electrical cords for home electrical devices. The wires at the service entrance for a residence may be as thick as one of your fingers.

The electrical engineer or contractor selects which type of wire or cable to use. The various forms of conductors—wire, cable, and bus bars—are sized according to the safe current capacity (ampacity) and the maximum operating temperature of their insulation. They are also identified according to voltage class, the number and size of the conductors, and the type of insulation. Insulation provides electrical isolation and some physical protection for the conductors. Where additional electrical shielding is desired, jacketed conductors are used. Noncombustible cable is required for most conditions. Special types of conductors include high-voltage cables, armored cables, corrosion-resistant jacketed cables, and underground cables. There are special rules for wiring in ducts, plenums, and other air-handling spaces.

When a very large quantity of current is carried at ordinary voltages, large rectangular copper or aluminum bus bars are used instead of wires, each of which is enclosed in a protective metal duct. Main bus bars are connected to local panels, with wires in conduits branching from panels to local fixtures.

Individual wires are run in protective coverings called conduits. Conduit types for fire-resistant construction include rigid metal conduit, electrical metallic tubing, and flexible metal conduit. Conduit is required for all exposed wiring. This may affect the interior designer's decision to remove a hung ceiling and expose the wiring and other equipment above, as the cost of rewiring into conduits can be substantial. For frame construction, armored or nonmetallic sheathed cable may be used. Underground wiring is enclosed in plastic tubing or conduits.

Conduits, busducts, panels, and communications wiring take up horizontal and vertical space as they travel throughout and between floors. Electricians must have access to wiring through doors, hatches, or removable panels. These access openings must be coordinated with the work of the interior designer.

LOW-VOLTAGE WIRING

Low-voltage wiring is usually 12V to 14V, and is used for doorbell circuits, thermostat circuits, and through relays for switching of lighting circuits, especially for complex switching or remote-control panels. Low-voltage

---

The cost of downtown office space was at record levels, and Anna's client had settled for a basement space in an older office building, with a ceiling tight against the structure above and only 7 ft, 6 in. off the floor. To make matters worse, the space had previously been used for storage, and the electrical conduit was running exposed on the ceiling and walls. The client was resigned to leaving the conduit exposed, but Anna felt that the folks who would be working in the basement deserved a finished space.

When Anna met with the architect and contractor at the site, they discussed whether new wiring should continue to be run in exposed conduits, or whether it could be run inside the walls and ceiling. Either way, the new design would require a substantial amount of electrical work. The existing concrete walls were unfinished, and the new drywall would be furred out, so there would be space inside the walls for wiring. However, the ceiling would have to be removed and replaced to hide wiring running to the lighting fixtures.

When the contractor checked with the building department, he discovered that they would be allowed to run BX cable within the walls and ceilings, as an alternative to steel conduit. This would cut the cost of new wiring significantly. Even with removing and replacing the existing drywall ceiling to run wiring horizontally, hiding the wiring within the walls would be less expensive than running the wiring in exposed steel conduit. Anna got her cleaned-up ceiling, and the client got a very nicely designed space.

wiring can't give shocks or cause fires, and can run through the building without cable or conduit. Because the amperages required are also low, the wire can be small and inexpensive. A small transformer connected to a 115V circuit produces the low-voltage current. Most telephone and communication wiring is low voltage, with the current provided by the communications company.

POWER LINE CARRIER (PLC) SYSTEMS

Adding sophisticated building management controls to an existing building would be very expensive if all new wiring had to be installed. Power line carrier (PLC) systems use existing or new electrical power wiring as conductors to carry control signals for energy management controls in existing large, complex facilities. Low-voltage, high-frequency, binary-coded control signals are injected into the power wiring. Only receivers tuned to a particular code react to the signals. In residential use, the control signal generator can be a small manually programmed controller. In commercial facilities, computers operate an energy management or lighting controller.

There are four types of receivers for PLC systems. A coded receiver and relay are added to a normal wall light switch for a wall switch module. Wall receptacle modules use a 20-A receptacle plus a receiver and relay to switch power on and off. Switching modules are connected to activate switches, small motors, and so forth from remote locations. The final type is a dimming module, which can be controlled locally or remotely.

PLC systems require high-quality power wiring installations to operate properly, so existing wiring must be tested. Interference from radio noise may be a problem, but it can usually be overcome.

CABLES

As an interior designer, you may find yourself involved in discussions about the type of electrical cables that can be run in a project. The type of cable that is permitted has a very significant effect on the cost of the electrical work. Contractors will frequently use these terms when discussing conditions on a site with you. There are actually many types of electrical cables, some of which are used only in specialized applications. Here are a few of the ones you are most likely to encounter.

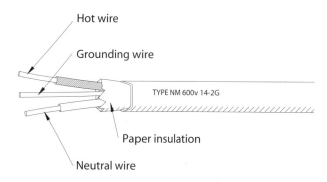

Figure 30-1 Nonmetallic sheathed cable (type NM or Romex).

The cable types designated NM and NMC (Fig. 30-1) by the *National Electrical Code* (NEC) are commonly known by the trade name "Romex." They are nonmetallic sheathed cables with a plastic outer jacket. The enclosing sheath is both moisture resistant and flame-retardant. The NEC limits the use of Romex cable to residential one- and two-family dwellings not over three floors in height. These are typically wood frame buildings. Romex cables are easier to handle but are more vulnerable to physical damage than BX cables.

The most common type of exposed wiring is probably BX cable, which is frequently used in residences and in rewiring existing buildings. Officially, BX cable is called NEC type AC cable (Fig. 30-2), and it is also known as flex cable or armored cable. Two or more conductors are wrapped in heavy paper or plastic and encased in a continuous spiral-wound interlocking strip of steel tape. BX cable is common in commercial applications. It is installed with U-clamps or staples against beams and walls. In new construction, the NEC requires BX cable to be secured at specified intervals. In existing construction, it can be fished through walls, floors, and ceilings for renovations. BX cable is often used to connect rectangular fluorescent lights in suspended ceiling grids to allow for flexibility in relocation. BX is allowed only in dry locations. BX cable is restricted in some jurisdictions even where the NEC allows it.

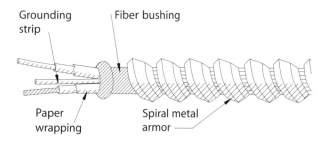

Figure 30-2 Metal-Clad Cable (type AC or BX).

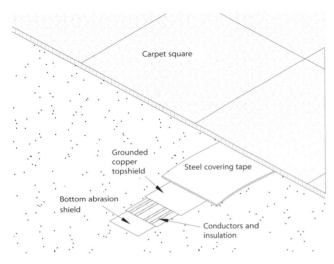

Figure 30-3 Flat conductor cable (NEC Type FCC) as installed under carpet squares.

Metal clad cable is NEC type MC, and is often used where BX cable is restricted. It looks similar to BX, but has an additional green ground wire, providing extra grounding protection. MC cable may be used exposed or concealed and in cable trays. When covered with a moisture-impervious jacket, it is permitted in wet locations and outdoors.

NEC type FCC is also called flat wire and flat conductor cable (Fig. 30-3). It is a small factory-assembled cable in a flat housing and, when used under carpet tiles, it doesn't make a bump on the surface. Three or more flat copper conductors are placed edge-to-edge and enclosed in an insulating material. The assembly is covered with a grounded metal shield that provides both physical protection and a continuous electrical ground path. The bottom shield is usually heavy polyvinyl chloride (PVC) or metal. The whole assembly is only about 0.76 mm (0.03 in.) high, and is essentially undetectable under carpet.

The use of easily removable carpet squares means that the flat cable system can be repositioned to meet changing furniture layouts with minimum disruption and no structural work. The cable is designed for use under office furniture and traffic without damage to its electrical performance. Accessories are available for connection to 120V power outlets. Flat cable systems are low cost and offer flexibility for open-plan offices. They are often used in new construction and to rework obsolete wiring systems in existing buildings. The NEC prohibits the use of flat cables in wet and hazardous areas and in residential, hospital, and school buildings. Flat cable layouts are usually shown on a separate electric plan.

BUSWAYS

Not all conductors are wires and cables. When larger amounts of current are carried from a source to a distribution point, cable assemblies are used. These come in a variety of forms. Some electrical distribution systems combine the conductor and enclosure in one piece. They include all types of factory-prepared and factory-constructed integral assemblies such as busways, busducts, and cablebuses. Flat cable assemblies and lighting track and manufactured wiring systems are also considered to be in this category.

The terms "busway" and "busduct" are often used interchangeably for assemblies of copper or aluminum bars in a rigid metallic housing (Fig. 30-4). Such assemblies are preferred when it is necessary to carry a large amount of current that can be tapped at frequent intervals along its length. Light duty busduct or busway is used for feeder or branch circuits. Connections can be changed easily.

Busways offer plug-in receptacles that can be positioned wherever needed. You have probably seen light-duty plug-in busways in countertops and along laboratory or workbenches, where it a less expensive alternative to installing many separate convenience outlets. Busways can provide 20 to 60 A at 300V in two- and three-wire constructions. Heavier 100-A power at 600V in three- and four-wire constructions is used for direct connection of machine tools, light machinery, and industrial lighting. A plug-in busway makes connection simple and quick with a plug-in device, and saves large amounts of expensive hand labor to connect to cables or conduit frequently, as in machine shops and workshops. A plug-in busway is used for direct connection of light machinery and industrial lighting. Heavy-duty busduct (Fig. 30-5) is used for the vertical feeders in high-rise buildings, for example, to connect a basement switchboard to a penthouse machine room.

Cablebus is similar to ventilated busduct with insulated cables instead of bus bars, rigidly mounted in

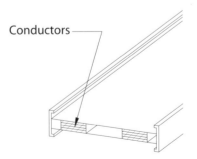

Figure 30-4 Busduct detail.

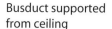
Busduct supported
from ceiling

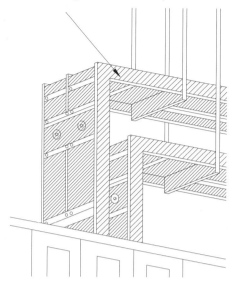

Figure 30-5 Busduct.

an open space frame. This allows overhead power distribution throughout a large open space. The circulation of open air carries off heat, permitting a higher ampacity. However, cablebus is bulky, and it can be difficult to make tap-offs.

CONDUITS

In most commercial construction and large multifamily residential construction, individual plastic-insulated conductors are placed in metal conduits. The NEC generally requires all wiring to be enclosed in a rigid metal corrosion-resistant conduit, which protects wiring from injury and corrosion and serves as a system ground. The conduit also protects against fire hazards due to overheating or arcing of conductors. In addition, it provides a corrosion-resistant support for the conductors. Wires are installed in the conduits after the conduit system has been inspected and approved.

Steel conduit (Fig. 30-6) protects the enclosed wiring from mechanical injury and damage from the surrounding atmosphere. It provides a grounded metal enclosure for wiring to avoid shock hazards, as well as a system ground path. Steel conduit protects its surroundings from fire hazard from overheating or acing of the enclosed conductors.

There are three types of steel conduit, differentiated by wall thickness. Heavy-wall steel conduit, also called

rigid steel conduit, is made of heavy-walled steel tubing joined by screwing directly into a threaded hub with locknuts and bushings. Intermediate metal conduit (IMC) and electric metal tubing (EMT or thin-wall conduit) are made of thin-walled steel tubing joined by compression or setscrew couplings. The inside diameters of IMC and EMT are larger than that of heavy-wall steel conduit, due to the thinner walls, which makes pulling wires through easier. They are also lighter and easier to bend in the field, but the NEC restricts their uses.

Steel conduit is fastened to the structure of the building with pipe straps and clamps. Banks of conduits hung from the ceiling use trapeze mountings. Conduit may also be installed in a concrete slab. The slab is covered with a concrete topping, which holds the conduit. The top of the conduit must be a minimum of 19 mm ($\frac{3}{4}$ in.) below the finished floor surface to prevent cracking.

Flexible metal conduit uses a helically wound metal conduit for connection to motors and other vibrating equipment. Flexible metal conduit is also known by the trade name "Greenfield." It consists of an empty, spirally wound, interlocked armored steel or aluminum raceway. Flexible metal conduit is used for motor connections and other locations for acoustical and vibration isolation of motors, ballasts, and transformers. It is also used for wiring inside metal partitions. Flexible metal conduit with a liquid-impervious plastic jacket for use in wet locations is known by the name "Sealtite."

Aluminum conduit is lighter than steel conduit, and resists corrosion better. Aluminum conduit loses less voltage over long distances, and will not spark. Aluminum conduit generally doesn't require painting. However, aluminum has several disadvantages that limit its use. When embedded in concrete, it may cause spalling and cracking, and it corrodes in earth. The threaded joints between sections freeze and the threads

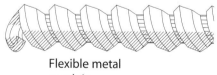

Flexible metal
conduit

Steel conduit

Figure 30-6 Conduit.

deform. In addition, it is difficult to make electrical contact with ground straps from aluminum conduit.

Nonmetallic conduit may be made of fiber, asbestos-cement, soapstone, rigid PVC, or high-density polyethylene. Nonmetallic conduit is used in nonhazardous areas, and must be flame-retardant, tough, and resistant to heat distortion, sunlight, and low temperatures. Many of the materials used have limitations. For example, PVC may be used for indoor exposed locations, but is limited to nonhazardous areas. Asbestos-cement, PVC, and fiber can be used outdoors or underground. Nonmetallic conduit requires a separate ground wire.

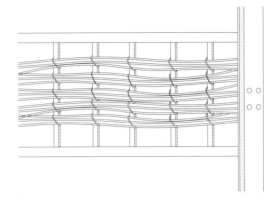

Figure 30-7 Cable tray.

RACEWAYS

So far, we have been talking about the electrical power system. For the moment, let's also consider the signal, data, and communication system as we look at the design of electrical raceways. When electrical engineers design the distribution paths for electrical wiring throughout a building, they design closed wiring raceways for both power wiring and for signal, data, and communication wiring. Raceways for communications cabling have become a major design item in almost all commercial businesses. Space requirements for communications often far exceed those for power cabling, and may be so large that they have a significant impact on the building architecture. Consequently, they should be considered early in the design process.

The sizing for power raceways can be figured out exactly, but communications cabling needs are constantly evolving with the rapid growth of networking and data interchange. It is especially difficult to estimate the needs of a future unknown rental client. Engineers try to accommodate these uncertainties by providing floor-level raceway space for the main cabling needs, and using add-on systems, like under-carpet wiring and surface or ceiling raceways, for additional needs.

The special design needs for data and communications may make it worthwhile to hire a design consultant familiar with the latest technology. The design will depend upon the number, type, and location of data processing terminals. The type of local area network (LAN) determines the communications medium, such as coaxial cable, shielded and unshielded wire, or fiber optic cables. This in turn determines the types of connections and floor outlets.

Another factor determining communications distribution layouts is the number, location, and types of major peripheral devices, such as mass storage, printing, and plotting equipment. Major subsystems for computer aided design/computer aided manufacturing (CAD/CAM) design spaces affect the layout. The location of presentation spaces requiring computers is another consideration.

In industrial uses, insulated cables are run in open raceways. Both the covering of the cable and the raceway tray provide safety while allowing access. Cable trays (Fig. 30-7) give continuous open support for cables. For general wiring system use, cables in cable trays must be self-protected. Since the cables are exposed to the air, which carries away excess heat, the wiring has a higher amperage rating. Wiring in cable trays is easy to install and maintain, and relatively low cost. However, the trays are bulky, and must either be exposed or accessible through a hung ceiling. While used primarily in industrial applications, they are also found in offices with heavy data and communications requirements.

All types of facilities use insulated conductors in closed raceways. The raceway is generally installed first, with wiring pulled in or laid in later. Raceways may be buried in the building's structure as conduit in the floor slab or as underfloor duct. They may be attached to the structure as surface raceways, including conduit and raceways suspended above hung ceilings. Wall and ceiling surface raceways (Fig. 30-8) are somewhat unsightly, but get wiring where it is needed with excellent access and without opening up walls or ceilings.

UNDERFLOOR DUCTS

In some buildings, especially office buildings and most computer facilities, special rectangular underfloor ducts with many access boxes for attaching fixtures allow wiring to be changed frequently. The ducts are installed

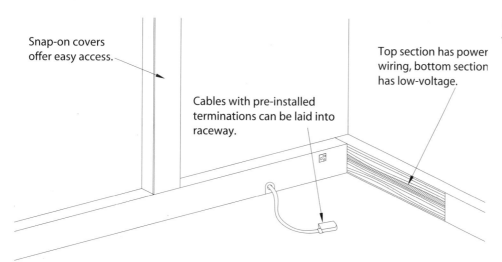

Snap-on covers offer easy access.

Cables with pre-installed terminations can be laid into raceway.

Top section has power wiring, bottom section has low-voltage.

Figure 30-8 Surface raceways.

below or flush with the floor (Fig. 30-9). In offices, underfloor ducts position power, data, and signal outlets close to desks regardless of the furniture layout. Parallel rectangular metal or heavy plastic raceways are laid on the structural slab and covered with concrete fill. Inserts connect the raceways to openings in the distribution ducts. Next, feeder ducts are installed at right angles to distribution ducts. The feeder ducts terminate in floor fittings for power and communications wiring.

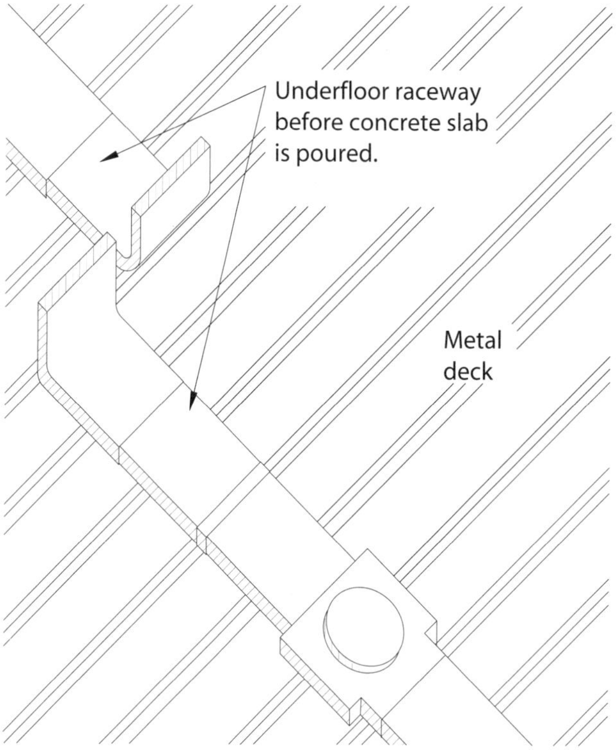

Underfloor raceway before concrete slab is poured.

Metal deck

Figure 30-9 Underfloor raceway.

Since they are cast in concrete, they are expensive. Their inflexible layouts sometimes result in underutilization in one area and inadequate supply in another.

Underfloor ducts were commonly used before the introduction of over-the-ceiling ducts and flat-cable wiring under carpets. Underfloor ducts are used with open floor areas that need to locate outlets away from walls and partitions. They are used when under-carpet wiring systems can't be used, and where outlets from the ceiling are unacceptable. Underfloor ducts may be a good choice where it is likely that furniture and other systems requiring electrical and signal service will be rearranged often within a set grid. Prestige office buildings, museums, galleries, and other display-case spaces, high-cost merchandising areas, and some industrial facilities may use underfloor ducts.

FULL-ACCESS FLOORS

In the recent past, installing raised access floors for underfloor delivery of power, data, and telecommunications services was considered suitable only for technology-heavy spaces like data centers and trading floors, because of the comparatively high cost of these floors. The revolution in desktop electronics and the increasingly fast turnover rates for offices combine to make underfloor delivery a much more cost-effective option for many offices, both because of the greater ease with which wires and cables can be distributed and the flexibility that access floors permit. Full-access floors (Fig. 30-10) provide space for both air supply and cabling.

Full-access floors accommodate very heavy cabling requirements and facilitate frequent recabling and re-

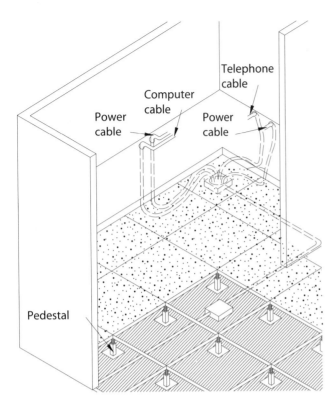

Figure 30-10 Full-access floor.

connection. Full-access floors were originally developed for data processing areas with requirements for large, fully accessible cable spaces and large quantities of conditioned air. The system allows rapid and complete access to an underfloor plenum.

 Lightweight die cast aluminum panels are supported on a network of adjustable steel or aluminum pedestals. The panels are 46 or 91 cm (18 or 36 in.) square, and the floor depth is normally between 31 and 76 cm (12–30 in.). Where air requirements are minimal, the pedestals can be as short as 15 cm (6 in.). The panels are made of steel, aluminum, or a wood core encased in steel or aluminum, or of lightweight reinforced concrete. They are finished with carpet tile, vinyl tile, or high-pressure laminates. Fire-rated and electrostatic-discharge-control coverings are also available. Access floor systems are designed for loads from 1220 to 3050 kilograms per square meter (250–625 lb per square ft, psf) and are available for heavier loads up to 5490 kilograms per square meter (1125 psf). Seismic pedestals are available to meet building code requirements.

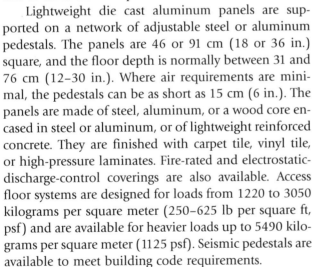 Electrical conduits, junction boxes, and cabling are run below the full-access flooring panels for computer, security, and communications systems. The space under the flooring panels can also be used as a plenum to distribute heating, ventilating, and air-conditioning (HVAC) air supply, with a ceiling plenum for air return. Ducts for conditioned air can also run beneath the floor. By separating the cool supply air from the warm return air, the system helps reduce energy consumption. The construction is usually completely fire-resistant. The ceiling height must be adequate to accommodate the raised floor. Ramps and steps are among the available accessories.

Access flooring systems are used in offices, hospitals, laboratories, computer rooms, and television and communications centers. They provide accessibility and flexibility in the placement of desks, workstations, and equipment. Equipment can be moved and reconnected fairly easily with modular wiring systems, which also cut down on labor costs.

FLOOR RACEWAYS

Individual floor raceways are sometimes installed to get power for computers, telephone lines, and other equipment at locations in open-plan offices away from the structure, without installing a complete floor raceway system. One labor-intensive process involves channeling the concrete floor, installing conduit in the opening (or chase), connecting the wiring to the nearest wall outlet, and patching the chase.

A second method uses a surface floor raceway, which is usually unsightly and may cause tripping and problems with cleaning the floor. Surface floor raceways can only be used in dry, nonhazardous, noncorrosive locations. Surface raceways are used where the architecture does not permit recessed raceways, for economy of construction and anticipated expansion. They offer outlets at frequent intervals and access to the equipment in the raceways. Surface raceways avoid the cutting and patching required to bury a raceway in the floor when rewiring.

Sometimes power is brought to remote locations by drilling the floor twice, and connecting a new outlet to a nearby floor outlet or wall outlet via conduit on the underside of the floor slab. Floor penetrations must be fireproof, and may disturb the occupants of the space below. Another method that requires drilling and running conduit on the ceiling below uses poke-through fittings designed to carry all the electrical services for a normal workstation. Connections are made to a multiservice floor outlet group, or into wired cubicle partitions. All four of these methods are inflexible and not a good choice where changes are likely.

CELLULAR FLOORS

Cellular concrete or cellular metal floors allow raceways to become part of an integrated structural-electrical system. Cellular metal floors have openings in their structures that will accept electrical conductors. Cellular floor systems allow for flexible placement of power, signal, and phone outlets in office buildings. Three separate wiring systems within separate floor cells and header ducts supply electrical power, data transmission wiring, and telephone and signal system wiring.

Precast cellular concrete floor raceways are similar to cellular metal floors, with the same advantages of large capacity, versatility, and flexibility for outlet placement and movement. Each cell is a single, enclosed tubular space in a floor made of precast cellular concrete slabs. Despite their high first cost, the life-cycle cost may be lower than a standard underfloor duct installation. The cells can also be used for air distribution and for piping.

FLAT CABLE ASSEMBLIES

Flat-cable assemblies use specially designed cable field-installed in rigidly mounted standard 41-mm ($1\frac{5}{8}$-in.) square structural channel. Flexible "pigtail" wires connect electrical devices or outlet boxes with receptacles to the channel. Flat cable assemblies are used for lights, small motors, and unit heaters served without hard wiring (conduit and cable).

Over-the-ceiling flat cable assemblies are more flexible than underfloor systems. They are used for lighting, power, and telephone, and can provide outlets for the floor above as well. Stores use ceiling systems to permit very rapid layout changes at low cost. They are easily altered for changes in functions of spaces as well as for furniture layout changes, making them very appropriate for educational facilities. Flat cable assembly systems use a metallic or nonmetallic surface-type raceway hung from the concrete slab above in the ceiling plenum. They are used with lift-out hung ceiling panels. Vertical poles carry the power from the top down to desk or floor level. The poles may be pre-wired with several power outlets, phone connections, and data cable outlets. Special conduit, raceways, troughs, and fittings are available for exposed installations. Many finishes are available, but the appearance of the poles usually gives away the system's low cost nature.

Lighting track is a factory-assembled flat cable assembly with conductors for one to four circuits permanently installed in the track. Tap-off devices carry power to attached lighting fixtures anywhere along the track. Lighting track is generally rated at 20 A, and may be used only to feed lighting fixtures. Taps to feed convenience receptacles are not permitted.

Chapter

Receptacles and Switches

Now that we have explored how electricity is distributed throughout a building, let's look at how it is controlled and accessed at the end point. Whether you are turning on a wall switch, plugging an appliance into a receptacle, or using a dimmer to dim the lights, you are using a wiring device installed in an outlet box. Even the attachment plugs (caps) and wall plates are considered to be wiring devices. Outlet boxes are also used where light fixtures are connected to the electrical system. Low voltage lighting control devices are considered wiring devices. Junction boxes are enclosures for housing and protecting electrical wires or cables that are joined together in connecting or branching electrical circuits. Commercial attachments that are not usually considered wiring devices include premise wiring, such as data and communications wiring and raceways.

Electrical equipment is given ratings for voltage and current. Voltage ratings indicate the maximum voltage that can be safely applied to the unit continuously. An ordinary electric wall receptacle is rated at 250V, but is only supplied with 120V in normal use. The type and quality of insulation used and the physical spacing between electrically energized parts determines the voltage rating. Current ratings are determined by the maximum operating temperature at which the equipment's components can operate at full load. This depends upon

the type of insulation used. Wiring devices are usually rated at 300 A or less and frequently at 20 A. They can be mounted in a small wall box.

Manufacturers classify wiring devices to indicate their quality and expected use. Wiring devices are manufactured in three quality grades. However, their grades are not standard across manufacturers, so if you specify by grade without a manufacturer named, you have little control over what you may actually get. The highest quality is hospital grade, which has a green dot on the device face. Hospital grade wiring devices are built to withstand severe abuse while maintaining reliable operation, and must meet Underwriters' Laboratories (UL) requirements for their grade. Federal specification grade is roughly equivalent to industrial (premium) and commercial specification grades, and is less stringent than hospital grade. Industrial specification grade is used for industrial and high-grade commercial construction. Commercial specification grade is used for educational and good residential buildings, so it isn't limited to commercial work only. The UL general-purpose grade corresponds roughly to residential grade, and is the least demanding quality. Standard or residential grade is used in low-cost construction of all types, but not necessarily in all residential work.

Each electrical receptacle, lighting fixture, or switch

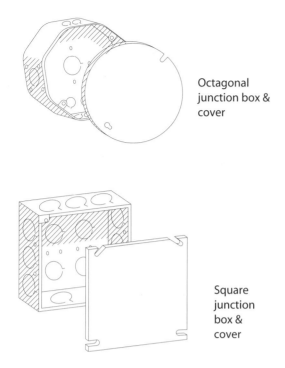

Octagonal junction box & cover

Square junction box & cover

Figure 31-1 Junction boxes.

is housed in a metal or plastic box that is fastened securely to the structure, supporting the device and protecting the box's contents. The cable or conduit serving the device is clamped tightly to the box where the wires enter. The bare neutral wire is connected to the box and to the frame of the device, ensuring that it will never cause shocks if the device becomes faulty. The black and white wires are stripped of insulation at their ends, and connected to the device with screws or clamps. The circuit is then tested for safe, satisfactory operation, and the device is screwed snugly to the box. A metal or plastic cover plate is attached to keep fingers out, keep electrical connections free of dust and dirt, and provide a neat appearance.

Outlet and device boxes are made of galvanized stamped sheet metal. Nonmetallic boxes may be used in some wiring installations. Cast-iron or cast aluminum boxes are used for outdoor work and in wet locations. Square and octagonal 10-cm (4-in.) boxes (Fig. 31-1) are used for fixtures, junctions, and electrical devices. Single switches and duplex outlets (one receptacle above another, as commonly found in homes) use a 102 by 57 mm (4 by $2\frac{1}{4}$ in.) box. Depths range from 38 to 76 mm ($1\frac{1}{2}$–3 in.).

Outlet boxes are wall- or floor-mounted for electrical receptacles. For lighting fixtures, they are wall- or ceiling-mounted. Floor boxes of cast metal are set directly into the floor slab. Switch boxes are typically

mounted on the wall to control a lighting outlet box. They are usually mounted within the wall on a stud. Installation of an electrical box usually just penetrates the wall surface, and does not require firestopping. The opening in the wall can't allow a gap greater than 3 mm ($\frac{1}{8}$ in.) between the box and the gypsum wallboard.

The *National Electrical Code* (NEC) specifies the minimum number of electrical boxes allowed for some building types, especially dwelling units. Most electrical codes specify the maximum distance between receptacles in a room, so that a lamp or appliance with a standard length cord can be placed anywhere around the room perimeter without using an extension cord. Codes also specify the number of receptacles per room and the maximum number of receptacles per circuit, to prevent overloading wires with excessive flows of current. The NEC and model building codes typically specify that no more than 645 square cm (100 square in.) of electrical boxes can be installed per 9.3 square meters (100 square ft) of wall surface.

When an existing electrical box is not being used, it must either have a cover plate installed or be totally removed, including the box and all its wiring, with the wall opening properly patched. In fire-rated walls, when boxes are used on opposite sides of the same walls, they must be separated by 61 cm (24 in.) horizontally.

Poke-through fittings (Fig. 31-2) are often used in existing commercial spaces to meet expanded desktop power and data wiring needs. They are fed through the floor from within a hung ceiling below. Poke-through fittings allow wiring relocations in rental office spaces. The NEC requires that electrical penetrations in fire-

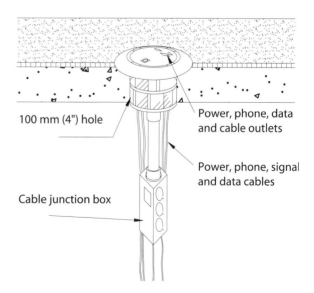

100 mm (4") hole

Power, phone, data and cable outlets

Power, phone, signal and data cables

Cable junction box

Figure 31-2 Poke-through electrical fitting.

rated floors, walls, ceilings, and partitions maintain the fire ratings, so poke-through fittings must be properly sealed to preserve the fire rating.

ELECTRICAL RECEPTACLES

The electrical outlet into which we plug an electrical cord is technically known as a convenience receptacle (Fig. 31-3). The number of poles (prongs) and wires, and whether they have a separate grounding wire or not, identifies the different types of receptacles. Grounded receptacles are used on standard 15-A or 20-A branch circuits.

An electrical receptacle is defined by the NEC as "a contact device installed at the outlet for the connection of a single attachment plug." This includes common wall outlets and larger, more complex devices. They are known as convenience receptacle outlets, receptacle outlets, or convenience outlets. Technically, the term "wall plug" is the name for the cap on the wire that carries electricity to an appliance—the part on the end of a line cord that is plugged into a wall.

A receptacle is by definition a single contact device. A normal wall convenience receptacle takes two attachment plugs, and is called a duplex convenience receptacle, or duplex convenience outlet. This is commonly shortened to duplex receptacle or duplex outlet.

Receptacles installed on a standard 15-A or 20-A branch circuit must be of the grounding type. Receptacles connected to different voltages, frequencies, or current types (alternating vs. direct current, AC vs. DC) on

the same premises must be polarized. Receptacles are typically 20-A, 125V, but are available from 10 A to 400 A, and from 125V to 600V. Locking, explosion proof, tamper proof, and decorative design receptacles are available. Some units, such as range receptacles, are designed for specific uses. Split-wired receptacles have one outlet that is always energized, and a second controlled by a wall switch. These are sometimes used for a lamp, with the switch near the entrance to the room.

Receptacles are normally mounted between 30 and 46 cm (12–18 in.) above the finished floor. In shops, laboratories, and other spaces with tables against walls, they are mounted at 107 cm (42 in.) above the floor. Receptacles above kitchen counters are mounted 122 cm (4 ft) above the finished floor. In accessible spaces, the *Americans with Disabilities Act Accessibility Guidelines* (ADAAG) requires a minimum 38 cm (15 in.) height for outlets, with outlets above kitchen counters at 107 cm (42 in.) above the floor. Where work areas are required to be accessible, as in public library carrels and office workstations, the receptacles should be located above the worksurface whenever possible, or alternatively under the front edge of the worksurface. This requires careful planning.

Modern electronic equipment is very sensitive to random, spurious electrical voltages, called electrical noise. Two special receptacles help eliminate electrical noise. One type with built-in surge suppression protects equipment from over-voltage spikes. Other receptacles with an insulated equipment-grounding terminal separating the device ground terminal from the system (raceway) ground eliminate much of the unwanted electrical noise. This latter type is connected to the system ground at the service entrance only, and is identified by an orange triangle on the faceplate.

POLARITY

As an interior designer working on a residential project, you are likely to encounter older lighting fixtures that have old cords and plugs, as well as houses with older outlets. You have probably noticed that newer plug-in fixtures with two-pronged plugs will fit into a modern convenience outlet only one way. One of the prongs will be wider than the other, and the outlet is designed to accept the plug in only one orientation. These newer plugs and outlets are designed to provide shock protection now mandated by the NEC. Plugs that fit into an outlet only one way, including three-prong plugs, are called polarized plugs.

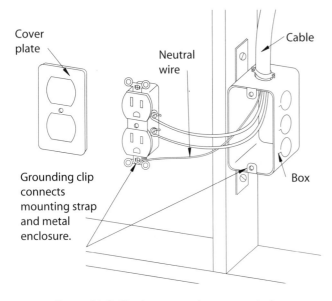

Figure 31-3 Duplex convenience receptacle.

Polarized plugs and outlets assure that the neutral wire in an electrical cord connects with the white neutral wire in the electrical system and that the hot wire in the cord connects to the black hot wire in the system. Remember, the black wire in the electrical system carries the power. The white neutral wire carries little power. When you flip a switch, you release the power in the black wire waiting to go to work spinning a motor or lighting a lamp.

Polarized plugs keep you from switching the hot and neutral wires around when you plug a cord into a receptacle. The wide blade that connects to the neutral wire will not fit into the narrower slot reserved for the hot wire, and the round prong on a three-prong plug fits only into the round opening in the outlet, which automatically positions the hot and neutral blades.

Normally, reversing the connection doesn't cause a problem. The lamp's internal wire connected to the hot wire of the cord runs through the switch and becomes exposed deep in the socket, where it makes contact with the bottom of the light bulb. It is virtually impossible to come into contact with this hot wire.

In many cases, however, the neutral side of the circuit in a lamp fixture is less well insulated than the hot side. The neutral wire connects to the screw base, which you are much more likely to touch. The insulation around the screw base often consists of little more than a cardboard tube that becomes brittle and cracks or even falls out as the fixture ages. With the cardboard worn or gone, the screw base can easily make contact with the outer metal socket. That contact is most likely to occur when you unscrew a bulb, holding the socket or another metal part of the lamp with your other hand. If the neutral wire is hot when you hold the lamp and contact occurs, causing a ground fault, you could get a dangerous shock. In fact, because the socket touches the rest of the metal lamp, the entire fixture could be electrically charged, even though the light isn't turned on.

People don't pay much attention to how they plug in their lamps. With nonpolarized two-prong plugs, the chances are 50/50 that the neutral side is actually hot, and many shocks occur with old light fixtures. Polarized plugs eliminate this hazard by keeping the hot wire properly connected. Even if the neutral wire accidentally touches the fixture while the light is on, you won't get a shock.

On residential interior design projects, you may be working with a client's older lighting fixtures, and may come across electrical plugs with two identical blades. These plugs were on equipment produced before the code change in the 1960s. You also will find nonpolarized two-prong plugs on some brands of new power tools. The NEC allows an exception to the polarized plug rule if the device is double insulated. In these devices, manufacturers encase the electrically conductive metal parts, such as the motor and wire connections, in an extra layer of nonconductive material, providing extra protection against shocks.

SWITCHES

You can turn a light on and off either by plugging a lighting fixture into an electrical outlet (receptacle) and turning the switch on the lighting fixture on and off, or by hard wiring the lighting fixture directly into the building's power supply system and using a wall switch to control the power. Switches up to 30 A that can be outlet-box mounted are considered wiring devices.

A common wall light switch is a type of general duty safety switch called a contactor. Contactors close an electrical circuit physically by moving two electrical conductors into contact with each other, allowing the power to flow to the lighting fixture. The contactor physically separates the two conductors to open the circuit, which stops the electrical flow and shuts off the light. Manual and remote pushbuttons use contactors to operate remote controls. Manual or remote pushbutton contactors can also be used with automatic devices such as timers, float switches, thermostats, and pressure switches. They are found in lighting, heating, and air-conditioning equipment, and in motors.

Contactors can be operated by hand, electric coil, spring, or motor. A wall switch is an example of a small, mechanically operated contactor. A relay is a small electrically operated contactor. The operating handles for contactors may be toggle, push, touch, rocker, rotary, or tap-plate types (Fig. 31-4). Mercury and AC quiet types of handles are relatively noiseless, while toggle, tumbler, and AC/DC types are not. A toggle switch has a lever or knob that moves through a small arc and causes the contacts to open or close the electric circuit. Keyed switches are used where access needs to be limited to authorized people. Tumbler-lock controlled switches are used where a keyed switch does not provide adequate security, as where keys may be stolen. Spring-wound timer switches are often used for bathroom heaters and ventilation fans.

General duty safety switches are intended for normal use in lighting and power circuits. Heavy-duty (HD) switches are used for high-fault currents subject to frequent interruption. They also offer ease of maintenance. Switches are installed in hot wires only. They disconnect an electrical device from the current, leaving the

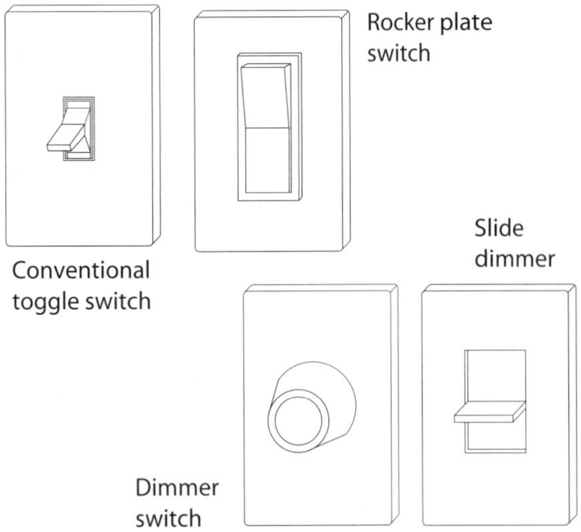

Rocker plate switch

Conventional toggle switch

Slide dimmer

Dimmer switch

Figure 31-4 Common types of wall switches.

device with no voltage going through it, and eliminating the possibility of shock when the switch is open.

A three-way switch is a switch used in conjunction with another switch to control lights from two locations, such as from the bottom and top of a stairway. An ordinary single-pole switch has "on" and "off" written on it. A three-way switch has three terminals, so the on and off positions may change, depending on the position of the other switch. Four-way switches are used in conjunction with two three-way switches to control lights from three locations.

Remote-control (RC) switches are used for switching of blocks of lighting or for exterior lights. They can control whole floors or whole buildings. They use electromagnets to operate fixtures from a distance without wiring. Ceiling fans and electrically operated window treatments often use remote controls.

Solid-state switches are beginning to replace the common wall switch. Solid-state switches use an electronic device with a conducting state and a nonconducting state, similar to a conventional switch in closed position and open position. The change between the two states is accomplished by a control signal in the voltage. The change is made instantaneously, noiselessly, and without sending a flash of electricity across a gap. With an electronic timing device added, you have a time-controlled electronic switch with no moving parts, acting independently of utility line frequency.

A switch with a solid-state rectifier makes it possible to switch incandescent lamps from high to low to off. They cost very little more than an ordinary switch, and can save energy where a lower illumination level is often acceptable.

Add a small programmable memory circuit—an erasable programmable read-only memory (EPROM) chip—and you have a programmable time switch. A programmable switch fits into a wall outlet box just like an ordinary switch. It uses miniature electronics for lighting, energy management, automated building control, and clock and program systems. For example, a read-only memory (ROM) chip can be programmed with the sunrise and sunset information for the latitude involved, thus becoming a "sun tracker," which can control circuits with dark-to-dawn control year round.

An even more sophisticated switch adds a microprocessor, giving it the ability to respond with a particular control plan to given input signals. This programmable controller uses programmable memory to store instructions that implement special functions. It amounts to a special type of computer that has a short program within its hardware for a specific type of function, such as logic, timing, counting, or other functions. Such switches are used in industrial controls, process controls, and elevators.

Wireless switching and control is undergoing extensive development. Wireless bandwidths are getting much bigger. The use of wireless devices will have a significant impact on building design. Wireless systems are finding a niche in facilities with fixed architecture, but in offices where the need for flexibility dictates partitions that can be quickly reconfigured, the benefits may be significantly reduced. For wireless systems to function properly, the locations of transceivers, the configuration of a space, and the number of users must all be coordinated. This can make a wireless office considerably less flexible than one with underfloor communications wiring distribution, which can be easily reconfigured.

To date, the trend toward the delivery of ever-larger amounts of information, at ever-greater speeds, directly to the desktop favors wired technologies over wireless devices. The bandwidth of today's wireless networks is narrow, which puts a limit on the amount of data that can be transmitted per second. Also, bandwidth is shared, which means that any one user's access is restricted as the number of users increases. These drawbacks, coupled with potential security problems inherent in wireless communication, make wireless systems a less desirable substitute for wire infrastructure in most office environments, except in very specific applications. However, all this may change as the technology continues to develop.

Interior designers often indicate the location of switches on their drawings. Switches to control lighting or receptacles are usually positioned on the handle side of the door of a room. The interior designer's drawings should show and identify plug-in strips on walls and special purpose receptacles. Use special symbols and notes to locate signal outlets for fire alarm, telephone and intercom, data and communication, radio and TV, and other equipment. The circuits for these types of equipment are not usually indicated on the floor plan, but are instead shown on a separate power plan. Lighting fixture outlets are usually included with wiring devices, unless this leads to a cluttered drawing, in which case they are represented on their own drawing. Motors, heaters, and other fixed, permanently installed equipment is shown and identified on power plans rather than on lighting drawings. Equipment with a cord and plug is not usually represented, but receptacles for plug-in equipment are shown and identified.

Lighting dimmers originated as large, expensive pieces of equipment for theater and display lighting. Today, modern wall-box dimmers are small electronic units. The simplest dimmers are rotary incandescent dimmers. Older units, and some inexpensive current units, produce annoying radio frequency interference and line harmonics that can affect computers and other electronic equipment. Newer dimmers use preset controls combining dimming and switching. They are used for smooth fan speed control, for remote and local controls, to provide automatic fadeouts, and to dim fluorescent lamps provided with dimming ballasts.

Dimmers, switches, receptacles, fan controls, cable TV, and telephone jacks are all available in a variety of colors. Be aware that cover plates specified in a bold color may have to be replaced if the wall color or other decor is changed.

Normal full-voltage switches are wired directly into the load circuit and operate at line voltage and full current. Common ratings include 15 A, 20 A, and 30 A; and 120V or 120/277V. Low-voltage switching is used for remote control switching. It uses light-duty, low-voltage 24V switches to control line voltage relays, which then do the actual switching. Low-voltage switching allows flexibility of location for the controls. Low-voltage, low-current wiring is less expensive than full-voltage wires and conduit. The system gives flexibility and makes changes simpler. The status of individual loads can be monitored at a central control panel by use of relays with auxiliary contacts. Low-voltage switching is also used for group load override by central control devices like timers, daylighting controllers, and energy management systems, and for individual load control override by local control devices, such as occupancy sensors and photocells. These are important elements of an energy conservation system.

Residential Appliances

Home appliances have come a long way in the last two centuries. For hundreds of years, there were no convenient local food stores, and the preservation and storage of food took a great deal of time and expertise. Cooking and washing dishes used to be the full-time jobs of cooks and scullions. Clothes were made, washed, and mended with the goal of lasting beyond the lifetime of the wearer. It is only in the past 200 years that home appliances began, as the advertisements used to say, to take the drudgery out of housework.

Today we have a constantly growing number of household appliances, designed for safe and efficient use. You have probably noticed the little tags glued incredibly durably onto the cords of household appliances and lighting fixtures, tags that read, "UL approved." That UL stands for Underwriters Laboratories, Inc., an organization that provides lists of inspected and approved electrical equipment. UL approval is referenced in electrical codes as a standard for electrical equipment safety. The UL tag is your assurance that the appliance is designed and manufactured for safe use.

Electrical equipment comes with several ratings that indicate wiring requirements. The voltage listing is a rating that gives the maximum voltage that can safely be applied to the unit continuously. An ordinary wall receptacle has a 250V rating, although it normally uses only 120V. It is therefore safe to use the receptacle even if the voltage should go above 120V. Some common household equipment normally requires 240V. These appliances include household electrical ranges and clothes dryers. Electric heaters that use more than 1500 W and window air conditioners using greater than 4.4 kW (1.25 tons) normally require 240V. They must be either directly wired into a circuit or plugged into a special receptacle designed for them.

Another wiring rating for appliances, the current-carrying ability, is measured in amperes. The maximum operating temperature at which components of the equipment (for example, a toaster) can operate continuously determines the number of amperes. Equipment with better electrical insulation inside can carry more current safely.

In 1987, the U.S. Congress passed the National Appliance Energy Conservation Act, over the objections of the Department of Energy (DOE) but backed by utilities, appliance manufacturers, and environmental groups. This law sets minimum efficiency criteria for heating, ventilating, and air-conditioning (HVAC) systems, refrigerators, freezers, and other appliances. When you specify any electrical equipment or appliance, look for the energy efficiency rating (EER) and the estimated yearly operating cost, listed on the yellow and black federal EnergyGuide label attached to every air conditioner, fan, dishwasher, dryer, refrigerator, or freezer sold in the United States. The EnergyGuide label gives you a way to compare one appliance with another. Higher energy efficiency results in lower energy use and lower operating costs.

As we discussed earlier, the U.S. Environmental Protection Agency (EPA) and the DOE have established the ENERGY STAR® label in voluntary cooperation with manufacturers and retailers to identify energy-efficient appliances, computers, lighting fixtures, and home entertainment equipment. Look for the ENERGY STAR label when specifying refrigerators, dishwashers, and clothes washers, as well as audio equipment, computers and monitors, and other office equipment. Local electric and gas companies may offer rebates for high-efficiency refrigerators and clothes washers.

When helping a client decide what type of equipment to purchase, it is important to determine the most efficient solution to the problem at hand. For example, a window fan may be a more energy-efficient choice than an air conditioner. Equipment that uses a timer, thermostat, or sensor can save energy without decreasing comfort. Photocells are available to control day and night operation. A timer on an air conditioner can turn it on or off depending on the occupant's presence, outside temperature changes, or on a preprogrammed time schedule.

Manufacturers are responding to the trend to include kitchen appliances in areas other than the kitchen, including dens and master bedroom suites, by offering very compact units. One such resembles a big wardrobe with overall dimensions of about 1.5 meters wide by 1.8 meters deep by 0.6 meters high (5 by 6 by 2 ft). It is suited for use in a small city apartment or large master suite. When the doors are opened, a full kitchen is revealed, including a refrigerator with freezer, a small dishwasher, a two-burner cook-top, a combination microwave/convection oven, a small sink and faucet, a recycling unit, and some storage.

PRESERVING FOOD

Before the nineteenth century, food was seasonal and had to be eaten immediately or preserved for leaner times. In England, through the nineteenth century, most small country cottage households had their own pig, and kept a dairy cow for milk, cheese, and butter. Prior to the eighteenth century, farmers didn't have access to winter feed for cattle, and thus most of the animals were slaughtered in the fall. Neighborhood shops didn't exist prior to the rise of the middle class, and isolated homesteads and manor houses relied on salting, smoking, freezing, and drying for meat, fruit, and vegetable preservation. Provisions were stored in larders, icehouses, and cellars.

Larders were rooms designed for meat to be potted into tubs and covered with lard, or salted or smoked for use through the winter. By the late nineteenth century, the larder was used to store not only meat of all kinds, but also vegetables, bread, cheese, and fruit. Larders were rooms near the kitchen, built to be as cool as possible, with windows covered with screen. Thick slate or marble slabs embedded deep in the walls served as cool shelves.

Frozen food goes back at least to the fourth century BC, when Alexander the Great had pits dug and covered with twigs and leaves to store ice and snow through the summer months. By the early seventeenth century, the French and Italians were routinely using long-term ice storage. In England, ice that was cut from ponds was stored in icehouses, where it could be kept for two years or more. By the mid-nineteenth century, small ice cellars were being built adjacent to houses, with insulated double walls and double doors to prevent the escape of cold air. Ice cellars were used to store cold water, butter, and other provisions. Thomas Masters patented an icebox for use inside the home in 1844. Ice chests and iceboxes were often designed as pieces of furniture, with taps for draining off melted ice.

Today, most people are dependent on refrigerators to preserve their food. Refrigerators use a lot of energy in order to stay cold and keep food fresh. However, there are many ways to keep food cool and fresh without the aid of electricity, ways that can be adapted to modern use.

A cool closet is an insulated storage cabinet on the north exterior wall of a house. Cool air from outside enters the closet through low vents, rises up the closet through slots in the shelves, and flows out of a top vent on the top of the house. Continuous airflow and heavy insulation lower the temperature and keep the food cold. Cool closets use no electricity, require low maintenance, and are easy to build.

Years ago, root cellars were used to keep meat, milk, cream, and other goods cold. A root cellar is a hole in the ground that is at least 3 meters (10 ft) deep. Because the earth stays at a temperature of about 10°C to 13°C (50°F–55°F), the humidity and temperature stay stable inside the root cellar. Cellars can be built into a hill or in a basement that has a dirt floor. The cellar is well insulated and has vents to circulate the air. Shelves are made from either rot resistant or pressure treated wood, and are kept a few inches away from the walls to help increase circulation around the food. The cellar is covered with a door, preferably made from two pieces of wood with insulation between them.

Mechanical cooling systems provided cold storage on a commercial scale long before they were adapted to home use. The first successful domestic refrigerator was the Domelre, marketed in Chicago in 1913, followed by Kelvinator in 1916, and Frigidaire in 1917. Electric refrigerators were common by the 1930s.

Refrigerators have been greatly improved in terms of energy efficiency. The average refrigerator made today uses about 700 kW-h per year, one-third of the energy of a 1973 model, and is larger and has better controls as well. Newer refrigerators have more insulation, tighter door seals, a larger coil surface area, and improved compressors and motors. Purchase of a newer model can provide a quick payback through energy savings. The larger the refrigerator, the more energy it will use, but one large refrigerator will use less energy than two smaller ones with the same capacity. The most efficient refrigerators are in the 16- to 20-cubic-ft range. Side-by-side models are less energy-efficient than styles with the freezer on top. Built-ins sometimes use more energy than freestanding models. Automatic icemakers and through-door dispensers are also somewhat more energy-intensive.

Energy Star refrigerators meeting the 2001 requirements must be 30 percent more efficient than required by 1993 standards. They accomplish this goal with more highly efficient compressors and condensers, and are available in side-by-side and freezer-on-top models.

When selecting the refrigerator style, consider the depth required when the door is open 90 degrees. The side-by-side models take up less space in front of the refrigerator. Refrigerators typically use a 115V, 60 Hz, AC, and 15 A grounded outlet. Some manufacturers offer counter-depth refrigerators that align with cabinets smoothly, providing maximum storage capacity without taking up a lot of space in the kitchen.

Special high-efficiency refrigerators are available that run on 12V DC electricity and are six times more efficient than a conventional refrigerator. Their efficiency is due to the location and design of the compressor and their thick insulation. In a traditional refrigerator, the compressor is located at the bottom, and the heat it generates rises and creates a blanket of warm air around the refrigerator. The high-efficiency refrigerator puts the compressor on top. The compressor lacks a fan and runs less often than standard models, contributing to exceptionally quiet operation.

Chest-style freezers that load from the top are 10 to 25 percent more efficient than upright, front-loading freezers, thanks to better insulation and the fact that air doesn't spill out as readily when they are opened, but chest freezers are more difficult to organize. Manual defrosting is more common than automatic defrosting for freezers, but automatic defrost may dehydrate food and cause freezer burn.

Icemakers that produce up to 50 lb of ice cubes every 24 hours are available in built-in or freestanding models. They require a water supply, and some models include a factory-installed drain pump. Electrical requirements typically include 120V, 60 Hz, 15- or 20-A service, with a three-wire grounded, fused electrical supply. Under-counter wine cellars are available that hold 60 bottles. They typically require a 120V, 60 Hz, 15- or 20-A, three-wire grounded, fused electrical supply.

Refrigerators and freezers should be located away from heat sources such as dishwashers and ovens, and out of direct sun. Allow a 25-mm (1-in.) space on each side for good air circulation. To avoid adding waste heat from a freezer to the house cooling load, consider locating the appliance in the basement or garage. Freezers won't work properly when located in spaces where the temperature goes below 7°C (45°F).

COOKING FOOD

The enormous hearth typical of medieval and Tudor kitchens was a multipurpose heat source for forging, dying cloth, and other trades in between mealtimes. A large hearth might accommodate a baking oven at each end and have multiple flues. A long horizontal bar up the chimney held pots and cauldrons, and meat was often smoked in the chimney as well. Before the advent of matches in 1831, a tinder-box and flint were used to light the fire, although once lit, glowing coals were preserved overnight to keep the fire going.

Such early kitchens had no sinks, since all the washing, food preparation, and other work involving water were done in the separate scullery. Kitchen furniture was easily movable, and included trestle tables and three-legged stools. Shelves on the wall held pottery and earthenware dishes, wooden bowls and chopping boards, and metal pots and platters.

By the early eighteenth century, kitchen fireplaces used mineral coal, allowing for smaller and shallower grates. Set in brickwork, built-in charcoal ranges began to take up the work no longer accommodated by the smaller, more decorative fireplaces. Iron baking ovens began to replace traditional clay or brick baking ovens set in the wall of the hearth. By the 1880s, charcoal-fired ranges were replacing open fires entirely.

As kitchens were freed of smoke from huge open hearths, and as messy tasks were diverted to adjacent sculleries, kitchen furnishings became more elaborate. Dressers, closets and cupboards, painted walls, and tiled floors were features of early nineteenth century kitchens.

The development of the kitchen range, which combined open fire, oven, and hot-water boiler, began in the 1780s. By 1850, even working-class English homes had open ranges that were set below an open chimney, and they persisted through the 1950s. The impressive-looking close range, which had a flue controlled by dampers that directed hot air around the ovens, the hot-water boiler, or the hotplate, is credited to George Bodley in 1802.

The compactness, cleanliness, and reliability of gas and, later, electric cooking stoves made it possible to reduce the size of kitchens and their adjacent spaces to the needs of twentieth century families. Gas ranges began to replace those using solid fuels in the 1890s, at least in cities where gas supplies were available.

Swedish scientist Gustav Dalen designed the Aga cooker in the early 1920s. The thickly insulated Aga has two ovens heated by coke from an internal firebox. One oven is always very hot, the other cool. The hot oven and hotplate are heated by radiant heat from the firebox, while the cool oven and warm-plate are heated by conduction. The economical Aga could also be used to keep a large tank of water constantly hot.

The original electric cookers were expensive and slow to heat water. Electric cookers increased rapidly in popularity in the 1920s with the spread of electricity, but still couldn't compete with the economy, convenience, and speed of gas.

Today, cook-tops are available as part of a standard range or as a separate unit, and are either electric or gas. New gas ranges are required to have electric ignition rather than wasteful pilot lights. Electric cooktops typically require single-phase AC, 240/208V, 60 Hz, 20-A or 40-A grounded electrical service. Some cooktops feature a modular design, with open bays that accept halogen, radiant, or coil element cartridges or a grill assembly.

Slide-in ranges provide a more solid, streamlined impression by removing frames and crevices. Freestanding and slide-in electric ranges require three- or four-wire, single phase, AC power. The 120/240V, 60 Hz service should be on a separate 50-A grounded electric circuit.

Electric cook-tops come with a variety of heating elements, including exposed coils, solid disk elements, radiant elements under glass, or high-tech induction or halogen elements. Solid disk elements are attractive and easy to clean. They heat up slowly, however, thus increasing their energy consumption. Radiant elements under ceramic glass are also very cleanable. They heat up faster than solid disks, but not faster than coils. However, they are more energy-efficient than coils or solid disks. Halogen elements use halogen lamps for instant heat and rapid temperature changes. They offer energy savings, but this is offset by the higher purchase price. Halogen elements heat food by means of the contact of the pan on the ceramic glass surface. All of these elements require that pans have good contact with the burners, so flat pan bottoms are a necessity.

Induction elements transfer electromagnetic energy directly to the pan. They are very energy-efficient, using about half as much energy as electric coil cook-tops. Induction elements work only with ferrous metal cookware, such as cast iron, stainless steel, or enameled iron, and not with aluminum pans. When the pan is removed from the heating element, almost no heat lingers on the cook-top. Induction elements are available on only the highest priced cook-tops.

Gas cooktops should have electric pilot lights, and often have sealed gas burners. They typically require single-phase AC, 120V, 60 Hz, 15-A grounded electric service. Gas cooktops are available in combination with gas grills. Those with sealed gas burners are easier to keep clean. Some manufacturers offer dual fuel models, combining sealed gas burners with an electric convection oven.

Gas cook stoves consume oxygen from room air and release carbon dioxide and water vapor. To make sure that gas combustion products are eliminated from the house, install a ventilation fan. The fan must exhaust to the outside when the stove is in use, and not just recirculate air. Avoid too large a fan, as it will waste energy, and may cause backdrafting problems. Large downdraft ventilation fans in cook-tops and ranges can suck in so much air that the house is depressurized, causing the heating system to fail to vent properly and creating a backdraft for combustion gases. Large fans need makeup air ducts, which are supplied by some fan manufacturers.

Conventional ovens with self-cleaning features have more than the usual amount of insulation, and are more energy-efficient, unless the self-cleaning feature is used more than once a month. A window in the door saves wasting energy when the door is opened to look at the progress of the food being cooked. Built-in electric ovens typically require a separate 208/240V, 60 Hz, 30-A grounded circuit. A time delay fuse or circuit breaker is recommended. Double ovens located one above the other get a lot of oven into a small amount of floor space.

Convection ovens are more energy-efficient than conventional ovens. Heated air continuously circulates around the food for more even heat distribution. Food can be cooked faster and at lower temperatures, saving about one-third of energy costs.

There are an increasing number of accessory cooking appliances available today. Warming drawers keep contents in the 3°C to 107°C (90°F–225°F) range. They offer removable serving pans, and the drawer itself may be removable. The electrical service required is 120V, 60 Hz. Rotisseries for residential use require electrical and gas connections, as well as an exhaust hood. They are heavy, weighing about 130 kg (290 lb), and must be supported adequately.

Microwave ovens use very high frequency radio waves to penetrate the food surface and heat up water molecules in the food's interior. Using a microwave can reduce energy use and cooking times, especially for small portions and for reheating leftovers, by around two-thirds over a conventional oven. They also contribute less waste heat to the kitchen. Temperature probes, controls that shut off when the food is cooked, and variable power settings also save energy. Microwave ovens are available in countertop, over-range, over-counter, and built-in models. Most specify a 120V, single phase, 60-Hz, AC, 15-A three-wire grounded circuit. Built-in microwaves may offer a drop-down door and a convection hood, and may require 120V or 240V, 20-A service. Microwave combination ovens come with a convection oven below, and may require 120/240V, 60-Hz, 40-A grounded service. Microwaves, toaster ovens, and slow-cook crock-pots, which combine an insulated ceramic pot with an electric heating element, can save energy when used to prepare smaller meals.

A new oven technology, currently under development and available in limited quantities at high prices, is designed to cook at five times the speed of conventional ovens. The oven works by using two-thirds convection heat and one-third electromagnetic energy (microwaves). The convection heat transfer pushes super-hot air down onto, around, and under the food. At the same time, microwaves are directed into the food, helping to achieve the perfect temperature and cooking time for any dish. Food cooks when the microwave energy couples with the water molecules inside the food, and the high heat flowing through the oven evenly wraps around the food to brown the surface. A catalyst at the base rapidly incinerates residue and drippings before they can cause odor or smoke. The oven can also be used as a regular convection oven or microwave. The oven's computer memory is preprogrammed for common foods, and lets you save recipes and custom-program the memory for cultural cooking styles.

Professional quality cooking equipment is sometimes specified for high-end residential projects. The allure of sleek finishes, large capacity, and added features promises that the home cook will accomplish chef-quality feats. It is important to remember that what happens in a real commercial kitchen is a world away from the experience of the home cook, and many of the features and much of the capacity of true professional equipment are beyond the scope of a residential project. Many high-end appliance manufacturers offer professional-style equipment that may be appropriate for a dedicated amateur chef, but often the issue is one of style more than substance. Brochures are replete with comments like, "Your decorator is going to love this. A sleek, elegant six-burner cooktop." As an interior designer, you can help your clients select equipment that fits their actual needs with a combination of good design and energy economy.

DISHWASHING

The dishwasher wasn't a glimmer in the inventor's eye as long as household labor costs were low. A basic model patented in the United States in 1865 consisted of a metal cupboard that was placed on the sink drain board and filled by a pipe from the tap. Metal plates turned by a hand crank forced water against plates in a wire rack. In 1885, a large Paris restaurant was using a machine invented by Eugene Daquin, which had eight artificial hands that gripped the plates. Plates were washed in a hot bath, vigorously brushed, and then dipped in cold water. In the 1890s, Mrs. Cockran of Indiana invented a dishwasher consisting of a wooden tub with a hand-cranked set of plungers that forced water over the dishes. It was filled by hand, but gained some success when fitted with a small electric motor. The first modern dishwasher dates to 1932, when the ancestor to the Kenwood dishwasher of the 1960s appeared. By 1951, only 1 million dishwashers had been sold in the United States, and problems weren't solved satisfactorily until the 1970s.

Heating water makes up 80 percent of the energy use of an automatic dishwasher, so using less water saves energy. Older dishwashers use 8 to 14 gallons of water per wash cycle. Since 1994, dishwashers have used between 7 and 10 gallons per cycle. By including a booster heater in the dishwasher, cooler water from the main water heater is raised to a temperature between 60°C and 63°C (140°F–145°F), optimum for dishwashing performance. Some dishwashers offer energy-saving wash cycles. No-heat drying circulates room air through the dishwasher by fans rather than using an electric heating element. The so-called "dirt sensor" technology touted by some manufacturers has shown uneven performance and is generally unreliable.

Energy Star dishwashers save both water and energy. Built-in sensors determine the length of the washing cycle and the temperature of the water necessary to clean the dishes. A speed cycle cuts wash time by 30 minutes, and a high-performance motor makes the unit run more quietly. Energy Star dishwashers minimize the amount of water needed, saving the energy required to heat that additional water. Energy Star dishwashers exceed minimum federal efficiency standards by at least 13 percent and by as much as 30 percent.

Dishwashers need both water supply and drain connections. Electrical connections are typically a 120V, 60-Hz, 15-A or 20-A fused electrical supply with copper wire on a separate circuit. A time delay fuse or circuit breaker is recommended. The outlet should be placed in an adjacent cabinet. Because of the heat they give off, dishwashers should not be installed near refrigerators. Unfaced fiberglass batt insulation added to the top, sides, and back, if permitted by the manufacturer, results in less noise and less energy use.

Compact dishwashers are usually 46 cm (18 in.) wide, and standard models are 61 cm (24 in.) wide. Compact models are often more expensive than standard models. The racks of some compact models are designed to hold full-size loads, which saves energy.

LAUNDRY

Before homes had running water piped into them, laundry was frequently an outdoor task. Clothes were beaten clean with wooden bats on a riverbank or in a communal washing cistern. Clothing was washed more often in warm spring and summer weather than in the winter, when drying was a major problem. Before the age of cheap cotton, clothes were laundered as little as possible. Originally, no soaps were used, and clothes were beaten to knock out the dirt. This was very hard on fine fabrics. Eventually, clothes were soaked in an alkaline solution called lye, made from furnace ash, bird dung, bran, or urine, all of which worked well to remove perspiration and greasy dirt that tended to rot fabrics. Soap, which was made from vegetable oils and animal fats, was expensive to buy and tedious to make.

In England, the size of a country-house laundry of the eighteenth century varied from a single washhouse separate from the main house, to a whole suite of rooms for bleaching, drying, ironing, and folding. Professional washerwomen in towns took care of clothing from surrounding estates as early as the fourteenth century. Traveling washerwomen teams stayed for a day or two in their customers' homes at the end of the eighteenth century. By the nineteenth century, cheaper cotton clothing generated more laundry, which was sent out each week or two by middle and upper-class city residents, or laundered by a professional washerwoman who came to the house once a week.

The old-fashioned laundry was a sweltering, damp place, steamy from the boiling coppers, the drying closets, and the iron-heating stoves or grates. Laundry was originally washed in large wooden troughs with washboards. By the early twentieth century, large glazed earthenware sinks replaced these. In addition, the washhouse was furnished with wooden tubs where laundry was churned by wash-sticks. A built-in boiling copper was filled and emptied with buckets and a dipper, and heated from underneath.

Hand-held agitators that were twisted or pumped up and down in a wooden tub inspired the first washing machines. The earliest washing machine patents date to 1752, while the first practical machines were those produced by Mr. Harper Twelvetrees in the 1850s. Clothes tended to get knotted around the legs of the agitators in this early equipment (Fig. 32-1). Other machines were patterned on washboards. Mr. Bradford of Saltram, England, patented the Vowel machines in 1861 (with A, E, I, O, and U models), which consisted of a hexagonal box that rocked and vibrated so that clothes rubbed against the ribbed wood lining inside. These machines were tiring to use and needed constant attendance.

C. 1850 washing machine

Horizontal action clothes washer

Figure 32-1 Clothes washers.

By the 1860s, piped hot and cold water was standard in newer homes. The first electric washers with motorized rotating tubs were developed around 1915 in both England and the United States. The motor under the machine lacked a protective casing, and water dripping on it caused frequent short circuits, fires, and shocks. Many of these early machines had to be filled manually with buckets and drained by hand. Clothes were removed wet, and the machine continued to run until the plug was pulled. Later machines had a central agitator and could spin clothes almost dry. It wasn't until 1939 that the first washer was manufactured with automatic timing controls, variable cycles, and preset water levels.

Today's washing machines are expected to wash clothes better with less water and less energy. Because they use less water, efficient washers also use less detergent and reduce the sewage treatment load. Heating water uses 90 percent of the energy consumed by washing machines. Appliance manufacturers met the 1993 DOE Standards by removing the option for hot water rinse from the regular cycle and by using better tub designs.

In 2001, the DOE announced new standards for clothes washers which, when fully implemented, will lead to approximately $48 in utility bill savings per year for consumers and save over 7090 gallons of water per year for the average consumer. The standard requires new clothes washers to be 22 percent more efficient by 2004 and 35 percent more efficient by 2007. Several clothes washer models currently offered on the market meet the standard outlined for full compliance in 2007. The energy and water savings result primarily from design innovations. More accurate sensors lead to more efficient use of hot and cold water. Higher spin speeds that remove more water from clothes result in less drying time, thereby saving energy.

Horizontal axis machines, which are usually front-loading, are generally much more efficient than vertical axis machines. Horizontal axis machines use about one-third as much water, thus saving about two-thirds of the energy use. They also clean more thoroughly than conventional machines. Because horizontal axis machines spin faster, less water is left in the clothes, which saves time and energy in the dryer. Front-loading machines may allow a dryer to be stacked on top for space savings. The money saved on energy and water may add up to around $100 per year, which along with the rebates often offered by manufacturers and utilities make the newer horizontal axis machines a wise choice.

Wash and rinse cycle options, especially cold water rinses, and water level settings save energy, as do machines that adjust automatically to the size of the load. Locate the washing machine as close as possible to the water

heater and insulate all hot water pipes for further savings. The washing machine should be located in a heated space if possible. Sound protection is sometimes a valuable option, although operating noises may let you know what stage the load is in. Washers usually require a 120V, 60-Hz, AC, 15-A or 20-A grounded electrical outlet.

Clothes were originally twisted dry, leading to the women's fashion for tight pleats in the eleventh century. In the late eighteenth century, mechanical wringers that squeezed clothes between rollers were screwed to sinks, and these became a standard feature of early washing machines. By 1880, rubber rollers pressed water out of clothes.

Once wrung out, clothes were spread on lawns in the sun to dry, or on rosemary and lavender hedges that scented the clothes as well. Only in wet or cold weather were clothes dried indoors, on drying rods suspended from the ceiling, or on airing racks hoisted overhead on pulleys. In France in 1800, M. Pochon invented a device called a ventilator. Hand-wrung damp clothes were put in a circular metal drum pierced with holes. Cranking the handle rotated the drum above an open fire. The clothes either dried slowly or burned, and smelled like soot. In the mid-nineteenth century, drying closets were constructed in large homes and institutions. Drying closets are brick enclosures built over furnaces or networks of hot pipes. Metal frames with racks pulled out from the drying closet to load and unload laundry.

Modern clothes dryers work by heating and aerating clothes. Gas dryers are much less expensive than electric dryers to use. Automatic shut-offs save energy and are easier on clothes. The best automatic shut-offs use moisture sensors in the drum, and don't just sense the temperature of the exhaust air. Cool-down and moisture sensing options also reduce the energy needed for ironing. Electric ignition, rather than pilot lights, is now required in gas dryers. Dryers should be located in heated spaces. Designing an area for air-drying delicate items protects clothes and also saves energy.

Some dryer models have drop-down rather than side-opening doors, making it easier to keep that loose sock from falling to the floor. Sound protection is a valuable option where a noisy dryer could be disturbing. Service requirements for electric dryers are typically a 120/240V or 120/208V, 60-Hz, AC, 30-A grounded electrical outlet. Gas dryers need a gas connection, of course, and a 120V, 60-Hz, AC, 15- or 20-A grounded electrical outlet.

Vent dryers—especially gas dryers—directly to the outside, with short, straight sections of metal duct. Flexible vinyl duct restricts airflow, and can be crushed. Vinyl duct may not stand up to high temperatures. Electric dryers may be vented inside the home during the winter if the house air is dry and the vent is properly filtered. Compact apartment or condominium dryers are sometimes vented indoors, but may cause condensation of moisture on windows. Dryer exhausts should have a vent hood that blocks air infiltration and seals the exhaust duct very tightly when the dryer is not running. Standard dryer vent hoods use a simple flapper, which is not as effective. Tightly sealing hoods cost a few dollars extra.

In this day of wash and wear, those of us who still iron our summer linens are a vanishing breed. The earliest piece of machinery to be used to iron sheets, tablecloths, and other flat linen was the mangle. The mangle combined pressure provided by a screw with a smoothing technique involving wrapping linens around smooth wooden cylinders and rolling them to and fro under pressure. For other items, flat irons in different sizes were used, often in pairs so that one could be in use while the other heated on a stove. Box irons were heated internally with slugs of hot metal or charcoal. Box irons are still in use in some parts of the world where power is unreliable and expensive. Beginning in the 1890s, paraffin, oil, and petroleum irons were available. H. W. Seeley of New Jersey patented the earliest electric iron in 1882, which dubiously featured flying sparks and weird noises. Today's irons are much safer, if less exciting. Models that will turn themselves off if left unattended are preferable.

FUTURE DEVELOPMENTS

A handful of companies are beginning to roll out a new generation of household appliances with Internet or network capability and a range of potential uses. Networked appliances are already available in Asia, and are expected to be available in the United States soon. Some appliances communicate with each other through the home electrical system, while most use the telephone line and an Internet service provider. Manufacturers are hesitant to bring products out, primarily in response to customer's concerns that the new products might not integrate with appliances from other manufacturers. Customers also worry that they may need to rewire their homes, or that their phone lines will be taken over by appliances. Manufacturers are still working out industry standards.

To date, wired microwaves, refrigerators, and washing machines are available that are designed to perform intelligent tasks such as collecting recipes from the Internet, tracking food inventory, and downloading new wash cycles from the Internet for different kinds of clothes. Each component connects to the Internet through telephone lines and built-in modems. Users may also be able to use appliance display screens to make two-way video telephone calls, watch TV, or send e-mail.

Part VI

LIGHTING

Chapter

Daylighting

• • •

Until recently, the workday ended when the sun went down. At the end of the day, everyone huddled around the fire, and then headed off to bed in the dark. Fires, candles, and oil lamps provided weak illumination, and were often too expensive for poorer people. People depended on daylight entering their buildings to give enough light for daily tasks. Architects and builders understood the role of natural light in buildings intuitively. Building orientations, configurations, and interior finishes were selected to provide sufficient levels of daylighting in interior spaces.

When energy is cheap, it is tempting to eliminate the variations inherent in daylight and supply all interior lighting with electric lighting supplemented by a few windows. Although daylighting offers significant opportunities for energy conservation, the budget for lighting operation and maintenance represents only a very small portion of total building costs over its entire life cycle. It is difficult to justify daylighting on cost savings alone. However, an energy-conscious approach is mandated by many building codes, and daylighting is one of the most effective ways to reduce energy use.

In addition to being an economical response to code-mandated energy budgets, daylighting can save businesses significant labor costs. The greatest costs for a business are related to the people who work in the building. In the last decade, daylighting has been linked to increased productivity. The promise of even a modest 1 percent increase in productivity is likely to appeal to a business owner more than a building that is 20 percent more energy efficient. The potential for a good daylighting design to improve productivity, even by a small increment, and thus to increase corporate profits, is a strong justification for a daylighting design.

PHYSIOLOGICAL EFFECTS OF DAYLIGHTING

In proper amounts, ultraviolet (UV) rays from the sun help our bodies produce vitamin D and keep the skin healthy. In addition, UV light dilates skin capillaries, causes blood pressure to fall slightly, creates a feeling of well-being, quickens the pulse rate and appetite, and stimulates energetic activity, perhaps even increasing work activity. On the other hand, overexposure to UV rays can damage the skin and cause malignant tumors and cataracts. We receive almost no UV in an artificially lit environment. There is almost no UV in incandescent and fluorescent lighting. Some new lighting sources include UV in their output.

Visible light affects our biological rhythms, hormonal activity, and behavior. We have already examined the importance of infrared (IR) radiation in radiant heating.

Anecdotal information supports claims of a link between daylight and productivity. When WalMart added skylights to their new Eco-Mart in Lawrence, Kansas, the company claimed significantly higher sales in the skylighted portion of the store. Similarly, managers at Lockheed's new daylighted Building 157 observed a 15 percent productivity increase and a decrease of 15 percent in absenteeism.

Studies are backing up these claims with data. When researchers at Heschong Mahone Group (HMG), an energy consulting firm in Sacramento, California, studied over a hundred stores in a chain, all in relatively sunny, southern locations, they observed that the stores with skylights had peak daylight levels two to three times the standard electric illumination levels of nearly identical stores without skylights. When they compared data from the two sets of stores, they determined that an average nonskylighted store in the chain would be likely to have 40 percent higher sales with the addition of skylights. After the number of hours open per week, the presence of skylights was the best predictor of the sales per store of all the variables that were considered. Shoppers tended not to be aware of the skylights themselves but commented that the skylighted stores seemed cleaner or more spacious than other similar stores. The study predicted that, were the chain to add the skylighting system to the remaining one-third of their stores, their yearly gross sales would increase by 11 percent.

The impact of daylighting on the performance of school children has been a subject of interest for many years. All schoolrooms were designed for daylighting until the advent of fluorescent fixtures. However, starting in the late 1960s, engineers concerned about energy conservation and air-conditioning requirements argued against the use of large expanses of glass and high ceilings. Facility managers sometimes considered that windows and skylights were a maintenance and security risk. The advent of flexible, open classrooms with solid exterior walls that avoided distracting views further limited daylight, and many schools were designed with little or no daylight.

More recently, the medical research community has linked light levels to human health. Recognition of Seasonal Affective Disorder, which is helped by exposure to daylight, increased pressure for reinstating daylight in schools. In a second study by HMG, three public school districts representing a wide range of climates and building types agreed to provide test score data to researchers. HMG reviewed a total of over 2000 second through fifth grade classrooms. The results for the Capistrano, California, classrooms were the most dramatic. Students with the largest window areas were found to progress 15 percent faster in math and 23 percent faster in reading. Students who had a skylight in their room that diffused daylight throughout the room and allowed teachers to control the amount of available daylight also improved 19 to 20 percent faster than those students without a skylight. However, skylight systems that allowed uncontrolled direct sun into the classroom showed a decrease in test scores for reading and no significant change for math. Students in classrooms where windows could be opened were found to progress 7 to 8 percent faster than those with fixed windows, regardless of whether they also had air-conditioning. Seattle, Washington, and Fort Collins, Colorado, studies also showed positive and highly significant effects from daylighting. High daylight levels in classrooms for these districts were shown to produce scores 7 to 18 percent higher than scores from classrooms with the least daylight.

Daylight helps us relate the indoors to the outdoors. Colors appear brighter and more natural in daylight. The variations in light over the course of a day and in varying weather conditions stimulate visual interest. People, like most living things, need full-spectrum light, which is a main characteristic of daylight. Without daylight, people tend to lose track of time, are unaware of weather conditions, and may feel disoriented. Even mail carriers who spend the majority of their day outdoors have expressed a clear preference for daylight in their indoor workplaces.

GLARE

Glare is a result of excessive contrast, or of light coming from the wrong direction. The contrast between the bright outside environment viewed through a window and the darkness of the interior space creates glare. Glare results in discomfort and eye fatigue as the eye repeatedly readjusts from one lighting condition to another. Direct sunlight or reflected sunlight from bright, shiny surfaces can be disturbing or even disabling, and should never be permitted to enter the field of view of the building's occupants. Windows or skylights within the normal field of vision of the building's occupants can appear distractingly bright next to other objects. A window next to a blackboard, for example, will create a glare situation.

There are two basic methods to avoid glare and reduce brightness contrasts: sensitive interior design and daylight light controls. We will cover daylighting controls shortly. As far as interior design strategies to control glare, you should assign tasks where adequate natural light is available but guard against glare. Orient furniture so that daylight comes from the left side or rear of the line of sight. A workstation should never face windows unless they are on a northern exposure and no exterior glare sources are in the line of sight. Windows should be placed away from internal focal points in a room. Factories use north-facing clerestories to reduce glare away from very bright views and to avoid glare accidents.

DESIGNING FOR DAYLIGHTING

By careful planning, daylight can be increased with a few carefully placed windows and appropriately selected interior finishes at a very moderate cost. The energy supply for daylight is free. Keeping windows and interior surfaces clean for better reflectance may add something to maintenance costs. However, because daylight is not available at night, artificial lighting sources must be provided as well.

Through centuries of trial and error and sensitivity to local sites and climates, indigenous builders historically have used daylighting effectively and well. Bill Lam, lighting designer and author of two classic texts on daylighting and architecture, cites Boston's John Hancock Tower as an example of how modern architects get it wrong. The building is mirrored to keep light out, with the long sides of the building facing east and west. The glazing extends from the floor to about one foot above the ceiling. To lessen glare and control overheating, interior blinds are lowered, and since people tend to be somewhat lazy, the blinds are left down—and the lights are left on—all the time.

Bill Lam believes that, particularly in North America, we have hardly begun to take advantage of the energy-saving potential of exploiting daylight. Now that the California energy crisis has created renewed interest in energy conservation, he believes that sunlighting and good energy design can regain a higher priority. He sets forth several principles for designing pleasant, delightful, luminous environments that are energy conserving and economical.

Basic daylighting can consist solely of making windows and skylights large enough for the darkest overcast days, as in many northern European buildings. True daylighting is more accurately defined as passive solar design. Daylighting involves the conscious design of building forms for optimum illumination and thermal performance. It is most challenging in workspaces such as schools, offices, laboratories, libraries, and museums with varied and demanding tasks, and least challenging in public spaces where comfort standards are less stringent and controlled lighting is less important.

Interior spaces need high ceilings and highly reflective room surfaces for the best light distribution. The light source—the sun—is constantly changing in direction and intensity. Ground-reflected light is ideal because it is both bright and diffuse, but adjacent buildings or trees often shade the ground. Light bouncing off the ground outside ends up on the ceiling.

Daylighting considerations affect the architecture of the building exterior, determining the amount of fenestration and its appearance on the building facade. The building orientation and shape should be designed with daylighting in mind.

In a daylighting design, heat and light are controlled through the form of the building. For example, in a Middle Eastern mosque located in a sunny climate, limited sunlight enters the building through small windows high in a decorated ceiling, and then is diffused as it bounces off interior surfaces. The large windows in a Western European cathedral, on the other hand, flood the interior with light, colored and filtered through stained glass. To take advantage of sunlight without an excess of heat or glare, the building should be oriented so that windows are on the north and south sides. Frank Lloyd Wright shaded the west and south sides from the most intense sun with deep overhangs. To study where light is coming from in an existing building, look at the shadows (this can be done with photographs).

Daylighting must be integrated with the view, natural air movement, acoustics, heat gain and loss, and electric lighting. Operable windows offer daylight and natural airflow, but allow in noise. Daylighting doesn't save any energy unless lights are turned off, so lighting zones must be circuited separately, with lights turned off or dimmed when the natural light is adequate and left on where proper amounts of daylight aren't available.

To be successful, the daylighting scheme must allow daylight to penetrate into the building, and ensure that daylight will be available whether the sky is overcast or clear. An atrium can be used to bring large quantities of direct or reflected sunlight down into a building interior. In some buildings over two stories high, light wells bring natural light into the interior building core. Light wells are smaller spaces than atriums that can be employed with skylights, clerestories, or window walls.

Sunlight is a highly efficient source of illumination, and a comparatively cool source. Daylight varies with the season, the time of day, the latitude, and weather conditions. More sunlight is available in summer than in winter, and the day's sun peaks at noon. An overcast day is very different from a day with a clear sky, and conditions can change several times during a day. Of course, sunlight is unavailable until dawn and after dusk.

On a bright day, sunlight provides illumination levels 50 times as high as the requirements for artificial illumination. Direct sun may be desirable for solar heating in winter, but the glare from direct sun must be managed. Indirect sunlight produces illumination levels between 10 and 20 percent as bright as direct sun, but still higher than needed indoors. Daily changes in daylight controls and seasonal adjustments in the size of daylight openings may help accommodate the changing nature of daylight and the overabundance of sun. Mirrored and low-transmission glass won't solve glare problems as well as shading does.

We can't look directly at the sun, and it is almost impossible to carry out fine visual tasks like reading or sewing in the glare of direct sun. The sky is brilliant with scattered sunlight, which is often bright enough to distract the eye. Direct sunshine bleaches colors, and the heat from direct sun in buildings is often intolerable, especially in summer. Clouds often obscure the sun's glare partly or completely.

The bottom line of daylighting design is to achieve the minimal acceptable amount of natural illumination when the available daylight conditions are at their worst, and to screen out excess illumination at other times. For example, the daylight available at 9:00 in the morning in December is used as the basis for the worst-case conditions. The designer also seeks to provide adequate daylight under average sky conditions, with artificial lighting supplying added light for less than average daylight conditions. The goal is to achieve adequate natural illumination during the majority of the daytime hours the space is occupied. The design is balanced with supplementary artificial lighting in dark areas rather than with an oversupply of daylight in lighter areas.

Daylighting relies mostly on diffused sunlight or reflected, indirect sunlight to illuminate building interiors. The amount of natural light available within a room depends on how much sky is directly visible through windows and skylights from a given point in that room. The amount of indirect light from the sky also depends on how bright the visible areas of sky are. The sky at the horizon is about one-third as bright as the sky directly overhead, so the nearer the window is to the ceiling, the more light it will gather, as long as it isn't blocked by trees or buildings. Skylights are very effective at collecting the brightest light.

The shape and surface finishes of a space have an impact on daylighting. Tall, shallow spaces with high surface reflectances are brighter than low, deep rooms with windows only at the narrow end and with dark, cold surfaces. It takes fewer bounces off the walls for light to get deep into a room when the windows are high on the wall. High windows distribute light more evenly to all walls and allow light to penetrate into the interiors of large, low buildings. The ceiling and back wall of the space are more effective than the side walls or floor for reflecting and distributing daylight. Remember that tall objects, such as office cubicle partitions or tall bookcases, can obstruct both direct and reflected light.

The level of daylight illumination diminishes as it goes deeper into the interior space. In order to reduce glare, you need to design a gradual transition from the brightest to darkest parts of the space. The amount of light about 1.5 meters (5 ft) from the window should not be more than ten times as bright as the darkest part of the room. In a room with windows on only one wall, the average illumination of the darker half of the room should be at least a third of the average illumination level of the other half with windows. By using windows on more than one side of the room, along with interior light wells, skylights, and clerestories, you can achieve more balanced daylighting. It is best to allow daylight from two directions for balance, preferably with the second source at the end of the room farthest from the main daylight source.

SIDELIGHTING

Daylighting is generally broken into two categories: sidelighting through windows in walls, and toplighting through skylights in roofs and clerestory windows very high up on walls.

Direct sunlight coming through a window and striking a worksurface can result in uneven light distribution and glare in the visual field. Light that arrives from a shaded area or on an overcast day is more acceptable.

The ground and nearby building surfaces may reflect sunlight into windows. Reflecting surfaces absorb most of the heat and scatter visual light at a much lower intensity than direct sunlight. Once inside the building, reflected light can reach indoor points directly or by reflecting further off other interior surfaces. These successive reflections can bring daylight more deeply into the space.

Openings for daylighting may also provide ventilation, views, and solar heat, but they should be considered potentially different from openings designed specifically for these other functions. The size and orientation of window openings and the transmittance of the glazing, as well as the reflectance of the room and outdoor surfaces, affect the quality of daylighting. As mentioned earlier, overhangs and nearby trees obstruct the sun. East and west windows must have shading devices to avoid bright early morning and later afternoon sun. In the summer, the low angle of the morning and evening sun creates glare and generates excessive heat. South-facing windows are ideal for daylight if they have horizontal shading devices that can control excessive solar radiation and glare. Windows and skylights facing north in northern latitudes receive little or no direct sunlight, and gather indirect light without significant heat gain.

The larger and higher the window, the more daylight enters the room. As a rule of thumb, you can use daylighting for task lighting up to a depth of two times the height of the window. By using the depth that light can penetrate into a given space as a guide, you can proportion rooms to take advantage of the maximum amount of daylighting. The ideal height from the top of the window to the floor should be about one-half the depth of the room if you want to get maximum daylight penetration and distribution without glare. The standard for daylighting of offices, lobbies, and circulation areas is for glazing to equal 5 to 10 percent of the floor area served. For display, drafting, typing, and factory work, the glazing should be about a quarter of the floor area. Sill height isn't critical, as the lower part of the window does not contribute much light to the inner part of the room.

Highly reflective surfaces absorb less light at each reflection, and pass more light to the room's interior. Surface brightness should change gradually from the outside to the inside. White exterior surfaces and window frames gather more reflected light in through the windows. Light-colored window frames, especially if splayed at an angle, help reduce uncomfortable contrasts between the bright outdoor views and darker interiors. Light-colored surfaces reflect and distribute light more efficiently, and dark colors absorb light. Large areas of shiny surfaces can cause glare. You can reduce contrast by using light colors and high reflectances for window frames, walls, ceilings, and floors.

Select interior surface colors and reflectances according to the primary source of incoming light. Direct and reflected sky light hits the floor first, while reflected sunlight hits the ceiling first. Light colors and reflectances on surfaces far from openings help increase the light in dim areas. By placing windows adjacent to light colored interior walls, reflected light goes through a series of transitional intensities rather than having an extremely bright opening surrounded by unlit walls.

TOPLIGHTING

Lighting from above offers the best distribution of diffuse skylight, with deeper penetration and better uniformity of daylight. Toplighting is best where light is desired but a view is not necessary. It offers better security and frees up wall space. Toplighting may eliminate the need for electric lighting on the top floors of a building during daylight hours. Unlike sidelighting, it is easy to distribute uniformly. Toplighting controls glare from low angle sunlight better than sidelighting.

Clerestories (Fig. 33-1) provide balanced daylight throughout the changing seasons better than do skylights. South, east, or west facing clerestory windows that are designed so that the light bounces against a vertical surface and is diffused on its way to the interior capture the maximum amount of sun in December and the minimum amount in June. The Johnson Controls building designed by Don Watson is an example. A light shelf (described later) and clerestories light the building during the day, and the sun striking a massive wall holds heat with only a slight difference in night temperature. Clerestories use standard weather-tight window constructions. In the northern hemisphere, south-facing clerestories provide the most heat gain in winter.

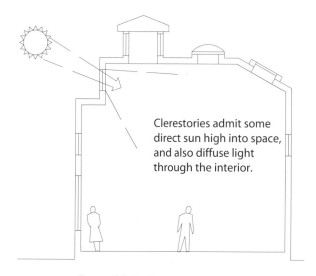

Clerestories admit some direct sun high into space, and also diffuse light through the interior.

Figure 33-1 Clerestory window.

Toplighting provides more light per square foot with less glare than sidelighting, and distributes the light more evenly. However, where the direct sun enters a skylight, it may strike surfaces and produce glare and fading. Unshaded skylights exposed to summer sun by day and cold winter sky by night lead to heat loss. High windows or toplights work best for horizontal tasks like reading at a desk, while lower sidelights (windows in walls) are best for vertical tasks like filing.

Skylights

Skylights (Fig. 33-2) allow daylight to enter an interior space from above. Skylights are metal-framed units pre-assembled with glass or plastic glazing and flashing. They come in stock sizes and shapes or can be custom fabricated. They are efficient and cost-effective sources of daylighting.

Skylights can be mounted flat or angled with the slope of a roof. Skylights that are angled on a north-facing or shaded roof avoid the heat and glare associated with direct sun. The angled sunbeams can be bounced off angled interior ceilings to further diffuse the brightness. Angled skylights can also sometimes offer a view of sky and trees from the interior.

Horizontal skylights get less of the low-angle winter sun than skylights on sloped surfaces, minimizing their contribution to cold weather heating. They also admit the most heat in summer, adding to the cooling load. Horizontal skylights need shades where artificial cooling is used. Controlling brightness and glare may also require louvers, shades, or reflector panels. Horizontal skylights don't collect much solar heat in winter, are covered by snow, and inevitably leak in rain. Horizontal skylights work best in overcast conditions. However, where an angled skylight may not be possible, a well-designed and installed horizontal skylight with a domed surface can bring daylight into an interior space and provide a view of sky.

Skylights are glazed with acrylic or polycarbonate plastic, or with wired, laminated, heat-strengthened, or fully tempered glass. Building codes limit the maximum area of each glazed skylight panel. Building codes also require wire screening below glazing to prevent broken glass injuries when wired glazing, heat-strengthened glass, or fully tempered glass is used in multiple-layer glazing systems. There are exemptions to these regulations for individual dwelling units. Double-glazing a skylight promotes energy conservation and reduces condensation. Skylights with translucent glazing provide daylight from above without excessive heat gain. The way that translucent materials diffuse light reduces contrast for a restful long-term environment, but the light appears as dull as that from an overcast sky. Clear glass should be used where you want the sparkle of sunlight.

Other Toplighting Options

Light pipes were first introduced in the early 1990s. They are basically a metal or plastic tube that delivers light from the roof into an otherwise dark room. The typical light pipe includes a roof-mounted plastic dome to capture sunlight, a reflective tube that stretches from the dome to the interior ceiling, and a ceiling-mounted diffuser that spreads the light around the room. There are a number of brands currently on the market. Most companies offer two sizes: a 33-cm (13-in.) model to fit between 41-cm (16-in.) on-center framing, and a 53-cm (21-in.) model to fit between 61-cm (2-ft) on-center framing. Tests done by the Alberta Research Council in Canada found a light pipe's output to be the equivalent of a 1200-W incandescent lamp. Light pipes won't give a view, but will bring light to spaces where a skylight won't, including walk-in closets, small interior bathrooms, and hallways. Installation is relatively simple.

Roof monitors (Fig. 33-3) reflect daylight into a space. The light enters a scoop-like construction on the roof, and bounces off the surfaces of the monitor opening and down into the space. Mirror systems using a

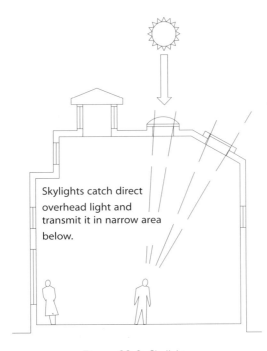

Skylights catch direct overhead light and transmit it in narrow area below.

Figure 33-2 Skylights.

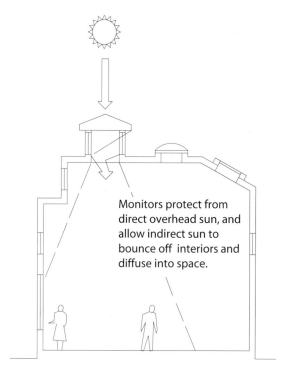

Figure 33-3 Roof monitor.

Monitors protect from direct overhead sun, and allow indirect sun to bounce off interiors and diffuse into space.

periscope-like device can bring daylight and views underground by reflecting them down through the space.

Roof windows are stock wood windows designed for installation in a sloping roof. They either pivot or swing open for ventilation and cleaning. They are typically 61 to 122 cm (2–4 ft) wide and 92 to 183 cm (3–6 ft) high, and are available with shades, blinds, and electric operators. Sloped glazing systems are essentially glazed curtain walls engineered to serve as pitched glass roofs.

Active techniques for daylighting include heliostats and tracking devices. A heliostat is a dish-shaped mirror that focuses sunlight onto a stationary second mirror. It dynamically readjusts the primary mirror to track the sun and maximize the capture and use of sunlight at all times of the day. Once the light is captured, it is distributed, often with a light pipe. The downside to this device is that it must be maintained to prevent dirt and dust accumulation from affecting its performance, and it requires a source of energy (perhaps solar).

DAYLIGHT CONTROL

A light shelf (Fig. 33-4) is a construction that cuts horizontally through a window and bounces sunlight into the room without glare. Light shelves shade glazing from direct sun, and reflect daylight onto the ceiling of the room. Both the direct sunlight and diffuse light from the sky are distributed indirectly deeper into the space. The light shelf shades the glazing below it from direct sun, but leaves ground-reflected light near the window. It increases uniformity of illumination by increasing daylight farther toward the back of the room while decreasing the amount of light near the window. Groups of parallel opaque white louvers are used in a similar way. Louvers and light shelves may let some sun filter in with lower winter angles, but cut glare. Light shelves can be used to keep light glare off computer screens.

Trying to resolve problems with the orientation of the building with mechanical shading devices rather than by proper building design is prone to problems. Bill Lam cites Oscar Niemeyer's Ministry of Education in Brazil, which faces east and west, as an example. Heavy exterior crank blinds were installed to block the intense sun, resulting in a very dark interior. The blinds ultimately rusted and had to be removed. Reliability is most important in selecting movable shading devices, or they won't be adjusted or used.

There are many types of shading and reflecting devices for controlling the sun's heat and glare. Trees and vines cool as well as shade, and deciduous plants admit more light in winter when they lose their leaves. Overhangs block or filter direct sunlight and allow only reflected light from the sky or ground to enter the window. Overhangs necessitate early planning and coordination between architects and interior designers. Awnings and shutters provide adjustable shade, and can be manually, mechanically, or automatically controlled.

Horizontal louvers on southern exposure windows work well to reflect light onto high-reflectance ceilings. Vertical louvers are effective for low sun angles on east and west facing windows. Eggcrate louvers, which have both horizontal and vertical elements, block both high and low sun angles, and reflect daylight into the space.

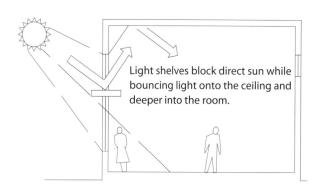

Light shelves block direct sun while bouncing light onto the ceiling and deeper into the room.

Figure 33-4 Light shelf.

Louvers convert direct sun to softer, reflected light and can reduce the apparent brightness of large areas of sky. Exterior louvers are usually fixed, but some can be raised up out of the way when not needed.

Venetian blinds adjust to changing exterior and interior conditions. Venetian blinds can block all daylight and view if desired. They permit light to enter the room by reflection back and forth between the slats, while still blocking glare. Venetian blinds can exclude direct sun and reflect light onto the ceiling, where it will bounce into the interior. When mirrored on one or two sides, they redirect daylight more deeply into the room. In the upper 61 cm (2 ft) of the window, they can beam daylight 9 to 12 meters (30–40 ft) into the space to provide illumination at the work surface. It is possible to rig blinds to cover only the lower half of the window. Units are available with slender blinds between two window panels, eliminating dirt and clumsy control strings.

Roller shades diffuse direct sunlight, eliminate glare, and increase the uniformity of illumination. When illuminated by direct sun, they can be so bright that they become a source of glare themselves. Off-white fabric colors or additional opaque drapery can be used to reduce brightness. If pulled up from the bottom of the window, opaque shades can eliminate glare while still permitting daylight into the room.

When blinds or shades are controlled individually and manually, blinds may be raised or lowered to different heights from window to window, and the appearance of a building facade may suffer. Automatic motorized shading systems that respond to sensors and constantly adjust the amount of daylight are usually impractical in all but the highest-end installations because of their substantial cost.

 The effectiveness of draperies for sun control depends upon the weave and the reflectivity of the fabric. Any amount of light transmission, from blackout through transparency, can be achieved. Even more flexibility is available with two separately tracked drapes over the same opening. Shades and curtains allow user adjustment and soften the interior environment. For maximum effectiveness, the exterior surfaces of shades, drapes, blinds, and insulating panels should be mirrored or highly reflective.

DAYLIGHTING AND HEAT

Daylight brings with it solar heat, which may be welcome as a part of the building's sustainable energy plan, or may raise energy use for air-conditioning. Some solar heating designs don't allow openings in the south wall for daylight. On the other hand, solar heating designs that allow direct sun through south facing walls may admit too much daylight and glare for visual tasks. Large glazed openings that let in daylight can lose heat through those same cold glass surfaces. Designs that limit openings on north, east, and west facing walls to keep heat within the building may shut out daylight from these directions. One design option is to use overly warm sun-heated air from southern exposures to warm the cooler north, east, and west facing perimeters of the building.

In the summer, shaded windows produce less heat gain than the electric lights they replace, resulting in decreased energy use for lighting and for cooling. Electrical lighting introduces around twice as much heat per unit of light into a space as daylighting. In the winter, there is some solar heat gain from south facing windows, but the use of daylighting eliminates some of the heat that would otherwise be generated by electric lighting, so supplementary heating may be needed.

GLAZING MATERIALS

Glazing materials, such as tinted glass or plastic, are used to control the amount of light that enters the interior. The materials are treated with metallic or metal oxide coatings or films that reflect light. They reduce the view into the interior from outside during the day. The tinted materials also change the way the exterior looks from inside the building. At night, the interior is put on display while occupants can't see out. Gray tinted glazing is a neutral tone, so interior colors are rendered fairly accurately. Colored materials, such as bronze, distort the appearance of interior colors. Light transmittance ranges from very dark at 10 to 15 percent to very light, with 70 to 80 percent of the light passing through. Tinted glazing materials transmit the IR spectrum, which contains the heat, at 10 to 15 percent below their visible light transmittance.

Lighting Design

Interior design schools routinely offer full semester courses on lighting design. It is not the purpose of this book to try to cover all the facets of lighting design to the degree that a lighting course would. Instead, we look at how our current approach to lighting developed, and how current lighting design practices affect the relationships between architects, engineers, lighting designers, and interior designers. We also look at some of the less glamorous aspects of selecting lighting sources and controls, and consider practical fixture requirements, lighting system maintenance, and emergency lighting.

After the sun went down, fire was our first source of heat and light, and it is still a major source in many parts of the world. Indoor lighting probably originated with the triangular stone oil lamp used by Cro-Magnon man around 50,000 years ago. A fibrous wick lying in a saucer-like depression was kept burning by rank-smelling animal fat. By around 1300 BC, the Egyptians burned less-odorous vegetable oil in their homes and temples. Their oil lamps had bases of sculpted earthenware and papyrus wicks. Later on, the Greeks and Romans used wicks of oakum (hemp or jute fiber) or linen. Wicks didn't consume themselves and had to be lifted and trimmed, and the lamps had forceps with scissors attached for this purpose.

Leonardo da Vinci can be credited with the first high-intensity lamp. He immersed a glass cylinder containing olive oil and a hemp wick inside a large glass globe filled with water. The water magnified the flame, and allowed Leonardo to work through the night.

The Romans preferred beautifully decorated oil lamps, but they also invented the candle sometime before the first century AD. Their candles were made of nearly colorless and tasteless animal fat tallow. This edible substance led starving soldiers to eat their candle rations. Centuries later, isolated British lighthouse keepers would do the same. By the eighteenth century, chandlers (candlemakers) used beef and mutton fat from small-town slaughterhouses to make the candles they sold to British housewives. Even the most expensive British tallow candles had to be snuffed every half hour, which entailed snipping the charred end of the wick without extinguishing the flame. Since matches had not yet been invented, once the flame was out, the candle was hard to relight. Unsnuffed candles generated less light and melted more tallow. Only about half of an unattended candle actually burned, and the rest ran off as waste. Castles that used hundreds of candles each week kept a staff of snuff servants solely for this purpose. Tallow candles could rot or be eaten by rats if not stored properly.

An inexpensive alternative to the tallow candle was the rushlight, made by soaking a reed (rush) in melted fat. Rushlights were held in the jaws of special holders, where they would burn, with constant care, for 15 to 20 minutes. Rushlights remained in use in rural England into the twentieth century.

By the late seventeenth century, the use of semi-evaporating beeswax candles was widespread. At three times the price of tallow, beeswax candles burned with a brighter flame, less smoke, and a much nicer smell. According to Charles Panati's, *Extraordinary Origins of Everyday Things* (New York: Harper & Row Publishers, 1987, 135), British diarist Samuel Pepys wrote in 1667 that with the use of wax candles at London's Drury Lane Theater, the stage was "now a thousand times better and more glorious."

By the eighteenth century, luxury beeswax candles were used by the Roman Catholic Church and by the rich. In 1765, household records indicated that one of Britain's great homes used 100 pounds of wax candles per month. Glossy white English beeswax, hard yellow vegetable tallow from China, and green bayberry-scented candles from the northeast coast of America were prized for their quality.

In the early eighteenth century, an oil from the head of sperm whales, called spermaceti, was used for candles that burned with a bright white flame. Vegetable oil candles with plaited wicks that didn't need snuffing were introduced in 1840 to celebrate Queen Victoria's wedding to Prince Albert. Cheap paraffin candles that burned as brightly as spermaceti were introduced in 1857.

By 1900, the availability of oil-lamps and gaslights was cutting into the market for candles. The simplest oil lamp hadn't changed much from Egyptian times. It consisted of a shallow dish with a lip that supported a wick made from rush or twined cotton, which gave about the same light as a candle. In 1784, French inventor Ami Argand enclosed a wick in a glass chimney below a large reservoir of oil. The result gave off the light of ten candles and would burn unattended for several hours. By 1836, the glass oil lamp with a key to wind the wick was a common sight.

Oil lamps used whale oil, and the aggressive hunting of whales would probably have ended in their extinction if petroleum hadn't been discovered in Pennsylvania in 1859. Petroleum was distilled into kerosene, and its clear, bright, and nearly smokeless light made it very desirable for lamps. Kerosene lamps appeared as elaborate chandeliers, functional kitchen lamps, and even tiny pressed tin lamps for servants' quarters. Unfortunately, the lamp oil had a very unpleasant smell and was highly flammable, so well-to-do households stored the lamps out of the way in a separate lamp room when not in use, and servants distributed them as the daylight faded.

Three thousand years ago, people in China burned natural gas to remove the brine from salt. Early European tribes erected temples around natural gas jets, to worship the eternal flames. In the seventeenth century, Belgian chemist Jan Baptista van Helmont manufactured coal gas. He believed in the use of the philosopher's stone to transform base metals to gold, and his invention was a bridge from alchemy to chemistry. His work inspired French chemist Antoine Lavoisier, who considered the possibility of lighting Paris streets with gas lamps, and invented a prototype lamp in the 1780s. Unfortunately, Lavoisier was guillotined during the French Revolution.

Before the invention of the electric lightbulb, gaslight supplied lighting for streets and buildings. The first gas company was established in London in 1813, leading to the advent of home gas lamps. By 1816, Westminster, England, boasted 26 miles of gas pipe. The heat and smell from gas fixtures relegated them to use outdoors until the middle of the nineteenth century.

German scientist Robert von Bunsen diminished the flicker of a pure gas flame by premixing the gas with air. In 1885, one of Bunsen's students invented the gas mantle, which greatly increased illumination. The mantle was made of thread dipped in thorium and cerium nitrate. When lit, the thread was consumed, and the remaining skeleton of carbonized compounds glowed a brilliant greenish white.

British inventors had been experimenting with electric lights for more than 50 years before Edison invented the lightbulb. When a current is passed through a filament in a glass chamber without air, the filament glows white-hot. Joseph Swan in England had the idea of using carbon for the filament, and patented a lamp in 1878, a year before Thomas Edison had the same idea and registered a patent in the United States. Edison then proceeded to set up a system of electrical distribution, and took the lightbulb out of the laboratory and into homes and streets. Swan and Edison sued each other, but eventually co-founded an electric company.

Edison's Pearl Street Power Station in New York City was the first to supply electricity on consumer demand. By December 1882, over 200 Manhattan individual and business customers were using more than 3000 electric lamps, each with an average bulb life of only 15 hours (compared to around 2000 hours today). By early 1884, Edison had perfected a 400-hour lightbulb, and increased that to 1200 hours in 1886.

Despite initial curiosity, the growth of electricity in homes was slow at first. It took seven years for Edison's initial 203 residential customers to grow to 710. Thanks to decreasing electric rates and word of mouth, however, by 1900, 10,000 people had electric lights. By 1910, the number was over 3 million.

In 1859, the French physicist who discovered the radioactivity in uranium, Antoine-Henri Becquerel, coated the inside of a glass tube with a chemical called a phosphor that fluoresced under electric current. His invention became the basis of the fluorescent tube. It took until 1934 for Dr. Arthur Compton of General Electric to develop the first practical fluorescent lamp in the United States. Operating at lower voltages, the fluorescent lamp was more economical than the incandescent bulb, which wasted up to 80 percent of its energy as heat. General Electric had white and colored fluorescent tubes on display at the 1939 World's Fair. By 1954, energy-saving fluorescent tubes had edged out incandescent lamps for commercial use.

Today, two electrical light source types dominate the lighting market. Incandescent and discharge lamps include tungsten-halogen types as well as the classic incandescent bulb. Fluorescent, mercury, metal-halide, sodium, and the more recent induction lamp are all gaseous discharge types. Plasma-type lamps are a third type; they use a microwave-powered sulfur lamp.

PRINCIPLES OF LIGHTING DESIGN

The goal of lighting design is to create an efficient and pleasing interior that is both functional and aesthetically pleasing. Lighting levels must be adequate for seeing the task at hand. By varying the levels of brightness within acceptable limits, the lighting design avoids monotony and creates perspective effects. Ambient lighting levels for general lighting should be at least one-third as high as task levels. Accent lighting levels that provide focus on a specific object should not be greater than five times the ambient level. In retail situations, ambient levels should be reduced as much as possible to allow accent lighting to remain within energy guidelines. Improve color rendition by going for as much of the full spectrum as you can.

In an open office, the advantages of nonuniform lighting increase as the space between workstations increases. Nonuniform ceiling layouts may appear chaotic. To avoid this, use uniform ambient lighting along with local task lighting for individual activities. By placing indirect luminaires carefully and making sure that they are the correct distance from the ceiling, you can avoid bright spots on the ceiling that show up as direct and reflected glare.

By grouping tasks with similar lighting requirements and placing the most intensive visual tasks at the best daylight locations, you can use fewer fixtures and less lighting energy. Movable fixtures work best for task lighting. Sometimes it is more energy-efficient to look at improving the way a difficult visual task is done than to provide higher levels of lighting.

Design with effective, high-quality, efficient, low-maintenance, thermally controlled fixtures. High-quality permanent finishes like Alzac, multicoated baked enamel, or aluminum finishes will retain their performance for eight to ten years. For energy efficiency, look for a high luminaire efficiency rating (LER). Low-maintenance fixtures remain clean for extended periods and are designed so that all reflecting surfaces are easily and rapidly cleaned without demounting. Fixtures should permit simple and rapid relamping, and you should locate them to provide adequate access.

Light-colored finishes on ceilings, walls, floors, and furnishings in workspaces reflect more light and make better use of lighting energy. Ceiling reflectances should be from 80 to 92 percent, those for walls from 49 to 60 percent, and for floors from 20 to 40 percent. Furniture, office machines, and equipment should have 25 to 45 percent reflectances.

Lighting equipment should be unobtrusive, but not necessarily invisible. Fixtures can be chosen to complement the architecture, and to emphasize architectural features and patterns. As you know, decorative fixtures can enhance the interior design.

THE PROCESS OF LIGHTING DESIGN

Until 1973, daylighting was considered part of architectural design, not part of lighting design. Since an artificial lighting system had to be installed anyway, the practice was to ignore daylight, even to the extent of shutting it out completely. However, when the energy crisis hit in the mid-1970s, the extensive use of electrical energy in nonresidential buildings for lighting drove designers to integrate the cheapest, most abundant, and in many ways most desirable form of lighting, daylighting.

In an interview with *Architectural Lighting* in March 2001 (p. 22), lighting designer and architect William Lam stated:

Lighting design is about design and not engineering. Fixture selection and calculations should be the last thing you do. . . . You have to understand about light and the physics of it, but mainly it's about having a vision. Lighting is applied perception psychology. . . . You have to understand the principles in relation to what makes something appear bright or dark, cheerful or gloomy—what makes a good or great luminous environment. It's not enough to have enough light and to avoid glare. Every room should be a positive experience for the activity with all elements of the space integrated.

The best lighting designs blend seamlessly into an overall interior design. Differences inherent in the objectives of the interior designer and the electrical engineer often lead to difficulties in achieving this goal. These differences have their roots in the training and functions associated with each profession.

The interior designer is trained to focus on aesthetics, to combine form with function, and to strive for an interior space that supports the client's image and facilitates the client's work process. Often, the electrical engineer's perspective may conflict with a design concept. Focused on technical issues, the electrical engineer's designs accentuate flexibility and efficiency. By standardizing lighting, fixture type, and fixture placement, and by minimizing the number of different light sources, the engineer promotes energy conservation and maintenance simplicity while providing enough light for the tasks at hand.

The designer and the engineer often have differing perspectives on their relationship with their client, and this can widen the gap between their approaches. The designer typically works with the client's executive management team to blend business objectives, work processes, and corporate image. The engineer might never meet this team, and frequently works with the facility manager, who may also be one of the interior designer's contacts. Facility managers are looking for a lighting scheme that is flexible, efficient, and low maintenance. A third client group is the users, including employees, whose needs focus on comfort and productivity. Unless the interior designer and the electrical engineer understand the needs of these three distinct client groups, they won't be able to work together effectively. When the interior designer and electrical engineer work well together, they help the client recognize and prioritize each client group's objectives, and achieve a design that integrates each discipline's strengths and meets the client's overall needs of all three groups—client, facility manager, and those who will use the space.

Professional lighting designers can help bridge the gap between the interior designer and the electrical engineer. With expertise in the technical aspects of lighting and strong resources in the aesthetic and functional aspects of lighting design, the lighting designer is able to see both perspectives. Add to this extensive knowledge of the fixtures available on the market and the ability to speak the electrician's language, and the lighting designer becomes an invaluable asset to the architect and interior designer.

Working through all these elements may add additional design costs to the project, but the results can be a significant benefit. When the design is based on a clear understanding and agreement about what benefits the client most, all parties involved will agree that an integrated solution, while it may sacrifice certain subgroups' objectives, will meet the project's overall objectives and serve the client's best interest.

Historically, the selection and location of lighting fixtures has been divided between architectural lighting and utilitarian lighting, with inadequate attention to the needs of specific visual tasks. Incandescent wall washers and other fixtures were used to emphasize architectural elements and provide form-giving shadows. Luminance levels, cavity ratios, foot-candles, and dollars dominated utilitarian lighting selection.

Fortunately, both trends have been largely eliminated. Thoughtful architects, engineers, and lighting designers led research into ways to satisfy real vision needs with minimal energy use. The 1973 Arab oil embargo spurred on the development of energy codes and of higher efficiency sources. The Illuminating Energy Society of North America (IESNA) is a research, standards, and publishing organization that develops stable scientific bases for lighting, while remaining aware of its artistic aspects. The combination of science and art make lighting design a truly architectural discipline.

The process of designing lighting for a large building involves an interaction between the designer of the lighting and other consultants. Central to the design is the connection between artificial lighting, the heating, ventilating, and air-conditioning (HVAC) system, and daylighting. From the owner's point of view, the initial and operating costs are key considerations. The architect will be concerned with the amount and quality of daylighting, and with the architectural nature of the space. The first step is to establish a project lighting cost framework and a project energy budget.

A quarter of the electrical power generated in the United States is used for lighting, an amount of energy equivalent to approximately 4 million barrels of oil per day. Of that amount, approximately 20 percent is used for residential lighting, 20 percent for industrial lighting, another 20 percent for lighting retail spaces, and 15 percent for school and office lighting. Outdoor lighting and other uses account for the other quarter of the energy used. Lighting comprises 20 to 30 percent of a commercial building's electrical energy usage; percentages are higher for residences and lower for industrial buildings. Good lighting design can save up to half of the electrical power used for lighting.

Lighting is a major contributor to the building heat load. Each watt of lighting adds 1 W (3.4 Btu per hour) of heat gain to the space. It takes about 0.28 W of additional energy to cool 1 W from lighting in the summer, but the added heat may be welcome in the winter. Reducing the lighting power energy levels to below 2 W per 0.09 square meters (1 square ft) in all but special areas results in less impact from light-generated heat on the HVAC system.

Fixture efficiency is directly affected by temperature. Fluorescent units operate best at 25°C (77°F), so removing heat is helpful even at low lighting energy levels. The most efficient way to remove heat is to connect a duct to the fixture itself, but this is expensive and immobilizes the fixture. An alternative is to use an exhaust plenum with air passing over the fixtures to pick up excess heat.

Lighting standards are set by a variety of authorities, depending upon the type of building, whether it is government owned or built, and where it is located. Two of the federal agencies that have specific requirements for lighting are the U.S. Department of Energy (DOE) and the General Services Administration (GSA). In addition to the National Fire Protection Association (NFPA) codes, which include the *National Electrical Code* (NEC), standards are set by the American Society of Heating, Refrigeration, and Air-Conditioning Engineers (ASHRAE), the Illuminating Engineering Society of North America (IESNA), and the National Institute of Science and Technology (NIST). In 1989, ASHRAE/IESNA Standard 90.1, *Energy Efficient Design of New Buildings*, set lighting power credits for lighting control systems designed with energy conserving controls. Credits like these can help a designer meet the requirements while providing the lighting needed for tasks and for aesthetic impact. Local authorities may refer to the requirements of these organizations.

Energy budgets and lighting levels set by these standards affect the type of lighting source, the fixture selection, the lighting system, furniture placement, and maintenance schedules. State codes may regulate the amount of energy permitted for lighting in various occupancies. New York State energy guidelines, for example, set a maximum level of 2.4 W per square ft. With good design, lighting levels can be even lower than limits set by codes.

Once the lighting energy and cost budgets are established, the next step is task analysis. Lighting must provide an appropriate quantity of light for a specific task in a given area. Activities requiring greater visual acuity require higher illumination. The repetitiveness, variability, and duration of the task are also taken into account. Another consideration is the health and age of the occupants. In addition, the cost of errors caused by inadequate illumination is considered.

The amount of light should relate to the difficulty of the task performed. This depends upon the size of the object viewed, the contrast between the object and its background, and the luminance of the object. Luminaires should not be more than 20 times brighter than their background. No place in the normal field of view should have a luminance ratio greater than 40 to one.

Electrical engineers usually determine the amount of light needed by using an analytical approach. They establish numerical requirements, and manipulate the variables of sources, fixtures, and placement of units. An alternative approach is referred to as brightness design. The designer labels surfaces with the desired brightness and designs the lighting accordingly. Brightness design is highly intuitive, and requires lots of experience on the part of the designer.

During the design stage, detailed suggestions are raised, considered, modified, and accepted or rejected. The interior designer or lighting designer typically prepares a lighting plan (Fig. 34-1) and schedule that indicates fixture locations and selections. The designer then must coordinate his or her selections with the HVAC engineers, who will monitor power loads. The result is a detailed, workable design that may involve relocating a space or changing lighting or HVAC system details.

The design stage progresses through several steps. A lighting system is selected, which involves analysis of the light source, the distribution characteristics of the fixtures, daylighting considerations, electrical loads, and cost. Next, the lighting requirements are calculated. A pattern of fixtures is established and the architectural effects are considered. The interaction of the color of the light source and the color of surfaces is evaluated. Supplemental decorative and architectural (built-in) fixtures are then designed. The physiological and psychological effects of the lighting should also be considered, especially in spaces that are occupied for extended periods of time. Finally, the design is reviewed, and checked for quality and quantity of fixtures, esthetic effect, and originality.

During the evaluation stage, the design is analyzed for conformance to the constraints of cost and energy use. The results are provided to the architect for use in the final overall project evaluation.

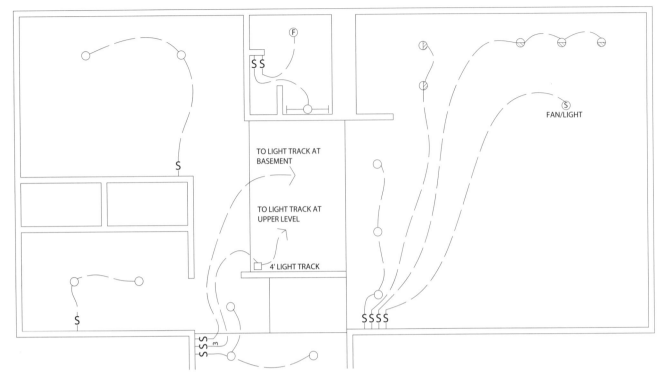

Figure 34-1 Reflected ceiling plan with lighting.

LIGHTING SOURCES

Our eyes perceive the longest visible wavelengths as red, then the progressively shorter wavelengths as orange, yellow, green, blue, and violet. White is a balanced mix of all the wavelengths, and black is the absence of light. Our eyes evolved to see in sunlight, and we perceive sunlight as normal in color.

The color appearance of any object is strongly influenced by the illuminating lamp's spectrum and color temperature. The spectrum is the range of energies or wavelengths that, when reflected or transmitted by materials, are interpreted by our eyes and brain as colors. When materials absorb these energies, they become heat.

A lamp's color temperature indicates its own color appearance, for example yellow, white, or blue-white.

Miguel was very excited about his new project renovating his client's home from top to bottom. However, there was one space that was problematic. The clients wanted to convert a section of the basement into a yoga and meditation room. The low ceiling wasn't too big a problem, since they would be sitting or lying on the floor much of the time. However, the space available was right next to the furnace room, and there were several large ducts running along one wall of the room. Miguel was struggling to find a design concept that would support the peaceful ambience the clients sought within this small, cluttered space.

Miguel talked the problem over with the lighting designer, Bill, and together they came up with a novel solution. They were bemoaning the limited space when Bill suggested that they borrow an aesthetic approach that celebrated the beauty of small spaces. The ductwork would be enclosed in a soffit, which would clean up its appearance and also help muffle any noise from the HVAC system. On the face of the soffit, they would build a ledge to hold a strip with small candelabra-style lamps. In front of the soffit, they would install narrow metal frames. The frames would hold a translucent material that looked like handmade paper but was made for lighting fixtures. The frames could be lifted off to change lamps. The result was a glowing panel, lit from behind, that suggested a traditional Japanese shoji screen. The yoga/meditation room became a delicate, minimalist, Japanese-style space.

The color temperature is also usually a guide to the colors in which it has the most energy. Color temperature determines whether the light source is regarded as warm, mid-range or cool. A candle flame has a warm color temperature of about 1750° Kelvin (K), compared to a standard incandescent lamp at between 2600°K and 3000°K. A cool white fluorescent lamp is about 4250°K. A clear blue sky is around 10,000°K. As you can see, the higher the color temperature, the cooler the source!

Along with other color-rendering considerations, the color rendering index (CRI) should be considered during the selection and specification of lamps. The CRI is the only color rendering rating published in lamp manufacturers' product literature. The CRI is a complex measurement of the color-rendering capability of a lamp, and is useful only in comparing lamps with the same or very similar color temperatures. A CRI rating of 80 or above indicates that there is very little shift in test colors when illuminated by the lamp, as compared to a reference source of the same color temperature.

Incandescent lamps, including halogens, with color temperatures of 2700°K to 3000°K and CRIs well above 90, are often used to enhance warm palettes. Although incandescent sources in general are rated as excellent in color rendering, standard incandescent types can distort cooler colors, especially at low light levels. Fluorescent lamps are available in a large variety of color temperatures, ranging from 2700°K to 6500°K, with CRIs ranging from 90 to the low 50s. For example, compact fluorescent lamps come in 2700°K and 3000°K for warm palettes, 3500°K for mid-range or mixed palettes, and 4100°K for cool palettes, all with CRIs of 80 to 85. Linear fluorescent lamps, such as T8 and T5 types, are the sources of choice today in retail and commercial installations where color rendition is important. High-intensity discharge (HID) lamps have a range of color temperatures from 1800°K to 6400°K and CRIs from 60 to 85.

Incandescent Lamps

The light from an open fire, a candle, or an oil lamp is incandescent, as is the glowing filament of a lightbulb. Incandescent light has fewer shorter wavelengths, and therefore appears redder than sunlight. Up to 90 percent of the electrical energy used by an incandescent lamp is lost to heat, and only the remaining 10 percent is emitted as light. The added heat increases the building's cooling load. Incandescent lamps generally have short lives, with about 750 hours being standard. At least one incandescent lamp is available that has a 10,000 hour long life.

Where incandescent lamps are used, limit energy use and increase the amount of overall light by using one larger lamp rather than several smaller ones. One 100 W-incandescent produces more light than three 40-W lamps, and uses 20 W less electricity. Three-way lamps are a good choice, as they can be switched to a lower wattage when bright light is not needed. Dimmers help add flexibility to the light load. Energy saving incandescent lamps replace standard types without a visible difference; 40 W lamps are replaced by 34 W, 60 W by 52 W, 75 W by 67 W, and so forth.

Fluorescent Lamps

Fluorescent lamps are sealed glass tubes filled with mercury. An electrical discharge between the ends of the tube vaporizes the mercury vapor and excites it into discharging ultraviolet (UV) light to a phosphor coating the inner surface of the tube. The phosphor glows, with the color of the light it emits depending upon the composition of the phosphor. Fluorescent light usually lacks the longer, warmer wavelengths, and thus appears bluer than sunlight, although fluorescent lamps are now available in 220 colors. Trichromic phosphor fluorescent lamps combine green, blue, and red for a highly efficient white light. They can be made cooler or warmer by changing the proportions of the primary colors. Compact fluorescent lamps have largely solved the problems of size and design of fixtures with a multitude of forms.

Fluorescent ballasts regulate the electric current flowing through the fluorescent. This activates the gas inside the fluorescent tube. Self-ballasted compact fluorescents have an electronic ballast as the part of the lamp that screws into the bulb socket. Modular compact fluorescent lamps have separate ballasts (adapters) that screw into standard lightbulb sockets. With a separate adapter, you don't have to replace the ballast when the lamp fails. A fluorescent lamp will last about 10,000 hours, while a fluorescent ballast will be good for 50,000 hours or more.

Fluorescent lamps provide three to five times more light for the same amount of energy than conventional incandescent lamps, lowering utility bills. By replacing a 75-W incandescent lamp with an 18-W compact fluorescent, you can save 570 kW-h of electricity and eliminate 1300 lb of carbon dioxide emissions over the life of the fluorescent lamp. Fluorescent lamps last up to 24,000 hours, decreasing the need for replacement. They also give off less heat, reducing energy needed for air-conditioning. If every home in the United States replaced one incandescent lamp with one fluorescent, the reduced air emissions would equal that produced by three major power plants.

Fluorescent T8 lamps and T5 lamps with electronic ballasts can help meet energy-efficiency code requirements. T5 lamps are highly efficient, and use an ultra-slim ballast case that can be hidden in slender fixtures. Because the T5 puts out the same light as a T8 with 40 percent less lamp wall area, its surface brightness is about 60 percent higher than that of the T8. This allows very efficient design, but is too bright to look at. New fixtures are being designed that take advantage of the T5's qualities while shielding glare.

Subcompact fluorescent lamps are smaller, brighter, and less expensive than earlier compact fluorescent lamps. With their subcompact size and screw-in bases, they fit in most lighting fixtures designed for incandescent lamps. Subcompact fluorescents offer the same energy-efficiency benefits as larger compact fluorescents, and meet stricter technical specifications for color rendition and light output. They are available with the ENERGY STAR® label.

Once you have selected a fluorescent fixture and checked size, lamping, finishes, and other options, you have to choose whether to specify an electronic ballast or a magnetic one. Magnetic (or electromagnetic) ballasts have been around for more than 70 years. They have a core of laminated steel plates surrounded by copper or aluminum wire coils; this assembly is then connected to a power capacitor and is placed in potting compound in a metal case. These components provide the proper conditions for starting and controlling the current flow to the fluorescent lamps. Magnetic ballasts generally operate the lamp at the line frequency of approximately 60 Hz.

Electronic ballasts usually have a solid-state construction and use semiconductor components to change the electrical frequency, along with other small components to provide the starting and regulating functions. These ballasts raise the line frequency at which the lamps operate to very high frequency levels, 20,000 to 60,000 Hz. These higher frequencies excite the gas mixture in a fluorescent lamp more efficiently, often increasing efficiency by about 10 percent.

Magnetic ballasts can be significantly less expensive than electronic ballasts, however, and are available for a wide variety of lamp wattages. Magnetic ballasts are durable and rugged, and withstand higher temperatures. Magnetic ballasts are also less likely to interfere with other electrical equipment, such as computers.

On the other hand, magnetic ballasts are larger and weigh more than electronic ballasts. As already noted, they are less efficient than electronic ballasts in most cases. Some magnetic ballasts produce an audible vibration and hum. Magnetic ballasts take longer to start two-pin fluorescent lamps that must preheat, or linear four-pin preheat types with starters, and lamps may flicker.

Electronic ballasts offer flicker-free lamp operation with low or no audible noise. They are energy-efficient, and help provide higher light levels with low energy use. They are smaller in size and weight than comparable magnetic ballasts, and produce less heat. Electronic ballasts are more suitable for dimming, especially continuous dimming. It is possible to extend lamp life with programmed start electronic ballasts.

Electronic ballasts are more expensive than magnetic ballasts. Electronic ballasts conduct more electrical noise through lines and produce more radiated electrical noise than magnetic ballasts, increasing the risk of interference with other equipment. If the ballast doesn't incorporate a means to detect the end of its useful life and to shut down, the ballast will continue to try and start burnt-out lamps. Large current spikes can lead to damage of connected electronic control devices unless the ballast is designed to limit them.

The DOE is implementing new regulations regarding the manufacture and sale of fluorescent lamp ballasts. Starting in 2005, ballast manufacturers must meet new minimum ballast efficacy requirements that currently can be met only with electronic ballasts. Metal halide fixtures also use electronic ballasts.

Mercury is used in fluorescent and HID lamps to generate the UV energy that energizes the phosphor and produces light. Mercury, however, is a toxic material that accumulates in fish and other species. Mercury has been regulated as a hazardous material since 1980. The U.S. Environmental Protection Agency (EPA) initiated a new test protocol in 1990, the Toxicity Characteristic Leaching Procedure (TCLP), and fluorescent and HID lamps failed this new test.

In 2000, the EPA established the Universal Waste Rule, which requires that building owners and management dispose of their old lamps in an environmentally sound manner. Conforming to the rule is easier if fixtures are relamped in a group rather than singly. Facilities may need to provide an area for storing spent lamps prior to disposal.

New nonhazardous TCLP-compliant lamps are now available in almost all fluorescent configurations, as well as in high-pressure sodium (HPS), lower-wattage metal halide, and in some compact fluorescent styles. Lamps that pass the TCLP either have reduced mercury content or have found other technological means of producing a passing result, and do not need special disposal procedures. They can be recycled along with noncompliant lamps, or disposed of otherwise. Specifying TCLP-compliant lamps reduces the environmental impact of the building on society. Their price is competitive with higher mercury content lamps, which they match in performance, lifetimes, output, and color properties.

Halogen Lamps

Tungsten-halogen lamps (commonly called halogen lamps) are an efficient, lightweight, compact, incandescent light source with a 2000-hour light span. A halogen lamp, like a standard incandescent lamp, produces light by heating a filament. The addition of a small amount of halogen gas to the bulb produces a brighter, whiter light than standard incandescent lamps and prolongs lamp life. These lamps are available in standard or low-voltage designs, with the standard design around 20 percent more efficient than a standard incandescent lamp. Low-voltage reflector lamps are about 40 percent more efficient.

Halogen lamps are available in a variety of designs and bases. They are smaller than standard incandescents of the same wattage, and are ideal for precision point sources. The light output of an aging halogen lamp is much better than that of an aging incandescent. Halogen lamps with reflectors offer a variety of high-intensity beams for professional spotlighting, task lighting, and accent lighting.

It takes a lot of heat for the halogen gas to heat the compact, high-temperature filament, and if the gas pressure inside the lamp becomes too great, the quartz lamp envelope can break violently and scatter hot quartz fragments. Consequently, fixtures with halogen lamps should be screened or shielded. The high lamp temperature can also be a fire hazard. These hazards are avoided when the lamp is encapsulated inside a sealed envelope. Encapsulated halogen lamps are available in a variety of shapes, and can replace standard incandescent lamps of the same shapes, with triple the life span.

High-Intensity Discharge (HID) Lamps

High-intensity discharge (HID) lamps are even more efficient than fluorescent lamps, and have a 24,000 hour life span. The overall efficiency of HID lamps is influenced by the design of the lighting fixture, the age of the lamp, and the regularity of cleaning. Their color properties formerly limited their use to outdoors or in-

dustrial spaces, but with over 60 colors now available, they are more often used to replace incandescent and fluorescent lamps indoors.

High-intensity discharge lamps come in three main types, named for the materials in the lamp's arc tube, and affecting the light color. Mercury lamps tend to be more blue-green. Metal halide lamps provide the most natural looking light, and are used in stores and public spaces. The third type, high-pressure sodium (HPS), tends toward the red-yellow wavelengths. Newer HPS lamps have a whiter color than incandescent lamps, and are good for retail applications. High-pressure sodium lamps are available with a color rendering index of 80—an outstanding rating—and a color temperature of 2700°K. They have a 10,000-hour life span and are highly energy efficient. These HPS lamps can be used as accents, and for display, wall washing, and downlights. Their warm crisp light has been described as being like sunshine on a clear day. At present, HPS lamps have some technical problems involved in fixture design, but these are being worked out, so we can expect to see more versatile high-quality HPS lamps on the market in the future.

LIGHTING CONTROLS

A good lighting control design gives you both flexibility and economy. It allows a variety of lighting levels and lighting patterns while conserving energy and money. Energy-efficient lighting control strategies can reduce consumption over uncontrolled installations by up to 60 percent without reducing lighting effectiveness. Money is saved by reduced energy use, reduced air-conditioning costs due to less heat from lights, longer lamp and ballast life due to lower operating temperatures and lower energy output, and lower labor costs due to control automation. In order to meet building code energy budget requirements, it is frequently necessary to employ energy-saving lighting controls that dim or shut off fixtures.

Lighting controls include all the ways that lighting systems can be operated, including both automatic and manual controls. You can help conserve energy by using occupancy sensors and automatic daylight compensation controls where appropriate. Dimming, stepped switching, and programmable controls are sometimes recognized for credits from utility companies. Control systems decisions are made at the same time as the lighting is designed, to assure that controls are appropriate to the light source and that the system arrangement and accessories are coordinated with the control scheme.

Light zones are defined to accommodate the scheduling and functions of various spaces. Ambient, task, and accent lighting are considered in laying out the zones. Each zone should be separately circuited, and each task light should have its own switch. Traffic patterns are analyzed, and an on/off switch is located at every entrance. Convenient, easily accessible lighting controls encourage the use of all possible lighting combinations. The extra initial expense of extra switches and extra cable is made up in energy cost savings. The result is good illumination where needed, and no wasted energy where a lower light level will serve just as well.

 When you are designing a complex multiuse space, like a hotel banquet room, it is essential to talk to the people who use the space daily to discover how the space is used. Audiovisual technicians and banquet crews, for example, will be aware of common problems. Often controls are located in places that are hard to reach during an event, or where you can't see the result of an adjustment in lighting level while you are making it.

The minimum number of lighting control points required by code is one per 40.5 square meters (450 square ft), plus one control point per task or group of tasks located in the space. Automatic controls are more effective than manual controls that depend on one person to select lighting levels for others, especially in open office spaces. Interior and exterior lighting systems in buildings larger than 465 square meters (5000 square ft) must have an automatic shut-off control, except for emergency and exit lighting.

The designer of the lighting control system selects the number of lighting elements to be switched together and establishes the number of control levels. Switching off entire fluorescent fixtures results in abrupt changes in light levels in a space. An option is to switch ballasts to allow four different light levels to be produced by a single three-lamp fluorescent fixture with a two-lamp ballast and a one-lamp ballast. Maximum illumination is produced when all three lamps are on. With just the two-lamp ballast on, lighting is at two-thirds. With only the one-lamp ballast, you get one-third of the fixture's output, and with all lamps off, no light at all. Switching ballasts allows light reduction in small steps at low cost.

Fluorescent lamps can be dimmed down to around 40 percent of their output without reduction in efficiency, even with conventional ballasts. A continuous fluorescent dimming from 10 percent to 100 percent is possible with special individual magnetic silicon-controlled rectifier (SCR) dimming ballasts, with triac dimmers, or with electronic ballasts. New high-efficiency electronic ballasts allow for linear fluorescent lamps to be dimmed from 100 percent down to 1 percent. Compact fluorescent lamps can now be dimmed from 100 percent down to 5 percent.

Manual lighting controls generally give employees a sense of control, leading to a feeling of satisfaction and increased productivity. Manual systems can also be wasteful of energy, as people tend to leave lights on at the maximum level even when daylight is sufficient or when leaving the room for an extended period. Manual dimmers in multioccupant spaces lead to personal dissatisfaction and friction. With remote-control dimming systems, occupants can adjust the lighting fixtures closest to their workstations without disturbing other employees, which can help them reduce glare on computer screens.

Static automatic lighting controls can be set for time schedules where there are regularly scheduled periods when task lighting is not required, such as coffee and lunch breaks, cleaning periods, shift changes, and unoccupied periods. Programmed time controls save between 10 and 20 percent of energy use. The payback period for the installation of these controls ranges from one to five years. A relatively simple programmable controller can be substituted for a wall switch. More sophisticated units allow remote control of loads and circuits on a preprogrammed time basis. With tight programming, the system can save up to half over uncontrolled installations. Because they do not detect actual space use patterns, they must have an override for special conditions such as dark, rainy days and evenings when people need to work late.

Dynamic automatic lighting control initiation uses an information feedback loop to respond to actual conditions that are indicated by sensors. Dynamic control systems consist of a programmable controller and field sensors plus wiring. Some systems use high-frequency signals impressed on the power wiring system to transmit control signals in a power line carrier (PLC) system. Completely wireless systems use radio frequencies and wireless transmitters and receivers.

You can change seamlessly from daytime to nighttime lighting environments with a dimming controls system. Dimming also increases the lamp life for incandescent lighting. When specifying a lighting controls system, you need to consider whether the system is flexible enough to expand for unanticipated needs. A reliable controls system manufacturer must be available to modify and adjust the system during the development and implementation of a project. The cost of lighting controls is always a consideration, with features balanced against competitive systems' costs. Lighting controls should be compatible with other related equipment, such as theatrical or themed entertainment industry standards.

Some lighting controls allow the user to create and recall custom preset scenes for common room activities. These systems are practical for restaurants, conference and meeting rooms, offices, hotel rooms, and homes. Scenes are set by adjusting a light or group of lights controlled together within a room or space for a specific activity. You can switch between scenes at the touch of a button.

Wireless lighting control systems for conference and meeting rooms give a presenter control of lights, motorized window shades, and projection screens at the touch of a button. Some wireless systems use a radio frequency tabletop transmitter that can be located anywhere inside a room. By pressing buttons on the transmitter, radio frequency signals are sent to controllers housed in the ceiling. These controllers then send signals to dimming ballasts to adjust the light levels, and also to optional motorized window shades and projection screens or other audiovisual equipment. Some systems offer control by simple slide dimmers, and are designed for use in classrooms and lecture halls, where presenters may not be as familiar with complex audiovisual equipment.

Simplicity of setup and use is also important. Walking into a conference room and not being able to turn on or control the lights is really an unnecessary challenge. Too many options can be a bad thing. Sophisticated engineering that will allow a system to do almost anything, while still making it all easy to understand and intuitive to use, has eluded most major manufacturers.

Occupancy Sensors

Between 9:00 a.m. and 5:00 p.m., offices in commercial spaces are occupied only one-third to two-thirds of the time, due to coffee breaks, conferences, work assignments, illness, vacations, and different work locations. Occupancy sensors can turn office lights off, or dim them to corridor lighting levels, after the space has been vacant for 10 minutes. Occupancy sensors can also turn off fan-coil air units, air conditioners, and fans. Relighting may be instantaneous, delayed, or manually operated by the occupant.

Passive infrared (IR) occupancy sensors react to the motion of a heat source within their range. The IR sensor creates a pattern of beams, and reacts when a heat source, such as a person, moves from one beam to another. These IR sensors don't react to stationary heat

sources. Small movements that don't cross to another beam may not be detected, and the lighting may shut off if a person just sits quietly. Very slow movements may not trigger the sensor. The IR sensor must have the heat source within its line of view, so heat sources blocked by furniture are not detected. If not carefully selected and located, the IR sensors may have dead spots in their detection patterns.

Ultrasonic occupancy sensors (Fig. 34-2) emit energy at between 25 and 40 kHz, well above the human hearing range. The waves of energy reflect and rereflect throughout the space in a pattern monitored by the sensor. The sensor detects any movement disturbing the pattern. Unlike IR systems, ultrasonic systems don't require a direct line of sight to the movement. They detect small movements, which means that curtains, or even air movement, can trigger action, and they must be frequently adjusted to reduce sensitivity to avoid false sensing. However, decreased sensitivity also decreases coverage.

Hybrid dual technology occupancy sensors use both IR and ultrasonic detectors for turning lights on. Once on, a reaction in either sensor keeps the lights on. Sophisticated electronic circuitry learns the space's occupancy pattern, and is programmed to react accordingly.

Occupancy sensors work best in individual rooms and workspaces. You can use wall-mounted sensors in any small office where there is direct line of sight between the sensor and the occupant. Private offices often use ultrasonic wall mounted occupancy sensors that are turned on manually, set for maximum sensitivity and ten-minute delay. Manual-on operation prevents lights from turning on unnecessarily when triggered by corridor activity, day-

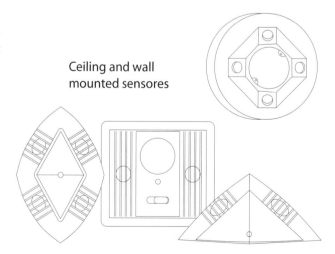

Ceiling and wall mounted sensores

Figure 34-2 Ultrasonic occupancy detectors.

light, brief occupancy, or when a task light is sufficient. The sensors may be wall or ceiling mounted, or placed in wall-outlet boxes in a combined sensor/wall switch configuration. The system should be tested before final installation. An IR detector can cover from 23 to 93 square meters (250–1000 square ft), and can save enough energy to pay for itself in six months to three years.

The Audubon Society Headquarters in New York, designed by the Croxton Collaborative, installed motion sensors to detect the presence of persons in a room, and to turn the lights off after a specified number of minutes without activity. The system produced an immediate 30 percent reduction in energy consumption and reduced the lighting-produced cooling load.

For open offices, ultrasonic ceiling mounted occupancy sensors are set to maximum sensitivity with a 15-minute time delay so that they will detect a single, quiet worker. In spaces with vertical files, partitions, or any other objects that create barriers higher than four feet, the standard coverage area given in manufacturer's literature may be too generous, and you may need more closely spaced sensors. Verify sensor spacing directly with the sensor manufacturer.

Some ceiling mounted ultrasonic sensors are specifically designed for linear corridor distribution. They are usually set to maximum sensitivity and 15-minute time delay. The narrow linear distribution patterns increase sensitivity at a distance, turning lights on well before a person reaches an unlighted area.

Daylight Compensation

Daylight compensation is another energy saving control system, one that works by automatic dimming. Daylight compensation reduces artificial lighting in parts of a building when daylight is available for illumination needs. The system's designer establishes zone areas, usually south exposures and sometimes east or west exposures depending on the latitude and climate. The northern exposure has only a narrow perimeter zone with adequate daylight, and doesn't usually need automatic dimming. The zone size is set at the maximum room depth that will receive a minimum of one half of its light from daylight for several hours per day. Photocells trigger dimming as required. Daylight compensation dimming can reduce energy use in perimeter areas by up to 60 percent, and will pay for itself in from three months to three years. As opposed to dimming, minute by minute changes caused by the constant switching on or off of lamp levels can by very annoying to the space's occupants, and is damaging to the lamps.

LIGHTING SYSTEM TUNING

Designing and specifying lighting is complex, and it is rare that the system functions perfectly in the field as designed. This is inevitable due to assumptions and imprecision in calculations, differences between the specified and installed equipment, and changes in equipment locations. The system is tuned in the field to adjust to these changes and achieve the designer's goals.

Tuning often results in the reduction of lighting levels in nontask areas, as spill light is frequently adequate for circulation, rough material handling, and other functions. Lighting system tuning can reduce energy use by 20 to 30 percent. Lighting system tuning is also required when the function of an entire space is changed, or when furniture movement or changes in tasks alter a single area. It can help with glare reduction and result in improved task visibility.

During the lighting system tuning, adjustable fixtures are aimed and their positions are modified. Incandescent lamps and fluorescent tubes are replaced with lower wattages. Ballast switching and multilevel ballasts are fine-tuned for efficiency, and dimmable fixtures are adjusted. Standard wall switches are replaced with time-out units, programmable units, or dimmer units. It is a good idea to include the lighting system tuning process as part of the lighting designer's complete scope of services.

LIGHTING FIXTURE REQUIREMENTS

Building codes increasingly require energy-efficient lighting. Energy restrictions commonly apply to all buildings over three stories, and to all building types except low-rise housing. These energy restrictions are relatively new code requirements, and continue to be modified and accepted in new jurisdictions. Minimum code requirements must be met to acquire a building permit. Codes usually allow trade-offs between energy-efficient building envelope components and energy use by HVAC or lighting. Interior lighting energy use can usually be calculated by either a building area method, or on a space-by-space basis. Code requirements typically apply to new construction and additions, and do not require alteration or removal of existing systems, although some efforts at relamping existing fixtures may be required.

The process of meeting the code requirements involves extensive calculations and reporting, provided by the electrical engineer or lighting designer using special software. Sometimes the contractor may be accepted as the designer of record, and contractors often provide the documentation. Since the lighting energy allowance meshes with building envelope and HVAC requirements, the entire architectural and engineering team is involved in meeting code requirements.

The energy-efficiency code requirements mandate automatic shutoff provisions for interior lighting. Incandescent lighting may effectively be eliminated for exit signs. Some types of facilities are not included in the total energy use calculations, for example, spaces specifically for the visually impaired, enclosed retail display windows, display lighting in galleries or museums, lighting integral to advertising or directional signage, and lighting for theatrical purposes, among others. The ENERGY STAR program includes lighting fixtures and lightbulbs, so look for the ENERGY STAR label when specifying fixtures to meet energy codes.

Lighting fixtures are marked for wall mounting, under-cabinet mounting, ceiling mounting, or covered ceiling mounting. Wall mounted lighting fixtures (sconces) must meet the Americans with Disabilities Act (ADA) maximum 4-in. projection limit where applicable. Each lighting fixture is manufactured and tested for a specific location. Those approved for damp locations are labeled "Suitable for Damp Locations." Lighting fixtures listed for a wet location can also be used in damp locations.

The method of attachment of a fixture to the outlet box is related to its weight and the type of fixture. The outlet box can usually support fixtures up to 22.7 kg (50 lb). Heavier fixtures require additional support.

The NEC has strict requirements for access to electrical components. All electrical boxes must allow access for repairs and wiring changes at any time. All lighting fixtures must be placed so that both the lamp and the fixture can be replaced when needed. This is especially important when fixtures are used with architectural elements such as ceiling coves.

Fire-tested and labeled lighting fixtures should be used on interior projects. Only certain types of fixtures are allowed in fire-rated assemblies. When a lighting fixture is placed in a wall or ceiling of combustible material, the mechanical part of the fixture must be fully enclosed. Usually, noncombustible materials must be sandwiched between the fixture and the finished surface. When typical 61 by 122 cm (2 by 4 ft) fluorescent ceiling fixtures are placed end to end, no gaps are allowed between fixtures. Side by side installation is not usually considered safe. Fixtures with air handling are typically allowed if they have provisions to stop air movement in the event of fire.

LIGHTING SYSTEM MAINTENANCE

Maintenance is often the last consideration when selecting a lighting fixture, and yet it is the one most likely to result in long-term negative feedback from building owners and facility managers. Premature failures are expensive and annoying for building owners and tenants, tarnish lighting designers' and contractors' reputations, and may cause fire danger or other hazards. Often the problem does not lie in the design, but in poor installation and maintenance practices. Within a short time after installation, the lighting system may be operated and maintained by someone with little training or experience with the latest equipment. Here are some common problems and their cures, which you can pass on to clients. They will welcome hearing from you before problems arise.

Replacing burned-out halogen lamps while the circuit is energized, a practice known as "hot relamping", jars the lamp's filament just as it makes contact with the line-voltage lamp base and receives a pulse of current. The stress of hot relamping can damage the filament and send it to an early failure at about 200 hours, rather than the rated 3000 hours. Hot relamping also violates the Occupational Safety and Health Administration (OSHA) safety regulations. Cold relamping (shutting the circuit off first) is more time-consuming and difficult, as it can require more trips up the ladder, a two-person relamping team, or working in dim light. Manufacturers recommend cold relamping for all types of screw-in lamps. A related problem occurs when workers screwing a lamp into a hot socket sometimes stop as soon as the lamp lights, and fail to make a firm connection at the base contact. This can cause resistive heating and damage to the lamp or fixture.

If an incandescent lamp fails early, even when an employee seated it carefully in a cold socket, the problem may be due to the socket's running at higher than the 120V standard. Running incandescent lamps even slightly above their rated voltage will significantly shorten their life, sometimes by as much as half. High voltage can occur for a number of reasons, including proximity to utility transformers, poor electrical system grounding, loose neutral wire connections, or unbalanced loads on multiple-phase or split-phase systems. Utilities are typically allowed a 5 percent tolerance either way on voltage they supply, but most will try to correct abnormally high voltage that occurs consistently throughout a facility, usually with a simple transformer adjustment. High voltage that occurs only in parts of a facility is probably caused by internal wiring problems, which may be difficult to correct and requires troubleshooting by an experienced electrician.

When a fluorescent lamp's pins are not fully rotated into the recessed grooves in the white lamp holders at their ends, enough electrical contact may occur to start the lamps, but high resistance across the poor connection will cause electrical heating that slowly cooks the lamp holders brown. Grooves or dimples on the metal end caps perpendicular to the axis of the pin connectors will be vertical when the lamp is properly rotated.

When fluorescent lamps in new fixtures flicker a few times per second for about the first hour and a half of use, the problem may be bad ballasts with poor soldering. Once the ballast is warmed up, the soldered connection has enough conductivity to allow normal operation. The ballasts should be returned, and an allowance added to the cost for relamping labor.

Storing fluorescent tubes on end in an unheated storage area can cause the mercury in the lamps to condense into small droplets and pool in the end caps of the lamps. The reduced vapor pressure in the lamps can result in bands of light and dark progressing along the length of the lamp, or in the lamp's not lighting at all. Generally, fluorescent lamps should be stored above 10°C (50°F). They will usually return to normal operation as the mercury becomes vaporized over a few days' use.

Other lamping problems can result if lamps and ballasts are not carefully matched, creating poor electrical conditions for lamps. Compatibility information is found on the ballast label.

Lamps deteriorate over time and emit fewer lumens as they are used. Dirt, dust, and foreign matter collect on lighting fixtures and on the reflecting surfaces of a room. The reflecting and transmitting materials in some luminaires undergo gradual chemical changes in the presence of air and light. These conditions result in a maintenance factor, also referred to as the depreciation factor or light loss, and used in design calculations for lighting systems. The maintenance factor reflects both the fixtures and the maintenance conditions of the space.

Access to fixtures helps them stay clean. The maximum ladder for a custodian is around 4.6 meters (15 ft) so many fixtures may be out of reach. A lampstick is used to reach conventional filament or mercury lamps in open reflectors up to 7.6 meters (25 ft) high. Crawl spaces above the ceiling, catwalks, and disconnecting hangers allow fixtures to be lowered to floor level.

EMERGENCY LIGHTING

Emergency lighting (Fig. 34-3) provides power for critical lighting systems in the event of a general power failure, the failure of the building electrical system, an in-

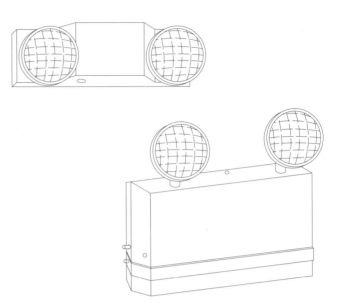

Figure 34-3 Emergency lighting units.

terruption of current flow to the lighting unit, or even from the accidental operation of a switch control or circuit disconnect. It is customary for the battery-powered units to be hard-wired into the building's electrical system, so that the battery can be recharged by the building power. Emergency lighting requirements are set by ANSI/NFPA 101, *The Life Safety Code*. This code, published by the American National Standards Institute (ANSI) and the NFPA, defines the locations within specific types of structures that require emergency lighting, as well as specifying the level and duration of the lighting. The *National Electrical Code* (NEC), also known as NFPA 70, mandates system arrangements for emergency light and power circuits, including egress and exit lighting. The NEC also discusses power sources and system design. NFPA 90, *Health Care Facilities*, dictates special emergency light and power arrangements for these occupancies. Requirements set by OSHA are primarily safety oriented and cover exit and egress lighting. Other industry standards are published by IESNA and the Institute of Electrical and Electronics Engineers (IEEE) as ANSI/IEEE Standard 446, *Recommended Practice for Emergency and Standby Power Systems*. There may also be additional local code requirements.

The general goals of emergency lighting are to avoid distress or panic and to provide lighting for egress from the building. The level of lighting required is related to the level of normal illumination and to the degree of hazard. Exit areas must maintain 50 lux (5 footcandles or fc), and stairs are required to have 35 to 50 lux (3.5–5 fc) of lighting. Hazardous areas like machine rooms are set at 20 to 50 lux (2–5 fc), and other spaces at 10 lux (1 fc). No point along the path of egress should have less than 1 lux (0.1 fc). Maximum to minimum illuminances along the egress path must not exceed a ratio of 40 to 1. These are low levels, but are sufficient to permit orderly egress once the eyes have adjusted.

Most codes require 50 lux (5 fc) on nonilluminated exit signs, internally illuminated signs, or self-luminous signs with light-emitting diode (LED) displays. Some exit signs are equipped with a battery and controls. Others illuminate the area beneath the sign, which is especially helpful for finding the way to an exit in a smoky room. Some have a flasher and/or audible beeper. Nonelectrical, self-illuminating signs are considered to be part of the emergency lighting system.

Exit lighting is required at all exits, and at any aisles, corridors, passageways, ramps, and lobbies leading to an exit. General exit lighting and exit signs must be lit at all times the building is in use.

Because it takes the eyes up to five minutes to adjust to the drop from normal lighting levels, bright spotlight-type emergency lighting heads must be very carefully arranged to avoid disabling glare and distorting shadows. It is best to provide some lighting at floor level, preferably of a type that aids direction finding, as people may crawl along the floor to stay below the level of smoke. Ceiling mounted emergency lighting sometimes fails to illuminate the floor in smoky areas, or may create a bright, fog-like condition. Some codes mandate adequate egress lighting at baseboard level.

Emergency lighting must remain at the minimum 10-lux (1 fc) level for at least 90 minutes. It can then be lowered to 6 lux (0.6 fc); higher levels may be required if quick evacuation is not possible.

The easiest way to provide emergency lighting is to put some of the existing light fixtures on a separate circuit designed for emergency lighting, one that is connected to a backup power source. You must make sure that if one fixture burns out, it will not leave an area in darkness. Use dual lamp lighting fixtures and fixtures with battery packs, and design overlapping lighting patterns.

Local emergency lighting arrangements include a rechargeable battery and charger and voltage sensing and switching equipment. For fluorescent lights, an electronic ballast is available that operates the lamp at high frequency and usually reduced output. Packaged units are available with integral incandescent lights. Equipment should be maintenance free for up to five years.

Chapter

Lighting for Specific Spaces

• • •

As indicated earlier, these chapters on lighting aren't intended to replace a comprehensive lighting course. The information in this chapter covers some of the basic requirements, in an effort to give the interior designer some insight into the way electrical engineers and lighting designers approach the design of the most common types of spaces. Lighting levels that are referenced by electrical engineers and lighting designers are given in the Illuminating Engineering Society of North America's (IESNA) *IES Lighting Handbook.*

RESIDENCES

Each area of a home should have multiple light levels. Through a multilayered design approach involving task, ambient, and accent lighting, a balanced, three-dimensional lighted environment is created that allows for a variety of settings or moods. The best approach is to first provide for the task lighting requirements, and then determine what ambient lighting, if any, is required to supplement this layer. Finally, provide appropriate accenting and highlighting to enhance artwork and architectural elements.

Provide low-level lighting in all rooms, including bathrooms. Use high-low switches, simple dimmers, multilevel ballasts or multilevel switching to allow mod-

ifications in lighting levels. Provide local task lighting for relatively difficult visual tasks like the kitchen menu planning area. Control accent lighting with dimmers and switches. Use programmable timers with photocell overrides for exterior lighting. Locate areas normally occupied during the day, such as the kitchen and living rooms, where they will receive daylight. Consider skylights with built-in artificial lighting for these areas. Area switching can be used to control lighting in work areas, children's rooms, and home offices.

Some spaces in the home are lighted during the day and often well into the evening, such as kitchens and home offices. For these areas, it is recommended to use fluorescent lights with a high color rendering index (CRI) or standard or infrared (IR) halogen incandescent lights. Electric light sources used in the home should be in the 2700°K to 3000°K color temperature range with CRIs of 80 or better. For exterior landscape and security lighting, consider high-intensity discharge (HID) sources.

Incandescent lighting is inefficient, but is frequently used in residential work to flatter skin color. It offers low first cost, small size, focusing ability, and uses simple and economical dimmers. Reserve tungsten-halogen lamps for highlighting and specialty requirements to avoid low efficiency and concentrated heat. Low-wattage (9–13 W) fluorescent lamps can replace incandescent lamps in frequently used dark corridors and stairwells. These small lamps can be left on for extended periods for low-level lighting without constant switching and lamp replacement. Compact fluorescent downlights are not as bright as incandescent downlights, but are good choices where they will be left on for more than three hours per use, if brightness isn't a major concern. Incandescent lamps are appropriate for quick on/off use in closets, pantries, and other similar spaces.

Kitchens

Kitchens should have natural light with an area of not less than one-tenth the floor area, or a minimum of 0.9 square meters (10 square ft). Building codes will typically allow completely artificial light if daylight is not available. Provide general lighting, plus task lighting over each work center and countertop. For energy efficiency, consider fluorescent sources with color temperatures from 2700°K to 3000°K in kitchens and work areas, to maintain a match with incandescent sources. Specify fixtures that are fitted with electronic ballasts to maximize energy efficiency and eliminate noise and flicker. Some kitchen spaces with a lot of wood and natural finishes look much better under incandescent light. Where incandescent sources are used, they should be either line- or low-voltage halogen for energy efficiency and longer life, and should have dimming controls.

Low-glare linear and nonlinear task fixtures mounted under wall cabinets at perimeter countertops can provide evenly distributed, shadow-free lighting on the task surface. Pendants, downlights, or track lighting can do the same over islands, peninsulas, and sinks, as can integrated lighting in ventilation hoods over cooktops.

In addition to daylight, ambient lighting in kitchens should be provided to fill in shadows, reduce contrast, and light vertical surfaces. Ambient lighting can be provided by indirect lighting mounted on top of wall cabinets, suspended indirect or direct/indirect linear fluorescent fixtures, low-glare overhead surface-mounted fixtures, coves and ceiling drops with integrated lighting, and carefully placed downlights. Carefully placed means laid out at a distance and configuration so as not to produce severe and off-center scallops on wall cabinets and appliances; remember that lighting must be designed in three dimensions.

Bathrooms

Natural lighting is desirable in a bathroom. Sunlight can also help warm the thermally massive materials such as tile, porcelain, and stone that are commonly used in bathrooms, providing a welcome warmth in an area where we are most likely to be undressed. Windows can also provide fresh air.

In the design of a bathroom, you should avoid directing sun onto the face. A mirror should not be located directly opposite a window. The goal is to light the face of the person, not the face in the mirror, without causing glare. The background behind the face should be no lighter than the face. It is helpful to have more light from one side than from another to model the face in three dimensions. This can be achieved with dimmable switches, or by daylight controls in windows.

A single overhead fixture is usually not acceptable for lighting a bathroom. Residential bathrooms should use dimmed halogen incandescent as a primary source. The traditional theatrical lighting approach of unprotected bulbs around a mirror is likely to cause direct glare. Lights above the mirror may cause shadows under the eyes, and lights too close to the face can produce glare.

An evenly distributed, shadow-free vertical light should be provided on the face by a vertically oriented linear fixture either flanking the mirror or integrated with the mirror. Other types of fixtures suitable for use with a mirror include wall sconces or luminous pendants flanking the grooming position at face height, horizontally oriented fixtures over the mirror with a lensed front and enough width to illuminate the face, or architectural soffits or valances with a direct/indirect distribution. As a general rule, do not use downlights for grooming tasks as they tend to cast unfavorable shadows on facial features. If there is no other alternative, place downlights as close as possible to the mirror, spaced on either side of the grooming position and used in conjunction with a matte white countertop for upward reflectance.

For many of us, the only time we get a good look at ourselves is in the bathroom. In addition to the standard mirror over the sink, a discretely located full-length mirror can help us face the naked truth. Good lighting should show us at our best and still provide enough light to remove a splinter. The quality of the light is important, to complement skin tones, and to help us notice when we (or our children) are really not looking well.

Showers and tubs should always be illuminated for grooming tasks. The most common fixture is a lensed downlight with a gasketed trim ring, usually limited to 40-W incandescent lamps due to heat restrictions. With the advent of smaller compact fluorescent lamps, the amount of light can be increased with the same or less wattage per lamp, although the initial cost may be higher.

In most cases, the task lighting system will also provide adequate ambient illumination in the space, especially in smaller bathrooms and powder rooms. Downlighting, indirect coves, adjustable accents, fan/light combination fixtures, and wall sconces offer additional ambient lighting.

Other Residential Lighting

Preset multiscene controls allow for a variety of lighted settings in dining rooms, from predining events to clean-up tasks. Family rooms, great rooms, and living rooms should achieve a relaxing, casual atmosphere through the use of a nonuniform, mostly perimeter lighting system. Ambient lighting is best provided by soft indirect lighting. Downlights, wall sconces, table lamps, or other accents can be used for higher task lighting levels. Artwork, sculpture, and other architectural features should be highlighted with recessed adjustable accents, surface monopoints, a track system, or a wire/rail system for maximum flexibility.

Besides sleeping, which requires an absence of light, other tasks in a bedroom space include dressing, grooming, reading, and where there are school-age children, homework. Smaller rooms, up to about 12 square meters (125 square ft), can be adequately illuminated with a multilamped lighting fixture that provides a uniform lighting pattern throughout the space. Larger rooms will require additional adjustable accents on one or more walls. Task lighting adjacent to the bed for reading is usually best provided with table fixtures.

Using the home as a work area creates special communications and equipment considerations that affect the sources, control, budget, and energy use of lighting. In home offices and dual-purpose areas combining work and recreation, design lighting for each use individually, with the maximum for common use. Fluorescent lighting is recommended for workspaces, as it provides a generally uniform distribution with relatively high task illuminances. Fluorescent fixtures for home workspaces can be in the form of downlights, surface-mounted direct fixtures, suspended indirect fixtures, or built-in indirect coves. Track lighting or other adjustable direct fixtures do not work well due to the shadows they cast. Task fixtures on work surfaces and accent lighting highlighting artwork help to balance the space.

Home theaters are becoming more commonplace both in high-end residences and in average homes. They should be lighted like a theater, using a multilayer lighting system with general space illumination, low-level lighting for moving about in the dark, and effects lighting for fun.

Residential Lighting Controls

In most living spaces, there is a need to adjust the light levels for varying tasks to provide different moods, to lower the color temperature, to increase or reduce contrasts on objects, or simply to provide a reduced level of illumination, and some type of dimming control is recommended. This is true not only for incandescent sources but for fluorescent lamps as well. High-quality electronic dimming ballasts are available for T8, T5, and compact fluorescent lamps for areas where dimming these lamps is appropriate.

Lighting controls can vary from relatively low-cost simple wallbox dimmers to remote panel dimming systems that use one-touch preset buttons and connect to other home automation systems.

For large residences, consider low-voltage or wireless controls for the convenience of remote control and energy savings. Automation also promotes energy conservation and safety. Equipment can report conditions at the house to the homeowner both on site and at a remote location. Low-wattage and wireless systems feature a wall mounted master at each entrance in the kitchen and home office, a bedside tabletop master in the master bedroom, and radio-operated switches and dimmers in all rooms.

LIGHTING PUBLIC TOILET ROOMS

With a large number of plumbing fixtures and high volume use, good lighting is essential for keeping public bathrooms clean and pleasant. Whether we are designing a restroom for an office building, where the same people will use it every day, or for a public space, creating a good impression with lighting enhances the interior design.

The lighting in a public toilet room should vary from the light levels in the rest of the building. Well-lit toilet rooms encourage the maintenance staff to keep the space bright and clean, and assure the users that it is safe and hygienic. The toilets, urinals, and lavatories benefit from a task-lighting approach. Other areas may be much less brightly lit, depending on whether the interior is in a nightclub or an office, for example. Good quality lighting near the mirrors enhances the user's appearance, which is especially important in restaurants and similar social environments. The guidelines provided under the section on residential bathrooms also apply to lighting fixtures for the mirror areas of public restrooms, with the proviso that all fixtures have to withstand the potential abuse of a public (but often isolated) space.

OFFICE LIGHTING

Designing lighting for the office means designing for change. Design flexibility into both the overall layout and the degree of control that the individual employee has over his or her workspace. One way to achieve individual flexibility is with addressable ballast technology, which can make use of either a handheld remote control device or a control window that appears on an employee's computer screen, allowing the employee to make adjustments to the ambient light conditions in the immediate area.

Light should be distributed relatively uniformly in a work environment, avoiding hot spots, shadows, or sharp patterns of light and dark. In larger offices or open-plan spaces, use more than one type of light fixture, each with specific distribution characteristics, to light the task and room surfaces most effectively. Select fixtures specifically designed for wall washing to light walls from top to bottom. Avoid locating fixtures closer than 1 meter (3 ft) from walls. If they are too close, they create harsh patterns and dark upper walls, resulting in a cave-like appearance.

Office lighting should feature energy conservation and good color. A good choice is the T8 3500°K to 4100°K triphosphor linear lamp or a similar compact fluorescent unit with high-frequency electronic ballast. High-intensity discharge lamps can be used for indirect lighting in spaces with high ceilings. Color-corrected high-pressure sodium (HPS) and metal-halide lamps with high CRI ratings can be used as well. Incandescent lamps may be used in storage areas, closets, and other spaces with short burning times. Incandescent and tungsten-halogen lamps are appropriate for illuminating displays.

The American Society of Heating, Refrigeration, and Air-Conditioning Engineers (ASHRAE), in conjunction with IESNA, have issued ASHRAE/IESNA Standard 90.1P, which sets power limits for office spaces at 1.5 W per square ft for private offices and 1.3 W per square ft for open plan offices. The limit for office corridors is 0.7 W per square ft, and 1.8 W per square ft for reception and lobby areas. Conference and meeting rooms are allowed 1.5 W per square ft. Active stairs are set at 0.9 W per square ft, and active storage is allotted 1.1 W per square ft.

The room surface reflectance levels for offices are critical to support the lighting design. The IESNA recommendations for office-type spaces suggest that ceilings should have 80 to 92 percent reflectance, with perforated ceilings being about 15 percent lower than their finish. Walls and partitions should average in the 40 to 60 percent range. The floor should be between 20 and 40 percent reflectance, and window blinds should be in the 40 to 60 percent range. Desktops, furniture, and office machines should have reflectances of 25 to 40 percent.

Glare and Lighting for Computer Monitors

In an office, glare occurs when bright light sources interfere with the viewing of objects or surfaces that are less bright. The contrast between very bright and less bright may be uncomfortable or disabling, both of which are undesirable in an office environment. Fixtures located to the front or side of the employee cause direct glare. Overhead glare is caused by excessive brightness directly above. Reflected glare can also occur on glossy paper from lights directly in front. Most glare can be controlled by either increasing the brightness of the surroundings or decreasing the brightness of the sources, or both.

Direct light sources, even when shielded by lenses or louvers, can cause reflected glare on computer screens from images of fixtures located behind the employee, although this is much less of a problem than it used to be since screen technology has gotten so much better at combating glare. The eye is drawn to the bright spot, which competes with the text or graphics on the screen, but is separated in depth by the thickness of the glass on the face of the computer monitor. Your eyes try to focus on both images and change the depth of focus constantly, resulting in eyestrain and severe fatigue.

Government agencies have issued guidelines for employees using computer monitors (also called video display terminals—VDTs) limiting work periods and monitoring physical effects. The health department of the state of New Jersey has issued guidelines for all state employees requiring 15-minute breaks every two hours and periodic eye examinations. Computer monitors are required to have adjustable tilting swivel mounts and separate adjustable angle keyboards.

Avoid reflections on the keyboard and other specular (mirrored) objects nearby by selecting matte finishes. Increasing room surface brightness by illuminating walls and ceilings and using lighter-colored materials reduces contrast. Increase the brightness around the glare source by using semispecular or white louvers, or by indirectly illuminating the ceiling. Reduce the brightness of the lamps by using more lamps of lower brightness, and compensate by using more fixtures if necessary.

Indirect lighting with a ceiling at least 3 meters (10 ft) high is recommended for lighting spaces with computer monitors. Semi-indirect and direct-indirect lighting may be used in spaces with ceiling heights between 2.75 and 3.36 meters (9–11 ft). With indirect lighting systems, ceilings and walls become the sources illuminating the room, and the space seems brighter and more alive. Indirect solutions generally work better if the occupant has some sense of where the light is actually coming from. Very evenly lit spaces tend to produce a slightly eerie, unreal, or disoriented feeling in the occupant. Diffusers, lenses, or perforated metal panels can provide a minimal sense of the light's origin. Some ceiling mounted indirect fixtures are designed for easy relocation without extensive rewiring.

Ceiling mounted indirect lighting fixtures don't work well in spaces with ceilings under 2.75 meters (9 ft), as they have to be dropped below the ceiling enough to shine up on it without creating hot spots. They also don't work well in extremely long spaces, even where ceilings are high. A large array of ceiling hung fixtures can create the impression of a second ceiling plane below the actual ceiling, and perhaps intensify the feeling of confinement in a low-ceilinged space.

Furniture mounted indirect lighting, attached to the wall or partition systems at 168 cm (5–6 ft) or so, allows plenty of room to achieve reasonable light distribution and avoid hot spots even in very low-ceilinged environments. However, because codes generally require that these fixtures be hard-wired and powered at 277V, they can't simply be plugged into the panels and moved easily around the space when the office is rearranged. Some municipalities, including Chicago, require that office buildings be wired at 120V, which means that a truly flexible furniture mounted lighting system is possible. A flexible furniture mounted system may also be an option in an older building that remains wired at 120V.

Ceilings under 2.75 meters (9 ft) should use direct lighting, with low-brightness luminaires to prevent reflections and direct glare. Low-luminance troffers with miniature parabolic wedge louvers or more efficient large-cell specular parabolic louvers are options. Specular louvers reflect lamps and appear as bright spots reflected onto monitor screens. This is not the case with the deeper fixtures designed for use with video monitors. Direct lighting fixtures must be well maintained, as dust shows up as a bright spot on a dark background.

The brightness of the computer monitor itself can create too much contrast with its surroundings. Where surrounding surfaces are lighter, the luminance of the monitor should be at least one-third as bright. The monitor should be in a ratio of three to one to darker surroundings. More distant areas of the room should be no more than one-tenth as bright as the monitor. The monitor should maintain a 17 to 1 ratio to lighter remote surroundings.

Other Office Lighting

Task lighting (Fig. 35-1) is often integrated with office furniture, eliminating problems with changes of furniture layout. Initial construction costs are reduced, as are energy requirements, since the light and task are close together. Each occupant has on/off control of task lighting, including the possibility of position control. Maintenance is easy, as fixtures are accessible from the floor. Fixtures mounted on furniture take advantage of higher depreciation rates than fixtures on building surfaces.

Furniture mounted fixtures may have trouble dissipating heat and minimizing magnetic ballast noise so close to the user, so electronic ballasts should be used. Veiling reflections from reflected glare are always present as the fixtures shine on the worksurface. The luminance ratios in the near and far surrounding areas may exceed recommended levels. It is difficult to light a freestanding desk with furniture-mounted fixtures, as most fixtures are under-counter or sidewall mounted. Lighting a large table or an L-shaped desk area is also difficult, as the fixtures tend to concentrate light. Control by automatic switching and dimming is not easy either. In addition, unless the light source can be repositioned, you may need fixtures on both sides of the work space to accommodate both right-handed and left-handed people.

Wall cabinets and cabinets attached to furniture partitions create disturbing shadows on the vertical surfaces they overhang. A low quantity of lighting should be provided to remove this shadow and maintain a balance of brightness. Undercabinet lights with opaque fronts are available commercially or sold as part of the furniture system. A single T8 lamp generally provides too much

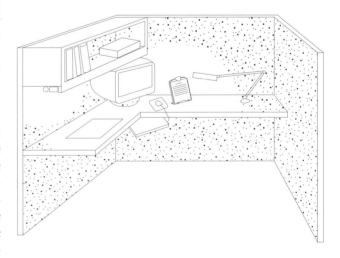

Figure 35-1 Open office task lighting.

light, so it should be coupled with a 50-percent-output ballast, which reduces the amount of light, reduces energy consumption, and balances the brightness.

Compact fluorescent desk lights allow workers to control their own lighting to meet individual needs. Articulated task lights, which allow adjustment in all three planes, are effective and inexpensive, and are preferable to under-cabinet lights for task lighting.

Private offices need a combination of task and ambient lighting. The ambient lighting may be spill light from the task, especially if a pendant unit with an uplighting component provides it.

Lighting Controls for Offices

Lighting controls save energy by dimming or turning off unnecessary lighting. We have already discussed ultrasonic occupancy sensors. By installing switching or automatic dimming for fixtures in the daylighted zone within 3.7 meters (12 ft) from a window wall, you can reduce lighting costs when adequate daylight is available. In rooms smaller than 37 square meters (400 square ft), an alternative approach is to provide separate switches for the light fixtures in the daylighted zone and connect them to a separate occupancy sensor. In daylighted zones greater than 37 square meters, consider electronic fluorescent dimming ballasts for continuous dimming down to 20 percent or less, automatically controlled by photosensors. Only smooth, continuous dimming should be used for office spaces to prevent distraction to the employees. The smoothness of the dimming depends on the quality of the dimming ballast more than on the controls.

EDUCATIONAL FACILITIES

The goal for lighting educational spaces is to conserve energy while supporting a rich learning environment through careful selection and location of lighting fixtures and controls. Institutional and educational buildings have tight budgets and require extremely hardy, vandal-proof, and low energy consumption lighting. Maintenance is generally poor and on a repair rather than prevention basis, so equipment should be as maintenance-free as possible.

Strive for uniform general lighting in workspaces such as classrooms. To avoid harsh shadows, locate parabolic louvered or lensed fixtures at least 1 meter (3 ft) from walls.

For good lighting and uniformity on vertical surfaces, the center of the vertical area should not be more than twice the brightness of the edges. Lighting should be located 0.6 to 1 meter (2–3 ft) away from the vertical surface. Most wall washer fixtures use internal reflectors so that light reflected from the wall is not a reflected glare source for students.

The most efficient lighting source for educational buildings is daylight, which is followed by high-pressure sodium (HPS), then fluorescent, then metal halide. Long-life sources require less maintenance, so fluorescent or high-intensity discharge (HID) fixtures should be used in corridors, stairs, and in any locations where relamping is difficult, like high-ceilinged gyms and assembly rooms. Where specific color lamps are called for, the color temperature and lamp type should be permanently stenciled in large letters on the lighting fixture for proper relamping.

Most schools are not air-conditioned, so there is less masking air noise. Ballasts and diffusers making noise or vibrating are likely to be noticed. Electronic ballasts are better, but cost more.

For vandal-proofing and low maintenance fixtures, look for captive screws (which can't be removed from the fixture), rust-preventive plated parts, and captive-hinged diffusers whose cleaning requires only one person. Ballasts should be replaceable without demounting fixtures, so use plug-in ballasts. Fixtures should be made of nonyellowing plastics, with high-quality finishes and assembly.

Light levels in corridors must be adequate for seeing into lockers and viewing student displays, as well as for security. Within these limits, a lower light level in corridors is not only refreshing, but also necessary to meet the energy code.

The power limits for school spaces set by ASHRAE/IESNA Standard 90.1P allow 1.5 to 1.6 W per square ft for private offices, classrooms, and auditorium spaces. Dining and cafeteria spaces are set at 1.4 W per square ft, and corridors and active stairs are allowed 0.7 and 0.9 W per square ft, respectively.

RETAIL LIGHTING

Good retail lighting can enhance a store's image, lead customers inside, focus their attention on products, and ultimately increase sales. Retail lighting must have good color, contrast, and balance. This can all be achieved with energy-effective lighting that is energy code compliant.

Lighting for Small Stores

 Although incandescent lighting is appropriate for use in a small retail store, other lighting sources should also be considered for ambient lighting, accent lighting, perimeter and valance lighting, and shelf and case lighting. Fixed location lighting using spotlights is often more effective than track lighting and floodlights. Plan carefully to avoid random fixture layouts or visual chaos, and stay away from too many shiny surfaces, and dark surfaces that reduce lighting effectiveness. Black ceilings will reduce indirect lighting levels, but can be used where this is not a problem. Lower level ambient lighting will allow attention to be focused on highlighted important elements. Ambient lighting must be adequate to clearly examine merchandise.

Put the light source close to the merchandise. For ambient lighting, use efficient, diffuse sources such as fluorescent. For accent lighting, use narrow beam spotlights. Using a limited number of lamp types reduces relamping mistakes and maintenance problems. Illuminate the aisles with spill light from accented merchandising areas or displays. Light colors on the interior surfaces of shelving reflect light onto merchandise. An organized pattern of light fixtures helps customers navigate merchandise displays. Use high color rendering lamps for both ambient and task lighting.

Lighting Intermediate-Sized Stores

For medium-sized stores that sell clothing, stationary, accessories, housewares, furniture, and/or small objects, ambient lighting is supplemented with limited accent lighting. Beauty shops and gourmet shops also fall into this category. The goal for lighting these types of shops is illumination that is uniform enough to see and examine product and read labels. Limited accent lighting is desirable to set products apart, to create highlights or enhance texture, and to attract attention to window displays. Partially conceal ambient light sources with louvers or baffles to create more emphasis on product. Locate accent lights close to displays. Use exposed or decorative accent lights to create attention or establish image.

High-End Retail Lighting

More expensive or exclusive higher-end stores include those selling jewelry, gifts, antiques, fine clothing, and accessories. Fine housewares and beauty salons are also included here. These stores have lower activity than other retail types and feature the most personalized attention and assistance from sales personnel. The lighting should establish image and enhance product color, sparkle, or texture. The lighting goal is to encourage lingering, examination of products, and impulse buying. Higher-end shops do not need to use more energy to be effective, and can provide more focus and highlights by decreasing the ambient light levels. Use fluorescent lighting for ambient lighting. White-painted parabolic louvers may be preferable in small spaces or low ceilings. For highest end applications, consider smaller diameter T5 or T2 fluorescent lamps for concealed applications such as coves, valances, and shelf lighting.

Use the best color rendering lamps with CRIs above 80 and a warmer color temperature of 3000°K to 3200°K for higher-end stores. For example, select fluorescent lamps designated 830. Since the eye is attracted to the brightest object in the field of view, and then to the next brightest object, provide the highest wattage or the tightest focus lamps on the most important items or areas of the store. Use exposed or decorative sources to attract attention to specific displays or areas of the shop.

Proper lighting controls assure that individual fixtures are on only when they are most effective. The display window lights should be controlled separately from the rest of the store lights. In addition, other fixture types should be on separate circuits, controlled by an astronomical time clock that adjusts to sunrise and sunset times. This way, only the most efficient fixtures will be used outside of business hours, for staff activities such as cleaning and restocking. This not only saves energy, but also greatly reduces maintenance for burned-out accent lights.

Lighting for High Activity Retailing

Mass merchandising and discount stores, along with hardware, video, fast food, and grocery stores, are identified as high activity retail establishments. Some service establishments and stores that sell bulk or large objects, such as appliances or furniture, are also included in this category. These destination stores don't require lighting to draw customers inside. The goal of the lighting design should be to light all objects uniformly, to provide good visibility for reading labels, and to create a bright, clean, stimulating environment. Exposed lighting sources help project a discount image. Fluorescent and metal halide sources provide the best value—they give good color rendering, are highly efficient, and provide long life. Use light-colored finishes on wall surfaces to increase overall brightness and reflected light.

HOTEL ROOMS

The lighting fixtures in hotel rooms make up a significant part of overall building energy use. There are generally five to six lights in each room, and as many as half of the 15 million hotel rooms in the United States are still using incandescent lamps. Researchers at the Lawrence Berkeley National Lab set out to measure how much energy could be saved with simple changes to hotel room fixtures. Replacing bathroom incandescent lamps with fluorescents would save $40 per year per room. Adding occupancy sensors to automatically turn off bathroom lights could save an additional $10 per year. Replacement of incandescent floor and table lamps with compact fluorescent lamps offers a simple payback time of just two years.

INDUSTRIAL BUILDINGS

Industrial lighting is principally designed for cost savings. However, improved lighting has been shown to reduce accidents, improve employee morale, and result in an improved product. In one instance, when a merely adequate lighting installation was improved, despite considerable cost, production jumped 15 percent, easily covering the 3 percent cost of the improvements. In another case, new inspection lighting reduced product failures, thus providing an economic gain.

Many industrial buildings are one story, and roof monitors, skylights, and clerestories can provide daylighting. These light sources must be accessible for cleaning. Artificial lighting sources should be highly efficient, retain their brightness over time, and offer long life. Fluorescent and HID lighting are the best choices. New induction and sulfur lamps may be good alternatives, with additional development and field-testing. HID is easier to maintain, store, clean, and relamp than fluorescent lighting. However, HID has a delay in restarting.

Minimal reflectances for industrial ceilings are between 75 and 85 percent. Walls range from 40 to 60 percent reflectances, with equipment at 25 to 45 percent and floors at around 20 percent.

OUTDOOR LIGHTING

Interior designers are sometimes called on to help select lighting fixtures for the landscaping and entry around a home. By lighting all exterior vertical surfaces from above—not below—whenever possible, you can reduce light pollution that limits our ability to see the night sky. If you select luminaires with shields for a sharp cutoff beyond the illuminated area, you can limit the intrusion of unwanted light onto neighbors' property and into windows. After the installation is complete, inspect the site at night to determine if there is a nuisance.

SECURITY AND COMMUNICATIONS SYSTEMS

Chapter

Communications and Control Systems

As the interior designer, you are likely to have the most detailed knowledge of your client's priorities, how your client will use the space, and where equipment will be located. You will be communicating information about the location of telephones, intercom systems, public address speakers, and computer terminals to the architect, electrical engineer, or contractor. For residential construction, this information is often shown on the construction floor plan.

For commercial construction, the interior designer or architect often draws a separate power plan. The electrical engineer uses the power plan to draw the electrical plan. The power plan usually shows telephone and communications systems along with power outlets. When the precise location of communications or security equipment is critical, the power plan will give exact dimensions. Interior designers sometimes show convenience outlets on the furniture plan if they relate to the placement of furniture. The electrical engineer or contractor usually determines the actual circuiting, wire sizes, and connections to central equipment.

SIGNAL SYSTEMS

All the signal, communications, and control systems that send and receive electronically coded information are considered to be signal systems. These include fire detection and alarm systems, telephones and intercoms, broadcast TV with UHF and VHF reception, and closed-circuit TV for security or educational use. Paging and sound systems, as well as master clock and bell systems, are also signal systems. Heating, ventilating, and air-conditioning (HVAC) controls are signal systems too, including everything from thermostats to computerized energy management systems. Data transmission is another major category. A building's signal system often includes several different functions.

Communications systems are signal systems and include intercoms, telephones, and computers. Television systems, including surveillance systems, cable services, and satellite hookups, are communications systems too. The assistive listening devices required by the Americans with Disabilities Act (ADA) in assembly occupancies are also considered to be communications systems.

The signals for communications systems are usually carried on small, low-voltage wiring. The *National Electrical Code* (NEC) and standards organizations set some requirements, but low-voltage communications systems have very few safety problems, so they are not as heavily regulated as other electrical systems. The primary problem is the fire hazard caused by the potential spread of fire along cables or circuits. The NEC regulates the type of cable or wiring, the clearance for power conductors, and proper grounding procedures. Recent code provisions may be added for the use and wiring of computers, and other requirements may exist at the local level, so it is best to keep up to date on code requirements.

You will almost certainly be working on projects with intercom, computer, surveillance, cable, satellite, building telephone, public telephone, or assistive listening systems. Although your client will probably contract directly with the company that supplies and installs these systems, it is a good idea for you, as the interior designer, to have contact information. It is common for questions to come up during the design and construction phases that you will need to answer, and you may discover that you are the key contact person between the general contractor and these outside suppliers. You need to be aware of the central location of the system and special considerations for system components, as they can affect the interior designer's work. The installer's work has electrical implications and must conform to local regulations, and an electrical engineer may be required on some projects.

The system of raceways, boxes, and outlets dedicated to all the types of communications systems, with the general exception of audio signals, is referred to as premise wiring. The small, low voltage wiring that is normally used to convey these signals may include fiber optic cabling, which offers increased bandwidth, freedom from interference, and high security levels. Communications and data wiring can't share a raceway with electrical power wiring because of interference problems. TV antenna cables and closed-circuit connections must be shielded, and are generally not grouped with phone lines to avoid signal interference.

Surface-mounted raceways are sometimes preferred for communications wiring because frequent access may be required. Data cables that have been preterminated may be difficult to pull into recessed raceways, and are easier to manage in surface-mounted ones. Large raceways are simpler to install on the surface.

TELEPHONE SYSTEMS

Telephone system equipment is either privately owned or is provided as part of the local phone service. Every building requires a central switching room or area where incoming telephone service is connected to the building's phone system. This is typically in the basement or on the ground floor as close as possible to the telephone service entrance. A small building may need only a small panel located in the mechanical room or closet. The number of phones serviced and the size of the switching panel determine the size of the room. We will look at telephone systems for residential buildings later on.

Commercial buildings require much more space for the telephone system equipment than residential buildings. Very large buildings have their own telephone terminal room. Within a finished space, phone equipment may be enclosed in a recessed cabinet. You can find out the size needed by consulting the company installing the phone service.

The type of cable used for telephone wiring depends on where it is used. Telephone cables must be fire-rated and appropriately labeled, and installed separately from electrical cabling. Typically, telephone cabling is not permitted in any raceway, compartment, outlet box, or junction box used for electrical lighting or power.

The transmission wiring for telephone systems is run in conduits or sleeves. Under-floor or ceiling raceway systems are often used. The system may need riser space or shafts for vertical wiring and vertically aligned closets with a sleeve through the floor for cables.

Telephone cable terminates at a telephone outlet, often installed adjacent to an electrical outlet. The ADA specifies that phone outlets where access is required for people with disabilities be at least 38 cm (15 in.) above the floor.

In buildings with more than one floor, each floor has its own telephone closet that feeds off the main phone switching room. Each area or floor in a large office building with telephone switching equipment must have its own telephone closet. Telephone closets provide service throughout the floor, either directly to each phone or to one or more satellite closets, and are often used within a tenant space to allow separation of utilities and easier distribution of cables in large buildings. They are stacked vertically to carry wiring from floor to floor. The interior of the closets is surfaced with plywood to mount cabinets, raceways, and fittings. Telephone closets must have adequate lighting and electrical service for phone company workers. Computers operate many of the newer telephone systems, and the switching room may need additional space to accommodate this equipment.

Private branch exchange (PBX) systems have a switchboard that accepts all incoming calls. This is the type of system that, for example, a hotel uses. An operator manually redistributes the calls to interior stations. A PBX system may need its own equipment room with ventilation and acoustic isolation for the noisy, hot equipment.

Public telephones include pay phones, public closed-circuit phones, and other phones for public use. Their installation is usually the responsibility of the telephone company. The NEC does not regulate public phone systems. Under Title IV of the ADA, some public telephones must be accessible to people with disabilities, and the ADA sets clearance and reach requirements for these accessible phones.

Not all public telephones have to be accessible for people with disabilities. Where one or more public phones are provided, at least one must be accessible. Where there are several banks of public telephones, additional phones may need to be accessible. The interior designer must be aware of ADA requirements and be able to specify the correct type of public phone.

Accessible public telephones must have either front or side access for people using wheelchairs, with a clear area of 76 by 122 cm (30 by 48 in.). The base, side enclosures, and fixed seats can't reduce these clearances. The mounting height of the phone depends on the way the phone would be approached by a person in a wheelchair and the depth of any obstruction such as a shelf. Accessible phones must be located on an accessible route. ADA requirements include volume controls, the number of text telephones to be provided, push button controls, the position of phone books, the length of the cord, and signage displays.

Emergency telephone systems (Fig. 36-1) use regular phone lines or PBX. Power supply or battery backup is not required. The user simply pushes the button once to call and speak, and units are able to notify the attendant of the location of the calling phone by a recorded message and digital display. ADA-compliant emergency phones have a light-emitting diode (LED) indicator for the hearing impaired, as well as raised letters and Braille signage for visually impaired individuals. Indoor models can be designed to fit limited spaces, like elevator phone boxes.

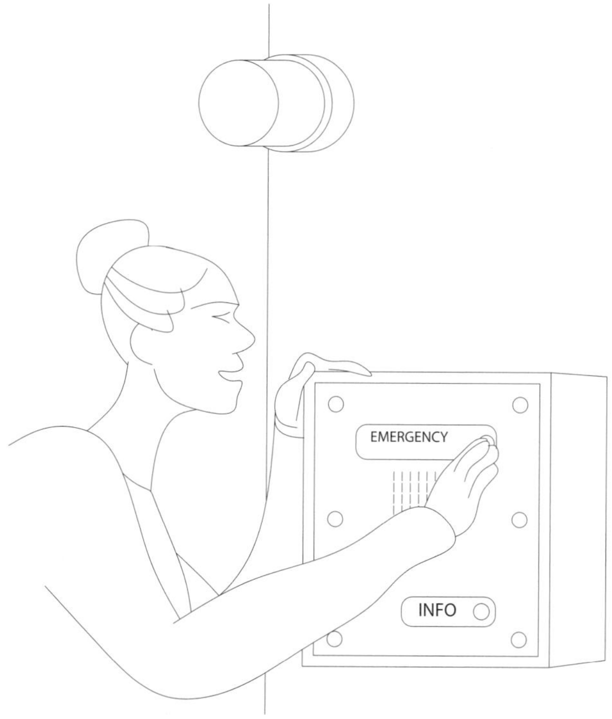

TELEVISION SYSTEMS

Closed circuit television is used for security in banks, retail stores, high-rise apartment buildings, and industrial complexes. Access to parking lots and garages and to elevators is often monitored with closed circuit TV. Closed circuit TV needs adequate uniform lighting without dark spots to operate properly. Systems are available with cameras that pan, tilt, or zoom; these may be directed automatically or from a central monitoring console. However, it is more common to simply add additional cameras to cover all contingencies.

Cable TV systems may receive signals from an outdoor antenna or a satellite dish, a cable company, or a closed circuit system. If several TV outlets are required in a space, a 120V outlet is supplied with a plug-in amplifier. Coaxial cables in a nonmetallic conductor raceway transmit the amplified signal to the various outlets. We look at requirements for television systems in residential buildings later on.

EMERGENCY CALL SYSTEMS

Emergency call systems are used in housing for people with disabilities, elderly people, and other residents. They alert outsiders to an emergency within an apartment and allow residents to call for help when ill or in distress. Housing and construction codes may include descriptions of equipment that is required.

Usually a call initiation button is mandated in each bedroom and bathroom, with an audible alarm and visible annunciator signal that is monitored at all times. Additional signals may be located in the corridor on each floor and at the entrance to each apartment to alert neighbors to a distress call.

INTELLIGENT BUILDINGS

Automatic building controls use a timing device, a sensor like an occupancy or daylight sensor, or a programmable device like a microprocessor or computer to con-

Figure 36-1 Emergency phone system.

trol building system equipment. Automatic control systems may be simple or complex. They are considered to be stand-alone systems because they are not integrated into a larger building automation system.

There are many names for intelligent building systems, such as building automation systems (BAS), computerized building control, integrated computer control, supervisory data systems, integrated building control, and facilities managements systems. An intelligent building is one that provides a productive and cost-effective environment through its structure, systems, services, and management, and that maintains relationships between these four elements. Solutions are matched to the needs of the building's occupants for convenience and efficiency.

Complex mechanical and electrical systems need a central point of supervision, control, and data collection. Office building control and automation systems control water, air conditioning, heating, ventilation, and electrical systems. They provide data on temperatures, pressures, flow, current, voltage, and mechanical systems for operational decisions and for programming automatic systems. They monitor all systems and act on all alarms automatically at a supervisory control center. Using computers for operations decisions results in the best system performance and in savings of operating and maintenance costs.

Intelligent building systems are part of the trend toward integrated system design and centralized monitoring and control of building systems. An intelligent building system might include HVAC, energy management, and lighting control. The system could also include security, life safety (fire alarm, fire control and suppression, and emergency vertical transportation control), material handling, and some communications systems. Previously only economical in large, owner-user facilities, intelligent building systems have become an economic necessity for some buildings, due to high labor costs and the relatively low cost of computer and microprocessor controls. The result is highly cost-efficient and environmentally appropriate facilities. Retrofitting older buildings with intelligent building systems is becoming a major industry. System components require good lighting and ventilation and extensive raceway space, but take up little floor space.

Chapter 37

Securing the Building

• • •

In order to address building security issues, the architect and interior designer must look at how people use the building. Most building security problems can be resolved with a combination of common sense and a little technology. Let's look at some common office building situations and their solutions.

Ideally, the lobby for an office (Fig. 37-1) should be visible from the reception desk. When the reception area doesn't have a view into the lobby, an intruder might be able to enter the building and, by gaining access to the stairwells off the lobby, move up or down to other floors. By adding glass to the stairwell exit doors, we can let people in the lobby see if someone is inside the stairwell. A continuously activated alarm system will allow cardholders free entry to the office, but will ring should anyone try to force the office door or prop it open. Another layer of security is added when a door with a card reader is installed at the corridor leading to the elevator.

If the doors to restrooms are out of sight of a receptionist and unlocked, an intruder could hide inside a restroom. Card readers (Fig. 37-2) or push-button combination locks on the restroom prevent entry by unauthorized visitors, while avoiding the need for employees to get a restroom key at the reception desk.

Where the office lobby has a thick glass wall with a view into the reception area, the receptionist can see vis-

itors while maintaining a secure barrier. The glass wall also provides a surface for attaching the metal strip required for a magnetic lock. For extra security when the reception desk is unoccupied, a detector can be added that registers the frequency of breaking glass and sends a signal to an alarm system. A camera can be installed in front of or behind the receptionist to identify interlopers after they've entered.

Elevators equipped with a card-reader system ensure that only authorized persons have access to a given floor. Although the system can be refined to limit an individual's access to certain times of the day or week, it is most practical for use after-hours, when fewer people need to gain entry.

Controlling access at a loading dock during the day and after-hours while providing egress to comply with safety regulations involves several strategies. There must always be a manned door that allows entry from the dock to the service elevators. This door must be lockable to restrict access from the street after business hours, with an alternative entry and egress point provided for authorized visitors. An intercom and camera can be positioned here for after-hours communications with a security guard at a desk. Ideally, a mailroom should be created off the ground or lower floor to reduce traffic through the lobby and other office areas. A

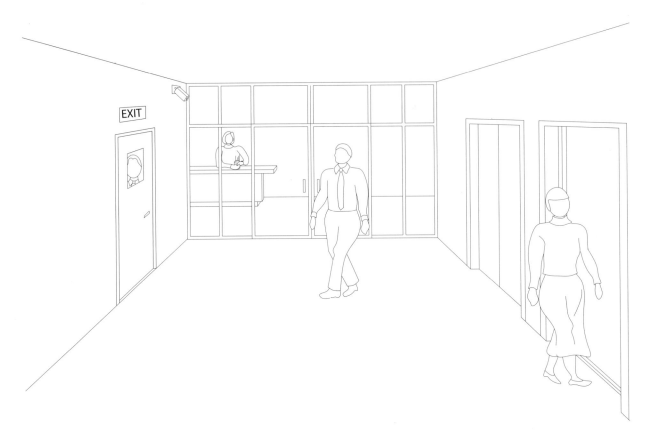

Figure 37-1 Office lobby security.

camera positioned at the street helps ensure that only authorized visitors will be admitted.

Burglary and vandalism cost owners of homes and commercial buildings many millions of dollars each year. Every effort put into making security improvements will be repaid many times in increased protection against loss and damage, and greater safety and

peace of mind. As a bonus, adding security measures may reduce owner's insurance premiums.

On many projects, your client will probably rely on security experts for advice. However, as the interior designer, you should be aware of the methods that may be used to detect intruders, prevent entry, control access to secure areas, and notify staff of unauthorized entry or emergencies. Some of these functions require special security systems, but the first line of defense involves the design of secure doors and windows.

SECURING DOORS

Interior designers often specify doors and their hardware, and sometimes prepare hardware schedules for residential and commercial projects. To help you understand the issues involved in specifying door hardware, here is a rundown of basic lock types and their related hardware accessories.

A good door lock is very important, but only if the door itself is strong and secure. You should specify only solid-core doors at least 44 mm ($1\frac{3}{4}$ in.) thick for exte-

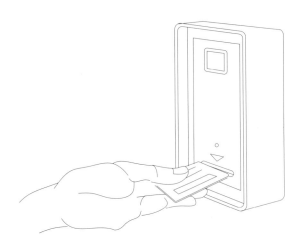

Figure 37-2 ID card reader.

rior entries, including an entry into an attached garage. Choose metal-clad doors if possible, especially for side and rear entrances. Many metal doors have designs appropriate for front entries. Specify solid doorframes that are securely mounted with long screws.

Residential basements often have sloped doors over the exterior basement step. These should be metal or metal-clad doors with the hinge barrels sunk flush in a concrete curb. The exterior basement doors need security crossbars at two points on their underside.

If you are involved in a renovation where increased security is a concern, you can opt to replace glass sidelights in doors, garage doors, and windows with shatterproof plastic. The insides of windows and sidelights can be covered to block the view of the interior. A peephole door viewer will allow the occupants to see who is at the door. Be sure that your client changes the factory-set frequency of a remote-control door opener.

If the barrels of ordinary hinges are on the exterior side of a door, the pin can be driven out and the door opened. Specify either hinges that have nonremovable pins or security stud hinges. With the latter, when the door is closed, a stud attached to one leaf projects into a hole in the other leaf.

Locks and Locksets

Control over unsupervised access into a building often relies on keys and locks, which have problems despite some technological advances. There are four major kinds of key-operated locks used on exterior doors: locksets, mortise locks, rim- or surface-mounting deadbolt locks, and cylinder deadbolt locks. Two other kinds, crossbar and brace locks, are more cumbersome and less attractive but offer even greater security.

Locksets for doors, also called cylindrical or key-in-knob locks, are manufactured assemblies of parts that make up complete locking systems. They include knobs, plates, and the locking mechanism itself. In a lockset, the entire mechanism is built into the doorknob. The outer knob has a key cylinder and the interior knob has a pushbutton or turn lever to operate a deadlatch. The deadlatch is a spring latch plus a deadbolt plunger that prevents opening the latch with a plastic card. A cylinder lock (Fig. 37-3) is housed within two holes bored into the door at right angles to each other, one through the lock stile of the door and the other through the door edge. Cylinder locks are relatively inexpensive and easy to install.

While very popular for their trim appearance, all but the most substantial and most expensive locksets offer only limited security. The outer handle containing the

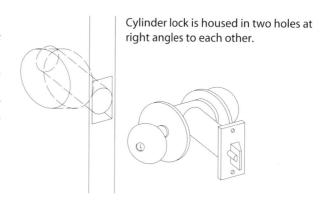

Cylinder lock is housed in two holes at right angles to each other.

Figure 37-3 Cylinder lock.

key cylinder can be sheared off with a few blows from a sledgehammer, and the mechanism can then often be operated with a screwdriver. An exposed key cylinder should be protected with a guard plate if possible.

A door is held shut by a spring latch that moves when you turn the handle or that is pushed back when its slanted face hits the strike plate on the jamb. The strike is a plate with a recess for the deadbolt that is mounted on the doorframe. A door can be locked securely only by a bolt that extends at least one inch into a substantial strike plate. A deadbolt has no spring and is moved by turning a key or lever in a cylinder lock.

A mortise lock (Fig. 37-4) is housed within a mortise cut into a door edge so that the door covers the lock mechanism on both sides. The lock is concealed except for a faceplate on the door edge, the knobs or levers, a cylinder, and the operating trim. The spring latch is operated by a doorknob on both sides, or by a thumb lever above a fixed handle on the outside. Pushbuttons in the edge of the door can block operation of the latch from

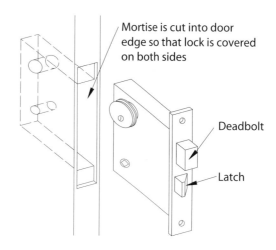

Mortise is cut into door edge so that lock is covered on both sides

Deadbolt

Latch

Figure 37-4 Mortise lock.

the outside. Security locking is provided by a separate deadbolt that is operated by a key from outside and a lever from inside. The pocket for a mortise lock can be a weak spot in the frame of a conventional wood door. Adding a reinforcing plate is a wise measure.

Unit and integral locks combine the security advantages of mortise locks with the economy of cylinder locks. Unit locks (Fig. 37-5) are housed within a rectangular notch cut into the edge of the door. An integral lock fits into a mortise cut into the door's edge.

A rim lock, also called a surface-mounting deadbolt, or night latch, fastens on the back side of a door stile and has a deadbolt that engages a strike mounted on the jamb. The rim lock is operated by a small knob (thumbturn) on the inside and by a key from the outside. The key cylinder extends through a hole in the door's stile. The deadbolt may move horizontally or vertically into the strike. A vertical bolt is more secure because it engages holes in the strike and cannot be popped out by prying the door away from the jamb. The strike should have an L shape that mounts with screws from two directions. Rim locks are easy to install and provide good security if bolted rather than screwed to the door, and if strike screws reach into the door studs.

A cylinder deadbolt lock is installed in the same manner as a cylinder lockset. A single-cylinder lock is operated with a key from the outside and a thumbturn from the inside. To open a double-cylinder lock from either the inside or the outside, you need to use a key. This prevents anyone from operating the lock after making a hole to reach inside. However, in an emergency anyone inside can be trapped unless the key is immediately available. For this reason, some communities ban double-cylinder locks in residences.

Cylinder deadbolt locks offer excellent security when they are properly mounted in a substantial door. Depending on the design of the lock and the thickness

of the door, some cylinders protrude on the outside. They must have tapered guard rings of casehardened steel to protect them from being gripped with a wrench or attacked with a hammer. A cylinder deadbolt or a rim lock is often used in addition to a mortise lock or a lockset for increased security.

A crossbar lock mounts on the back of the door, with a key cylinder in the center. Turning the key or an inside knob extends two hardened metal bars into metal braces bolted to the framing on either side, or above and below. A brace lock or so-called police lock mounts on the lock stile of the door, above the handle. A removable, heavy-duty metal rod fits into a socket on the floor to provide triangular bracing. A key from the outside and a lever from the inside operate the brace lock. Both kinds of lock offer substantial security, but they are very large and quite ugly.

Interior chain locks or door guards permit opening the door only partway, but offer no security. Surface-mounting sliding bolts offer various degrees of security depending on their size, design and materials. The same is true of padlocks in hasps, which may be suitable where appearance is not important.

Additional Fittings

A hardened metal guard plate or escutcheon is a cover over a flush-mounted key cylinder on the outside of a door. It is secured with round-head bolts or tamperproof screws.

Extra long or L-shaped replacement strike plates can hold a deadbolt more securely than a standard, short plate. So can a strike box, which has a metal box that fits into the deadbolt mortise. All mount with screws long enough to reach into the door studs. Various wraparound reinforcing plates fit over the edge of the door to protect the area where a lockset, mortise lock, or deadbolt lock is installed.

Some homeowners install keyed sets on two or more doors. These are locks with matching cylinders, so that the same key operates them all. This does not increase security, but avoids having to keep track of separate keys for each entrance. You can buy keyed sets, or purchase matching key cylinders and install them in existing locks of the same make.

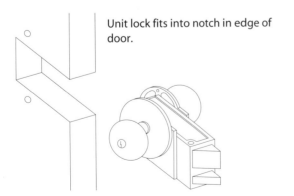

Unit lock fits into notch in edge of door.

Figure 37-5 Unit lock.

SECURING WINDOWS

Most people focus on doors and their locks for build- ing security, but windows are the weakest points in the security of most homes. They are often left open or unlocked and the typical locks or latches offer little resistance to a burglar. In addition, they are made of glass that is easily broken. Whether you are involved in specifying windows for new construction or helping a homeowner improve their existing windows, it is important to understand how to secure this weak point.

The center latch on a double-hung window will hold it shut against weather, but do not depend on it for security. Many types of window latches can be operated with a knife blade from the outside, and the narrow sash rails do not permit using long, substantial screws to mount them.

One way to secure a double-hung window is to fasten the top sash with angle brackets and then cut a rod to fit between the bottom sash and the top jamb. However, this prevents the top sash from being lowered for efficient ventilation. For more flexibility, install a pin that locks the meeting rails in the center of the window together. Use an eyebolt for the pin, so that it can be easily grasped in emergencies. To lock the sashes partway open for ventilation, drill a second hold five or six inches higher in the upper sash stile. Instead of an eyebolt, you can use a keyed lock with a pin or a window vent guard.

To secure a single-sash casement window, install surface bolts at the top and bottom that slide into reinforcing plates and mortises in the frame on the latch side. For a double-sash casement window, install bolts on both center stiles that extend into plates on the header and sill.

Sliding Windows and Doors

Security problems with sliding windows and doors are similar to those with windows. The outer fixed panel must be securely fastened with inaccessible screws from the inside. The simplest way to lock the moving panel is to put a stick in the bottom track, cut just long enough to fit between the frame and the jamb. For large panels, specify a bar that is hinged to the jamb and drops into a catch on the moving panel. It can be locked into the catch with a pin, or held in a bracket against the jamb when swung up out of the way. Another commercially available bar telescopes to length and has a pressure-sensitive siren that sounds if the panel is moved.

The two panels of a sliding door or window can be pinned together for security. Use an eyebolt through holes in the frame, or a pin with a bracket and chain. A keyed lock with a pin that enters a hole drilled in the window frame can also be installed. A number of different locks are available that mount on the moving

panel or on the lower track. A track lock allows the panel to be opened partway for ventilation.

Grates and Grilles

No matter how they are locked, glass windows can be broken. Metal bars or grilles on the outside can protect easily accessible windows. At least one window in each room must have a quick-release security latch on the inside for exit in an emergency.

Exterior window guards should be professionally installed with one-way screws or welded in place. Vertical bars should have welded crossbars at the top, bottom, and center to prevent their being spread apart with a simple screw jack. Adjustable burglar grates and folding gates that are installed inside the window may be less expensive.

The installation of security bars to protect a building from intrusion can result in harm to residents during a fire. In July 2001, a woman and three of her children were killed when fire broke out in their house in Houston, Texas, where doors and windows had been blocked with security bars. Rescuers beat on the windows, but the bars were locked. The bars apparently didn't have a quick-release mechanism, and it is possible that in the heavy smoke from the fire, the victims couldn't find the key to unlock the bars.

Alternatives to Glass

Ordinary window glass can be broken virtually noiselessly if a burglar puts tape on the glass. Tempered safety glass cannot be cut or easily broken, but can be shattered with a strong hammer blow. The alternative is to glaze vulnerable windows with plastic or a plastic-glass laminate or to protect glass with a security film.

Acrylic plastics (Lucite, Plexiglas, and similar products) resist impact but can be burned through with a torch. They are easily scratched and tend to yellow with age. Polycarbonate plastics (Lexan, Lexiguard, and others) in 4.8 mm ($\frac{3}{16}$ in.) or thicker single or laminated sheets are virtually indestructible, but can be burned or melted. Plastic materials are flexible and often can be pushed out of standard glazing. To prevent that, they should be through-bolted into window frames.

Laminated glass consists of a sheet of plastic sandwiched between two layers of glass. This provides the scratch resistance of glass and the impact resistance of plastic. If the glass is broken, the plastic will hold it in place. Existing glass can be laminated by having a plastic security film applied to it by a professional.

DETECTING INTRUSIONS

We have already discussed the use of occupancy detectors to control lighting and heating, ventilating, and air-conditioning (HVAC) systems. They are also among the devices used to alert building owners and occupants to intruders.

Simple normally closed contact sensors include magnetic contacts for doors and windows, window foil, and pressure/tension devices. When the contact is broken, they transmit an alarm signal, thereby detecting an intrusion or damage to the system.

Mechanical motion detectors are used where window foil or fixed contacts are not practical. Mechanical motion detectors use a spring-mounted contact suspended inside a second contact surface. Motion on the surface on which the device is placed causes the contacts to come together momentarily and triggers an alarm. Mechanical motion detectors are very sensitive, and may be activated by sonic booms, wind, or a heavy truck passing the building.

Photoelectric motion detectors use a beam that opens a contact and initiates an alarm when it is interrupted. Modern photoelectric devices use lasers or infrared (IR) beams, which can be arranged to tell the difference between an intruder and other disturbances. Signals can be picked up, amplified, and retransmitted in a new direction, forming a perimeter security fence from a single source.

Passive infrared (PIR) presence detectors (Fig. 37-6) use the principle that all objects emit IR radiation (heat). Because objects change temperatures slowly, IR radiation changes very slowly in an undisturbed area.

Thus a rapid change in an IR reading indicates an object entering or leaving the space, and an alarm is triggered. PIRs are used as occupancy sensors to turn off lights when a room is unoccupied. They can also be used when motion in a monitored area is unavoidable. Rapid temperature changes caused by the sun, a cold breeze, or a heater turning on, however, can cause false alarms.

Some motion detectors operate at microwave or ultrasonic frequencies. When a moving object changes the frequency of a reflected signal, an alarm sounds. Motion detectors work best when located so that the path of an intruder is directly toward or away from the detector, not sideways to it. Ultrasonic detectors are cheaper than microwave detectors, but are disturbed by strong air turbulence and by very loud noises. Microwave detectors penetrate solids, and therefore may be affected by motion outside the protected area.

Acoustic detectors emit an alarm when the noise level exceeds a preset minimum. An acoustic detector may also respond to a particular range of frequencies, such as those of breaking glass or forced entry. They are also used as occupancy sensors for switching and lighting.

Using multiple detectors with differing techniques that can verify each other reduces the number of false alarms. Passive infrared and ultrasonic detectors are available installed in a single housing for this reason.

LIMITING ACCESS

Since the late 1980s, building personnel access control is a specialty that has grown into an independent profession. There are a large number of identification technologies that are controlled and supervised by computers. The type of control depends on the importance of limiting access at a specific portal (entrance).

At the entrance to a large multipurpose space, many people gather quickly. To avoid the delay of a physical barrier, one or more guards are used to inspect a badge with a photo ID quickly. Physical barriers are slower, as the user must physically open a door. The identification process with a physical barrier may also involve human intervention.

At barrier-free optical turnstiles, the user presents an access card to an electronic reader. These turnstiles can pass a maximum of about one person per second. They can form pedestrian passageways to controlled areas, and are typically used in up-scale lobby entrances where the ability to move people through quickly with a high level of security is important. Optical turnstiles are mon-

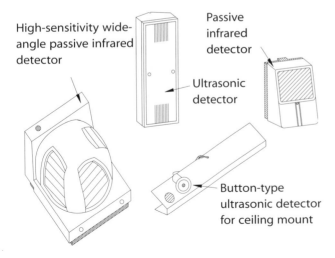

High-sensitivity wide-angle passive infrared detector

Passive infrared detector

Ultrasonic detector

Button-type ultrasonic detector for ceiling mount

Figure 37-6 Intrusion detection equipment.

itored through a visual display and audible alarms. They ensure that only one individual per valid card presented is granted access, preventing a second person from tailgating through. An attempt to enter without presenting an authorized card sets off an alarm locally and alerts security personnel. Optical turnstiles can be finished to match the interior finishes of the lobby.

Unattended barriers use magnetic, bar-coded, or proximity-reader cards. Electronic locks can be pro-grammed for varying conditions and to prevent access to certain cards. Within buildings, they can limit access to copy and fax machines, phone lines, and other office facilities, preventing personal use.

Newer technologies include biometric identification systems that compare physical characteristics such as eye patterns with a reference image. Biometric identification systems can also be used to scan crowds for facial proportions that match a database of criminal suspects.

Systems for Private Residences

High-speed telecommunications wiring, video cabling, and low-voltage wiring are becoming increasingly important technological upgrades in both new homes and remodeling projects. Prewiring a home in this way provides flexibility and offers the potential to turn any room into a home office, connect any TV to a cable or satellite hookup, or control both inside and outside lighting from one central location. Adding high-tech wiring for advanced communications, entertainment, and security systems can involve a number of major wiring systems.

It is important to plan thoroughly before rewiring, mapping out where to put new televisions, home theaters, speakers, or computers. The interior designer should try to look ahead and plan for a possible office, a need for faster Internet connections, or more computers. It is valuable to try to predict what the client will want in five years so that the wiring will be available. You can reduce the number of walls that need to be removed or replastered in older homes by running wires through ceiling or floor moldings.

The Internet requires fast speed and high bandwidth (information carrying capacity) to enable users to download photos, graphics, and music. In addition to the Internet, high-definition TV requires high bandwidth wiring to transmit crystal clear signals into a home, whether it has cable service or a satellite dish.

Low-voltage wiring is used for whole-house lighting control, for control of heating and air-conditioning systems, and for integrating security systems into the other low-voltage systems in a home. Having all of these low-voltage systems create a unified network makes it possible to control the systems in a home whether a person is sitting in the living room or is miles away in a car sending commands over a cellular telephone.

Prewired cables from the main entertainment center to other rooms in a home can direct both video and audio signals to outlets in every room. Home run wiring, where every wire or cable starts from one central distribution box inside a home and radiates out to each room, has several advantages. Each outlet or jack has its own wire or cable, independent of any other connection, so it's easier to make changes in the future. It is simpler to diagnose problems with home run wiring, and when problems do occur, they're isolated to that one wire or cable. Finally, home run wiring provides the best signal quality, and this is of critical importance for getting the best performance from the Internet and high-definition TV signals.

Signal systems for private residences add to the value of the home. Sophisticated automated systems are available in the residential market that combine security, fire alarm, and time functions. A single panel can control multiple residential systems, using an annunciator to display the location and type of the alarm. We discuss these residential systems in more detail shortly.

RESIDENTIAL TELECOMMUNICATION AND DATA SYSTEMS

The telephone company normally follows the route of the electrical service, either overhead or underground to the building's service entrance. A separate service entrance must be provided for telecommunications wiring, either overhead through a sleeve in the wall, or underground with a separate entrance conduit. Unless the residence has many entering lines, no source of power is required for phone service. Wiring for telephone service inside the home can be done either by the telephone company or by the homeowner's electrician.

 The huge increase in the number of private residences with multiple phone lines, dedicated fax lines, and special high-speed data transfer lines to home office outlets makes telephone system planning a necessity in a residential design. Unsightly surface-mounted cables will be visible if telecommunications wiring is left until after completion of construction of a residence. Prewiring cables on the wall framing and into empty device boxes to which instruments are connected later on can avoid objectionable visible cable. The designer must provide for multiple lines with adequate raceways. A local phone company technical representative can be very helpful.

RESIDENTIAL INTERCOM SYSTEMS

In large private residences, intercom systems allow occupants to monitor other parts of the house and communicate with one another. One or more master stations and several remote stations, including the front door, allow the intercom system to be answered from various points in the home. Visual identification at the entrance is achieved with the addition of closed-circuit TV. When left on, the intercom system can be used to monitor sounds in a baby's room. Low-voltage, low-power wiring uses multiconductor color-coded intercom cable, which is run concealed in walls, attics, and basements. The system may also use the house power

wiring to carry voice signals. This eliminates separate wiring and allows portable remote stations to plug into a power outlet.

Voice/music intercoms allow you to answer the door from any intercom speaker as well as to communicate within the building. The system can include a battery backup for up to 30 hours. Wireless radio remote control is also an option.

Video door-answering systems give the security of screening callers by sight and sound. The system includes a video monitor and door camera.

OUTDOOR SECURITY LIGHTING

Effective outdoor lighting is a major component of good security. The primary security function of exterior lighting is to deny would-be intruders the shroud of darkness and to scare them away. Additional functions are to ensure good visibility if occupants should have to exit in an emergency, and to illuminate the building number clearly to aid emergency response personnel. Good lighting is also a convenience and safety factor. For example, exterior lighting is helpful when you come home after dark with a trunk load of groceries, or late at night when no neighbors are likely to be awake if you should need help.

All entrances to a home, garage, and outbuildings, as well as areas not clearly visible from the street or neighboring homes, should become well lighted as soon as anyone comes near. High-wattage floodlight lamps are best for illuminating areas directly below a fixture. Spotlight lamps are useful to reach an area from any height or distance. Specify exterior or weather-resistant lamps, to minimize the need to replace them.

Ordinary entrance lights with 40- or 60-W lamps are usually mounted just above the door or alongside it. Locate security lighting fixtures high enough on walls or poles to be out of reach. Protect bulbs at any level against breakage with wire cages or tamper-resistant plastic housings.

Because security lighting could be expensive to operate and bright enough to annoy neighbors, many homeowners prefer to have inexpensive low-voltage, low-intensity lighting for convenience and safety along sidewalks and steps. This is supplemented with bright security lighting in areas such as the back door and garage and the concealed sides of the house. The security lighting is controlled by sensors and comes on only when triggered by someone entering a protected zone. This will surprise and scare off most prowlers.

The bright lights used for outdoor security lighting are usually powered by 120V household current. Codes require that exposed 120V wiring must run through metal conduit, which also protects wires from being cut. To ensure lighting even if household power is lost, you can specify lights powered by conventional batteries that must be replaced periodically, or by batteries that are recharged by the sun. Solar-charged batteries do not have to be replaced, but are not effective where sunlight is scarce in the winter or where they might become covered with snow.

A hard-wired switch, a timer, a remote radio-frequency switch, or a sensor can activate outdoor lighting. The most widely used and effective sensors are a photoelectric cell, a passive infrared (PIR) sensor, and a microwave sensor. A photoelectric cell acts as a switch to turn on a light when the surroundings become dark. Timer controls respond to whatever schedule is set. For lighting that comes on only when someone enters a protected zone, choose an infrared (IR) or microwave sensor. As with photocells, you can specify fixtures with built-in sensors, or install separate sensors that connect to existing fixtures. Most include a photocell so that they will operate only after dark.

A PIR for outdoor security lighting detects heat sources, such as people or car engines, within an unobstructed field of coverage. A microwave sensor detects any movement within a field of high-frequency energy that it emits. Many units can be set to either flash on and off or to remain on continuously for a preselected length of time. You also can adjust the sensitivity so that a passing cat or swirling leaves will not turn on the light. The exterior units that are least prone to false triggering use a combination of PIR and microwave sensors.

An exterior security fixture can power an alarm as well as lights, or exterior fixtures can be connected to a whole-house electronic security system to activate when triggered by sensors inside or outside the house. Some systems also let you operate the lights from a central control panel or by remote control.

INTERIOR SECURITY LIGHTING

The primary security function of interior lighting is to make a house look occupied when the occupants are away. That means having lights come on and go off in various parts of the house in what seems to be a normal pattern of use. Equipping a lighting fixture with a screw-in photocell socket into which the lightbulb is screwed will leave a light on all night, but for a more normal, varied pattern of light use, specify a timer control.

A basic lighting timer uses a rotating dial with pegs that trip the switch on and off. A receptacle timer plugs directly into an outlet, and the device to be turned on and off plugs into the timer. A socket timer plugs or screws into an outlet or fixture and has a socket for a bulb.

Some mechanical-switch timers can be set for only one on and one off time, while others permit two or more pairs of settings. Many operate at exactly the same set times every day, but better models have optional random operation that varies the times by up to 20 minutes a day for a more normal pattern. Almost all have an override switch so you can turn the light on or off independently without disturbing the timing.

Electronic timers can be programmed for multiple settings. They have a control ring, pushbutton, or keypad for entering timing settings, which are recorded on a magnetic chip that controls switch relays. Some provide a digital display of the settings as they are made. One such device is a timer switch that mounts in a wall box, in place of a standard switch, for automatic control.

A solid-state master unit that controls individual appliance modules throughout the house provides the most versatile and sophisticated timing. From a central location, it can operate lights or appliances plugged into the modules without the need for special wiring. The control unit is plugged into any electrical outlet. Lights or other appliances are plugged into individual modules, which in turn plug directly into existing outlets. Various control units can handle from four to ten or more modules. Settings for each module are entered on the keypad of the control unit. At the programmed times, the control unit transmits on/off signals either over the existing electrical wiring or by a radio frequency. Override switches on the modules permit manual operation of the lights when desired, and the control unit permits independent manual operation as well.

INTRUSION ALARM SYSTEMS FOR RESIDENCES

Magnetic switches are commonly used for door and window intrusion alarm systems. Motion and/or PIR detectors are also common. The installation of a manual switch at the end of a long cord allows the occupant to set off an alarm when an intruder is heard.

Commercial security services will wire a home with sensors and alarms and monitor the system for a monthly fee. The residential system is linked to a central monitoring station by telephone or radio. In most systems, one or more alarms go off in the building and a signal is flashed to the center if a sensor is tripped. If there is no answer, or if whoever answers cannot provide the code number that identifies the building, the center notifies the local police, who then investigate.

An alternative to commercially monitored systems consists of individual units located wherever the building owner wants to protect against intrusion. Systems for small buildings can be either wireless or wired. In one kind of wireless system, the sensors are connected to transmitters that are plugged into convenience outlets and communicate with the control unit over the building's electrical circuits. The system is wireless in the sense of not requiring any new, special-purpose wiring, but an outlet must be near each sensor location.

In another kind of wireless system, the sensors are connected to transmitters that exchange signals with the control unit by short-range radio. These transmitters may use building power or batteries.

In a hard-wired security system, the sensors are connected to the control unit by low-voltage wires. This is far less expensive than a wireless system, but it involves running wires throughout the building and connecting them. There is no complex electrical work to be done and the thin, low-voltage wires are easy to handle, but holes for running wires must be drilled and concealed.

The control unit is the component that determines whether a security system is reliable and easy to use. The best units have extension keypads. The control unit is located in a safe, concealed place, often in a closet. The keypads are located by the front and back or side exits. They give the occupants time to arm and disarm the door sensors as they come and go. Window sensors respond immediately, however, since it is unlikely that it is one of the building residents coming in through the window.

In addition to sensor/alarm controls, a controller may have timing circuits for turning lights or appliances on and off. When power is lost, the best controllers will switch to built-in batteries, and revert to building current to recharge the batteries when power is restored. They also will silence an alarm after several minutes and reset the sensors automatically if no one is in the building to deal with the situation. Some controllers also respond to signals from smoke detectors wired into the system.

How the control unit communicates with the user is important. Some units present messages in words on a display panel, indicating the room name. Some controllers that send signals through the household wiring can be set or activated by telephone. A controller that is linked to the telephone will also accept commands from an outside telephone, or let the user check the status of the system while away from the building. With an auto-dialing unit, the system can even signal the user at an-

other location or call the police or any other programmed number.

INTELLIGENT RESIDENCES

The security system described above can be one part of an intelligent residence. Intelligent residences are also referred to as smart houses or automated homes. They coordinate control of lighting, sound systems, home theaters, heating and cooling equipment, and security systems. Touch-screen computer controls (Fig. 38-1) or portable plug-in programmable microprocessors are used to set the system. The best and most expensive systems can be controlled by the user's phone.

At least one system is available with intuitive speech recognition that allows the homeowner to control the system by phone or a home computer. The system uses existing phone and power lines, and no rewiring is necessary. The user can talk to the computer from the home or anywhere else to manipulate lighting, thermostats, and other devices, or to retrieve information in real time. Groups of commands for specific lighting settings, security, home theater, and so forth can be preprogrammed in batches so that an entire home can be transformed with one verbal command. The system is designed to be easy to install, simple to use, and affordable.

It is preferable that the components of an intelligent home system, such as the security system or lighting controls, are each wired to run independently of the central control system. If something goes wrong and the central controls fail, each system will continue to operate on its own.

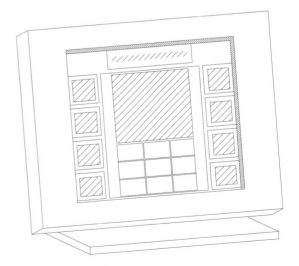

Figure 38-1 Touch-sensitive control panel.

Chapter

Other Security and Communications Applications

Communications and security systems for buildings are continually increasing in variety and complexity. Each type of occupancy has its own special challenges, and consequently its own types of security and communications equipment. It is important for the interior designer to discuss security and communications needs with the client. Individual suppliers often install these separate systems, and it is imperative to coordinate their installation with the general contractor. Otherwise, they are likely to be added on at the last minute, resulting in either exposed wiring or difficult snaking of wires through finished walls. Here is a rundown of some of the more common types. Many of these systems are applicable to other building types as well.

SYSTEMS FOR MULTIPLE RESIDENCES

The problems of security in a residential setting are greatly magnified when many people share housing. Monitoring who is at the door becomes much more complex when the door serves hundreds of residents. Interior designers coordinate the appearance and location of lobby entry system panels and plan for the lo-

cation of speakers or phones within each residential unit.

Entry and Security Systems

The simplest entry and security systems for multiple dwellings consist of a series of pushbuttons in the lobby with an intercom speaker or phone to connect with residents (Fig. 39-1). The tenant has a speaker microphone and a lobby door opener button. These systems can use the regular telephones of the residential units. Where there are a large number of units, an alphabetical roster with an apartment button panel is used to locate the tenant's name. Even larger systems employ an alphabetical panel and a phone. With the addition of a closed-circuit TV, tenants can see and hear the caller.

Some multiple residences use emergency call buttons within each apartment, in case an intruder gets past a lobby security check. In housing for elderly people, the emergency button unlocks the door so that help can reach the resident.

Luxury apartments may have apartment doors monitored from a central security desk. The security personnel at the desk investigate any unscheduled door

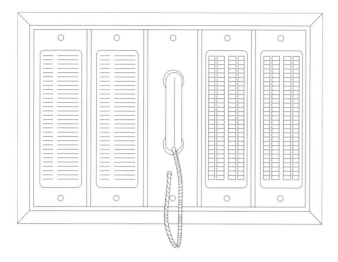

Figure 39-1 Apartment building intercom.

movement. These systems are custom designed to the needs and requirements of the building owner.

Television Systems for Multiple Residences

All modern multiple residences supply each room with one or more TV/FM jack outlets. TV signals are transmitted from a rooftop satellite dish and the house VCR, or by cable TV with pay TV as an option. The systems are always subcontracted, so new buildings are constructed with a system of empty conduits connected to cable pulling points in cabinets. The raceways are sized liberally to accommodate constant expansion in the electronic entertainment field. Surface mounted raceway with a removable cover is the most versatile solution, but is generally unsightly, so that many installations specify concealed raceway.

Telephone Systems for Multiple Residences

Service entrance space requirements for phone service in multiple dwelling buildings vary with the size of the building and the telephone capacity. A small apartment house three stories tall needs a clear wall space of between 122 and 180 cm (4–6 ft). A terminal (equipment) room is required only in large residential buildings. Where multiple telephone companies have the right to offer service to residents, there may be stiff competition for basement space.

In rental apartment buildings and dormitories, the

plans of all floors are similar, making it easy to run risers between floors. Cable is run in risers extending through vertically aligned closets in apartments. In a shaft other than a closet, conduit is used for easy installation, protection, and repair.

HOTEL AND MOTEL SECURITY SYSTEMS

Keys provide little more than a psychological barrier to unauthorized room access in a hotel. Electronic room locks allow the opening code to be changed with every guest in most modern hotels. They use coded pushbuttons, magnetically or punched-hole coded cards, or programmable electronic locks with coded keys.

Guest rooms often have a television and possibly a VCR. Meeting rooms may be equipped with a TV, VCR, projectors, and computer terminals. Consultants specializing in theft control have developed a number of methods to provide equipment security. One system type senses the disconnection of equipment from the power connection (wall outlet) and transmits an alarm over the power lines to an annunciator at a central location, notifying authorities immediately upon the removal of the equipment.

Hotel and motel telecommunications and data systems are important and complex. Hotels for business guests provide computer terminals and modems in an increasing number of function and guest rooms. These constantly increasing needs require adequate raceways and cabling facilities.

Business meetings and technical conferences in hotels entail very heavy electronic equipment use in conference and meeting rooms. This equipment must be installed and rearranged quickly. Access flooring and modular cabling help facilitate quick changes.

SYSTEMS FOR SCHOOLS

Intrusion alarms and security systems are now routinely part of normal school requirements. Sensors on doors and windows are arranged to trip local alarm devices and to notify police headquarters. Vandals may be frightened off by an alarm system that lights up exterior and interior building areas. Perimeter alarm detection systems are used for particularly vandal-prone areas to prevent after-hours entry. They are expensive to install, but very frequently cost-effective in preventing building damage.

Exit control alarms in schools lock doors from the outside but must be able to be opened from the inside in an emergency. When the door is opened, an audible, visible or remote alarm is triggered. Exit control alarms may have a timed bypass for keyed operation by authorized personnel that prevents the door from being held open without alarming. One type gives an immediate alarm, but takes 10 to 20 seconds of pressure before opening. This gives time for the staff to investigate who is using the door, but increases the time it takes for people to leave the area in an emergency.

Clock and Program Systems

Class-change signals are part of a master clock system. A programmable clock can control clock signals, audible bells, and other switching functions. Large-faced analog clocks are easiest to read in all ambient light situations. Digital clocks using light-emitting diodes (LEDs) must be viewed directly, not at an acute angle.

Audible devices include bells, gongs, buzzers, horns or tones reproduced on classroom loudspeakers. Tones from classroom loudspeakers are preferred, as they are clearly audible in each classroom and adjustable to the noise level in the room. The loudspeaker's sound will not be confused with fire alarm gongs or other emergency signals. The classroom loudspeaker has multiple uses and complete flexibility of programming so that special programs can be directed to selected groups of students.

Intercom Systems

In a small school, a simple wired intercom system connects various offices and outside phones in the administration offices with the paging system integrated into the school sound system. In larger buildings, a private phone system can be connected with the school sound system. This provides an intercom between staff members and offices and direct communication with classrooms either selectively or all at once. Larger systems offer paging zones, group calls, and conference calls, and can be connected with outside phone systems. Combination program/intercom controllers use direct push-button dialing and programming, eliminating switchboards and operators.

Sound Systems

A sound-paging-radio system provides the means to distribute recordings via CDs or tapes, broadcast AM/FM, or live sound to preselected areas of the school. In a simple system, a CD player with a single microphone input and single channel is distributed to all the speakers in the school. More complex systems might use three simultaneous input signals distributed to six different areas of the school.

Conventional systems use a control console with most of the input units, amplifiers, switching devices, and connections to remote loudspeakers. The inputs may be one or more AM/FM tuners, a VCR, a CD player, a tape deck, or microphones. Usually, one microphone will be located at the console, one in the principal's office, and others in the auditorium, the school office, and so forth. Microphone outlets may be placed throughout the school so that a microphone and stand can be plugged into any outlet. Loudspeakers are located in classrooms, the gymnasium, the auditorium, the cafeteria, and outdoors. Loudspeakers can be mounted flush or in surface baffles. Loudspeakers for large areas have volume controls, and can be specified with a locking cover.

Small systems can be installed in a compact desktop console. Larger systems require a console that is usually built into a desk arrangement. The interior designer should provide adequate space for the console and the person who operates it.

Electronic Teaching Equipment

The use of electronic media for teaching is growing and changing rapidly. A differentiation is generally made between passive mode and interactive mode educational computer use. Passive-mode usage makes all recorded material available to students via some form of information retrieval technology, including printing, audio, and video means. Passive-modes include both conventional and electronic library forms.

In interactive modes, each student uses a computer-teaching terminal to study at his or her own pace. The computer acts as a one-on-one tutor. Modern teaching programs sense a student's weak points and emphasize these areas in the program. By providing adequate electrical power, cable raceway, lighting, and heating, ventilating, and air-conditioning (HVAC) provisions, the building designer can try to accommodate the rapid change in computer technology.

Office Communications Systems

 Interior designers are often called upon to help update the finishes or reorganize the layout of an existing office. Within short order, it becomes obvious that the critical factor in deciding whether to rearrange the cubicles is not the aesthetic or functional issues, but the difficulty of wiring the multitude of workstations and peripheral equipment. Even the decision as to whether to replace the carpet may depend on how hard it is to move the cubicles and all their wiring out of the way. Discussions of planning options turn into arcane conversations about "UTP cables." (If you don't yet know, that's "untwisted shielded pair cables," and they're explained below.) The location of the service closets can end up driving the space plan's design. Here is an introduction to the world of office communications systems. Although new technology is always being developed, many existing facilities are making do with wiring technology from the past.

Office building communications require large amounts of space in critical locations. Planning for communications must be done simultaneously with other space planning, although exact amounts of space needed are usually not known at the planning stage. Planning must take into account changes in space use and increases in communications and data transmission services that are likely in the future. Estimates for planning are based on usable office area. Fiber optic and other technical advances reduce the equipment size and space requirements. Systems are designed for current requirements with reasonable estimates for the future based on expert advice. Some types of offices, like brokerage houses, are especially heavy users of communications systems.

The user can purchase or lease as much of the office communications system as desired, so the system may be all privately owned, owned completely by the telephone company, or some combination. Some instruments and switching equipment are used for both intercoms and outside connections.

Typically, an office building has a service entrance room or equipment room where the incoming cable or network cable enters. The service entrance room contains terminated empty conduits for expansion and data cables and a network cable splice box. Connection (network interface) cabinets connect building equipment, including phones, modems, and faxes. The service entrance room should be dry, well ventilated, and well lighted for close work in wiring and color recognition. A minimum of two 20-A duplex convenience circuits on a separate circuit should be supplied. Larger equipment rooms need space for circulation and egress as well as emergency lighting and power.

When Yelena met with the prospective client to discuss the scope of work for the office renovation, the client emphasized that the project's chief goal was to replace the patchwork of carpeting throughout the space and to repaint the walls. Other aspects included new artwork, and possibly some reorganization of the waiting area and conference rooms. Once Yelena got the job, she realized that replacing the carpet was much more complicated that she had anticipated.

The space was organized with a perimeter of enclosed and semi-enclosed offices surrounding a large central open area full of cubicles. The high-tech client had linked just about every workstation with data and power cabling, which was run through the cubicle partitions. To complicate matters, various types of cabling had been installed at various times, and connections had been spliced repeatedly. To remove and replace the carpeting, the cubicles would have to be disassembled and moved, along with their wiring.

The office technical wizard wanted to rip the whole system out and install new, state-of-the-art wiring. He was concerned that the terminations wouldn't accept another round of cutting and splicing. When the client started running some numbers, however, he realized that the budget for such a major rewiring job didn't exist. Suddenly the prospect of new carpet was gone, and Yelena found herself trying to spruce up the space with paint and artwork that accommodated the existing mismatched carpets.

Riser spaces (shafts) and riser closets are stacked vertically to carry the main cables through the building's floors. Sleeves that can be sealed and fireproofed are set in floors to connect vertically aligned closets. Communications closets are preferably separated from electrical power closets.

Cables from the riser system are connected to switching and power equipment in zone closets, also called apparatus closets. These closets need a switched ceiling light and a separate 20-A, 120V circuit with two duplex receptacles. A source of emergency power is a good idea, as it prevents phone service outages during power outages.

Satellite closets are distributed on floors as required. Satellite closets don't contain any switching or power equipment. They supply a cable-connecting and terminating facility in large, complex buildings where the riser closet space is not sufficient.

Auxiliary equipment rooms are used for extensive cross-connection or when tenants have their own private switchboard (PBX) equipment. Auxiliary equipment rooms are relatively small alcoves or closets. They need a 20- to 30-A, 120/208V circuit, plus a 20-A, 120V outlet, and a grounding point. Adequate equipment space, good lighting, and ventilation are required. The room should have absorptive acoustic material on the ceiling and on at least one wall.

Wiring is distributed horizontally between the closets and the end devices through conduit, boxes and cabinets, underfloor raceways, and over-ceiling systems. Distribution is often located in ceiling and plenum spaces and under carpets. Large volumes of wiring are required, and conduit is not often used.

OPEN OFFICE CABLING

The growth of computers and their peripheral equipment has resulted in increasing needs for connections within offices and with the rest of the world. Local area networks (LANs) are commonly found in offices to connect computers, fax modems, printers, and scanners. The proliferation of LANs has increased the need for more flexible, cost-effective cable systems with greater data capacity.

Wireless technology is becoming more common, but cabling is still the primary way office computer equipment is connected. New cable types and better ways of transferring information provide more information more quickly than before. Standardized preinstalled cable systems are widely used. The importance of handling and managing cables correctly is often overlooked, leading to serious and costly information system problems. These problems may become chronic and difficult to diagnose.

In the past, office furniture systems have been an impediment to effective cable management. Recently, the office furniture industry has begun to address the critical need for handling greater volumes of complex, vulnerable cables.

Standards for the design and installation of cable infrastructure in the United States recognize three types of communications cables. The most common is Category 5 unshielded twisted pair (UTP) cable. A second type is shielded twisted pair (STP) cable. The third type, optical fiber, is becoming more common as demand for ultra-high-speed information transfer rates increases and costs for fiber optics decrease.

Unshielded Twisted Pair Cable

Category 5 rated UTP cable has four pairs of unshielded, insulated copper wires (Fig. 40-1). Each wire is insulated, and the wires are then twisted together in pairs. The twisting limits electronic signal interference between adjacent pairs of copper wires, an effect known as crosstalk. An outer jacket covers all four pairs. UTP is relatively strong and physically durable. It can be damaged if manufacturer's instructions aren't followed, or if it is improperly installed.

Category 3 twisted pair copper cable was the unshielded cable standard for office wiring for many years. Shielded twisted pair cable (STP-A) has a higher bandwidth than Category 5 rated cable, and is less susceptible to electromagnetic interference than UTP cabling. However, STP-A cable is larger and more expensive than alternatives like optical fiber.

Electromagnetic Interference

All copper wires are susceptible to electromagnetic interference (EMI) from electric motors, generators, transformers, ballasts in fluorescent lighting fixtures, and power cables. Photocopiers and 110V circuits can also cause EMI problems. Electromagnetic interference results in computer problems, including the loss or corruption of signals.

Communications and data cabling should be kept away from transformers, large motors as found in elevators and utility rooms, and photocopiers. The cables should be spaced at least 15 cm (6 in.) from parallel 110V cable, and from laser printers and scanners, and at least 30 cm (1 ft) from fluorescent ballasts. Have the electrical engineer review the initial design drawings to ensure that all potential EMI sources are identified prior to cable installation.

Coaxial Cable

Coaxial cable (Fig. 40-2) is very resistant to electronic interference or noise. Coaxial cable typically contains a

Figure 40-2 Coaxial cable.

single wire conductor, surrounded by a layer of insulation, outer shielding conductor, and a second layer of insulation. Coaxial cable is used for high bandwidth analog systems like cable TV and radio frequency LANs. It is rarely used for desktop communications, due to its basic incompatibility with voice systems.

Fiber Optic Cables

Fiber optic cables are used for installations with very heavy transmission loads, with video systems, and for applications needing high-security, low-noise, and broad bandwidths. Fiber optic cable has a core of glass or plastic filament encased in a protective sheath. It is used to transmit data that have been converted into light pulses, as opposed to the electrical signals carried by Category 5 and other copper cables. It has an exceptional capacity for carrying high volumes of data at very high speed. The two major classifications of fiber optic cables are multimode and single mode.

Single-mode fiber optic cables are primarily used for long distances, greater than 2 km (1.2 miles), and high bandwidth applications. Multimode fiber optic cabling (Fig. 40-3) is used for shorter distances of less than 2 km (1.2 miles) and applications that have multiple connection requirements. Multimode fiber optic cabling is the most common fiber optic cabling used within commercial office buildings.

As fiber optic cables transmit light impulses rather than electrical energy, they are immune to EMI. This characteristic also provides a level of security from electronic eavesdropping. There is no risk of fiber optic cable generating static electricity or sparks, which can be an important safety consideration in some factory office environments or clean rooms. Like Category 5 cable, fiber optic cables are susceptible to damage when improper installation practices are employed. Fiber op-

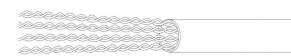

Figure 40-1 Category 5 unshielded twisted pair (UTP) cable.

Figure 40-3 Multimode fiber optic cable.

tic cable has the capacity to transmit data over great distances without any appreciable attenuation or loss of signal. Fiber optic cable is becoming the norm in new facilities or in situations where faster, higher capacity communications platforms are in use or planned for the future. Fiber optic cabling is currently more expensive than other types of wiring, but costs are going down as it becomes more common.

Wireless Systems

Wireless systems allow mobile communications inside buildings. As we discussed earlier, wireless systems currently have limitations that make them less adaptable than wired systems. Products are coming on the market with built-in antennas that make wireless technology a part of the building finishes and reduce the need for communications cabling. Ceiling panels with high-performance, low-profile antennas embedded inside provide invisible connections in buildings and full capability for voice and data applications.

CABLING OPEN OFFICE FURNITURE SYSTEMS

In designing an open office space and selecting a furniture system, the interior designer should look for the ease and flexibility of cable entry into furniture from the floor, ceiling, perimeter walls, and building support columns. Look for the ability to lay cables into the furniture, even at corners and intersections, without risk of damaging by pulling through apertures or grommets within the furniture. A good internal panel construction will have the facility to manage safely a variety of cables that require generous bend radii and adequate horizontal support.

Select furniture that provides the ability to route large quantities of cabling horizontally and vertically, with storage capacity for excess cable. Cables should be able to route into panels connected at right angles, off-module. Look for internal panel thicknesses that are deep enough for surface-mounted terminals, consolidation points, and preterminated cables.

Look for panels with methods for separating copper data cables from electrical power conduit to avoid EMI. Access to cabling and distribution points should be convenient and not require special tools or disruption of the workplace.

Specify an office furniture system that can accommodate the installation of preterminated data cables, particularly those with oversized or unusually shaped terminals or connectors. The system should meet requirements for hoteling, shared offices, and teaming by providing immediate access to voice, data, and networks connections. Data terminals accessible at any height are a desirable feature.

For cost-effective open office layout changes, seek generic or nondedicated components that can be reused in other applications. Look for systems with a minimal number of parts or pieces, or with universal parts required to attach panels in different configurations. Select systems that have the ability to change partition height to increase privacy or increase visible interaction without removal of panels, cabling, and ceiling feeds. Add-ons that accept ceiling power feeds and carry cables horizontally and vertically are a good feature.

Seek out the ability to substitute panels of different dimensions without cutting or disconnecting cables. Systems that allow a change from glazed to fabric-covered panels with cabling are also desirable. Easy installation of new cabling for new equipment and the safe removal of terminated cables without disconnection or cutting out jacks and boxes also add flexibility.

The ability to store extra cable runs inside the panels for future expansion may save 50 to 100 percent in additional costs for adding them later. Look for easy access to cables and consolidation points housed within the furniture, and acceptance for fiber optics to be added later.

Office Cabling Distribution

The permissible distance from the telecommunications closet to each workstation determines how office cubicles can be arrayed. Voice and data communications are run between the telecommunications closet and individual workstations in an open office by either home run wiring, which is hard wired, or by zone distribution, where the individual equipment is wired back to a local control area, which in turn is wired to the telecommunications closet. Home run cable distribution provides an uninterrupted cable connection between the telecommunications closet and the outlet or connector that connects an electronic device. Home run distribution minimizes the risk of signal loss due to bad connections. However, the signal decreases with the increasing distance from the telecommunications closet (attenuation), so home run distribution has very specific standards for the maximum length of cable runs in open offices. This affects the office layout and placement of equipment.

Underfloor systems are undergoing changes in the way that cabling is connected in a number of important ways. Currently, it is standard practice to home run the cable connecting each and every PC to a network within the office back to a telephone or communications closet. As electronics become smaller, it may be possible to place network devices directly below the floor, and to zone groups of computers together, running a single fiber optic or copper cable from a group of adjacent workstations, rather than eight, ten, or more separate cables, back to the closet.

The increasing standardization of cable across all the telecommunications industries, coupled with the increasingly widespread use of underfloor systems in office buildings and other facilities, is likely to produce yet another important change. Standardization and acceptance will push manufacturers of underfloor products to develop and market fully integrated, modular systems, which will reduce the expense of access floors and eliminate many wire-management problems.

Zone cable distribution is an alternative for offices that require frequent workstation reconfiguration to accommodate new equipment, changes in work patterns, and individual user needs. The zone creates an intermediate distribution point between the telecommunications closet and the computer or other end device. Modular patch cords connect the distribution point to the device. This avoids pulling longer or additional cables from the telecommunications closet when equipment is added or moved. The result is less cost and disruption after the initial installation. However, the multiport connections at distribution points create a risk of signal interference.

The zone cabling distribution point is a multiuser telecommunications outlet assembly (MUTOA) between the telecommunications closet and the electronic device. A MUTOA is located close to the cluster of workstations it serves. A distribution point is installed on a perimeter wall, a building column, in a raised floor, or in the systems furniture panel if there is room. The distribution point must be readily accessible, and can't be above the ceiling, where access is limited and there is a risk of exposure to interference from power cables and fluorescent lights.

 Wall-mounted distribution points may be unsightly. Using a systems furniture panel with removable surface tiles that can be mounted flush against the wall can hide them, improving both access and aesthetics. When the distribution point is within systems furniture, the furniture must be permanently attached to the building surface by anchoring to a permanent wall or building column. The preferred location is in the same panel as the wall or ceiling feed, avoiding disruption if other adjacent panels are later moved.

Connecting the Building to the Systems Furniture

The cabling from the telecommunications closet is connected to the systems furniture through the ceiling, the floor, a perimeter wall, or an interior structural column. In general, the amount of exposed cable should be minimized to avoid inconvenience and possible injuries. Mechanical covers can be installed to shield cables running across floors. Nylon or plastic spiral wrap can be used to protect cables at furniture exit points. This also simplifies removal, maintenance, and installation of new cables.

Ceiling Entry

Data cables are often routed horizontally through the ceiling plenum. Fire-rated jackets may be required by building codes. The cables are supported in trays or cable managers. They must be more than 30 cm (1 ft) from fluorescent ballasts to avoid EMI. Ceiling cables gently drop vertically into the furniture through a conduit housed in a pole or ceiling feed (Fig. 40-4), which is usually integrated into furniture and which may be supplied by the furniture manufacturer. Ideally, all panels should be able to accept a ceiling feed. When

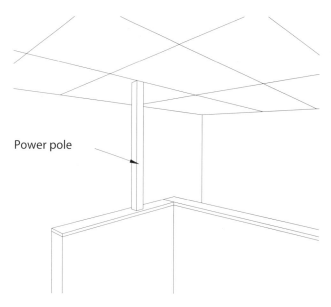

Figure 40-4 Ceiling entry.

Power pole

the ceiling feed is restricted to a dedicated panel, corner connection point, or end of panel run, flexibility is limited. For example, the entry point may end up directly below a ceiling light fixture, heating, ventilating, and air-conditioning (HVAC) register, ceiling support, or other obstacle. Entry near one end of a panel allows the panel to be turned 180 degrees to give a choice of two positions.

Apertures (portholes) in ceiling tiles and panels can kink or stretch cable, even when grommets are used. The number of openings needed to avoid tight entries must be carefully considered. A lay-in cable entry using poles with snap-off covers avoids this problem and also helps with preterminated cables with jacks or boxes. Poles must include a physical barrier between power conduit and communications cabling.

One way to get wiring from the ceiling to the desktop is through stacked sections of frames that rise to just below the ceiling. This offers a very large area for cable to enter the panels. Well-designed stacked panel sections can be installed around the existing ceiling feed pole without having to disconnect communications and power cables. Selecting furniture systems with good ability to distribute cable horizontally and vertically can minimize the number of ceiling connections, allowing large clusters to be fed from a single pole.

Floor Entry

Cabling can enter systems furniture from a floor monument fixed by the building architecture. Buildings with cellular or similar floor feed systems tend to limit the entry points to a specific building grid. Access is often not according to the floor plan, and outlets end up several inches from the location designated on the plans.

Raised floor systems offer flexibility with access at almost any point (Fig. 40-5). Horizontal distribution in the systems furniture is consequently less important, but good vertical distribution is still required. Select panels with flexible cable entry points, preferably through the bottom of the panel. Ideally, all panels should be able to accept cable entry.

Cable can be poked through the floor slab, but this is severely limited by building obstacles, is expensive, and can cause structural damage if too many holes are poked. Service access may have to be provided from the floor below, disrupting other departments or tenants.

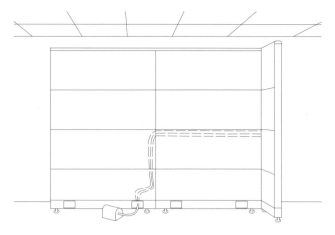

Figure 40-5 Floor entry.

Perimeter Wall and Column Entry

Cable entry into systems office furniture from perimeter walls is very common and may be cost-effective. In some cases, however, entry through walls may be difficult. It may be hard to position a run of panels parallel to the wall if they are connected to a wall outlet. If the panels don't have removable tiles, they must be set back from the wall by several inches to allow room for plugging into the outlet and to accommodate the bend radii of the entering cables. This wastes floor space.

Removable panel tiles (Fig. 40-6) with ample internal cavities allow panels to be positioned against the wall, with access from the other side of the panel. If the panel is perpendicular to the wall, it can be connected through the nearest side or bottom. Panels with base raceways typically permit cable entry at a fixed point,

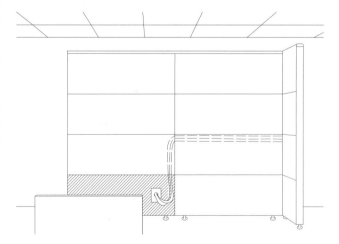

Figure 40-6 Panels with removable tiles.

and may not be ideal for a wall outlet. Entry from a structural column is similar to that from a perimeter wall. Some manufacturers offer partial-width tiles for exposed areas of entry panels.

CABLE TERMINATION AND TESTING

Cables are terminated with an appropriate jack or connector at both ends. At the workstation end, they are typically installed in cover plates or in various surface mounted housings. Both ends of all communications cables should be labeled to simplify future identification.

Terminated cable is run through the furniture and dropped into the worksurface through an opening in the panel surface. The opening has a faceplate in a prepunched cutout on the panel surface or tile, or a surface mount concealed within the panel, accessed by removing a surface tile. Terminations should be located where they are not likely to be damaged by coffee, feet, or vacuum cleaners. They should not be mounted face-up.

Many varieties of surface terminal plates are available from systems furniture manufacturers for Category 5 cable termination in furniture panels. Furniture manufacturers usually have optional prepunched knockouts in surface tiles or raceway covers. Some furniture allows surface mounted cover plates and office box type housing, which are preferable to attaching surface mounted units to the surface with double-sided tape or screwing them directly into the surface. Brackets may be available to mount housings inside panels.

The panel should be thick enough to preserve the minimum bend radii of terminated cables, especially behind the data plate. Some panels in systems with mechanically fastened construction can accept oversize wall-mounted boxes. Grommets avoid cuts and abrasions to the cables.

Terminations for optical fibers are also mounted on or inside furniture panels. The technology for optical fiber termination has improved to make it easier, quicker, and somewhat less expensive than in the past, which will help increase the use of fiber optics.

CORD MANAGEMENT

Not all offices consist of large arrays of cubicles. Alternative offices and hoteling often have flexible, free-standing furniture arrangements. Many home offices and private business offices have a computer, fax, copier, printer, and a couple of telephones perched on or next to the desk. Inevitably, a jungle of cables drapes down the back of the desk and onto the floor below, inviting entire communities of dust bunnies to take up residence. Sometimes the cables snake out across the room to trip up the unwary. Switching cables in and out of equipment can be a nightmare.

Keeping cables neat and accessible is a challenge, and safety is always an issue when electricity is involved. The safest way to keep cords out of reach is to place the computer workstation or desk against a wall, so that the cords are not in traffic paths. Grounded outlets and surge protection are essential, and an uninterruptible power source is good protection against data loss.

Several products are on the market that address this tangled issue. One is a canvas bag that holds all the cords neatly together. Another consists of a long plastic bar that attaches to the back of the desk to lift cords out of the way. Each of these accessories will hold about six cords. A coil that wraps itself around bundles of cables keeps them visible and organized but tidy.

Whenever possible, the number of cords should be reduced. Cords can often be shortened, or at least wound up and secured. Labeling cords will help when equipment is unplugged and reconnected, and little books of number stickers are available for this purpose. Sometimes you can write the name of the equipment directly on the cord.

Any cords with broken insulation must be replaced. Avoid winding cords together, as this can lead to undesirable heat build-up caused by an electromagnetic field being created in the cords. It is best to keep computer cables away from other electric wires to avoid interference. Be sure not to overload a circuit, which will cause the circuit breaker to trip repeatedly.

Many furniture manufacturers are addressing the need for flexible furniture configurations that deliver the power and route the wiring in an organized and tidy way. One option for controlling cable clutter is a corner power column that is installed below the work surface. The column plugs into a wall or floor receptacle or is hard-wired. The outlet panel rests on the desktop. Corner power columns can also be installed vertically above the work surface top. Another option is a power/communication dome, which is a small dome that sits above a grommet in a desktop, with electrical and data outlets on four sides. Strips of power and data outlets can also be mounted below a desktop or behind a modesty panel.

CONFERENCE ROOMS AND MULTIMEDIA

Computer video and other audiovisual (AV) presentation equipment is widespread in hotel meeting rooms, office conference spaces, and educational facilities. Internet access is becoming standard, especially in educational facilities. Frequently, the presenter is from outside the organization and may not be familiar with the equipment. We probably have all seen the befuddled efforts of a guest speaker faced with unknown and unpredictable AV equipment. Here are some guidelines on making the controls for the ever-growing collection of equipment easy to find and use.

In corporate conferencing centers, presentation equipment is being designed to facilitate computer presentations and networking. Wireless keyboards can be placed on lecterns. The keyboards use labeled touch panels rather than buttons, which are easier to see, understand, and hit accurately in a darkened space. The keyboard combines all of the controls for the varied equipment in a unified way. Lighting controls should be included with the other controls but also mounted on the wall, with both sets of controls tied together. Large rotary knobs for volume control for both live speech and recorded programs are easier to operate than small buttons. The lectern can include a preview screen for the presenter. Pop-up controls in the main screen panel are simple to understand, and don't get lost. Some of the less-often adjusted backup equipment can be hidden out of the way

Meeting and conference rooms are designed for effortless conversing with or without a sound system. Here the goal is to control reverberation, with no flutter from parallel hard surfaces and no focusing from concave hard surfaces. These rooms may also have special equipment for teleconferencing and equipment for projection from slides, film, videotape, or television. Liquid crystal display (LCD) projectors are now bright enough to be used without substantially dimming out the room. Front projection screens generally still need a lower light level than rear projection screens.

Conference rooms should have sound-absorbent material applied to walls between seated and standing heights. On the ceiling, limit absorption to the perimeter so that the center can reinforce and distribute sound. Meeting and conference rooms usually use a distributed loudspeaker system recessed in the ceiling.

Teleconferencing and videoconferencing rooms operate like broadcast studios. Acoustic control is produced through the use of sound-absorbent materials applied so that there is some in each of the room's principal axes. Unequal application results in coloration of the sound, which favors certain frequencies over others. All walls and ceilings should have a similar average absorption coefficient when two surfaces of a pair are taken together. The acoustic treatment and its facing should be uniform and visually acceptable for digitized video transmission. Special low-frequency absorption may be needed, especially in small rooms with relatively thin sound-absorbing materials.

Data/digital projectors for conference rooms are frequently used to show presentations, spreadsheets, and video clips to large groups. Also known as LCD projectors, they can be permanently installed, sometimes along with a networked computer. Ceiling mounts are installed into the ceiling to hold a projector. This option is more expensive than using a table, but it hides cable mess and can reduce shadows.

Computer-based tools include interactive whiteboards, electronic whiteboards, and room-control systems. Interactive whiteboards combine a computer and LCD projector with a traditional whiteboard. A computer presentation can be projected onto the board and marked or changed on a touch-sensitive screen. A whiteboard application allows notes and markings to be captured as electronic data and then saved into a file, reducing the work of transcribing and distributing notes. Electronic whiteboards record the notes written on the whiteboard surface to a PC. They typically do not have computer-control capabilities.

A plasma display panel (PDP) is a flat-panel display that allows you to view your computer image on a larger scale than a standard monitor, without the depth. The PDPs are only about 13 cm (5 in.) deep, and range in size from 107 to 127 cm (42–50 in.) on the diagonal. They produce a crisp, bright, distortion-free image. An interactive overlay adds touch control and annotation capabilities to the PDP.

Advanced room-control systems allow the operation of a wide range of electronic equipment from a single, integrated system. Audio, video, projection, lighting, screens, shades and blinds, and security and communications systems can all be controlled from one central location (Fig. 40-7). Audiovisual devices located in conference and meeting rooms can be networked through a control system, connected to the Internet, and controlled from a touch screen. Teleconferencing broadcast rooms can be linked into the system. Touch panels can also be controlled through radio-frequency wireless systems, allowing freedom of movement through walls, indoors, or outside.

Audioconferencing phones include a telephone and often several microphones strategically placed through-

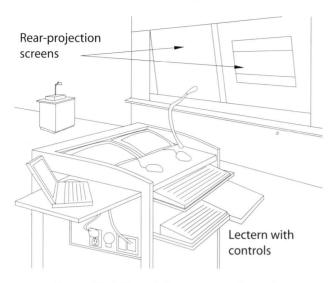

Rear-projection screens

Lectern with controls

Figure 40-7 Presentation room equipment.

out the room. These phones typically provide full-duplex audio, which means that a natural, multiparty conversation can occur (as opposed to half-duplex audio on a standard phone, which often clips one party's conversation). Data conferencing allows computer users to share text, images, and data in real time.

A videoconference connects two or more participants at different sites linked via telephone or data lines to transmit audio and video. Videoconferencing cameras must be located to see and be seen by all participants. Light colors and low reflection finishes are best for videoconferencing.

The design problems for multimedia conference rooms are similar to those for office systems. The location of the equipment and the length of cable runs are important planning issues. The cable from the presenter's computer to a ceiling-mounted LCD projector is very thick, with a big bend radius. Good quality cables, which have higher quality shielding, give a better picture but are expensive.

Audiovisual equipment includes audio amplifiers and speakers that can be connected to a computer to enhance a presentation, and VCRs or DVD players that are useful for showing videos or DVDs. A VCR or DVD player can be attached to a projector for a larger image. Technician desks provide a central location for the audiovisual tech and control equipment for presentations.

It is common for multimedia presentations to be scheduled in rooms that were not designed with AV equipment. Sometimes the equipment is wheeled in on a cart, with wires dangling and spare parts rolling around. Multimedia cabinets are designed to integrate meeting, classroom, or presentation equipment into a

compact and well-organized unit. More advanced than the standard AV cart, mobile multimedia cabinets are aesthetically pleasing and come prewired to simplify installation and use.

Boardroom tables are generally impressive in both size and design. They are often the featured element of the meeting room for the business' top people. Boardroom tables frequently include microphones and are set up for AV presentations (Fig. 40-8). The integration of the electronic equipment into the table itself allows the space to retain its impressive appearance.

The design of boardroom tables requires knowledge of the number of people, the sight lines to presentations, the size of the chairs, and the viewing angles. The design process must begin early in the design of the AV system. Boardroom tables and desks can be prewired with electrical outlets and network hubs to eliminate untidy cords and provide ready access to required connections. Connections to tables are made through floor boxes, bases, legs, or wire access doors. Tabletop access doors allow electric, data, phone, microphone, and control panel connections under the table. Pop-up spring mechanisms provide tabletop access for electricity, microphone, and data, and disappear into the table when not in use. Conference tables can be fitted with gooseneck microphones that pull out of the table. Raised center sections are used to accommodate speakers when they can't be located in the ceiling. Tables are wired after installation. Some lightweight tables click together to allow reconfiguration without disturbing electrical connections.

Although some speaker's lecterns are quite simple, they can also be very complex pieces of furniture, with controls for lights, clocks, and microphones. Wiring is

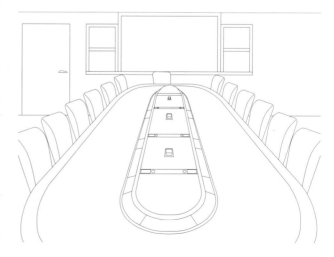

Figure 40-8 Boardroom table.

usually through a floor box. A lectern can be fitted with a monitor and mouse for each presentation screen, as well as multiple pullout keyboards to support PC, Macintosh, and Unix platforms. Plug-in receptacles located near a foldout panel allow laptops to be connected. A slide-out door can hide a document camera.

Custom designed wall units can unify monitors, plasma screens, speakers, lights, cameras, and other equipment. Wall units require good ventilation, as they get very hot inside. It is imperative to get technical information on the equipment early enough for these units to be designed.

When designing a multimedia conferencing space, consider that too tight a program can limit flexibility later on. Spaces are often used in unexpected ways, so a multipurpose space should not have fixed seating and risers. The design should be changeable, flexible, and modular, to accommodate technological changes. Acoustics and lighting must be integrated into the design from the start.

VIII
Part

FIRE SAFETY

Principles of
Fire Safety

● ● ●

Each year, 12,000 lives are lost in building fires in the United States. An additional 300,000 people are injured, often seriously and painfully. According to the National Fire Protection Association (NFPA), residential fires lead all other categories of building fires, both in the number of blazes and the cost of property lost. The latest available statistics show an annual total of 407,000 residential fires in the United States. Nationwide, there were more than 3500 deaths and 16,000 injuries from residential fires in 1999. Annual property losses from residential fires amount to $4.5 billion.

Poorly designed interiors, and in particular their materials, have been responsible for many lives lost. The 1942 Cocoanut Grove Club fire in Boston, Massachusetts, killed 491 people, most from toxic fume inhalation. Eighty-four people died (82 from smoke inhalation) and 679 were injured at the MGM Grand Hotel fire in Las Vegas, Nevada, in 1980. Of the 52 pieces of evidence that the NFPA collected from the MGM, 34 were interior finish or furniture materials.

We tend to be most aware of fires in large, high profile buildings. However, people in low-income neighborhoods are 20 times more likely to be injured or die in a house fire than people in higher income areas, according to a study in the *New England Journal of Medicine*. A Dallas-based study by Dr. Gregory Istre revealed that chil-

dren, African-Americans, and the elderly suffer the greatest risk in house fires. Poor residents in small, wood-framed, single-family houses are the most susceptible to fire. Poor people are also more likely to use space heaters and less likely to have smoke detectors. Where wood-framed houses are less common in poor communities, single-family homes are less regulated than multifamily housing units and the source of more fire problems.

When people are caught in a fire, their lungs and respiratory passages may be burned by hot air and their skin severely damaged by thermal radiation. Some deaths occur when panic causes people to push, crowd, and trample others. Other times, panicking people make irrational decisions, like running back into a burning building to save belongings.

Even though we think of burns as the primary injury resulting from a fire, the most common cause of death by fire is suffocation or carbon dioxide poisoning due to the dense accumulation of smoke. Victims of fires are often suffocated by air depleted of oxygen and full of poisonous gases. Normally, oxygen constitutes about 21 percent of the air we breathe. When other gases replace the oxygen consumed by the fire, we suffer from progressively serious symptoms. If the oxygen is reduced to 15 percent of the air, we experience diminished muscular skills, making it harder for us to get out of the building. Faulty judgment and fatigue set in when oxygen is only 10 to 14 percent of the air. When a mere 6 to 10 percent of the air is oxygen, physical collapse occurs, but we can still be revived with oxygen if we are rescued in time.

Buildings concentrate fuel that can sustain a fire. Wood building structures, wood paneling, and plastic insulating materials all will burn. Buildings often contain oil, natural gas, gasoline, paints, rubber, chemicals, or other highly flammable materials.

Buildings offer many possible sources of ignition for a fire. Defective furnaces, sparks from a fireplace, leaky chimneys, and unattended stoves can all start fires. Loose electrical connections and overloaded electrical wiring are common sources of fires.

Many fire deaths are caused by careless use of matches and cigarettes. Cigarettes cause an estimated 1,000 deaths and 2,400 injuries annually in the United States.

People often believe that they can heat their home more cheaply with an inexpensive portable electric space heater than by purchasing expensive home heating oil. Many people are unaware of fuel-assistance programs that could help them pay heating bills. Even though electricity is expensive, and often inefficient, the low purchase price of a space heater offers a convenient alternative. The U.S. Consumer Product Safety Commission says that heating devices cause 12 percent of residential fires. In 1997, portable heaters caused 5400 of the 406,500 fires nationally, killing about 130 people and injuring 430. In four days in November 2000, the misuse of space heaters resulted in three fires that killed six people in communities surrounding Boston, Massachusetts.

A building is like a stove in that it contains the fire and encourages its growth. The building concentrates heat and flammable combustion gases. Vertical passages through the building that are open to the fire create strong convective drafts that fan the flames. As the fire spreads up through the building, it finds new sources of fuel.

Buildings often hold dense concentrations of people and can subject them to the heat and gases from the fire. The design of the building may restrict their ability to escape. The building's design may also serve as a barrier to firefighters. Firefighting ladders can only reach up seven stories, so in tall buildings, firefighters must use the stairs. Very broad, low buildings can put the fire beyond the reach of fire hoses. Firefighters are exposed to excessive heat, poison gases, and explosions. They are in danger of great heights, toppling walls, and collapsing roofs and floors. The loss of firefighter's lives is a tragic result of fires.

COMBUSTION

For a fire to exist, you need three things: fuel, oxygen, and high temperatures (Fig. 41-1). Fires begin when supplies of fuel and oxygen are brought together at a sufficiently high temperature for combustion. The fire consumes fuel and oxygen as it burns, and gives off gases, particles, and large quantities of heat.

Oxidation is a process in which molecules of fuel are combined with molecules of oxygen. The result is a mixture of gases and the release of energy. Oxidation is how our bodies turn food into energy. Rust is the oxidation of iron. The process of combustion involves a chemical change that releases energy as heat and light. When oxygen mixes with a combustible substance rapidly and continually, you have a fire. Smoke is produced when incompletely burned particles are suspended in the air.

The best way to avoid a tragic fire loss is to prevent fires from starting. Fires need fuel, heat, and oxygen. Break that fire triangle, and a fire can't ignite. Limiting one element of the fire triangle (fuel, oxygen, or high temperature) prevents the fire from starting or puts it out. Fire suppression systems can work by covering the fuel or by displacing the oxygen with another gas, thus limiting the supply of oxygen. High temperatures can be controlled by cold water from sprinkler systems. However, the primary way that we strive to prevent and control fire in a building is by controlling the fuel: the building's structure and contents.

There are a variety of ways to ignite a fire. Chemical combustion, also known as spontaneous combustion, occurs when some chemicals within a building reach the point where they can ignite at ordinary temperatures. Chemical combustion happens when combustible ma-

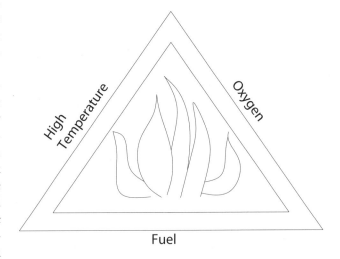

Figure 41-1 The fire triangle.

terials are saturated with chemicals and rapidly produce heat. The process of chemical combustion depends on having enough oxygen to support the fire but not enough to lower the temperature. When the chemical-saturated materials are protected by their immediate surroundings, as for example oily rags in a metal garbage can in the sun, the fumes are contained while the temperature rises to reach combustible levels.

Electrical fires are usually caused by resistance heating appliances or space-heating equipment, although induction, arcing, static electricity, or other electrical processes ignite some electrical fires. Heating specialists blame most fires in which space heaters play a role on the building's wiring. Low-income housing stock, in particular, often has old, inadequate wiring, and people tend to overload the outlets they have. Extension cords running all over the house can result in a lot of problems. The situation is compounded when a space heater draws a huge amount of amperage and overloads old wiring. Fires can also start when a space heater is placed too close to combustible material like curtains or bedding. The heaters should never be left on when everyone is asleep or has left the building.

Lightning is an infrequent source of ignition, but is enormously destructive. Tall buildings and buildings in exposed locations are particularly vulnerable. A lightning strike averages 200 million V and 30,000 A. It goes through a grounded object in less than one one-thousandth of a second.

A lightning protection system safeguards a building in the event of a lightning strike by providing a continuous metallic path for the high-voltage static electrical charge into the solid ground. A typical residential lightning system consists of three parts: air terminals (lightning rods), conductors, and ground terminals. In many areas, it should be supplemented with a surge arrester installed at the electrical service panel. Manufacturers of lightning protection equipment sell only to Underwriters Laboratories (UL) listed installers.

Building codes and zoning ordinances regulate the combustibility of materials in different areas of a city, and also the conditions for storage of flammable and explosive substances in or near buildings. Building maintenance personnel must make sure that rubbish is stored safely and removed frequently. Firefighters and fire underwriters (insurers) inspect buildings periodically, looking for accumulated combustible materials. Heating devices, chimneys, electrical systems, electrical devices, and hazardous industrial processes are controlled especially tightly. Smoking is now prohibited by law in many kinds of places, including gas stations, some industrial plants, and auditoriums.

PRODUCTS OF COMBUSTION

The thermal products of a fire are flame and heat, and people exposed to them are subject to burns, shock, dehydration, heat exhaustion, and the blocking of the respiratory tract by fluid. Flames and heat are responsible for about one-quarter of the deaths from building fires.

Most fire deaths, however, result from the nonthermal products of combustion, including smoke and other gases, which can usually be seen or smelled. Smoke is made of droplets of flammable tars and small particles of carbon suspended in gases. Smoke irritates the eyes and nasal passages and sometimes blinds or chokes a person.

In addition to displacing oxygen, the gases produced by a fire may be poisonous. These gases are sometimes invisible and other times make up part of the smoke we see. Gases that occur without visible smoke are difficult to detect. Some of these are directly toxic and all are dangerous, as they displace oxygen. As you know, carbon monoxide is a deadly, invisible, odorless gas. It is often the most common product of combustion.

Carbon dioxide gas is produced in large quantities in fires. It rapidly overstimulates breathing and causes the lungs to swell. Other gases found in smoke are hydrogen sulfide, sulfur dioxide, ammonia, oxides of nitrogen, cyanide, and phosgene. Burning polyvinyl chloride (PVC) produces hydrogen chloride gas.

Smoke from burning plastics presents special problems. Burning PVC produces up to 500 times as much smoke per square foot of exposed surface area as red oak during the first three minutes. Most plastics are synthesized petroleum distillates. This "molded gasoline" burns faster and hotter than other materials. A smoldering plastic can decompose and emit poisonous gas before combustion occurs and without people being aware that there is a fire.

Burning chemicals present a danger to firefighters, who must protect themselves with breathing apparatus. A fire with decomposing plastics can cause lung and pulmonary damage, and may cause disorientation and loss of the sense of smell. Respiratory failure can follow. Toxic chemicals whose individual levels are below lethal can still be deadly in combination. Repeated exposure is especially dangerous. Some chemicals are still a danger after a fire is out.

Plastic materials are found in furniture, carpet, draperies, wall coverings, plumbing systems, electrical wiring, and other products and equipment. About 10,000 new chemicals are introduced each year, and the hazards related to their behavior in a fire are unknown.

Polyvinyl chloride is a plastic used for electrical wiring insulation, electrical fixtures, interior plastic plumbing, and in office copy machines and other equipment. Decomposition of PVC produces over 60 gases, including hydrogen chloride, phosgene, and some carcinogens. Hydrogen chloride incapacitates a person, who may then succumb to carbon dioxide poisoning from smoke. Phosgene gas, a gas used in chemical warfare, is produced when PVC wiring insulation is subjected to electrical arcing in transformers and control panels during fires in commercial buildings.

Urea formaldehyde foam doesn't combust readily unless subjected to the intense heat of an extensive fire. However, when it does burn, it produces hydrogen cyanide gas in large quantities.

FIRE SAFETY CODES

In your practice as an interior designer, you will certainly find many occasions when you have to check the building codes for fire safety requirements. Whether you are specifying a fabric for a commercial project or checking a floor plan for the number, size, and location of exits, you will rely on applicable state and local code requirements. Fire safety codes govern how spaces are planned and how materials are used. They dictate the location and number of fire alarms and exit signs. Sprinkler system requirements affect the layout of ceiling designs and lighting. In fact, fire safety provisions are probably the most common building code requirements that an interior designer will need to respect.

Modern building codes first evolved as responses to devastating fires and have gradually come to include many other health and safety issues. Codes require a permit before construction. Plans are submitted, checked, and approved by the building department. Depending upon the size, type and location of the building, an architect or engineer's stamp may be required for approval. In many communities, fire department officials also review the plans before the building permit is granted. Inspections during construction by the building inspector verify that the construction meets the code. Fire department inspectors also visit the site. The design professional in charge of the project is ultimately responsible for making sure that the design meets all applicable codes. As the interior designer, you must be familiar with the codes for your project's location, and must make sure that your design complies. Failure to do so can result in costly mistakes, delays in construction, and a very unhappy client.

As we discussed earlier, there are three established model building codes in use in different regions of the United States; and a fourth, the new *International Build-*

ing Code (IBC), was recently introduced by the International Code Council (ICC). The *National Building Code* (NBC) is primarily used in the northeast United States. The *Uniform Building Code* (UBC) is used in the central and western United States, while the southeastern states use the *Standard Building Code* (SBC). The IBC is the first uniform U.S. code, but its adoption by all the states may take some time.

Each model code organization has its own fire prevention code. The *Life Safety Code®*, also known as NFPA 101®, is the most widely used fire code in the United States and in several other countries. It is revised every three years, but some jurisdictions may use older editions. The *Life Safety Code* is not a building code. Its purpose is to establish minimum requirements to provide a reasonable degree of safety from fire in buildings and structures. It concentrates on problems involving the removal of all persons from a building fire zone. NFPA 101 references additional standards publications, including NFPA 80, *Standard for Fire Doors and Windows*, and NFPA 220, *Standard on Types of Building Construction*.

The first part of the *Life Safety Code* discusses occupancies, means of egress, and fire protection. The rest of the text is divided by occupancy classifications for both new and existing buildings. There is an appendix that expands on the code's provisions and offers additional valuable information. Some states and cities in the United States have stricter standards than the *Life Safety Code*. These include the Boston Fire Code, and the fire codes of California, Massachusetts, New Jersey, New York City, and New York State.

Another code that is important for fire safety is the *National Electrical Code* (NEC), which is also produced by the NFPA. The NEC ensures the safety of persons and the safeguarding of buildings and their contents from hazards arising from the use of electricity for light, heat, and power. Fire safety provisions are also found in the *Safety Code for Elevators and Escalators* published by the American National Standards Institute (ANSI).

Building codes may differ in detail, but most are organized in the same way. They begin by defining categories of use or occupancy. They also define types of construction according to the building's degree of fire resistance and combustibility. The classification of the building's construction is given according to the fire resistance of major components, including the structural frame, exterior bearing walls, and nonbearing walls. Interior bearing walls, permanent partitions, floor, ceiling and roof assemblies, stairways, and shaft enclosures are all considered.

Interiors projects that are affected by construction types and building sizes include ones that relocate walls or add a stairway or other structural work. Each construction type assigns structural elements a minimum fire protection rating. This is the number of hours the structural element must be able to resist fire without being affected by flame, heat, or hot gases. It is essentially a fire endurance rating. We look at these ratings in more detail shortly.

The primary structural element that an interior designer may be involved with is an interior wall, either load-bearing or non-load-bearing. The designer's work may also affect firewalls and party walls, smoke barriers, and shaft enclosures. Interior designers frequently work with columns, floor and ceiling assemblies, and roof/ceiling assemblies.

To be classified a certain construction type, a building must meet the minimum standards for every structural element in that type. When you change existing interior structural elements or add new ones, you need to know the construction type of the building. If the additions aren't consistent with the existing building materials, they could reduce the entire building classification. This would reduce building safety and could affect building insurance and liability.

The goal of the code requirements is to protect the building from fire and to contain the fire long enough for people to evacuate the building safely. Building codes set forth height and area limits in relation to the occupancy or use of the building and the type of construction. They establish standards for structural design and for the construction of walls, floors, and roofs. The codes detail requirements for fire protection systems and means of emergency egress. Building codes specify minimum standards. They can't cover all the possible aspects of a building's design, as there are simply too many variables.

Where construction is required to be fire resistant, it must have one-hour fire-resistant construction throughout. Unprotected construction has no requirements for fire resistance, except for shaft and exit enclosures or where the building code requires protection of exit walls due to the proximity to the property line.

Building codes are generally performance-based, stipulating how a particular component or system must function without necessarily specifying the means to be employed to achieve the required results. They refer to standards established by the American Society for Testing and Materials (ASTM), ANSI, and various other technical societies and trade associations to indicate the properties required in a material or component, and the methods of testing to substantiate the performance of products. The American National Standards Institute (ANSI), establishes product standards that are often cited in product specifications. The American Society for Testing and materials (ASTM) also establishes tests, and publishes thousands of test procedures that describe how the test must be set up, how materials are to be prepared, and the length of the test. The results for ASTM tests are frequently listed in a product's specifications. The Underwriters Laboratories (UL) performs testing, approves building materials and assemblies, and publishes the results in the *UL Building Materials Directory*. As you already know, the UL label is frequently found on electrical appliances.

Codes often relax prescriptions when an active fire suppression system is designed into the building. Size limits may be exceeded in a sprinklered building, or when a building is divided by firewalls into separate areas, none of which individually exceeds the size limit. Detailed computer analysis of fire spread and occupant evaluation for a given design may also allow greater distances to exits, larger open floor areas, and alternative construction methods. This performance-based analysis approach to design requires close cooperation between designers and fire code enforcement officials.

There are variations among jurisdictions about the need for fire safety systems that provide redundant levels of protection. Some jurisdictions require sprinklers in almost all buildings, and others allow trade-offs in the codes for sprinklered buildings. New products and more advanced tests and computer simulations may bring about more accuracy in representing what would happen in a real fire. This could streamline the type of fire protection and prevention that is possible.

Design for Fire Safety

When we design a building to resist the start and spread of a fire, we not only protect the building itself and its contents but, more importantly, we protect the lives of the people who occupy the building. To react safely to a fire emergency, you need early warning, the means to extinguish a small fire, and at least two ways out of the building. Once a fire has started in a building, you may have only a few minutes to get out safely. A fire can spread at the rate of 4.6 meters (15 ft) per second. Smoke spreads fast and can overcome people in moments. You may not be able to see because of the smoke, and you could be having trouble breathing. Other people in the building might be panicking, and you know you need to get to a door immediately. Will the design of the building help you, or lead you into an inferno or dead end?

OBJECTIVES FOR FIRE SAFETY

In older buildings, the goal of fire safety design decisions was to keep the fire from spreading to other buildings. With increased fire-resistant construction and control by building codes, fires are now usually confined within a single building. The addition of fire suppres-

sion systems has contained most fires to one or two floors of a building. With technically advanced automatic detection and suppression systems, fires can be contained to a single room or even smaller area. In the United States, most fires are now extinguished using five or fewer sprinkler heads, limiting damage from water as well as fire. Fire protection systems are designed to minimize the size of the fire fighting system and to retard the spread of smoke and fire. The average size of fires within buildings continues to decline, with the emphasis increasingly on minimizing water and smoke damage.

Fire protection requires the coordination of the architecture and interiors, the mechanical, electrical, and plumbing systems, and the signal system. The best design for fire safety is also good design for lighting, thermal, acoustic, and water systems. Most thermally massive materials don't burn easily, and thermal mass also benefits passive heating, cooling, and acoustic isolation of airborne sound. High ceilings allow large quantities of smoke to collect before reaching the occupant's level and allow smoke and flames to be seen from a greater indoor distance. High ceilings also aid daylight distribution and ventilation. Windows provide firefighting and rescue access and escape routes and dilute smoke with fresh air. They also offer daylight, ventilation, and view. Solid, noncombustible overhangs above windows that discourage the vertical spread of fire over the building face can serve as an emergency exterior refuge and also double as sun shading. Elevated water tanks provide water for firefighting before the arrival of firefighters, and assure adequate water pressure for plumbing fixtures.

Fire safety concerns can conflict with other building design issues, however. High ceilings and low partitions in spaces without sprinklers can allow fire and smoke to spread. Fire builds up faster in small, enclosed rooms that retain heat. Buildings without operable windows or with sunscreens covering windows block access by firefighters and escape by occupants. Broken windows can fall and hit people below.

In some buildings, continuing operations during a fire is a priority. Special fire alarm and suppression systems are available for especially critical operations areas such as control rooms. The heating, ventilating, and air-conditioning (HVAC) system of the building can be designed to take in only outside air to purge the building of smoke. Floors should be waterproofed for speedy removal of water dumped on the fire by the sprinkler system, but rarely are. Waterproofing should continue up walls, columns, pipes, and other vertical elements for a distance of 10 to 15 cm (4–6 in.).

Creating a safe building starts with the design of fire-resistant exterior walls. How close a building is to its neighbors governs both the types of building materials and the extent and treatment of windows and doors. Protection from exterior fire sources is provided by using noncombustible materials for the building exterior or by erecting firewalls between the building and its neighbor. Exterior doors with properties that delay fire and windows with fire-rated shutters that close automatically at high temperatures also protect the building. Wired glass, which holds together against flame for a considerable time, is usually required in windows facing nearby structures.

PROTECTING THE STRUCTURE

The structure of a building is protected to prevent collapse of the building within the time the fire runs its course or to delay the collapse of low buildings until all occupants have escaped and firefighters have had a reasonable chance to save the building. The building may survive to be salvaged rather than being demolished after the fire. Protecting the structure maintains the value of the building. It protects the occupants, firefighters,

and neighboring buildings. Tall buildings present a significant danger if all or part of the building falls.

The most important elements of the structure to be protected are the columns (Fig. 42-1). Next in importance are the girders and the beams, and lastly the floor slabs. Most large buildings are constructed of either reinforced concrete or protected steel. Steel doesn't burn but loses much of its structural strength in a fire and will sag or collapse at the sustained temperatures frequently reached by ordinary building fires. Steel reinforcing bars in concrete beams and columns are buried a specific distance within the mass of the concrete and are protected by its thermal mass and natural fire-resistant properties.

Brick, tile, and mineral fibers that are unaffected by fire can be used to protect the building structure. Brick and tile are made using the intense heat of a kiln, and are not weakened by fire. However, mortar joints may disintegrate, and the construction can fail.

Concrete is more resistant to fire than steel. Because concrete and plaster are largely made up of hydrated crystals, they will absorb very large quantities of heat during a fire before the water of crystallization is evaporated. Consequently, concrete and plaster provide a barrier to the fire as they slowly disintegrate. If the fire lasts long enough, though, concrete or plaster will not be able to prevent serious structural damage.

Both solid brick and poured concrete are expensive and add to the structural load and the cost of the building's structure. Today, steel beams and columns are encased in lath and plaster and surrounded with multiple layers of gypsum wallboard (drywall). They are also sometimes sprayed with lightweight mineral insulations in cementitious binders or have preformed slabs of mineral insulation attached to them.

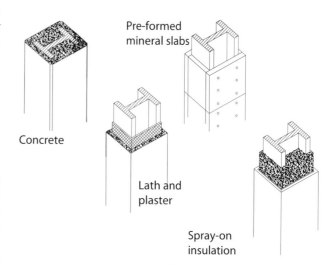

Concrete

Pre-formed mineral slabs

Lath and plaster

Spray-on insulation

Figure 42-1 Protecting columns from fire.

In the past, asbestos was used to insulate steel columns. We now know that loose asbestos fibers can get into our lungs. Other forms of spray-on materials or slabs of mineral insulation are now available. Intumescent coatings, in the form of paint or a thick coating that is put on with a trowel, soften when exposed to heat and release bubbles of a gas that expands the coating to create an insulating layer.

Low industrial and commercial buildings of unprotected steel are considered to be incombustible, but there is an unlikely possibility that they may collapse rapidly in a hot fire before occupants have time to escape. Buildings constructed of heavy timber are considered to be slow burning buildings, and are permitted to be one to two stories higher than unprotected steel buildings. Plaster or plasterboard walls and ceilings offer one-half hour of protection for smaller wooden buildings.

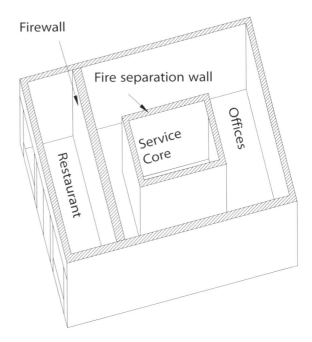

Figure 42-2 Firewalls.

COMPARTMENTATION AND FIRE BARRIERS

An entire building or a large space can be divided into two or more separate spaces, each totally enclosed within a fire barrier envelope of floor/ceiling assemblies and walls. This compartmentation prevents the spread of fire, smoke, and heat beyond a restricted area of the building. Compartmentation protects the building's occupants and property by confining the fire, heat, smoke, and toxic gases to the area of their origin until the fire is extinguished or until it burns itself out completely. It stops the spread of fire by hot combustion gases. In row houses, fire-resistant walls separate dwellings. Compartmentation is required between different types of functions within a building. Compartmentation is also used to provide areas of refuge for occupants and firefighters.

Building codes set maximum floor areas for various constructions and occupancies. Using sprinklers usually increases the limits on floor areas. Larger areas must be subdivided with fire-rated walls and doors. In one-story factories and warehouses where firewalls are not practical, incombustible curtain boards are hung from the roof to catch and contain rising hot gases. Self-opening roof vents in each compartment allow hot gases to escape before they can spread the fire. Doors of the roof vent are held closed against springs by a fusible link of a metal with a low melting point, which melts and releases the doors when heat builds up.

Fire barriers are fire-rated structural elements. They include wall, ceiling, or floor systems that prevent the spread of flame and heat through the use of fire-rated structural materials with fire-resistant (FR) ratings. Building codes limit the number of penetrations in a fire rated wall. Fire barriers can be divided into three types. Firewalls (Fig. 42-2) have the highest fire ratings and are usually part of the building shell. Fire separation walls are used to create fire-rated compartments within a building. The fire ratings of the third category, floor/ceiling assemblies, depend on the walls they surround.

Firewalls, also called party walls, are used for occupancy separations. Firewalls provide continuous protection from the foundation of the building to the roof and to each exterior wall. They are built so that if one side of the wall falls, the other side would remain standing. Firewalls typically have three- to five-hour ratings. Firewalls are often used to subdivide a building into two separate types of construction. They are also used to separate one occupancy from another in a mixed-use building. Interior designers generally aren't involved in designing firewalls, but our work may involve possible penetrations. All openings in a firewall are limited to a certain percent of the wall's length, and must be protected by self-closing fire doors, fire-rated window assemblies, and fire and smoke dampers in air ducts.

Fire separation walls, which include tenant separation walls (demising walls), corridor walls, vertical shafts, and room separations, are more likely than firewalls to be added or changed during an interiors project. Tenant separation walls create fire-rated compartments within a building that separate two tenants or dwelling units. They typically require one-hour ratings, depending on the occupancy and whether sprinklers are used. Interior designers often work with fire separation walls.

Corridor walls must have ratings of from one to two hours, depending upon how corridors are used, the occupancy, and whether sprinklers are used. Corridor walls that are used as exits must usually have a two-hour fire rating, and corridors used as exit accesses generally require one-hour ratings. We look at all the components of exits in more detail shortly. Typically, codes require that corridor walls be continuous from floor slab to floor slab, and that they penetrate suspended ceilings. Some corridor walls may also act as demising walls, and then the stricter requirements apply.

The walls that create vertical shaft enclosures for stairwells, elevators, and dumbwaiters are usually continuous from the bottom of the building to the underside of the roof deck. Stairs used as part of an exit have requirements for fire ratings, can have only limited penetrations, and may require that the enclosure be smokeproof. Stair enclosures are required to have a one-hour fire rating for up to three stories, and two-hour ratings for four or more stories. Where stairs connect only two floors within a single occupancy, the space may be considered to be an atrium, and the enclosure restrictions may be less restrictive.

Most rooms within a space do not require fire rated walls. Where the contents of the room may be hazardous, however, codes may specify that they be separated from the rest of the building by a fire-rated wall. Construction costs are reduced if spaces with similar requirements, such as boiler rooms, furnace rooms, and large storage rooms, are located adjacent to one another.

Fire-rated floors and ceilings are rated as either floor/ceiling or roof/ceiling assemblies. The assembly consists of everything from the bottom of the ceiling material to the top of the floor or roof above. This includes all the ducts, piping, and wires between the finished ceiling and the finished floor above it. If you are adding a ceiling to a space, you need to determine the ratings of the surrounding walls and use the same rating at the ceiling.

Fire can spread quickly in concealed spaces over suspended ceilings, behind walls, within pipe chases, in attics, and under raised floors. Specify noncombustible materials in these and similar spaces. Automatic fire detection and suppression systems and oxygen deprivation systems can be used in concealed spaces. Fire stops and firewalls may be required to break up continuous concealed spaces.

AREAS OF REFUGE

Refuge areas, called areas of rescue assistance by the *Americans with Disabilities Act Accessibility Guidelines* (ADAAG), are provided in high-rise buildings and for wheelchair users in multistory buildings. In large buildings, not everyone can evacuate in time, and refuge areas provide a place to wait that is protected from smoke. Ideally, refuge areas should remain free of smoke, gases, heat, and fire throughout the fire and until rescue. The structure and essential services in refuge areas are intended to be maintained at all times, but these goals are almost impossible to achieve in practice.

Areas of refuge are commonly located adjacent to a protected stairway, and are protected from smoke. They are provided with communications devices to summon firefighters to rescue the people in the refuge. When a stairway is used as a refuge area, it is designed to hold all the building occupants, allowing 0.28 square meters (3 square ft) per person. Horizontal exits (which we define later) can be areas of refuge, as can smoke-protected vestibules or enlarged landings adjacent to exit stairways. The Americans with Disabilities Act (ADA) sets minimum requirements for accessible spaces in refuge areas, and mandates a specific type of two-way emergency communications system. The ADA requires specific identifications for accessible spaces in refuge areas.

In an exit stairwell, the landings at the doors entering the stairs can be enlarged so that one or more wheelchairs can wait for assistance without blocking the means of egress. An alternative arrangement provides an alcove for wheelchairs in a portion of an exit access corridor located immediately adjacent to the exit enclosure. Another possibility is to provide space immediately adjacent to an exit enclosure by creating an enclosed exit discharge, such as a vestibule or foyer.

Limited refuge areas are built from noncombustible materials around double-vestibule, pressurized stairwells. These can normally serve other functions, such as libraries, conference rooms, restrooms, and so forth. They resemble other building rooms, but have direct access to stairs, self-closing fire doors, and voice-activated intercom systems connected to the master fire control center on the ground floor.

HORIZONTAL EXITS

A horizontal exit does not lead to the exterior of the building. Instead, it provides a protected exit to a safe area of refuge in another part of the building or an adjoining building without a change in level. The horizontal exit uses fire-rated walls and doors to subdivide a building into separate areas, which are then treated as separate buildings. Occupants escape from a fire on one side by moving horizontally through self-closing fire doors to the other side.

When you pass through the door of a horizontal exit, the whole space beyond is considered an area of refuge where you can either wait for assistance or use exit stairs to leave the building. Horizontal exits can provide refuge for very large building populations in healthcare, detention, and educational buildings.

Horizontal exits can be used in any occupancy classification, and are most commonly found in Institutional occupancies. Hospitals use horizontal exits to divide a floor into two or more areas of refuge. This allows a patient bed to be rolled into a safe area protected by a rated firewall in a fire emergency. To reduce the danger of smoke inhalation, self-closing doors are installed on nursing home and hospital patient rooms where evacuation is impossible. Prisons use horizontal exits to contain the fire without evacuating the entire prison. They are also used in large factories, storage facilities, and high-rise buildings.

A horizontal exit consists of the walls enclosing the area of refuge and the doors through these walls, all of which must be fire-rated. The walls must be continuous through every floor to the ground or be surrounded by a floor and ceiling with a fire rating.

Doors in a horizontal exit must be fire-rated and swing in the direction of travel to the exit. If the horizontal exit has an area of refuge on either side, it must have two side-by-side doors, each swinging in an opposite direction, so that occupants can push through the doorway in either direction.

Horizontal exits may reduce the number of other types of exits required, but codes place limits on the total number of horizontal exits a building can have. They are only allowed when two or more exits are required, and can't constitute more than one-half of the total required exit widths.

VERTICAL OPENINGS

Because the vertical spread of a fire through a building is the biggest problem, compartmentation requirements around vertical openings tend to be especially strict in order to prevent the convection of fire and combustion products through the building. Open vertical

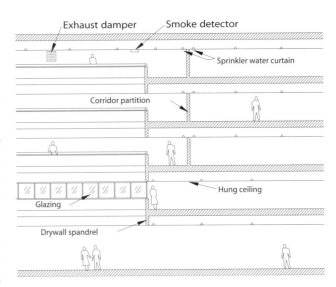

Figure 42-3 Atrium fire protection.

shafts of any kind, including stairs, elevators, ductwork, and electrical wiring and piping chases, must be enclosed with fire-rated walls with self-closing fire-rated doors at each floor.

The only exception to the enclosure requirement for vertical shafts is a vertical atrium (Fig. 42-3). An atrium is defined in many codes as a roofed, occupied space that includes a floor opening or a series of floor openings connecting two or more stories. Atriums are often found in shopping arcades, hotels, and office buildings. Balconies around the atrium may be open to it, but surrounding rooms must be isolated from balconies and from the atrium by fire-rated walls. An exception is made for any three floors selected by the building's designer, so that lobby spaces on several floors can be continuous with the atrium.

Codes require a 1.8-meter (6 ft) deep curtain board (smoke barrier) at the opening to the atrium at each floor. Smoke detectors and motorized dampers in ducts are required. A building with an atrium must have sprinklers throughout. Sprinklers located 1.8 meters on center at the lobby level, the atrium floor level, and where office floors open to an atrium, create a water curtain. The frames for glazing at the perimeter of the atrium should be designed for thermal expansion so that they don't break their glass when they get hot, with sprinklers on the office side of the glazing. Fire-rated frames are listed for both heat resistance and water pressure from the hose stream. The atrium must be provided with fans with dampers that open and turn on automatically in case of fire to bring fresh air into the space at ground level and exhaust smoke at the ceiling level.

CONSTRUCTION ASSEMBLIES

Construction assemblies have been assigned one-, two-, three-, and four-hour ratings by ASTM E-119. Assemblies that are tested this way include permanent partitions, shaft enclosures for stairways and elevators, floor/ceiling constructions, doors, and glass openings. Doors and other opening assemblies also receive 20-, 30-, and 45-minute ratings.

Any opening that pierces the entire thickness of a construction assembly is referred to as a through-penetration. Codes require that penetrations in fire-rated assemblies be protected with fire assemblies in the form of fire doors, fire windows, firestops, and fire dampers. These opening protectives or through-penetration protection systems must have fire protection ratings. Usually, no opening greater than 11 square meters (120 square ft) is permitted. The combined width of all openings must not exceed 25 percent of the length of the wall. Any assembly that passes the required tests must have a permanent label attached to it to prove it is fire-rated.

DOORS

Fire doors are actually entire door assemblies. The typical fire door includes the door itself, the frame, the hardware, and the doorway (wall opening). Fire door assemblies are required to protect the openings in fire-rated walls. The whole assembly is tested and rated as one unit. Standard methods of fire tests of door assemblies are provided by ASTM E-152. The test results are used in the selection of doors for fire-resistive constructions. For example, exit access corridor enclosure walls require a one-hour construction assembly rating, and doors in those walls require at least a 20-minute rating. For a firewall with a required four-hour assembly rating, a door with a three-hour rating is required.

Many types of doors are regulated as fire doors by building codes, including swinging and vertical sliding doors as well as accordion folding, Dutch, and bi-parting doors, among others. Fire doors are typically flush, either solid-core wood or metal, with mineral composition cores. A few panel doors may meet fire door requirements, and some fire doors may have applied finishes to improve their appearance. Frames are wood, hollow metal steel, or aluminum. The doorframe and hardware must have a fire rating similar to that of the door itself. The maximum fire door size is 122 by 305 cm (4 by 10 ft).

Hardware includes hinges, latches and locksets, and pulls and closures. Hinges, latchsets, and closing devices are the most stringently regulated, as they must hold the door closed securely during a fire, and must withstand the pressure and heat the fire generates. Hinges must be steel or stainless steel and a specific quantity is required for each door.

The door must be self-latching and equipped with a closer. Fire-rated exit doors also require a specific type of latch. The most common is called fire exit hardware (Fig. 42-4), and consists of a door-latching assembly that disengages when pressure is applied on a horizontal bar spanning the interior of an emergency exit door at waist height. The push bar should extend across at least one-half the width of the door leaf on which it is installed. The term panic hardware is also used, but technically panic hardware is not tested and should not be used on fire-rated doors. On the other hand, fire exit hardware is tested and rated. Fire exit hardware is typically required in Assembly and Educational occupancies, and is often used on other exit doors. The codes also regulate the width, direction of swing, and location of required exit doors, according to the use and occupancy of the building. The ADA requires that the force necessary to push open or pull open a door be no greater than 5 lb.

Door closers are hydraulic or pneumatic devices that automatically close doors quickly but quietly. They help reduce the shock a large, heavy, or heavily used door would transmit upon closing to its frame, hardware, and

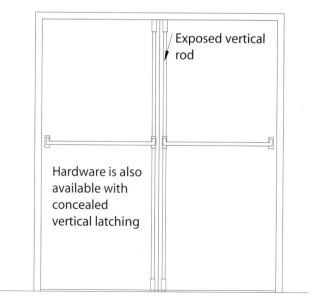

Figure 42-4 Fire exit hardware.

the surrounding wall. Building codes require the use of self-latching, self-closing doors with hardware rated by the Underwriters Laboratories (UL) to protect openings in firewalls and occupancy separations. For doors that are normally kept in an open position, an automatic closing device uses a fusible link that is triggered by heat or activated by the smoke detector to close the door. Other doors with lower ratings may require self-closing devices to close the door after each use.

The doorway, including the lintel and sill, also has rating requirements. Fire doors are typically specified and sold by the manufacturer as a whole assembly. You can generally use a door of a higher rating than required, but you should check with the jurisdictional authority.

B-label doors have one-hour or one and one-half hour UL-approved ratings. C-label doors have a three-quarter hour rating. B and C label doors are permitted to have louvers with fusible links, up to 0.37 square meters (576 square in.). No glass and louver combinations are allowed. Doors with Class C and 20-minute ratings are the most common on interior projects. Class A and B doors are also used on interiors.

 Glass entrance doors are required to have 13 or 19 mm ($\frac{1}{2}$ or $\frac{3}{4}$ in.) safety glazing. Building codes require the glazing for sliding glass doors to be tempered (heat-strengthened) safety glass. For energy conservation, units are glazed with insulating glass.

The leaves of revolving doors must be of tempered glass in metal frames. The revolving door enclosure must be of metal or of tempered, wired, or laminated glass. Some building codes may credit revolving doors for up to half of the legal exit requirements, while others require adjacent hinged doors for emergency exits.

WINDOWS

The types of windows that are covered by building code fire regulations include casement, double hung, hinged, pivot, and tilting windows. Stationary windows, sidelights, transom lights, view panels, and borrowed lights are also included. Glass blocks are also covered by fire regulations.

 Building codes regulate the clear opening of any operable window that serves as an emergency exit for a residential sleeping space. Typically, the minimum area permitted is 0.53 square meters (5.7 square ft), with a minimum clear width of 508 mm (20 in.), and clear height of 610 mm (24 in.). The sill must be no more than 1120 mm (44 in.) above the floor. Codes may restrict the location of glazing.

Wire glass has a wire mesh embedded in the middle of a glass sheet. The wire distributes heat and increases the strength of the glass. The codes set size limits for wire glass.

Windows with fire ratings typically consist of a frame, wire glass, and hardware. They are used for openings in corridors, room partitions, and smoke barriers. Window ratings are similar to those of doors, with hour classifications usually not greater than one hour. The glass product most often associated with fire rating is polished wired glass. It has provided fire protection for more than 100 years, and is frequently seen in schools, hospitals, and other high occupancy facilities. In North America, wired glass is typically rated for 45 minutes in lite (glass pane) sizes up to 0.84 square meters (9 square ft). In a fire door, glazing can't exceed 0.065 square meters (100 square in.) of wired glass, and no single dimension can be greater than 254 mm (10 in.). The biggest advantage of wired glass may be its low cost. However, its relatively low impact safety resistance and the institutional look of the wire are sometimes considered drawbacks.

Another type of fire-rated glazing is glass ceramic. It is made from a ceramic material or a transparent gel between several sheets of glass. This provides a heat shield and additional insulating protection. Fire-rated glazing is available with 60- and 90-minute ratings. European manufacturers have a glazing assembly that meets the requirements of a two-hour rated wall assembly. Higher ratings allow larger sheets to be used, and these larger sizes may exceed the current maximum listings found in building codes. Work with local code officials and the glazing manufacturer. Fire-rated glazing must pass the appropriate tests and standards and have a permanent label etched into the glass.

Once installed, this wireless product looks similar to window glass. Glass ceramic products offer fire ratings from 20 minutes to three hours, in sizes ranging up to 2.23 square meters (24 square ft) per lite. Like wired glass, the glass ceramics are able to withstand the thermal shock of water thrown by sprinklers or a fire hose. Glass ceramic products offer great design flexibility. Products are available that offer at least four times the impact resistance of wire glass. Products can also have beveled edges and be sandblasted for artistic effect.

Glass ceramic is also available made into insulating glass units with two layers of glass with an air space between them. Depending on which components are used, they can provide not only fire protection but also comply with energy codes, and can be used for sound reduction applications.

Another emerging category of fire-rated glass could be called transparent wall units. Although widely used in Europe for a number of years, they are just now becoming popular in North America. These units are special, multiproduct assemblies that block the transfer of heat. While appearing to be regular glass, the thicker composition of the units allows them to perform similar to a fire-rated masonry wall. With proper framing from wall to wall and floor to ceiling, these large expanses of glass have obtained fire ratings of up to two hours. They are typically used to block the transfer of heat through the glass while allowing visibility, light, and security. These products, like wired glass and glass ceramics, withstand thermal shock. They meet high levels of impact safety as well.

A final category of fire-rated glazing is specially tempered glass. However, these products only carry ratings of 20 or 30 minutes, and cannot withstand the thermal shock of water thrown from sprinklers or a fire hose. Such products are sometimes used in 20-minute rated doors.

Glass block typically has a 45-minute rating, with newer types available with 60- to 90-minute ratings. Codes limit the number of square feet of glass block permitted as an interior wall. They also limit glass block used as a view panel in a rated wall, where it is required that it be installed in steel channels.

Safety glazing is required for any window that could be mistaken for an open doorway. Any window area greater than 0.84 square meters (9 square ft) and located within 61 cm (24 in.) of a doorway, or less than 152 cm (60 in.) above the floor must be safety glazed with tempered glass, laminated glass, or plastic. The type and size of glazing allowed in fire-rated walls and corridors is also regulated.

STAIRS

The design of stairs is strictly regulated by building codes and by the ADA. We consider the additional requirements of stairs used as part of a fire exit later. Building codes may allow limited use of curved, winder, spiral, switchback, and alternating tread stairs. This depends upon the occupancy classification, number of occupants, use of the stairs, and the dimension of the treads. Most stairs must have a clear minimum width of 112 cm (44 in.). With an occupant load under 50, a 914-cm (36-in.) minimum width is permitted.

Most stairs require handrails on both sides, except in individual dwelling units, when stairs are less than 1120 mm (44 in.) wide, or when there are fewer than four risers. Extra-wide stairs also require intermediate handrails. Handrails must be between 914 and 965 mm (36–38 in.) above the leading edge of treads or nosings. Handrails may project a maximum of 89 mm ($3\frac{1}{2}$ in.) into the required width. Stringers and trim may project a maximum of 38 mm ($1\frac{1}{2}$ in.). They must be continuous without interruptions by a newel post or other obstruction. The handrail should extend a minimum of 305 mm (12 in.) beyond the top riser, and a minimum of 305 mm plus one tread width beyond the bottom riser. Handrail ends should return smoothly to the wall or the walking surface, or continue to the handrail of an adjacent stair flight.

Landings must be at least as wide as the stairway width, and a minimum of 1118 mm (44 in.) in length measured in the direction of travel. In dwelling units, a minimum of 914 mm (36 in.) is allowed. Doors must swing in the direction of egress, and cannot reduce the landing to less than one-half of its required width. When fully open, doors must not intrude into the required width by more than 178 mm (7 in.).

A guardrail is required when the side of a stair is exposed and not enclosed by a wall. Guardrails are usually 107 cm (42 in.) high, and must not allow a ball with a 10-cm (4-in.) diameter to pass through.

Codes set requirements for stair treads, risers, and nosings. A minimum of three risers per flight is recommended to prevent tripping. The ADA sets a minimum tread depth at 28 cm (11 in.), and a riser height between 10 and 18 cm (4–7 in.). Risers and treads must maintain uniform dimensions, and open risers are not permitted. Nosings are limited to a maximum protrusion of 38 mm ($1\frac{1}{2}$ in.) and a maximum radius of 13 mm ($\frac{1}{2}$ in.). They should be sloped, or their undersides should have a 60-degree minimum angle from the horizontal.

FIRE DAMPERS AND DRAFT STOPS

Fire dampers are used in HVAC ductwork. The fire damper automatically interrupts the flow of air through the duct system during an emergency. It restricts the passage of smoke, fire, and heat. Fire dampers must be installed whenever a duct passes through a wall, ceiling, or floor that is part of a fire-rated assembly. They can be installed within a duct or on the outside as a collar fastened to the wall or ceiling. A fire damper includes a fusible link on either side of the assembly the duct penetrates. This link melts during a fire, causing the fire damper to close and seal the duct.

Draft stops are required in combustible construction to close off large concealed spaces. They are not required to be noncombustible themselves. Draft stops are placed between the ceiling and the floor above, in attic spaces, and in other concealed spaces. They create separate spaces and prevent the movement of air.

FIRESTOPS

Firestops restrict the passage of smoke, heat, and flames in concealed spaces. They seal and protect openings for plumbing pipes, electrical conduit and wire, HVAC ducts, cables, and so forth passing through walls, floors, and ceilings. Firestops may also be required in concealed spaces between walls and in connections between horizontal and vertical planes. Firestops are required at through penetrations in fire and smoke barriers.

Firestops consist of silicone foam, mortar, fire resistive board, wire mesh, and collars or clamp bands. The most common way to create a firestop system is to fill the open space with a fire-rated material and finish it with a sealant. Firestop devices are factory built and are typically installed as part of a penetration through a wall or ceiling/floor assembly.

DESIGNING TO HELP FIREFIGHTERS

Firefighters often have to use the stairs to reach parts of the building above the seven-story limit of their ladders. One exit stairway in a taller building must be placed in a smoke proof enclosure. This stairway is connected to the main spaces of the building only by open-air balconies, or is automatically pressurized by a fan in case of fire.

Each exit stairway in a multistory building must have a standpipe to connect fire hoses at any floor. A Y-shaped Siamese connection is provided at street level for firefighters to supply water continuously through the standpipe. One to two fire trucks can maintain pressure and volume in the standpipe if city water mains can't keep up with demand during the fire.

SMOKE MANAGEMENT

Smoke kills more people in building fires than heat or structural collapse. Even if a person is not killed by smoke, smoke inhalation can result in memory loss and lingering physical effects. Before a flame is visible, smoke may move more than 25 cm per second (50 ft per minute) from the point of origin to kill people who are unaware of the fire. Once the flame is visible, smoke may move more than 50 cm per second (100 ft per minute) before the flame starts to spread. Fires in modern buildings usually last less than 30 minutes, but smoke problems can be present for hours. Smoke inhalation leads to unclear thinking. You might claw at a doorknob instead of turning the handle. Hot smoke washing over people leads to panic as logic vanishes and fear overwhelms them.

The goals of smoke management are to reduce deaths and property damage and to provide for continuity of building operations with minimum smoke interference. A barrier's effectiveness in limiting smoke movement depends on how smoke can leak through it and the pressure differences on each side of it. Pressure depends on the stack effect, the buoyancy of warm air, the presence of wind, and the operation of the HVAC system.

Smoke Barriers

The heat of a fire changes the air's pressure and buoyancy, which in turn spreads the smoke. As temperature increases during a fire in a low building, gases in the smoke expand, and convective air motion moves the smoke around. In tall buildings, these effects are compounded by the stack effect as heated air rises rapidly within vertical shafts. Wind forces outside and the forced-air system increase the stack effect.

Wall assemblies that are continuous from outside wall to outside wall and from floor slab to floor slab are good smoke barriers. This type of construction is mostly used in Institutional occupancies between areas of refuge.

In tall buildings, vertical shafts for stairs, elevators, and waste and linen chutes can be designed to be smokeproof. Smokeproof enclosures require ventilation or pressurization systems. All openings must automatically close on detection of smoke. Smoke-stop doors that close tightly may be required.

Vestibules adjacent to smokeproof stairwells or elevator hoistways and between the shaft and an exterior exit door are subject to special size requirements. Doors must be fire-rated and have closers and drop sills. The ceiling must be high enough to trap smoke and heat. Natural or mechanical ventilation is required.

When doors in stairwells that are pressurized to exclude smoke are opened for people to escape, they are sometimes left open. Keeping the outside air at a lower pressure than the air in the stairwell prevents smoke from getting through the open door.

Smoke control systems are required in all buildings of over six floors. The exit access corridors must be continually pressurized. The NFPA requires that every patient sleeping room in a hospital have an outside window operable from the inside to vent the products of combustion. An exemption is provided for buildings with an engineered smoke control system.

Smoke Confinement

 Smoke should be confined to the area of the fire and excluded from refuges. Firewalls and smoke barriers confine smoke. Even firewalls have leaks around doors and other openings. A large open space above dividing walls can hold a great deal of smoke while the building occupants evacuate. Smoke barriers, sometimes called curtain boards (Fig. 42-5), are suspended from the ceiling to trap hot air and smoke. They help to set off fire detection and suppression systems more quickly. Curtain boards lose their effectiveness quickly when the smoke layer becomes too thick to contain.

Smoke dampers are similar to fire dampers, but are activated by smoke. They are rarely required, except in large Educational occupancies and at smoke barriers in Institutional occupancies. Smoke dampers have a smoke detector located inside the duct that causes the smoke damper to close off the duct.

Smoke Dilution

Diluting smoke with outdoor air helps people evacuate a burning building. Dilution alone is not enough to control smoke, however, especially when toxic fumes are present. Smoke dilution is usually combined with confinement and an early detection/suppression system.

Providing a large quantity of fresh air in refuge spaces creates higher pressures, which in turn helps resist smoke entering through cracks. However, fresh air alone is not usually enough to keep smoke from entering an open door. In stairways, the fresh air should not be supplied entirely from either the top or the bottom of the stairs. Doors open near the only fresh air source can mean that no fresh air reaches other floors.

Fans that bring in outside air must be located so that the fire does not affect their operation, and so that their intakes remain smoke free. Locating the fan's intake below the level of smoke accumulation keeps smoke above people's heads.

Exhausting Smoke

Special exhaust systems that function only in fires are becoming more common. They use a combination of air velocity and air pressure to control smoke. Smoke exhaust systems work well in large-volume atriums, removing smoke at the ceiling and supplying fresh air below. They involve significant initial expense for special fans and smoke exhaust shafts.

Smoke exhaust systems remove toxic gases from refuge areas. They help firefighters by providing better air quality near the fire, and by creating air currents that help control the fire's direction. Exhaust systems remove unburned combustion gases and prevent backdraft or flashover smoke explosions. By creating higher pressure in refuge areas and lower pressures in fire zones, exhaust systems keep smoke out of refuges, even when the door is open. They also prevent the stack effect from overcoming smoke management efforts, and remove smoke after the fire is over.

Figure 42-5 Curtain board smoke barrier.

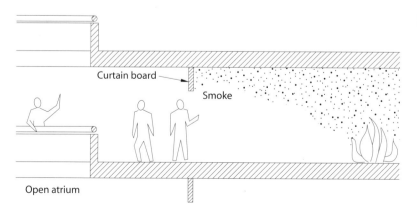

Other Smoke Controls

Automatic ventilation hatches vent heat and smoke without fans. They are suitable for smaller buildings and one-story buildings such as shopping malls. Heat and smoke trigger the controls and the hatches open individually. Ventilation hatches improve conditions near the fire for firefighters, and help firefighters on the roof locate the fire inside the building.

Coordination of the HVAC, fire detection/suppression, and smoke exhaust systems is essential to smoke management. The fire detection/suppression system activates the smoke exhaust and overrides HVAC controls. Sprinklers can conflict with a smoke exhaust system. The curtain of water from the sprinklers can inhibit the movement of smoke. The water cools the smoke, and the resulting reduction in buoyancy causes it to descend to the level where people are. Fire suppression with oxygen-replacing chemicals can conflict with fresh air from the smoke exhaust system. Using both sprinklers and fire suppression may mean there is less need for the smoke exhaust system, however.

Escape Routes

●●●

In order to design safe exits from a building, we must first create safe exit paths. We construct stairs and corridors along the path to slow down the fire while guiding occupants out of the building. We locate exits to offer more than one route out, and limit distances to safe exits. Finally, we limit the number of people allowed to occupy the building at one time so that the building can be emptied quickly.

At least 30 percent of fire deaths are the result of fire cutting off paths to exits. Although people can panic in a fire, most of the time they initially respond to clues to the fire, like the smell of smoke or the sounds of breaking glass, sirens, and alarm bells, more or less calmly. It is rare for people to actually see flames as the first warning of fire. Open plans show the signs of fire more easily to more people. Next, the occupants decide how serious the situation is. The reactions of other people influence their behavior. Without signs of fire, an entire group of people may refuse to evacuate the building in the early stages. Finally, people start to cope with the fact that the building is on fire and they must get out. The fight or flight reaction takes over. At this point, occupants must be able to see exit paths clearly and have access to firefighting equipment.

For residential buildings, the *One and Two Family Dwelling Code* requires a minimum of one regulated exterior exit door per residence 92 by 203 cm (3 ft by 6 ft, 8 in.), with a specified type of landing on each side. Minimum widths are specified for hallways and exit accesses. Most homes rely on exterior windows as a means of egress during an emergency, and codes restrict the size, height, and operation of windows used as exits. Stairs and ramps are regulated, but not as strictly as in the model building codes for commercial buildings. Smaller tread and riser sizes are allowed, and a single handrail is permitted.

In a low-rise building, the primary goal is to evacuate all occupants in the time between the detection of the fire and the arrival of the firefighters. We have already looked at some of the ways building codes keep the route to safety clear, including stairwell enclosures and horizontal exits.

Firefighting equipment normally reaches up to only seven stories, around 229 cm (90 ft). In many high-rise buildings, only two exit stairways are provided. With only two exit stairs, a small 15-story building with 120 people per floor can be evacuated in around nine minutes. By comparison, in a large 50-story building with 480 people per floor, evacuation with two exit stairs would take a minimum of two hours and eleven minutes. On top of that, firefighters must be able to move up while the occupants move down. Sometimes occupants will try to reenter the stair to rescue family members, pets, and valuables, further complicating the flow.

When doors are held open on each floor to admit people to the stairwell, smoke can enter the stairs. In the past, people have commonly refused to evacuate high-rise buildings because they felt they would rather trust the fire extinguishing equipment than go down many stories of stairs.

The interior designer must plan the means of egress carefully on interior projects and coordinate the means of egress requirements with fire and smoke separation requirements. Once a building occupant enters the protected portion of a means of egress, the level of protection can't be reduced or eliminated unless the code authorities allow an exemption.

OCCUPANT LOADS

Building codes use the occupant load (or occupancy load) to establish the required number and width of exits for a building. The occupant load determines the maximum number of people allowed in a specific occupancy at any one time. We should emphasize that the occupancy load is not the same as an occupancy classification. An occupancy classification indicates the use of the space, rather than the number of people. There may be more than one occupancy within a single building if there is more than one use.

The code assigns a predetermined amount of space or square feet that is required per occupant within specific occupancies and building uses. This amount of space is called the occupant load factor. Occupant load factors allow for furniture and equipment, and sometimes for corridors, closets, and other areas, in setting the number of square feet per person for various occupancies.

The occupant load of a space is the total number of persons that may occupy a building or portion of a building at any one time. It is determined by dividing the floor area assigned to a particular use by the square feet per occupant permitted in that use. It is calculated using the area inside of the exterior walls. Some load factors are calculated in gross square feet, including interior wall thicknesses and all miscellaneous spaces in the building as a whole. Others are based on net square feet of actual occupied space, not including corridors, restrooms, utility closets, and other unoccupied areas. Sometimes fixed items that take up space, such as interior walls, columns, built-in counters, and shelving are deducted from the number of square feet used in the calculations.

The minimum total egress widths per floor is the number of inches of width for all the exits from that floor added together. To determine the minimum total egress width for a floor, you first calculate the net or gross floor area (whichever the code is using), and then divide that floor area by the occupant load factor. This gives you the number of occupants per floor. You then look in the code to get the number of inches of egress width required for each occupant of the floor. You multiply this number of inches per person by the number of occupants per floor to get the minimum total egress width for that floor. Then you divide up that total egress width into the number of exits you plan to have from the floor, based on each exit's clear width. What you end up with is a minimum number of exits and their minimum sizes.

MEANS OF EGRESS

A means of egress is a continuous and unobstructed path of travel from any point in the building to its exit or a public way. The means of egress is also the path of travel an occupant uses to obtain a safe area of refuge within the building.

Any means of egress has three components: the exit access, the exit, and the exit discharge. A means of egress is comprised of both vertical and horizontal passageways including doorways, corridors, stairs, ramps, enclosures, and intervening rooms. The model building codes and *Life Safety Code* set most egress requirements. The Americans with Disabilities Act (ADA) should also be considered for related requirements.

EXIT ACCESS

The exit access is that portion of a means of egress that leads to an exit. We define an exit in the next section. An exit access leads from the room or space to the exit, and can include doors, stairs, ramps, corridors, aisles, and intervening rooms. The exit access doesn't necessarily require a fire rating or need to be fully enclosed. When a fire rating is required, it is usually one hour.

Doors in an exit access are regulated as to type, size, and swing direction, depending upon where they are located. Doors along a corridor must be fire-rated. Those between smaller tenant spaces or rooms don't require a rating. A minimum height of 91 cm (6 ft, 8 in.) is typically required. The *ADA Accessibility Guidelines* (ADAAG)

requires a minimum of 81 cm (32 in.) clear width, and 91 cm (36 in.) doors are generally used, to allow for the thickness of the door and its hardware. The finished floor surface on either side of a threshold must be within 13 mm ($\frac{1}{2}$ in.) of the top of the threshold, or else the threshold must be beveled.

An exit access corridor is any corridor leading to an exit in a building. The typical corridor is not required to be fire-rated, or may require a one-hour rating. The width and length of travel of the corridor are limited by codes and by accessibility requirements. Corridors in a means of egress that must allow the passage of two wheelchairs at one point must be a minimum of 2.6 meters (8 ft, 6 in.) wide. Clearances can be smaller if a wheelchair can change direction, or if passing spaces are provided in long corridors. The exit access for low-rise buildings must have at least 81 cm (32 in.) of clear width to permit wheelchair use. The depths of objects protruding into the corridor are limited. If possible, a horizontal or ramped route should be provided for wheelchairs to exit a building in an emergency.

An aisle is a pathway created by furniture or equipment, with a maximum wall height of 1.75 meters (5 ft, 9 in.). If the furniture or equipment is any higher, the pathway is considered a corridor. Tables, counters, furnishings, equipment, merchandise, or other obstructions can create aisles. The pathways between movable panel systems in offices are considered aisles, as are the paths between tables and chairs in restaurants and display racks in stores. Check the ADA for specific dimension requirements. Rules for aisles that are part of an exit access are similar to those for corridors.

Assembly occupancies sometimes have fixed seating for large numbers of people. Codes restrict aisle widths depending upon the size of the occupancy, the number of seats served by each aisle, and whether the aisle is a ramp or a stair. The minimum distances between seats and where the aisles terminate are also regulated.

An exit access should be as direct as possible. In some projects, the access path may need to pass through an adjoining room or space before reaching a corridor or exit. This may be allowed if the path is a direct, unobstructed, and obvious means of travel toward the exit. The code allows smaller rooms to empty through larger spaces to access a corridor. Reception areas, lobbies, and foyers are allowed, as long as they meet code requirements. Kitchens, storerooms, restrooms, closets, bedrooms, and other spaces subject to locking are generally not allowed as part of an exit access except in a dwelling unit or where there is a limited number of occupants. Rooms with a higher susceptibility to fire are also restricted.

Elevators may not be used as part of a means of egress because of their inherent unreliability in a fire. Specially equipped elevators are required to assist firefighters in gaining quick access to upper floors of tall buildings. These special elevators must comply with elaborate precautions for reliable smoke control, secure electrical supply, and complete isolation from the effects of the fire.

Most of the stairs that we deal with in buildings are exit stairs. Another category covered by codes is the exit access stair. Exit access stairs are not as common as exit stairs. They are usually used within a space when one tenant occupies more than one floor of a building or where there is a mezzanine. Exit access stairs usually don't need a fire-rated enclosure unless they connect more than two floors.

No single floor should have steps or stairs within a means of egress. Ramps can be used wherever there is a change of elevation and access is required for people in wheelchairs. Ramps have width and clearance requirements similar to those of corridors. Ramps require landings at certain intervals and with certain dimensions depending on the length of the ramp and the number of changes in direction. Landings are also required at the top and bottom of the ramp. The ramp and landings require specific edge details and a rough nonslip surface. Handrails are typically required when ramps exceed a certain angle or rise, and guardrails may also be required.

EXITS

At last we come to the exit. The exit is the portion of a means of egress that is separated from all other spaces of a building. The exit leads from the exit access to the exit discharge, and must provide an enclosed, protected means of evacuation for occupants of the building in the event of fire. There are specific requirements for the quantity, location, and size of exits, along with other code and accessibility requirements similar to those for the exit access. The exit must be fully enclosed and fire-rated with minimal penetrations. Exits are typically required to have a two-hour fire separation, as compared to the exit access and exit discharge, which usually require up to one hour.

The exit must open either into another exit, into an exit discharge, or directly onto a public way. The exit may be a door opening directly to the outside from a ground floor room or corridor. It may be an exit passageway with walls of fire-rated construction. When the exit arrives at the door from above or below grade, you have an exit stair.

Exit Stairs

Exit stairs are the most common type of exit (Fig. 43-1). An exit stair includes the stair enclosure, any doors opening into or exiting out of it, and the stairs and landings within the enclosure. The stair enclosure must meet fire-rating requirements. All doors in an exit stair must swing in the direction of discharge.

When an exit stairway is enclosed by walls of fire-rated construction and is accessible by a vestibule or open exterior balcony, you have a smokeproof enclosure. An exterior balcony is defined as a landing or porch projecting from the wall of the building and serving as a required means of egress. The smokeproof enclosure must be ventilated by natural or mechanical means to limit penetration of smoke and heat. Stairs in smokeproof towers have direct access to outdoor air and to

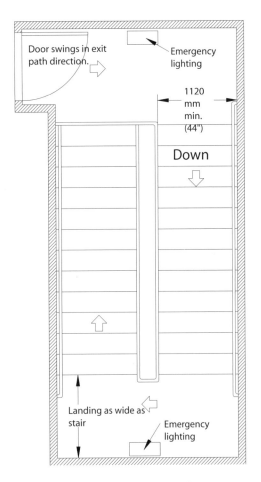

Figure 43-1 Fire exit stairs.

firefighting equipment at each floor, and are therefore the safest stairs. Building codes usually require one or more of the exit stairways of a high-rise building to be protected by a smokeproof enclosure.

 Enclosed exits may create some security concerns. An enclosed stair may allow an unauthorized person to gain entry to the building. They can provide an easy escape route for thieves. People may use enclosed stairs to travel to prohibited floors, or to avoid questioning by a receptionist or security guard. Enclosed exits can't be locked in the direction of exit travel, but can be locked from the exterior with emergency exit hardware and an alarm to deter unauthorized exits. Keeping the area adjacent to enclosed exit stairs easily visible to receptionists and security personnel will help control access. Glass in exit stair doors will let people see if someone is inside.

Exit Passageways

An exit passageway is a fully enclosed, fire-rated corridor or hallway. It provides the same level of protection as an exit stair. The exit passageway consists of the surrounding walls and the doors leading into it.

An exit passageway is most commonly used to extend an exit. If an enclosed exit stairway is not located at an exterior wall, the exit passageway can connect the bottom of the exit stair to an exterior exit door. Its length is limited to the maximum dead-end corridor permitted by code.

An exit access, such as a corridor, can also exit into an exit passageway. This may occur on the ground floor of a building when secondary exits are required, as in malls and office buildings with center building cores. The exit passageway is created at the building perimeter between two tenants, so that an exterior door can be reached off the common corridor.

An exit passageway can be used to shorten the distance to an exit by adding an enclosed, fire-rated corridor leading to a door at an exit stair. This gives a new end point for measuring the distance to the exit, and can help comply with code requirements for travel distances to an exit.

EXIT DISCHARGES

All exits must discharge to a safe place of refuge outside the building, such as an exit court or public way at ground level. An exit court may be a courtyard, patio,

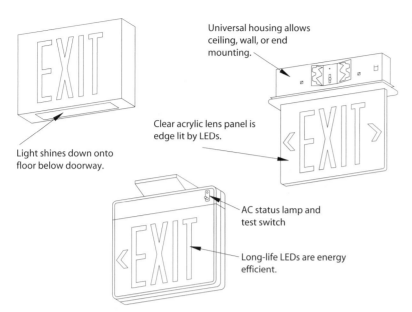

Figure 43-2 Exit signs.

Universal housing allows ceiling, wall, or end mounting.

Clear acrylic lens panel is edge lit by LEDs.

Light shines down onto floor below doorway.

AC status lamp and test switch

Long-life LEDs are energy efficient.

or exterior vestibule, connecting the exterior exit door to the public way. A public way is a street, alley, or similar parcel of land open to the sky and permanently available for free passage and use of the general public. Small alleys or sidewalks less than 3 meters (10 ft) wide are not considered public ways, and become exterior exit discharges connecting the exterior exit door to a larger alley, sidewalk, or street.

The exit discharge is the part of a means of egress that connects the exit with the public way, typically on the ground floor of a building. The width of the exit discharge is determined by the width of the exit it supports and the handicapped access requirements. If more than one exit opens into an exit discharge, the width is the sum of the various exits' requirements. A minimal ceiling height of 244 cm (8 ft) is typical.

 In the main building lobby, the distance between the door of an exit stair and the exterior door is considered to be an exit discharge. A foyer or vestibule—a small enclosure on the ground floor of a building between the end of a corridor and the exterior exit door—can be part of an exit discharge. If the size of such an enclosure is kept to the minimum, the codes may not require a high fire rating. A larger enclosure may be considered an exit passageway, requiring a higher rating.

Sometimes, in older buildings, an exit stair empties into the ground floor without a fire-rated exit passageway connecting the exit stairs to the exterior door. In this case, a corridor may become an exit discharge. This is not recommended, and is allowed only in a sprinklered building.

EXIT SIGNS

Exit signs (Fig. 43-2) are usually required wherever two or more exits are mandated by code. Exit signs are located at the doors of all stair enclosures, exit passageways, and horizontal exits on all floors. An exit sign is placed at an exterior exit door and at any door exiting a space or area when the direction of egress is unclear. An exit sign is usually required at a door, with directional signs at other places. Some smaller occupancies may not require exit signs.

Within an exit access, the maximum distance from an exit sign is limited to 30.5 meters (100 ft). Exit signs may be required by code to be mounted 20 cm (8 in.) above the floor in some occupancies, in addition to ceiling or wall mounted signs.

Chapter

Limiting Fuels

Many of the fatal fires throughout history have been due to flammable finishes and upholstery. In 1942, the fire in Boston's Cocoanut Grove Nightclub killed 492 people. This triggered the enactment of the Boston Fire Code, which established requirements for interior finishes. Some of the most rigid requirements are in the states of California, Florida, Massachusetts, New Jersey, and New York. Boston and New York City also have strict codes, and other cities now also have their own requirements. The model building codes and the *Life Safety Code* have sections on interior finishes. The *Life Safety Code* is usually stricter than the model building codes.

The *Life Safety Code* has a table for finish materials. Some occupancies have additional finish restrictions or requirements, and you may need to do further research in the *Life Safety Code* or the model building codes under the occupancy in question. Typical occupancies with special requirements include health care, detention or correctional institutions, hotels or dormitories, and apartment buildings. Theaters, where combustible scenery and temporary electrical wiring fill the backstage area, require provision of a fire-rated curtain, which is held rolled-up above the proscenium under normal circumstances, but which drops in a fire and seals the stage from the audience. Buildings with unusual structures may also have special requirements.

Stricter finish requirements usually apply where occupants are immobile or have security measures imposed on them restricting their freedom of movement, or in overnight accommodations. Industrial and storage buildings generally have more relaxed requirements because they generally have fewer occupants, who tend to be alert and mobile. Sprinklers throughout a building can change the finish class ratings, so it is important to know if a building has sprinklers and where they are located.

TERMINOLOGY

By definition, noncombustible materials will not ignite and burn when subjected to fire. Noncombustible materials are used in a building to prevent the substantial spread of fire. Noncombustible building materials are composed of steel, iron, concrete, and masonry. Their actual performance in a fire depends on how they are used.

Combustible materials will ignite and continue to burn when a flame source is removed. Wood can be chemically treated for some fire resistance. It is then called fire-retardant treated wood (FRTW). Heavy timber of a large enough diameter is considered fire resistant. This includes columns a minimum of 20 cm square (8″ × 8″), and beams a minimum of 152 by 254 mm (6″ × 10″).

Flammable and inflammable both mean the same thing: tending to ignite easily and burn rapidly. Both are the equivalent of highly combustible, so we will use that less confusing term.

We really shouldn't use the term "flameproof," as very few materials are truly completely resistant to flame. The proper terms are "flame retardant" and "flame resistant" or "fire resistant." Fire-resistant materials include gypsum wallboard, gypsum concrete, plaster, and mineral fiber products.

"Fire-rated" means that a product has been tested to obtain an hourly fire rating. Manufacturers must label tested products to ensure that they have passed the tests. Most manufacturers typically test products before putting them on the market. They know their products must meet code requirements to be specified. You must know how to find and obtain the required test results. Many manufacturers list test results on samples and products, or can provide the information on request.

 As an interior designer, you need to keep current on the testing and code requirements. Even where the jurisdiction may have lower standards, try to specify the most advanced tests and materials. If you are ever held legally liable, you must prove you used the most advanced requirements at the time of the project design.

Don't start selecting the finishes and furniture for a project until you determine what tests are required for each area. Make copies of the information in manufacturers' labels. If you have fabric treated for fire retardance, be sure to follow up with the fire-retardant treatment companies to make sure they send certificates to your client, and keep copies for your own records. Double-check requirements for spaces where people are seated for extended periods of time and areas that permit smoking. These include transport terminals, cocktail lounges, restaurants, and the lounge areas of public buildings, among other spaces.

 Various professional organizations publish lists of tested assemblies for walls and partitions, floor/ceiling systems, and roof/ceiling systems. They set standards for protection of beams, girders and trusses, columns, and window assemblies. The *Fire Resistance Directory* published by the Underwriters Laboratories (UL) covers beams, columns, floors, roofs, and partitions in Vol. I, and through-penetration firestop systems in Vol. II. Two other publications are also referenced in model codes, the Gypsum Association's *Fire Resistance Design Manual*, and the Factory Mutual *Specification Tested Products Guide*. To rate an assembly in an existing building, de-

termine the fire rating required by the building code, then use these publications to find a fire-rated assembly that is most similar to the existing condition. Use the file number of this assembly in your specs for new construction in the building. You must specify building materials with the correct fire rating for interior partitions. Too low a rating can reclassify the whole building into a lower category.

Be aware that test results and ratings of materials and assemblies can become invalid if the products are not used and maintained properly. In such an instance, the product or assembly must be retested or have added fire protection. If the construction of joints between each assembly, such as wall to wall, wall to ceiling, or wall to floor, is substandard, fire and smoke can penetrate regardless of the quality of the assembly. Some assemblies are tested with conventional openings, but some are not. Wall electrical switches and outlets, electric raceway, or pull boxes in the floor or ceiling can affect the system's endurance. Fire can impair the stability of a structural assembly. If an assembly is exposed to flame and heat, the strength and structural integrity of the building materials can be affected. Consequently, the original fire rating may not be accurate after a fire.

The interior designer should ask suppliers how materials have performed in real fires. Modern polymer materials have a complex response to fire. They may have good fire retardance, yet have high toxicity and smoke. Wallcovering that is not flame resistant can spread a fire down the length of a corridor in seconds, igniting other highly combustible materials and producing smoke, heat, and toxic fumes. Be cautious if the manufacturer is unresponsive or doesn't know the answers to your questions.

USING MATERIALS SAFELY

Many finishes and furnishings that an interior designer will specify are subject to fire code restrictions. Interior wall finishes include exposed interior surfaces applied over fixed or movable walls, partitions, columns, and other constructions. Interior ceiling finishes include exposed interior surfaces, such as suspended ceiling grids, and coverings applied to fixed or movable ceilings, soffits, and space frames. Fire code provisions regulate exposed interior surfaces including coverings applied over finished or unfinished floors, stairs (including risers), and ramps.

Until recently, in all but the strictest jurisdictions, codes regulated only interior wall, ceiling, and floor finishes, and didn't set requirements for furnishings or their finishes. Requirements continue to grow stricter, however, and to spread to more jurisdictions. It is the interior designer's responsibility to check requirements and to select furnishings with knowledge of codes and standards. Codes affecting furnishings cover exposed finishes found in furniture and window treatments, such as fabrics, wood veneers, and laminates. Also included are nonexposed finishes like the foam in seating and the linings in draperies. Furniture includes whole pieces of furniture and upholstered seating, as well as panel systems.

Many jurisdictions share a number of common rules for determining what is covered, although some localities use older code editions with less restrictive rules. The 10-percent rule for trims and decorative finishes that usually have lower fire ratings states that they must comprise less than 10 percent of the surface, and be evenly distributed and not concentrated in one area. This means that crown molding or wainscoting distributed throughout a project and amounting to less than 10 percent of the wall surface may be allowed, but paneling concentrated wall to wall and ceiling to floor in a law office may run into code problems.

The $\frac{1}{28}$-in. rule states that most interior finishes, such as paint and wallpapers, applied to noncombustible building materials (gypsum wallboard, brick, concrete) don't have to be rated if they are less than 0.9 mm ($\frac{1}{28}$ in.) thick. This rule does not apply when finishes are layered on top of each other. Vinyl wallcovering is regulated in all thicknesses, due to its burning characteristics and high smoke density. When a finish is applied to furring strips rather than directly on a noncombustible material, the total thickness is permitted to be a maximum of 44 mm ($1\frac{3}{4}$ in.) thick. Spaces between the furring strips must be filled with a fire-rated material or fire-blocked at 2.4-meter (8-ft) intervals.

In some jurisdictions, the presence of sprinklers may lower the permissible fire rating enough to allow finishes without ratings. This may not be allowed by the model building codes, however, and is not acceptable for new health care facilities.

All exits and paths of travel to and from exits must be clear of furnishings, decorations, or other objects. No drapes or mirrors are allowed to obscure exit doors, and mirrors are prohibited next to exit doors. Attention must not be drawn away from the exit sign.

Wood columns, heavy timber beams, and girders are typically allowed to remain exposed, because they are spaced relatively far apart and do not provide a continuous surface for flame spread. This is specified in the structural sections of the building code.

Foam plastics and cellular materials can't be used as wall or ceiling finishes unless they pass a test or comply with the 10-percent rule. There may be some small exceptions to this requirement.

Try to specify office furniture that is as noncombustible as possible, and specify steel filing cabinets. Choose wall coverings that are either noncombustible or low hazard. Everything in a plenum should be noncombustible or encased in noncombustible materials. In many major fires, combustible materials in hidden spaces resulted in injuries, deaths, and property losses. The way a material or system is oriented in relation to the environment also affects how readily it will burn.

Even though deaths occur more often in residential fires, the codes are much stricter for commercial projects. You have the option of choosing to design residential projects to the higher commercial standards. All wall and ceiling finishes for a residence, except for trims and materials less than 0.9 mm ($\frac{1}{28}$ in.) thick and wallpaper and paint, are required to meet the American Society for Testing and Material's ASTM-E84 testing requirements. Some finishes, such as wood veneer and hardboard paneling, must conform to other standards as well. Finishes in showers and bath areas are also regulated, and must be smooth, hard, and nonabsorbent, such as fiberglass, vinyl, or ceramic tile.

It is important to determine if you are selecting a finish or a furnishing. The same items take on different meanings depending on the jurisdiction and the project. Carpet may be considered a furnishing if installed over a finished floor. Movable walls and panel partitions may be furnishings or temporary walls, depending upon the jurisdiction. The majority of window treatments are not regulated by codes unless they cover large portions of a wall. Codes consider draperies a finish only if they cover more than 5 to 10 percent of the wall area, and consider tapestries in the same way. Be aware that some jurisdictions do have requirements for draperies and wall hangings.

Built-in cabinetry and seating with continuous expanses of plastic laminates and wood veneers are considered interior finishes by many jurisdictions. Highback upholstered restaurant booths can be restricted in certain jurisdictions.

FINISH CLASSES AND TEST RATINGS

Fire-resistance classes become stricter as you move closer to the exit, with the strictest ratings at the exit itself. The *Life Safety Code* and the *Standard Building Code* (SBC) use A, B, and C class ratings for wall and ceiling finishes. The *National Building Code* (NBC), and the *Uniform Building Code* (UBC) use I, II, and III designations.

Classes A, B, and C are wall and ceiling finish classifications based on flame spread and smoke development. Flame spread is the speed at which fire may spread across the surface of a material. Smoke-developed ratings indicate the amount of visibility in a given access route when a material is on fire and creating smoke.

Class A is the strictest and includes any material classed at a flame-spread rating of less than 25 with a smoke-developed rating below 450. Class B includes materials with flame-spread ratings between 25 and 75, and smoke test ratings below 450. Class C includes flame spreads from 76 to 200, and still limits smoke ratings to below 450. For example, labeled wood that has been treated with fire retardant usually qualifies as a Class A interior finish. Most untreated wood has a Class C flame-spread rating.

The Steiner tunnel test, ASTM E-84, determines both the flame-spread and smoke-developed ratings for wall and ceiling materials, as well as rating the surface burning characteristics of interior finishes and other building materials. During the test, a sample piece is placed in a tunnel test chamber that has a controlled flame at one end.

The *Life Safety Code* rates interior floor finishes as either Class I or Class II. Floor finishes are tested to determine the minimum energy required to sustain a flame. The test measures a floor covering's tendency to spread flames if located in a corridor and exposed to flame and hot gas from a fire in an adjacent room. The flooring radiant panel test, NFPA 253, ASTM E-648, or NBS IR75-950, tests a sample of carpet in a horizontal position. Class I requires a minimum critical radiant flux of 0.45 W per square cm. Class II requires a rating of 0.22 W per square cm.

Not all occupancies require that floor treatments be tested. If testing is required, only exits and access to exits are usually regulated. Finished floor coverings, like wood floors and resilient floor coverings, are unlikely to be involved in the early growth of a fire.

All carpets manufactured for sale in the United States since 1971 have been required to meet the *Federal Flammability Standard*, also known as the methenamine pill test. This is a pass/fail test that regulates the ease of surface ignition and surface flammability. A test sample of carpet is placed in a draft-protected cube, and held in place with a metal plate with a 20-cm (8-in.) diameter hole. A timed methenamine pill is placed in the center of the hole and lighted. If the sample burns to within one inch of the metal plate, the carpet fails the test.

Wall-to-wall carpet is regulated by a separate test, DOC FFI-70, and area rugs are covered by DOC FF2-70. Carpets used for purposes other than being placed on floors require additional tests.

Smoke density tests determine whether a solid material will hold a flame or smolder, and how much smoke it will emit. They also measure how thick and dark the smoke is to determine the amount of visibility during a fire and give a rating based on the results. The two best-known smoke density tests are NFPA 258 and ASTM E-662. The smoke density chamber test, NFPA 258, measures the optical density of the smoke on a scale of 0 to 800. Many codes require a smoke-developed rating of 450 or less for finish materials.

Toxicity tests are fairly new and are currently required only in a few states. The test used was developed by the University of Pittsburgh, and is known as the Pitts Test or LC50. It measures the amount of toxicity a material emits when burned, and tests wall, ceiling, and floor finishes. Upholstered furniture, mattresses and mattress pads, electrical wire and conduit, mechanical ductwork, thermal insulation, and plumbing pipes are also tested. The higher the LC50 rating, the less toxic are the emissions.

Finish and furnishing tests are constantly changing, and codes have improved older tests and added new tests. It is critical for the interior designer to keep abreast of changes so that the specified finishes and furnishings can pass the correct tests. There are currently tests that measure ignitability, flame spread, smoke density, and smoke toxicity. Some fabrics need additional or different tests depending on their use as drapery, upholstery, or wall coverings.

VERTICAL TREATMENTS

Vertical treatments, such as curtains, draperies, window shades, and large wall hangings or tapestries are tested under NFPA 701. Any vertical finish exposed to air on both sides may be covered. NFPA 701 encompasses two separate pass/fail tests. A small-scale test is used for straight hanging pieces. A large-scale test applies to fabrics used in folds, like gathered drapery. When vertical treatments cover a large area, they may also be required to pass the Steiner tunnel test.

When napped, tufted, or looped textiles or carpets are used on walls and ceilings, a corner test (or a similar test under another name) is used. This is a pass/fail test for flame spread, burning drops, flashover, and net peak heat.

UPHOLSTERED FURNITURE

Some cities and states have their own regulation standards for upholstered furniture. Among the strictest states are California, Massachusetts, and New York. New York City and the Port Authority of New York and New Jersey are two other jurisdictions with strict regulations.

A cigarette ignition test analyzes the smoldering resistance of an upholstered finish. This nonflame test uses a lit cigarette to see how a product will smolder before either flaming or extinguishing. It is used to test individual samples and mock-ups, and is especially important for seating using padding or foam.

Most smolder tests, including NFPA 260 and CAL 116, are pass/fail tests that measure the char size left on the fabric. CAL 117 is a smolder test that assigns a rating from A to E to a furniture mock-up. There is a similar test for mattresses and mattress pads, the *Standard for the Flammability of Mattresses* (FF4072), which is a federal government regulation.

California Technical Bulletin #133, more commonly known as TB 133 and CAL 133, is one of the most innovative and restrictive tests to date; CAL 133 is a pass/fail test of a whole piece of furniture (Fig. 44-1). It originally applied to furniture used in public spaces in California, including any area or room with ten or more articles of seating furniture, but requiring CAL 133 is becoming more common throughout the country and in more occupancies.

California Technical Bulletin #133 is a flame-resistance test that measures the carbon monoxide, heat generation, smoke, temperature, and weight loss of an entire piece of furniture. It aims to eliminate the flashover of a fire's second phase, when the fire may explode and simultaneously ignite surrounding rooms and corridors. Manufacturers are responsible for having their furniture tested and labeled. The test does not approve individual materials for individual uses.

The interior designer must select furniture passing CAL 133 when required. California, Illinois, Massachusetts, Minnesota, New Jersey, Ohio, Washington, and Wisconsin are among the states requiring furniture to pass CAL 133. Required spaces include public spaces and occupancies classified as high risk where occupants have limited or restricted mobility.

Some upholstered furniture may require only a smolder resistance test. Some jurisdictions that require CAL 133 for new upholstery accept CAL 117 for reupholstered pieces and built-in seating. Both smolder test and CAL 133 test results improve with certain fabric back-coatings, interliners, fire blockers, and specially rated foams.

Many manufacturers offer CAL-133 compliant products. All members of both the Business and Institutional Furniture Manufacturers (BIFMA) and the American Furniture Manufacturers Association (AFMA) are required to do so. Buildings with sprinklers are not always required to have CAL 133 tested furniture. If a fire occurs, the lack of tested furniture may, however, be a liability issue. Hence it may be appropriate to use a CAL 133 compliant product even when it is not required.

Manufacturers must decide how to assemble furniture to meet CAL 133. They may provide a fire block liner between the foam and the upholstery, or use flame-retardant foam. A fire block liner may reduce the price, so specifying one may help. Specifying a special fabric or customer's own material (COM) will change CAL 133 test results on a piece of furniture. The cost of retesting by the manufacturer may be passed on to the interior designer. The lead-time or length of production may be extended.

NONTESTED FINISHES

Sometimes finishes geared to residential use or from smaller manufacturers with specialty items have not been tested. The interior designer must then have the finish tested or make sure it is properly treated to meet code requirements. Depending on the situation, testing companies can be very costly to use, as they may have to simulate actual installations.

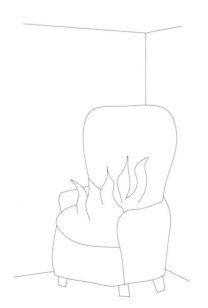

Figure 44-1 CAL 133 tests an entire piece of furniture.

It is often more cost effective to have a finish treated for fire retardance. Flame-resistant finishes add fire-retardant coatings to materials that haven't passed tests. Local manufacturers' representatives know the local requirements and where to get materials treated. Treatment may be applied to the material's surface, or as a fire-resistant coating used as a backing. The treatment delays the ignition of the material and slows the flame spread without changing the basic nature of the material. It may also lower the smoke development value.

The interior designer sends the fabric or other finish to the treatment company and tells them which tests the finish must pass. The treatment company adds the appropriate fire-retardant coating. Treatments can usually upgrade nonclassed finishes, and can even improve the performance of some rated materials to a higher class. The treatment company sends the interior designer a Certificate of Flame Resistance that indicates which tests the fabric will pass.

Some fabrics are not suitable for treatment. Flame retardant treatments can alter finishes and furnishings and cause a variety of possible problems when added to fabric. The fabric may shrink or decrease in strength so that it tears more easily. The hand or feel of the fabric may become stiffer. If the fabric has a texture, it may be flattened or distorted by the treatment. The treatment itself may cause the fabric to give off toxic fumes, especially in the presence of fire. If a wet treatment is used, the dye in the fabric may bleed or possibly change color or fade in the future.

You should check with the company doing the treatment, and submit a sample for testing prior to purchasing or treating the entire amount of fabric. The results of the treatment will depend on the content of the fabric and the type of treatment. It is best to have the fabric treated before applying it to the surface or furniture where it will be used, in case of problems.

Fire Suppression

In high-rise buildings and buildings with large areas, there are places that can't be reached by firefighters' ladders and hoses. While most fire deaths occur in smaller, often residential buildings, larger commercial, industrial, and institutional buildings create a potential for many deaths and injuries from a single fire. High-rise buildings require an inordinate length of time to evacuate. Stack effects can be created in high-rise buildings over 23 meters (75 ft) tall. Such buildings must have their own firefighting system. This is usually an automatic sprinkler system.

Everybody knows that water will put out a fire. Water cools, smothers, emulsifies, and dilutes the fire. But it also damages building contents, and can conduct electricity when used as a stream (less so as a spray). Water will not put out burning oil; the flammable oils will float and burn on the surface. When water hits a hot fire, the steam can harm firefighters. Despite these disadvantages, water remains one of the main ways to suppress a fire.

The earliest sprinkler system consisted of a bucket of water suspended over the likely location of a fire by a black powder fuse. When a fire lighted the fuse, it blew up a powder keg and dispersed water, theoretically in the direction of the fire.

Automatic sprinkler systems extinguish incipient fires before they have a chance to get out of control. The sprinkler system (Fig. 45-1) consists of a network of pipes in or below the ceiling. The pipes are connected to a water supply and have valves or sprinkler heads that are made to open automatically at a certain temperature. Each sprinkler head is controlled by a plug or link of fusible metal that melts at a temperature of around 66°C (150°F). Sprinkler heads are so efficient that one to two heads can usually put out a fire.

Building codes commonly allow sprinklered buildings to have greater distances between exits, eliminating one or more stairways in a large building. By allowing larger floor areas between fire separations, some fire-resistant walls and doors may be eliminated. Buildings may be allowed to have greater overall areas and heights. Some structural elements may need less fire protection, and the building may be able to contain greater amounts of combustible building materials.

Fire insurance rates are much lower for sprinklered buildings. Most fire underwriters refuse to insure a high-hazard building with no sprinkler system. However, insurance rates may increase if water damage is a big risk.

OCCUPANCY HAZARD CLASSIFICATIONS

Building codes classify various occupancies according to fire hazard. These classifications are used to determine the design of sprinkler systems.

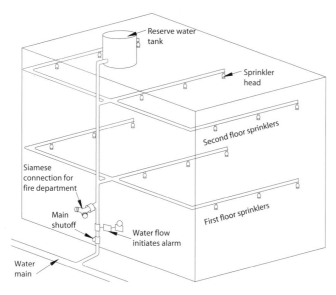

Reserve water tank

Sprinkler head

Second floor sprinklers

Siamese connection for fire department

Main shutoff

First floor sprinklers

Water flow initiates alarm

Water main

Figure 45-1 Sprinkler system.

The light hazard classification is used for buildings where it is relatively easy to provide effective fire protection. The quantity and combustibility of the building's contents is considered to be low, and a low rate of heat release is expected from possible fires. Light hazard occupancies include apartments, auditoriums, churches, hospitals, hotels, libraries, museums, nursing homes, office buildings, restaurants, schools, and theaters. A light hazard occupancy is required to have one sprinkler head per 18.6 square meters (200 square ft), with a maximum of 4.6 meters (15 ft) between supply lines and between the heads on each line. The sprinklers don't have to be staggered along their lines.

Ordinary hazard occupancies are considered to have moderate to high quantities of combustible materials, where the level of combustibility is relatively low to high. A moderate to high rate of heat release is expected. The materials may cause rapid fire development. Automotive garages, bakeries, laundries, and machine shops are considered ordinary hazards, as are manufacturing facilities, paper mills, print and publishing establishments, warehouses, and other industrial properties. Ordinary hazard occupancies require one sprinkler per 12 square meters (130 square ft) where there is a noncombustible ceiling, and one sprinkler per 11 square meters (120 square ft) for combustible ceilings. The maximum distance between lines and between sprinkler heads on a line is 4.6 meters (15 ft). Sprinklers are required to be staggered if the distance between heads exceeds 3.7 meters (12 ft).

The quantity and combustibility of materials in extra hazard (severe) occupancies are both very high. Rapid fire development and high heat release rates are expected where volatile flammable materials are processed, stored, mixed, or dispensed. Extra hazard occupancies include aircraft hangers, chemical works, explosive plants, linoleum manufacturing plants, paint shops, and shade cloth manufacturers. One sprinkler head is required every 8.4 square meters (90 square ft) with a noncombustible ceiling, and every 7.4 square meters (80 square ft) with a combustible ceiling. Sprinkler lines and heads must be no more than 3.7 meters (12 ft) apart, and heads must be staggered if they are more than 2.4 meters (8 ft) apart.

Generally, sprinkler systems are required for Factory, Hazardous, and Storage occupancies, or where large groups of people are present, as in Assembly, Institutional, and large Mercantile and Residential occupancies. The requirements are based on the number of occupants, the mobility of the occupants, and the types of hazards present.

Sprinkler systems are also commonly used in basements, windowless buildings, and high-rises. Sprinklers are often found in furnace and boiler rooms, at incinerator, trash, and laundry collection areas, and at the tops of chutes. They are required in kitchen exhaust systems and at spray painting shops or booths. Sprinklers are used in vertical openings, duct systems that exhaust hazardous materials, drying rooms, and atriums.

Residences generally don't have a water supply adequate for a standard sprinkler system. Toxic gases and smoke fill small residential rooms quickly, so a rapid response is essential for life safety. Many codes now require fast-response sprinklers with tested ability to enhance survival in the room where the fire originates in all residential occupancies. Such sprinklers are listed for protection of dwelling units. They are sensitive to both smoldering and rapidly developing fires, and open quickly to fight a fire with one or two heads.

Most codes exempt residential bathrooms under 5.1 square meters (55 square ft), closets with a minimum dimension of less than 91 cm (3 ft), open porches, garages and carports, and uninhabited attics and crawl spaces not used for storage. Entrance foyers that are not a sole means of egress are also exempted.

Residences use a special water distribution pattern, with water sprayed to walls and high enough to prevent the fire from getting above the sprinklers. They cool the gases at the ceiling level, so that fewer sprinklers need to open. The cost of residential sprinkler systems can be recovered through reduced fire insurance rates, but there is a long payback time.

DESIGNING FIRE SUPPRESSION SYSTEMS

The plumbing engineer or a sprinkler system specialist usually details the requirements for spacing sprinklers and references the appropriate codes. The design of the system considers the degree of hazard to the occupants. The maximum floor areas per head are set by hazard level. The areas covered by various types of sprinkler heads determine their approximate locations. Heads are located to detect fire readily and to discharge water over the greatest area. The sprinkler system designer considers obstacles such as joists, beams, and partial height partitions. The design of the hydraulic piping that supplies the sprinklers is a complex process.

 The interior designer should work closely with the sprinkler system designer to verify sprinkler head locations and provide adequate clearance at each sprinkler. Typically, a minimum of 46 cm (18 in.) must be left open below the sprinkler head deflector. The interior designer should be especially observant of this requirement where wall cabinets or shelving are used, as in storage rooms, kitchens, and libraries.

SPRINKLER SYSTEM COMPONENTS

Sprinkler systems are designed to start to put out the fire and to send out an alarm simultaneously. When water flows through a sprinkler head, an alarm gong goes off outside the building. The gong alerts people outside the building to the fire, and allows the occupants to make additional firefighting arrangements to minimize loss and to speed the end of the fire. Turning off sprinklers as soon as possible prevents water dam-

Figure 45-2 Siamese connection.

age. The alarm is often connected to a private regional supervisory office that calls the municipal fire department. All public buildings and some other buildings are required to have a fire detection and alarm system with an indicator of the location of the fire in the custodian's office.

Sprinkler systems need an adequate water supply, and standby power for water pumping. Siamese connections (Fig. 45-2) allow fire engines to pump water into the system from outside the building. They are installed close to the ground on the exterior of a building and provide two or more connections through which the fire department can pump water to a standpipe or sprinkler system. Tall buildings may have elevated water storage tanks that can help supply water for sprinklers.

Sprinkler systems require very large supply pipes, valves, and fire pumps. The valves are used to shut the system off for maintenance, system modification, or replacement of heads that have operated after a fire. An improperly closed valve is the major reason for sprinkler system failure. Fire pumps provide required water

Ted's client wanted to add a direct entrance from the street to his new retail store. The site, however, was a historic building, and the Landmark Commission insisted that the new door exactly mirror the appearance and location of the existing door to the building on the opposite end of the facade. This posed a problem because a big brass Siamese sprinkler system connection was located right in front of the proposed new door. The placement of the door was critical to the interior design of the store, and Ted needed to have the problem settled before he could finish his design.

Once the contractor got into the building, he discovered that the piping for the sprinkler connection was tight against a granite foundation wall. The connection could be moved off to one side, but not completely out of the way. By moving the connection as far to the side as possible, and by widening the door's framing detail, Ted and the contractor were able to install the new door where it would work from the inside, while still being acceptable to the Landmark Commission on the outside. The result looks like it has always been there.

pressure in a standpipe or sprinkler system when the pressure in the system drops below a preselected value.

Many code authorities will accept combining sprinkler piping with the heating and cooling system, heat recovery system, hot and chilled water thermal storage system, or solar energy system, permitting construction cost savings.

Sprinkler Heads

The sprinkler head keeps the water in the system by a plug or cap held tightly against the orifice (opening) by levers or other restraining devices. The levers are held in place by the arms of the sprinkler body. In the past, the restraining device was usually a fusible metal link that melted at a predetermined temperature. More recently, a glass bulb with colored liquid and an air bubble is used. Heat expands the liquid, which compresses the air bubble until it is absorbed. Expansion continues with rising temperature until the bulb bursts at a predetermined temperature and releases water in a solid stream through the orifice.

The deflector on the sprinkler head converts the solid stream to a spray. It is more efficient to direct the spray down and horizontally rather than up, for better water distribution near the head and more effective coverage below.

Sprinkler head types include upright heads that sit on top of exposed supply piping (Fig. 45-3), and pendant heads that hang below the piping (Fig. 45-4). Sidewall sprinklers (Fig. 45-5) are usually located adjacent to one wall of smaller rooms, as in hotels or apartments, and throw a spray of water across the room, allowing

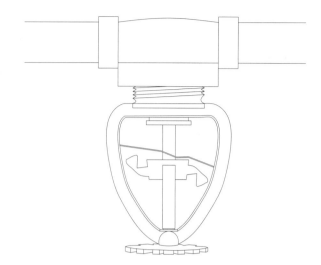

Figure 45-4 Pendant sprinkler head.

an entire small room to be covered by one sprinkler head.

Pendant heads may be recessed, with part of the sprinkler body concealed above suspended ceilings and the deflector below the ceiling. Flush heads have only the heat-detecting element below the ceiling. Concealed heads are entirely above the ceiling, with a cover plate that falls away in a fire. Sprinkler head finishes are available in plain or polished brass, satin or polished chrome, stainless steel, and gold. The manufacturer may be able to coat ornamental pendants to match a desired decor, but sprinkler heads are never permitted to be field coated.

The air around a standard sprinkler may reach around 538°C (1000°F) before the standard 175°F-rated sprinkler opens, causing a lag time. Quick-response sprinkler heads are now required throughout light hazard occupancies, including office buildings, motels, and

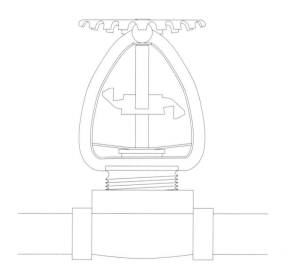

Figure 45-3 Upright sprinkler head.

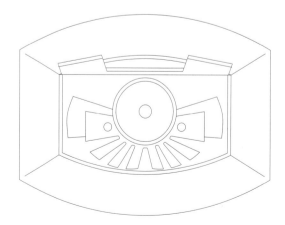

Figure 45-5 Sidewall sprinkler head.

hotels. They are more thermally sensitive and open sooner than older styles, and are able to fight a fire with fewer open heads, causing less water damage. The quick-response sprinklers track air temperature rise. The earlier operation is considered to offer superior life protection. They may, however, open for extraordinary heat that is not fire related.

Early suppression fast-response (ESFR) sprinklers are used for specific challenging fire hazards, for example where storage is piled high. The sprinkler's higher pressure and flow penetrate the fire's base faster. Quick-response, early suppression (QRES) sprinklers are similar to ESFR sprinklers, but with a smaller orifice for light-hazard occupancies. They are expected to be available soon for business, retail, public assembly, and educational applications.

Extended coverage sprinklers are used for unobstructed construction with flat smooth ceilings and no projecting lighting fixtures or grilles. Extra-large orifice sprinkler heads emit large quantities of water where water pressures are low. Multilevel sprinklers use sprinklers at lower levels in a space that has other sprinklers at a higher level. Normally, the lower sprinklers would be inhibited by the action of the higher sprinklers. Flow control sprinklers close automatically when ceiling temperatures are reduced, saving water and damage. A new development is a single head that may provide multiple types of sprays. Larger droplets penetrate the fire while a finer spray cools ceilings.

Sprinkler System Piping

The most common and simplest piping system for sprinklers is a wet-pipe system. Wet-pipe systems contain water at a sufficient pressure to provide immediate, continuous discharge through the sprinkler heads that open automatically in the event of a fire. They are used in spaces with air temperatures above 4°C (40°F). The affected sprinklers are opened by sensitive elements in the heads and immediately emit water. Wet-pipe systems must be drained in order to change the location of a sprinkler head, adding expense and inconvenience to the project.

A dry-pipe system contains pressurized air or nitrogen that is released when a sprinkler head opens, allowing water to flow through the piping and out the opened nozzle. Dry-pipe systems are used in unheated areas where wet-pipe systems might freeze, such as loading docks, cold-storage areas, and unoccupied buildings. Dry-pipe systems require compressed air, a heated main control valve housing, and pitched piping to allow drainage after use.

A preaction system is a dry-pipe system with air in the pipes, with water flow controlled by a valve operated by separate heat or smoke detection devices more sensitive than the ones in the sprinkler heads. The preaction valve holds water back until heat or smoke opens it, sounding an alarm and filling the pipes with water. Preaction systems are used where building contents are sensitive to water damage. The early alarm allows the fire to be extinguished manually without using the sprinklers in computer rooms, retail stores, and museums. The delay can allow the fire to grow rapidly, however, by as much as 30 percent within 60 seconds, thus requiring 30 percent more water to extinguish it.

A deluge system uses open sprinklers on dry pipes. When a heat and smoke detection system opens the deluge valve, the system floods with water and all heads emit water. This releases a huge quantity of water. Deluge systems are used for areas with a risk of extremely rapid fire spread, like aircraft hangers and places where flammable liquids are stored or used.

A circulating closed-loop system is a wet-pipe system with larger sprinkler piping. The system circulates water for the heating, ventilating, and air-conditioning (HVAC) water heat pumps. Temperatures must stay between 49°C (120°F) and 4°C (40°F).

Sprinkler System Damage Control

The space with sprinklers should have adequate water drainage during and after the fire. When fire hoses and sprinklers overshoot the fire area, the building and its contents sustain water damage even where there is no fire. The water drains to lower building levels, so floor drains should be provided to safely carry this water away from the building.

Provisions for drainage of water can include scuppers in exterior walls, which are less likely to clog than floor drains. Scuppers should have hoods to control birds and insects. Salvage covers can protect sensitive objects and direct water toward drainage points. A readily accessible outside valve that controls all the normal sources of supply to the system can cut off water promptly when it is no longer needed.

STANDPIPES AND HOSES

Standpipes are water pipes that extend vertically through the building to supply fire hoses (Fig. 45-6) at every floor. Wet standpipes contain water under pressure and

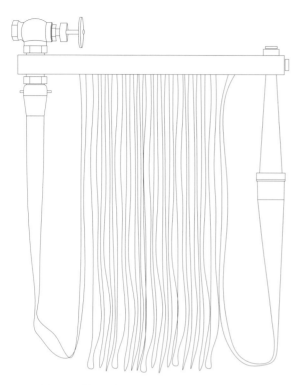

Figure 45-6 Standpipe system hose rack.

are fitted with fire hoses for emergency use by building occupants. Dry standpipes do not contain water, but are used by the fire department to connect fire hoses to a fire hydrant or pumper truck.

Separate water reserves, upfeed pumping, or fire department connections feed standpipes. They provide emergency firefighting before the fire department arrives, and are also used for full-scale firefighting. The water supply can be turned on automatically or manually.

OTHER FIRE SUPPRESSION SYSTEMS

For buildings where water would cause irreparable damage to the building contents, expensive systems are available that discharge an inert gas or powder over the flames. These systems are used in libraries, museums, and art galleries.

Commercial kitchens use dry chemical systems for grease fires. The exhaust plenum and duct system becomes grease coated and the kitchen's high operating temperatures create a fire hazard. A flash fire in a cooking appliance can ignite grease in the duct. A dry chemical system with a sodium bicarbonate base is sprayed into the plenum chamber and ducts, extinguishing the

fire in seconds. The system automatically cuts the supply of heat to the stove or appliance, whether it is gas or electric. Grease fires can distort a duct, allowing grease to spill into concealed spaces in walls and ceilings. As a result, fire suppression nozzles are located in hoods over cooking areas and in ducts.

Systems that don't use water are available for electronic data storage areas, paint dip tanks and spray booths, petroleum storage, securities vaults, and transformer rooms. These systems use carbon dioxide, halon, high-expansion foam, or dry chemicals.

Mist systems have been used for shipboard fires in the past, and are now being considered for other uses as well. A mist system allows a faster initiation of the alarm and a quicker response to the fire than a sprinkler system. By using smaller volumes of water, they reduce damage. The mist poses no safety threat to firefighters and allows more building ventilation during the fire. It eliminates residues from clean-agent gases such as halon. The system doesn't have to be refilled with expensive gases, and can be returned to service more quickly after use. Mist system heads are spaced more closely together and are more sensitive to heat than sprinkler heads. They operate by heat extraction and oxygen displacement and block radiant heat.

Intumescent materials, which expand rapidly when touched by fire, create air pockets to insulate the surface from the fire, or swell material to block openings through which fire and smoke could travel. Intumescent paints, caulks, and putties are available, as are 6-mm ($\frac{1}{4}$-in.) thick sheets with a variety of facing materials.

FIRE SUPPRESSION AGENTS

We have already mentioned some of the fire suppression agents that are used in these various suppression systems. Here is some more information on the subject.

Halon

Halogenated hydrocarbons, commonly known as halons, are flame-extinguishing gases that are stored as liquids. Until the mid 1990s, the most common was Halon 1301, which provided lightweight, space-saving fire suppression for commercial aircraft, computer rooms, museums, libraries, telephone exchanges, and kitchens. Halon 1301 extinguishes fire without leaving a residue to damage electronic components. Because it doesn't displace oxygen, it causes little harm to people.

Halon 1301 is now known to be a long-lived and significant threat to the stratospheric ozone layer, and production was phased out in 1994. Mists, foams, and inerting gases and clean agents have replaced it. The inerting gases and clean agents protect building contents more than the building structure and leave no sticky residue.

Clean Agent Gases

Replacements for Halon 1301 are being developed that use hydrochlorofluorocarbons (HCFCs) and hydrofluorocarbons (HFCs). These chemicals are confined to vital spaces such as control rooms, computer and communications facilities, and emergency response centers.

FM-200® works like halons but does not cause ozone depletion. It has a much shorter atmospheric lifetime and presents less of a threat of greenhouse gas and global warming. FM-200 leaves practically no particulates or oily residue to damage electronic instruments and does not conduct electricity. It is noncorrosive and colorless. FM-200® displaces only around 7 percent of the air in a space, and has acceptable toxicity levels, making it relatively safe for firefighters.

Foams

Fire suppression foams consist of masses of gas-filled bubbles. Because they are lighter than water and flammable liquids, they float on the surfaces of burning liquids to smother and cool fires and seal in vapors. The foam won't harm aircraft or delicate machinery.

Low-expansion foam extinguishes burning combustible liquid spills or tank fires. High-expansion foam and medium-expansion foam are used for indoor fires in confined spaces. They fill enclosures such as basement room areas and the holds of ships. They also can be used to control liquefied natural gas spill fires and to help disperse the resulting vapor cloud.

Fire suppression foams will conduct electricity, and can't be used for electrical fires. Firefighters need to use self-contained breathing apparatus and a lifeline to enter a foam-filled passage.

Carbon Dioxide

Carbon dioxide prevents the ignition of potentially flammable mixtures and extinguishes fires involving flammable liquids or gases. It absorbs combustion energy, and reduces the temperature of the flame and vapor mixture below the level necessary to sustain combustion.

Carbon dioxide smothers fires by displacing oxygen, and is limited to use in tightly confined spaces without people or animals. It is appropriate for use in display cases, mechanical and electrical chases, and unventilated areas above suspended ceilings or below raised floors. Carbon dioxide is used in data centers, telecommunications equipment spaces, and electrical equipment rooms where water would damage the contents.

Carbon dioxide is stored as a liquid in cylinders under great pressure. It is noncombustible and won't react with most substances. It does not conduct electricity, and doesn't normally damage sensitive electronic equipment. There is no residue to clean up after use.

After use, the carbon dioxide gas escapes to the atmosphere at levels that pose a significant danger to building occupants and firefighters. Smoldering embers may ignite again after being suppressed by carbon dioxide.

PORTABLE FIRE EXTINGUISHERS

Since portable fire extinguishers are movable and don't require access to plumbing lines, they are usually specified by the interior designer on interior projects. Portable fire extinguishers are used to extinguish fires at an early stage. They are rated for the class of fire they are designed to fight. How many are required and where they must be located depend on the hazard classification of the occupancy. They must be located in conspicuous places along ordinary paths of egress. Fire extinguishers may be surface mounted or recessed within the wall using a special cabinet with a vision panel. The extinguisher must be visible at all times, must be tested regularly, and must have an approved label. This presents a challenge to the interior designer, since fire extinguishers and related equipment are bright red and in highly visible locations. It may be a good idea to show this equipment on your interior elevations, so that your client (or you yourself) isn't surprised by the final appearance of the room.

The typical home fire extinguisher is not designed to fight large or spreading fires, because it will run out in eight seconds or less. A fire extinguisher must be rated as the correct type for the fire that you need to put out. The extinguisher must have adequate force to fully extinguish the fire. Locate the extinguisher where it is both quick and safe to get in case of fire. Someone who has the strength and knowledge to use it properly and without hesitation must handle the fire extinguisher.

Building codes specify which occupancies and types

of building uses require fire extinguishers. Most occupancies do require extinguishers, and some specific areas within buildings have special requirements. Commercial kitchens and smaller kitchens and break rooms in commercial spaces require extinguishers. NFPA 10, *Portable Fire Extinguishers* provides guidelines for types and locations of extinguishers. Generally, no occupant may be more than 22.9 meters (75 ft) from a fire extinguisher where they are required.

The interior designer needs to be familiar with the codes and related Americans with Disabilities Act (ADA) requirements for portable fire extinguishers. If a fire suppression system is to be used by the building's occupants, it must be mounted at accessible heights and located within accessible reaches from a front or side wheelchair approach. Fire suppression equipment may not protrude more than 102 mm (4 in.) into the path of travel. This requirement may eliminate bracket-mounted fire extinguishers and surface mounted fire protection cabinets in some areas.

Fire extinguishers are classified by types represented by letters. They also have force ratings indicated by numbers. The higher the rating number, the more extinguishing agent the unit contains, and therefore the larger the fire it should be able to put out. A higher force number also means a heavier extinguisher.

Type A devices are exclusively for use on ordinary combustibles such as wood, cloth, or paper. They are quite dangerous if directed at burning grease or energized electrical equipment. Type A units use water, foam, or multipurpose dry chemicals to put out the fire. They vary from Class 1A to Class 40A.

Type B extinguishers are for use on flammable liquids, including oil and grease. They employ carbon dioxide, dry chemicals, or wet chemical foam to suffocate flames. In the past, they also used halogenated agents. They include Class 5B to Class 40B.

Type C units are for energized electrical equipment. They use nonconductive dry chemicals or carbon dioxide. A combination type BC extinguisher is available for use in kitchens and other locations where both flammable liquids and electrical wiring might be involved in a fire.

Type ABC is a multipurpose dry chemical extinguisher that usually uses ammonium phosphate. ABC extinguishers can be used on any kind of fire, but are not ideal for electrical fires, as they leave a hard residue that causes damage to electrical equipment.

Type D uses dry powders such as graphite or sodium chloride to put out fires in combustible metals. The specific combustible metal the extinguisher is to be used on is printed on the nameplate.

Fire Detection and Alarms

●●●

We have looked at how we can design to prevent fires from starting and spreading. We have explored the ways that we can get people safely out of a building in the event of a fire. We have also examined how to put out a fire once it starts. Now let's explore the systems that detect fires and alert us to their presence.

FIRE DETECTION

A fire progresses through four stages: incipient, smoldering, flame, and heat. Different types of fire and smoke detectors are designed to indicate problems at each of these stages.

Incipient Stage Detectors

Combustion produces microscopic particles when a fire is just starting. Ionization-type particulate detectors (Fig. 46-1) are designed to detect these particles by noticing a reduction in the electrical current flow and to set off an alarm. Ionization-type detectors work best indoors where there is stagnant air, where the air

velocity is low, and where there is little visible smoke with large particles. Ionization-type detectors respond best to fast-burning flaming fires, which need a fast response and produce less smoke. They should not be installed on warm or hot ceilings, or in kitchens, bakeries, workshops with open flames or burners, or where there are concentrated engine exhaust fumes. They need periodic cleaning to remove dust, and regular recalibration. Because the incipient stage of a fire also changes the gas content of the air, gas sensing fire detectors are often used along with particulate detectors. Incipient stage detectors cover between 14 square meters (150 square ft) and 84 square meters (900 square ft), depending on the type of detector and the situation.

Wilson cloud chamber type detectors are sensitive to microscopic particles in the early stages of a fire but insensitive to dust. They use continuous air sampling and give few false alarms. Wilson cloud chamber detectors require piping and are expensive in small installations. The price becomes competitive when over 30 detection points are needed. These detectors are used in high-value installations like museums, data processing spaces, libraries, clean rooms, and facility control rooms.

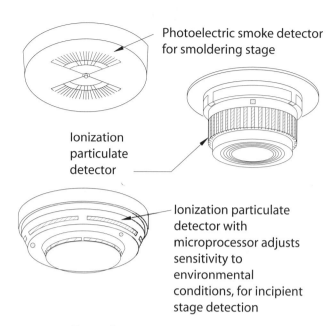

Photoelectric smoke detector for smoldering stage

Ionization particulate detector

Ionization particulate detector with microprocessor adjusts sensitivity to environmental conditions, for incipient stage detection

Figure 46-1 Automatic fire detectors.

Smoldering Stage

Smoke detectors have become increasingly important as finishes and furnishings become more flame resistant and therefore more likely to smolder for a long time without flame at temperatures too low to trigger sprinklers. NFPA 72, *Household Fire Warning Equipment*, and NFPA 101, Chapter 22 regulate the use of residential smoke detectors. The goal should be to provide sufficient time to evacuate residents and to take countermeasures.

The particles in smoke at the smoldering stage are large enough to be visible to the eye. Photoelectric smoke detectors use a beam of light projected to a photo-sensor. When the beam is broken by smoke, the alarm goes off. Dust, dirt, or heavy fumes can obscure both the photocell and the lamp, which along with aging of the lamp results in false alarms. Photoelectric smoke detectors require continuous maintenance and periodic recalibration. They are used for smoldering fires and smoky fires from plastics and chemicals.

Projected beam photoelectric smoke detectors (Fig. 46-2) can cover even greater distances. They use a beam transmitter and beam receiver mounted on the walls on opposite sides of the space somewhat below the ceiling. They are used in spaces with high ceilings, such as atriums, churches, malls, and auditoriums, where spot-type detectors are difficult to reach for maintenance. Projected beam detectors can be physically shielded for use in very dirty, corrosive, humid, hot, or cold areas. The range from the transmitter to the receiver is from 9 to

92 meters (30–300 ft). Units are spaced 9 to 18 meters (30–60 ft) apart. Projected beam photoelectric smoke detectors are expensive. They must have an unobstructed view, which may be a problem with exposed ductwork or pendant lighting fixtures.

Scattered light photoelectric smoke detectors are also called photoelectronic or Tyndall-effect detectors. A beam of pulsed light-emitting diode (LED) light is directed at a photocell. If the light is scattered by particles, it strikes an alarm cell. Scattered light detectors are not sensitive to normal dust, dirt, or light source depreciation and do not require continual maintenance. They are used for commercial and high-quality residential construction.

Laser beam photoelectric devices are scattered light type detectors that use a very high-sensitivity laser diode source. They are able to differentiate between smoke and dust particles, but work best in clean environments.

Air sampling detection systems sample air throughout a space by using piping with holes at sampling points. A fan powers them, and the piping is zoned to indicate the area of the problem.

A basic residential system places a listed smoke detector outside and adjacent to each sleeping area, in each sleeping room, and at the head of every stair, with at least one on every level including the basement. Combined smoke and heat detectors are recommended in the boiler room, kitchen, garage, and attic. An alarm in any detector should set off an alarm in all audible and visible units.

Codes specify which occupancies require smoke detectors but don't always give specific locations, so the

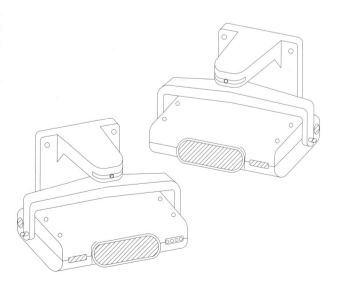

Figure 46-2 Pair of projected beam smoke detectors.

interior designer must then determine the best placement. Smoke detectors are subject to false alarms from moisture and particles in the air. The greater the sensitivity of the detector, the more false alarms. Choosing the appropriate type and avoiding placement where conditions cause problems will limit false alarms. If you must locate a smoke alarm in a poor location, use more than one type of detector, specify extra maintenance, and provide for verification of alarms.

Kitchens, laundries, boiler rooms, shower rooms, and other spaces with high humidity and steam create problems for smoke detectors. Repair shops and laboratories with open flames used in their work and garages and engine test facilities with exhaust gases affect sensors. Smoking rooms and areas near designated smoking areas can be a problem, as can areas with heavy accumulations of dust and dirt. High volumes of air movement near loading docks, exit doors, and discharging ducts and registers are also problems.

Avoid putting smoke detectors where normal cooking processes will activate the alarm in kitchens. Units are usually placed 15 to 30 cm (6–12 in.) from the ceiling when mounted on a wall. If the alarm is too close to the intersection of the wall and ceiling or too near a doorway, the air currents may carry smoke and heat past the unit. If you are unsure of proper placement, check with the manufacturer or with code officials.

Most jurisdictions require installation and hard wiring of smoke detectors in residential occupancies and hotel or motel units. Interconnected detectors tied into the building electrical system and with a battery backup are required in many new homes and homes with new additions or alterations. Other homes are required to have at least battery-operated units. Residences are usually required to have smoke detectors outside each sleeping area and on all habitable floors. Townhouses have even stricter requirements.

 Smoke detectors in apartment houses, dormitories, hotels, motels, and rooming houses are governed by NFPA 101 and NFPA 72. Alarm systems are designed to provide early warning and orderly egress at times when the building occupants may be asleep. Audible and visual alarms are positioned so that all sleeping persons, including those with sight or hearing impairments, will be wakened. Be aware that living rooms may be regularly used as sleeping areas. There should be an alarm light over the door of each apartment or suite to indicate the alarm location, especially if the central panel only shows a zone location. In high-rise residential buildings, an emergency voice alarm communication system should be provided.

Smoke detectors should be located in the corridors of multiple dwelling buildings, and in service spaces and utility and storage rooms. Battery powered detectors are not permitted in multiple dwellings. All fire alarm circuits should have standby power. All alarms must be identifiable by addressing or annunciation, which indicate the location of the alarm. Annunciator panels that have a map and lights can be located at a system control panel in the building management office or at the lobby desk of a hotel or dormitory. Lobby annunciators are helpful to firefighters.

In apartments, false alarms are common from kitchen smoke and excessive dust. Some apartment building alarm systems give only a local alarm for evacuation of the apartment. A separate central heat detector system sounds a remote alarm. This reduces the number of false alarms but increases the risk of a fire growing before activation of the fire-suppression system or before firefighting crews are dispatched.

Flame Stage

The presence of a flame leads to the almost immediate buildup of heat and the rapid spread of flame, creating a large increase in hazard. Fire suppression and evacuation must be very rapid.

Ultraviolet (UV) radiation detectors react to the UV radiation (heat energy) produced by flames. They are used indoors or outside for storage or work areas with highly flammable or explosive contents. A UV detector does not need a clear view of the flame, as it can respond to reflected radiation from walls and ceilings. They operate long-range, are very sensitive, react in milliseconds, and respond to most types of fires. Unfortunately, thick black smoke can block their view of UV radiation.

Infrared (IR) radiation detectors are most sensitive to radiation at the level emitted by hot carbon dioxide, and thus IR detectors are used for fires that result in rapid flaming combustion and production of carbon dioxide, such as petroleum products, wood and paper products, coal, and plastics. They are effective for only about half the range of UV detectors, and react in seconds rather than milliseconds. Because they are subject to frequent false alarms, they are usually used only in enclosed spaces like sealed storage vaults. Detectors that combine UV and IR are available to reduce the risk of false alarms (Fig. 46-3).

Heat Stage

Heat is the last and most hazardous stage, when the fire is burning openly. Great heat, incandescent air, and smoke are all present. The heat stage follows the smoke

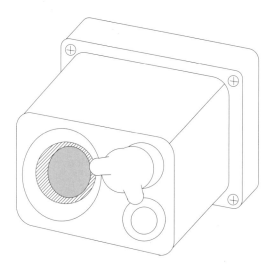

Figure 46-3 Combined UV–IR flame detector.

stage, and since smoke is responsible for most fire deaths, waiting for heat is dangerous. Heat-actuated detectors, also called thermal, thermostatic, or temperature detectors, operate like the fusible link in a sprinkler head. They are used to detect rapid temperature rise fires.

Spot units are mounted in the center of a space, such as separated, unoccupied areas. Linear units are cable-like elements that sense heat along their entire length. They can sense the overheating of an object without fire, and are used in cable trays and bundles, and for large, long equipment.

FIRE ALARM SYSTEMS

The goal of a fire alarm system is first to protect life, and secondly to prevent property loss. Systems are tailored to specific building types and uses. A fire alarm system includes equipment for signaling that there is a problem, for processing the signal, and for alerting people as to the situation. A fire alarm system can initiate fan controls, smoke venting, smoke door closers, rolling shutters, and elevator controls as part of an overall fire protection plan.

Signaling the Problem

Sometimes an automatic fire detector first detects the fire, as we have just discussed. Other times, a person is the first to notice the fire, and gives the alarm by using a pull station (Fig. 46-4) or telephone.

Manual fire alarm initiation stations must be placed in the normal path of egress to be used by a person exiting the building. Manual stations must be well marked and easily found. Do not place them in nooks, corners, or camouflaged cabinets to avoid spoiling the decor. Never paint over smoke detectors or other fire safety equipment, as this may hamper their effectiveness by keeping fusible links from melting.

New handicapped-accessible types of pull boxes are available that are actually pushed and that take minimal effort to operate. Both regular pull boxes and the newer accessible boxes must be red.

The architect or designer of the fire alarm system must ascertain which current regulations have jurisdiction before designing the system. The codes generally specify where manual or automatic fire signaling systems or fire alarm systems are required. The codes specify required systems and provide testing data. An electrical engineer will be involved in the design of an extensive fire alarm system.

With a protected premises fire alarm system, the alarm sounds only in the protected building. Protected premises systems are used for privately owned facilities. If a building were unoccupied, the fire department would be notified only if a passerby happened to report the fire.

An auxiliary fire alarm system is a local system with a direct connection to a municipal fire alarm box. Auxiliary systems are used in public buildings such as schools, government offices, and museums.

With a remote station protective signaling system, an alarm is transmitted via a phone line to a police facility or telephone answering system that is manned 24 hours a day. The notice is then phoned to the fire de-

Figure 46-4 Manual pull station.

partment. Remote station protective signaling systems are used for private buildings like offices and stores that are unoccupied for longer periods and where the owners don't want to rely on outside observers for notification.

Proprietary fire alarm systems are found in large, multibuilding facilities, like universities or manufacturing facilities. A visual display of the fire's location along with other information and a printed record is sent automatically to an on-site, manned central supervisory station that receives signals from all buildings in the system. The fire department is notified manually from the on-site station. The central station can also be used for security and other control functions.

A central station fire alarm system is like the proprietary system, but the system supervision and equipment is owned and operated by a service company. A central station supervises many individual, unrelated locations for a fee.

Fire alarm systems may have circuit supervision alarms that warn of malfunctions in the wiring of an alarm. The signal for this is separate and distinct from the alarm signal itself. Circuit supervision may be required by code, so that a single break in the alarm system will not prevent fire alarms from going off.

A public emergency reporting system may be located in key egress and public gathering areas. Building occupants report fire or police or medical emergencies to qualified operators within a facility, who then act to deal with the problem.

Processing the Signal

In a conventional fire alarm system, detectors and manual stations transmit alarm signals only. All signals are the same, so you don't have any way to tell if an alarm is false or due to a malfunction. False alarms happen with all types of detectors. In places like hospitals, theaters, office buildings, and large dining facilities, they can cause serious disruption, property loss, personal injury, and even death. Constant maintenance checks to verify that all alarms are working properly are expensive and time-consuming.

Fire alarm signal processing uses a control panel to start the audible and visible alarm circuits, illuminate the annunciator panels, and control fans and door releases. Control panels can be both simple and reliable. However, with system growth, they can become heavy, complex, and expensive. Panels can become large and bulky, and changes may be difficult. Troubleshooting is often faulty and time-consuming, and false alarms may

be difficult to locate quickly. Because of these problems, addressable control systems were developed.

With an addressable fire alarm system, each detector is a separate zone that can be identified centrally, with up to 100 detectors on one line. The detectors are continually checked from a central panel to see whether they are working and on standby, giving an alarm, or experiencing trouble. It is easy to confirm an alarm with an addressable system, so false alarms are reduced. The system records any decrease in detector sensitivity or malfunction. The initial hardware costs are higher than with a conventional control panel, but maintenance costs are lower.

For a residential building, the central panel should show the location of the alarmed device and be arranged to shut off the oil and gas lines and attic fan to prevent spread of smoke. The central panel should also turn on the lights inside and outside the residence, and automatically ring a neighbor's or a commercial central station's telephone and give a distinctive alarm sound when answered. An outside bell to transmit the alarm is an important feature. A supervised storage battery can provide backup power. Wiring should be on supervised circuits with a trouble alarm for faults that is distinct from the fire alarm.

Large facilities are difficult and dangerous to evacuate, so most of them have fire and evacuation plans that include some type of alarm verification before a general evacuation alarm sounds. Some fire codes permit or even require alarm verification. Verification systems require activation of a minimum of two detectors in a single area. The detector on a remotely set alarm must repeat its alarm after being reset. By requiring a minimum alarm time, false alarms due to smoke puffs are eliminated. A physical visual inspection of the site may be required to eliminate the possibility of a false alarm. This requires knowing the exact location of the detector, so detectors need to be grouped in zones with an annunciator that indicates the location.

The firefighter's command post, which is usually in the building lobby, should have two-way communications active to a minimum of one fire station per floor, all mechanical equipment rooms, the elevator machine rooms and air-handling fan rooms. The system should include visual display of all fire alarm devices, including sprinkler valves, fire pump status, emergency generator status, and water flow indicators. The control center houses controls for any automatic stair door locking system that provides security access. The location indicators and operation and capture controls for the elevators and controls for smoke doors and dampers should also be included. The system should provide a means to test circuits and devices.

Firefighters communication systems that provide communication between the fire command center and firefighters are generally required for high-rise construction. They are required in large structures where a portable radio carried by a firefighter may not reliably penetrate the building. The communications system is a simple intercom system at all stair tower doors and at each elevator lobby, and may include a telephone jack for the firefighter's phone.

Indicating the Alarm

Each required exit must have a fire alarm not more than 1.5 meters (5 ft) from the entrance to the exit to help occupants locate the exit during an emergency. Water flow switches in sprinklers can be used to set off an alarm and can show up on a sprinkler alarm panel.

Audible signals have minimum sound levels for public and private spaces. Setting these levels is highly technical and requires acoustic analysis of the space, the occupancy, and the characteristics of various devices. Alarm bells must not be placed inside a hung ceiling.

Visible signals are required primarily for hearing-impaired people. These may be lighted signs that flash "FIRE" above alarm bells, or rotating beacons or strobe lights. Different manufacturers use a variety of names for visible fire alarms, including visible alarm signals, visible signal devices, visible signaling appliances, and visual notification appliances. Strobe lights are usually Xenon flashtubes flashing at an interval that minimizes problems for people with photosensitive epilepsy. Careful placement also helps avoid problems. Visible signals must be visible from any point in the space regardless of the viewer's orientation. The maximum distance between strobes is 30 meters (100 ft). Where visible alarms are required, they must be placed in more locations than audible alarms, as they require direct sight lines.

 The Americans with Disabilities Act (ADA) requires accessible warning systems to be both audible and visual (Fig. 46-5), and sets requirements for the type and specific locations. Where required, alarms must be provided in each restroom, hallway, and lobby, and in other common use areas such as meeting rooms, break rooms, examination rooms, and classrooms. In occupancies with multiple sleeping units, a percentage of the units must be equipped with a visible alarm as well as an audible alarm.

Because fire truck ladders can't reach the upper floors of tall buildings and travel down stairs filled with many people is very difficult, voice alarm systems are required by almost all major cities for high-rise con-

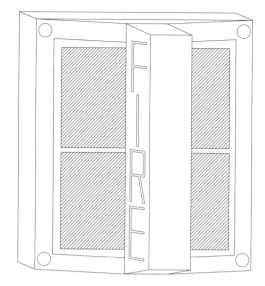

Figure 46-5 Audio and visual fire alarm signal.

struction. The voice alarm issues specific instructions to occupants of each part of the building about safe refuge areas and the progress of rescue efforts. Voice alarms are also very good in any large building where people may not be familiar with the building, evacuation procedures, or the alarm system. This includes hotels and convention centers, where visitors often ignore or misunderstand bells and horns.

High-rise office buildings require emergency voice alarm communication systems. The system should allow full control of transmission and building-wide distribution of all tones, alarm signals, and voice announcements on a selective or all-call basis. Alert tones, signals, and prerecorded messages on independent channels should be distributed to selected areas over a building-wide system of loudspeakers. A voice alarm system can use a standard public address system independent of the fire alarm system, or the voice alarm can be electronically supervised and an integral part of the fire alarm system. Messages may be prerecorded or live. The system must have adequate sound quality for clarity.

In schools, and especially in elementary schools, rapid orderly evacuation is most important. Fire gongs should not be similar to program gongs, and the system must be arranged to allow fire drills.

In factories, large storage facilities, and other hazardous occupancies, fire alarm systems are tied to an audio system. This intercom system directs occupants out of the building, and may also give the location of the emergency. Industrial facilities have manual stations at points of egress, and horns instead of bells or gongs because of the high noise level.

Part IX

CONVEYING SYSTEMS

Chapter

Elevators

Any multistory building needs ways to get people and objects from one floor to another. Stairs are the most basic means of vertical transportation, of course, and are included even in very tall buildings as secure exits in the event of fire. But nobody wants to walk up 20 flights of stairs or carry furniture and supplies up them, which is where elevators and escalators come in.

The design of the elevators has major implications for the architecture and structural engineering of the building. Elevators and escalators are an important factor in determining the building's shape, core layout, and lobby design. Although, as the interior designer, you won't be deciding how many elevators will be in the building, or even where they will be located, these decisions will affect your space planning, as elevators take up a great deal of space at critical locations and are focal points for circulation paths.

Interior designers are often involved in selecting the finishes for elevator cabs and lobbies, and for the buttons and indicators in the cab and at each floor landing. Because people congregating at elevator lobbies are often forced to stand around waiting for an elevator, the design of these areas can have a great impact on the comfort of building occupants and visitors, and on the impression they have of the building and the businesses within it. This is especially important for people who have to use the elevators every day, when unpleas-

ant, unsafe, or uncomfortable surroundings become a dreaded part of the daily routine. The design of elevators and their lobbies also has implications for security, fire safety, and maintenance of these semipublic areas.

The ground floor elevator lobby is also called the lower terminal, and is usually located close to the main entrance, with a building directory, public telephones, elevator indicators, and possibly a control desk nearby. Lobbies are designed to be large enough for the peak load of passengers, with 0.5 square meter (5 square ft) of floor space allowed per person waiting for one or more elevators. The same allowance should be made for hallways approaching the lobby. If the elevator's main lower terminal is on a mezzanine due to varied elevations of street entrances, escalators offer a good connection to a single main lower elevator terminal.

The size of the elevator car and the frequency of trips determine the car's capacity. This is independent of the number of cars in the elevator bank. In practice, according to actual counts in many existing installations during peak periods, cars are not loaded to maximum capacity but are only 80 percent full.

Manufacturers and elevator consultants supply standard layouts for elevators, including dimensions, weights, and structural loads. The average trip time is determined by the time spent waiting in the lobby plus the time it takes to travel to a median floor stop. For a commercial elevator, a trip of less than one minute is highly desirable, with 75 seconds considered acceptable. A trip time of 90 seconds becomes annoying, and anything over 120 seconds exceeds the limits of toleration. For residential elevators, users often spend a minute or more of the trip time just waiting for the elevator.

PARTS OF AN ELEVATOR

The parts of an elevator are spread through the building from top to bottom (Fig. 47-1). The landing is the part of the floor adjacent to the elevator where passengers and freight are received and discharged. The elevator's rise or travel is the vertical distance traversed by the elevator cab (also called the car) from the lowest to the highest landings.

The cab rides up and down in the elevator shaft or hoistway. The hoistway is the vertical space for travel of one or more elevators. There are guide rails—vertical steel tracks that control the travel of the elevator car or the counterweight (see below)—on the side walls of the shaft. They are secured to each floor with support brackets. Guide shoes on the sides of the cab fit onto the guide rails and guide the cab vertically in the shaft. The elevator pit is the part of the shaft that extends from the level of the lowest landing to the floor of the hoistway.

The cab is lifted in the shaft by cables, which connect to the top beam of the elevator. The cables are steel wires that pass over a motor-driven cylindrical sheave at the traction machine, then down to the counterweights. The hoisting cable is a wire cable or rope used for raising and lowering the elevator car. A traveling cable is an electrical cable connecting the elevator car to a fixed electrical outlet in the hoistway.

Counterweights are rectangular cast-iron blocks mounted in a steel frame, and attached to the other end of the hoisting cable to counterbalance the elevator cab. The counterweights ride in two guide rails on the back wall of the shaft. Their weight equals the weight of the cab plus an allowance for the people in the cab. The counterweight creates traction at the sheave and balances the weight of the cab. There are also cables attached to the bottom of the cab and the counterweight, to balance the weight of the hoist cable.

At the top of the shaft is a structural platform for the elevator machinery. A penthouse or elevator machine room on the roof houses the elevator machine that turns the sheave, which lifts or lowers the cab. The penthouse rises one or two levels directly above the shaft. Heavy steel beams support the hoisting machin-

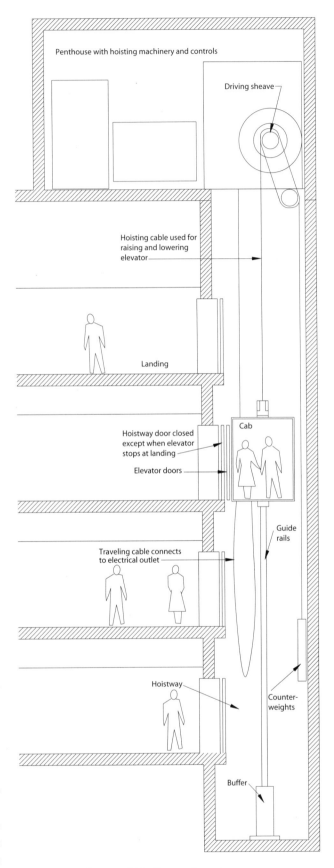

Figure 47-1 Parts of an elevator

ery. A control panel with switches and buttons regulates the hoisting machine. The drive or motion control governs velocity, acceleration, position determination, and keeping the car level with each floor.

The elevator includes a speed governor to detect excessive speed or freefall and signal brakes to clamp onto guide rails to slow down and stop the elevator car. A limit switch automatically cuts off the current to an electric motor when the elevator passes a point near the top or bottom of its travel. The buffer is a piston or spring device that absorbs the impact of the descending car or counterweight at the extreme lower limit of travel.

The hoistway door between the elevator landing and hoistway is normally closed except when a car is stopped at a landing. Hoistway doors are typically 214 cm (7 ft) or 244 cm (8 ft) high.

Operating controls for the elevator control the car door operation and the function of car signals. Car signals include floor call buttons and other indicators. Supervisory controls allow group operation of multiple car installations.

Elevators can be noisy. Noise-sensitive areas, such as sleeping rooms, should be located away from elevator shafts and machine rooms. Using vibration isolators between guide rails and the structure can reduce elevator noise. Properly designed controls also reduce system noise. Solid-state equipment eliminates the clatter and whirring sound of older machine rooms.

GEARED TRACTION ELEVATORS

Geared traction elevators are found in medium-rise buildings. Geared traction machines use a worm and gear between the driving motor and hoisting sheave that permits them to use a smaller, cheaper, high-speed motor. This simpler motor is then geared down to provide car speed up to 137 meters (450 ft) per minute. Geared traction elevators are limited to a maximum rise of 107 meters (350 ft). With the appropriate drive and control system, geared traction elevators can offer almost the same high quality, accurate, smooth ride as gearless traction elevators, which we look at next.

GEARLESS TRACTION ELEVATORS

High-rise buildings use gearless traction elevators, which can operate at 360 meters (1200 ft) per minute. Gearless traction motors are powered by a motor with its

shaft connected to the brake wheel and driving sheave. The elevator hoist ropes go around the sheave. Because there are no gears, the motor must run at the same relatively low speed as the drive sheave. Gearless traction motors are used for medium- and high-speed elevators that run from 153 meters (500 ft) per minute to 610 meters (2000 ft) per minute.

Gearless traction elevators are used for passenger service, where their speed makes them the first choice for taller buildings. They are more efficient, quieter, need less maintenance, and last longer than geared traction elevators. Gearless traction elevators provide a very smooth, high-speed ride for rises above 76 meters (250 ft). However, they are more expensive than geared traction elevators.

HYDRAULIC ELEVATORS

In a plunger hydraulic elevator, a plunger attached to the bottom of the car pushes against oil that is under pressure. Hydraulic elevators do not need penthouses. Because of the lower speeds and piston length limit, hydraulic elevators are used only in buildings up to six stories in height. A machine room containing the hoisting equipment, control equipment, and sheaves for raising and lowering the car is located at or near the bottom landing. The elevator has no cables, drums, traction motors, controllers, safety devices, or penthouse equipment, and is consequently relatively inexpensive.

Hydraulic elevators are used for low speed, low-rise applications where the construction of a plunger pit is a desirable alternative to a penthouse. Only the guide rails project above the car, so a hydraulic system can be used with a glass-enclosed observation cab. The hoistway is smaller than that of conventional elevators. Hydraulic elevators are available with telescoping plungers that don't require a plunger hole. The ride on telescoping plunger elevators, however, is jerkier than that of other hydraulic elevators.

Hydraulic elevators are expensive to operate. The ride is not great, but is adequate for residential, merchandise, and industrial uses. Oil can leak into the ground, leading to groundwater pollution, which may violate U.S. Environmental Protection Agency (EPA) regulations.

Hydraulic elevators are used for office and residential buildings, generally under four stories in height. Low-rise department stores, malls, basement and garage shuttles, theater elevators, stage lifts, and freight applications are also common, especially where heavy loads are involved. Handicapped accessible elevators may also be hydraulic.

Roped hydraulic elevators have a smoother rise, made possible because of a single moving jack section. They are simple and reliable and the most common choice for low-rise, light- to medium-duty hydraulic elevators.

PASSENGER ELEVATORS

 The architect makes the final decision on the type of elevator equipment for a building, based on the required passenger handling capacity, the trip time, and the cost. Usually, the architect consults with an elevator expert, either an independent consultant or a representative of a major elevator manufacturer. The interior designer and architect select finishes and details for the elevator cab and lobby. The cab interior is often selected from the manufacturer's stock finishes, but custom designs are common.

The cab and elevator lobby should be comfortably lighted and have a pleasant atmosphere. The cars and shaftway doors pass from floor to floor, and their design reflects the architectural image of the building. As an elevator rises from an impressive lobby up through the building, it may open onto floors with well-designed tenant lobbies as well as on more mundane spaces. The cab and shaftway door designs must be compatible with the variety of conditions that can occur throughout the building.

Codes and Standards

Building codes heavily regulate elevator design, installation, and signals. These codes affect the interior designer's choices for elevator cabs and lobbies.

The American National Standards Institute (ANSI/ASME) Code A17.1, *Safety Code for Elevators, Dumbwaiters, Escalators and Moving Walks*, sets strict installation requirements for vertical transportation equipment. The states of Massachusetts, Wisconsin, Pennsylvania, and New York, and the cities of Seattle and Boston, among others, have their own, stricter codes. The National Fire Protection Association's NFPA 101, *Life Safety Code*, sets fire safety requirements for elevators and escalators, and NFPA 70, the *National Electrical Code* (NEC) governs the electrical aspects of elevator construction. Other localities and states have additional requirements.

The Americans with Disabilities Act (ADA) and ANSI A117.1 set barrier-free provisions for access by people with disabilities. Manufacturers follow the ADA access requirements as a minimum, and may add additional conveniences as a particular project or local code requires. The main concerns of accessibility requirements are mobility, vision, and hearing.

Elevator Doors

Code requirements indicate that the clear opening for elevator doors should be at least 107 cm (42 in.), with 122 cm (48 in.) preferred. Smaller doors are appropriate only in residential or small, light-traffic commercial buildings. With a door only 91 cm (36 in.) wide, two people can't pass each other at the same time, so loading is delayed until unloading of passengers is complete, affecting the speed and quality of the service (Fig. 47-2). For elevators with small cars and a short rise, a swing-type manual corridor door is permitted. Larger cars need power-operated sliding doors.

Doors must have delayed door-closing capacity, and detection beams that reopen a door without contact when they sense a passenger. Delayed door closings increase travel time, so in buildings with traffic peaks, one or more elevators can be designated for use by people with disabilities during busy periods.

Elevator Cabs

According to the ADA, the inside car dimensions must permit a wheelchair to turn (Fig. 47-3). Accessible elevator cars with doors opening to one side must have a

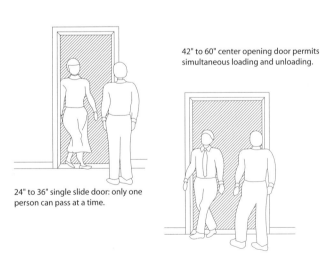

42" to 60" center opening door permits simultaneous loading and unloading.

24" to 36" single slide door: only one person can pass at a time.

Figure 47-2 Elevator doors.

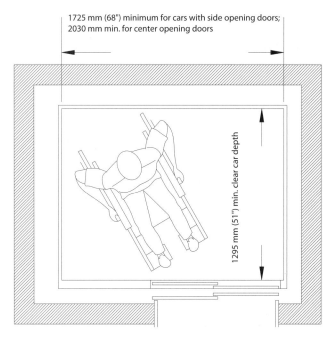

1725 mm (68") minimum for cars with side opening doors; 2030 mm min. for center opening doors

1295 mm (51") min. clear car depth

Figure 47-3 Accessible elevator floor plan.

minimum width of 173 cm (68 in.). Cars with center opening doors must be a minimum of 203 cm (80 in.) wide. The minimum clear depth is 130 cm (51 in.).

To aid people using wheelchairs as well as those who are walking, the ADA requires excellent car leveling, which means that the elevator car will come to rest at the same level as the floor onto which it is opening.

The elevator cab interior is a virtually inescapable, highly intimate, and extremely visible place. It is important for an elevator cab in a commercial or institutional building to create a positive impression. Interiors must deal with physical abuse, gravitational stress from rapid acceleration and deceleration, and shifting and vibration through constant movement. In addition, people in elevators are sometimes uneasy about traveling in a confined space and in close contact with strangers. The problem is that standard original equipment manufacturer choices are not very compelling, and a custom-designed elevator interior can be costly, time-consuming, and subject to cancellation. Elevator manufacturers offer their own standard cab interior dimensions that vary from those of their competitors, making standardization of design difficult.

The interior designer is likely to be involved in the decor of elevator cabs and the styling of hallway and cab signals. The normal elevator specification describes the intended operation of the equipment, and includes an amount to cover the basic functional decor of the cabs. The type and function of signal equipment speci-

fied, along with finishes and styling, are options that the architect and interior designer specify.

Elevator cab interiors may be finished in wood paneling, plastic laminate, stainless steel, and other materials. The choice of material depends on the architectural style of the building, the budget available, and the practicality of the material for the elevator's intended use. One set of protective wall mats is usually provided for each bank of elevators, especially if there is no separate service car, and many elevators have small pegs high on the cab walls to hang these mats.

Ceiling coves, ceiling fixtures, or completely illuminated luminous ceilings provide lighting for the cab. Lighting fixtures may be standard or special designs. If you start noticing the lighting in elevator cabs, you will see that many designs cause glare and unflattering shadows. The goal in lighting the cab should be to provide pleasant, even illumination from sources that are resistant to vandalism and abuse.

Pre-engineered systems exist for designing and installing elevator cab interiors, offering architects and interior designers a well-designed product at a reasonable price. The systems come complete with panels, handrails, trim pieces, and ceiling that offer a wide range of optional features in a fixed price range. The solution places a framework of mullions in the raw shell of the cab that have enough dimensional latitude to accept a range of panel sizes, shapes, and materials. The emphasis is on the panels, which tend to be of more concern to architects and interior designers than the mullions, which appear as a grid. Designed to present a strong visual statement along with economy and durability, these pre-engineered systems offer affordable prices, easy installation, reduced labor costs, rugged components, and fast delivery times.

Car finishes should be appropriate to use by people with disabilities. Many people with vision problems can see with sufficient, nonglaring lighting. Sturdy handrails and nonslip finishes help people who have mobility problems. Well-designed signals and call buttons avoid confusion for everyone, including people with perceptual problems.

Cab and Hallway Signals

Cab and hallway signals and lanterns are designed to fit with the decor of cabs and corridors. The ADA specifies requirements for signals appropriate for people with disabilities. Codes mandate the location of visible and audible hall call signals or lanterns within sight of the floor area adjacent to the elevator. These signals must be centered a minimum of 183 cm (72 in.) above the floor at each hoistway entrance. Both jambs of the elevator hoistway entrances must have signage with raised characters and Braille floor designations, centered 152 cm (60 in.) above the floor. Hall call buttons are to be centered 107 cm (42 in.) above the floor in each elevator lobby.

Hall call buttons indicate the direction of travel, and confirm visually that the call has been placed. A hall lantern at each car entrance gives a visible indication of the direction of travel of the arriving elevator, and can also indicate its present location. An audible signal of the car's imminent arrival allows people to move to the arriving car and speeds up service. Hall stations may have special switches for fire, priority, and limited access service.

Cab Operating Panels and Signals

Within the elevator cab, signals indicating the travel direction and present car location are either part of the cab panel or separate fixtures. A voice synthesizer may announce the floor, direction of travel, and safety or emergency messages inside the car. Voice synthesizers are very helpful for people with vision problems.

The ADA mandates that buttons and emergency controls must be within easy reach from a wheelchair. Easily seen and understood visible signals in the car and at landings should be accompanied by audible signals. Signals should indicate that the call has been registered, when a car is approaching the landing, the direction of travel, the floor, and the car position. Car floor buttons are required to have adjacent Braille plates. Use large, easily recognized symbols adjacent to emergency controls for passenger use. The best designs are easily distinguishable from the call buttons themselves, avoiding embarrassment for those of us who tend to push the Braille plates rather than the call buttons. People with hearing impairments also benefit from large visual signals that visually indicate when a call is placed, and turn off when the call is answered.

The car's operating panel must have full-access buttons for call registry, door opening, alarm, emergency stop, and firefighter's control. An intercom connected to the building control office provides added security. Sometimes a door-closing button is provided if hand operation is anticipated.

Controls that are not to be used by passengers are grouped in a locked compartment. These include a hand operation switch as well as light, fan, and power control switches. Other security and emergency controls are also included. Still other controls are located in a cab compartment accessible only to elevator technicians. These include devices controlling door motion, car signals, door and car position transducers, load-weighing controls, door and platform detection beam equipment, the speech synthesizer, and visual display controls.

Fire Safety

In the elevator, a fireman's return emergency service is required by ANSI and other local fire codes. Emergency personnel should have a means of two-way communication with cars and the control center. Other emergency controls allow switching of power between cars during emergency generator use.

Building codes generally require elevator shafts to have smoke vents at the top, allowing the hoistway to become a smoke evacuation shaft in an emergency. If there is a fire on a lower floor, the shaft fills with smoke, which helps clear smoke from the area of the fire. However, this prevents firefighters and other people from using the elevator.

People have died riding elevators down through smoke-filled shafts or becoming trapped in cars midshaft, so codes require that in the event of a fire, all elevator cars close their doors and return nonstop to the lobby or another designated floor, where they park with their doors open. They can then be operated only in manual mode with a firefighter's key in the car panel. All car and hall calls are canceled and car signals turned off. This way, firefighters can be sure that all elevator cars are secured and that no one is trapped in an elevator. In the event of an emergency, a light or message panel in each car is activated to inform passengers of the nature of the alert and that the cars are returning to the designated terminal. Traveling cars stop at the next landing without opening their doors, and then proceed to the designated terminal. Door sensors and in-car emergency stop switches are deactivated to prevent the cars from stopping and opening at potentially burning floors. Once at the terminal, cars may then be used by trained personnel to transport fire personnel and equipment, and to evacuate people from the building.

The lobby control station can override false alarms and return the system to normal use. This is especially important in large buildings with hundreds of fire, smoke, and water-flow detectors and automatic fire alarm systems. The frequency of false alarms or alarms responding to a very limited threat would immobilize a system without overrides.

Elevator Security

If someone is being attacked in an elevator, the attacker can render the enclosed space of the elevator cab inaccessible by pressing the emergency stop button. An attacker can then restart the elevator and escape at any floor. To try to counter this danger, alarm buttons are provided that alert building occupants and security personnel.

Elevators must be equipped with communications equipment by code. A two-way communication system with hands-free operation is good for security in the car. Security improves with a closed-circuit television monitor with a wide-angle camera in each car. Such systems require continuous monitoring at a building security desk.

Sometimes it is necessary to restrict access to or from a given floor or elevator car. Pushbutton combination locks and coded cards may work, but a second person can follow an authorized person into the car. The best system uses automatic monitoring and access devices, plus continual supervision by persons who know the appropriate action to take in an emergency.

Elevator System Controls

Large elevator systems use very sophisticated controls. The controls for small systems may be much simpler. Solid-state systems are universal now on new elevators.

The simplest elevator control system is the single automatic pushbutton control. It answers one call at a time with one uninterrupted trip per call. Calls are registered at each floor only when the car is not in motion. Single automatic pushbutton controls are used only for private residences and light-use freight elevators.

Selective collective operation systems are used in apartment houses, small office buildings, and professional buildings with moderate service requirements. They may tend to bunch cars, resulting in long waits. The system collects all waiting "up" calls on the trip up, and all "down" calls on the trip back down. The operation of more than two cars with this system is not recommended, and operating more than three cars is not feasible. Long lobby waiting times are seen as a major drawback when a company is considering renting space in a building. Modern group supervisory systems treat any call that has been waiting more than 50 seconds as a priority call. Elevator computerized system control uses a central computer to collect and process enormous amounts of data. The system must continually monitor demand and control each car's motion. The system analyzes all possibilities and answers each call in the most efficient manner.

Lobby elevator panels used to be wall-mounted adjacent to the related elevator bank. Now, however, one or more computer screens are usually located at a lobby desk. Sometimes an information-only screen is wall-mounted next to the elevators for passenger information. The monitors provide information on car locations, movement direction, waiting corridor calls, and other status data.

In very tall buildings, an attractively decorated lobby with a good view can break the long trip. This sky lobby is used where a building has office areas below and residences above, and most of the lower section occupants never use the upper lobby. The upper level users can use a shuttle that goes from the entry level to the sky lobby.

Elevator Maintenance

Elevator controls and mechanisms are complex, diverse, and subject to heavy wear. They are designed with large safety factors, and require thorough and frequent maintenance.

Specialists associated with manufacturers must service elevators at close intervals. Local municipal representatives inspect them regularly for safety.

SERVICE ELEVATORS AND ELEVATORS FOR SPECIAL USES

In office buildings, one service car is provided for every ten passenger cars. A service car has a door 122 to 137 cm (48–54 in.) wide for furniture, and should have access to a truck door or freight entry, as well as to the lobby. Service cars can serve as passenger cars at peak times. Service elevators for bulky furniture should be designed for up to 1816 kg (4000 lb), with a 122-cm (48-in.) door and a high ceiling.

Because hospital elevators must accommodate gurneys, wheelchairs, beds, linen carts, and laundry trucks, the cabs are much deeper than normal. A hospital elevator can hold more than 20 people, and service is slow. Large hospitals generally have some passenger-only elevators. Dumbwaiters are also common in hospitals, so that food carts, laundry, and pharmaceuticals can be kept out of busy elevators.

Retail stores generally have one to two elevators for use by staff and to provide service for people who are unable to use escalators. They are commonly located off the main circulation paths.

SPECIAL ELEVATOR DESIGNS

In an observation car, a glass-enclosed car is attached at the back to a traction lifting mechanism behind the car. The back is treated as a screen to hide the equipment. Observation cars can also be designed with hydraulic lift mechanisms and cantilevered cars. When located on an outside wall, no shaft space is used within the building, increasing usable interior space and saving costs.

Inclined elevators are cars that ride up a diagonal path on inclined rails, pulled up by a traction cable. The St. Louis Gateway Arch, for example, has a ten-passenger inclined elevator on each side.

Rack and pinion elevators ride up or down a rack. They are simple and safe, providing for an unlimited rise with low maintenance and operating costs, and they use little space. A rack and pinion system was used for a 64-meter (210-ft) rise in the 1986 renovation and rehabilitation of the Statue of Liberty in New York. The elevator is used to evacuate heart attack victims as an alternative to carrying them down 171 spiral stairs from the observation platform in the crown to the main upper landing. Rack and pinion elevators are used indoors and outdoors in industrial environments for vertical transport of passengers and materials.

PLATFORM LIFTS AND RESIDENTIAL ELEVATORS

Vertical platform lifts are safe, economical, and space conserving ways to overcome architectural barriers up to 12 ft high. These lifts are an alternative to an elevator for limited rises. They are manufactured with a stationary enclosure, including gates and doors, as needed

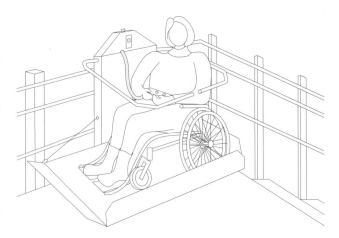

Figure 47-4 Inclined platform lift.

for each application, as compared to the stair-mounted lifts described below. These units do not require a hoist-way or runway. Enclosures may be made of steel panels or clear or tinted acrylic panels, which allow the user to have a view from the lift during operation. They can be enclosed overhead when used outdoors. Designs can be customized to fit special decorative requirements. Most platform lifts are not allowed as a means of egress, although the ADA does provide exceptions.

One way to get a person who uses a wheelchair from one floor to another is to install a platform lift on a stair. Winding drum platform lift designs can only traverse straight runs of stairs. Inclined platform lifts (Fig. 47-4) with a rack and pinion drive are able to make turns on stairs, so they can accommodate landings and longer floor-to-floor distances. The rack and pinion driven unit protrudes less than 32 cm ($12\frac{1}{2}$ in.) from the wall when folded. Pressing a button unfolds the platform lift. The safety barrier arm goes up to the vertical position and the access ramp folds down to allow the

---

Tina had worked for architects for quite a few years before going off on her own. She remembered the days just after the ADA took effect and before manufacturers had developed appropriate solutions to wheelchair access problems in small businesses. In particular, Tina remembered the time her boss had asked her to do some research on elevators. His client was hoping to expand her restaurant from one floor to two, and they needed to figure out how to make the second floor accessible. Tina's research revealed that the cost of installing an elevator in the restaurant and the space that it would take up would both be prohibitive.

Her next task was to help her boss prepare an appeal to the state's Architectural Access Board, which would rule on whether the upstairs dining areas would have to meet accessibility requirements. The board ruled that the upstairs spaces were required to be wheelchair accessible. As a result, the client decided not to expand the restaurant to a second floor.

Fortunately, this problem now has a solution. A limited use/limited application (LU/LA) elevator could be installed without a separate elevator room or overhead drive equipment, with only a small pit below. If LU/LA elevators had existed back then, Tina and her boss would have been able to proceed with the design of the restaurant, and their client could have expanded her business.

user to enter the lift. Upon reaching the destination level, the safety barrier arm rises to a vertical position and the access ramp lowers to allow the user to exit the lift. Pressure sensitive features stop the unit if it encounters an obstruction. Platforms are available up to 81 by 122 cm (32 by 48 in.), which accommodates a great variety of wheelchairs.

Since the enactment of the ADA, there has been a need for another type of vertical transportation, the limited use/limited application (LU/LA) elevator. In general, LU/LA elevators were created to fill the void between the commercial elevator and the vertical platform or wheelchair lift. Typical applications include schools, libraries, small businesses, churches, and multifamily housing. They are available with cabs measuring 91 by 152 cm (36 by 60 in.), 107 by 137 cm (42 by 54 in.), and 107 by 152 cm (42 by 60 in.) cabs. Phones and control panels that are ADA-compliant are available accessories. An LU/LA elevator uses a roped hydraulic drive system, which does require additional space for a machine room. The pit depth varies from 33 to 97 cm (13–38 in.).

Residential elevators (Fig. 47-5) are available with laminate or wood cab interiors. The doors, which can be designed to look like residential wood doors, have concealed safety locks. Cabs can have a single opening or two openings opposite each other or at right angles. Separate machine space is required. Small private-residence elevators are also used as wheelchair lifts. Because they require overhead equipment space, standard traction elevators are uncommon in private residences. Similarly, hydraulic elevators must have a plunger bore hole below.

A special section of the American Society of Mechanical Engineers (ASME) elevator code A17.1b, part

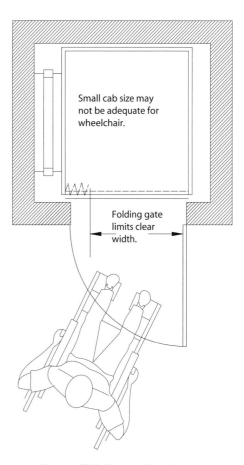

Figure 47-5 Residential elevator.

XXV, *Limited Use/Limited Application Elevators,* limits the size of private residence elevators to 1.67 square meters (18 square ft) and the load to 635 kg (1400 lb). They may not rise more than 7.6 meters (25 ft) or go faster than 9.15 meters (30 ft) per minute. These and other safety, drive, and space limitations result in lower costs.

Chapter

Escalators

An elevator is an efficient way to move people from one floor to another without taking up an excessive amount of floor space. However, nobody likes to stand and wait for an elevator. Escalators move more people more quickly. You can't be trapped on an escalator in a power failure, and escalators don't require emergency power; in the event of a power interruption, you simply walk up or down the stationary escalator as though it were a stairway.

An escalator is a power-driven stairway consisting of steps attached to a continuous circular belt. They move large numbers of people efficiently and comfortably through up to six floors, although they are most efficient for connecting two to three floors, with elevators preferred for rises over three floors. Their decorative design allows users to observe panoramic views.

Escalators require space for floor openings and for circulation around the escalator. In many buildings, escalators and elevators are used together, with the elevators providing transportation for people with mobility problems.

Let's look at the parts of an escalator (Fig. 48-1). A truss (a welded steel frame) supports the escalator and provides space for mechanical equipment. Escalators require support on both ends, and in the middle if the rise is over 5.5 meters (18 ft). The tracks are steel angles that are attached to the truss and that guide the step rollers. The drive system consists of sprocket assemblies, chains, and a machine, and works in a way similar to a bicycle chain drive. Escalator drive machines are efficient up to a 7.6-meter (25-ft) rise, and can be modified up to an 18.3-meter (60-ft) rise with a separate machine room. Machine controls are contained in a control cabinet.

An emergency control button is located at both ends of the escalator. When pressed, it stops the drive machine and applies the brake. A key to start, stop, and reverse the direction of the escalator operates the control switch at the top and bottom newels (the posts supporting the handrails at its ends). The Americans with Disabilities Act (ADA) requires elongated newels with a minimum of two horizontal treads before the landing plate, to allow people to adjust before stepping off the escalator.

The handrails are synchronized with tread motion. The balustrades, or side panels of the escalator, may be made of fiberglass, wood, or plastic. Crystal balustrades are made of tempered glass. In addition to the standard straight escalator, special escalator designs include curved escalators.

Escalators are preferred over elevators by storeowners, as the customers see merchandise while changing

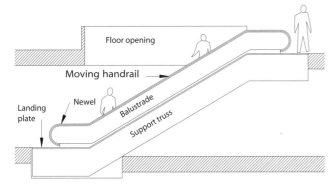

Figure 48-1 Parts of an escalator.

levels. They are located on the main line of traffic so users can see them readily and identify the escalator's destination. When laying out a retail space, you should avoid blocking the line of sight to the escalator with large displays. Customers should be able to move toward the escalator easily and comfortably.

SIZE, SPEED, CAPACITY, AND RISE

In the United States, all escalators rise at an angle of 30° from the horizontal. There must be 2.14 meters (7 ft) clearance overhead for passengers. Escalators move at a standard speed of 30.5 meters (100 ft) per minute.

The dimension between balustrades gives the size of an escalator, while the width is the tread width. Thus, an 81-cm (32-in.) size escalator has a tread width of 61 cm (24 in.), while a 122-cm (48-in.) size has a 102-cm (40-in.) tread width.

A tread 102 cm (40 in.) wide could theoretically accommodate two people. In reality, for psychological and physical reasons, one person per tread in an alternating diagonal pattern is the most common use. One half of the treads on a 61-cm (24-in.) wide escalator are unused.

LANDINGS

An escalator needs an adequate queuing space at each loading and discharge point. Backups are dangerous when people are constantly exiting the escalator, especially in theaters and stadiums with peak traffic flows. You can avoid backups by providing well-marked escalators with enough capacity. Collecting space at inter-

mediate landings relieves pressure. Physical divisions at intermediate landing turnaround points guide riders away from the discharge points. Dividers provide adequate space and time for riders to leave at that level or follow the guide around to continue the trip. A setback for the next escalator eases a 180-degree turn, so that people don't have to bunch up where they step onto the next escalator.

Escalators should exit to an open area with no turns or change of direction necessary. If turns are needed, large clear signs should direct users. The landing space for an 81-cm (32-in.) wide escalator should be a minimum of 244 cm (8 ft). For a 122-cm (48-in.) wide escalator, the landing should be a minimum of 3 meters (10 ft). If the escalator reverses direction, landings must be provided at both ends.

SAFETY FEATURES

Handrails and steps are supposed to travel at exactly the same speed of 30.5 meters (100 ft) per minute. Large, steady steps prevent slipping, as do proper step design and leveling with comb plates. Close clearances at comb plates and step treads also lower the risk of items being caught in the escalator. A proper balustrade design prevents clothes or packages from catching. Escalators need adequate illumination at landings, comb plates, and down stairways. Some escalators have built-in lighting.

An automatic service brake stops the escalator if the equipment breaks down or if an object becomes jammed into the handrail or steps. The escalator will also stop when the emergency stop button at either end of the escalator is pressed. Escalators will stop in power failures, when fire safety devices operate, when a tread sags, rises, or breaks, or when the drive motor malfunctions. If the escalator is traveling over or under the proper speed, a governor shuts it down. The governor also prevents a reversal of direction and operates a service brake. Passengers then have to walk up or down the steps.

Escalators are typically not allowed as a means of egress. Some exceptions are made for escalators in existing buildings if they are fully enclosed within fire-rated walls and doors. Codes may also require specific sprinkler system configurations.

Escalators must have adequate lighting for safety, especially on the comb plate at the end. In addition, as a featured part of the decor, lighting should enhance the visual focus on the escalator.

ESCALATOR FIRE PROTECTION

When an escalator pierces more than two floors, there are several methods to prevent a fire from spreading through the escalator opening. One approach calls for a fire shutter, activated by temperature and smoke detectors, to shut off the wellway of a given floor, thus preventing drafts and the spread of fire up through the building.

In a second method, fireproof baffles surround the wellway and hang 51 cm (20 in.) from the ceiling, creating a smoke and flame deflector. An automatic curtain of water from sprinkler heads on the ceiling then further isolates the escalator.

Another way to isolate the fire is with a spray-nozzle curtain of water similar to a smoke guard. The close-spaced, high-velocity water nozzles create a compact water curtain, preventing smoke and flames from rising through the wellways. Automatic thermal or smoke relays open all the nozzles simultaneously.

In a final method, a sprinkler-vent fire control system uses a fresh air intake on the roof. A blower drives air down through the escalator floor openings, and an exhaust fan on the roof creates a strong draft upward through the exhaust duct. This draws air from just under the ceiling of each floor opening. The system includes spray nozzles on the ceiling.

ARRANGEMENT OF ESCALATORS

The most common arrangement for escalators places the entrances and exits to their upper and lower ends at opposite ends of the escalator. This is known as a crisscross arrangement. Escalators arranged in this fashion can be built for less money, take up the minimum amount of floor space, and have the lowest structural requirements. A spiral crisscross arrangement (Fig. 48-2), where the stairs nest into each other, offers a rapid and pleasant trip, and is very economical of space. Spiral crisscross arrangements can be used for up to five floors without the user feeling inconvenienced. A walk around crisscross arrangement (Fig. 48-3) requires floor construction around the escalator, which offers an opportunity to display merchandise.

Separated crisscross arrangements consist of only an up or a down escalator in one location. They allow space at the end of the run for merchandise. If the distance to the next run is over 3 meters (10 ft), or if the next escalator is not in sight, users become annoyed at the walk

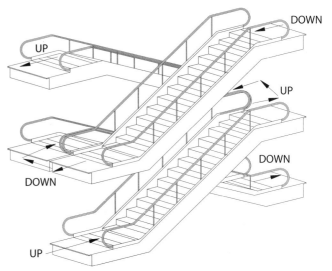

Figure 48-2 Crisscross spiral escalators.

and confusion, and the result is resentment. This is made worse when the floor space for the trip between escalators is inadequate, resulting in crowding, pushing, and delays. If passengers traveling over three floors don't have access to an elevator, the problem is even worse.

Parallel escalators face in the same direction. They use more floor space than crisscross arrangements but have an impressive appearance. They are less efficient and more expensive than crisscross escalators. Parallel escalators can use spiral arrangements or stacked parallel arrangements. Spiral parallel arrangements (Fig. 48-4) allow the user to continue on simply by turning around at the end of the ride.

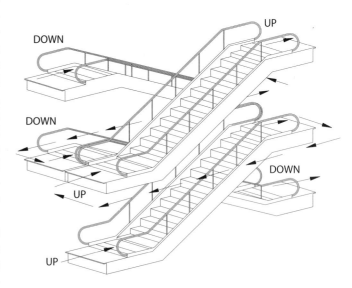

Figure 48-3 Crisscross walk-around escalators.

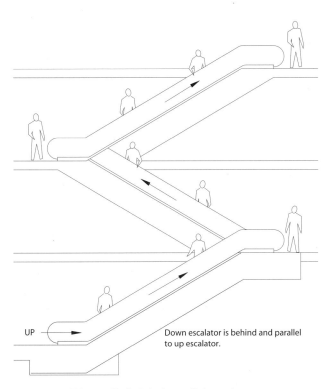

Figure 48-4 Spiral parallel escalators.

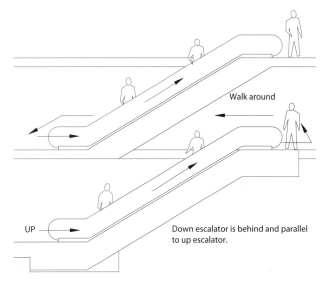

Figure 48-5 Stacked parallel escalators.

The stacked parallel arrangement (Fig. 48-5) forces users to walk around, and if the trip is too long, users become annoyed. Stacked parallel arrangements are used in mass-purchasing facilities and malls, and are mostly limited to two stories. In public buildings, transportation buildings, and other heavy traffic areas, they are easy to see, and may all go in the same direction. Stacked parallel escalators offer the option of reversing direction during rush hours when everyone is going the same way.

MOVING WALKS AND RAMPS

Moving walks eliminate the need to walk long distances in a building, and are also used to speed up walkers. They eliminate congestion and force movement along a designated path. They consist of power-driven continuously moving surfaces similar to a conveyor belt. Moving walks can be used to transport large, bulky objects easily. They allow parking to be located away from airports and rail and ship transportation terminals. They are also useful for people with mobility problems. A moving walk must not incline more than five degrees from the horizontal.

A moving ramp is a moving walk that inclines between 5 and 15 degrees. Moving ramps offer a way for wheeled vehicles and large, heavy packages to move vertically and horizontally through a building. Moving ramps are an option for people who would have trouble using an escalator. Multilevel stores use moving ramps to transport shopping carts to rooftop parking lots. Transportation terminals use them to carry luggage carts that can't easily negotiate escalators.

Moving walks and ramps are limited to about 305 meters (1000 ft) in length. Their construction is similar to that of an escalator, but with a flattened pallet instead of a step. The depth of the supporting truss is 107 cm (3 ft, 6 in.), which would impinge on the ceiling of the floor below.

Materials Handling

Until the late 1970s, materials were transported within commercial and institutional buildings primarily by hand, with some mechanical assistance. Office messengers carried mail. Hospitals used dumbwaiters, service elevators, conveyors, or chutes. Large stores used pneumatic tubes to carry money. Most of these tasks can now be done automatically and usually much more rapidly. The initial cost of automatic systems is high, but the reduction in labor and increased speed result in a short payback period and a rise in efficiency.

There are four major types of systems for material handling in commercial and institutional buildings. They include vertical lift car-type systems, horizontal and vertical conveyors, pneumatic systems, and automated and track-type container delivery systems.

VERTICAL LIFTS

Vertical lifts are related to elevators. They include freight elevators, dumbwaiters, and ejection lifts.

Design factors for freight elevators include the amount of weight that must be transported per hour, the size of each load, the method of loading, and the distance of travel. The type of load, type of doors, and speed and capacity of cars is also considered.

For low rises below 18 meters (60 ft), hydraulic elevators provide accurately controlled, smooth operation and accurate automatic leveling. Cabs are made of heavy-gauge steel with a multiple-layer wood floor designed for hard service. Ceiling lighting fixtures must have guards against breakage. Freight elevator gates slide up vertically and are at least 1.8 meters (6 ft) high. Hoistway doors lift vertically or are center opening, and are manually or power operated.

Hydraulic and mechanical vertical lifts are available for warehouse and industrial use. They are open frameworks custom-fit to the application, ranging from simple two-level applications to sophisticated multilevel, multidirectional systems.

Manual load-unload dumbwaiters are used in department stores to transport merchandise from stock areas to the selling and pickup centers. Hospitals use dumbwaiters to transport food, drugs, and linens. Restaurants with more than one floor carry food from the kitchen and return soiled dishes in dumbwaiters. Dumbwaiter designs include traction or drum styles.

Automated dumbwaiters (Fig. 49-1) can carry loads of up to 454 kg (1000 lb) at speeds up to 107 meters (350 ft) per minute. The maximum cart size is around 81 cm (32 in.) wide by 173 cm (68 in.) long by 178 cm (70 in.) high.

Figure 49-1 Automated dumbwaiter.

Automated dumbwaiters are also called ejection lifts. Institutional and other facilities use them for rapid vertical movement of relatively large items. They can deliver food carts, linens, dishes, and bulk-liquid containers, for example. Each load is carried in a cart or basket, which is manually or automatically loaded.

Some dumbwaiters have programmable controllers for automatic loading, dispatching, and ejection. Electronic sensors determine if space is available for a load, and the system automatically returns unloaded carts. Automated dumbwaiters are relatively expensive, and require a large shaft area.

CONVEYORS

Industrial facilities and commercial buildings like mail-order houses use horizontal conveyors. They are relatively low cost and can carry large quantities of merchandise. However, they demand an inflexible right-of-way, are noisy, and may be dangerous if misused.

A selective vertical conveyor picks up and delivers tote boxes (also called trays) that are carried along a continuous chain. The operator puts up to 27 kg (60 lb) in a tote box, electronically addresses the box, and places it at a pickup point. The chain picks up the box and delivers it. The process is monitored by a microprocessor. Vertical conveyors are available at a moderate cost. They require a large shaft, and are noisy. It is difficult to switch from a horizontal conveyor to a vertical one.

PNEUMATIC SYSTEMS

Pneumatic tubes continue to be used for the physical transfer of items, although electronic data transfer is replacing their use for carrying information on paper. Pneumatic tube systems are reliable, rapid, and efficient. They are relatively low cost if installed during the initial building construction. Pneumatic tube systems consist of single or multiple loops of tubes 57 to 152 mm ($2\frac{1}{4}$–6 in.) in diameter.

A single large, noisy compressor pressurized older systems. Newer systems are computer controlled with a small blower in each zone. They operate on a combination of vacuum and pressure and are relatively quiet. The newer systems can be of unlimited length. The carriers within the tubes travel at 7.6 meters (25 ft) per second.

Pneumatic trash and linen systems provide for rapid movement of bagged or packaged trash and linen from numerous outlying stations to a central collection point. Health codes require separate systems for trash and linen. Linen systems are commonly used in hospitals. Trash systems are found in many types of buildings, often along with trash compactors.

The pneumatic trash or linen system consists of large pipes under negative pressure, with loading stations throughout the building. The pipes are 41, 46, or 51 cm (16, 18, or 20 in.) in diameter. They carry one load at a time at 6 to 9 meters (20–30 ft) per second.

The compressors for trash and linen systems are large and very noisy. The system requires a main vacuum system, a high pressure line for the doors, and sprinkler heads every few floors. The cost of such systems is low to moderate.

AUTOMATED CONTAINER DELIVERY SYSTEMS

In an automated container delivery system, containers are locked onto a motorized carriage, which is in turn locked onto the track system. Containers can be moved at 37 meters (120 ft) per minute horizontally or somewhat slower vertically. Containers come in various sizes, and can carry up to 9 kg (20 lb).

The container delivery route may be either a simple point-to-point or loop system with simple controls or a complex system with loops and branches operated by a centralized computer. Automated container delivery systems are easy to retrofit into a building, due to their small size and flexible track layout.

In another variation, floor tapes below the carpet invisibly route robotic battery-powered vehicles. The vehicles can connect to elevators for vertical transport. The sensing, instruction, power, and vehicle control are all on the vehicle. These automated self-propelled vehicles can carry up to a 136-kg (300-lb) load, and can operate for an eight-hour day without recharging, at speeds from 6 to 37 meters (20–120 ft) per minute. They are used for pickup and delivery of parts in industrial settings, for food and supplies distribution in hospitals, and for mail and document pickup and delivery in offices.

Part X

ACOUSTICS

C h a p t e r

Acoustic Principles

Our training as interior designers develops an intense awareness of the visual qualities of the spaces we occupy. We notice and comment on the colors, materials, lines, forms, and patterns we see. In our work, we select and manipulate materials for their visual effect. We design beauty for the eye of the beholder.

Our experience of the world is strongly visual, but we are often deeply affected by messages received by our other senses as well. Perhaps the most critical of these is our sense of hearing. Sound in a well-designed space reinforces the function of the space and supports the occupant's experience. A poorly designed acoustic environment hinders both function and enjoyment of the space, and can even damage the health of the user.

Acoustics is the branch of physics that deals with the production, control, transmission, reception, and effects of sound. Acoustical design is the planning, shaping, finishing, and furnishing of an enclosed space to establish an acoustic environment necessary for the distinct hearing of speech or musical sounds. Understanding how we hear sound and how sound interacts with the built environment helps us design spaces that are as acoustically pleasing as they are visually rich.

Sound is defined as the sensation that is stimulated in our ears by radiant energy transmitted as pressure waves through the air or another medium. Sound is in-

duced through the ear by means of waves of varying air pressure emanating from a vibrating source. In order for sound to exist, there must be a source, a transmission path, and a receiver. So, technically, if a tree falls in a forest and no one is there to hear it, there is no sound.

WAVELENGTHS AND FREQUENCIES

A vibrating object radiates sound waves outward from the source equally in all directions until they hit a surface that either reflects or absorbs them (Fig. 50-1). The sound waves have peaks and valleys, similar to the waves in water. The distance between the peak of one wave and the peak of the next is called the wavelength. Wavelengths of sounds we can hear vary from more than 15.25 meters (50 ft) for very low pitches to less than 25 mm (1 in.) for very high pitches.

Whether we perceive a sound as high or low depends on its frequency. The peaks in sound waves will pass a stationary point at different rates. A higher pitched sound has peaks that pass at a higher frequency (more frequently), while the peaks of a lower pitched sound pass at a lower frequency (less frequently). The frequency with

Sound pressure waves radiate in all directions.

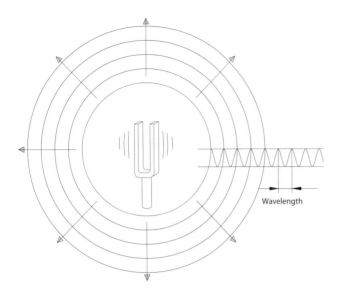

Figure 50-1 Wavelengths.

which these peaks pass a given point is measured as the number of cycles completed per second. A sound wave's frequency is measured in hertz (Hz). One hertz equals one cycle per second, so a wave whose peaks pass at 50 cycles per second has a frequency of 50 Hz.

As we've already noted, high-pitched sounds have higher frequencies, and high frequencies correspond to short wavelengths. Bass notes have lower frequencies; low frequency and long wavelengths go together. Frequency is an important variable in how a sound is transmitted or absorbed, and must be taken into account in designing the acoustics of a building.

THE EAR

If you have ever tried to draw someone's ear, you will have noticed that our ears are as individual as our fingerprints. They are small or large, simple or convoluted, smooth or fuzzy, or even hairy, but all healthy ears have the same parts.

The structures of the ear (Fig. 50-2) enable us to collect sound waves, which are then converted into nerve impulses. The outer ear is a sound-gathering funnel. The outer ear in humans is a more efficient sound gatherer than the nonexistent external ear in many reptiles and birds, but lacks the collecting and focusing capacity of a cat's ear. Sound travels from the outer ear through the auditory canal, which is also called the external ear canal, and into the middle ear.

Within the middle ear, sound waves set the eardrum (tympanic membrane) in motion. At the threshold of hearing, the displacement of air molecules on the eardrum and the eardrum movement is equal to about the diameter of an atom. If our ears were one order of magnitude more sensitive, we could hear thermal noise. The sensitivity of our ears is close to the practical limit for sound reception. The average human ear can withstand the loudest sounds of nature, yet be able to detect the tiny pressures of barely audible sounds.

The middle ear is an air-filled space surrounded by bone and bounded by two membranes, the eardrum on the outer side and a flexible membrane separating it from the inner ear on the inner side. The main job of the middle ear is amplification. The vibrations from the eardrum are transmitted across the middle ear space by three tiny levers of bone to the extraordinarily sensitive inner ear mechanism (cochlea). These three bones, called the ossicles, are the malleu (hammer), incus (anvil), and stapes (stirrup). The movement of each bone increases the amplification of sound. The footplate of the stirrup bone is attached to a flexible membrane that covers an opening into the inner ear called the oval window. Moving back and forth like a piston, the stirrup bone sets in motion the fluids of the inner ear. In the short but intricate journey from eardrum to inner ear, the sound wave is amplified as much as 25 times.

The inner ear is where the sound vibrations are converted to electrical nerve impulses for interpretation by the brain. The rhythmic waves in the inner ear fluid are set in motion by the stirrup bone's pressure on the oval window. They excite a highly delicate organ that is at the heart of sound reception. Coiled like a snail shell

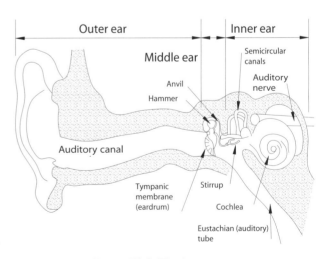

Figure 50-2 The human ear.

(its name, cochlea, is from the Latin word for snail), it is sometimes described as a spiral piano keyboard. Hair cells at one end of the keyboard respond to sounds at high frequencies, up to 20,000 cycles per second; those at the opposite end respond to low ones, down to 16 cycles per second. The receptors for low tones are at the innermost turn of the spiral. The basilar membrane in the cochlea resonates at one end at a frequency of 20 Hz (Hertz), and at the other end at 20 kHz (kilohertz). This range of 20 Hz to 20 kHz establishes the range of frequencies that the human ear can hear.

As the vibrations of the hammer shake the hair cells of the cochlea, anvil, and stirrup, they initiate an electrical impulse that is transmitted to the nerve fibers, which then merge into the auditory nerve. These impulses are carried into the central auditory pathways of the brain and ultimately to the cerebral cortex, where their pattern is interpreted as sound.

If you are young and your ears are in excellent physical condition, you can hear sounds in the 20 to 20,000 Hz range. You will be most sensitive to frequencies in the 3000 to 4000 Hz range. Very high frequencies may be uncomfortable for young listeners, who may be very sensitive to the sound of high-speed dental drills. Our ability to hear upper frequencies decreases with age. By middle age, the typical upper limit is around 10 kHz to 12 kHz. Upper range hearing loss is usually more pronounced in men than in women.

Our ears can pick out specific sounds to which we want to pay attention, but more frequently it combines sounds distinct from each other in frequency and phase, as chords in music, for example. Most sounds are actually complex combinations of frequencies. Musical tones combine fundamental frequencies with harmonics (overtones). A trained conductor can pick out one single instrument in a 120-piece orchestra. Amazingly, we have the ability to pick out one voice in background noise much louder than that voice, a phenomenon known as the cocktail party effect.

SPEECH

The vibration of our vocal cords produces human speech. These vibrations are modified through the throat, nose, and mouth. Each sound that makes up speech lasts only one-fiftieth to one-thirtieth of a second.

Speech is composed of fundamental frequences in the 100 to 600 Hz range, with many important overtones up to about 7500 Hz. Most of the information in speech is carried in the upper frequencies, which is why we tend to listen most attentively to higher pitches. Most of the acoustic energy is in the lower frequencies (think of the way you can feel the beat of a bass drum in your stomach). For sounds of equal energy, the human ear is less sensitive to low frequencies than to middle and high frequencies.

Many consonants, however, have the most energy at much higher frequencies. We must hear frequencies from 300 to 4000 Hz clearly for maximum intelligibility. In English, most of the information is carried in the consonants, not the vowels.

The sounds "s" and "sh" have their greatest energy above 2 kHz, and both are important in conveying information. Male voices center around 500 Hz, while female voices are usually around 900 Hz. Higher frequencies carry sound with a greater sense of direction, and can be heard around a barrier more easily. High frequencies are the most easily absorbed.

Telephone and radio signals use frequency bands smaller than our ears can hear. The loss of information due to the limited frequency range results in loss of voice quality and intelligibility.

LOUDNESS

Loudness is a measure of the power of sound. The human ear is sensitive to a very large range of sound power. The way we experience a change in loudness is subjective; it is not related in a linear way to sound power, which is measured in watts. A sound we perceive as twice as loud as another sound is actually much more than twice as powerful.

The loudness of sounds is measured in a way that relates actual sound intensity to the way humans experience sound. Loudness is measured according to a mathematical logarithmic scale of decibels (dB). A decibel is a unit for expressing the relative pressure or intensity of sounds on a uniform scale, from 0 dB for the least perceptible sound to around 130 dB for sound loud enough to result in the average threshold of pain. We hear a doubling of sound pressure and intensity, not as being twice as loud, but as a barely perceptible change.

The decibel scale uses whole numbers to measure the increase of sound levels. Ten decibel units equal a doubling of perceived loudness, so 30 dB is twice as loud as 20 dB, and 70 dB is twice as loud as 60 dB. When the change of decibels is 20 dB, the loudness is doubled twice, so 30 dB is four times as loud as 10 dB. The scale is set up in this way to account for the way we perceive loudness.

Our perception of a sound's loudness depends both on the power of the sound and on the distance from the source of the sound to our ear. Every time the sound power is doubled, the actual sound intensity level changes 3 dB. When the distance from the source of the sound is doubled, the sound intensity level changes 6 dB. Decibel levels from two sound sources can't be added mathematically. For example, 60 dB + 60 dB equals 63 dB, not 120 dB. If all this sounds confusing, be assured that you will soon get used to relating decibels to sound levels and will cease to be bothered by the math.

Because we are not equally sensitive to all frequencies within our audible range, we can hear only certain frequencies at the lowest levels of loudness. Where we are most sensitive, in the range of 3000 to 4000 Hz, we can hear sounds even at −5 dB. The most information in human speech is found between 3000 and 4000 Hz, so we are good at listening for very quiet speech. Our sensitivity drops off at low decibel levels, especially at low frequencies. This is why most stereo amplifiers provide a boost for bass sounds at lower volumes. At the threshold of hearing at 0 dB, we can hear only at 1000 Hz.

The upper limit for loudness is 120 to 130 dB. This level of sound intensity is high enough to produce a sensation of pain in the human ear, and thus is called the threshold of pain. At this level, we experience pain in all frequencies.

SOUND WAVES

Sound waves travel at different velocities, depending on the medium through which they are traveling. Sound travels through air at around 0.3 km (1087 ft) per second at sea level. Sound travels through water more rapidly than through air, at around 1.4 km (4500 ft) per second. Through wood, sound moves at about 3.6 km (11,700 ft) per second, and through steel at around 5.5 km (18,000 ft) per second.

Sound waves radiate spherically from a point source. A point source, like a tuning fork, is relatively small compared to the wavelength produced. A line source, like the string of a violin, creates cylindrical waves. Large vibrating surfaces, like the head of a large drum, create plane waves. When sound originates from a source like the human voice, it radiates more strongly in some directions than in others.

Sound energy, like heat energy, can be absorbed or reflected by an object. The ground, building surfaces, and other objects interact with sound waves with which they come in contact. Because of the complexity of these interactions, sound fields in the real world can't be described by simple mathematical expressions.

How much sound energy is absorbed and how much is reflected by a surface has a significant effect on what one hears within a space. Where little sound is absorbed and much is reflected, sounds are mixed together. When steady sounds are mixed together, they accumulate into a reverberant field, and you have a noisy space. Speech becomes less intelligible, but music may sound better in a reverberant space. Where much of the sound energy is absorbed and little is reflected, the room sounds quiet for speech but may sound dead to music.

REFLECTED SOUND

The lengths of sound waves for audible frequencies vary from 15 meters (50 ft) for very low pitches to less than a few millimeters (less than 1 in.) for very high ones. When a sound wave strikes a surface that is large compared to the wavelength, a portion of the sound energy is reflected (like light from a mirror) and a portion is absorbed. The harder and more rigid the surface a sound wave strikes, the more sound is reflected. Reflected sound leaves the surface at an angle equal to the angle at which it strikes it.

Reverberation

Reverberation (Fig. 50-3) is the persistence of sound after the source of the sound has ceased, as a result of repeated reflections. Reverberation affects the intelligibility of speech and the quality of music. The reverberation time of a space is the amount of time that sound bounces around a room before dying out to an inaudible level. It is defined as the time required for sound energy to decay 60 dB, or to one millionth of its initial intensity.

The sound in a room is a combination of direct sound from the source and reflected sound from walls and other obstructions. Our ears sense reverberation as a mixture of previous and more recent sounds. The reverberation time is longer in a room with a larger volume, as the distances between reflections are longer. When sound-absorbing materials are added to a space, the reverberation time decreases as sounds are absorbed.

The reverberation time of a room should be appropriate to the use of the space. For speech in offices and small rooms, a reverberation time of 0.3 to 0.6 second is desirable. The reverberation time for auditoriums ranges from 1.5 to 1.8 seconds. You can control the quality of the sound by modifying the amount of absorptive or reflective finishes in a space.

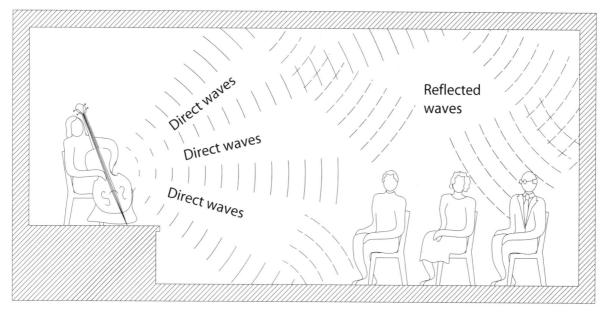

Figure 50-3 Reverberation.

The reverberation of sounds in lecture halls, theaters, houses of worship, and concert halls sustains and blends sounds, making them much smoother and richer than they would be in open air. Short reverberation times are best for speech, as they allow clarity for consonant sounds. However, some reverberation enriches a speaker's voice, and gives the speaker some sense of how well the voice is carrying to the audience.

Music benefits from longer reverberation times that extend and blend the sounds of instruments and voices. Music sounds dead and brittle with too short a reverberation time, but loses clarity and definition when the reverberation time is too long.

Attenuation

Sound energy lessens in intensity as it disperses over a wide area. Attenuation is the decrease in energy or pressure for each unit area of a sound wave. Attenuation occurs as the distance from the source increases as a result of absorption, scattering, or spreading in three dimensions.

Sound Reinforcement

Natural (as opposed to electronic) sound reinforcement is the amplification of the sound being heard from various reflections as well as directly from the source. Covering the ceilings of meeting rooms, classrooms, and auditoriums completely with sound-absorbing material eliminates the potential for sound reinforcing reflections off the ceiling, and may result in inadequate sound levels in the rear of the room. You may be able to avoid having to install an electronic sound reinforcing system by leaving the center of the room as a reflecting surface.

Echoes

In very large halls, the delay in receiving the sound from multiple reflections may cause echoes and produces confusing sound. Echoes result when repetitions of a sound are produced by reflection of sound waves from a surface, loud enough and received late enough to be perceived as distinct from the source. A clear echo is caused when reflected sound reaches a listener from 50 to 80 milliseconds after the listener has heard the direct sound. Echoes are undesirable even if they are not distinct, as they make speech less intelligible and cause music to sound mushy. Auditoriums frequently produce echoes between the back wall and the ceiling above the proscenium. Echoes may occur when parallel surfaces are more than 18 meters (60 ft) apart.

Echoes can be avoided by careful planning of the room's geometry, or by the selective use of absorptive surfaces. Absorbing the sound energy in echoes wastes energy that can be redirected to places where it becomes useful reinforcement. It is useful to allow nat-

ural sound reinforcement along short paths, while absorbing sound at excessive distances.

Flutter

When sound waves are rapidly reflected back and forth
between two parallel flat or concave surfaces, you can
have an effect called flutter. Flutter is a rapid succession
of echoes with sufficient time between each reflection
for the listener to be aware of separate, discrete signals.
We perceive flutter as a buzzing or clicking sound. Flutter often occurs between shallow domes and hard flat
floors. The remedy for flutter is to change the shape of
the reflecting surfaces or change their parallel relationship. An alternative solution is to add absorptive materials to the space. Which answer is best depends on the
reverberant requirements of the space, the cost of cor-
rections, and the aesthetics of the result.

Standing Waves

Standing waves operate on the same principle and have
the same cause as flutters, but are heard differently. Standing waves are perceived as points of quiet and of maximum sound within a room. Certain frequencies of voice
or music are exaggerated as they bounce back and forth
repeatedly between opposite parallel walls. When the walls
are exactly one-half wavelength apart, the tone is very loud
near the walls and very quiet halfway between them, as
the waves cancel each other out in the center of the space.

Standing waves must be avoided in rooms for music performance, but the problem presents only an annoyance for speech. Standing wave problems in rooms
with parallel walls are improved by slightly tilting or
skewing two of the walls, or by adding acoustic absorptive material to one of the walls. Rooms for music
rehearsal and broadcast studios often have nonparallel
walls, and undulating ceilings can also help. The proportions of the room can minimize the effect, which is
especially noticeable for bass frequencies.

Focusing and Creep

When sounds are reflected from a concave surface, they
may converge at a single point. This is called focusing
(Fig. 50-4). The sound is greatly reinforced at the focal
point and is less loud elsewhere. Spaces with concave
domes, vaults, or walls focus reflected sound into certain areas of rooms. Focusing deprives some listeners of
useful sound reflections and causes intense sound spots
at other positions.

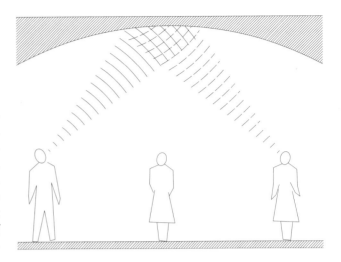

Figure 50-4 Focusing.

The reflection of sound along a curved surface from
a source near the surface is called creep (Fig. 50-5). The
sound can be heard at points along the surface but is
inaudible away from the surface. A space with concave
surfaces can become a whispering gallery, a room in
which two people can stand at two related focal points
of curved surfaces and hear each other's whispers with
startling loudness and clarity while remaining unheard
by other people in the space.

Diffusion and Diffraction

Convex surfaces scatter sound, reinforcing sound levels
in all parts of a room. Diffusion (Fig. 50-6) occurs where
sound is reflected from a convex surface. Flat horizontal and inclined reflectors produce some diffusion as

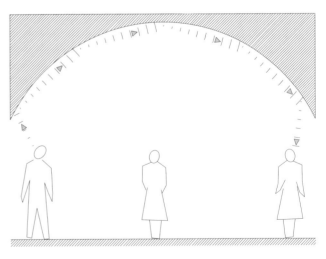

Figure 50-5 Creep.

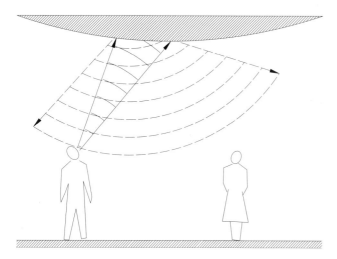

Figure 50-6 Diffusion.

well. Diffusion results in the sound level remaining fairly constant throughout the space, a very desirable quality for music performance.

When a sound wave strikes an object smaller than or similar in dimension to its wavelength, it is diffracted, and the wave is scattered around the object. Diffraction is the ability to be heard beyond a barrier, and is measured by the amount that airborne sound waves are bent by moving around an obstacle in their path.

ABSORBED SOUND

 Absorbed sound is one of the chief acoustic techniques used by interior designers. Soft porous materials absorb a large proportion of the sound energy that strikes them. When sound is absorbed, the sound energy flows through the material as heat. Greater thicknesses of porous materials are required to absorb lower frequencies. Thin fabric wall coverings absorb only frequencies near or above the top of the audible range of the human ear. Padded carpet and thick drapery absorbs the majority of sound waves in a higher proportion of the audible range.

MASKING SOUND

Studies confirm that poor office acoustics in open plan offices is the number one barrier to the productive use of office space. People are sensitive to sounds that are louder than the background sound, and especially aware of speech that is intelligible over the rest of the sounds in the room.

When two separate sources of sound are perceived simultaneously, they tend to obscure each other. This phenomenon is called sound masking. Sound masking introduces a nonintrusive, ambient background sound into the environment that renders speech unintelligible, so that it doesn't grab our attention. Sound masking helps to ensure speech privacy, reduces stress and absenteeism, and creates a better work environment.

Masking is most effective when two sounds are close in frequency, as it is then harder for the ear to tell them apart. Background noise that is used for masking unwanted sounds is broadband (containing many frequencies), continuous, and without intelligible information. This helps to cover both lower and higher frequency sounds.

MUSICAL SOUNDS

Musical sounds are usually of longer duration than speech sounds. Especially in instrumental music, they encompass a much broader range of frequencies and sound pressures. Musical instruments often produce very high frequencies in high-pitched overtones. Some large pipe organs produce pitches with frequencies near the extreme lower end of the hearing range.

Musical sound often depends on resonance. Sometimes a vibration in one object produces sympathetic vibrations of exactly the same period in a neighboring body. Resonance occurs when sound is intensified and prolonged by sympathetic vibration.

NOISE

Noise is simply defined as any unwanted sound. This is a subjective judgment; one person's noise is another person's music. Children yelling while they run around the yard playing is reassuring and welcome to the parent who is keeping track of their whereabouts, but is a disturbing noise to the neighbor trying to get some sleep before working the night shift. The amount of annoyance produced by unwanted sound is subjective, psychological, and proportional to the loudness of the noise. The most annoying sounds are high frequency rather than low frequency and intermittent rather than continuous noise. Pure tones are more conspicuous than broadband sounds. When a sound is moving and not locatable rather than from a fixed location, it tends to distract us. Finally, sounds bearing information are harder to ignore than no-sense noise.

The types of sound that can constitute noise are extremely varied. Speech or music may sometimes be considered noise. Natural sounds like wind and rain may be pleasant or disturbing. We are surrounded by mechanical sounds that are commonly considered to be noise: engines, gears, fans, tires on pavement, squealing brakes, buzzing electronic equipment, and banging pipes.

Engineers use noise criteria curves to represent how much sound pressure at various frequencies is acceptable for background noises in various environments. Higher noise levels are permitted at lower frequencies, since the human ear is less sensitive to sounds in lower frequencies.

Acoustic Design

The history of modern acoustics begins with the design of the Fogg Art Museum Lecture Hall at Harvard University in Cambridge, Massachusetts. When the building was first built in 1895, the acoustics of the main Lecture Hall space were a disaster, and the space could not be used for lectures. A 27-year-old new assistant professor in the Physics Department, Wallace Clement Sabine, was asked to find a solution. He started by considering the age-old problem of why the acoustics of some rooms were good, while others were mediocre or impossible.

Sabine isolated himself from his colleagues in the Physics Department, and worked with two lab assistants late in the evening and early in the morning to avoid the impact of street noise and the vibrations from the newly constructed Harvard Square subway line. He had promised to university authorities to return everything to normal each morning by class time, so he and his assistants dragged hundreds of upholstered seat cushions from the nearby Sanders Theater to the Fogg Lecture Hall after midnight each night and back again at dawn. Sabine studied and measured the sound quality of similar spaces. He used his ears and a stopwatch to measure the length of reverberations from organ pipes.

From his efforts, Sabine developed reverberation equations and absorption coefficients for many common building materials. He discovered that the reverberation time of a room is directly proportional to the cubic volume of the room, and inversely proportional to the sound absorption provided at the room's boundary surfaces and by the room's furnishings. His equation uses the simple dimensions of the room and absorption coefficients of materials to determine the acoustic effect of the space, offering an easy method for architects to determine favorable room proportions and treatments.

Thanks to Sabine's recommendations to add absorbent hairfelt to parts of the rear wall and ceiling, the Fogg Lecture Hall was reopened in 1898. Sabine then went on to work as acoustic consultant for Boston Symphony Hall. His input resulted in one of the world's best concert halls.

Incidentally, the Fogg Lecture Room satisfied Sabine, but remained unpopular with the faculty who lectured there. In 1912, the room was reduced in size from around 400 to 200 seats and redesigned with a semicircular wall and a flat floor. By World War II, much of the curved wall was covered with hair felt and perforated asbestos board. In the 1960s, the floor was carpeted, but students complained of a whispering gallery effect and difficulty hearing at some locations. In 1972, the wall was covered with highly absorbent glass fiberboard and a large canopy was added at the front, which finally improved intelligibility. Ironically, the space was demolished in 1973. It was tested first, and the curved wall and domed ceiling were found to be the cause of the intelligibility problems.

The Fogg Lecture Hall is a lesson not only in the development of the art and science of acoustics, but a reminder of how difficult it can be to remedy a space that is initially built with poor proportions, and how inexact the process of acoustic design can be. It is much, much easier to design a well-proportioned and properly finished space than to remedy a bad design once built. It is difficult, if not impossible, to retrofit proper acoustic design without substantial structural alterations. Solutions to acoustic problems depend on experienced judgment and common sense, along with at least a conceptual understanding of the basic properties of sound, how it is propagated throughout the building spaces, and how various building materials and construction systems influence it.

ROLE OF THE DESIGNER

When designing a building, the architect and interior designer must recognize potential noise problems and take steps to solve them. The acoustic design of the building should be integrated with other architectural requirements. By carefully planning the building's siting and structure, the architect can reduce noise penetration into the building. The overall building design and function ought to be reviewed in terms of desirable acoustic qualities. Noise sources should be placed as far as possible from quiet areas. The internal acoustics of individual rooms must be reviewed. For special acoustic issues, an acoustic consultant should be brought into the process at the earliest possible time.

By limiting sources of noise, the amount of necessary acoustic treatment can be reduced. When designing for an existing building, the architect and interior designer must first define the character of the sound problem. For new buildings, they have to imagine what noise sources can be anticipated. All parts of the building and its surfaces are potential paths for sound travel. The design team can compare the costs and coordinate the work of the construction trades to get the most cost effective combination of modified sound sources and acoustic treatments.

Acoustic consultants are most commonly called in for buildings where loud noise is a special problem, or where the quality of interior sound is critical. Opera houses and concert halls, as well as theaters and places of worship, have essential acoustic criteria. Educational classrooms, lecture halls, libraries, and music practice rooms benefit greatly from good acoustic design. All types of residential structures, including apartment buildings, hotels, and multifamily and single-family residences, are improved by sensitivity to acoustic problems. Airports and other transportation structures need to block noise from outside, and athletic buildings and sports stadiums should control the noise produced within. Other commercial and industrial buildings also benefit from the expertise of an acoustic designer.

Acoustic consultants play a role in selection of materials and the detail of construction components. They also influence the selection and use of interior surface materials. Their work has direct implications for the interior designer. Acoustic consultants also design and specify sound and communications systems, and detail components for noise and vibration controls in mechanical systems.

Ongoing interdisciplinary research in architecture, neuroscience, psychology, music, theater, engineering, speech, and other fields is developing methods to evaluate, model, predict, and simulate the acoustic qualities of a building. These methods should soon be available for evaluating specific rooms within the building through acoustic modeling and aural simulation. New materials are being developed to diffuse sound in predictable ways.

Modern instrumentation and extensive testing of building materials and construction details are giving us better information on their ability to block sound transmission. New methods for testing noise from impacts on flooring systems are also being developed. Studies of how to reduce plumbing system noise are underway. Duct linings, which reduce heating, ventilating, and air-conditioning (HVAC) system noise, are being studied for their effect on health. The acoustic qualities of air-conditioning noise are being studied to refine the design criteria for acceptable equipment noise. Advances in sound system components and design continue to improve quality while in many cases reducing the size of equipment.

BLOCKING EXTERIOR NOISE

The sounds of cars, trucks, airplanes, and trains outside the building vary with the time of day and volume of traffic. Traffic noise ranges from higher pitched horns and squealing brakes to low-frequency truck motors. Other noise sources coming from the building's neighborhood might include construction noise, playgrounds, industrial plants, and sports arenas. On-site noises can include children's play areas, refuse collection, and delivery or garage areas. Sound can also be reflected from other buildings.

Sound energy lessens in intensity as it disperses over a wide area, so outdoor sound control starts with placing the building as far from the noise source as possible. Locating physical mass, such as earth berms or the irregularities of the natural terrain, between a noise source (for example, a highway) and the building blocks unwanted sound. Heavy walls of concrete or masonry can block noise along direct sight lines between a quiet space and the source of noise if the walls are high and wide enough. To avoid sound that is diffracted around the edges of the barrier, the barrier must be close enough either to the source of the noise or to the protected room. Light wood fencing does not help much. Dense plantings of trees and shrubs diffuse and scatter sound, but single trees don't make much difference. Planting grass or other ground covers provides more sound absorption than hard, reflective surfaces.

The interior of the building can be screened from outside noise sources by using mechanical, service, and utility areas as sound buffers. Activities with higher noise levels should be located on the noisier side of the building. It is best to locate quieter rooms as far as possible from sources of noise such as busy streets. Building configurations with a central court or U-shaped buildings can create an echo chamber, where noise bounces from one wall to another.

Building materials and construction assemblies designed to reduce transmission of airborne and structure-borne sound help control both exterior and interior noise sources. The walls, floor, and ceiling of the protected room should be heavy and airtight. Window and door openings can be oriented away from the sources of undesirable noise. Multiple glazing of windows can also help.

ADDRESSING INTERIOR ACOUSTIC DESIGN ISSUES

Acoustic attenuation is the term used for the reduction of the magnitude of a sound signal by any of a variety of means. This reduction may be a result of separating a sound source from the listener, enclosing the source to isolates the sound, absorbing the sound with materials that change the sound energy to heat, or canceling sound waves by electronic means.

Changes in the ways buildings are designed and built have had an effect on the amount of noise produced and transmitted indoors. The weight of building materials has been reduced over the years to reduce construction costs, but lighter materials allow sound to be transmitted more easily through the structure. Offices are becoming smaller and more densely packed with people, increasing the human and equipment noise levels. Open office plans eliminate barriers to sound and create challenges for speech privacy. Mechanical systems also add to the noise.

How sound behaves in a given room depends on the shape, size, and proportions of the room. The amounts of sound of various frequencies that are absorbed, reflected, and diffracted from the room's surfaces and contents also determine acoustic effects. The room's shape determines the geometry of the paths along which sound is reflected, and can alter the sound quality, sometimes in unexpected ways.

What you hear at any point in a room is a combination of sound that travels from the source directly to your ear and sound reflected from the walls and other obstructions. If the reflections are so large that the sound level becomes uniform throughout the room, you have what is termed a diffuse acoustic field.

Most rooms have a variety of acoustic fields. The area within one wavelength of the lowest frequency of sound produced in the room is called the near field. For the male human voice, that distance would be about 3.36 meters (11 ft). The reverberant field is the area close to large obstructions such as walls, where conditions approach a diffuse acoustic field. The free, or far, field falls between the near and reverberant fields.

Ideally, every listener in a lecture hall, theater, or concert hall should hear the speaker or performer with the same degree of loudness and clarity. This isn't possible using only direct sound paths from the source to the listener, so the acoustic designer reinforces desirable reflections and attempts to minimize and control undesirable ones to even out the sound in the space. Designers usually only consider the first acoustic reflection, as the second and third times the sound bounces is less noticeable. When sound reflects off a hard polished surface, the result is termed a specular reflection, the same as with light. Acoustic designers sometimes place a reflecting panel above theater seats, sized to a minimum of one wavelength at the lowest frequency they are considering, to bounce the sound from the stage to the audience.

The design of a space such as a concert hall for good listening conditions starts with developing a room shape that distributes and reinforces sound evenly throughout the audience. The distribution of sound is predicted by plotting the paths of the sound waves and their reflections on plan and section drawings, or with computer graphics. The process can also involve electronically testing a scale model of the hall.

Especially when rehabilitating an existing building for a new use, the designer may not be able to achieve the optimal configuration and proportions for a space. Electronic acoustics, consisting of a system of speakers and amplifiers, can remedy the problems created by the natural acoustic conditions. Electronic acoustics can focus additional sound into acoustically dead areas by adding a fraction of a second of reverberation time.

Computer software can predict in advance what the acoustic properties of a space will be, and can model it with electronic equipment to simulate what music will sound like from any location in the hall. This allows the designers to try out the hall before construction, propose changes that address problems, and then hear the results.

ACOUSTICS AND BUILDING CODES

City and town regulations or zoning bylaws set standards, regulations, criteria, and ordinances for noise. Agencies also set standards for specific industries, including limits on sound produced by a source. Building codes have recently added limits on noise as well. The Building Officials Code Administrators International (BOCA), the International Conference of Building Officials (ICBO), and the Southern Building Code Congress International (SBCCI) all include acoustic standards. Federal Occupational Safety and Health Administration (OSHA) regulations require that workers be protected from high noise levels. Continual exposure to high noise levels results in a degree of temporary deafness in the majority of people. Long periods of exposure, such as an eight-hour workday, result in permanent hearing impairment. OSHA sets the safe upper limit at 85 dB. A continual 75- to 85-dB level produces or contributes to physical and psychological ailments such as headache, digestive problems, heart problems, anxiety, and nervousness.

Several organizations set standards for building industry acoustic analysis and test methods. The American Society for Testing and Materials (ASTM) has established methods for measuring, analyzing, and quantifying noise. The American National Standards Institute (ANSI) sets scientific parameters and criteria used in acoustic analysis. The American Society of Heating, Refrigeration, and Air-Conditioning Engineers (ASHRAE) determines sound levels for mechanical systems in buildings.

REDUCING NOISE

The noise inside a building comes from the activities of the building's occupants and the operation of building services. As we have already seen, additional sound comes in from outside the building.

The first principle of noise reduction in a building is to reduce the noise at its source. This usually involves proper selection and installation of mechanical equipment. The second step is to reduce noise transmission from point to point along the transmission path by selecting appropriate construction materials and construction techniques. Finally, noise can be reduced at the listener's end by acoustic treatment of the space.

To keep mechanical system noise out of inhabited spaces, engineers may use duct silencers. Duct silencers are sound traps that are designed to fit round or rectangular ducts of various sizes. They contain fiberglass baffles to absorb sound and attenuate duct-borne noise. Duct silencers perform like duct lining, but are more efficient. They offer fair performance at low frequencies, are best for mid-frequency sounds, and quite good at high frequencies.

The acoustic design of variable air volume (VAV) ceiling diffusers can be coordinated with the expected air velocities and any requirements for masking noise in the space. Partially closing dampers on ceiling diffusers produces very high noise levels.

MASSIVE MATERIALS

Many of the structural materials used in building construction attenuate airborne sound very well. Heavy, dense materials (Fig. 51-1) prevent outdoor sound from carrying to the inside of the building.

Brick has substantial mass, and is good at attenuating sound. When a wall is made of two layers of brick used side by side, but without connection, the level of sound attenuation is very high. Brick walls absorb very little sound, and reflect sound at all frequencies.

Normal weight concrete is one of the best materials for attenuating sound. Lightweight concrete is less effective. Concrete absorbs virtually no sound. Concrete will carry and transmit impact sounds, however. Aerated concretes are porous, and absorb sound fairly well.

Concrete masonry units (CMUs) with hollow cores can attenuate sound quite well, especially when the CMU is of normal weight concrete, and when the hollow cores are filled with concrete, sand, or grout. Walls of two unconnected CMU layers have exceptionally high attenuation.

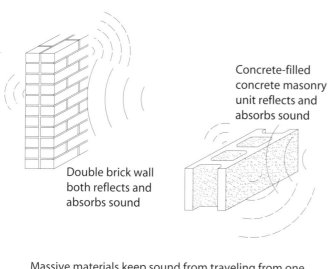

Massive materials keep sound from traveling from one side to the other.

Figure 51-1 Massive materials.

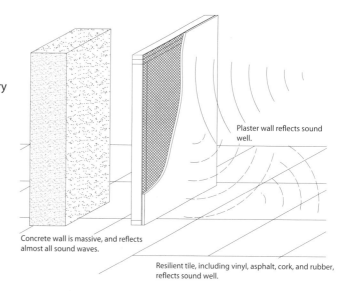

Reflective materials bounce sound back into the space of its origin.

Figure 51-2 Reflective materials.

CMUs, especially cinder blocks, are slightly porous unless painted or sealed. If sealed, CMUs can reflect all frequencies well. Other forms of masonry vary, but are similar to brick, concrete, and CMUs.

Stone, including reconstituted materials such as terrazzo, can be used for massive, load-bearing walls, stone veneer facing, or paving. Thick, well-sealed stone walls attenuate sound very well. Marble is among the most acoustically reflective materials. Some stone is naturally porous, and therefore less reflective.

Plywood has a modest amount of mass, and is relatively ineffective for attenuating sound. Thin plywood furred out from a solid wall is a good absorber of low frequencies. Plywood is quite reflective at high frequencies.

Glass is massive but thin, so its ability to attenuate sound is marginal. Well-separated double-glazing offers superior sound attenuation, as do some types of laminated glass. Laminated glass consists of two or more sheets of glass with interlayers that provide damping as the glass sandwich is flexed. Some types of laminated glass have substantially better attenuation than equal thicknesses of glass alone. Glass reflects higher frequencies almost completely. Because glass resonates, it will absorb good amounts of low frequencies.

When designing interior glazing, glass lights with laminated glass set in resilient framing have more mass and offer better damping than plain glass in rigid frames.

REFLECTIVE MATERIALS

A smooth, dense wall of painted concrete or plaster absorbs less than 5 percent of the sound striking it, therefore making an almost perfect sound reflector (Fig. 51-2). Applying a skim coat of plaster makes very little improvement on the ability of masonry to absorb sound, except at low frequencies when suspended or furred out from the solid surface. Concrete is a massive material that reflects sound. Resilient flooring, such as vinyl, cork, asphalt, or rubber sheet or tile, also reflects sound, although it is acoustically useful to cushion impact noises.

ACOUSTICALLY TRANSPARENT SURFACES

Soft, porous, acoustically absorbent materials are often covered with perforated metal or other materials for protection and stiffness. These coverings are designed to be acoustically transparent except at higher frequencies. With even smaller holes, the higher frequencies can also pass through. Staggering the holes improves absorption. Open weave fabric is almost completely transparent to sound, and provides a decorative cover on absorbent wall coverings.

Sound Absorption Within a Space

● ● ●

If your noise problem is not coming from outside the room but is a result of the sound inside the room bouncing around, you need to address noise reduction within the space. The acoustic treatment of a space starts with reducing the source of the noise as much as possible. Next, try to control unwanted sound reflections. Speech privacy is another major acoustic concern for the interior designer. Sometimes it is also necessary to decrease or increase reverberation time for sound clarity and quality.

Noise is reduced within a building by intercepting the sound energy before it reaches your ears. This is accomplished by changing acoustic energy into heat energy. The amount of heat energy produced by sound is miniscule; 130 dB of sound, which is loud enough to cause pain, produce only one one-thousandth watt of heat. Most of this heat can easily be absorbed by the room contents and wallcoverings, and by the structure of the building itself.

The contents of the space control the noise levels within the space, while the structure of the building controls the transmission of noise between spaces. In a normally constructed room without acoustical treatment, sound waves strike walls or the ceiling, which then transmit a small portion of the sound. The walls or ceiling absorb another small amount, while most of the sound is reflected back into the room. The amount of transmission to an adjoining space is determined primarily by the mass of the solid, airtight barrier between the spaces, not by the surface treatment. However, the amount of sound that is reflected off the surfaces back into the room is greatly decreased by absorptive materials. When acoustic material is applied to a wall or ceiling, some of the energy in the sound wave is dissipated before the sound reaches the wall, and the portion that is transmitted is reduced slightly.

Adding absorptive materials to a room changes the room's reverberation characteristics. This is helpful in spaces with distributed noise sources, like offices, schools, and restaurants. The acoustics of a space with hard surfaces can be improved by adding absorptive materials. In spaces with concentrated noise sources, the noisy equipment should be enclosed, rather than trying to treat the entire space.

ABSORPTION COEFFICIENTS

Materials are neither perfect reflectors nor absorbers of sound. The coefficient of absorption measures how efficiently the material absorbs sound. When all of the sound energy striking the material is absorbed, and none of it is reflected, the absorption coefficient is 1.0. This is what happens when sound flies out an open window; the window opening is said to absorb (not reflect) all the sound.

Rooms are constructed and furnished with a mixture of materials, each with a different absorption coefficient. For most common materials, the ability to absorb sound varies with the frequency of the sound. In order to give a useful and general idea of a material's ability to absorb sound at a variety of frequencies, the absorption coefficients at 250, 500, 1000, and 2000 Hz are averaged together for the noise reduction coefficient (NRC). The NRC is useful as a single-number criterion for measuring the effectiveness of a porous sound absorber at midrange frequencies. It does not accurately indicate the material's performance at high or low frequencies. Because it is an average, two materials with the same NRC may perform differently.

INSTALLATION OF ABSORPTIVE MATERIALS

The way materials are installed affects their ability to absorb sound (Fig. 52-1). Installing absorptive materials directly on a wall or ceiling gives the least effective sound absorption. A layer of air between the absorptive material and a rigid surface works almost as well in midrange frequencies as if the same cumulative thickness of absorptive material were used, which is useful to know

because air is cheaper than other materials. To get the best low-frequency absorption, you need a deep air space on the ceiling, and you should treat the walls as well. A hung ceiling 41 cm (16 in.) below the structural slab is too shallow to even absorb midrange frequencies well. The absorption coefficient ratings for materials are always given with mountings corresponding to American Society for Testing and Materials (ASTM) requirements.

Hanging the absorptive material below the ceiling and supporting it away from the walls works better than attaching material firmly to walls or ceilings. The best way to install acoustically absorbent material is to hang cubes or tetrahedrons from the ceiling. When you use very thick blocks installed at a distance from each other, the edge absorption is very large, especially in the high frequencies. However, these objects become major architectural elements in the space. As this may not be appropriate for all uses, louvers or baffles offer a somewhat less effective but simpler option.

For best results, treat the ceiling, floor, and wall opposite the sound source approximately equally. Treating the ceiling alone may miss highly directive high-frequency waves, which may not reach the ceiling until the third reflection off a surface.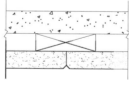

Materials absorb high frequencies better than lower frequencies. The amount of absorption is not always proportional to the thickness of the material, but depends on the material and its method of installation. Beyond a certain point, added thickness does little to increase absorption, except at very low frequencies. The lowest musical frequencies can't be absorbed efficiently by ordinary thicknesses of porous material. Let's look at how some specific materials absorb sound.

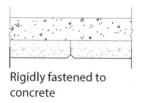

Rigidly fastened to concrete

Nailed to furring

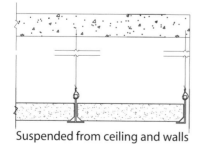

Suspended from ceiling and walls

Figure 52-1 Installing absorptive materials.

FIBROUS MATERIALS

Materials absorb acoustic energy by the friction of air being moved in the tiny spaces between fibers. A material's sound absorption depends on its thickness, density, porosity, and resistance to airflow. Paths must extend from one side of the material to the other, so that air passes through. Sealed pores don't work for sound absorption, and painting may ruin a porous absorber such as an acoustic tile ceiling. If you can blow smoke through a porous, fibrous, thick material, it should make a good sound absorber.

One type of acoustical deck consists of a structural deck of perforated steel backed with an absorptive material, usually fiberglass. Acoustical deck is usually used exposed, when it has an NRC of around 0.50 to 0.90. These acoustical panels are available in widths up to 1.22 meters (4 ft) and lengths up to 3 meters (10 ft). Acoustical deck can greatly reduce noise and reverberation in gyms, factories, and workshops.

Acoustical deck can also be made entirely of fibrous materials. Fibrous plank is a rigid material usually made of coarse wood fibers embedded in a cementitious mix. Some planks can be used as structural roof decking. The fibrous surface absorbs sound, with performance depending upon thickness. A 25-mm (1 in.) plank has an NRC of around 0.40, with up to NRC 0.65 for 76 mm (3 in.) thick planks. If the surface is exposed to a room, fibrous planks will reduce noise and reverberation in the room.

Acoustical foam comes in a number of forms, usually made of polyurethane cells. Acoustical foam can have open or closed cells. Air can be blown into and through open cell acoustical foam. Each cell in closed cell acoustical foam is sealed, and the material is airtight. Acoustical foam is an excellent sound absorber if thick enough. Foam 6 mm ($\frac{1}{4}$ in.) thick has an NRC of 0.25; 51 mm (2 in.) thick foam has an NRC of up to 0.90. Acoustical foam is used as padding for upholstered theater seats, where it stabilizes reverberation time in the space regardless of whether seats are empty or full.

Fibrous batts and blankets of fiberglass or mineral fiber are commonly used for acoustical or thermal insulation. They may be exposed to the room as a wall finish behind fabric or an open grill, or as a ceiling finish behind perforated pans or spaced slats. Fibrous batts and blankets absorb sound to reduce noise and reverberation in the room. Their performance depends on their thickness and the properties of the facing. The NRC rating can be as high as 0.90.

Fibrous batts and blankets improve attenuation when used between the two faces of a partition in a stud space, or above a suspended ceiling between the ceiling and the floor above. They absorb sound as it passes through the partition's cavity. Their ability to absorb sound is limited when the wall is tied rigidly together with wood studs, but sound transmission loss is significantly improved with use of light gauge steel studs. The performance of fibrous batts and blankets depends on their thickness. Fibrous batts or blankets should never completely fill a cavity.

Fibrous board works like batts or blankets, but has a higher density. Rigid or semirigid boards, especially those made of fiberglass, offer excellent absorption. They are available with a variety of sound-transparent facings, including many fabrics, and are used as wall or ceiling panels. Ratings for 25-mm (1-in.) fiberglass board are around NRC 0.75, and around NRC 0.90 for 51-mm (2-in.) board.

Fiberglass comes as batts, blankets, and boards with excellent sound absorption. The manufacturing process for fiberglass creates consistent, very fine sound-absorbing pores. Fiberglass is used for many applications, including insulation in stud walls and ducts, and for industrial noise control. Compressed blocks or sheets are used to form resilient supports or hangers, or as joint fillers instead of rigid ties. The absorption of fiberglass depends on the airflow resistance, and is affected by the material's thickness and density, and by the diameter of the fibers. The thickness of the board or blanket is usually the most important element.

Loose acoustical insulation is similar to fibrous batts and blankets, but is blown or dumped in place. Loose insulation reduces sound transmission through the partition.

Cellulose fiber is a sound absorbing material that is the basis of acoustical tile, wood wool, fibrous sprays and other acoustical products. Fibrous sprays include a variety of spray-on insulation materials that are often specified for fire resistance, instead of asbestos fibers. Fibrous sprays are inherently porous, and therefore absorptive. Their performance depends on their thickness and on the application technique used. A well-applied 25-mm (1-in.) thick coat can achieve an NRC of 0.60 or higher.

CEILING TREATMENTS

The ceiling is the most important surface to treat for sound absorption. Some of the fibrous materials we discussed above are used for ceilings, either openly or covered with acoustically transparent fabrics or perforated panels. There are also products designed specifically for the acoustic treatment of ceilings, the most common of which is acoustical ceiling tile.

Acoustical Ceiling Tile

Acoustical tiles are excellent absorbers of sound within a room, where they help lower noise levels by absorbing some of the sound energy. Their extreme porosity and low density, however, offer no reduction in the passage of noise from room to room through a ceiling or wall. To improve resistance to humidity, impact, or abrasion, tiles are available factory painted, or with ceramic, plastic, steel, or aluminum facing.

Acoustical tile is made of mineral or cellulose fibers or fiberglass. Mineral fiber tiles have NRC ratings between 0.45 and 0.75. Faced fiberglass tiles are rated up to NRC 0.95. Acoustical tiles are both lightweight and low density, and can be easily damaged by contact. Consequently, they are not recommended for walls and other surfaces within reach. The main purpose of acoustical tile is sound absorption. Membrane-faced tiles absorb less high-frequency sound than porous-faced tiles.

Tiles are available in a variety of modular sizes: square tiles range from around 31 cm (12 in.) to 61 cm (24 in.). Rectangular tiles are often 61 by 122 cm (24 by 48 in.). Tiles are also available based on 51-, 76-, 122-, and 153-cm (20-, 30-, 48-, and 60-in.) dimensions. Typical thicknesses include 13, 16, and 19 mm ($\frac{1}{2}$, $\frac{5}{8}$, and $\frac{3}{4}$ in.). The thicker the tile, the better the absorption. Edges may be square, beveled, rabbeted, or tongue-and-groove. Acoustical tiles come in perforated, patterned, textured, or fissured faces. Some tiles are fire-rated, and some are rated for use in high-humidity areas.

Acoustical tile is usually suspended from a metal grid, but can also be glued or otherwise attached to solid surfaces. Suspended applications absorb more low-frequency sound than glued-on tiles. Suspended grids create space for ductwork, electrical conduit, and plumbing lines. They allow lighting fixtures, sprinkler heads, fire detection devices, and sound systems to be recessed. The grid consists of channels or runners, cross tees, and splines suspended from the overhead floor or roof structure. The main runners are sheet metal tees or channels suspended by hanger wires from the overhead structure, and are the principal supporting members of the system. The cross tees are secondary sheet metal supporting members, carried by the main runners. The grid may be exposed, recessed, or fully concealed. Most systems allow acoustical tiles to be removed for replacement or access.

In addition to absorbing sound within a room, many acoustical tiles also attenuate sound passing through to adjacent rooms. This can be critical where partitions stop against or just above the ceiling to create a continuous plenum. Tiles for sound attenuation in this use are usually made of mineral fiber with a sealed coating or foil backing.

An integrated suspended ceiling system includes acoustic, lighting, and air-handling components. The grid is typically 152 cm (60 in.) square, with flat or coffered acoustical panels. Air handling can be integrated into the modular luminaires to disperse conditioned air along the edges of the lighting fixtures, or it may be part of the suspension system and diffuse air through long, narrow slots between ceiling panels.

Metal-Faced Ceilings

Perforated metal pans backed by fibrous batts (Fig. 52-2) are an alternative to acoustical tile ceilings. Similar panels may be used on walls to absorb sound. Perforated metal-faced units are available for use with suspended ceilings. The metal panels have wrapped mineral wool or fiberglass fill, and receive somewhat lower NRC ratings than acoustical tile. They are available in sizes from 31 by 61 cm (12 by 24 in.) to 61 by 244 cm (24 by 96 in.). Baked enamel finishes are available in a variety of colors. Metal panels are easy to keep clean, have a high luminous reflectivity, and are incombustible. With the acoustic backing removed, a perforated unit can be used for an air return.

The size and spacing of the perforation—not just the percentage of openness—affect the performance. Depending on the perforation pattern and type and on the thickness of the batt, the NRC of perforated metal pans can reach 0.50 to 0.95. If the batts are encased in plastic, as required in some states, the high-frequency absorption is impaired. Metal pans won't reduce sound transmission unless they have a solid backing.

Linear metal ceilings consist of narrow anodized aluminum, painted steel, or stainless steel strips. Slots

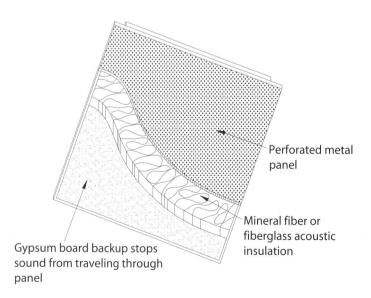

Perforated metal panel

Mineral fiber or fiberglass acoustic insulation

Gypsum board backup stops sound from traveling through panel

Figure 52-2 Perforated metal ceiling panel.

between the strips may be open or closed. Where they are open, a backing of batt insulation in the ceiling space allows sound absorption. Linear metal ceilings are usually used as part of a modular lighting and air-handling system.

Slats and Grilles

Wood or metal slats or grilles in the ceiling are often believed to have acoustic value, but in fact serve only to protect the material behind them, which is typically absorbent fiberglass. The absorption value is maintained if the grilles or slats are small and widely spaced. Increasing the size of the dividers or reducing the space between them will cause high frequencies to be reflected.

Acoustical Ceiling Panels

Acoustical ceiling panels (Fig. 52-3) or boards of treated wood fibers bonded with an inorganic cement binder are available in a range of sizes, from 31 by 61 cm (12 by 24 in.) to 122 by 305 cm (48 by 120 in.). Available thicknesses range from 25 to 76 mm (1–3 in.), and they come with a smooth or shredded finish. Acoustic ceiling panels are installed in ceiling suspension systems or nailed or glued to walls and structural ceilings. They receive NRC ratings from 0.40 to 0.70.

Acoustical ceiling panels have high structural strength and are abuse resistant. They have an excellent flame-spread rating. Panels can be used across the full span of corridor ceilings, or as a long-span finish di-

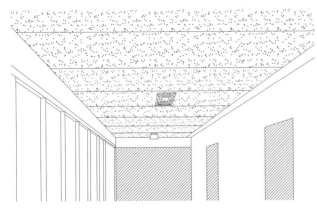

Acoustical panels made of wood fibers in a cement binder can span lengths up to 3.66 meters (12').

Figure 52-3 Acoustical ceiling panels.

rectly attached to the ceiling. They are appropriate for wall finishes in school gyms and corridors. Although they are usually resistant to humidity, check high-humidity use with the manufacturer, especially for panels with reveal edges.

Acoustical lay-in panels are fabricated of steel or aluminum with textured and embossed facings to give a cloth-like appearance. With acoustical fiber fill, the panels offer sound absorption as high as 1.10 NRC and meet fire safety standards.

Acoustical ceiling backer is available in 61 cm (2 ft) square or 61 by 122 cm (2 by 4 ft) sizes. Ceiling backer can easily be placed on top of an existing ceiling tile system that is not providing enough sound attenuation. The barrier material is a reinforced aluminum and fiberglass construction.

Perforated steel or aluminum panels with finished edges provide both absorptive and reflective surfaces for environments where a variable reverberation time is desirable, such as music rooms, concert halls, performing arts centers, and restaurants. The units are 61 cm (24 in.) wide closed and hinge open to 122 cm (48 in.) wide for additional absorption.

Acoustic baffles are available in 51 mm (2 in.) fiberglass and a variety of standard heights and widths. These panels are designed to acoustically upgrade existing spaces such as cafeterias, auditoriums, pool areas, and anywhere where high ceilings and poor acoustics require more sound absorption. The facing of the baffles is stretched to provide a smooth surface free from wrinkles or other distortion.

Cloud panels are used when ceiling heights are too low for traditional baffle installations, and perform the same acoustical functions without sprinkler or lighting interference. A 25 or 51 mm (1 or 2 in.) fiberglass core acts as an absorber and is contained within an extruded aluminum frame. The panels are available up to 122 cm (48 in.) square, and are finished with fabric.

Perforated galvanized steel or aluminum panels that can be individually attached to ceilings or walls offer an economical sound absorbing and fire-resistant approach to acoustic control. The panels are hung on metal brackets and backed with high performance acoustical fill. Panels can be cleaned in place without removing the acoustic fill. Optional protective plastic or fiberglass wraps are available. Perforated metal panels are appropriate for gymnasiums, swimming pools, weight rooms, and similar facilities, and can be used in auditoriums, theaters, libraries, and food service operations where noise is a problem and cost is an issue. They are also appropriate for industrial applications.

WALL PANELS

Acoustical wall panels are used in offices, conference rooms, auditoriums, theaters, teleconferencing centers, and educational facilities. Wall panels have wood or metal backing and mineral fiber or fiberglass substrates. Fabric coverings are usually fire-rated. Fabric covered panels are available from 25 to 51 mm (1–2 in.) thick. The NRC ratings vary from 0.5 for direct-mounted 25-mm mineral fiber panels to 0.85 for strip-mounted 38-mm ($1\frac{1}{2}$-in.) fiberglass panels. Panels are available from 46 to 122 cm (18 to 48 in.) wide, and up to 305 cm (120 in.) long. Reveals at the ceiling and base help assure a good fit. Openings for wall plates and thermostats can be field cut.

Acoustical wall panel systems can also include tack boards that are used as accessory panels in cubicles, conference rooms, break rooms, reception areas, and lobbies. Tack boards may be attached using hook and loop attachments.

At least one European designer has created a collection of acoustic wall panels made of felt-like recyclable molded polyester fiber or molded plastic. Easily installed and adjusted with self-adhesive hook and loop tape, the panels can be used as room dividers or mounted on walls.

CARPET

Carpet is the only floor finish that absorbs sound. Carpets in almost any degree of density, looping, and depth, especially when used with additional padding depth, produces a high degree of absorption in the middle- to high-frequency range. Carpet can be glued to a floor or installed over an underlayment of hair felt or foam rubber. The absorption is proportional to the pile height and density, and increases with the thickness of a fibrous pad, unless the carpet has an airtight backing. Carpet earns an NRC of between 0.20 and 0.55, mainly for high frequencies.

Carpet is sometimes installed on walls where drapery is not feasible and wall panels are impractical. It should be installed on furring strips with an enclosed air space behind to increase absorption over the entire acoustical spectrum, especially in the low frequencies, where glue-down application performs poorly. Carpet on walls may have different fire-rating requirements than carpet on floors.

Carpet does not reduce the passage of sound from room to room, but it can prevent noise that originates when an object makes hard contact with the floor. Using a thick carpet with pad, along with a resilient layer within the floor construction, will reduce impact noise.

DRAPERIES, FABRICS, AND UPHOLSTERY

Curtains absorb sound if reasonably heavy—at least 500 gm per square meter (15 oz per square yard)—and, more importantly, if the resistance to air flow is sufficiently high. The curtain fabric must severely impede but not stop the airflow through the material. Drapery fabrics at 100 percent fullness vary between 0.10 and 0.65 NRC, depending on the tightness of the weave. A light curtain has an NRC of around 0.20. Heavy flow-resistant drapery covering up to one-half of the area can achieve an NRC greater than 0.70. Sound absorption at all frequencies is increased when the drapery encloses an air space between the wall and the drape. Venetian blinds, by comparison, have an NRC rating of 0.10. Curtains do not reduce the passage of noise from room to room through a ceiling or wall.

Fabrics attached directly to hard surfaces don't absorb sound. However, fabric that is not airtight and is stretched over fiberglass or other absorbent materials creates an excellent finish that fully preserves the absorption of the underlying material. Deep, porous upholstery absorbs most sounds from midrange frequencies upwards.

OTHER FINISH MATERIALS

Acoustical plaster is a less well-known, porous, plaster-like product that was originally intended to create joint-free surfaces that absorb sound. Acoustical plaster consists of a plaster-type base with fibrous or light aggregate material on top. It is useful for curved or nonlinear surfaces and can be applied up to 38 mm (1.5 in.) thick. It is fire-rated.

Unfortunately, the performance of acoustical plaster depends upon the correct mixing and application techniques. Under controlled conditions, acoustical plaster can achieve an NRC of 0.60. Field installations are usually much less effective, however, so acoustical plaster can't be relied upon as a sound absorber. Acoustical plaster is very easy to abuse, and not resistant to humidity.

As mentioned earlier, resilient tile made of vinyl, asphalt, rubber, cork, or similar materials, is almost as sound reflective as concrete. If it is foam backed, resilient flooring can attenuate high frequencies.

Relatively thin finishes of wood boards or panels, usually attached to furring, are generally little better than a basic wall. Wood paneling absorbs low frequencies by resonance, and can result in a serious bass

Remember Harry and the hair salon he designed? The shampoo sink wasn't the only difficult design issue. When his client explained that it cost $1 every time he sent a towel out to a commercial laundry service and that the salon used hundreds of towels a week, Harry understood why the client wanted a commercial-size washer and two dryers on site. Fitting the huge machines into the tight space was hard enough, but Harry knew that they would be noisy, and their exposed location (the only possible one) could be readily seen by customers and made acoustic control a serious issue. Not only that, but staff had to be able to get to the machines frequently throughout the day.

Harry decided to install heavy curtains from the ceiling to near the floor. He selected an inherently flame-resistant velvet fabric in a soft green. Working with the curtain fabricator, he decided on a hospital cubicle-type curtain track mounted on the ceiling just in front of the machines. The track had to jog horizontally around the machines. Because of ductwork soffits and structural beams, the curtain was made in several panels, with some shorter where the ceiling was lower. The curtain was lined to provide extra sound absorption.

The final design not only camouflages the machines, but also effectively reduces the noise level. It also provides a lovely, soft vertical surface in an otherwise hard-surfaced space.

deficiency in music rooms unless it is thick or attached directly to the wall without an airspace.

RESONATOR SOUND ABSORBERS

Sound can create a resonance in hollow constructions whose natural frequencies match that of the sound. Air within the hollow acts as a spring, oscillating at a related frequency. Because a resonating body absorbs energy from the sound waves that excite it, resonating devices can absorb sound energy. Resonators are easiest to construct for lower frequencies. They are often used in modern concert halls, and are constructed as concealed hollows in the walls.

Volume or cavity resonators, also known as Helmholtz resonators, consist of an air cavity within a massive enclosure connected to its surroundings by a narrow neck opening. Sound causes the air in the neck to vibrate, and the air mass behind causes the entire construction to resonate at a particular frequency. The result is almost total absorption at that frequency.

Cavity resonators can be tuned to different frequencies, for example to 120 Hz for electrical transformer hum. Concrete blocks can be used as cavity resonators by tuning their openings and adding absorptive materials. The use of a fibrous filler in the block increases high-frequency absorption.

Resonator sound absorbers come in a wide variety of shapes and sizes. Some are manufactured in standard sizes, but most are tailored to a specific job using standard designs. They are generally large, and must be integrated into the architectural design of the space.

Panel resonators consist of a membrane of thin plywood or linoleum in front of a sealed air space that usually contains an absorbent material. The panel is set in motion by the alternating pressure of the sound wave. The sound energy is converted to heat. Panel resonators are used for efficient low-frequency absorption, and when middle- to high-frequency absorption is not sought or is provided for by another acoustic treatment. They are often used in recording studios.

SPECIAL ACOUSTIC ABSORBERS

Space units are blocks of fibrous and porous material made of mineral fibers or fiberglass. They look much like acoustic tile and are typically 50 mm (2 in.) thick. Space units are applied to hard wall and ceiling surfaces. They absorb sound efficiently, helped by the exposure of their thick sides.

Functional absorbers are free-hanging cylinders used in industrial applications. They employ both surface absorption and tuned resonances to absorb sound and help reduce noise and reverberation in a room.

Quadratic-residue diffusers consist of a series of narrow wells of unequal depth separated by even narrower plates. Typical depths are 10 to 41 cm (4–16 in.) or more. This results in an attractive ribbed appearance. Quadratic-residue diffusers work by spreading the sound reflections over a wide arc at an angle to their wells. They are used in broadcast and recording studios, control rooms, and wherever specular reflections off plain surfaces are to be avoided. They can be made of any hard material and may be engineered to work over a wide range of frequencies.

Chapter 53

Sound Transmission Between Spaces

Sound travels through other materials as well as air. It can be transmitted through steel, wood, concrete, masonry, or other rigid construction materials. The sound of a person walking is readily transmitted through a concrete floor slab into the air of the room below. A metal pipe will carry plumbing noise throughout a building. A structural beam can carry the vibrations of a vacuum cleaner to an adjacent room, or the rumble of an electric motor throughout a building.

Buildings generate their own sounds. Rain and sleet pound and clatter on building surfaces. Doors slam and old wood floors creak. Heating and plumbing systems, elevator machinery, and machines like garbage disposals produce mechanical noises. When the structure of the building is pushed and pulled by the wind, heat, or humidity, the building creaks, groans, and crackles.

CONTROLLING BUILDING SYSTEM NOISE

A lot of the noise in a building comes from mechanical systems. Machines cause noise by vibration. Enclosing the noise at the source with materials that reduce noise by absorption and block airborne sound limits

the problem. The equipment supplier can often provide prefabricated partial and full enclosures. Curtains and panels may also help isolate the machinery.

Laundry machines, mixers, bins, chutes, polishing drums, and other machinery with sheet metal enclosures that vibrate can create a lot of noise. The vibration can be dampened by permanently attaching a layer of foam to the vibrating metal, which converts the noise energy to heat. Adding a heavy limp barrier material to the outside of the foam creates a composite damping barrier material and further reduces the noise.

The first step in quieting machine noise is to select quiet equipment and install it away from inhabited parts of the building. Mount equipment with resilient fittings to eliminate structure-borne noise, and house noisy equipment in sound-isolating enclosures to cut down on airborne noise transmission. Damping is accomplished by rigidly coupling the machine to a large mass, called an inertia block.

Decoupling the vibration from connections that would carry it throughout the building can reduce airborne machine noise. Breaking the connection from the vibration source to the building structure will also keep noise from spreading. Using flexible joints in all pipes and ducts connected to the machine accomplishes this. Flexible conduit connections are used for all motors, transformers, and lighting fixtures with magnetic ballasts.

Elevators, escalators, and freight elevators are localized sources of noise, and generally run at fairly low speeds. If the spaces around them are located judiciously, their noise should not be a major problem. However, the motors and controls can be noisy.

Higher-priced upper floors in a building may be near noisy elevator machine rooms, mechanical equipment rooms, and cooling towers. An acoustic expert should be called in during the equipment design phase, as these problems are almost impossible to solve later.

Plumbing and Mechanical System Noise

The piping for a building's plumbing system can also be a source of noise, both from the normal sounds of water rushing through uninsulated pipes and from water hammer in improperly designed systems. Pipes and flushing toilets should be kept away from quiet areas.

In many buildings, 40 percent of the construction budget is spent on the mechanical system. Mechanical equipment in the building has many noise-producing components. The air-handling system includes fans, compressors, cooling towers, condensers, ductwork, dampers, mixing boxes, induction units, and diffusers, all of which can either generate noise or carry it to other locations. In one east coast hotel, the roof-mounted chiller causes clearly audible vibration in the meeting room chandeliers below. Systems also include pumps and liquid flowing through piping.

Roof mounted heating, ventilating, and air-conditioning (HVAC) units are very economical but very noisy. The vibrating equipment, short duct runs, and acoustic sound reflections all lead to problems. Use of vibration isolators, sound mufflers, and careful location of equipment all help.

Electrical System Noise

Most noisy electrical equipment produces a low-frequency 120-Hz hum that is difficult to reduce. Mounting the transformer on vibration isolators, hanging it from a wall with resilient hangers, or placing it on a massive slab can minimize electric transformer noise. When transformers are located near acoustically reflective surfaces, the sound can be amplified. Sound-absorbent material behind the unit is not useful at 120 Hz; only cavity resonators will work at that low frequency. Flexible conduit connections should be used. Be aware of transformer locations so that they don't end up adjacent to or immediately outside quiet areas or directly below a window.

Magnetic lighting fixture ballasts for fluorescent and high-intensity discharge (HID) sources also produce a 120-Hz hum. Magnetic ballasts are being replaced by electronic ballasts in fluorescent sources, but are still used in HID fixtures. When the ballast is attached to the fixture, the sound is amplified. A large number of fixtures in a plenum can lead to a serious noise problem. Absorbent materials in plenums, flexible conduit, and resilient fixture hangers can help. Ballasts can be remote mounted if necessary.

Weatherstripping on windows and doors will reduce wind noises. This will also cut the transmission of outdoor noises into the building, and reduce heat loss as a bonus. Rain and sleet noises can be reduced with heavier roof and window construction.

Structural noises in a building may be inevitable and are difficult to remedy, as building components slip past each other during sporadic releases of built-up stresses. If the source is precisely located, the component can be nailed or bolted more tightly. Blowing graphite particles into a moving joint as a lubricant sometimes helps.

AIRBORNE AND STRUCTURE-BORNE SOUND

Airborne sound originates in a space with any sound-producing source, and changes to structure-borne sound when the sound waves strike the room boundaries. The noise is still considered airborne, however, because it originated in the air. Structure-borne sound is energy delivered by a source that directly vibrates or hits the structure. In practice, all sound transmission involves both airborne and structure-borne sound.

When airborne sound hits a partition, it makes the partition vibrate, generating sound on the other side (Fig. 53-1). The sound will not pass through the partition unless an air path exists. If the partition is airtight, then the sound energy causes the structure itself to become a sound source by vibrating the partition. The partition vibrates mostly in the vertical plane, but also causes some energy to pass into the floor and ceiling, resulting in structure-borne sound.

When a mechanical contact vibrates or hits a struc-

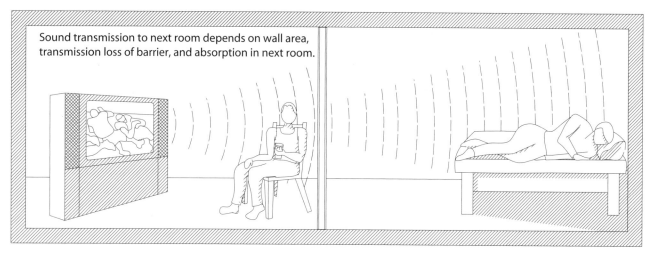

Sound transmission to next room depends on wall area, transmission loss of barrier, and absorption in next room.

Figure 53-1 Sound transmission between rooms.

ture, the sound travels along the structure causing vibrations, which then become airborne sound. Rigid wall-to-floor connections result in sounds that can be heard clearly through the building structure. A rigid structure with rigid connections offers a good sound path even in a massive concrete structure with masonry walls. The approach then becomes one of absorbing impacts with heavy carpet and resilient floor-wall connections.

When there is no air cushion between a noise source and the building's structure, high-intensity energy is introduced into the structure, where it travels at great speed with minimal attenuation. The sound in the structure is attenuated only by breaks in the structure. The structure must have structural integrity to carry loads, so breaking the structure to stop noise is complex and expensive.

With structure-borne sound (Fig. 53-2), the entire structure becomes a network of parallel paths for the sound. Partial solutions are useless, as sound finds flanking paths. The entire building structure must be soundproofed. Adding mass does not usually block structure-borne sound, especially in buildings with long spans. The floor becomes a diaphragm, improving structure-to-air noise transfer efficiency like a drumhead. Exposed structural ceilings further reduce the attenuation that would occur in a plenum. As most structure-borne sound is carried by floor structures, the sound radiates up and down into the rooms above and below.

Airborne sound is usually less disturbing than structure-borne sound. The initial energy is usually very small and attenuates rapidly at the room's boundaries. Air-

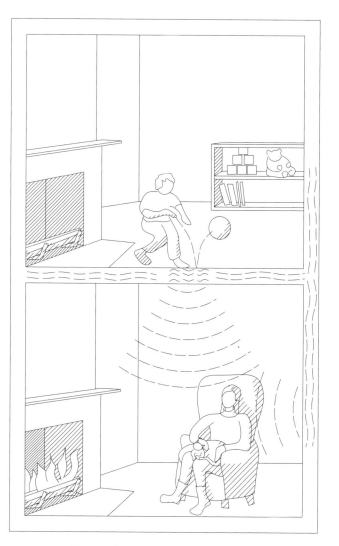

Figure 53-2 Structure-borne sound.

borne sound changes directions (diffracts) easily. Low-frequency sounds are the most flexible, and can get around barriers.

Structure-borne sound has a higher initial energy level, and attenuates slowly through the structure, thereby disturbing large sections of the building. Structure-borne sound is magnified by the sounding board effect, like the handle of a tuning fork placed on a table. The sound appears to be amplified, although it actually is just a case of more efficient energy transfer from the tuning fork to your ear. Similarly, a vibrating pump may make little sound, but will transfer a large amount of energy to the structure, resulting in audible sound at each partition, floor, or wall rigidly coupled to the structure. Soft or damping connections prevent energy transfer, so less energy is transferred into the connecting efficient radiation surfaces.

Structure-borne sound travels much more rapidly than airborne sound. Sound traveling along a massive structure will radiate outward from the structure only minimally, though enough to be very annoying. The large mass minimizes vibration in the outward direction, but focuses the speed along the direction of the structural members.

DIFFRACTION

Diffraction (Fig. 53-3) is the physical process by which sound passes around obstructions and through very small openings. Any point on a sound wave can establish a new wave when it passes an obstacle. When most of the wave is blocked, the portion that gets through a small opening starts a new wave. A small hole, there-fore, can block long wavelengths (low frequencies) more than short ones (high frequencies).

Sound diffracts around or over a barrier. The best location for a barrier is either very close to the source or close to the receiver. The worst position is halfway between source and listener. A massively thick barrier is only slightly better than a moderately thick one, so there is a practical limit to thickness. Absorptive material on the source side of the barrier will reduce noise reflected back to the source, but will not help the receiver much.

FLANKING PATHS

Sound will find parallel or flanking paths, sort of like an acoustic short circuit. It is important to avoid locating doors and windows where they will allow short cuts for sound. The most common flanking path is a plenum with ductwork, registers, and grilles. A plenum will make an excellent intercom unless it is completely lined with sound absorbent material. Even then, low-frequency sound will still get through.

Air turbulence in HVAC ductwork creates noise, which increases with increasing velocity and at sharp bends. Sound travels as easily against the flow of air in an HVAC duct system as with the airflow. Both supply and return ducts should be lined with absorbent duct lining to control the transmission of fan noise. Duct lining is acoustical insulation that is usually made of fiberglass impregnated with rubber or neoprene compound to avoid fibers from coming loose in the air current. Duct lining is available from 13 to 51 ($\frac{1}{2}$ in. to 2 in.) thick. In high-velocity ducts, the duct lining may be faced with perforated metal to prevent deterioration of the lining. Duct lining is typically installed only in rectangular ducts. Round ductwork requires an internal perforated screen to hold the lining in place. There are now proprietary products available that help solve the problem for round ducts more simply and at less expense by mechanically fastening the lining to the interior surfaces of the ducts.

There are current investigations going on into the breakdown of duct lining, which releases particles into the air in the duct. Most past problems have been due to misuse of the duct lining in situations where there is high airflow velocity. Small glass fibers may get into the air stream. Laboratory tests have produced cancer from fiber implanted in an opening in the abdomen of a test animal, and research is continuing into the possible dangers from glass fibers.

Duct linings should not be used in areas like humidifiers or cooling coils, where the air may be very

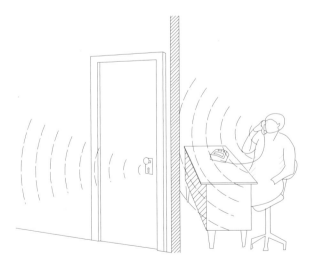

Figure 53-3 Diffraction.

moist. Moisture can condense on linings from cool air moving through the ducts, creating environments for the growth of mold, spores, and bacteria that can then be blown throughout the building. The mechanical engineer must provide adequate air movement and control the moisture content of the air. Duct linings should be avoided where the airflow is contaminated by lab hood exhausts or in some types of industrial or laboratory environments. Duct linings should also not be used in health care areas like burn units where bacteria present an exceptional problem, unless the air is filtered before entering the room.

Duct lining absorbs sound and attenuates noise as it moves along the ducts. Duct lining doesn't work as well for low frequencies as for high ones. When the ducts themselves are made of fiberglass, the attenuation is similar, but the lightweight construction allows sound to escape into the surrounding space. Duct lining is inexpensive and takes up little room.

In addition to lining ductwork to reduce noise, designing smooth transitions between ducts of different sizes reduces noise. Keeping adjacent ducts as far apart as possible can also minimize cross talk between rooms and between ducts. Damping material glued on the outside prevents thin metal duct walls from resonating. Mufflers and silencers on fans can reduce high-frequency noise, but don't help much with lower frequencies.

TRANSMISSION LOSS

Transmission loss (TL) is a measure of the performance of a building material or construction assembly in preventing transmission of airborne sound. It is equal to the reduction in sound intensity as it passes through the material or assembly, when tested in a laboratory at all one-third octave band center frequencies from 125 to 4000 Hz.

The TL indicates the sound-insulating quality of a wall. The TL of a wall is related to the wall's physical characteristics, mass, rigidity, materials of construction, and method of construction and attachment.

SOUND TRANSMISSION CLASS

The sound transmission class (STC) is a single-number rating of the performance of a building material or construction assembly in preventing transmission of airborne sound. The STC is derived by comparing the lab-

oratory TL test curve for a material or assembly to a standard frequency curve. The higher the STC rating, the greater is the sound-isolation value. An open doorway has an STC value of 10. Normal construction has STC ratings from 30 to 60. Special construction is required to achieve an STC rating over 60.

STIFFNESS AND RESONANCE

The stiffer a barrier, the more it will be set in motion by sound energy. The stiffness of a barrier is determined by its material and the rigidity of its mounting. In a stiff material, the sound energy motion is passed from molecule to molecule, conducting sound very efficiently. Less stiffness results in high internal damping. The motion of the molecules is not transmitted well, so less stiff materials are good sound insulators. The rigidity of a mounting is like a drumhead: the tighter it is, the more sound is transmitted. Stiffness transmits the most sound at low frequencies.

Lead sheet is sheet metal made of lead or a lead alloy. It is available combined with other materials, such as in leaded vinyl. Lead sheet is used to close off a plenum above a room where the partitions extend only to the suspended ceiling. Lead sheet is good at cutting down sound transmission, as it is both heavy and limp. It is easily shaped to conform to irregularities, avoiding holes in tightly sealed barriers.

Steel joists and trusses are structural members used to support floors and roofs. They do not aid in sound attenuation, but their spacing and rigidity can affect vibration isolation. Steel structural components don't generally absorb sound but may help diffuse sound if they are exposed.

COMPOUND BARRIERS

Most partitions are built of light, upright framing members with plaster or gypsum wallboard surfaces attached to both sides. This construction does not provide a very good sound barrier. Adding layers of gypsum wallboard to one or both sides increases the wall's mass and improves acoustic performance.

Gypsum wallboard consists of fire-rated sheets of gypsum, which has been heated to a high temperature, plus additives. These are then sandwiched between sheets of special paper. Gypsum wallboard is not very heavy or thick but provides fair sound attenuation. The best construction detail for blocking sound uses multiple layers of gypsum wallboard with a resilient separation between the two faces of the partition, and with absorptive material in the stud space. The wallboard joints must be perfectly sealed. Gypsum wallboard will resonate unless it is attached directly to a solid substrate without an air space, so that it will absorb low-frequency sounds. It is highly reflective of higher frequencies.

Compound barriers or cavity walls improve transmission loss when the void between the two sides of the wall is filled with porous, sound-absorbent material. This decreases the stiffness of the compound structure, and absorbs sound energy reflecting back and forth between the inside wall surfaces. Steel channel studs are used to frame partitions and are covered with gypsum wallboard. Light gauge steel studs are lightly resilient, which helps the wall attenuate sound. Heavy gauge steel studs and wood studs are stiffer and offer less sound attenuation. Steel or wood studs do not add significantly to the wall's sound absorption.

When one layer of gypsum wallboard is attached to the framing with resilient metal clips instead of tight screws, structure-borne transmission of sound through the partition is reduced substantially. Resilient clips and channels (Fig. 53-4) are usually made of light-gauge sheet metal, and are used between studs or joists and the finished gypsum wallboard or plaster surface. They are highly effective with wood joists and studs. By breaking the rigid connection between the two faces of the partition, resilient channels and clips permit room surfaces to vibrate normally without transmitting vibrating motions and the associated noise to the supporting structure. They reduce the sound transmission through the partition or ceiling.

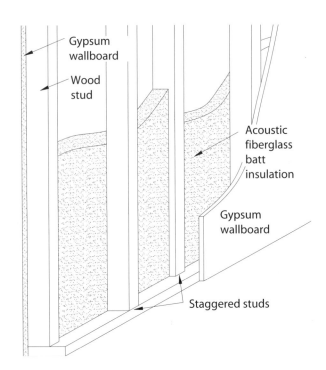

Figure 53-5 Staggered-stud partition.

Where the studs are used in two unconnected rows, their stiffness isn't an issue. Staggered-stud partitions (Fig. 53-5) for reducing sound transmission between rooms are framed with two separate rows of studs arranged in a zigzag fashion and supporting opposite faces of the partition. This type of wall is often used in recording studios. A fiberglass blanket is often inserted between the rows of studs. A stud wall with staggered studs is better than a single-material or common stud wall.

SOUND TRANSMISSION BETWEEN ROOMS

Wherever an opening exists—even a keyhole, a slot at the bottom of a door, or a crack between a partition and the ceiling—sound will move from one room to another. Weatherstrip cracks around ill-fitting windows and doors, and close all other cracks and openings with airtight sealants. Avoid using telephones with mechanical ringers or wall-hung phones with electronic ringers that vibrate through to the adjacent unit. Mount sound-system speakers on resilient padding to minimize transmission of low-frequency noise. Install closers on all cabinetry to decrease impact vibration that reradiates as sound to the adjacent space.

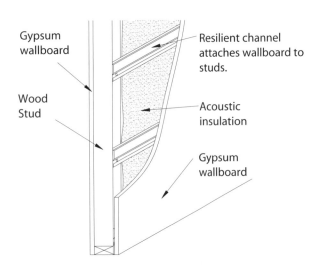

Figure 53-4 Resilient channels.

Partitions from the top of the floor slab to the underside of the next floor provide maximum sound isolation. For best results, partitions should be built in as massive and airtight manner as possible. Acoustic mass resists the transmission of sound by the inertia and elasticity of the transmitting medium. In general, the heavier and more dense a body, the greater is its resistance to sound transmission. Thick brick walls provide a good sound barrier between rooms. A partition of concrete blocks is not as good, as it is somewhat porous and allows sound to penetrate. Adding plaster on one or both surfaces results in a better, airtight wall. However, as we have already discussed in the section on structure-borne sound, an impact on a massive wall can be transmitted throughout the building if the structure is rigid.

The overall acoustic performance of composite walls—those walls with a window, door, vent or other opening—is strongly affected by the element with the highest sound transmission. The acoustical quality is harmed less if the poor-performing element is much smaller than the better performing parts of the wall, but even a very small opening seriously degrades the ability to keep sound within the room.

Doors

Doors in residential buildings, including private homes, apartments, dormitories, and hotels, and in commercial offices, should not be located directly across from each other. Louvered and undercut doors are useless as sound barriers. The most important element in the soundproofing of doors is a complete seal around the opening. In the closed position, the door should exert pressure on the soundproofing gaskets, making the joints airtight.

Two gasketed doors, preferably with enough space between them for a door swing, are used to create a sound lock. All surfaces in the sound lock are completely covered with absorbent materials, and the floor is carpeted. A sound lock will increase attenuation by a minimum of 10 dB, and by as much as 20 dB at some frequencies.

Special sound-insulated wood flush doors have their faces separated by a void or a damping compound. They are installed with special stops, gaskets, and thresholds.

Windows

Exterior walls usually have a high STC, but windows are the weakest part. Sound leaks through cracks in operable windows are more critical than the type of glazing in keeping sound out.

Weatherstripping for thermal reasons also helps acoustical performance. The manner of opening and the window placement also affect transmission loss.

Plate glass 13 mm ($\frac{1}{2}$ in.) thick has an STC in the low 30s, while laminated glass of the same thickness may approach an STC of 40. Double-glazing with a wide air gap also improves performance. A narrow air gap, which works well for thermal insulation, acts as a stiff spring and transmits sound almost completely.

Steel decking is sheet steel that is corrugated for strength. It is highly sound reflective unless it is free to vibrate, when it will absorb low frequencies. It is used for noise barriers along highways. Steel decking is often used as a base for other materials, but the combined mass of the deck and the concrete topping are not much better at reducing sound transmission than the concrete by itself.

DEMOUNTABLE PARTITION SYSTEMS

Lightweight operable or demountable partition systems have many panel joints, floor and ceiling tracks, and side wall intersections where sound can escape. It is relatively easy to seal a fixed partition, but the seals for operable or demountable partitions must also be operable, and must be durable enough to last the life of the installation with minimal maintenance. The details of the materials, system, and specifications must assure that panel joint seals will last.

CUSHIONING IMPACTS

Impact noise is often the greatest acoustic problem in buildings with multiple residents. Reducing the sound of footfalls and other impacts on the floor can be done in a variety of ways. Kitchens and bathrooms should be stacked and not located over living rooms or bedrooms. Specify felt sliders for chairs and other movable furniture.

Cushioning the initial impact that produces a noise will frequently eliminate all but severe problems. The impact isolation class (IIC) is a rating for floor construction, similar to STC ratings for walls. It is based on tests of actual construction using a tapping machine. The results are compared to a standard. The IIC rating is influenced by the weight of the floor system and of the suspended ceiling below, the sound absorption in the cavity between the floor and ceiling, whether the floor is carpeted or not, and the type of building structural system. Wood structural components and wood bearing walls lower the IIC as compared with post- and slab-type steel buildings.

Floor finishes can increase IIC ratings. Resilient tile has little effect on the sound attenuation of the floor construction, but will help reduce the sound generated by high-frequency impacts, especially if it is foam backed. Vinyl tile 1.6 mm ($\frac{1}{16}$ in.) thick has an IIC rating of 0. Linoleum or rubber tile 3 mm ($\frac{1}{8}$ in.) thick is rated between 3 and 5. Cork tile 6.4 mm ($\frac{1}{4}$ in.) thick is rated between 8 and 12.

Floor/ceiling assemblies with relatively low STC ratings may have high IIC ratings, especially if the floor is carpeted. This means that sound may be transmitted through the wall from an airborne source, yet direct impact on the floor will be muted.

Living units above other occupied living units should probably be carpeted. Carpet with padding provides excellent impact isolation. It is most useful where the floor structure is exposed to the space below, and in buildings with wood bearing wall construction. Low-pile carpet on a fiber pad has IIC ratings between 10 and 14. With a foam rubber pad, the rating increases to 15 to 21. High pile carpet with a foam rubber pad earns ratings between 21 and 27. Condominium covenants often require carpets in hallways and foyers and over half of the other living areas to remove most of the objectionable footfall noise.

ISOLATING SOUND IN FLOOR/CEILING SPACES

Another approach to controlling impact noise is to suspend the ceiling and use an absorber in the cavity. The most disturbing noise tends to be that which radiates down from the ceiling. A flexibly suspended ceiling with an acoustically absorbent layer suspended in it is effective if paths leading into walls and reradiating into the space below don't flank it. The insulation is usually 76 to 152 mm (3–6 in.) thick and not packed into the space. Insulation may lie on the ceiling or be attached to the underside of the floor. Blown-in insulation can be used if it evenly covers the area and is not packed into the cavity.

Two or more layers of gypsum wallboard on a metal channel frame suspended from vibration isolation hangers can replace or be added to an existing ceiling. A double-layer gypsum wallboard ceiling can also be installed on resilient channels or clips, with fiberglass insulation in the cavity.

Installing a resilient layer between the structural floor and a hard finish floor treatment like marble, ceramic tile, or wood will help cushion impacts. Resilient products are often installed beneath lightweight gypsum concrete or other lightweight leveling materials. Floor underlayments are used to control sound transmission of both impact and airborne noise in floor systems, and consist of precompressed molded glass fibers. The sound matt is installed between a plywood subfloor and the floor's finish material. Floor underlayments provide a system stiff enough to prevent grout cracking in tile floors while being resilient enough to greatly reduce noise.

Wood decking, supported by beams or trusses to form a floor or roof, is often used for exposed ceilings. Wood decking has a relatively low mass, and does not attenuate sound well unless it is ballasted with heavier materials. Wood decks are generally reflective, but cracks between boards will absorb a fair amount of sound. Increasing the weight of the structural floor may help, but this is often not feasible and requires a significant increase in mass to be effective.

FLOATING FLOORS

Floating floors (Fig. 53-6) reduce transmission of impact noise and increase the sound transmission loss (TL) rating of a structure. They are used in condominiums, apartments, and commercial buildings for the control of impact noise produced by footfalls or other impacts. In recording studios, sound rooms, television or movie studios, floating floors reduce the transmission of external noise into the studio. Floating wood floors are used for dance and exercise floors with resiliency requirements.

The floor can be separated from the structural floor by a resilient element, such as rubber or mineral wool pads, blankets, or special spring metal sleepers. The effectiveness of such a system depends on the mass of the floating floor, the compliance of the resilient support, and most importantly, the degree of isolation of the floating floor, which must avoid flanking paths at the borders.

The mass of the floating floor must be large enough to spread loads properly, or the padding underneath will compress, deform, and transmit impacts. The total construction must be airtight, and consequently sound tight. Where partitions rest on a floating floor, they must not compress it. Flanking paths at walls or penetrations are to be avoided. The construction should be consistent throughout, as mixed construction types create flanking paths.

First, isolation pads are placed on the floor, separated

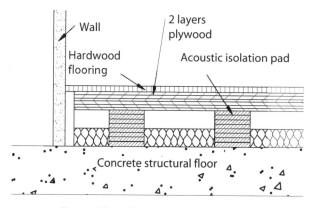

Figure 53-6 Floating wood floor detail.

by low-density acoustical fiberglass. Continuous wood nailers or steel channels are then installed and a plywood subfloor is constructed. Depending on the design requirements, multiple layers of plywood or a combination of plywood and gypsum board may be specified. A floating wood floor is completed with the installation of parquet, hardwood, vinyl tile, or other finish flooring.

Roll out floating concrete floor systems consist of 51 mm (2 in.) thick high-density pre-compressed molded fiberglass isolation pads, separated by low-density acoustical fiberglass. Mechanical equipment noise, loud musical instruments, and industrial noise can all be significantly attenuated with floating concrete floors. The floating floor material is laid over the structural concrete floor, and topped with a floating layer of concrete.

Another type of floating device for a concrete floor is used for areas with regular perimeters and light or uniform loads. Isolation mounts are placed up to 122 cm (4 ft) on center each way on top of polyethylene that has been laid on the structural floor. Reinforcing bars are then installed across rows of isolators and the concrete is poured. After curing, the slab is raised to operating height using built-in jack screws or spring lift slabs.

SPECIAL ACOUSTIC DEVICES

When the building design calls for the placement of quiet spaces such as executive offices, conference rooms, theaters, or recording studios next to, under, or over noisy mechanical equipment rooms, kitchens, or manufacturing spaces, additional measures must be taken to assure that quiet spaces will remain quiet. Double partitions and a high mass ceiling are used to create a room within a room with a floating floor. Acoustical product manufacturers have developed systems for gypsum wallboard that isolate the partitions from the structure while

providing lateral restraint to prevent toppling or collapse. The systems include resilient, load-bearing underlayment, vertical joint isolation material, sway braces, and top wall brackets.

Air springs are manufactured and used for strictly acoustical purposes. They are probably the most effective vibration-isolating devices available today. Air springs are custom designed for critical applications where only extremely low levels of vibration can be tolerated. They work by trapping a volume of air in an inflexible jacket. The spring is installed to eliminate any mechanical ties between the building structure and what is to be isolated. Compressible air gives the spring, and air pressure plus the jacket provide stiffness.

Resilient hangers include a variety of spring-like devices designed to support suspended ceilings or to suspend pieces of mechanical equipment, or ducts or pipes connected to equipment. Resilient hangers are steel springs, pieces of rubber-like materials, or compressed fiberglass. Resilient ceiling hangers improve attenuation even better than resilient clips. Resilient equipment hangers are also known as vibration isolators.

Resilient mounts are similar to resilient hangers, and are used as vibration isolating supports for mechanical equipment. They are also used to support floating floors, where they are typically 51 mm (2 in.) tall and made of solid neoprene or neoprene-covered fiberglass. Double floors with a structural slab and floating slab provide exceptionally good sound attenuation.

Flexible connections consist of flexible inserts of canvas or leaded vinyl that are located between two pieces of metal duct. Flexible conduit or flexible hose are also considered flexible connections. Flexible connections offer resilient breaks in ducts and pipes to attenuate vibrations. They are essential in all duct, pipe, and conduit runs between a piece of vibration-isolated equipment and the building structure.

Sway braces are another variety of resilient connectors that allow the structure to be supported without any rigid ties. Neoprene or fiberglass insulating material is attached to steel clips or angles. Sway braces allow construction of freestanding walls in double-wall construction where rigid braces would hurt sound attenuation. Small angle braces lend stability to masonry walls whose tops must be kept free of the slab above for sound isolation reasons.

Gaskets are airtight seals of pliable neoprene or vinyl designed for acoustical doors and sound-rated partition systems. Gaskets eliminate air leaks to provide maximum attenuation in sound locks. A perfect fit is required if the attenuation capabilities of the door or other panel are to be realized.

Chapter

54

Acoustic Applications

• • •

Now that we have explored the basic principles and tools of acoustic design, let's look at some specific applications. Probably the most common acoustic problem confronted by interior designers is keeping conversations in offices private and nonintrusive.

SPEECH PRIVACY

When you want to keep the sounds of conversation contained within an office, a good place to start is with the use of absorbent materials, which will lower sound levels within the room. This reduces the level of sound that is available to pass to adjacent spaces. Next, designing barriers between spaces with heavy, airtight construction cuts down on the amount of sound transmitted to the adjoining rooms. Providing masking noise in neighboring spaces helps to disguise the information carried by speech and makes it less intrusive.

Enclosed Offices

Some offices require more intense efforts to assure speech privacy than others. The level of acoustic treat-

ment within the room where the sound originates depends on the loudness of the speech, the effect of the room's sound absorption on the speech level, and the degree of privacy required.

The amount of privacy is also affected by the acoustic isolation of the receiving room. This depends on the sound transmission class (STC) rating of the barrier between the rooms, the noise reduction factor, and the background noise level in the receiving room. Greater sound absorption in the receiving room reduces the reverberation buildup of sound for the listener, lowering the speech level and intelligibility. The larger the size of the listener's room as compared to the source room, the lower the speech level will be in the receiving room.

Acoustic consultants use a speech privacy analysis method that quantifies the principle acoustic factors into a single privacy rating number. This method is used to analyze existing spaces and to design new spaces.

Open Offices

Open offices create a multitude of problems for achieving speech privacy. Open office spaces are more densely populated with office workers, with fewer buffering spaces like storerooms between people. The trend to-

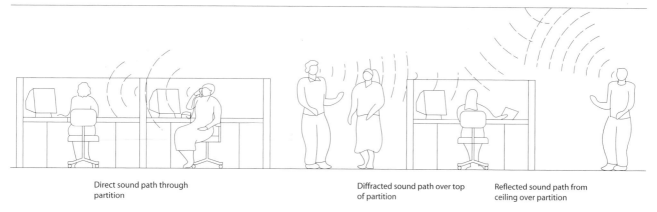

Direct sound path through
partition

Diffracted sound path over top
of partition

Reflected sound path from
ceiling over partition

Figure 54-1 Sound paths in an open office.

ward more employees working at computers or desks results in open office plans with increasingly smaller cubicles for one or two people.

The amount of speech privacy required within an open office varies. Acoustic consultants identify three levels of speech privacy: normal, confidential, and transitional. Normal speech privacy levels allow normal voice levels from an adjacent cubicle to be heard, but without intelligibility unless the listener concentrates on the sound. Raised voices will generally be intelligible. Where overall noise levels are low, background noise levels should remain within 6 dB of the intruding sound so that speech doesn't stand out.

Confidential speech privacy requires that normal voice levels be audible but generally unintelligible. Raised voices may be partially intelligible. The noise level should be minimal. The background noise level should be no more than 2 dB less than the intruding sound, and a maximum of 3 dB more. In such a space, 95 percent of the people don't sense sound as intrusive and disturbing, and are able to concentrate on most types of work.

Transitional speech privacy levels are also referred to as minimal or marginal privacy. Transitional speech privacy levels are considered intolerable by around 40 percent of people, and the number whose productivity would suffer is even higher. Speech at normal voice levels in adjoining open offices is readily understood most of the time, and the overall noise level is average. Intruding speech levels may be 10 dB or more than the background level. Offices with two occupants or one office receiving noise from three adjacent offices have transitional levels of speech privacy. It is almost impossible to have adequate speech privacy in a cubicle shared by two people.

 Sound in open offices can travel directly from the source to the listener (Fig. 54-1). It may also be dif-

fracted by objects in its path, or reflected off ceilings or walls. The architectural arrangement of the space has a great impact on speech privacy. When designing an open office, group spaces according to their speech privacy requirements. Confidential areas should be at the edge of open areas that serve as a buffer zone, with low overall sound levels including any background noise. Speech in perimeter offices with reflective surfaces may bounce out into areas occupied by other workers (Fig. 54-2). High noise production areas should be grouped and placed on the perimeter at a maximum distance from confidential areas.

Open areas within an open office plan should be as large as possible with acoustic insulation on the perimeter walls. Ceiling height should be no lower than

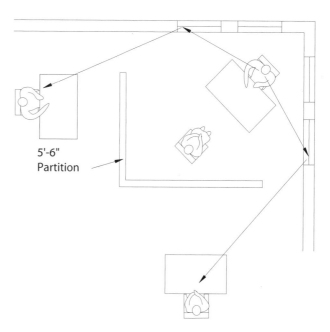

5'-6"
Partition

Figure 54-2 Speech privacy issues in a corner office.

2.75 meters (9 ft), with a 914-cm (3-ft) plenum above. Ductwork should be acoustically treated.

Try to keep individual office cubicles as enclosed as possible, with the maximum possible partition height. Occupants should be at least 3 meters (10 ft) apart, which increases to 3.7 meters (12 ft) for normal privacy and 4.9 meters (16 ft) for confidential privacy. Check desk locations for speech path privacy; desk orientations need not be the same in all cubicles (Fig. 54-3).

The absorption characteristics of the ceiling are the most important factor in designing open office speech privacy. Metal air pan diffusers and flat lighting fixtures provide strongly reflective speech paths, which bounce sound rising from one cubicle down into another. Highly absorptive baffle strips on equipment perimeters help to block sound paths.

The angles of reflection of sound waves from the ceiling depend on the location and height of the source of the sound, and on the ceiling height. The majority of angles formed by sound hitting and bouncing off the ceiling are between 30 and 60 degrees. Ceiling materials are available with high absorption at these angles. Minimal absorption coefficients at angles between 30 and 60 degrees should be 0.65 for 250-Hz frequency sounds (around the lower range of a male voice), 0.65 to 0.75 at 500 Hz, 0.85 at 1000 Hz (both of these encompass men's and women's voices), 0.90 at 2000 Hz (women's voices), and 0.90 at 4000 Hz (electric office equipment).

An articulation class (AC) rating indicates the absorption efficiency at angles of incidence between 45 and 55 degrees, and AC ratings should be at least 220, with the higher the number the better. Ceiling material manufacturers have tested and can supply accurate absorption data on their products. Light fiberglass ceiling tiles have an absorption coefficient at voice frequencies of 0.95. Mineral fiber tiles range from 0.8 to 0.85.

If you place flat-bottom lighting fixtures directly over low office partitions, they provide a speech path between the offices. The best fixture from an acoustic standpoint has deep reflector cells with parabolic bottom surfaces (which is what reflects both light and sound) in a 31 by 122 cm (1 by 4 ft) or 61 by 122 cm (2 by 4 ft) format.

Because sound always finds the path of least resistance, very little sound actually passes through low office partitions, as it usually goes over the top. Where a seated speaker is 112 to 122 cm (44 to 48 in.) high and about a meter (3 ft) away from the partition, the partition should have an STC of 25 to 26. With greater distance and a higher partition, an STC of 20 to 22 is permissible. The AC ratings should be in the 200 to 220

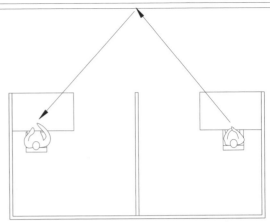

Sound bounces off corridor wall and into adjacent office.

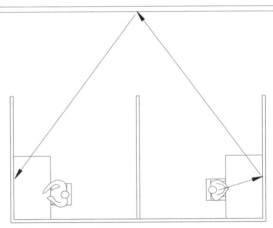

Sound bounces off office wall, then into corridor, before entering adjacent cubicle. Result: Less sound transmitted

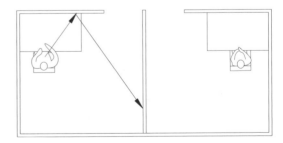

Front closure partition eliminates reflection off corridor wall.

Figure 54-3 Open office layouts.

range. Joints between partitions should be carefully sealed, as even small openings lower efficiency. For acoustic isolation, partitions should reach the floor, although lower areas don't have to be insulated in low speech privacy areas.

Partitions must be high enough to block direct line-of-sight voice transmissions. The median height of the mouth of a standing American male is 160 cm (63 in.), so partitions should not be lower than 165 cm (65 in.), and preferably 168 to 183 cm (66–72 in.) when located between cubicles. Because the greater 183-cm height also blocks vision, tall partitions are generally only used between departments, with 160 to 168 cm high partitions between cubicles.

Team work areas should be located away from normal working spaces, or be completely enclosed in full-height fixed or demountable partitions. Areas where raised voice levels would be common, like video conferencing rooms, telecommunications spaces, and areas with speakerphones or voice activated computers, should be sited carefully or completely enclosed.

Glass is very reflective of sound, and windows are often located in managers' offices where confidential discussions routinely take place. Windows and walls that lack absorptive treatment will reflect sound out of the space at an angle. To preserve privacy in these offices, use full-height partitions and fixed glass vision panels, with doors in openings. If windows are present, heavy drapes can be used to eliminate reflections. Locate confidential spaces in groups, and buffer them from open office spaces with unoccupied storage areas.

Floors in open offices do not affect the overall sound absorption very much. However, cushioned floors do greatly reduce the noise of chair movements and footfalls. For this reason, all floors in open office areas should be carpeted, but pile depth makes only a minimal difference. Using a polyurethane pad rather than jute gives the same positive difference as a thicker pile.

Masking Sound

In a busy room full of people, so much noise is generated in the frequency range of human speech that only the closest, most attentive listener can understand what you say. A spy will turn up the radio before holding a conversation in a possibly bugged room for the same reason. Background sound that is close to the frequency of speech reduces the intelligibility of speech.

Noise that carries information reduces the productivity of office workers. What we hear depends on the level of attention to what we are doing and to the in-trusiveness of the outside sound. In a very quiet space with no background noise, any sound is distracting. With a constant ambient sound level in the listener's room, sound transmitted from another room is masked, becoming inaudible, or simply less annoying.

Where it is too costly or too difficult to treat a building for a persistent or distracting noise source, low-level masking noise may help. Masking sounds are also useful in rooms that are so quiet that heartbeats, respiration, and body movement sounds are annoying, as in a bedroom where small noises disturb would-be sleepers. Natural sounds, like waves against a shore, wind through trees, an open fire crackling, the sound of rain on a roof, or a brook or fountain splashing are sometimes used. Sometimes, a slightly noisy ventilation system works, but most systems run irregularly and can themselves be distracting.

Because heating, ventilating, and air-conditioning (HVAC) system background sound levels rarely provide the consistency and spatial uniformity necessary for speech privacy, practically all open-plan office installations use carefully designed electronic masking systems to provide uniform background sound at the proper level and with good tonal characteristics. These masking systems are usually operated at or near the upper limits of acceptability for average building occupants, around 50 dB. Higher masking sound levels make the masking sounds themselves a source of annoyance.

A masking system consists of a signal (noise) generator, an equalizer for shaping the signal, an amplifier and controls, and a distribution system for feeding the speakers, which can be hung above a suspended ceiling, mounted in the ceiling, or wall-mounted. Volume is controlled remotely and can be automatically reduced after-hours to a level that won't bother the few remaining workers.

The sound produced by an electronic masking system is white noise, which has been described as the noise of air rushing through an opening, the noise of water in piping, or a whooshing sound. It can be tailored to the user's preference with filters in the equalizer. The sound is usually tuned to emphasize lower frequencies, which avoids high-frequency hissing noises.

For use in offices, electronic sound-masking units are often hung above the ceiling where they are completely out of sight. The sound masking fills the plenum area and then gently filters down through the ceiling tiles into the office space below to unobtrusively raise the background sound level. The speakers can be adjusted to the individual acoustical comfort requirement in any given area. The units are about 15 cm (6 in.) in diameter and about 20 cm (8 in.) tall with a chain for

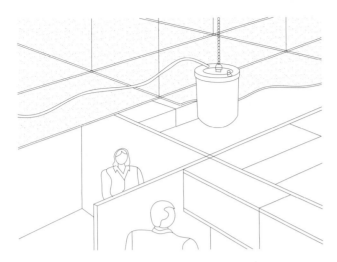

Figure 54-4 Sound masking speaker canister.

hanging (Fig. 54-4). The number of units required depends on the size of the area to be masked. On average, one unit can cover approximately 21 to 23 square meters (225–250 square ft). The units are easy to install, maintenance free, and have negligible operating costs. Sound-masking systems cost about $1 per square foot of space covered.

Some sound-masking systems also offer paging and music, but this is not recommended, especially if the masking sound shuts off during announcements, as it will be noticed when it is turned back on. The masking sound should blend into the background, and its hidden quality should not be disturbed.

Suspended ceiling systems are now available that not only incorporate wireless systems for office communication, but also include sound systems that deliver sound masking, paging, and music simultaneously, without shutting off the masking sound. All three modes are delivered through the same set of speakers that blend invisibly into the ceiling plane. This eliminates the need for redundant systems.

The Public Building Service of the U.S. General Services Administration (GSA) sets criteria and standards for the design, specification, and evaluation of systems and components for open office spaces in federal buildings. The GSA's speech privacy potential (SPP) rating is a summary of background sound level and attenuation between typical source and listener locations. You may encounter this rating when doing work in federally owned buildings, and when specifying materials that are marketed to government agencies.

 Ceiling-mounted masking system loudspeakers should not be visible, as they attract interest and eventually become annoying. They can be placed face-up in a plenum to increase dispersion and improve uniformity, but should not be mounted face down in the ceiling. Most ceiling tiles will allow masking sound to penetrate to the office area below.

SPACES FOR MUSIC AND PERFORMANCE

The design of spaces for music performance is both an art and a science. For concert halls and other important music spaces, the services of an acoustical consultant are essential. In the last half of the twentieth century, progress was made in the design of spaces for critical listening. Previously, the acoustics in places of listening was left to chance, or spaces were modeled on buildings with known characteristics.

Although the architectural character of a performance space is usually worked out well before the interior designer becomes involved in the project, the finishes and details of the hall's interior are critical to its acoustic success. A relatively long reverberation time is needed for music, so the amount of sound reflection and the liveliness of the space matter a great deal. Brilliance of musical tone is primarily a function of high-frequency content, so spaces that are too absorbent will dull musical sounds. A good sound path for musical tone is equivalent to a good visual path, which means that a seat where you have a good view of the performers is likely to also be a good seat acoustically.

When we listen to music, we want a sense of the direction of the source. This sense, called directivity, declines if a reinforced signal is excessively delayed by too many reflective surfaces.

Diffusion is desirable for music performances as it spreads the sound evenly over a wide seating area. Sound reflected from convex (outward curving) surfaces is diffuse, producing a constant sound level throughout the space.

The acoustic design of a space for the performance of music, theater, or other presentations starts with control of all undesired sounds from exterior sources, adjacent spaces within the building, the HVAC system, and other noise sources. Next, all sounds that the audience has come to hear are controlled so that they are adequately loud and properly distributed without echo or distortion throughout the space. Typical paths from the sound source to the receiver are studied, usually using computer-aided design and analysis procedures.

In order to assure that the sound source is loud enough, major room surfaces can be reinforced naturally to direct reflected sound to the audience. Sound reinforcement is coordinated with the basic acoustics of the room. Electronic reinforcement systems are used in large rooms or for weak sources. Very large auditoriums and sports arenas use electronic amplification systems.

Concert Halls

 It is important for the architect to spend time with the acoustic consultant early in the design of a concert hall, to get acoustic qualities into the architectural design. The shape of the building is critical to the quality of the music heard there. The design should proceed from the outside in, and then the materials should be selected. The interior designer must work closely with the architect and acoustic designer to create a design that will accommodate a variety of musical styles and instrumentations.

The project architect may or may not understand basic acoustic considerations. There has been a history since 1945 of concert halls with long reverberation times, where the tone drops after the high frequencies are absorbed on the first reflection. The resulting poor acoustics have alerted architects to the importance of calling in an acoustic designer earlier in the process. Acoustic designers know what needs to be done, and are taking a stronger role.

After researching 54 concert halls, acoustical expert Leo Beranek developed a list of essential acoustic attributes of a concert hall. They include reverberence, loudness, spaciousness, clarity, intimacy, warmth, and the ability to hear on stage. Clarity involves intelligibility, articulation, and definition. The quality of the sound, spaciousness, and enhancement are part of the room's audible effects or ambiance. Good sightlines, which often are also good listening paths, are critical as well. The hardest place to get good sound is in the center, middle seats, which ironically are the most expensive seats.

The sense of being enveloped by the music, especially when listening to large groups playing symphonic music, depends largely on reflections received from the side (lateral reflections). Where the audience sits in a fan-shaped area, side reflections are limited. A saw-tooth shaped wall or reflector panels along the wall help create the desired reflections. Nonhorizontal ceiling reflector panels also create some lateral reflections, especially for people sitting in the balcony.

The traditional European shoebox-shaped hall developed along with Western classical music, and the two influenced each other. During the fourth century under Constantine, churches were modeled after the Roman civic basilica. The very long reverberation times of these buildings literally turned speech into music. This had a profound effect on the development of European music. Monophonic chant developed from speech, and the rhythm was provided by the Latin text. Eventually, harmony and polyphony were added. The evolution of the organ for religious music occurred along with the architecture of the cathedrals it fills with sound. Traditional European concert music was developed from this environment.

Through the Renaissance, secular music evolved in rooms not designed specifically for musical performance. Music was performed in small oratories with a rectangular shape, and in rectangular palace ballrooms. Eventually, with the evolution of a middle class with leisure and money, concerts moved out of oratories into new concert halls with the same rectangular shape. The construction methods, aesthetics, and the ability for patrons to see and be seen influenced the design. Composers wrote music for the acoustic qualities of these specific spaces.

Traditional shoebox-shaped concert halls were successful due to their narrow, tall shape which provided plenty of lateral reflections. Understanding how lateral sound reflections work has been a catalyst for radical designs of concert halls, particularly in the 1970s and 1980s. Some of the major work on the importance of lateral reflections was done by a British acoustician, Mike Barron.

Outdoors, we receive sound straight from the orchestra, there are no reflections from the walls, and the sound appears distant. When we play music inside, reflections from the walls, ceiling, and floor embellish the sound. When sound reaches the listener from the stage, the same sound signal is received at both ears. This is because the head is symmetrical and the sound to both ears travels an identical path. When reflections come from the side, the sound at each ear is different. Sound to the farther ear has to get around the head. This means the sound arrives later and is significantly altered. The brain senses it is in a room, and a feeling of being enveloped by the music occurs.

Halls that are too wide and low lack these important lateral reflections. The basic shoebox shape works well for up to 2000 people (2500 maximum). The surfaces of these shoebox-shaped spaces are not smooth or slick in either older or new halls, with side and rear balconies breaking up the geometry. Details such as niches and statues in older buildings or deliberate architectural manipulations in the ceilings and walls of new concert halls create diffusion. Chandeliers, however, do not add to good diffusion.

Boston's Symphony Hall remains one of the world's favorite concert halls, and Wallace Clement Sabine, the father of acoustic design, along with the building's architect, recorded the design process in great detail. The rectangular box shape with irregularities compounded by the coffered ceiling was calculated to create a reverberation time that supported the music while allowing clarity. The building needed 1-meter (3-ft) thick masonry bearing walls to span the ceiling height without columns. The heavy wall material and small cushiony seats don't diminish the lively bass response.

High stage ceilings can create on-stage communication problems by absorbing sound directly above the performers. The configuration of the performance area has both functional and acoustic implications. A large sound-reflecting surface suspended over the performing area improves the ability of musicians on stage to hear one another.

Sound reflecting panels were first used to cure focusing effects and improve sound distribution in domed auditoriums. They have also been used to improve the distribution of reflected sound in concert halls. A clear space above the panels adds to the reverberant volume. Sound reflecting panels allow the use of nonshoebox shapes, like the large fan plan at Tanglewood, in Lenox, Massachusetts. In-the-round stages have problems, since musical instruments and the human voice are directional sound sources, and most classical music was written for performance in conventional rectangular spaces. Circular and elliptical shapes risk focusing sound on hot spots.

Concert halls are designed for a minimum of 80 percent full audience. Performers like a nearly full hall, so the size of the hall shouldn't be over-designed. However, it can be difficult to rehearse in an empty hall, and sometimes spaces are tuned with movable curtains and banners to avoid this problem during rehearsals.

Where audiences are seated behind the performers, nondirectional percussion, trombones, and some other instruments are clearly heard. Even directional instruments like horns can be heard from behind, and seats behind the stage are generally good seats, except for oratorios, cello concertos, or piano pieces, where the directionality of the source prevents good acoustics in all directions.

The major additions to acoustic knowledge and technology since 1980 have made it possible for problems to be avoided before construction. When Lincoln Center's Avery Fisher Hall, home of the New York Philharmonic, was built in the 1960s, there was no way to measure the acoustic effect of the lack of diffusion produced by smooth walls at the front and back. The problems had to be corrected by adding diffusing panels af-

ter the hall's opening. The Royal Festival Hall in London, built in 1951, originally lacked adequate bass response and reverberation. The room volume was too small, and there were too many sound-absorbing elements. The hall was improved by a subtle and sophisticated electronic system, known as assisted resonance, designed by P. H. Parkin. With modern digital technology, electronically synthesized acoustics can be of exceptionally high quality.

As new types of spaces evolve, music continues to evolve that takes advantage of the acoustics of the space. The combination of electronic and acoustic sources for live music performance adds a whole new layer to the acoustic complexity of concert spaces.

Opera Houses

Opera houses, with singers onstage and the orchestra in the pit, require both reverberation and clarity for speech and song. Acoustics and visibility both necessitate a good line of sight from all seats to the stage. In addition, both the proscenium arch separating the performers from the audience, and the tall stage tower behind the proscenium for rapid scene changes make it harder for people on stage to be heard. The design of an opera house is further complicated by the fact that the pit may be raised for events that don't use an orchestra, so that more seating can be added. Added to this are concerns with the reverberant and absorbent qualities of finish materials and the details of the design that determine lateral sound reflections.

In the 1920s, almost all opera houses were designed to double as concert halls. The stage tower can do double duty as a concert shell, and part of the tower can be used to add to the reverberation, but it is better to design a separate space for concert performances, as the sound is otherwise compromised for economy. Many of these older halls have been redesigned in response to an increased awareness of quality concert hall sound.

Opera houses have their own personalities and regional characteristics. The musicians, conductors, and administrators of an opera house must form a consensus on what constitutes good acoustics. La Scala, the famous Italian opera house, is small, tall, and narrow, while the Metropolitan Opera House in New York, a huge, barn-like structure seating 3800 people, can hire only singers with strong voices. The design goals for an opera house will vary with the character of its performances and the goals of its supporting constituency.

Recital Halls

Small halls for the performance of chamber music are often also used for a wide range of other activities. Adjustable absorption, such as draperies on tracks, allows control of reverberation time and loudness with flexibility. Stage areas can be adjusted for various sizes of performances using movable stage wall elements and batten-hung ceiling elements.

Other Listening Spaces

In addition to concert halls, recital halls, and opera houses, many other types of rooms have acoustic requirements for the performance of music. Large rehearsal rooms, ensemble rooms, faculty studios, music classrooms, practice rooms, and recording facilities all have special acoustic requirements. Prefabricated and pre-engineered sound isolation rooms are available for use as music practice rooms and for laboratory testing. Medical facilities use sound isolation rooms for diagnosing hearing problems. Industrial spaces use hearing protection booths to isolate workers from extremely loud processes.

Musical instruments can be uncomfortably loud in a small room, so sound-absorbing materials are necessary. Instrumental rooms need more acoustic treatment than choral rooms, as the music is louder. Adjustable absorption devices allow the treatment to change to fit the use. Absorptive material should be installed on the walls, at least between sitting and standing height. This minimal amount is appropriate for small practice rooms, but large or high rooms need more coverage. Absorption should take place in all three dimensions.

 Spaciousness is desirable in ensemble and rehearsal rooms, which are usually one and one-half stories high, and ideally two stories for larger rooms. Ensemble and rehearsal rooms often use suspended sound reflecting panels. They should have sound-absorbing materials for reverberation control, loudness reduction, and to avoid the possible flutter-echo paths between parallel walls.

Evenly dispersed sound reflections are critical for optimum sound quality and consistency. Geometric sound diffusers are used for band and choral rehearsal rooms, where the shaped surfaces of the diffusers break up direct sound reflections and disperse them evenly throughout the listening space. Made of heat-molded plastic and available in two standard shapes, geometric diffusers are commonly used in conjunction with acoustical wall panels for a combination of sound diffusion and absorption that improves overall room acoustics.

SPACES FOR SPEECH PLUS MUSIC

Interior designers are often involved in the design or renovation of spaces that do double duty. Auditoriums and theaters are often used by multiple and diverse community groups with varying levels of acoustical sophistication. Lecture rooms in schools, colleges, and other institutions often combine unamplified verbal presentations with electronic visual presentations. Churches, synagogues, mosques, and other worship spaces vary in size, function, and the combination of music and voice.

Auditoriums

Auditoriums must accommodate many activities, including concerts. Their acoustic quality depends on the design concept, the budget, and the availability of auditorium staffing to adjust movable acoustic treatments. The varied activities in an auditorium have differing acoustic requirements. Solutions therefore must be either a compromise between the disparate needs, or be adjustable for varied circumstances. The acoustic design of an auditorium involves room acoustics, noise control, and sound system design.

Changing the volume of the space, moving reflective surfaces, or adding or subtracting sound absorbing treatments can alter the acoustic environment of an auditorium. The size of the audience, range of performance activities, and sophistication of the intended audience influence the acoustic design. Once the basic floor area is determined by the size of the audience, the volume of the space is determined by the reverberation requirements.

The ceiling and side walls at the front of the auditorium distribute sound to the audience. They must be close enough to the performers to minimize time delays between direct and reflected sound. The ceiling and side walls also provide diffusion.

To allow adjustments to the acoustics for different events, large areas of tracked sound-absorbing curtains can be installed along the room's boundaries. The curtains can retract into storage pockets to maximize the reverberation time. For movies and lectures without music, permanent sound absorption on the ceiling, rear, and side walls results in a low reverberation time.

By enclosing the orchestra with special movable surfaces, less sound is lost backstage, and full-range sound is efficiently transferred and distributed to the audience. Orchestra enclosure surfaces offer good balance between parts of the orchestra and good on-stage communication for the musicians. The simplest, most economical modular surfaces allow leakage and reflect sound imperfectly at lower frequencies. Custom designs are heavier, more complex, and more expensive, but they work better.

 Fully upholstered seating minimizes the difference between the times when the room is full of people and when it is almost empty, such as during a rehearsal. Upholstery covered with an open weave material is particularly effective.

Reflector panels are used on the ceilings of auditoriums, performing arts centers, lecture halls and churches. They are designed for large spaces that require improved sound reinforcement and timing of sound reflections to improve listening quality. The sound reflective and diffusive surface of the flat panel is bowed and positioned in the field to the architect's or acoustical consultant's specifications. The panels are made of a plywood core faced with a fiberglass gel coat finish, and are available in widths up to 30.5 meters (10 ft) and lengths up to 12.2 meters (40 ft). Panels are mounted with wire rope or cables.

Theaters

In a theater, the effortless perception of speech is the most important acoustic goal. Sound reinforcement is essential in large theaters seating over 1000 people, and in theaters in the round seating over 600 people. A moderate fan plan keeps a larger number of people closer to the stage than a rectangular plan. Balconies also bring people closer to the performers.

Monumental, high-ceiling spaces don't work well for theaters, as they have long reverberation times and need strong reinforcement for speech. All wall and ceiling surfaces that don't produce quick reflections should be treated with efficient sound-absorbing material to control echo and reverberation.

Lecture Rooms

Lecture rooms are similar acoustically to small theaters. The boundaries, especially the ceiling, should be shaped for good natural reinforcement of the speaking voice. Applied sound-absorbent treatments control reverberation, echo, and flutter. The rear wall, the perimeter of the ceiling, and the side wall areas—especially where parallel—between seating and standing height are the most important to treat. Acoustic tile ceilings with hard walls are not an adequate solution for a lecture room.

Classrooms linked through interactive video networks for distance learning are treated similarly to teleconferencing rooms.

Worship Spaces

Houses of worship combine speech and music during the same service, so changing draperies to accommodate either is not an option. The type of music varies from amplified gospel choruses that favor shorter reverberation times to traditional boys' choirs and organs that benefit from longer reverberations. Liturgical music from medieval times to the present has depended on long echoing interiors for much of its emotional effect. To deal with this complexity, the acoustics are usually designed for music, with special assistance for speakers.

Where the preaching is the most important element of the service, the space should be designed for short reverberation times. A sound-reflecting canopy over the pulpit directs the speaker's voice to the congregation. A loudspeaker may be added over the canopy. Chanted liturgy may have derived from the need for clarity in early religious buildings with enormously long reverberation times.

The materials in worship spaces are often hard and sound reflecting, like those in concert halls. Wood paneling absorbs low-frequency energy unless it is very thick or bonded to a massive surface. Brick, stone, and concrete reflect sound well, as does thick plaster. Carpet is generally not used, except in large evangelical churches. No sound-absorbing materials are used on the ceiling. Pew cushions are sometimes needed to compensate for missing sound absorption in empty pews.

In the past, too much sound-absorbing material in large cathedral spaces sometimes resulted in acoustically dead spaces that were very poor for music and not very good for speech. The remedy was often the addition of an expensive sound system. The contemporary approach to acoustic design for churches is to design a spacious room with hard, sound-reflecting surfaces that effectively distribute the sound of music through the space, allowing the congregation to hear themselves sing and producing ample reverberation. This is coupled with a sophisticated sound amplification system to place amplified speech energy into the sound-absorbing seating area without directing large amounts of amplified energy at wall and ceiling surfaces. The process requires coordination between the architect and interior designer, the acoustic consultant, and the sound system contractor.

Small, low, meetinghouse-type churches may have a medium-sized pipe organ or an electronic instrument.

The style of architecture eliminates a long reverberation time, and favors the more intimate types of music. Speech will probably be clear without amplification.

Medium-sized churches and many synagogues and mosques can have good concert hall acoustics. Typically, such houses of worship will have a moderate- to large-sized pipe organ. They often have hard, sound-reflecting surfaces. There is usually a relatively simple sound system with a central cluster of speakers.

Large evangelical churches are like large auditoriums with an amplified chorus, electric instruments, and television. Carpet is used in large evangelical churches, especially near the choir and organ. Pew cushions are always needed with amplified music.

Because of the need for a high level of intelligibility in a space with a long reverberation time, some houses of worship use speakers distributed in the backs of the pews. Wireless microphones accommodate mobility, with automatic microphone mixers for simplicity of operation.

SCHOOLS

Schools have a variety of spaces and a variety of acoustical environments. Auditoriums need sound systems for some activities. Integrating loudspeakers into the design without creating large obstructions can be architecturally difficult, and they should be designed early in the process. Some schools use a modified gym or cafeteria for musical and theatrical presentations. If the space includes large areas of sound-absorbing materials, it will work poorly for use as an auditorium.

 Classrooms are usually around 9 meters (30 ft) square with 3-meter (10-ft) high ceilings. Use sound-absorbing materials to reduce noise levels. The ceiling tile should have a noise reduction coefficient (NRC) rating of at least 0.7. Design walls for adequate privacy between classroom spaces, and be especially aware of sound leaking through doors between classrooms. Partitions should be full height from floor to ceiling slab or roof construction. The air-handling system and ductwork should be designed to avoid excessive noise. Unit ventilators within the room can provide adequate background noise, but only when they are operating.

School dining areas are especially noisy. Keep the kitchen and serving areas separate from the eating area so that kitchen noise doesn't add to the clamor of hundreds of kids. The ceiling and walls should have sound-absorbing materials. The ceiling tile should have a minimum NRC of 0.8.

Nothing will quiet the excessive noise in a gymnasium, but noise is expected. The ceiling should be sound absorbing, with an NRC of 0.7. If there is a sound amplification system, the walls should also have sound absorption to prevent echoes. Swimming pools are chaotically noisy. Special moisture-resistant acoustic materials are available for wet areas like swimming pools and shower rooms.

Workshops have noisy machines and manual tools that produce airborne and structure-borne sound. Isolate these noisy activities from quiet areas. Use ceiling and wall treatments with an NRC of 0.75.

RESIDENTIAL BUILDINGS

Understanding how to control noise in a residential building is a critical part of your work as an interior designer. Whether you are trying to separate a home office from a blaring radio in a teenager's bedroom, or isolate the sound of a toddler's almost constant footfalls from the retired couple's apartment on the floor below, your sensitivity to acoustic design issues will help keep the peace between family members and neighbors.

The acoustic design of apartment buildings and other buildings with multiple residents strives to protect privacy and reduce annoyance. Plan the locations of convenience outlets, medicine cabinets, mechanical services, and direct-exhaust duct connections between apartments carefully.

Use rugs or carpets with pads to limit footfall noise. Group quiet spaces together and away from noisy activities. Bedroom ceilings should have ceiling mounted absorptive materials with an NRC rating of at least 0.6. A mechanical system with a continually operating fan can help mask sound from adjacent residential units.

The U.S. Department of Housing and Urban Development (HUD) and the Federal Housing Administration (FHA) publish *A Guide to Airborne, Impact and Structure-Borne Noise Control* and other publications for multiple-residency buildings. They set grades based on building location for sound transmission class (STC) and impact isolation class (IIC) levels.

Grade II covers residential urban and suburban areas with average noise environments. Airborne sound insulation in wall partitions between dwelling units in Grade II buildings should have an STC greater than 52. Floor and ceiling assemblies should be rated higher than 52 IIC. Grade I is a suburban quiet environment, and Grade I ratings are three points higher than Grade II.

Grade III, for noisy environments, has STC and IIC ratings four points lower than Grade II.

Acoustic Privacy in Bathrooms

Residential bathrooms are inherently reverberant spaces (which is why we sound so good when we sing in the shower) that demand acoustic privacy. The sounds of flushing toilets, spraying showers, running water, and whirring fans can be difficult to isolate inside a bathroom. In addition, we prefer to keep our bathroom activities acoustically private and separate from adjacent spaces. Separating the bathroom from bedrooms by intervening closets and hallways isolates the sound.

The construction of doors, walls, ceiling, and floors can be modified to reduce the passage of sound. Eliminating undercut or louvered doors (which are often used to improve ventilation) and providing acoustic treatment around the doorframe keep sound within the bathroom. Avoid back-to-back electrical outlets between the bathroom and bedroom. Air grilles should not open into ducts and then out into a bedroom. Do not locate another open window near the bathroom window.

The sound of water in pipes can travel from the bathroom throughout the house and end up next to the dining table. Wrap and resiliently mount pipes. When planning the layout of the house, locate fixtures so that piping is inside less acoustically critical walls.

ACOUSTIC PRIVACY IN PUBLIC TOILET ROOMS

You should not be able to hear the noises from toilet rooms in adjacent spaces. When designing toilet rooms within service cores, surround them with corridors and mechanical spaces. Avoid seating people adjacent to a wall with plumbing, where they will hear the rush of water through the pipes. Ventilating openings and access ways carry sound to other spaces. Interior designers should discuss this with the mechanical engineer or contractor.

Within the toilet room, a lack of acoustic privacy results in repeated flushing, which is wasteful and noisy. Use a steady masking sound to obscure sounds. A higher-sound-level ventilating system, for example a noisy fan, solves the problem and is less expensive too, although its sound can carry through ductwork to other spaces. Music can disguise sounds very well. Another option is a recirculating fountain. One very clever Italian restaurant played the sound tracks to Italian soap operas in the restrooms!

Electronic Sound Systems

• • •

The goal of sound reinforcement is to adjust acoustic problems and to assure that everyone in the listening space can hear well. The ideal sound reinforcement system would give every listener the same loudness, quality, directivity, and intelligibility. Speech would be as clear as if the speaker were 61 to 91 cm (2–3 ft) away, with a longer distance acceptable for music. Sound reinforcement systems should be designed to provide adequate sound levels without distortion. Loudspeakers can't completely correct poor acoustics, but they can improve a bad situation.

DESIGN OF SOUND REINFORCEMENT SYSTEMS

The designer of a sound reinforcement system needs a clear understanding of the functions that the system is intended to perform. The size and placement of loudspeakers can strongly influence the interior design, and therefore needs to be coordinated with other interior features. Space for the controls has to be located where they are accessible but unobtrusive. Signal processing and amplification equipment needs adequate space and ventilation, and electrical supply of adequate capacity.

Wiring for the sound system should be run as discretely as possible, preferably within walls. Sometimes sound wiring is shielded from interference in metal conduits, and when this isn't done, interference from other wiring can produce hum in the sound system. In order to get sound wiring into conduits and inside walls, the design of the sound system should be coordinated early on with the electrical and other construction. Specialists in sound system design are sometimes certified members of the National Council of Acoustical Consultants. Others may operate independently, and it is always wise to check into their experience and previous work.

When a sound system is well-designed, carefully installed, and properly operated, the sound it provides has a pleasant, natural quality, without being disturbed by distortion or coloration. The quality of the frequency response should bear the same relationship between frequencies as the original sound. Distortion happens when a system changes the shape of the acoustical signal that it receives; some stages of the amplification are overloaded and some frequencies are incorrectly amplified. Distortion usually results from a mismatch between the size of the signal and the size of the equipment that is processing it. If a system was designed for a single person giving a speech and is used for a rock band, the undersized equipment will probably distort the excessive signal. If the equipment that was purchased and installed was inadequate for the designated use, you will also get distortion from the undersized equipment.

Sound coloration occurs when a reproduced sound loses its naturalness and acquires unpleasant, ringing quality. Coloration may be caused by certain frequencies being amplified more than others. When this situation is extreme, usually because the system is turned up too loud, there will be acoustic feedback or howling. Both of these problems can be corrected, but may require changes or adjustments in the equipment or system design.

The sound should appear to be coming from the original source, so that the loudspeakers are not identifiable by location. Speakers are placed so that the reinforced sound arrives at the listener's ears with a slight delay following the sound directly from the natural source. This allows the listener to localize the sound as arriving from the direction of the source, not the loudspeaker.

The power of the human voice is strongest between 500 and 600 Hz, and decreases rapidly above 1000 Hz. The sounds of consonants are more important than those of vowels for intelligibility, but are relatively weak and easily masked by noise. Most of the energy in consonant sounds is in the higher frequencies. At high frequencies, the human voice is highly directional, so the intelligibility of speech drops off rapidly when a speaker turns away from the listeners. This produces problems during conferences and in the theater, where the speaker or actor doesn't always face the audience.

Intelligibility can be restored through amplification of speech sounds at frequencies greater than 500 Hz, but the result doesn't sound natural. To create a more natural effect, a high quality sound system starts amplification around 125 Hz.

A sound reinforcement system is usually required for spaces larger than 1400 cubic meters (50,000 cubic ft). That is about the space occupied by 550 people in a lecture room with a 4.6-meter (15-ft) high ceiling, or a 325-person theater with an average 6-meter (20-ft) ceiling height. The normal speaking voice can maintain a volume of 55 to 60 dB in a room this size. With limited background noise, the speaker will be heard, but in a noisier space, the speaker's voice will be less intelligible. Strong speakers will be heard clearly in smaller rooms for about 100 people, but people with weaker voices will require sound reinforcement even in a room that size. The voice level should be a minimum of 25 dB above the background noise. The intelligibility of sound in rooms with a long reverberation time is im-

proved with a sound system that directs sound at the listener's position.

SOUND SYSTEM COMPONENTS

A sound reinforcement system consists of three parts: the input, the amplifier and controls, and the loudspeakers. The input can be a microphone, any of a variety of types of commercial broadcasts, or one of many means of reproducing recorded material in common commercial formats, for example, compact discs. In sophisticated systems, the input is connected to local computers and computer networks.

Microphones convert acoustic energy into electrical energy. They convert sound waves into electrical signals, which are further amplified, transmitted, and processed as required in the sound system. Microphones may be hand held or on stands, or miniature lavaliere types that allow more movement by the speaker. Small wireless transmitters are available for any type of microphone, and are especially helpful for theatrical plays.

Preamplifiers reinforce the signal of the microphone for further processing and feed it to the other components of the sound system. A control console or mixer does the same job as a preamplifier, but is more complex and allows for more flexible control of the sound.

Power amplifiers provide a signal output with sufficient power (voltage and electrical current output) to feed the loudspeakers connected to the system. The amplifier is rated to deliver sufficient power to produce 85 to 90 dB for speech, 95 dB for light music, and 100 to 105 dB for symphonic music, in situations where the background sound level is 60 dB. Systems for rock bands produce sound pressure levels above 110 dB, and exposure to this level of loudness for extended periods will damage hearing. The amplifier's power can be reduced in quieter spaces. An acoustic specialist or a sound engineer usually specifies the amplifier. Amplifiers have controls for volume, tone mixing, and input-output selection.

Signal processing equipment includes equalizers, limiters, electronic delays, feedback suppressors, and distribution amplifiers. Equalization controls allow the signal to be shaped to increase or decrease specific frequencies. After the system is installed, portions of the overall audio frequency spectrum are adjusted. This process tailors the system to the acoustical properties of the space. Without equalization controls, the system will howl, sound rough, or give insufficient and poorly distributed sound. A competent sound engineer should do equalization after completion of installation and construction.

Limiters protect the amplifiers and speakers from overload by restricting the level of the signal applied to the system inputs. Electronic delays retard signals to amplifiers serving supplementary loudspeakers closer to the listener, and are also used with distributed loudspeaker systems to delay the sound to distant seats. This delay is necessary in a large space, where the electronic signal, which travels at the speed of light, may have to be delayed on its trip to the loudspeaker to match the speed of the direct sound, which travels at approximately one-millionth that speed. Feedback suppressors are used with weak-voiced speakers or with long-range microphone pickups in the theater. Distribution amplifiers are used in large systems to provide division of signals to many amplification tracks while isolating the source from the receivers.

Loudspeakers convert the electrical signal supplied from the power amplifier into air vibrations that the ear perceives as sound. The design and placement of the loudspeaker system must be coordinated with the architectural design. The speaker placement of conventional distributed loudspeaker systems has to be coordinated with the locations of lights, sprinklers, and air-handling system diffusers. Central loudspeaker systems require architectural enclosures and adequate supports. Loudspeakers must be of the same high quality as the rest of the sound system.

It is not physically possible to produce a simple loudspeaker with a satisfactory reproduction over the entire audio-frequency range from a single unit. Usually, different speakers reproduce separate frequency bands. Manufacturers of loudspeaker equipment offer packaged modular loudspeakers systems designed to meet the requirements of a range of typical, frequently encountered applications. This simplifies installation and integrates more easily with the interior design.

The most common loudspeakers are electromagnetic direct-radiator types that range from 7 cm ($2\frac{3}{4}$ in.) in diameter for high frequencies to 45 cm ($17\frac{3}{4}$ in.) in diameter for low frequencies. They are housed in cabinets to cancel the radiation of sound from the back of the cone. Smaller speakers are not as efficient as larger types at low frequencies. Directional speakers focus high-frequency sounds into a narrow beam, whereas coaxial designs offer a better high-frequency dispersion angle, and work better for distributed loudspeaker systems. Systems are available with two loudspeaker arrays with controlled directivity, a bass enclosure, and an electronic controller that shapes frequency response of the system. Only two loudspeaker arrays are needed for speech, with the bass speaker added for music. Recently, much smaller units have become available for high-power, high-quality low-frequency sound reproduction.

Depending on the application, loudspeakers are arrayed in either a centralized system or a distributed pattern. Centralized systems are used in large spaces with high ceilings to project sound with strong directionality from a focal point such as a stage or pulpit. Distributed loudspeaker patterns are used in spaces with lower ceilings where the sound is distributed evenly and without a strong sense of source through many smaller speakers, as in offices or restaurants.

A conventional central loudspeaker system (Fig. 55-1) uses a carefully designed central speaker array of high-quality, sectional (multicell), directional, high-frequency horns and less directional low-frequency large-cone woofers to provide directional realism with a relatively simple design. The array is placed slightly in front of the primary speaking position, or above the source of the live sound. In most theaters, this is just above the proscenium arch on the centerline of the room. These components are very large, and the architect and interior designer must be aware of the dimensions to be accommodated. Smaller units are available with folded horns, but they are less responsive in low frequencies, making them acceptable for speech but not appropriate for music. Supplemental speakers may be added for coverage of the balcony and under-balcony areas.

Central loudspeaker systems provide directional realism for medium to large auditoriums. Where the audience is deep, the coverage of the front and distant parts of the audience is likely to be uneven, and supplemental speakers are used. Deep balconies and areas under balconies, as well as wide first rows, often need supplemental speaker coverage. Delayed signals help preserve the sense of direction of the sound.

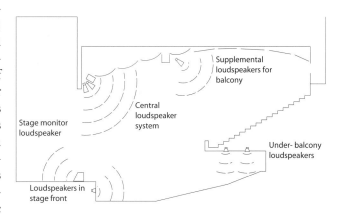

Figure 55-1 Auditorium with central loudspeaker system.

In large meeting, convention, and exhibition halls, distributed loudspeaker systems (Fig. 55-2) offer flexibility in seating arrangements and reinforce sound from any position in the room, even when the room is divided by movable partitions. Distributed systems provide flexibility in spaces where the source and the listener locations vary according to the use of the space. They don't provide directional realism, but offer very good clarity and intelligibility. Distributed systems are not appropriate for rooms with very high ceilings.

Distributed loudspeaker systems use a series of small low-level speakers, 10 to 31 cm (4–12 in.) in diameter, located throughout the space. These are often ceiling mounted or recessed in the ceiling and send sound directly down, so that each speaker covers a small area. Speakers may also be located in the backs of seats or pews. Distributed loudspeaker systems are used in areas with low ceilings where a central loudspeaker cluster can't provide the proper coverage. They are also used for public address functions if directional realism is not essential, as in exhibition areas, airline terminals, and offices. In public areas with highly reflective surfaces, careful speaker positioning and volume levels are critical, or the result is extremely loud but unintelligible speech.

Individual loudspeakers in a distributed system can be easily switched on or off for proper coverage. Ideally, a listening position gets sound from only one loudspeaker. If the speakers overlap, loudness and garbled speech results. Another significant advantage of a distributed system is that the speakers nearest the microphone can be switched off, which is important in deep rooms with low ceilings. Speakers should not be placed on each side of a proscenium opening, and rows of speakers should not be located on one or both sides of a room.

Whatever the loudspeaker arrangement, the sound system operator should be within the covering pattern of the speakers. This means that space must be provided within the audience seating area or in a control room with a large opening located at the rear of the space. The best location for the sound control room or position is in the rear of an auditorium, where the operator can directly hear the sound and follow activity. The sound control room should either be fully open to the volume of the space, which is practical only for small systems without much equipment, or in a separate sound control room with a large operable sound control window. Using a monitor loudspeaker or working from a remote location control room produces unsatisfactory results for live performances. Many performing arts sound reinforcement systems use control facilities located entirely within the audience area.

SYSTEMS FOR SPECIFIC SPACES

Interior designers are routinely involved in coordinating the many details of an installation, and this sometimes includes the sound system. There is a tendency to think of the sound reinforcement system for a smaller project as an add-on, and leave it to the end of the design and construction process. Doing so risks last minute crises when sound wiring, speaker locations, and space and wiring for control equipment has to be retrofit into locations for which it was not planned. Running wires within walls is much easier before the walls are closed in and finished. Although sound reinforcement design may not properly be a part of an interior designer's work, ignoring these details creates difficulties that definitely affect the appearance of the project and the smoothness of the construction process. A familiarity with the equipment required for specific types of spaces will help you anticipate conflicts with the details of the interior design and head off last minute problems.

Home Listening Rooms

In a small living room, all sound reflecting from the room's boundaries arrives at the listener in very quick succession, following the direct sound by only a few thousandths of a second. The amplified sound is consequently easily integrated with the direct sound, so loudspeakers with a wide dispersion of sound are used, rather than highly directional ones. In rooms with small volumes used for private listening, background noise can be kept at low levels. Consequently, the efficiency of loudspeakers is of little concern, and the speakers should be selected for high fidelity over the widest possible range of frequencies.

Small residential listening rooms can experience significant coloration and poor spatial imaging of repro-

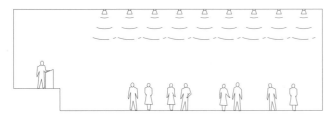

Figure 55-2 Distributed loudspeaker system.

duced sound if they are not extensively and uniformly treated with broadband sound absorbing materials. The goal is to suppress the sound of the room itself, but not to totally deaden it. This requires large areas of effective sound-absorbing and sound-diffusing treatments on all surfaces. Treat surfaces so that the average noise reduction coefficients in pairs of surfaces are the same. For example, if each side wall is 50 percent absorbent and the wall behind the front loudspeakers is 100 percent absorbent (which is commonly done to keep reflected sound waves from affecting waves from the loudspeakers), the rear wall then should be 100 percent hard, and shaped to diffuse the sound waves. The treatment must be totally symmetrical on the left and right sides of the main listening axis, so that sound transmission paths for left and right playback channels are identical. Surround sound channels have special placement considerations.

Office Spaces

When we specify a good-looking or comfortable chair, we show our client a sample, and they can see the tangible benefits of the expense. When we select durable finishes, we can offer information about long-term savings. However, the benefits of good acoustics are difficult to demonstrate to a client in advance.

Research has been performed on the benefits of good acoustic design, showing that paying attention to the acoustic qualities of a workspace can increase productivity and save money. Surveys of office workers show that noise is a bigger distraction than inadequate lighting or poor air quality, and that background conversation is the biggest distraction of all. In one study, improved acoustics resulted in a 13 percent improvement in productivity. The biggest cost of doing business is manpower, so improved productivity is worth money, and the expense of improved acoustics pays off.

Except for conference and meeting rooms, sound reinforcement in offices is limited to announcements or background music. Distributed loudspeakers for announcements are either recessed in ceilings or concealed in the ceiling plenum behind sound-transparent ceiling panels. As we discussed earlier, open offices usually have masking sound systems for speech privacy.

High-rise office towers may include a sound system designed for life-safety announcements and transmission of warning signals. Emergency sound systems are normally separate from other systems and use fire-rated equipment, wiring, and installation materials.

Auditoriums and Lecture Halls

In very large spaces, the background noise from the audience is not well controlled. The sound system needs to deliver at very high output with very high efficiency. In very large rooms, sound reflections from the walls follow the direct sound with very long delays, and do not integrate well with the direct sound. This is generally harmful to the intelligibility and clarity of the sound. By using loudspeakers that radiate sound within a narrow angle and pointing them at the audience, the directivity reduces the amount of harmful sound reflections from the walls. The best speech intelligibility occurs when most of the sound reaches the listener directly without reflection from walls or ceiling, so loudspeakers are placed close to listeners and radiate the sound in a highly directional way. In medium to large auditoriums, it is important to have a sense of directional realism, that is, to have the loudspeakers create the sense that the sound is coming from the source.

In auditoriums and lecture halls, the controls for sound, projection, and lighting are frequently located within the listening room. It is good to have a provision for remote controls for projection, volume control of the sound, and dimming of lights at the lecturer's position.

Large assembly halls may have central or distributed speakers, depending on the configuration of the space and the requirements of the users. Where the audience or delegates participate from the floor, microphone arrangements vary from simple to very complex.

Assembly halls for multinational conferences must have a system for simultaneous translation. A signal from the speaker's microphone is sent to the translators' booths. The translated signals are reinforced and distributed to the delegates' seats. The delegates select a language channel with a switch, and listen with headsets with individual volume controls. Simultaneous translation is also possible using wireless transmission and individual receiver/headsets. This allows freedom of movement, and is required where seating arrangements are flexible with movable seats. Translators' booths must have sound isolation from each other, be located so that translators can see the lips of the speaker, and must accommodate two interpreters sitting side by side.

Concert Halls

High-quality, full range sound reinforcement systems are used in concert halls with multiple functions. In order to reinforce speech with high intelligibility in spaces with long reverberation times, the central loudspeaker system with high directivity is suspended in free space or integrated into the architecture. Sound reflectors or canopies above the orchestral platform are part of the system. Concert halls also use backstage performance monitoring and paging systems and production intercoms.

Theaters and Opera Houses

Theaters and opera houses may reinforce vocals over orchestral sounds, but some music fans prefer the sound without amplification. Amplification is more of a necessity in larger theaters.

In order to provide directional realism, the central loudspeaker system is usually located at the proscenium. There may also be supplemental speakers. Microphone receptacles are located in the footlights at stage front, and may also be in the wings.

Theaters often use program monitoring and stage manager paging systems for the cast offstage. Productions communications systems are provided for lights and sound technicians, projection rooms, and similar functions. These may be special intercom systems with mobile wireless remote stations.

The sounds of an organ can be produced electronically in buildings without pipe organs, but since organ pipes can produce sounds as low as 16 Hz, few sound systems will do this well. The normal frequency range for a high-quality sound reinforcement system is 40 to 12,000 Hz.

Exhibition Halls

Exhibition halls use sound reinforcement for announcements and for background music. If the hall includes a permanent or demountable platform for stage presentations, it will typically include a central loudspeaker system located above the front of the platform to provide sound reinforcement with directional realism.

Hotel Ballrooms and Banquet Halls

Hotel ballrooms and banquet halls are often divided for smaller groups of people, and microphone pickup may be required from any location on the floor. The overhead speakers are distributed throughout the rooms. If the room contains a stage platform or projection screen, it should include a central loudspeaker system.

Hotel banquet rooms are used for many types of activities, from medical conferences to bar mitzvahs and fashion shows. The sound design should consider including production communication facilities for lighting, projection, and sound control technicians. The controls for these functions are usually in wall-mounted boxes, which should be integrated into the room design rather than being stuck onto the walls during construction. During renovation projects, it is a good idea to check and see whether existing equipment mounted on the walls is actually in use. In one hotel, microphone antennas that had not been used for 12 years would have been given special treatment when the wallpaper was installed if an alert technician hadn't noticed and alerted the designer.

Sports Facilities

Indoor sports arenas with up to 15,000 seats use a directional loudspeaker system located in the center of the arena. If there are additional performance stages, each platform needs its own system. Multipurpose arenas have a performance monitoring and paging system, plus an intercom system for stage management, lighting, and sound. They need a great deal of acoustic treatment for low-frequency sound, or the noise becomes uninterrupted and speech clarity and intelligibility suffers. Systems can limit the signal to exclude the lowest frequencies without harming the quality of speech.

Sports facilities with over 5000 seats are also used for large public events and popular music concerts. The surfaces are too far from the performers and listeners for sound reinforcement from reflected sound energy without echoing. Massive applications of acoustical treatments with high absorption coefficients in the speech frequency range, especially between 250 and 4000 Hz, are used to make the boundary surfaces sound absorbent.

In concrete structures, thick sound-absorbing foam boards can be left in place on the underside of the concrete. Steel surfaces can be made of perforated metal roof decks with glass fiber in the middle. Inflatable domes use a special sound-absorbing fabric that sags below the dome fabric.

Wall and ceiling surfaces should be acoustically treated. Upholster seats if possible, or use perforated metal seat bottoms with an absorbent material inside the seats. Sound absorbing material also helps control crowd noise, and allows the sound system to communicate emergency information over the noise.

Motion Picture Theaters

Movie theaters use amplified sound and cushion the space with highly absorbent materials, so the shape of the space is not acoustically important. The most important consideration is the reflectivity of the room boundary. A large quantity of wall and ceiling mounted broadband sound-absorbing material should be used to control reverberation. A minimum of half of the walls and between half and the entire ceiling should be treated. The loudspeakers are located in the front of the theater behind a perforated screen. Baffling is used to capture the sound radiating to the rear of the screen.

Special Sound System Installations

Paging and voice alarm systems are used in power plants and other industrial facilities, where high levels of ambient noise and long reverberation times overwhelm public address systems. Paging and voice alarm systems also cost less and are smaller than public address systems. Lights or sirens are used for simple messages, and headsets can be used with earmuffs.

The Americans with Disabilities Act (ADA) requires assistive listening systems in some assembly areas, and specifies the types and placement of systems. Listening devices are often provided at selected seats in auditoriums by an outlet jack that accommodates a headset, and an individual volume control under the chair's armrest. Wireless systems can cover all auditorium areas. In transient lodging accommodations, such as hotels and motels, a certain number of rooms must be accessible to people with hearing impairments.

As the interior designer, your awareness of acoustic concerns that affect the health, safety, and enjoyment of the public is an important part of your role as a member of the building design team. Your knowledge of all the systems that make a building work will enhance the quality of your design work, the value of the building to those who use it, and your own enjoyment of your work as an interior designer.

INDEX